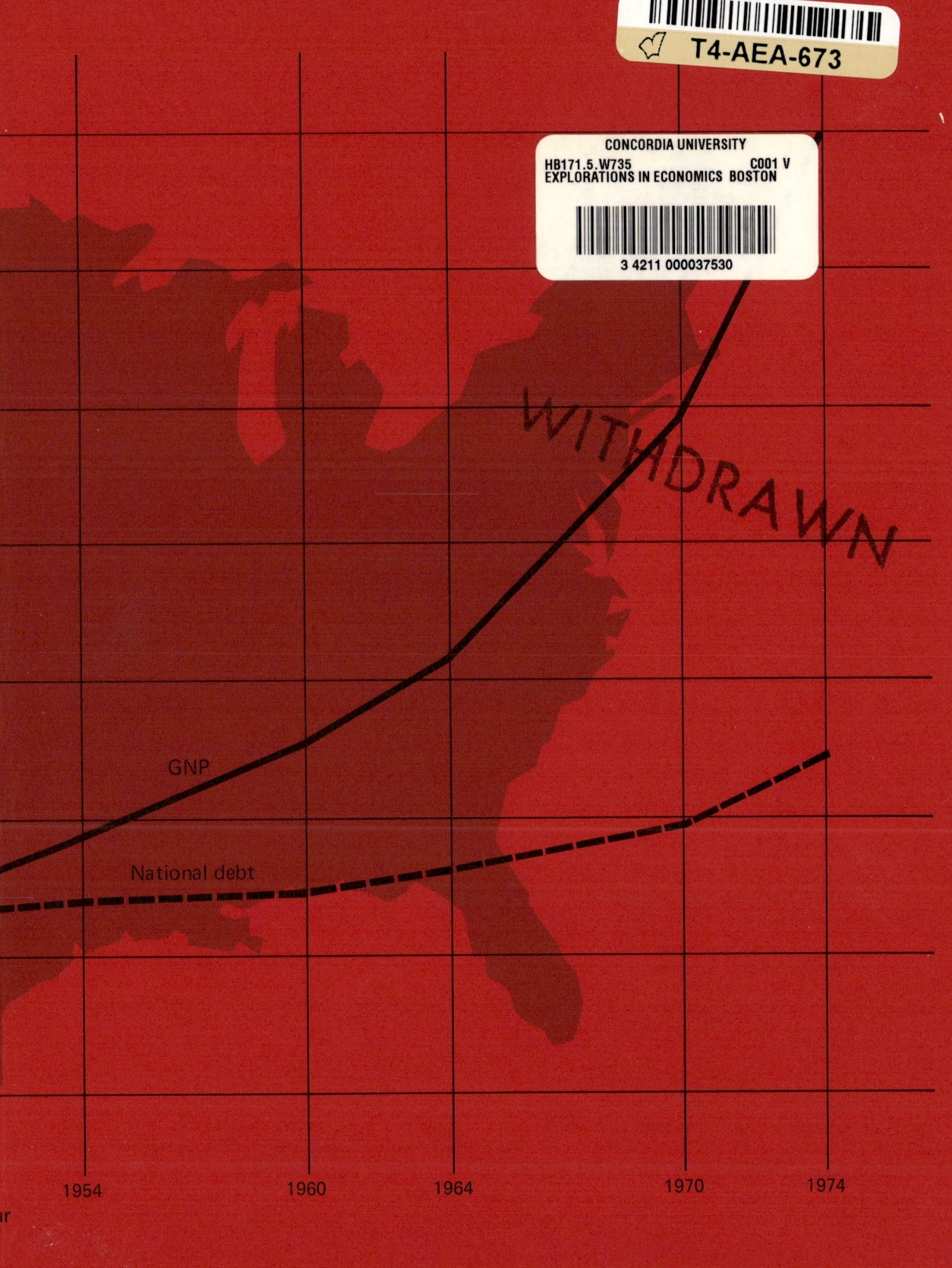

Explorations in Economics

Explorations in Economics

James F. Willis   Martin L. Primack
San Jose State University

Houghton Mifflin Company, Boston
Atlanta   Dallas   Geneva, Illinois
Hopewell, New Jersey   Palo Alto   London

Acknowledgments

Quotations in Chapter 1, Chapter 7, and Application 13 from John Maynard Keynes, *The General Theory of Employment, Interest, and Money*, Harcourt, Brace & World, New York, 1936. Reprinted by permission of Harcourt Brace Jovanovich, Inc., and Macmillan London and Basingstoke.

Quotation in Application 1 from John G. Gurley, "Maoist Economic Development" (from *America's Asia*, edited by Edward Friedman and Mark Selden, Random House, New York, 1971) in *Economics, Mainstream Readings and Radical Critiques*, 2nd ed., edited by David Mermelstein, Random House, New York, 1973. Reprinted by permission of the author and Random House, Inc.

Quotations in Application 4 from Joel F. Henning, "Corporate Social Responsibility: Shell Game for the Seventies?" in *Corporate Power in America*, edited by Ralph Nader and Mark J. Green, Grossman, New York, 1973. Copyright © 1973 by Ralph Nader. All rights reserved. Reprinted by permission of Grossman Publishers, a division of Viking Penguin, Inc.

Quotations in Application 5 from Robert B. Pettingill and Jogindar S. Uppal, *Can Cities Survive? The Fiscal Plight of American Cities*, St. Martin's Press, Inc., New York, 1974. Reprinted by permission of the publisher.

Application 10, "First Steps in Banking," from *Punch*, April 3, 1957, pp. 440–441. © Punch (Rothco). Reprinted by permission of the publisher.

Table 16-2 from "Electronic Watches for the Mass Market," *Business Week*, April 22, 1972. Reprinted from the April 22, 1972 issue of *Business Week* by special permission. © 1972 by McGraw-Hill, Inc.

Quotations in Application 19 from Charles McCarry, *Citizen Nader*, Signet Books, New York, 1972. Copyright © 1972 by Charles McCarry. Reprinted by permission of the publishers, Saturday Review Press/E. P. Dutton & Co., Inc., and William Morris Agency, Inc.

Quotations in Application 22 from Seymour Melman, ed., *The War Economy of the United States*, St. Martin's Press, Inc., New York, 1971. Reprinted by permission of the publisher.

Material paraphrased in Application 25 from Hollis B. Chenery, "Comparative Advantage and Development Policy," *American Economic Review* 51:1 (March 1961). Reprinted by permission of the author and the American Economic Association.

Quotation in Chapter 26 from Friedrich Engels, "Socialism: Utopian and Scientific," in *The Marx-Engels Reader*, edited by Robert C. Tucker, Norton, New York, 1972. Reprinted by permission of the publisher.

Quotation in Chapter 26 from Robert Owen, "A New View of Society," in *Masterworks of Economics*, edited by Leonard D. Abbott, McGraw-Hill, New York, 1946, vol. II, p. 79. Copyright 1946, renewed 1974, by Copeland & Lamm, Inc. Reprinted by permission of Copeland & Lamm, Inc.

Quotation in Chapter 26 from Burnett Bolloten, *The Grand Camouflage*, Burns & MacEachern, Don Mills, Canada, 1961. Copyright © 1961 by Burnett Bolloten. Reprinted by permission of the author and Praeger Publishers, Inc.

Endpapers: The National Debt and Gross National Product, 1929–1974.

Copyright © 1977 by Houghton Mifflin Company. All rights reserved.
No part of this work may be reproduced or transmitted in any form or by any means, electronic or mechanical, including photocopying and recording, or by any information storage or retrieval system, without permission in writing from the publisher.

Printed in the U.S.A.

Library of Congress Catalog Card Number: 76-13973

ISBN: 0-395-24524-9

To Marianna, Jim, and my parents.
J. F. W.

To my three girls, Marlene, Renee, and Ellen.
M. L. P.

Contents

Preface xxiv

Alternative Plans for Using the Text xxviii

1 Breaking the Ice 1

The Aims of the Economist 1
What Is Economics? 2
What Is the Economist's Method? 4
The Citizen and Economic Policy 6
Applications: Concrete Examples of Abstract Ideas 6
End-of-Chapter Summaries 6
Mathematics De-emphasized 7
Positive Versus Normative Economics 8
A Word About Words 9
Summing Up 10
Questions 11
Suggested Readings 12

Application 1 Self-interest: Endangered Motivation? 13

Self-interest: Key to All Characters 13
Homo economicus 15
Private Citizens Want Private Profits 15
Do Corporations Value Profits Above All Else? 15
The Economic Citizen: Voices of Dissent 15
Summing Up 16
Questions 17
Suggested Readings 17

PART ONE   Macroeconomics with Micro Foundations   19

2 Scarcity and Economic Development   20

Scarcity: Source of Basic Economic Questions   20
  An Unreal World: No Scarcity
  Back to the Real World: Basic Questions
  Is Scarcity Meaningful Today?
Viewing the Choices: The Production-Possibilities Curve   22
  The Production-Possibilities Table
  Graphing the Production-Possibilities Curve
Employment, Full Employment, Unemployment, Underemployment   25
A Word of Caution   27
What Is Economic Integration?   27
Increasing Costs: Why Is the Curve Shaped That Way?   28
Mental Reservations   30
A Classical Explanation of Growth   31
Institutions Play a Part in Decision Making   32
Summing Up   32
Questions   33
Suggested Readings   34

Application 2 The Rich Countries and the Poor Countries   35
Economic Development: Problems of Closing the Gap   35
Economic Determinism   36
Basic Questions About Economic Development   37
  How Do You Measure Well-being?
  How Great Is the Income Gap?
Resistances to Growth and Development   39
  Social and Cultural Resistances
  Technological and Technical Resistances
What About Natural Resources?   42
Is the Income Gap Widening or Closing?   43
A Note About China   44
Is There Hope for Underdeveloped Countries?   44
How Long Will It Take?   45
Summing Up   45
Questions   46
Suggested Readings   46

3 Supply and Demand: Price Determination in Competitive Capitalism   47

What Is Competition?   47
How Are Prices Set? Supply and Demand   48

  DEMAND   49
An Individual Demand Curve   50
Changes in Quantity Demanded Versus Changes in Demand   51
Demand: Summing Up   53
Market Demand   53

  SUPPLY   54
What Is Supply?   55

What Do Supply Data and the Supply Curve Tell Us?   57
    What Causes Physical Efficiency to Decrease?
Market Supply   58
Difference Between Movements Along and Shifts in Curves   58

    COMPETITIVE PRICING   59
Conditions for Competitive Pricing   61
Summing Up   62
Questions   64
Suggested Readings   65

Application 3   Should We Let Supply and Demand Work? The Price of Gasoline   **66**
First Shortages, Then Price Hikes   66
What Can We Do?   67
What About Supply?   68
Strategies   69
Summing Up   69
Questions   70
Suggested Readings   70

4 Components of an Economic Society: Households, Business Firms, Governments   71

The Circular-Flow Model   71
    The Simple Model
    The Complex Model
What Does the Model Show?   74

    HOUSEHOLDS   74
The Sources of Income: Functional Distribution   75
The Way Households Allocate Their Income   76
The Way Personal Income Is Distributed   76
Economic Implications of Inequality in Income Distribution   79

    BUSINESS FIRMS   80
Sole Proprietorships   80
    Advantages of a Sole Proprietorship
    Disadvantages of a Sole Proprietorship
Partnerships   81
    Advantages of a Partnership
    Disadvantages of a Partnership
Corporations   81
    Advantages of a Corporation
    Disadvantages of a Corporation
Big Business: Is It a Threat?   84

    GOVERNMENTS   86
Expenditures: What Do They Spend All That Money On?   86
Taxation   87
    Principles of Taxation
    Types of Taxes
    Composition of Taxes

    Who Pays the Tax?
Government and the Rules of the Game   92
Government and Regulation   92
Summing Up   93
Questions   95
Suggested Readings   96

Application 4 The Social Responsibility of Business: The Invisible Hand Versus the Good Corporate Citizen   97
The Effect of Competition on Business Morals   97
The Social Responsibility of Business   97
Suggested Readings   98

Application 5 The Cities: Our Society's Stepchildren?   99
Where Has All the Money Gone?   99
What Cities Spend Their Money On   100
Where Cities Get Their Money   101
Alternative Solutions to the Cities' Money Crisis   101
Some Conclusions   102
Question   103
Suggested Readings   103

5 Measuring Economic Activity   104
Background: Why Is National Economic Accounting Important?   104
The Expenditure and Income Approaches   105
Gross National Product and Gross National Income   107
    Gross National Product (GNP)
    Gross National Income (GNI)
Net National Product and Net National Income   111
    Net National Product
    Net National Income
National Income   113
Personal Income   114
Personal Disposable Income   115
Circular Flow: Another View   115
Final-Value and Value-Added Methods   116
Current, Constant, and Per Capita GNP   119
Output Excluded from GNP   121
Economic Transactions Excluded from GNP   121
Summing Up   122
Questions   123
Suggested Readings   125

Application 6 Is GNP Growth a Measure of Human Well-Being?   125
What GNP Does Not Include   125
What Does Contribute to Well-being?   126
Is Growth Evil?   127
Alternatives to Using GNP as a Yardstick   128
A Possible Conclusion   128

Summing Up   129
Question   129
Suggested Readings   129

6 Business Fluctuations   130

Fluctuations: Characteristics and Clues   130
  Kinds of Business Fluctuations
  Phases of a Business Cycle
  Do Business Cycles Follow a Regular Pattern?
  Durable- Versus Nondurable-Goods Industries
  Leading Economic Indicators
Unemployment   135
  Kinds of Unemployment
  Problems That Accompany Unemployment
  Economic Costs of Unemployment: The GNP Gap
  Psychological and Social Costs of Unemployment
Prices and the Problem of Inflation   139
  Kinds of Inflation
  What Effect Do Price Changes Have?
Employment and Prices   146
Summing Up   148
Questions   150
Suggested Readings   151

Application 7 Who Is Hurt by Inflation?   **152**

The Story of One Inflation   152
Taxes and Inflation   153
Does Anyone Come Out Ahead?   154
Summing Up   155
Question   155
Suggested Readings   155

7 Income and Employment: The Beginnings   156

  THE NEOCLASSICAL THEORY   157
Say's Law   157
The Abstinence Theory of Interest   159
Wage-Price Flexibility   161

  THE KEYNESIAN CRITIQUE   162
What About Say's Law?   162
The Abstinence Theory of Interest: Not True   162
Lack of Wage-Price Flexibility   164

  THE KEYNESIAN CONCLUSIONS   165
The Consumption Function   166
The Savings Function   169
A Change in Consumption and Savings   169
The Intended Investment Function   172
  What Determines Autonomous Investment?

    How Much Investment Will People Make?
    Instability of Investment
  How Does Investment Fit into Our Model?   175
  Summing Up   176
  Questions   179
  Suggested Readings   180

8 Income and Employment Without Government   181

    THE SIMPLE MODEL   182
  Savings Equals Intended Investment   182
  Ex-Ante and Ex-Post Investment   186
  Aggregate Demand Equals Aggregate Supply   187

    THE MULTIPLIER   190
  Average and Marginal Propensities to Consume and Save   190
  How Changes in Aggregate Demand Affect Changes in Income   192
  Why a Multiple?   193
  The Multiplier Formula   194
  Instantaneous Multipliers Versus Periodic Multipliers   194

    THE ACCELERATOR PRINCIPLE   195
  The Paradox of Thrift   197
  Summing Up   198
  Questions   201
  Suggested Readings   201

  Application 8 The U.S. Economy: Ups and Downs   202
  The Depression of 1921   202
  The Prosperity of the 1920s   202
  The Depression of 1929-1933   203
  Weak Recovery: 1933-1937   205
  The Recession of 1937-1938   205
  The Early Forties and World War II   205
  The Postwar Boom: 1945-1948   206
  The Recession of 1949   206
  The Korean War and the Expansion of 1950-1953   206
  The Recession of 1954   207
  The Expansion of 1955-1957   207
  The Recession of 1958   207
  Weak Recovery: The Recession of 1960-1961   207
  The Expansion of the 1960s: 1962-1969   207
  Inflation and Unemployment: The Recession of 1970-1971   208
  The New Nixon Economic Policy: 1971-1973   208
  Inflation and Unemployment Again: 1974-   209
  Summing Up   210
  Questions   212
  Suggested Readings   212

9 Completing the Model: Adding Government and Fiscal Policy   213

  Adding Government Expenditures to the Simple Model   213

 One Approach: Savings Equals Intended Investment Plus Government Expenditures
 Another Approach: Aggregate Demand Equals Aggregate Supply
Adding Taxes to the Simple Model   217
 One Approach: Savings Plus Taxes Equals Intended Investment
  Plus Government Expenditures
 Another Approach: Aggregate Demand Equals Aggregate Supply
Deflationary and Inflationary Gaps   222
 The Deflationary Gap
 The Inflationary Gap
The Balanced-Budget Multiplier   224
Fiscal Policy   225
 Discretionary Fiscal Policy
 Functional Finance
How Functional-Finance Economists Handle Recession   227
 How Are Deficits Financed?
How Functional-Finance Economists Handle Inflation   228
Government Expenditures   229
Taxes   231
Balanced Budget   232
Faults in the Keynesian System   233
A Crisis in Policy?   233
Summing Up   234
Questions   236
Suggested Readings   237

10 Automatic Stabilizers and the National Debt   239

 AUTOMATIC STABILIZERS   239
The Employment Act of 1946   240
A Longer Horizon   240
Increased Size of Government Expenditures   241
Progressive Taxes   241
Expenditures That Stabilize   241
Stabilizers Versus Today's Dilemma   242
The Full-Employment Budget   243

 THE NATIONAL DEBT   244
The Size of the Debt   245
Qualitative Significance   246
Who Pays for Wars?   248
Some Problems   248
Conclusions   250

Summing Up   251
Questions   252
Suggested Readings   253

Application 9 Wage and Price Controls: Effective Tools or Market Distortions?   **253**
Wage and Price Guidelines: Please Cooperate   254
Wage and Price Controls: Obey the Law   255
 Disadvantages of Controls

When Controls Work
Summing Up   258
Questions   258
Suggested Readings   258

11 Money in the Modern Economy   259

A Barter System of Exchange   259
A Money System of Exchange   260
The Functions of Money   261
Characteristics of a "Good" Money   263
The Supply of Money   263
Money Is Debt   265
Savings Accounts, Near Money, and Credit Cards   266
The Origins of Commercial Banking: Goldsmith Banking   267
The Future of Money, or Can the Computer Replace Currency and Coin?   269
The Economy and the Supply of Money   269
The Equation of Exchange   270
The Velocity of Exchange, V 270
Output, Prices, and M (for Money)   271
The Demand for Money: An Alternative   272
Summing Up   273
Questions   274
Suggested Readings   275

12 Commercial Banking and the Creation of Money   276

The Simple Economy: Four Assumptions About a Simple Model   276
Money Creation in the Simple Model   278
Enter Currency and Coin   280
Enter the Government   283
Reserve Requirements   284
Enter Many Other Banks   286
The Federal Reserve and Clearing Checks   286
Lending by Individual Banks: A Little Goes a Long Way   287
But There Are Leakages   290
A Final Word About Excess Reserves   292
Summing Up   292
Questions   294
Suggested Readings   295

Application 10 First Steps in Banking   295

13 The Fed Again: Monetary Policy and the Role of a Central Bank   297

The Structure of the Federal Reserve   297
General Powers of the Federal Reserve   299
  Open-Market Operations
  The Discount Rate
  The Required Reserve Ratio
A Review: How the Fed Nudges the Banking System   305

Specific Powers of the Federal Reserve   305
  Margin Requirements on Stocks
  Regulations X and W
  Regulation Q
  Moral Suasion
Functions of the Federal Reserve   307
  The Fed Regulates the Supply of Money
  The Fed Acts as a National Clearinghouse for Checks
  The Fed Issues Paper Currency
  The Fed Regulates and Examines Member Banks
  The Fed Acts as a Banker's Bank
  The Fed Is a Fiscal Agent and Bank for the U.S. Treasury
  The Fed Is a Fiscal Agent for Foreign Central Banks and Treasuries
Monetary Policy   310
  Varying the Supply of Money
  Varying Interest Rates
Some Recommendations on Monetary Policy   310
  What to Do When Recession Hits
  What to Do When Inflation Hits
Weaknesses of Monetary Policy   312
Monetarism   314
Summing Up   314
Questions   316
Suggested Readings   317

Application 11 Does Money Really Matter? Monetarists Versus Keynesians   **318**
The Monetarist Position   318
The Keynesian Defense   319
A Conclusion   319
Summing Up   319
Questions   320
Suggested Readings   320

Application 12 Fiscal Policy, Monetary Policy, and Debt Management: Too Many Cooks?   **320**
The Economy: Many Hands Make Heavy Work   320
Fiscal Policy   321
Monetary Policy   321
Debt Management   321
Question   322
Suggested Readings   322

14 Expansion and Growth   323
Sources of Expansion   323
Increasing Efficiency and Growth   325
Decreasing Efficiency and Growth   326
The Classical View   327
Has the Malthusian Nightmare Already Started?   328
  Technological Change
  Population Increase
Full-Employment Growth   331

Growth at Full Capacity: How Fast Should It Be?   333
Full Employment Versus Full Capacity   334
Capital Formation: The United States and Other Nations   335
Summing Up   336
Questions   337
Suggested Readings   338

Application 13 Can We Have Growth Without Massive Military Spending?   **338**
Do Wars Keep the Economy Healthy?   338
What About Reaching Potential?   339
Defense Spending: Does It Encourage or Retard Technological Change?   341
What About the 1970s?   342
Question   342
Suggested Readings   342

Application 14 More Growth Versus a Clean Environment   **343**
The Economists' View   343
How Population Enters the Picture   344
As Ecologists See It   344
As Economists See It   344
Summing Up   345
Questions   346
Suggested Readings   346

PART TWO   Microeconomics   349

15 The Demand Side of the Market   350
What Is Demand?   350
Income and Substitution Effects   351
Utility: Another Way to Explain Demand   354
  Diminishing Satisfaction
  Maximization of Utility
  An Arithmetic Illustration
Deriving a Demand Curve   357
Market Demand   358
Elasticity: Responsiveness of Quantity Demanded to Changes in Price   358
Different Elasticities of Demand   360
Summing Up   362
Questions   364
Suggested Readings   365

Application 15 Will Redistributing Income Make People Happier?   **366**
The Distribution of Satisfaction   366
The Distribution of Income   366
Governments and Income Distribution   367
Questions   368
Suggested Readings   368

16 The Supply Side of the Market   369
What Is Supply?   369

What Determines Economic Costs?   369
  Explicit and Implicit Costs
  Profits
Four Kinds of Time Periods   371
  Market Period
  Short-Run Period
  Long-Run Period
  Historical Period
Costs and Supply in the Market Period   373
Costs and Supply in the Short-Run Period   373
  The Law of Variable Proportions
  Short-Run Supply
  Long-Run Supply
Supply Curves for a Whole Industry   381
Elasticity of Supply   382
Some Final Words About Supply   382
Summing Up   383
Questions   384
Suggested Readings   385

Application 16 Markets for Illegal Goods   **386**
Pricing Illegal Goods   387
Effect of Illegality on Demand   387
Effect of Illegality on Supply   388
Summing Up   388
Questions   388
Suggested Readings   389

17 Private Versus Public Costs and Benefits: Are They Always the Same?   390
Equilibrium Price   390
Private Equilibrium   392
Social Equilibrium   392
Spillover Effects   393
A Tax to Create Public Equilibrium   394
Can Externalities Be Internalized?   395
Government and Property Rights   396
How Much Government Intervention Is Enough?   397
Spillovers and Government Production   398
Summing Up   398
Questions   400
Suggested Readings   400

Application 17 How Much Clean Air Do We Want to Buy?   **400**
Dire Predictions and How to Live with Them   401
Business: Culprit or Savior?   401
The Price of Breathing   401
Enforcing Limits on Air Pollution: Hard Choices   402
Summing Up   403

Questions   403
Suggested Readings   404

18 Pure Competition: One Extreme   405

Market Classifications   406
Characteristics of Pure Competition   406
  Pricing Decisions
  Output Decisions

PURE COMPETITION IN THE SHORT RUN   408
Total Revenue and Total Cost   409
Profit Maximization: Marginal Cost Equals Marginal Revenue   411
  Situation 1: Economic Profit
  Situation 2: Normal Profit
  Situation 3: Economic Loss with Production
  Situation 4: Economic Loss Without Production
Pure Competition, Short Run: A Summary   416
Marginal Cost: The Competitive Firm's Short-Run Supply Curve   417

PURE COMPETITION IN THE LONG RUN   417
Increasing-Cost, Constant-Cost, and Decreasing-Cost Industries   418
  Increasing-Cost Industries
  Constant-Cost Industries
  Decreasing-Cost Industries

THE ADVANTAGES OF PURE COMPETITION   423
Most Efficient Level of Cost   423
Most Efficient Combination of Products   424

THE DISADVANTAGES OF PURE COMPETITION   425

THE RELEVANCE OF PURE COMPETITION   426
Summing Up   427
Questions   429
Suggested Readings   429

Application 18   Do We Really Want Competition? The Farming Mess   430
Origins of the Agricultural Support Program   430
No Bed of Roses: Agricultural Economic Problems   431
  Demand
  Supply: Short Run
  Supply: Long Run
  Continuity of Production
  Technological Change
The Agricultural Support Program   434
  Critique of the Agricultural Support Program
  Did the Agricultural Support Program Help All Agriculture?
Since 1972: Where Have All the Surpluses Gone?   438
  Wheat and the Soviet Union
  Anchovies
  Substitutes
  Exports

Legislation to Help the Farmer in the Mid-1970s   439
Summing Up   440
Questions   441
Suggested Readings   441

19 Pure Monopoly: The Other Extreme   442

Pure Monopoly: A Definition   442
Barriers to Entry   444
Pure Monopoly MR, AR, and D 447
Elasticity of Demand   448
Pure Monopoly: Short Run   449
Pure Monopoly: Long Run   452
Pure Competition Versus Pure Monopoly   454
Technology and Monopoly   456
Regulated Monopoly   458
Price Discrimination   460
    Conditions Necessary for Price Discrimination
    Graphic Analysis of Price Discrimination
Summing Up   463
Questions   464
Suggested Readings   465

Application 19 A National System of Nader's Raiders: Whose Interests Are Represented by Public Regulation?   **466**

Regulatory Commissions: Imperfect Guardians of the Public Interest   466
Who Watches the Watchdog   467
A Conclusion   469
Question   469
Suggested Readings   469

20 Monopolistic Competition: Most Small Firms   470

What Is Monopolistic Competition?   470
Monopolistic Competition: The Short Run   474
Monopolistic Competition: The Long Run   476
Monopolistic Competition: Economic Consequences   477
Summing Up   479
Questions   480
Suggested Readings   480

Application 20 Is This as Close as We Can Get to Competition?   **481**

Monopolistic Competition: A Definition   481
Forms of Differentiation   481
    Location
    Quality of Service
Conclusions About Competition   482
Questions   483
Suggested Readings   483

21 Oligopoly: Much of the Real World   484

Definition of Oligopoly   484

Number of Firms: Small   485
Product: Both Homogeneous and Differentiated   486
Barriers to Entry: Substantial   486
Behavior of the Oligopolistic Firm   486
Kinked-Demand Oligopoly   487
Price Inflexibility in a Kinked-Demand Oligopoly   489
Collusive Oligopoly: If You Can't Lick 'em, Join 'em   491
    Covert Collusion
    Price Leadership
Nonprice Competition   494
    Styling
    Services
    Quality
    Advertising
Profit Maximization: Fact or Fancy?   499
Administered Prices   501
Oligopoly Evaluated   502
Countervailing Power   503
Summing Up   504
Questions   506
Suggested Readings   507

Application 21 Oligopoly Behavior: Some Cases   **508**
Patents, Brand Names, and the Drug Industry   508
The Predatory Use of Monopoly Power: The Bakery Industry   510
Covert Collusion: The Case of the Electrical-Equipment Manufacturers   512
Summing Up   513
Questions   514
Suggested Readings   514

Application 22 The Military-Industrial Complex: Myth or Reality?   **515**
Ten Propositions About the Military-Industrial Complex   515
The Military-Industrial Firm: Is It a Free-Enterprise Firm?   515
Growth: Is It Parasitic or Productive?   516
Some Conclusions   517
Questions   517
Suggested Readings   517

22 The Factor Markets: Not Only Products Are Sold   518
What Are Factor Markets?   518
Factors: Supply and Demand   519
What Determines the Demand for Factors?   520
An Example of Factor Demand   521
To Maximize Profit, Minimize Cost   524
Demand for a Resource by the Market as a Whole   524
Elasticity of Demand for a Resource   525
Income Distribution: Fair or Unfair?   526
Demand for Resources Among Monopolistic Firms   527
Summing Up   529
Questions   531

Suggested Readings   532

Application 23 How Much Education Should We Buy?   **533**
Summing Up   536
Questions   537
Suggested Readings   538

23 How Prices of Factors Are Set   539

Wages: Competitive Versus Noncompetitive   539
Why Not a Single Wage Rate?   542
  Different Skills and Different Supplies of Skills
  Different Wages and Same Skills
How Wages Are Set: Competitively Priced Labor   544
How Wages Are Set: Noncompetitively Priced Labor   546
  Monopsony
  Collective Bargaining
  The Government Steps In
Other Factors of Production   551
  Land and Its Rent
  Rents as Signals: Valid or Not?
  Capital and Interest Rates
  Government and the Capital Market
  Entrepreneurship and Profit
  Is Profit Earned?

Summing Up   558
Questions   561
Suggested Readings   562

Application 24 Wages, Incomes, and Economic Discrimination   **563**
What Is Economic Discrimination?   563
Understanding Discrimination   564
What Are the Consequences of Crowding?   564
Unequal Wages for Equal Jobs   564
A Note of Caution   566
What Can Be Done About Discrimination?   567
  Public Action
  Private Action
  Unions
  Creating Entrepreneurs
Summing Up   568
Questions   569
Suggested Readings   569

PART THREE   And Now the Rest of the World   571

24 Patterns of International Trade   572

What Is Trade?   572
How Important Is Trade?   573
Is Trade as Important to Us as to Others?   575

The Gains from Trade   576
Trade and Comparative Advantage   576
The Terms of Trade   578
What Determines Comparative Advantage?   579
Increasing Costs and Other Cautions   581
The Means of Protection   582
   Tariffs
   Quotas
Arguments in Favor of Protection   585
   The Infant-Industry Argument
   The National-Security Argument
   The Cheap-Foreign-Labor Argument
   The Macroeconomic-Employment Argument
Free Trade: A Reprise   588
Summing Up   588
Questions   591
Suggested Readings   592

Application 25 Does Trade Create Development?   593
The Relation Between Trade and Development   593
   The Classical View
   Reservations About the Classical View
The Implications for Trade Policies   595
Summing Up   597
Questions   597
Suggested Readings   598

25 Paying for International Trade   599
An Example of Money Exchange   599
A Good International Monetary System   600
Determining Equilibrium Exchange Rates   601
   Freely Floating Exchange Rates
   Fixed Exchange Rates
Adjusting Economies to Fluctuations in the Exchange Rate   605
The Gold Standard   607
Postwar International Exchange Arrangements   610
The Rambouillet Conference   611
The Balance of Payments   611
   The Balance-of-Payments Statement
   The Balance of Payments in Summary
The U.S. Balance-of-Payments Deficits   615
Summing Up   616
Questions   619
Suggested Readings   619

Application 26 Politics and the Balance-of-Payments Problem   620
Reasons Behind Import Restraints   620
Who Pays and Who Benefits?   621
The Big Push: The Burke-Hartke Bill   621

1975: How a Deficit Becomes a Surplus   622
What Happened to Protectionism?   622
The Lesson to Be Learned   622
Summing Up   622
Questions   623
Suggested Readings   623

26 Other Economic Systems in Theory   624

CAPITALISM   624
Economic Advantages Claimed for Capitalism   625
Economic Disadvantages of a Market System   626

SOCIALISM   627
Utopian Socialism   627
  Saint-Simon
  Fourier
  Robert Owen
  The Kibbutz Movement and A. D. Gordon
  B. F. Skinner
Communes of the 1960s and 1970s in the United States   630

MARXIST SOCIALISM   632
Dialectical Materialism   632
Class Conflict   633
Social Production and Surplus Value   634
Falling Profits and the Reserve Army of the Unemployed   635
Recurring Business Cycles   635
Marx's Gloomy Prediction: The Collapse of Capitalism   635
Why Haven't We Had a Revolution?   636
Leninism   636
Democratic Socialism   637

ANARCHISM   638
Summing Up   640
Questions   643
Suggested Readings   643

27 Economic Planning: The Soviet Union   644
Emergence of the Planned Economy   644
What to Produce: Central Planning   645
  Setting of Goals and Priorities
  The Planning Process
  Input, Output, and Planning
  Implementing the Plan
How to Produce: State Ownership   649
Who Receives Output: The Wage System   650
The Distribution of Real Income   651
Prices in the Soviet Union   652
Problems of Soviet Planning   653
Libermanism and Decentralized Decision Making   654

Soviet Economic Growth   655
   Basis of Russia's High Rate of Growth
   Russia's Declining Rate of Growth
Summing Up   658
Questions   660
Suggested Readings   661

Application 27 Mainland China: A Different Communism?   **661**
Differences Between the U.S.S.R. and the People's Republic of China   661
China's Progress Since the Revolution   662
Structure of China's Planned Economy   663
An Evaluation of China's Experiment   663
Questions   664
Suggested Readings   664

Application 28 Ideological Convergence: The New Melting Pot?   **664**
The United States and the U.S.S.R.: How Far Apart?   665
Technology: Pathway to Common Cause   665
A Note of Caution   666
Question   666
Suggested Readings   666

Glossary   667

Index   685

Preface

> An educated person is one who has finally discovered that there are some questions to which nobody has the answers.
>
> Anonymous

From our own observations as teachers and from recent developments in the field, two facts about the principles of economics course are apparent. First, enrollments are growing, and second, they are growing not just because students want to learn about economics, but also because they are *required* to take the course.

On the one hand, this boom gives those of us who teach economics a greater opportunity to expose students to our way of thinking, to economists' ideas on how to approach the understanding and solution of problems. On the other, it means that we have to provide students with some good reasons for learning about the subject, especially if we expect them to retain what they learn. It is our hope that this book will help students understand how economists think, and how applicable an economic perspective is to the problems of the real world. Furthermore, the basic questions facing our students, as political creatures in a democracy, are economic ones. This text should prepare them to understand policy debates in such areas as economic stabilization, the crisis of the cities, poverty, and agricultural policy. Obviously, an understanding of economics is also useful, if not necessary, for careers in such areas as business administration, sociology, psychology, history, and the administrative end of many types of engineering.

We have therefore tried to do two things. First, we have reduced the principles of economics in both volume and complexity to the point at which our students can grasp (and, we hope, *retain*) them. Second, we have applied the basic principles to problems that our students can recognize. We have tried to address particularly those students who are more concerned with a J.O.B. than a Ph.D. Many of the problems these students will face concern economics to some degree. And, although there are some questions in economics to which nobody knows the answers, there are even more for which there are *many* answers. Our students need to be able to analyze the alternatives, choose the most feasible one, and—perhaps most important—*know the basis on which the choice rests*.

Scope and Approach

In our experience, the greatest criticism of the principles of economics course is that we instructors try to do too much. Using the average textbook of 900-plus pages crammed with solid, valuable materials, an instructor naturally has to race in order to cover the ground. Furthermore, students tend to become swamped with the detail and diversity of the subject matter. They often become confused about what is most important. We have tried to avoid this situation.

Of necessity, we could not include in this text everything that our colleagues wanted us to—although we are grateful to them for their suggestions. We included those principles and problems that seemed most important *to us*, including what we did because both of us are teachers. In other words, we put in materials that work with our students. We have included the essential materials dealing with income determination, banking and money, government stabilization policy, supply and demand, the theory of the firm, and pricing of factors of production. In addition to this basic core, we have added materials on economic development, international trade, and other economic systems. We realize, however, that different instructors may wish to delve more deeply into an issue or expand on a problem in a particular chapter. Therefore, we have listed, at the end of chapters and applications, a number of additional sources.

We feel that this principles of economics text has several distinct advantages over many others in the field:

1. It is not an encyclopedia of economics but, rather, contains enough theory to equip the student with a *permanent* level of economic literacy.

2. Theoretical chapters are immediately followed by applications that use the economic principles just covered in analyzing practical economic problems.

3. The use of mathematics has been limited to the practical minimum by avoiding complex algebraic manipulations and difficult derivations of relationships, and by using, instead, simple two-dimensional diagrams to illustrate principles.

4. Every attempt has been made to communicate in the everyday language of the student rather than in the technical language of the economic journal.

5. Special attention has been given to chapter summaries, end-of-chapter materials, and the glossary in order to help the student review and to reinforce the concepts presented in each chapter.

Organization

This book is traditional in the sense that it contains an initial chapter on what economics is about, a section on macroeconomics (Part One), a section on microeconomics (Part Two), and finally, a section on the rest of the world which deals with international trade and comparative economic systems (Part Three). Some instructors prefer to begin with microeconomics and then proceed to macroeconomics. The book is so organized that this ordering of subject matter should present no problem (see our suggestions on page xxviii and in the Instructor's Manual). The detailed Glossary at the end of the book should also help overcome any problems of definition that result from taking this route. In any case, we recommend beginning with the introductory chapter, proceeding either to Part One or Part Two, and then finishing off with Part Three, which draws together the principles presented and sets them in perspective.

We have stated the principles in each chapter and followed them immediately with relevant applications. (Three of these applications—2, 8, and 18—are so long that they are practically minichapters themselves, but the subject matter in these cases demanded in-depth treatment.) There is a distinct separation of functions. The chapters are used to state and expand on basic theory. The applications are used to apply this theory to economic problems. We have tried very carefully to keep these two functions separate.

The Study Guide

To help students obtain some drill in economic problem solving and find out how well they are grasping the material, we have prepared a study guide: *Individual Explorations in Economics*. Each unit of this guide starts with a review of the chapter and its accompanying applications. It then moves on to a review of key terms, and essay questions and problems that are designed to make students rethink the material just learned. It ends with a self-test consisting of true/false, multiple-choice, and matching questions. After the self-test are all self-test answers and occasional problem answers.

We regard the study guide as an important supplement to *Explorations in Economics*. Since economics requires a lot of concentration and going over material again and again, we strongly advise that students arm themselves with this learning aid.

Acknowledgments

We benefited from the advice and assistance of many people in preparing *Explorations in Economics*. While it is not feasible to acknowledge our debt to each one, we do want to note some very special acknowledgments to those who made major contributions. Many economists, including our colleagues at San Jose State University, contributed either formal reviews or helpful suggestions about the book at various stages in its preparation. We are indebted to them all. Four economists—James V. Koch of Illinois State University, R. D. Peterson of

Colorado State University, Joseph M. Perry of the University of North Florida, and Joseph Domitrz of Western Illinois University—reviewed the entire manuscript. For their many useful suggestions, most of which are incorporated in the book, we are grateful. We accept responsibility, of course, for any errors that remain. Most of the typing and marshaling of resources to complete the manuscript was done by Virginia Ayres and Geri Brandt. For their excellent work and their cheerful willingness to help us meet deadlines, we are very grateful.

James. F. Willis
Martin L. Primack

Alternative Plans for Using the Text

One-term (semester or intensive quarter) course

Chapter 1	Breaking the Ice (plus Application 1)
Chapter 3	Supply and Demand (plus Application 3)
Chapter 4	Components of an Economic Society (plus Applications 4 and 5)
Chapter 5	Measuring Economic Activity (plus Application 6)
Chapter 7	Income and Employment: The Beginnings
Chapter 8	Income and Employment Without Government (plus Application 8)
Chapter 9	Completing the Model
Chapter 10	Automatic Stabilizers and the National Debt (plus Application 9)
Chapter 12	Commercial Banking and the Creation of Money
Chapter 13	The Fed Again: Monetary Policy and the Role of a Central Bank (plus Application 12)
Chapter 16	The Supply Side of the Market
Chapter 17	Private Versus Public Costs and Benefits (plus Application 17)
Chapter 18	Pure Competition (plus Application 18)
Chapter 19	Pure Monopoly
Chapter 20	Monopolistic Competition
Chapter 21	Oligopoly (plus Application 21)
Chapter 22	The Factor Markets
Chapter 23	How Prices of Factors Are Set (plus Application 24)
Part Three	And Now the Rest of the World (selections as desired)

Two-term course beginning with microeconomics

Chapter 1	Breaking the Ice (plus Application 1)
Chapter 2	Scarcity and Economic Development (plus Application 2)
Chapter 3	Supply and Demand (plus Application 3)
Chapter 4	Components of an Economic Society (plus Applications 4 and 5)
Part Two	Microeconomics (Chapters 15 through 23 plus applications)
Part One	Macroeconomics with Micro Foundations (Chapters 5 through 14 plus applications)
Part Three	And Now the Rest of the World (selections as desired)

Breaking the Ice

The Aims of the Economist

Economics has had a bad press ever since the nineteenth-century Scottish essayist Thomas Carlyle referred to it as "the dismal science." Carlyle had in mind the gloomy predictions about the future welfare of the human race that many economists were making at the time. This was about a hundred years ago, when economists were still being referred to as "political economists"—an apt name for them, calling to mind Lenin's remark that "political institutions are a superstructure resting on an economic foundation."

Economics has changed in the hundred years since Carlyle called it a dismal science. It has become more scientific and less dismal. The subjects that economists deal with—jobs, the distribution of income, the growth of industrial output, the prevention of inflation—have remained the same, but what *has* changed are the methods we use to investigate them, and the amounts and kinds of information we have. Our view of the future has also changed: most economists today are optimistic about the *ability* of people to solve problems.

Economists do differ greatly on *how* to solve particular economic problems. There are radical economists, like Paul Sweezy and John Gurley, who argue that the economic problems of the United States stem from the capitalist nature of its institutions—especially private ownership of the means of production. Some mainstream economists, like Robert Solow, feel that the radical critique is not based on sound scientific methods, which dictate traditional economic approaches. Still others feel that socialist economists fail to take into account human acquisitiveness and self-interest. They point to the failure of many socialist ventures, such as the Soviet Union's problems with agricultural production, and say that such failures would not happen if there were a freely operating market system and if Soviet economists were to take account of the human urge for private ownership of land.

These wide divergences of opinion prevent economists from reaching agreement—at least agreement on *how* to solve problems. Economists, nonetheless, do have a lot in common: concern for certain problems, for example. Also, certain tools and methodology, such as quantitative methods and model building, are widely accepted. Most economists accept a basic procedure for looking at aggregate economic problems, like unemployment, and at nonaggregate market problems as well. So in spite of differences about solutions to specific economic problems, economists often agree as to the *approach* to the analysis of problems. American economists, for instance, often voice the view that government action is necessary to achieve employment goals. However, there are great differences of opinion between one economist and another about *how* this government role should be fulfilled.

The fact that today's economists are, in the main, optimistic about the future may seem strange. After all, today the United States—and most of the rest of the world—is beset with problems of unemployment and inflation. However, we have come far during the last hundred years, if we consider the enormous increase in material well-being for much of the world's populace. The most famous economist of this century, John Maynard Keynes (rhymes with *gains*), writing in 1930 and looking ahead to the next hundred years, put it this way:

> I draw the conclusion that, assuming no important wars and no important increase in population, the *economic problem* may be solved, or at least be within sight of solution, within a hundred years. This means that the economic problem is not—if we look into the future—*the permanent problem of the human race.*

Keynes wrote this in the early years of the Great Depression of the 1930s. He was wrong, of course, in assuming that there would be no major wars after 1930, but his assumption about no major increase in population may turn out to be correct, at least for the more developed industrial countries. Keynes's statement illustrates two things: (1) economists of the twentieth century are no longer dismal about the future, and (2) economists develop economic principles not for the sake of abstract exercise, but to be able to analyze and propose solutions to problems that plague the human race. Economists are, in short, deeply concerned with *people*.

What Is Economics?

Now let's define economics in terms of the "economic problem" to which Keynes referred.

Economics is the social science that deals with the analysis of material problems. It identifies the various means by which people can satisfy their desires for goods and services by using the limited re-

Economics is concerned with using theory to find solutions to worldwide problems. (J. P. Laffont/Sygma)

sources available to produce them. This is a very general definition, but a useful one, because it points out certain basic features of economics.

1. *Economics is a social science.* It deals with the actions of groups of people in relation to society. Economics differs from physical science, which has laws established in the laboratory, where conditions can be controlled. The laboratory of economists is the world, in which nothing is certain and nothing can be controlled with any surety. Economists base their principles on what they observe about people—their willingness to spend money or to save it, for example—and on what they observe about the economic institutions that people have created, such as private property, government planning, and the banking system.

2. *Economics is analytical.* Economists use the principles of economics to diagnose various problems, such as unemployment and poverty, and propose solutions to them. Instead of choosing one solution and saying, "Here's what to do," economists set forth the available alternative solutions to a given problem and point out the costs and benefits of each.

3. *Economics is concerned with the material well-being of people.* Economists study figures on what is produced and consumed now and try to

project figures for the future. This does not mean that they feel it is *only* material well-being that counts, but they do insist that it takes the use of limited material resources (land, labor, capital) to solve nearly all social problems. Solving economic problems is closely tied to efforts to solve other kinds of problems.

What Is the Economist's Method?

Even though economics is a social science, its method is scientific and based on facts and logic. An economist's starting point, like a chemist's or physicist's, is a hypothesis, or a statement about a relationship between two things (or ten or twenty things). At this point, however, the economist steps outside the safety of the laboratory into the unpredictable realm of people. We can best demonstrate the three stages of the economist's job with an example.

Suppose that you are a young economist, a consultant to the President's Council of Economic Advisers, and are called to a meeting of the council. Everyone looks grave. The chairman explains that the country's economy is showing some alarming tendencies. Personal incomes in the last year have risen, but for some reason, consumer spending has fallen. People just aren't buying, and business is beginning to hurt. The President is deeply concerned, and so is Congress. You are to find out what has happened and tell the government what to do about it.

Now you begin on stage 1 of the economist's three-stage process (see Figure 1-1). First you gather all the data you can that might explain what has happened. Exactly how much did incomes grow in this past year? Did spending on consumer goods change in any way, and if so, how? How do the figures for this past three-month period compare with the figures for the same quarter a year ago? Has there been a change in the relationship between income and spending? What have people been doing with all the money they haven't been spending? Have they been saving it? Have they been using it to pay taxes?

FIGURE 1-1 The Three Basic Stages in Economic Analysis

Stage 1	Stage 2	Stage 3
Gathering facts	*Formulating and testing theory*	*Making economic policy*
The economist gathers data that are relevant to the hypothesis or statement (this is called *descriptive economics*).	On the basis of the data, the economist sets forth a general theory about economic behavior and tests the theory (this is the *theorizing* stage).	The policy maker, who is not necessarily the same person as the economist, formulates measures to deal with economic behavior and its consequences (this is the *policy-making* stage).

After you have finished this fact-finding or *descriptive* stage, you embark on stage 2, the *theorizing* stage. You try to formulate a theory that will explain the way behavior changes as income changes. You want to express not only what is happening now, but also what is likely to happen a year from now, two years, or five years from now, given certain incomes, populations, and supplies and prices of goods. The theory you evolve may be a simple one (people have lost faith in material things and are giving all their money to churches), or very complex (people are afraid of inflation and at the same time distrustful of anything modern, so they are putting all their money in gold, Renaissance paintings, and pre-1914 Rolls Royces). In any event, you spend days writing up your version of the situation, using all the facts at your command and expressing your opinion in the clearest manner possible.

On the basis of the data you have collected, you form the hypothesis that short-term changes in consumer spending depend not only on changes in income but also on changes in other factors such as taxes and expectations about the future. You can use various statistical techniques—the most common is called *regression analysis*—to isolate the effect of one factor (short-term income changes) on another (consumer spending).

When you are setting up these theoretical interrelationships, you construct a **model,** a systematic analogy to real consumer behavior. This model enables you to interpret the statistical results.

Suppose you find that there is a weak (perhaps nearly zero) correlation, during any six-month period, between changes in people's incomes and changes in their spending habits. In other words, even if their incomes go up, their spending changes little, or perhaps not at all. Then you must explain the decline in consumer spending in terms of changes in other factors.

Your model may include the expectations people have about future changes in prices and in taxes (income taxes, excise taxes). Suppose your data show that taxes (and other important factors that might offer some explanation) have not changed in the past six months. Then you conclude that the decline in spending must be due to *expectations* about the future. People are putting off buying things until later in the year. They're waiting for inventory-reduction sales, for the crops to come in, for an expected drop in the interest rate. For many reasons, they're just holding onto their money and waiting. You incorporate all these ideas in your report to the chairman of the President's Council of Economic Advisers.

The third stage is the *policy-making* stage. This stage is out of your hands, because the people who decide on the economic policy act on their own, although they base their decisions on the economists' recommendations. The policy maker may be Congress, or the President, or the President and the Cabinet acting together. But bear in mind that a nation's economic policy is part of its overall social policy (including diplomatic, military, and political policies). Your role as an economist has been only to identify to the policy makers the nature of the problem, tell them how serious it is, and point out alternative solutions, with the costs and benefits of each.

(For a fascinating view of how economists may try to sway the President or may even dictate policy decisions, read *Economics on a New Frontier*, by E. Ray Canterbery, published by Wadsworth in 1968 as a paperback. This book describes the economic transformation of Presidents Kennedy and Johnson.)

The Citizen and Economic Policy

The above example is fairly simple and clear-cut. The policy maker here may decide on the basis of reports prepared by you and others that no change in economic policy is required. It appears in this case that consumer spending is going to rise in the long term, as prices fall and as people adjust to their higher incomes.

From this illustration, you might conclude that economic investigation and policy making are processes reserved for experts in politics and economics. This is not so. Whether the issue is local or federal taxes, or local or national economic policies, the United States needs an enlightened public. The *non*economist, *non*politician, just plain citizen can review, criticize, and in the long run even change economic policy. People can do this by discussion and by the way they vote.

We write this book with the conviction that (1) the economic principles a person needs to know to make intelligent decisions on economic issues are simple, and that (2) such positions should be founded in fact and logic.

Applications: Concrete Examples of Abstract Ideas

Much of economics consists of abstractions, theories, and discussions of curves and trends. But, as we pointed out at the beginning of this chapter, it isn't all just theories; you already know a lot about economics. So we have tried to use the knowledge you already have to illustrate the theoretical part of economics. You will find sections called "applications" scattered throughout this book. They show you the practical application of the theory or principle that has just been explained. For example, after the chapter that introduces the theory of supply and demand, there is an application that discusses a concrete example of supply and demand: the price of gasoline. These applications can serve as beacons to help you fix your position in unfamiliar surroundings as you explore the economic way of thinking.

End-of-Chapter Summaries

At the end of each chapter, you'll find a section entitled "Summing Up." (Some applications carry these postscript sections too.) These sections repeat, in condensed form, what the chapter or application is about. Even if you feel you understand the chapter as you read it, read "Summing Up" carefully. The repetition will help to imprint the material in your mind.

Mathematics De-emphasized

One reason why economics has a reputation for being a tough subject is that many people are afraid of mathematics, and they associate economics with it. However, as you work your way through this book, you will realize that it contains very little mathematics. When economists write articles in professional journals, they may use very advanced mathematics, but you do not need to know advanced mathematics to learn the basic principles of economics.

This book does contain a number of graphs and tables of data. The data serve to ensure that we are using facts as the basis for our discussions, and the graphs are simply devices to help you visualize abstract ideas. Figure 1-2 is an example of a graph.

Nearly all the graphs we use are two-dimensional. That is, they measure the relationships between two factors. They have *height* (measured along the vertical axis) and *length* (measured along the horizontal axis). The picture of the first factor to change (called the **independent variable**) comes from the vertical axis. The picture of the factor whose change depends on the first factor (the **dependent variable**) comes from the horizontal axis.

As we go along, we will use graphs to chart the progress of a number of dependent and independent variables: prices of goods, quantities sold, demand for goods and services, jobs, wages, and so forth. In each case, the rule about reading graphs will remain the same.

Now look at Figure 1-2, on the next page, and we'll discuss some of the kinds of relationships that may occur between dependent and independent variables. The lines drawn on this diagram are called *curves*, even though in this case they are straight lines.

1. Curve *A* is a case in which the relationship between independent and dependent variable is *inverse*. This means that as the independent variable increases (moves up the vertical axis), the dependent variable decreases (moves toward zero). As the independent variable decreases, the dependent variable increases. We say that curve *A* is *negatively sloped*, or that it *slopes downward*.

2. Curve *B* is a case in which the independent variable doesn't change at all. All change occurs in the dependent variable. The dependent variable responds almost without limit at the given value of the independent variable.

3. Curve *C* is a case in which the relationship between independent and dependent variable is *direct*. As the independent variable increases, so does the dependent one. As the independent variable decreases, so does

FIGURE 1-2 An Illustration of Graphing

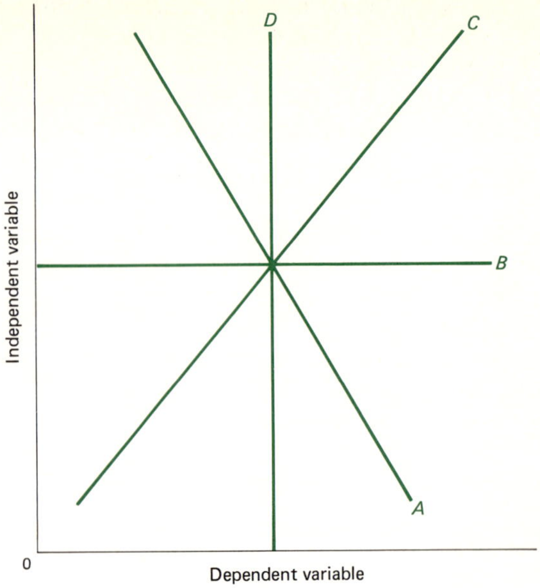

the dependent one. We say that curve C is *positively sloped,* or that it *slopes upward.*

4. Curve D is a case in which the dependent variable doesn't change at all. All change in D takes place in the *in*dependent variable. The independent variable responds almost without limit at the given value of the dependent variable.

If you keep these four cases in mind, you won't be confused by the graphs in this book. Indeed, the graphs will help you to visualize and understand relationships that might otherwise be hard to grasp.

Positive Versus Normative Economics

A person starting out in a first course in principles of physics or chemistry usually does so with no preconceived notions. Since we don't feel at home talking about subnuclear particles, we're willing to leave that subject to the physicists and take anything they say as the truth. However, most people approach economics with a considerable amount of built-in expertise. We have biases about economics, as we do about any social science. We cannot avoid having them, since from an early age we have all had considerable experience with economics. We get jobs, spend income, pay taxes, and watch the government spend.

But we should not simply leave economic issues to the economists and the politicians. Citizens who are *not* economists, who are *not* politicians, are the ones who must in the long run make choices, through voting or in other ways. Citizens must choose among alternative solutions to economic problems, and they often have to approve or turn down choices that have already been made by some governing body. To be a good citizen, to make intelligent choices on voting day, one needs an understanding of economic principles, backed up by a knowledge of how those principles work out in actual application.

When you come to the point of choosing among alternative solutions, you enter the area of **normative economics**, or making judgments about what *should* be.

Positive economics, on the other hand, consists of determining what *is*. It involves stating facts. We have pointed out that when you gather facts and apply economic principles in an attempt to find a solution to a problem, you do not find just one answer, one unique "right" way; you find that there are several alternative solutions. Normative economics involves looking at these various solutions and applying personal or collective value judgments, to decide what *should* be. (Generalizing about economic behavior naturally has some normative aspects. Therefore, in writing a book about economics, we cannot avoid a few judgments here and there. We have tried to keep them to a minimum. When they do appear, we try to point them out and you're free to agree or disagree.)

To be sure that you understand the difference between positive and normative statements, let's take an example. You go to a party and find an economist who is talking about food stamps and their economic impact. The following conversation takes place.

Economist: The United States spent $4 billion in 1974 on the food stamp program. *(Positive)*

You: But a lot of people are still going hungry because they have to present the food stamps at stores in person, and many elderly or disabled people are too feeble to go to the store. It isn't fair. *(Normative)*

Economist: A family of four with an income of $6,000 a year or less can qualify for $150 a month in stamps. *(Positive)*

You: A family of four can't *live* on $6,000 a year—not what *I'd* call living. *(Normative)*

See how hard it is to keep from being normative? *(Normative)*

A Word About Words

Economists sometimes speak what seems to be a language all their own. In fact, someone once defined an economist as a person who states the obvious in terms of the incomprehensible. When economists speak of contrived versus natural scarcities, implicit factor returns, and maximum-profit monopoly equilibrium, you sometimes wonder if they're really speaking English. Throughout this book, we have tried to avoid speaking "economese," or what William F. Buckley calls "econospeak." However, we could not weed out *all* the economese, because economics is a complex subject, full of difficult language. When we introduce a term, we put it in italics and define it. Boldface color means that you can find the word in the Glossary at the back of the book. As you go along, whenever you are not certain of the meaning of something, don't look back through the book for the definition. Just turn to the Glossary and look it up. Definitions are important in economics, because often a word means one thing in everyday usage and another in the language of economists. This book is designed to teach you economics, in the clearest and most painless way possible.

SUMMING UP

1. Economics has acquired the reputation of being extremely difficult, abstract, and mathematical. This book attempts to make the difficult understandable, to give concrete examples to demonstrate the abstractions, and to de-emphasize the mathematics so that people without an extensive mathematics background can readily grasp the ideas.

2. In the nineteenth century, people referred to economists as "political economists." They also called economics "the dismal science," because of the pessimistic views of the future many economists held. We have come a long way in the past hundred years. Technology and economic organization have caused many modern economists to have an optimistic view of the ability of people to improve their material well-being.

3. Economists differ greatly among themselves about how to *solve* economic problems, but less about how to *study* them. They disagree about both the sources of the problems and which solutions are the right ones to adopt. For example, radical and orthodox economists have fundamental differences in their ideology and philosophy, but their methods of analyzing problems are relatively similar.

4. *Economics* may be defined as the social science that deals with the analysis of material problems. Economists perform their functions by identifying alternative means through which people can provide for their material well-being.

5. Economics differs from physical science, in that physical science proves its principles by means of controlled experiments. The laws of economics are derived from observations of human behavior. As behavior changes, so must economists' rules.

6. When economists identify the alternative solutions to economic problems, they also point out the costs and benefits of each.

7. Economists are not necessarily more materialistic than other people. They do, however, insist that solutions to noneconomic questions require material resources (land, labor, capital). Thus these solutions are based in economics.

8. An economist's work is in three stages: (a) gathering facts, (b) theorizing and testing theory, and (c) making economic policy.

9. Gathering of facts is necessary to ensure that concrete information (not hearsay or superstition) is the basis for economic investigation and decisions. Theorizing is necessary to enable the economist to construct a systematic analogy to real life (a *model*), since reality itself is too complex to be described fully. Policy making is often out of the economist's hands.

10. This book is written with the following convictions: (a) people need to know economic principles in order to understand economic issues and these principles *can* be stated in a clear, understandable way; and (b) discussions about economic issues should be founded in logic and fact.

11. This book contains very little mathematics. However, it does use many graphs to help you visualize certain concepts. In a graph, the vertical line represents the *independent variable*. The horizontal line represents the *dependent variable* (it depends on the independent one).

12. Lines (called *curves*) come in four varieties: (a) the relationship between the dependent and the independent variable is inverse; (b) the independent variable does not change and only the dependent one changes; (c) the relationship between the dependent and the independent variable is direct; and (d) the independent variable changes, but the dependent variable does not.

13. In *normative economics*, value judgments form the basis for choosing solutions to economic problems. Normative economics states what *should be*. *Positive economics* states what *is;* no value judgments are made. This book tries to avoid making normative statements. When they do occur, we have identified them, and the reader is free to agree or disagree.

14. The book makes a strong effort to avoid the use of "economese," or complex ways of wording economic principles. When more technical terms first occur, they are defined at once, and they are defined again in the Glossary at the end of the book.

QUESTIONS

1. Suppose that a nation considers fighting a war on crime in the streets. Is this an economic question? If so, in what ways?

2. Is it possible to solve noneconomic problems without answering economic questions? Why?

3. Consider the following statements and decide whether each is normative or positive.
    a. There are too many unemployed in the United States today.
    b. Unemployment among black teen-agers in the United States is 30 percent.

    c. A federally guaranteed annual income is a good idea.
    d. Federally guaranteed annual incomes involve a transfer of income from one group to another.
    e. The distribution of wealth in the United States is not equal.
    f. The distribution of wealth in the United States should be equal.

4. Why is it that economists cannot conduct their experiments in controlled laboratory surroundings the way physical scientists do?

5. Do you think Keynes was right in believing it possible to solve the economic problem? Why?

6. What is an economic model? Why do economists construct models rather than just trying to describe reality?

7. Why do economists differ so much on solutions to economic problems when they differ relatively little on the way to analyze these problems?

8. Suppose that you are the personal assistant to the President of the United States on economic matters. The President calls you in and says, "For my main campaign plank this year, I am going to promise to solve the nation's economic problems. I want your advice, though, on whether this is a realistic promise." What advice would you offer?

SUGGESTED READINGS

Canterbery, E. Ray. *Economics on a New Frontier*, Wadsworth, Belmont, Calif., 1968.

Friedman, Milton. *Essays in Positive Economics*. University of Chicago Press, Chicago, 1953.

Galbraith, John Kenneth. "Power and the Useful Economist." *American Economic Review*, March 1973.

Heilbroner, Robert L. "On the Limited Relevance of Economics." *The Public Interest*, Fall 1970.

Keynes, John Maynard. "Economic Possibilities for our Grandchildren." In *Essays in Persuasion*. Norton, New York, 1963.

Schultze, Charles. "Is Economics Obsolete? No, Underemployed." *Saturday Review*, January 22, 1972.

Solow, Robert M. "Science and Ideology in Economics." *The Public Interest*, Fall 1970.

Sweezy, Paul M. "Toward a Critique of Economics." *Monthly Review*, January 1970.

Application 1

Self-interest: Endangered Motivation?

> The public is merely a multiplied "me."
> — Mark Twain

> There is only one class in the community that thinks more about money than the rich, and that is the poor. The poor can think of nothing else.
> — Oscar Wilde

These quotations illustrate two points: (1) what happens to the economy as a whole depends on the economic actions of individuals, and (2) economic forces vitally affect and concern each of us. Economists and noneconomists alike have long sought to understand the basic motivations that determine how we play our roles as consumers, producers, or planners on the economic stage. In this application we are going to examine some views on this subject.

Self-interest: Key to All Characters

One of the first people to theorize about economic motivation was Adam Smith, author of *The Wealth of Nations* (1776), who is often considered the founder of modern economics. Smith contended that people were not moved primarily by love of their fellow humans; they ordinarily acted in their own self-interest. Smith said, "It is not from the benevolence of the butcher, the brewer, or the baker that we expect our dinner, but from their regard to their own interest." He said that he never knew business people to get together in the social interest. Rather, they sought some "nefarious purpose."

If Adam Smith were alive today and could see laborers banding together to form unions, co-ops, and consumer-protection societies, he would probably attribute the same motives to these groups. Such ventures, he'd probably say, would result in conspiracies against the public interest. This view of human nature led Smith to argue that the economic role government should perform is to create conditions under which the individual's pursuit of self-interest results in maximizing the public welfare. But Smith did not make clear what *kind*

"I wish all I had to worry about was the world—not taxes, mortgages, rising prices, the cost of college..."

of political system would do this. What would prevent public officials from acting in their own interest rather than in the public's? This problem, as we shall see, comes up again and again. See, for example, Application 22, which deals with the so-called military-industrial complex.

Samuel Butler wrote in his notebooks: "The world will always be governed by self-interest. We should not try to stop this; we should try to make the self-interest of cads a little more coincident with that of decent people."

And Dostoyevsky, describing the vicious Fyodor in *The Brothers Karamazov*, summed up the essence of the self-interested person: "He was one of those senseless persons who are very well capable of looking after their worldly affairs, and, apparently, after nothing else."

The economic citizen in action (James Nachtwey)

14   Application 1

Homo economicus

After Adam Smith, other philosophers continued to name self-interest as the dominant force moving people. Jeremy Bentham (father of the **hedonist**, or self-satisfaction, school) carried this idea to new heights in his concept of *Homo economicus*, or economic man, who was not only motivated by self-interest, but was literally a walking calculator of pain and pleasure. *Homo economicus* measured every action in terms of the amount of the self-satisfaction that could be derived from it, precisely maximizing personal pleasure or minimizing pain.

Private Citizens Want Private Profits

Economists today no longer hold such an extreme hedonist view. They no longer believe that people either can, or always try to, maximize their pleasure or minimize their pain with precision. However, they do still believe that all people are motivated by self-interest. Alfred Marshall, considered by many to be the originator of modern economic methods, put it this way in his path-breaking book *Principles of Economics:*

> The steadiest motive to ordinary business work is the desire for the pay which is the material reward of work. The pay may be on its way to be spent selfishly or unselfishly, for noble or base ends; and here the variety of human nature comes into play. But the motive is supplied by a definite amount of money; and it is this definite and exact money measurement of the steadiest motives in business life, which has enabled economics far to outrun every other branch of the study of man.

In other words, Marshall, although admitting to a higher nature in humans, still argued that people's basic economic nature is one of self-interest, the desire for monetary gain. Chapter 1 quoted Keynes as saying that he foresaw an end to the economic problem. But Keynes, too, felt that an appeal to the acquisitive motives of people would be necessary, at least into the twenty-first century, in order to get them to save, invest, and assure economic growth.

Do Corporations Value Profits Above All Else?

Most orthodox economists today still accept the concept of the "economic citizen," especially as it relates to the decisions of business people. Some of them have attacked the idea that business firms seek to maximize profits. However, Robert Solow has defended it in these words:

> Does the modern industrial corporation maximize profits? Probably not rigorously and single-mindedly, and for much the same reason that Dr. Johnson did not become a philosopher—because cheerfulness keeps breaking in. Most large corporations are free enough from competitive pressure to offer a donation to the Community Chest or a fancy office building without a close calculation of its incremental contribution to profit. The received doctrine can survive if businesses merely *almost* maximize profits.

Solow also feels that consumers are more likely "almost" to maximize satisfaction than "almost" to do anything else and argues that the idea of firms maximizing profits comes closer to explaining and predicting their behavior than any other assumption. His beliefs probably represent the position of most American economists.

The Economic Citizen: Voices of Dissent

Several economists, however, have attacked the idea of *Homo economicus*. John Kenneth Galbraith, for one, in his books *The New Industrial State* and *Economics and the Public Purpose* says that the view is outmoded. He feels the power of individuals has been eroded by a corporate system in which "technocrats" in big corporations control the system. These technocrats seek to maximize a larger set of *corporate* (not stockholder) interests (growth, security, their own salaries, and so on). Galbraith maintains that, through advertising, technocrats cause consumers to want what they (the technocrats) *wish* them to want.

One example of the technocrats at work is the advertising campaign by television manufacturers in the late fifties. The campaign was designed to sell televisions to those people—and there were many of them—who had been resisting buying a TV set, on grounds that they did not want their children to watch it. They apparently wanted them, instead, to play outdoors, read books, study, and talk to the family. In addition, many people deplored the preponderance of commercials and prepackaged entertainment, which they feared would stifle their children's creativity.

So the television industry initiated an advertising campaign to change people's tastes. The makers of TV sets ran full-page ads in newspapers throughout the nation, showing two miserable-looking children in a corner, who seemed close to tears. The caption was, "But gee, Dad, all the other kids have one," followed by a hard-sell paragraph addressed to the parents, beginning with the words, "If you *really* loved them, you'd buy a television set...." There were cries of outrage, angry letters to the editor, and disgusted comments on editorial pages from coast to coast. (Within a week, the ad campaign was canceled.)

Galbraith believes that government should use controls and planning to replace much of this (distorted) profit-maximizing behavior of the markets. But if this came about, public bureaucrats might replace market technocrats. One can imagine government agencies imposing their own ideas on what was socially correct on private decision makers. Galbraith's plan, in other words, would transfer the locus of *Homo economicus* to public agencies.

A second attack on economic self-interest has come from radical economists, who say that, in an industrial or capitalist society, *Homo economicus* is at best an endangered species and at worst a myth. Marxist theory holds that the concentration of power and ownership in private hands (which exists in a capitalist society) leads to alienation of workers and deprives consumers of their right to consume as they wish. It also deprives producers of their right to produce as they wish, because, according to the Marxists, it means that fewer and fewer people make decisions about production. Some radicals have argued for the creation of *Homo communista*, communist man, in place of *Homo economicus*. John Gurley, in an essay entitled "Maoist Economic Development," puts it this way:

> The Maoists' disagreement with the capitalist view of economic development is profound.... The profit motive is officially discouraged from assuming an important role in the allocation of resources, and material incentives, while still prevalent, are downgraded.... Development is not likely to occur unless everyone rises together.... Selflessness and unity of purpose will release a huge reservoir of enthusiasm, energy and creativity. Maoists believe that each person should be devoted to "the masses" rather than to his own pots and pans.

Which is the dominant feature of reality? Economic self-interest or community concern? If both exist now, will both survive? Or should one or the other be on the endangered-species list? For answers to these questions, we may have to wait until at least the twenty-first century, for only the future will tell the story.

SUMMING UP

1. Adam Smith, considered by many the founder of economics, thought that self-interest and acquisitiveness were the primary economic motivations of people. Smith thought that the appropriate economic role of government would be to provide a system within which individual self-interest could be harnessed to accomplish the public good.

2. The *hedonists* (Benthamites), or self-satisfiers, thought that people were walking calculators who measured every act in terms of the pain or pleasure it would bring. Benthamites thought that people would always precisely maximize the amount of pleasure they could achieve. This view is now discredited.

3. Modern economists, beginning with Alfred Marshall, assume that people are motivated in their economic actions primarily by a desire for money and a desire to achieve maximum satisfaction. They are not able, however, to measure satisfaction or pain precisely, even though they can measure profit.

4. Although Keynes thought that the economic problem was on its way to being solved, he too believed that until this solution is reached, we must rely on the economic citizen's primary desire; that is, the desire for money.

5. Most orthodox economists (such as Robert

Solow) regard the idea of the economic citizen (the profit- and satisfaction-maximizing person) as the best long-term view of human behavior, and believe that this view explains people's economic actions more accurately than any other assumption.

6. John Kenneth Galbraith says "technocrats" (who hold the power in large corporations) maximize corporate interests and manipulate the tastes of consumers through advertising. He feels that the technocrats have replaced the old competitive economic citizen. Galbraith proposes a system of public controls and planning to replace these distorted (noncompetitive) market forces.

7. Some radicals, especially Maoists, argue that *Homo communista* is evolving in China and may replace *Homo economicus* in future societies.

QUESTIONS

1. Whether self-interest basically motivates people is a question of human behavior. Why can't we simply observe human behavior to answer the question easily?

2. What is wrong with the hedonistic view of an individual as a walking calculator of pain and pleasure?

3. If people don't exactly maximize their satisfaction or their profit, how can assumptions that they do lead to a satisfactory basis for explaining and predicting economic events?

4. Was Keynes right in saying that, until the economic problem is solved, we need to rely on the acquisitiveness of people? Why?

5. Which do you think is more likely to be the economic motivation of the future: self-interest or community interest? Why?

SUGGESTED READINGS

Burck, Gilbert. "The Myths and Realities of Corporate Pricing." *Fortune*, April 1972.

"Can Capitalism Survive?" *Time*, July 14, 1975.

Easterlin, Richard. "Does Money Buy Happiness?" *The Public Interest*, Winter 1973.

Galbraith, John K. "A Reply to Critics." In *Economics, Mainstream Readings and Radical Critiques*, 2nd ed. Edited by David Mermelstein. Random House, New York, 1973.

Gurley, John G. "Maoist Economic Development." In *Economics, Mainstream Readings and Radical Critiques*, 2nd ed. Edited by David Mermelstein. Random House, New York, 1973.

Marshall, Alfred. *Principles of Economics*. Macmillan, London, 1948.

Smith, Adam. *An Enquiry into the Nature and Causes of the Wealth of Nations*. Modern Library, New York, 1937.

Solow, Robert. "Science and Ideology in Economics." *The Public Interest*, Fall 1970.

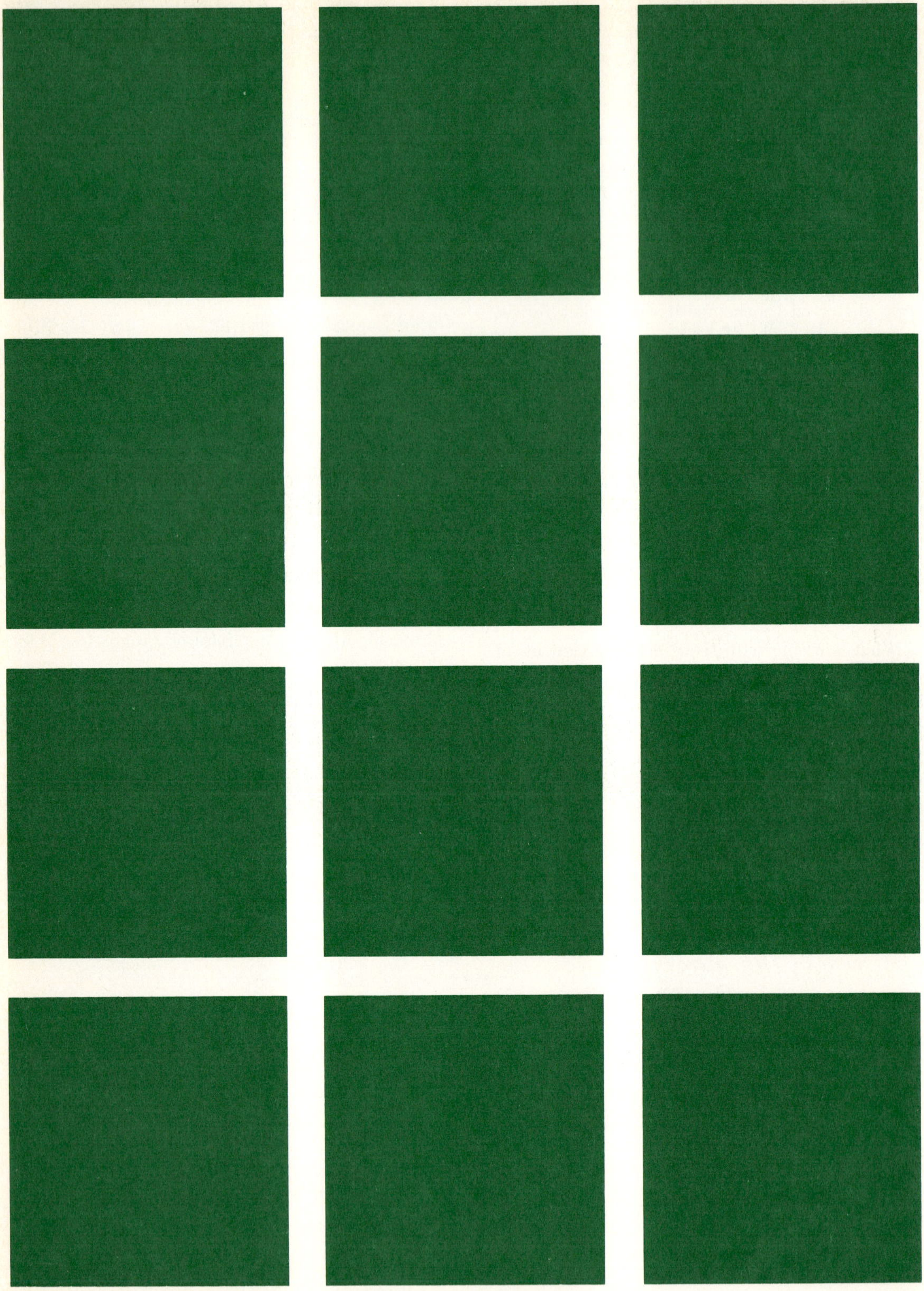

PART ONE

Macroeconomics with Micro Foundations

Part One deals with macroeconomics, or the study of the forces that determine the level of income and employment in a society. Macroeconomics gives us the big picture of a society, or what economists call its aggregate performance. We will focus on the origins of economic scarcity, the problems of economic development, and how households and business firms make economic decisions. We will use economic principles to analyze the problems of rich and poor nations. Starting with a simple model, we will gradually add the components that make up our complex economic world: government spending, gross national product, business cycles, the level of employment, the level of income, the money supply, banking, and expansion and growth.

2

Scarcity and Economic Development

In Chapter 1 we defined economics, related it to other subject areas, and talked about its methods of investigation. Now let us look at the overall operation of an economic system. At the outset, let us assume that the economy we are discussing is basically a free, private-enterprise economy and that it is capitalist in organization. This means that most of the means of production—land, labor, capital, and entrepreneurship—are allocated as a result of many private decisions made by buyers and sellers in that economy's marketplaces.

Before moving on to look at this allocative process, let us define the term *market system*. All of us have had experience with markets. We tend to think of them as places such as stores or auction houses in which commodities are sold or exchanged. Although these places are markets, a market need not have a specific physical location. In fact, a market exists whenever buyers and sellers have means to make exchanges. Thus a **market system** is the set of means by which buyer-seller exchanges are made. For example, today we can all make exchanges as readily by telephone as by going to an auction house. Whatever form they may take, market transactions provide answers to vital economic questions in the capitalist society.

Scarcity: Source of Basic Economic Questions

Why do people need to find answers to economic questions? For that matter, why do economic questions arise at all? To understand this, consider two important facts:

1. At any given time, the resources available to a society are limited. There is only so much oil, gold, timber, or wheat, just so much capital, just so much labor. **Resources**—the inputs we use to make consumer and producer goods—are limited.

2. People—individuals, families, or larger groups—have needs, wants, and desires which have to be satisfied, as much as they can be, by the goods and services produced by employing the society's limited resources. However, wants and desires—unlike resources—appear to be virtually unlimited. History and psychology show us that they may never be satisfied, since satisfaction of some wants only seems to lead people to acquire new wants.

As we move along, we shall look at each of these considerations in greater detail. For now, let's stress the fact that resources are *limited*, human wants are *unlimited*, and this means that our society, and every other society, no matter how rich or how poor, has to face the problem of **scarcity**, the inability to satisfy all people's wants for goods and services. We can best see why this is so by considering the hypothetical case of a country without scarcities.

An Unreal World: No Scarcity
If there were no scarcity, there would be no need for social organizations (government welfare departments, the Red Cross, and so forth) to allocate resources among competing potential users. But of course there always is scarcity, so assuming a world of nonscarcity would not be a satisfactory basis on which to learn about economic reality. If there were no scarcity, all wants could be satisfied. You and I would be able to choose among a vast number of **free goods** to satisfy ourselves. Free goods would exist in unlimited supply, and thus command no price. Air—under most conditions—is an example of a free good. We certainly would not buy anything that existed in unlimited quantities. If beef, for example, were available in unlimited quantities, we would not pay today's prices for it. Indeed, we would not pay for it at all, since our nation would be giving up nothing to produce enough beef to satisfy our wants. Buyers and sellers of beef would not have to organize a market system. And if there were unlimited supplies of labor, no one would pay a wage for labor. Indeed, labor, in the traditional sense of the word, would be a free good too.

Back to the Real World: Basic Questions
But in the real world that we all know there *is* scarcity, and social organizations are needed everywhere to allocate a society's limited resources. In the United States, a system of markets, established over several centuries, is mainly responsible for arbitrating the problem of resource allocation.

Consider the vast array of goods and services to be produced in the United States this year. Will there be nine or ten million automobiles? How many black-and-white and how many color television sets? Will automobile production be even more automated this year than last? Who will "consume" the automobiles and television sets? These are the kinds of questions each resource-using society must ask. The basic questions are:

1. *What* shall be produced? Out of all the combinations of goods that

present technology makes possible, what combinations of cars, television sets, vacations, medical services, and so on, shall we choose?

2. *How* shall the goods be produced? There are many questions contained within this big question, which encompasses not only the technology of production, but also the *system* by which production is organized. Will markets be privately or publicly controlled? Will there be competition? How much consolidation of producers will there be? (That is, large firms that produce a certain good, as opposed to small, mom-and-pop producer units.)

3. *For whom* shall output be produced? In other words, who is going to have the satisfaction of consuming the goods? This is the basic *distributive* question. Will the income of the society be distributed equally, or will there be a few who are rich and a majority who are poor? Or will there be some other distribution?

Are the solutions to these questions interdependent? Clearly they are. The technology and organizational structure of a society heavily influence who will receive satisfaction as consumers. When a society's industry tends toward monopolistic firms, the markets that result are likely to create a more unequal distribution of income. Why this is so will become clear later.

Is Scarcity Meaningful Today?

In many of the applications, we'll talk about debates in the United States that involve scarcity and its effects on choice making. As we will see, in many ways the debates have centered on differences in definitions and ideologies. In spite of these differences of opinion, it is clear that, in the sense of unlimited wants pursuing limited resources, scarcity exists even for supposedly well-off Americans, and that even this affluent society must make choices about how to use its limited resources.

Viewing the Choices:
The Production-Possibilities Curve

At this point a numerical example will help. Suppose that a hypothetical society, Ruritania, must economize, that is, choose between producing two goods: beef and all-purpose machines. (These all-purpose machines produce television programs, build roads, churn ice cream, dry wet hair, dig wells, light buildings, type letters, sew shoe uppers to soles, and drive people to work.) Obviously this is a great simplification of choice making. In the real world, two things are obvious: (1) choices are in *many* dimensions, with thousands of alternatives among which to choose, and (2) choices change almost continuously as technology changes. But in order to simplify the description of the process and make it easier to visualize what we mean by choices, we chose just two commodities. Let these two represent, in microcosm, the more complex process of choice making in the real world.

Scarcity in the real world: For whom shall output be produced? (George Malave/Stock, Boston)

One way to visualize Ruritania's choices is to look at the **production-possibilities curve**, a useful device, derived from the **production-possibilities function**, which is defined as follows:

The production-possibilities function *shows those combinations of goods that the full-employment use of a society's resources can produce during a particular period of time (using the best available technology).*

In other words, this represents a kind of frontier, or outer limit to the capacity both to produce and to make choices among production possibilities.

The *static* (timeless) picture we get from the production-possibilities function approximates the reality of *dynamic* (changing through time) choice making. However, the image is useful for many purposes.

The Production-Possibilities Table

Suppose that Table 2-1 represents the various combinations of beef and all-purpose machines available to Ruritania at a given time, within the limitations set out above (full employment and the best use of existing technology).

What does this table show? Let's look at it as a set of tradeoffs; that is, it's like a menu, except that the diner can't buy *all* the items on it. Consider combination A. This shows that when Ruritania employs all its resources and the best technology, it can produce 20,000 machines, providing it produces no beef. Alternatively, if Ruritania chooses to produce 2,000 tons of beef, it can produce only 18,000 machines. In the second case, it must give up 2,000 machines for 2,000 tons of beef. These tradeoffs may continue until the situation evolves into combination E. At this point, Ruritania can devote all its resources to producing 8,000 tons of beef, but then it can't manufacture any machines.

Which of these various combinations will (or should) Ruritania produce? There is no way for us to find out from this table. Answering this question is very complex, and the mechanisms by which societies make such choices vary greatly. Remember that we assumed that Ruritania is a private-enterprise capitalist society, and so the decision is made in its marketplaces. But we don't know which decision its producers and consumers will make. The data in Table 2-1 simply indicate the possibilities. (In some societies, these decisions might be made by both markets and government. In others, the decision may be made by government fiat.)

Graphing the Production-Possibilities Curve

Graphs, being pictures, not only adorn, but also tell stories. For many people, a graph—in this case a picture of certain economic relation-

TABLE 2-1 Production Possibilities for Beef Versus Machines, Ruritania, 1977

Product	\multicolumn{5}{c}{Production rates}
	A	B	C	D	E
Beef (thousands of tons)	0	2	4	6	8
Machines (thousands)	20	18	14	8	0

FIGURE 2-1 Production-Possibilities Curve, Ruritania, 1977

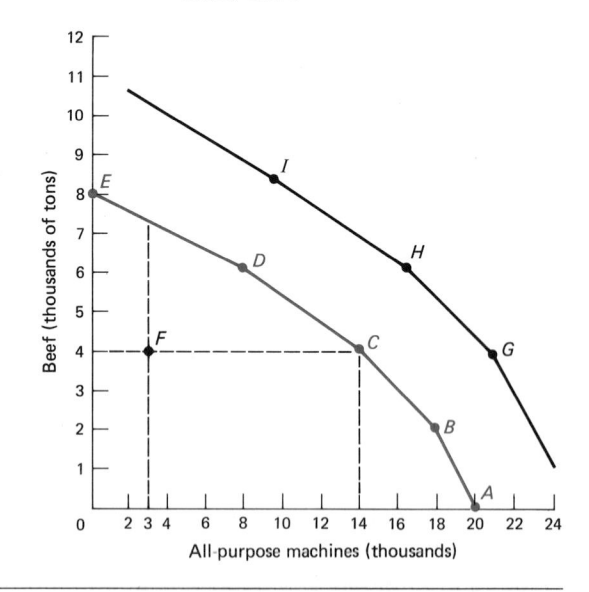

ships—can be worth a thousand words. For clarification, refer back to the basic data which it portrays. Figure 2-1 is a visual image of the data in Table 2-1.

Point *C* in Figure 2-1, for example, represents a combination that is a maximum attainable output: 4,000 tons of beef and 14,000 all-purpose machines. Each of the combinations *A*, *B*, *C*, *D*, and *E* is possible for Ruritania. The curve that has been drawn through these points is the production-possibilities curve (PP curve).

Why are points *F* and *G* not on the 1977 PP curve? Point *F* represents less production of *both* beef and machinery than some combinations that are on the curve. In other words, *F* does not represent a maximum attainable output. To see this, follow the dashed line that goes through point *F*. If Ruritania chose to produce 3,000 machines (possible at *F*), it could produce approximately 7,400 tons of beef, much more than the 4,000 indicated at *F*. In other words, if Ruritania picked combination *F*, it would not be maximizing output, and it would not be employing its resources fully.

We could apply the same logic to all such points (combinations) below or to the left of the production-possibilities curve. On the other hand, points such as *G* and *H*, which lie beyond or to the right of the current PP curve, are by definition not attainable. They would involve Ruritania turning out more of *both* products than it possibly could, given the combinations on the current production-possibilities curve. Since we are assuming full employment and best use of existing technology, points *G* and *H* are clearly unattainable. (However, they may be available in a later period, with different technology and resources.)

Employment, Full Employment, Unemployment, Underemployment

In Application 2, on economic development, we will use concepts of employment, including full employment and underemployment. Therefore, we must define some terms. The person in the street probably uses the word *employment* most often in connection with people's jobs. Here, however, we want to relate employment to all the resources available to a society. So for our purposes, we define **employment** as that condition in which a unit of resource (labor, land, capital, entrepreneurship) is used in some economic activity. In other words, as soon as a resource becomes an *input* in a process that results in the *output* of economic goods, it is considered *employed*.

Now this means that **unemployment**, on the other hand, is the condition in which a unit of resource that would otherwise become an input is unable to find use as such. In the case of labor, this means that a person can't find a job. Land, capital, and entrepreneurship can also be unemployed.

Today all societies—especially in developed nations—give high priority to achieving an employment goal. Frequently, this goal is full employment, or something near it. In other words, the society seeks to

Unemployment in the real world (Gary Settle/NYT Pictures)

ensure that each person who is looking for a job can find one (provided that he or she abides by certain institutional and legal restrictions, such as acceptable age of entry into the labor force or not working longer hours than the maximum workweek). When a society attains full employment, it is reaching the maximum on its production-possibilities curve. Each unit of resource is not only employed, but is employed in conjunction with other resources to create the greatest output of goods and services possible at that time, with existing technology.

Achieving a full-employment (maximum-output) position—that is, reaching any point on the PP curve—is extremely difficult and unlikely. We shall deal later with some of the reasons why. As we shall see, the PP curve is a *limit*, an ideal bench mark against which the deficiencies of *actual* economic performance can be assessed.

What is likely to occur in any society is that there is always **underemployment**, which means that some units of the nation's resources are not employed in their most productive uses. For reasons we shall explore in Application 2, physicists may be tending shops and journeyman carpenters may be mowing lawns for a living. Although they are employed, these people would be more productive if society provided more appropriate job opportunities; therefore, underemployment exists even though the nation may attain full employment.

A Word of Caution

Resist the temptation to read too much into a picture or graph. When we look at a Picasso painting, we may each read into it something different if we wish. On the other hand, what one may legitimately see in a graph is determined by the definitions and assumptions underlying the graph. In Table 2-1, we can see what the alternatives are (at full employment and using the best technology). We do not, however, know which choice Ruritania will make. There are social, political, moral, cultural, and legal aspects to be taken into account.

One thing is evident: What Ruritania produces today will influence what it can produce in the future. Let us assume that Ruritania is an underdeveloped (low-income) country (about which we will say more in Application 2). Ruritania—like many nations—has a ten-year plan by which it hopes to increase productivity from point C (in 1977) to point H (in 1987). Refer again to Figure 2-1. This means that Ruritania has to shift its production-possibilities curve to the right. To do this, it must have more productive capacity, which means more all-purpose machines. Thus politico-economic objectives in 1977 may dictate more machines (at the cost of less beef) to increase capacity for tomorrow's output. We say that movement from C to H is Ruritania's planned growth path.

What Is Economic Integration?

We have built our model of Ruritania's development on the assumption that its economy has a single set of social and technological conditions—in other words, that Ruritania is a country with a single economic standard for all its people and that all its resources are allocated by the same process. We are implying that all people who own resources in Ruritania have the same information and the same objectives and that Ruritania's potential users of resources also have the same information and the same objectives. For Ruritania to reach the PP curve, both groups must want to use those resources with maximum efficiency. We are also implying that there is a set of known choices—reflected in the production-possibilities curve—open to all of them. If all these conditions were fulfilled, the economy would be operating under full **economic integration**. In other words, it would be using all its resources in the most efficient manner. (Technically speaking, one has **perfect integration** in a market society only when all units of resources are employed and a given resource is paid the same in all its uses. Can you imagine why?) Such a society would be one in which there was no significant resistance to the goal of maximum efficiency, given the full use of resources with the best available technology. (We shall discuss later the reasons why maximum efficiency might be opposed.)

In reality, however, many influences stand in the way of integration in an economy, influences that reduce the likelihood of the economy's achieving full efficiency. Particularly in underdeveloped countries, these influences may be so strong that the system becomes characterized by **economic dualism**, which means the coexistence within a society of two or more different economies. The two that most often exist together in a dualistic society are (1) a modern exchange economy and (2) an indigenous (or native) *non*exchange economy.

Coexistence of a modern economy and a usually primitive, subsistence economy complicates any explanation of economic development in terms of the production-possibilities model. So let us introduce two modifications to the model:

1. In the modern sector of the economy, reaching the PP curve is no longer solely a question of increasing efficiency. Ruritania may now seek to make the indigenous nonexchange sector part of the modern exchange economy.

2. The resulting economy, which will be much larger, will have different resources from which to choose, and thus many more paths along which it can grow toward greater development.

Suppose that the nation making these choices is not Ruritania, but Urbania. Let's say that Urbania is a mature industrial economy whose chief problems include environmental pollution and hard-core unemployment. You can see that Urbanians would choose a different combination of alternatives on the production-possibilities curve. They might choose a combination of factors that would enable them to move from underemployment or unemployment (for instance, at point *F*) to full employment. Under these conditions, Urbania's equilibrium choice might be *D* rather than *B*, because Urbanians would give low priority to economic activities that would result in more machinery and thus more pollution.

Increasing Costs: Why Is the Curve Shaped That Way?

You have of course noticed that the PP curve is concave to the origin of the diagram. This is so because there is a hidden assumption underlying the choosing of the numbers and the construction of the curve. The assumption is that of *increasing opportunity cost*. To define this concept, let us go back to Ruritania and its twin industries, beef and all-purpose machines. Figure 2-2 shows Ruritania's production-possibilities curve.

We can illustrate **opportunity cost** by referring to movements along the PP curve. Suppose that the Farmers Party gains power in Ruritania, and the government decides to produce fewer machines (producer goods) and more beef (consumer goods). It decides to move from the machine-beef ratio at point *C* on the PP curve to the ratio at point *D*. This means that Ruritania gives up 5,000 machines in order to get 2,000 more tons of beef. The machines it gives up are the *real opportunity cost* of the beef. Opportunity cost is the alternative goods given up when a choice is made to produce a certain thing.

FIGURE 2-2 Production-Possibilities Curve, Ruritania

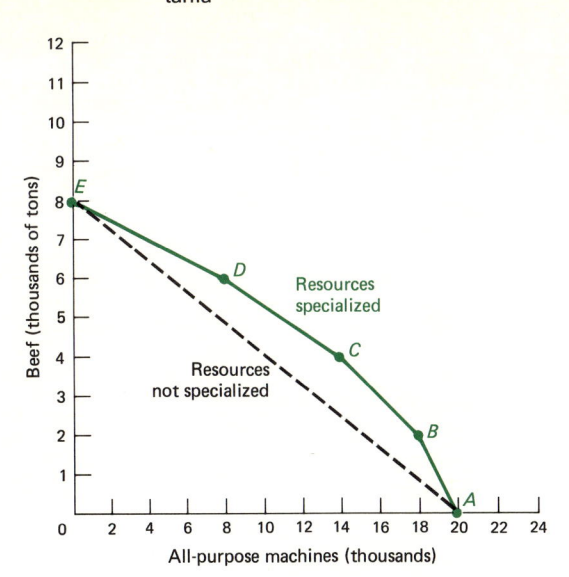

[Figure: Production-possibilities curve with Beef (thousands of tons) on y-axis and All-purpose machines (thousands) on x-axis. Points E(0,8), D(6,6), C(14,4), B(18,2), A(20,0). Solid green curve labeled "Resources specialized" connects the points; dashed line labeled "Resources not specialized" connects E to A.]

For example; suppose the average car costs $5,000, burns 755 gallons of gas per year, and carries one person to work. And suppose the average bus costs $80,000, burns 2,165 gallons of gas per year, and carries sixty people to work. If those sixty people all choose to buy cars to go to work in, the extra amount of money for the cars ($300,000 versus $80,000) plus the excess gas (45,000 gallons versus 2,165), to say nothing of the excess insurance cost and wear and tear on the highways of sixty vehicles versus one—all this is the opportunity cost those people are paying to go to work by car. (And 82 percent of Americans do commute to work by car.)

Now suppose that Ruritania decides to produce *no* all-purpose machines and instead uses its resources to produce *only* beef. The effect is that Ruritania moves to point E from point D on the PP curve. What has Ruritania given up? As you can see, the 2,000 additional tons of beef cost 6,000 machines. In other words, the real opportunity cost—as measured by the increasing slope of the PP curve[1]—is becoming larger. This would also be true if Ruritania chose to produce more machines instead of

---

[1] The absolute slope of the PP curve,

$$\frac{\Delta Y}{\Delta X} = \frac{\text{Change in output of beef}}{\text{Change in output of APMs}},$$

represented in the slope, therefore, is how much beef one loses in order to produce more machines, and vice versa. This is the *real opportunity cost*.

Increasing Costs: Why Is the Curve Shaped That Way?

more beef. In moving down the PP curve, Ruritania would be forced to give up more and more beef for each additional machine produced.

Why does relative cost ultimately increase as a full-employment society chooses to reallocate its resources? Why aren't resources completely *substitutable* in all uses, so that the PP curve looks like the straight dashed line *AE* in Figure 2-2? There are complex factors involved. We shall examine some of these in Application 2. Fundamentally, the reason is this:

Resources are relatively more productive in some uses than in others.

Imagine what would happen in Ruritania as it tried to produce more beef. Beyond some point, Ruritanian farmers would have to start turning their cows out into pasture land that is less well suited for cattle raising. Of course, if resources were adaptable to any use, all land could be used just as well for one thing as for another. In other words, it would be technically homogeneous in application. In such a case, the curve would be a straight line, such as the dashed line *AE* in Figure 2-2. But in real life this is not usually the case, though occasionally one does find either perfect substitutability or perfect lack of it. In fact, sometimes resources gain in efficiency as they are reallocated from one use to another. As we explained in Chapter 1, however, we want our economic models to clarify reality. Therefore, if models are to help us analyze general economic problems, they must be based on valid assumptions. For this reason, we shall assume a **diminishing rate of transformation**, which means that the rate at which one good may be traded off or transformed into another ultimately decreases—for a single firm, for an enterprise, or for an industry. In our illustration, this rate is shown as always decreasing.

Mental Reservations

You may have some mental opposition to these working assumptions about scarcity and increasing relative cost and may ask why you should accept them. In your own experience with producing something or your reading of economic history, you may have observed the following cases: (1) Sometimes, as a production process is speeded up or modernized—that is, as more inputs are used—output increases more rapidly than input. Consider automobile production after 1914 and the emergence of the assembly line. (2) In the twentieth century, U.S. resources have become much more productive, thus shifting the PP curve. Actually, both these observations may be correct, and yet neither invalidates the law of increasing opportunity costs. In making these assumptions, we can't hope to describe *all* facts of the real world. We can only hope to present the key aspects.

A Classical Explanation of Growth

Consider case 1. Efficiency does increase as a result of specialization of resources and division of tasks, as markets expand and firms produce more and on a larger scale. This improvement of technique, which means more output from the same inputs, results in the shifting of the PP curve, not in movements along it. Economists have noted such growth in efficiency ever since Adam Smith, who published *The Wealth of Nations* in 1776. Smith wrote about a pin factory in England in which, as specialization increased, labor became much more productive and output increased accordingly, just as it has in twentieth-century automobile-assembly plants.

In the same way, steel output has increased. In the 1950s and 1960s the use of automation and improved techniques expanded greatly within the steel industry, resulting in increased production in the 1970s. Steel productivity in the United States went up by 10.8 percent in 1973 alone, and in 1974 there were record-breaking performances everywhere in the industry. This, coupled with the devaluation of the dollar, enabled the steel industry in the United States to prove that it is more than cost-competitive with foreign producers.

Obviously, increasing efficiency, tied to growth, is an important aspect of economic development. Nonetheless, for the society as a whole, given existing technology, moving resources from one activity or industry to another (moving along the PP curve) ultimately decreases efficiency, because beyond some point (and with given technology and resources), people use inputs that are less and less well adapted to the new employment. Thus the industry will ultimately experience increasing relative cost. People will have to sacrifice more and more of one good to obtain a greater output of another.

As for case 2, twentieth-century economic history does bear out this observation. Resources have indeed become much more productive since 1900. On the other hand, the static assumptions of the PP curve about fixed supplies of resources and given technology clearly do not hold true. Since 1900, the PP curve has shifted dramatically to the right. Except during depressions, such as that of the 1930s, the shifts have been fairly continuous. According to the Department of Agriculture, in a report issued in 1961, a farmer in the 1960s, using modern machines, improved seeds, fertilizers, modern pesticides, and so forth, could turn out almost four times as much product for each hour of work as a farmer did in the years just preceding 1914. We can conclude from the assumptions of our production-possibilities model that the shifts have resulted from two factors:

1. Productivity has increased as a result of technological changes (new tools, new processes, and larger-scale activities). These changes have resulted, at least in part, from (a) increased economic integration, (b) market growth, and (c) specialization and division of use of resources.

2. Amounts and varieties of resources have increased. Our producers today possess many resources not even considered potential inputs in

1900 (including a labor force that is much more productive, partly as a result of investment in education).

Institutions Play a Part in Decision Making

The *rate* at which productivity has grown has also been influenced by changes and refinements in **economic institutions**, the social arrangements through which economic decisions are made.

An example of a public institution is the Federal Reserve System, or the Central Bank of the United States. Control over the supply and composition of money, as exerted by the "Fed," can drastically affect saving and investment, technological change, exploration of resources, and practically all decisions that influence a nation's growth in productivity.

As an example of a private institution, consider the modern corporation. Corporations today come in all sizes and forms, including the big multinational ones that cut across national boundaries and reach their roots into capital markets throughout the world.

Let us sum up. Any changes in such giant institutions as these, whether for good or ill, can change the economic climate in which decisions are made. And naturally the pace of development—the shifting of the PP curve—can be altered as a result.

Economic development—such as that experienced by the United States—is a long-term, dynamic process, stemming from a complex set of economic, political, and social changes. This is discussed more fully in Application 2, which concerns problems of economic development in the poor nations.

SUMMING UP

1. In a competitive private-enterprise economy, owners and employers of *resources* determine the uses of resources. Thus, decision making about markets is a decentralized process.

2. A society has to decide which resources to use, and how to use them, because (a) At any given time, resources are limited, and (b) Human wants for economic goods are virtually unlimited. The conjunction of these two factors gives rise to *scarcity*. This relative scarcity forces an economic society to choose among alternative uses of its resources.

3. Deciding what to do about resources involves answering the fundamental questions facing all economies: (a) *What* shall be produced? (b) *How* shall it be produced? (c) *Who* shall consume the output? (d) How do we recognize and act on the interdependencies in the first three questions?

4. The production-possibilities curve derives from static considerations. Nonetheless, if we understand the basis on which it is built, studying it can provide insight into the problems of economic development connected with *employment, unemployment, underemployment,* and related factors.

5. The production-possibilities curve can help one visualize the impact of *economic dualism* (or lack of *economic integration*) in a society. Dualism, which is the coexistence of multiple economies with different social and technological conditions, influences the way a society moves onto and shifts the PP curve to meet development objectives.

6. A useful means for visualizing the resource dilemma is the *production-possibilities function and curve*, which reflect the choices that affect full employment, most productive technology, and maximum output. Drawing the curve usually involves assuming *increasing opportunity cost*. This is another way of saying that resources are partially specialized in their uses and, beyond some point, become less efficient as they are reallocated to other uses.

7. The production-possibilities curve shows that a nation must give up some thing(s) if it is to produce other things. What the society forgoes in order to do so is called the *real opportunity cost* of production. The PP curve naturally does not tell us which choice a nation will make in using its resources.

8. We can make the production-possibilities curve more useful as a device for explaining economic growth by bearing in mind the classical idea that as economic activities expand, growth depends on efficiency, which is tied to specialization and division of tasks.

9. To complete our model, we must recognize that changes in *economic institutions* engender more efficient decision making, which in turn leads to both economic integration and faster growth, or shifting of the PP curve. These relationships are examined in Application 2.

QUESTIONS

1. In what ways have modern communication and transportation changed the ways in which markets function?

2. Will scarcity, as economists define it, always be a part of the human condition? Why?

3. Why are resources not perfectly substitutable? Why, for example, can we not easily move resources from an industry that isn't employing them fully to an industry that is booming, and that needs them?

4. What are some of the economic institutions that have changed or come into being in recent years? Why has this happened?

5. Does economic dualism exist at all in the United States? If so, where?

6. Suppose that the Secretary of Labor says to you, "We're having a lot of trouble getting people in areas such as Appalachia and the urban ghettos to seek and find jobs in commerce and industry. It almost seems as though these people are part of a different economy. Do you suppose they really are?" How would you answer the question in terms of economic integration and economic dualism?

SUGGESTED READINGS

Copeland, Morris A. *Our Free-Enterprise Economy.* Macmillan, New York, 1965.

Hecht, Reuben, and Eugene McKibben. "Efficiency of Labor." In *Power to Produce: The Yearbook of Agriculture, 1960.* Department of Agriculture, G.P.O., Washington, D.C., 1961.

Kaminsky, Ralph, ed. *Introduction to Economic Issues.* Doubleday, Garden City, N.Y., 1970. Part I.

Mundell, Robert A. *Man and Economics: The Science of Choice.* McGraw-Hill, New York, 1968.

Nozick, Robert. *Anarchy, State and Utopia.* Basic Books, New York, 1974.

Smith, Adam. *The Wealth of Nations.* Edited by Edwin Cannon. Random House, New York, 1937. Chapters 1, 2, 3, 4.

Zimmerman, Erich. *World Resources and Industries: A Fundamental Appraisal of the Availability of Agricultural and Industrial Materials.* Harper, New York, 1951.

Application 2

The Rich Countries and the Poor Countries

Economic Development: Problems of Closing the Gap

In Chapter 2, we talked about scarcity and about the knottiest decision of all: How should one best use resources? Through the device of a production-possibilities curve, we explained the impact that both factors—scarcity and allocation of resources—have on economic growth. Now we can employ these concepts to examine what is perhaps every nation's most basic economic problem: **economic development**. It is one topic on which nearly everyone—expert and layman—has an opinion. Interest in economic development was intense during the Industrial Revolution in the nineteenth century, when people were losing their jobs to machines, but interest waned in the early twentieth century. Since World War II, the subject has generated interest again—not only for economists and other academicians, but also for politicians and the person in the street. It's easy to see why if we examine the definition of economic development.

Economic development is the process by which the material well-being of a society's people is significantly increased.

Why does the definition deal only with *material* well-being? Basically because, as students of economics, we are concerned with goods and services. We know that goods and services are necessary to supply people's needs and wants, although having more of them doesn't necessarily make people better off or happier. On the other hand, people who are very poor, unless they can create the potential to produce more, cannot choose among alternatives. Their lives are hemmed in by necessity. They cannot choose whether they prefer more automobiles to more leisure, prefer more coal furnaces to cleaner air, or anything else. It is the freedom to make such choices that is a great value of economic development, and the main reason why we are concerned with it. The person who must toil for fourteen hours a day just in order to live and the society that can barely keep this year's output the same as last year's small output have very little economic freedom. Without economic freedom—the freedom to choose among many alternatives—can there ever be much social and political freedom?

"Sure, sure, I can see labor-saving possibilities. But how do we cope with all the leisure time it's bound to produce?"

The above definition of development raises questions as well as answering them! How do you measure well-being? How much increase is significant increase? How long does the process of economic development take? Let us deal with each of the questions in turn. As a generalization, however, our definition is enough base for the study of the characteristics of development.

1. *Economic development is an evolutionary process, a set of interdependent actions.* Consider the development of synthetic rubber. Prior to World War II, most developed countries had to import raw rubber from Malaysia and South America, because despite a hundred years of research,

Economic Development: Problems of Closing the Gap   35

chemists had been unable to produce a synthetic rubber molecule. At the beginning of the war, enemy warships cut off U.S. supply lines of natural rubber, just as the United States was gearing up its war machine and desperately needed rubber for truck, plane, and tank tires, for waterproof clothing and footwear for soldiers, and for hundreds of civilian uses. The U.S. government stepped in and combined forces with industry to search for the optimum combination of ingredients and for improved technology for making synthetic rubber. (The same thing was happening in Germany.) Finally, chemists abandoned the search for chemical equivalence and concentrated on trying to find materials with the same physical properties as rubber. And they succeeded. Today the world uses *twice* as much synthetic as natural rubber, and the United States produces almost half the world's supply. If it had not been for the war and for the incentive created by the government, chemical engineers might not have made that all-out effort, and still might not have developed synthetic rubber.

2. *Actions resulting in development have multiple origins, both economic and noneconomic.* For example, world food shortages and the population explosion led to the development of new strains of wheat, rice, and corn. Searching for a new wheat strain, Norman E. Borlaug, a plant breeder at the Rockefeller Foundation research station at Chapingo, Mexico, began in the 1950s to cross various strains of hybrid wheats until eventually he developed a new dwarf type that had much higher yields than the usual varieties and would flourish in many climates. This hybrid made possible year-round plantings in parts of the subtropics and tropics. Mexico was the first country to grow Borlaug's new wheat extensively, with astonishing results. Until the mid-1950s, Mexico had been importing a large percentage of its wheat, but with the new dwarf wheat, Mexico was able, by 1964, to export a sizable amount of wheat. Borlaug won a Nobel Prize for his accomplishment.

3. *The results of development are broad, and are both economic and noneconomic.* For example, the success of the dwarf wheat strains led rice researchers at the University of the Philippines College of Agriculture (founded jointly by the Ford and Rockefeller foundations in 1962) to try to increase rice production in Asia. They used the same crossbreeding techniques as the wheat growers, and found a new dwarf variety of rice—IR-8—which grows approximately forty inches high (compared to seventy inches for the traditional Asian rices), yields 6,000 to 8,000 pounds pounds of rice per acre (versus about 4,600 for the older rices), and is ready to harvest only four months after it is sown (versus five to six months for the traditional rices). Where the weather is warm enough and water is plentiful, farmers can raise two or three crops of it a year. Thus IR-8 has become known as the miracle rice, since it can double farmers' per-acre yields. Even tradition-bound Asian peasants were quickly won over to these new high-yielding varieties. By 1969 they were planting 34 million acres of the miracle rice.

However, this rapid switch has brought problems. More labor is needed for more frequent planting, and there must be continuous weeding, frequent irrigation, and vastly increased storage and transportation facilities to store and market the greatly increased crops. In many cases Asian farmers have had to store their grain in open fields or in public buildings such as schoolhouses. Another problem has been consumer resistance. Many peasants don't like IR-8 rice because it doesn't stick together when cooked. Agronomists have been continuing their experiments, crossbreeding further, trying to alter the grains to suit local preferences.

As a result of the development of IR-8 rice and Borlaug's dwarf wheat strain, many people who would have starved to death are now alive—and having more babies.

Economic Determinism

Our investigation of the problems of developing nations will naturally have to be very broad. We will emphasize people's economic motives, but also, of necessity, we will cover certain social and cultural factors bearing on the development process, factors that are not solely economic. If we were to examine the long-term evolution of a nation or people from a strictly economic standpoint, it would involve assuming **pure economic determinism**—in other words, assuming that the actions of people and institutions are mere reactions to changing economic reality, or economic opportunities. Not only is such a notion simplistic, but it ignores, for example, the relationship between social-cultural patterns and economic behavior.

Progress catches up with a less-developed country (Alain Nogues/Sygma)

Basic Questions About Economic Development

How Do You Measure Well-being?

To some people, just having enough rice to fill their empty stomachs is material well-being. To someone else, owning a car that runs well enough to drive to work is material well-being. To a third person, having a chalet in a fashionable ski area is material well-being. Clearly there is no single number or index that is adequate for this measure. However, many economists feel that growth in *real per capita income* ($Y/P \div N$, where Y = income and P = prices) is the best approximation. To obtain this index, divide the total national income (Y) by the population (N) of the country in question (the derivation of Y is explained in Chapter 5). Obviously, to get "real" income figures, we should be sure to leave out of our accounting mere price increases. For example, if prices go up 8 percent this year and national income rises by 8 percent, then for a given population there is *no* increase in real per capita income.

To sum up:

1. Total national income − price increases = real national income.

2. Real national income ÷ population = real per capita national income.

3. Growth in real per capita national income is the best single representation of development.

Thus, in order to estimate what is happening to an individual's ability to buy goods and services as national income grows, we must sort out both *population* increases, which reduce the per capita effect of income increases, and *price* increases, which do not represent more goods.

How Great Is the Income Gap?

Table A2-1 shows something about the income gap between the developed and underdeveloped nations.

We must be cautious in interpreting the differences too strictly. Biases are introduced when we convert figures in Indian rupees, for example, into dollars. Also we don't know what the distribution of income in India is or what nonmarket services the Indian government provides for its people.

Having said this, however, we can conclude from the data the following:

1. The income gap between the "rich" nations (for example, the United States and Sweden) and the "poor" nations (for example, India and Haiti) is very great—so great that we must conclude that, whatever the distribution of income and nonmarket services provided by government, the average citizen is much better off in the rich than in the poor nations.

2. Many countries with low per capita income have very small total income bases, which in turn are related to small national populations. Bolivia, for example, has a population of about 5.5 million and a 1970 national income of $864 million. Similar relationships can be found elsewhere in nations in Latin America, Africa, and Asia.

This is important because for even a well-integrated nation to adopt modern technology, it must have a market large enough to make specialization and division of resources economically feasible. With its small population and a per capita income of only $150, Bolivians find it hard to build the modern plants and install the processes that would enable them to reap the benefits of specialization and division of labor. Unless countries like Bolivia undergo economic integration (either internal or with other countries) to enlarge their markets, the large scale of modern industry may well remain beyond their reach. Imagine how few nations can afford the $500 million investment necessary to build a fully efficient steel plant!

3. In almost every part of the world, there are wide income gaps between nations. Per capita income is highest in Europe, North America, and Australasia. Even in these areas, however, there are nations that are pockets of poverty. See, for example, the income data for Portugal in Europe and Mexico in North America—where it belongs geographically, if not culturally.

TABLE A2-1 Estimates of Per Capita National Income, 1970

Country	Per capita national income (dollars)
Africa	
United Arab Republic	170
Ethiopia	70
Southern Rhodesia	220
Nigeria	70
Ghana	170
Liberia	210
North America	
United States	3,980
Canada	2,460
Caribbean and Latin America	
Bolivia	150
Brazil	250
Guatemala	320
Haiti	70
Mexico	530
Venezuela	950
Argentina	820
Middle East	
Iran	310
Iraq	260
Israel	1,360
Asia	
India	100
Indonesia	100
Japan	1,190
Pakistan	100
Philippines	180
Europe	
France	2,130
Germany (Federal Republic)	1,970
Italy	1,230
Portugal	510
Sweden	2,620
United Kingdom	1,790
U.S.S.R.	1,110
Oceania	
Australia	2,070
New Zealand	2,000

Source: Statistical Office of the United Nations, Department of Economic Affairs, New York, 1973.

A Nobel laureate in economics recently said that poverty rather than plenty is the international human condition. And Jesus said two thousand years ago, "The poor we have always with us." Even though the world has experienced two hundred years of industrialization and diffusion of technological information, all these advances have failed to raise significantly the economic well-being of perhaps 2 billion to 2.5 billion of the 3.5 billion people in the world today.

What Is a Significant Increase in Real Per Capita National Income?
Will the percentage increase in Y/P (real per capita national income) necessarily be the same, for example, in China as in India? This is unlikely because significant income growth is reached only when development becomes self-sustaining. In other words, the development process must build up a permanent momentum. For this to happen, the pace of development, reflected in the growth of per capita income, must be great enough to overcome whatever resistances there are to development in individual societies. These resistances, which often differ in kind and intensity from one society to another, fall into two categories.

Resistances to Growth and Development

Social and Cultural Resistances
Social and cultural resistances are those aspects of the social organization and cultural practice that influence the society's kinds and levels of economic activities. Such influences are too numerous to list, but some examples may help.

In India, the Hindus, who comprise the majority of the people, believe that it is sacrilege to slaughter cattle for beef. Even if people are starving, their bony cows wander the streets. Why is this important to India's development? Economists generally agree that an agricultural surplus—producing more than is consumed—is a necessary precondition for urbanization and industrial development. The Indians and their sacred cattle are an example of a poor nation deliberately, for religious or cultural reasons, depriving itself of a source of potential surplus.

Consider another example of cultural resistance to growth. In some Latin-American nations, middle-class families have for centuries clung to culturally ingrained biases against their sons getting jobs in commerce or industry. Families wanted sons to enter the legal profession, the clergy, and the military because these professions were—and to some extent still are—considered more prestigious than working in business or trade. The importance of this sort of social resistance is that it is likely to affect the supply of *effort* in a society. Because bright, energetic people raised in comfortable surroundings are needed to run a nation's businesses, the social stigma attached to commerce may downgrade both the amount and composition of entrepreneurial activity. Since **entrepreneurship**—the organization of diverse resources into producing units—is vital to technological change and development, such social foot dragging may retard growth in productivity or even prevent it entirely.

Perhaps the greatest resistance to income growth in underdeveloped countries is offered by hugely increasing populations. The facts that women begin in their early teens to bear children and the large size of families make development all the more difficult. (You may wonder why, since in the twentieth-century United States, population growth has meant more prosperity because of dollars spent on everything from baby buggies to education.) If a country sets aside only enough to take care of what is used up *(depreciated)* in current production, future output is at best likely to be no greater than what it is now.

As W. Arthur Lewis has put it, the development of a nation depends on knowledge, capital, and the will to economize. A part of knowledge is that the future can be better than the present; this prospect induces people to save and form capital.

Remember, however, that the United States, like other developed nations, has a large surplus. It does not consume everything it produces, while merely setting aside something to make up for depreciating plant and equipment. One of the basic economic questions in Chapter 2 was how much of current output one should set aside to invest in machinery and other facilities with which to produce for the future. Now, suppose that an underdeveloped country, because of foreign aid or some internal "bootstrap" operation (a feat achieved by its own efforts), generates a surplus and uses this surplus initially to increase productivity. It cannot necessarily maintain this surplus, or even expand it. Suppose that the higher productivity induces people to have larger families. Or suppose that the surplus is used to reduce the death rate. In either case there are more people of nonproductive (not in the labor force) ages to be fed, housed, and clothed. Supporting these people may literally eat up the surplus.

Therefore the resistance to income growth may be so strong that development does not occur or is not self-sustaining. How serious is this kind of resistance? Table A2-2 indicates that it may be severe.

Several things stand out in these data. Population throughout the world has grown since 1920—even in the depression years of the 1930s. It has grown much more rapidly since 1930 in the developing (low-income) regions than in the more developed regions. This population boom has put heavier pressures on the ability to create and effectively use surpluses in the underdeveloped countries than in the developed nations. However, the economic backwardness of the underdeveloped countries cannot be attributed to this population increase alone, or even primarily to it. Indeed, not all such countries have high population-growth rates. And some, such as Mexico, have shown rapid income growth even while maintaining high rates of population growth. In most cases, however, a burgeoning population has exerted a negative effect on development.

Technological and Technical Resistances

Figure A2-1 shows the PP curves of two nations: one a developed country and the other an underdeveloped country. Shown are tradeoffs between present goods (such as beef in our Chapter 2 example) and future goods (such as the all-purpose machines used earlier). The curves in Figure A2-1 represent—for the same points in time—a country with a high per capita income (Sweden) and a country with a low per capita income (India). Note that both curves reflect, in their slopes, *increasing opportunity cost*. In other words, each country's development comes not from ability to substitute resources for various present uses, but from the ability to substitute future goods for present goods. If a country wants future capital, it has to forgo some consumption today. (This is hard to do if the country's populace is unable to read and write, and if many of them are half-starved.)

Clearly, the more a country moves out the future-goods axis—in other words, trades off present for future consumption—the greater its stock of capital, including human capital, will be. More rapid diffusion of knowledge about technical change will shift the PP curve and development will take place. This is the difference between the two curves.

The underdeveloped country (India) runs into the resistances we mentioned above and finds it hard to use its surpluses productively. Notice in Figure A2-1 that the slope of India's supposed PP curve—in other words, the rate at which it may substitute future for present consumption—increases quickly. This means that the underdeveloped country quickly approaches a zero rate of transformation, or a point beyond which no amount of giving up present consumption increases future output. The rate of substitution, or of giving up present consumption, is shown by the

TABLE A2-2 Percentage Annual Growth Rate of Population

Year	World	More developed regions	Developing regions
1920–1930	1.0	1.2	1.0
1930–1940	1.0	0.8	1.2
1940–1950	0.9	0.4	1.2
1950–1960	1.8	1.3	2.0
1960–1965	2.0	1.3	2.3
1965–1970	2.0	1.0	2.4
1970–1975	2.1	1.0	2.5

Source: Population Division, United Nations, New York (reprinted in Morgan and Betz, *Economic Development, Readings in Theory and Practice*, Wadsworth, Belmont, Calif., 1970). More developed regions include North America, temperate South America, Europe, Japan, Australia, and New Zealand. Developing regions include Africa, East Asia (except Japan), South Asia, Latin America (except temperate South America), Melanesia, Polynesia, and Micronesia.

FIGURE A2-1 Production-Possibilities Curves for Developed and Underdeveloped Country

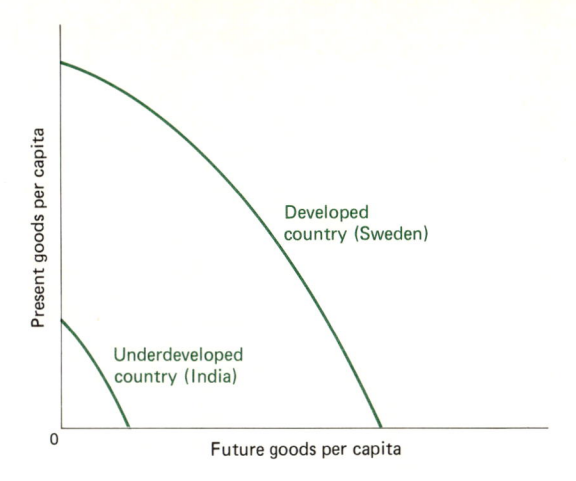

slope of the PP curve. In other words, it is equal to the *rate of change in present goods per unit change in future goods* per capita.

The developed country (Sweden) is able to substitute future consumption for present consumption more effectively and in larger per capita amounts. The developed country generates a larger surplus and reinvests more of it in future growth in productivity. Thus, the rich get richer while the poor get (relatively) poorer.

What are the major technological barriers the underdeveloped countries must overcome? Indeed, is the argument for the existence of such barriers valid? Some students have argued that low-income countries actually have certain technological advantages over high-income parts of the world. Two of the principal building blocks of this argument are:

1. Progress is a matter of degree. Underdeveloped countries for the most part have relatively simple capital requirements. Introducing an inexpensive, manually operated irrigation pump may constitute a major technological leap forward in a low-income country, whereas to get the same degree of impact in an industrial nation, major changes in technology would have to be introduced. This amounts to saying that the underdeveloped countries have a relatively low ratio of additional capital needed to produce additional output **(incremental capital-output ratio)**.

2. Underdeveloped countries, unlike high-income nations, can import modern goods from the vast menu of technological choices developed in the industrial nations. They do not have to use their resources to develop sophisticated processes such as continuous-rolling steel mills, automated assembly plants, and the like. According to this reasoning, these underdeveloped countries, which are on the receiving end of the generosity of the developed countries, stand to inherit the benefits of the historic labors of the industrial nations.

We, however, specifically reject these two arguments, on grounds that the costs involved in realizing the benefits are likely to outweigh the benefits themselves. In many cases, the benefits are illusory; that is, they only seem to be benefits. Let us see why.

1. It may well be that underdeveloped countries need only (technically) simple changes in capital equipment. But how productive will these changes be? One economist estimated that in the United States, between 1929 and 1957, about 43 percent of growth in real income was the result of (a) *increased education of labor* and (b) *advances in technical and managerial knowledge*. The study maintained that only 15 percent of such growth came from increased amounts of physical capital, such as factories and machines. Underdeveloped countries invest much less in their **human capital**—that is, in people—than developed countries do. Poor countries spend much less than rich nations do on education, health care, and the like. The fact is that simple attainable capital improvements—such as the water pump—may not rapidly increase productivity, unless the country has already made major investments in its human capital.

Instances of such barriers abound in the underdeveloped countries. Some years ago, an American economist doing research in Central Mexico met a state planning official who told him of a program to distribute steel plows to the owners of small nonmarket farms in the region. The program was good in theory, but some time after the plows had been handed out, a team of officials, who had returned to assess the results, found that most of the steel plows were sitting in corners, unused. The native owners of the small plots said that they had not used the steel plows because the cold of the steel—as opposed to the warmth of the wooden plow—would offend the

Resistances to Growth and Development 41

earth god. In other words, the steel plow—which had a strong positive effect on agricultural productivity in the United States in the nineteenth century—had no effect in this Mexican setting because there had been no prior investment in education. Nobody had come along before the plows were handed out and tried to overcome the peasants' religious-cultural bias. This is an example of *interdependency*, an important principle in economics.

In many cases, such **complementary investments**—those that increase the productivity of other investments—lie beyond the capacity of the underdeveloped countries, which often cannot substitute a present good (time and money spent on education) in favor of a future good (an educated populace).

2. In part, the impact of importing advanced technology depends on the complementary investments outlined in reason 1. Will a modern oxygen-process, continuous-rolling steel mill built in Egypt have the same productivity (output per hour of labor employed) as one built to the same engineering specifications, but designed and built in West Germany? Studies indicate that it will not, in the absence of the complementary investments discussed above—especially in education. There are also other reasons to believe that the advantages that imported technology offer to the undeveloped countries are partly illusory. Modern technology is not completely divisible. Egypt cannot build *half* a modern steel mill. Even if it built a *whole* one, in order to use the mill's output to best advantage it would have to develop simultaneously metal-fabricating mills, a freight transport system, an automobile industry, and so forth. Thus, in order to internalize the efficiencies of modern technology, a nation must often adopt that technology in toto. So Egypt and other societies that are not *fully integrated* (using their resources in the most efficient manner) may not find the appropriate technology in the industrial countries. The cost of adapting advanced technology to the skill levels, market sizes, and degrees of economic integration in the underdeveloped countries may outweigh the seeming benefits.

As a further point, consider that the technological processes of industrial nations are almost always **capital-intensive**. That is, they use relatively more capital than labor or land. In most underdeveloped countries, *labor* is the surplus factor. (Exceptions are the oil-rich sheikdoms, such as Kuwait, which we won't consider here because, although they have high per capita income, they have yet to demonstrate the kind of economic balance among agriculture, industry, and commerce that goes along with being developed countries.) In countries such as India, **labor-intensive processes**, those that use relatively more labor than capital or land, yield the greatest relative advantage.

Let us summarize: Technological advantages for poor nations are difficult to find. Adapting modern technological marvels to their peculiar problems and characteristics is likely to be a costly process and one that involves far more than merely using their surpluses to import technology.

What About Natural Resources?

Let us return to the production-possibilities model outlined in Figure A2-1. Remember that a shift factor—one that can move the curve to the right to reflect increased productive capacity—means an increase in endowment of resources. Many poor nations are rich in resources. Why has the development of these natural resources not been effective as a device for accelerating their growth?

Basically, we must go back to the saying by the late Erich Zimmerman: "Resources are not, they *become*." Consider the example of oil. Prior to the late nineteenth century, oil was not a major resource for the United States. It only became so with the rise of the automobile—a complementary development—and related changes in the American economy.

For Brazil, the riches of the Amazon basin fall into the same uncertain category. Without complementary investments in human capital and transportation, Brazil's rich mineral resources remain merely potential riches.

In Application 25 we shall discuss the development problems peculiar to economies that export raw materials. For the time being, let us say only that for most poor nations, exporting natural resources has failed to boost their economies to rapid growth. An exception would be the exports of cotton by the United States prior to 1860. However, in the case of the United States, much internal integration and investment in human capital accompanied that increase in exports of cotton.

Is the Income Gap Widening or Closing?

An enormous income gap exists between the poor majority of the world's population and the affluent minority. As Simon Kuznets put it in his Nobel Prize address in 1971:

> At present, about two-thirds or more of the world population is in the economically less developed group. In 1965, the per capita gross domestic product (at market prices) of 1.72 billion out of a world total of 3.27 billion was less than $120, whereas 0.86 billion in economically developed countries had a per capita product of some $1,900.

Given this wide gap, we must ask a follow-up question. Is the gap closing or widening? In other words, is the development problem being solved, or is it growing more acute? The data in Table A2-3 shed some light on this.

Interpretation of these data unfortunately does not yield hopeful answers to our question. Except for the Near East—which contains a relatively small percentage of the population of the low-income areas—in the 1950s and 1960s the underdeveloped countries grew less rapidly than the developed countries in terms of per capita GNP. (Per capita **gross national product** is the value, at current market prices, of a nation's total output of final goods and services, divided by the nation's population. It differs from national income only in that it encompasses depreciation, or the using up of resources in that year's output.) This is true even when one includes the United States, which grew much less rapidly than Europe and other developed areas in the 1950s. The Near East appears to be an exception to the general rule about relative income growth. It is too early yet to know whether the exporting of the oil riches of the Near and Middle East will result in long-term structural change and economic development for that part of the world. If it does, this region may join the ranks of the rich nations in the twentieth century.

It is particularly distressing to note the rate of growth of GNP of South Asia (1.5 to 2.1 percent in the 1950–1960 period); Africa (1.1 to 2.4 percent from 1960 to the present); and Latin America (1.6 to 2.9 percent in the same period). These are precisely the areas that hold most of the world's population and harbor most of the world's suffering. If we exclude the United States from the developed countries and the Near East from the poor

TABLE A2-3 Percentage Increase in GNP Per Capita, Less-developed and Developed Countries

	1950–1955	1955–1960	1960–1966	Current rate of population growth
Less-developed countries				
Latin America	2.3	2.0	1.6	2.9
Near East		3.3	3.9	2.4
South Asia	1.5	2.1	1.4	2.5
East Asia (Indonesia)		1.3	2.3	2.7
Africa			1.1	2.4
Total	2.8	2.1	2.3	2.5
Developed countries				
United States	2.6	0.5	3.4	1.2
Europe	4.3	3.7	3.5	0.9
Other developed countries	4.6	4.6	5.6	1.4
Total (including U.S.)	3.5	2.2	3.8	1.1

Source: Gross National Product, Growth Rates and Trend Data, Agency for International Development, Statistics and Reports Division, RCW-138.

nations, the per capita increase in GNP of the developed countries in the sixteen-year period grew almost twice as rapidly as that of the underdeveloped ones. In other words, the gap has widened, not closed.

Will population pressures in the underdeveloped countries be reduced as even modest economic growth continues? No one really knows, but reduction in population appears unlikely. Note that, as of 1966, population was growing more than twice as fast in the poor as in the rich nations (2.5 percent versus 1.1 percent). The zero-population-growth movement has made very little headway in low-income countries.

A Note About China

You've probably noticed that we haven't given any data or made any comments so far about mainland China. The People's Republic, a vast but undoubtedly poor nation, encompasses about one-fourth of the world's population, and our lack of detailed knowledge about its productivity, population, and income growth is a serious deficiency. Until recently, there were few contacts between outside economists and mainland Chinese economists, and no access to economic data. (Later on, we shall have more to say about China's "new road.") At this juncture, we have to rely for our information about China's progress on the personal observations of those few economists who have recently been allowed to visit this huge country. Professor Lynn Turgeon, whose field is comparative economic systems, visited China in 1972, and commented:

> The standard of living is low by East European standards but, except for Japan, high by Asian standards. Much of this standard is invisible, in the form of free education, free or very inexpensive medical services, very good care for retired persons. As in all socialist countries, there is no begging and few, if any, signs of disguised unemployment (shoe shines, street lotteries, etc.). The Chinese economy, especially in agriculture, seems to be booming.

No verdict is in with respect to the success of the Chinese experiment, particularly in emphasizing agricultural development rather than heavy industry. In Application 27, we'll take a look at some of the recent evidence regarding the Chinese economy. Until much more of the evidence is in, however, we should be cautious in generalizing about the future of poor, heavily populated nations.

Is There Hope for Underdeveloped Countries?

If by now you feel discouraged about the prospects of the poor nations, you have good reasons. We have argued that shifting the PP curve in the underdeveloped countries will require a combination of the following factors:

1. Basic structural or institutional change.
2. Economic integration.
3. Technological change through adaptation.
4. Specialization and division of resources.

Achieving these goals is obviously going to take a lot of doing. It will involve much more, as Simon Kuznets has put it, than "merely borrowing existing tools, material and societal, or of directly applying past patterns of growth." The political and social changes the underdeveloped countries will have to make to achieve these goals will be traumatic and, in some cases, probably violent. Economic development involves basic changes, and since it alters basic social, political, and economic power relationshps, it destabilizes a society. Any student of American history knows that this has been the case in the United States. Consider the redistribution of income away from landowners and in favor of owners of capital. This and many other changes in political and economic power create resistances and struggles. (Some believe that the American Civil War was the result of just such struggles.) It would be unrealistic of us to expect economic development to be otherwise in the underdeveloped nations.

One thing is clear, however. Economic development in the underdeveloped countries *is* possible, in spite of the disadvantages these countries face today in comparison with the way things were in Europe, the United States, Japan, and Australasia when those countries were on the verge of *their* big climb in economic development.

When will this climbing process begin? And in which underdeveloped nations? Will it require extensive economic planning? And will industrialization bring in its wake the problems of urbanization? Some economists have begun to question the accepted arguments for extensive central planning and industrialization as a basis for economic development. There can be no question that most of the world's people want improved material well-being. As they realize more and more the gap between their own economic reality and what is socially and technically possible, pressure for the above four aspects of change will increase. It may well be that this pressure for change will be the primary fact of our international future. If so, the impact on the economic and social positions of all the developed nations will be intense.

How Long Will It Take?

There is no answer to the question of how long because development, at least in the way we have defined it, is an open-ended process. Any society, no matter how affluent, is capable of further economic development. The underdeveloped countries must bring their population-growth rates down to at least the level of the developed countries. Then the productivity in use of their surpluses will depend on the awesome power of compound interest. Assuming modern economic institutions to use it, a per capita income that has a 6 percent compound rate of growth will double in twelve years. In this sense, even supposing that the people in a given underdeveloped country begin with only $100 annual per capita income, that nation can significantly improve the material well-being of its people in a quarter of a century. And this, after all, represents but a brief moment in the history of human beings.

SUMMING UP

1. *Economic development* is the process by which the material well-being of a society's people is significantly increased.

2. The concern for material well-being derives, at least in part, from its relation to social and political well-being and to *economic freedom*, which enables people to choose among growing numbers of alternatives.

3. *Pure economic determinism*, the idea that social and political decisions depend only on changing economic opportunities, fails to reflect the interdependence of these three kinds of influences.

4. The best single measure of economic development is growth in real per capita income. But this does not take into account public services and income redistribution, which also affect the material well-being of people.

5. Economic development in an underdeveloped country initially generates resistances, both sociocultural and technological. Sociocultural patterns affect the kinds and amount of effort needed to cause an economy to develop. Advanced technology is difficult to adapt to the peculiar conditions of the underdeveloped countries.

6. Population growth is a major impediment to economic development. The beginnings of development brought about through the use of surpluses may be eaten up by a larger population in the form of food, clothing, and housing. Data indicate that population growth is a greater disadvantage to the underdeveloped than to the developed nations.

7. The developed nation can shift its PP curve by substituting future for present consumption much more effectively than the underdeveloped country can; that is, over a much wider range of its PP choices. This ensures that output will continue to grow in the future.

8. For an underdeveloped country, importing advanced technology is difficult, not only because of its indivisibilities, but also because technology is not as productive in the underdeveloped as in the developed countries. Statistics show that productivity brought about by technological improvements depends heavily on *complementary investments*, especially investments in *human capital*, achieved by education and health care. Also, many underdeveloped countries, in the absence of economic integration, constitute markets that are too small for large-scale modern technology and the benefits due to specialization to be economically feasible.

9. Natural resources are potentially abundant in many underdeveloped countries. The productivity of these countries, however, depends again on complementary investments, especially the formation of human capital.

10. Data suggest that recently the income gap between the underdeveloped countries and the

rich nations has grown rather than diminished. With the exception of the Middle and Near East, most underdeveloped countries are not growing rapidly (in terms of economic development). More than two-thirds of the world's population lives in underdeveloped countries, in which the annual per capita income is $120 or less.

11. Statistics about the growth of per capita income in mainland China, the world's most populous country (850 million people), are hard to obtain. Some recent observations suggest that the standard of living of this one-fourth of the world's population has improved.

12. Natural resources are not distributed evenly around the globe. The best example is oil. Because many underdeveloped countries have no oil of their own and have to import it at the high prices set by the *OPEC* (Organization of Petroleum Exporting Countries), these underdeveloped countries have been plunged further into poverty by their desperate need for oil.

13. Economic development for the underdeveloped countries is possible, in spite of barriers against it. However, basic structural changes in society within these countries will be needed to bring it about. Where such development does take place, it will be the power of compound interest that will make it possible.

QUESTIONS

1. How does one define economic development? Would a broader definition be more useful? If so, what additional factors (or measures) do you think should be added?

2. Do you agree that pure economic determinism should not be used as the basis for explaining economic decisions and development patterns?

3. Why is it important to subtract price increases from data on income growth in order to measure economic development in a given country?

4. What is an economic surplus? What factors do you think determine how large the surplus must be to permit economic development?

5. What are the basic resistances to economic development? Are they purely economic?

6. What role does the size of a nation's market play in the classical explanation of growth and development?

7. How would you explain the fact that, after two hundred years of industrialization, two-thirds of the world's people are still very poor?

8. Construct an economic argument that industrialization is not necessary to the economic development of India, and that agricultural development may advance India's prospects just as well.

9. Why is investment in human capital so important to the economic development of a country such as Egypt?

10. What are the principal advantages to the developed nations in substituting future consumption for present consumption?

11. Given that many underdeveloped countries, such as Zaire, are rich in natural resources, why have these nations not used them more effectively to bring about economic development?

SUGGESTED READINGS

Healey, Derek. "Development Policy: New Thinking About an Interpretation." *Journal of Economic Literature*, September 1973.

Hirshman, Albert. *The Strategy of Economic Development.* Yale, New Haven, Conn., 1960.

Kuznets, Simon. "Modern Economic Growth, Findings and Reflections." *American Economic Review*, June 1973.

Ohlin, Goran. "Population Control and Economic Development." In *Economic Development* by Theodore Morgan and George W. Betz. Wadsworth, Belmont, Calif. 1970

Reynolds, Lloyd G. "Making a Living in China." *The Yale Review*, Summer 1974.

Rivkin, Arnold. *Nations by Design.* Doubleday, Garden City, N.Y., 1968.

Schultz, T. W. "Investment in Human Capital." *American Economic Review*, March 1961.

Turgeon, Lynn. "Notes on the New China." *The Center Magazine*, November–December 1972.

Ward, Barbara. *The Lopsided World.* Norton, New York, 1968.

3 Supply and Demand: Price Determination in Competitive Capitalism

In Chapter 2 we saw that the operation of society necessarily involves making choices and that these choices derive from three basic queries common to all societies: (1) *What* should be produced? (2) *How* should output be produced? (3) *For whom* should it be produced?

Let us now examine the means by which such choices—implicit in the production-possibilities curve—are made under a competitive private-enterprise system.

Economic reality is so complex that it cannot be described completely. What we can do, though, is to establish principles and build models in order to draw analogies to reality. First we are going to set forth some building-block principles that will serve to explain a few things about a competitive capitalistic society. Who is in control? Who or what sends out the signals that determine how we are going to use our resources? Is there some sort of giant power that decrees that some of us shall be poor and hungry, and others of us rich?

A private-enterprise system, based on competition, is much more complex. For the moment, we will not discuss the influence that big institutions—government, business, labor—have on the making of economic decisions. We will focus on competition and then, as we go along, add in the complexities introduced by big institutions and measure their effects by comparing them to the effects of competition.

What Is Competition?

A single word can have many different meanings. Take the word **competition**. If you think of competition as a contest between rivals (as the dictionary defines it), then it describes how the rivals interact. For economists, such a definition has two defects: (1) It is too general to use in analytical questions. (2) It contradicts real life, in which **price rivalry**—the contest in which sellers watch what prices others charge, and then react to those prices—*frequently is inversely related to the number of contestants*. If you are one seller among ten thousand others and you raise your prices, it affects the others little or not at all. If you are one seller among four and you raise your prices, the others may follow suit. Thus, for economists:

Competition *is the market form in which no individual buyer or seller has influence over the price at which she or he buys or sells.*

Unorganized single buyers bid for the available goods, and this determines demand. Unorganized single sellers make offers to sell, and this determines supply.

How Are Prices Set? Supply and Demand

If no single seller can set prices and no single buyer can either, how do prices become set, and how are resources allocated in competitive markets? The answer is that there are two independent influences—supply and demand—that determine prices in a competitive market. Let's look at these two components separately.

"This town isn't big enough for both of us—let's merge."

48 Supply and Demand: Price Determination in Competitive Capitalism

DEMAND

Demand is another word that has many meanings. For one thing, demand is not desire alone, but desire plus the purchasing power to back up that desire. The newspapers may say that the demand for cars is expected to reach 9 million cars this year. A worried business executive may say that demand for the firm's product is "not good" or is "weak." Both these statements mean something to the person making them. To economists, however, they lack one or both of the ingredients needed for analyzing markets: (1) the timing of the demand and (2) the range of prices for which the demand is expected to hold. The statement about automobile demand does indicate the time period (this year) but not the price range for which this estimate will hold. The worried executive, on the other hand, is summing up his or her judgment about the state of the market, rather than analyzing the general demand for the product. So let's define demand in a way that includes both necessary ingredients.

__Demand__ is a set of relationships showing the quantities of a good that consumers will buy over a specific range of prices within a specific period of time.

Let's take as an example a good that most people consider desirable: T-bone steak. What will be your demand this year for T-bone steak? You'll probably say, "That depends on what happens to the price of T-bones." Exactly! The price of a product—and changes in that price—are the main factors that determine how much of that product the public will buy. For example, an upswing in car sales followed the offer of price rebates by car manufacturers in 1975.

Of course, there are other factors that influence demand:

1. Income of buyers.

2. Tastes and preferences of buyers.

3. Prices of other products, both *complements* (products used in conjunction with T-bone steaks, such as potatoes) and *substitutes* (products used in place of T-bone steaks, such as ground round).

4. Consumers' expectations about future prices and market conditions.

These factors determine how many T-bones you or any other individual will buy, within any given price range. So when you say that your demand for T-bones depends on what happens to price, you are saying that this is true for your income and tastes, given prices of other products and given your expectations about future prices and conditions. In addition, there is a fifth factor that influences the total demand for a product, or for all products. That factor is *population*, or the number of consumers. (Remember from Application 2 that a problem of underdeveloped countries is that some have such small populations that there is inadequate demand to justify large-scale industries.) Let's hold these factors constant and establish demand for T-bone steaks in terms of the relationship between price and quantity demanded. This amounts to the same thing as holding certain variables constant and permitting *key* variables to change. This is called the ***ceteris paribus*** ("other things being equal") condition. It is an assumption that is common to much economic analysis, and in fact to analysis in other fields too.

An Individual Demand Curve

Let's take a week as the time period for which we're going to analyze your demand for T-bone steaks. Table 3-1 shows the number you will buy at various prices (given your income, tastes, prices of other products, and your expectations about the future).

What do these data on demand tell us?

1. The quantity of T-bones you buy increases as the price falls and decreases as the price rises.

2. There is a price ($2.50) above which you will buy no T-bones; in other words, above that price you will be excluded from this market (or you will exclude yourself).

3. Although you may buy more T-bones as the price falls, the strength of your taste for them probably declines beyond some number consumed per week; one reaches a saturation point.

When we plot the relationship of price to quantity (Table 3-1), we obtain the **demand curve** shown in Figure 3-1, which shows price on the vertical axis and quantity on the horizontal axis. (Remember that economists call a diagonal line of this sort a curve, even though it is a straight line.)

Point A (price = $2.50, quantity = 0) is the upper limit to your demand. For you, $2.50 is the price at which (or above which) you will stop buying. Point B represents three T-bone steaks per week (price, ($1.75); and point C, seven T-bone steaks (price, 75 cents). As price falls, quantity demanded increases and approaches a maximum (at point C).

The fact that demand curve D in Figure 3-1 slopes down and to the right reflects the **law of demand**: *Consumers buy more at low prices than at high prices.* There are two reasons why:

1. As prices in general fall, the purchasing power of your income increases, which causes you to buy more of a desirable good (the **income effect**).

2. As the price of a desirable good falls (other prices being unchanged), the good becomes relatively cheaper than other goods (the **substitution effect**).

Each effect tends to reinforce the other. Under normal conditions, both tend to cause consumer demand for a greater quantity of a desirable good as its price goes down.

There are exceptions to this normal pattern. There are some **Veblen goods** whose appeal to consumers increases with higher prices (Russian caviar, sable coats, large diamonds, and so on).

And then there are **income-inferior goods**, such as beans and rice, which people in poor countries eat because prices of these goods are very low and their cheapness permits people with low incomes to eat them. Compared to meat, milk, and other high-protein goods, beans and rice are very cheap. When the prices of these income-inferior goods drop sharply, people may eat less of them and use their greater purchasing power (income) to diversify their diet, by buying meat, for example.

Changes in Quantity Demanded Versus Changes in Demand

So far, we have been talking about a single demand curve, a curve charting the demand for a desirable good and showing that *movements along* that curve are the result of changes in the price of that good. The only thing that can cause a **change in quantity demanded**, therefore, is a change in the price of the good. Remember that we are holding four factors constant: income and tastes of the consumer, prices of other goods, and consumers' expectations of the future (plus population, for total demand). If even one of these factors changes, the entire demand curve will *shift*. There will be a **change in demand** itself.

But people's incomes and tastes often do change, and so do the other factors. If we are to analyze the operations of markets and the

TABLE 3-1 Demand Schedule for T-bone Steaks

Price per pound	Quantity bought per week
$2.50	0
2.25	1
2.00	2
1.75	3
1.50	4
1.25	5
1.00	6
.75	7

FIGURE 3-1 Demand Curve for T-bone Steaks

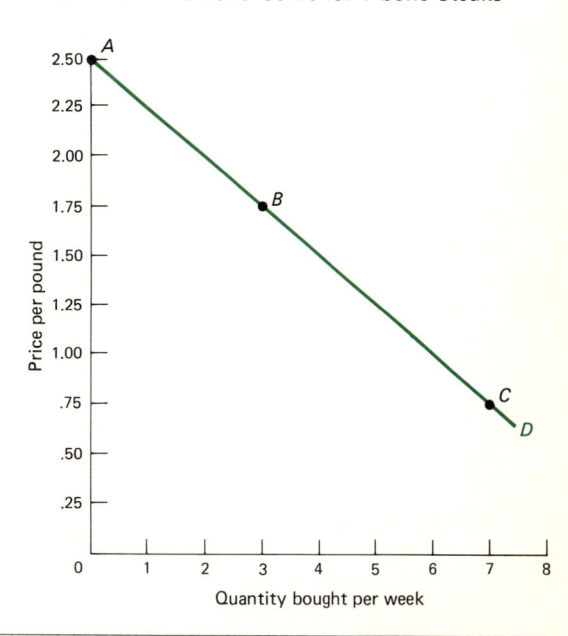

pricing of goods and services, we must account for variations in these aspects, in addition to variations in price. Figure 3-2 shows the difference between a change in quantity demanded and a change in demand. The movement from A to B along demand curve D_1 (caused by a reduction in price from $2.00 to $1.75) is called a *change in quantity demanded*. The movement from B to C is caused by a change in consumers' incomes or tastes, prices of other goods, or consumers' expectations for the future (or all of these). This movement involves a shift in the entire demand schedule.

First let's see what effect a change in income will have on changing demand. In Figure 3-2, D_1 is a curve showing your original demand for T-bone steaks. All points on it represent the original price-quantity relations. Now suppose you receive a raise in pay. Since we are assuming that T-bone steaks are a good you want, your demand curve will shift to D_2. Now that you have more money, you buy approximately three more steaks per week, at any price per pound between 75 cents and $2.50. Of course, if you were to have a pay cut, your demand curve would shift to the left as your income decreased. If we now take your income increase away, we expect that you will buy approximately three fewer steaks per week. In other words, your demand curve will shift back to D_1—unless, at the same time, your tastes or your expectations of the future, or the prices of other goods, change to offset the decrease in income.

Change in Other Prices. Suppose that the price of ground round doubles. Since T-bone steaks and ground round are to some extent substitutes for each other, your demand for the now relatively cheaper

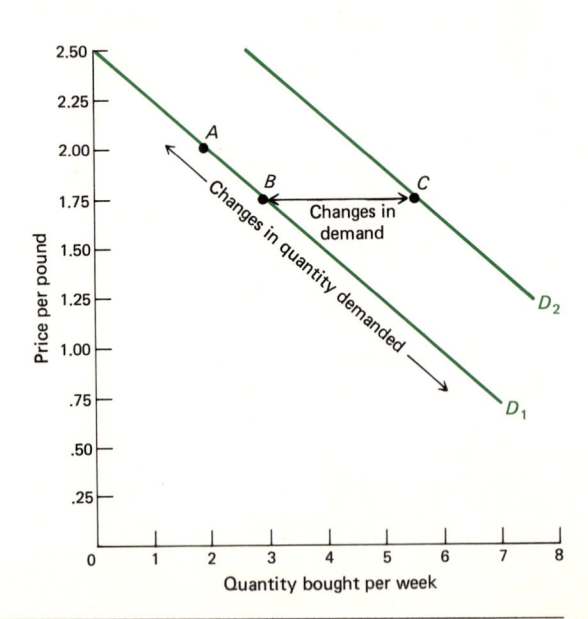

FIGURE 3-2 Demand for T-bone Steaks

52   **Supply and Demand: Price Determination in Competitive Capitalism**

T-bone steaks will increase, perhaps to D_2. But if the price of ground round falls, your demand for the now relatively more expensive T-bones will decrease, perhaps from D_2 to D_1. The same thing might happen if potatoes suddenly went up to $5.00 per pound: since potatoes are a complement to steak, you might consume less steak along with fewer potatoes.

Change in Tastes. Suppose that your demand for T-bone steaks is at D_2, and you develop a yen for pizza, which weakens your taste for T-bones. Your demand for T-bones will shift to the left (perhaps to D_1).

Changes in Expectations About Future Prices. Suppose that you read in the newspaper that there is a failure in the grain crop and that there will soon be big increases in the price of steak and other beef because of a jump in the price of feed grains. Your demand curve for T-bones may shift to the right (you may decide to buy a dozen steaks and freeze them). In other words, D_1 is your demand curve only as long as your current expectations about prices remain the same.

Demand: Summing Up

There are four things to remember about demand.

1. Demand curves slope downward to the right. In other words, consumers buy more of a good at lower prices than they buy at higher prices (the *law of demand*).

2. Only changes in the price of a good can cause changes in the *quantity demanded* by the public. Such changes result in *movements along* a demand curve.

3. The only one of the five demand factors that cannot cause a change in the demand for a good is a change in its own price.

4. Factors that may singly or jointly change people's demands are changes in their incomes or tastes, changes in prices of other commodities, and changes in expectations for the future.

Market Demand

So far, we have looked only at one person's demand. But competitive markets are made up of many unorganized buyers expressing their individual demands. How do we figure the total market demand? We must add up the demand schedules of many individuals, assuming that there are no interdependencies of demand, such as a desire to keep up with the Joneses.

Figure 3-3 illustrates the principle involved, since it shows the sum of your and my demand curves at each price, which gives a picture of market demand. My demand schedule is plotted from the same kind of data as in Table 3-1. Thus, when T-bone steaks are selling at $2.00 a

FIGURE 3-3 Market Demand for T-bone Steaks

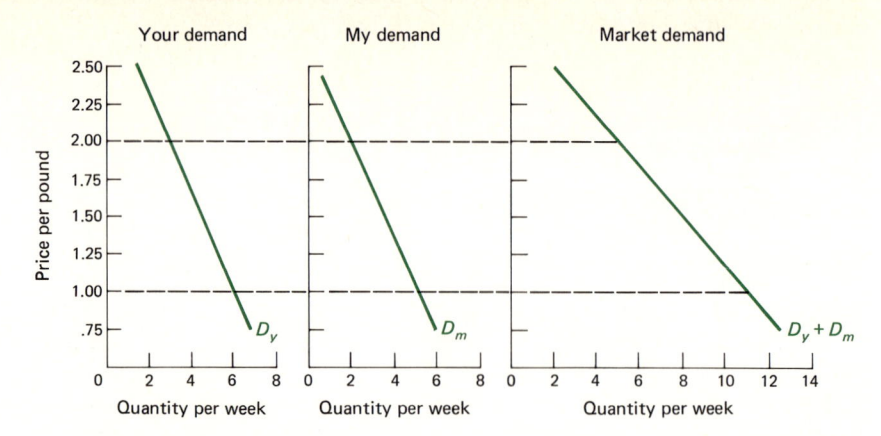

pound, you buy three and I buy two. Let's assume for simplicity that we are the only two consumers who are buying them. Market demand at this price is then five T-bones per week. Similarly, when T-bones are selling at $1.00 a pound, you demand six per week and I demand five, making market demand eleven T-bones per week.

Here are some general remarks about market demand.

1. People's demand curves are not the same, since everyone has different incomes, tastes, and expectations for the future.

2. Market demand curves, like the demand curves of individuals, slope downward to the right, since they derive their slope from the slopes of the demand curves of individuals. Of course, the market demand curve represents a larger quantity of a given thing, because many people buy more than one person does.

3. *Number of buyers* (population) is a determinant of market demand. As the number of buyers increases, so does demand (with other relevant factors constant).

SUPPLY

As we know, there are two sides to a market: demand and **supply**. Now we want to set up the same kind of curves for supply as we did for demand. We can use the same techniques.

You may think that the wellspring of the world's supplies—the business firm—has no objectives in common with the consumer who demands the output of the firm, but each *maximizes* (that is, builds up to the maximum) some aspect of self-interest. Consumers maximize satisfaction and business firms maximize profit or return on investment.

Supply and demand at work during the 1973 gas shortage (Arthur Grace/Stock, Boston)

What Is Supply?

Supply is the set of relationships showing the quantities of a product that a firm will offer for sale at each possible price within a specific period of time.

We set up the picture of the supply situation on the assumption that certain other factors are constant or unchanged—the *ceteris paribus* or other-things-being-equal assumption mentioned earlier. The other factors, which if they did change could affect the firm's supply curve, are:

1. The technology of production.
2. The prices of inputs or resources.
3. The prices of other goods.
4. The firm's expectations about future prices.

Who is the source of supply? In our competitive market, many small firms do the supplying. Enough firms participate in the market so that no one firm can influence the price of a good in the market as a whole.

To illustrate, let's go back to T-bone steaks. Table 3-2 sums up the quantities supplied versus prices of T-bone steaks for a typical competitive meat market. See what happens to quantity as price goes down. Why should butchers haul in all those steaks, store, and then sell them, if they cannot profit?

The **supply curve** of a firm shows the relationships between the various prices of a product and the quantities of it the firm supplies. A change in the price of a product is the only thing that can cause the firm to change the quantity supplied. Such changes are reflected in movements along the supply curve, as shown by the arrows parallel to S in Figure 3-4, which shows the relationship between price per pound and quantity supplied. Note that the supply curve goes up to the right. The vertical bar at the upper right of the graph means that a given firm—here the ABC Meat Market—eventually runs out of storage space, counter space, or sales clerks to sell all those steaks. In other words, after a certain maximum is reached, it becomes inefficient for the supplier to supply any more.

Suppose that the price of T-bone steaks goes up from $1.50 to $1.75 per pound. The ABC Meat Market will increase the quantity it supplies from two to three T-bone steaks per week. All such price changes are reflected in movements along a given supply curve, and are called **changes in quantity supplied**.

What happens when there is a change in one or more of those "other factors" we mentioned? An improvement in the technique of production (a new meat-slicing machine), a lower resource price (price of feed grains goes down), a change in the firm's expectations (a rumor that

TABLE 3-2 ABC Meat Market: Supply of T-bone Steaks

Price per pound	Quantity supplied per week
$2.50	5
2.25	5
2.00	4
1.75	3
1.50	2
1.25	1
1.00	0
.75	0

FIGURE 3-4 ABC Meat Market: Supply Curve

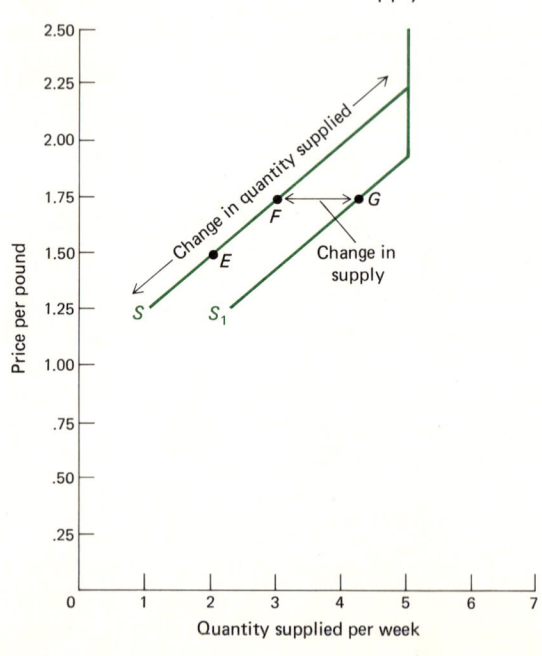

56   Supply and Demand: Price Determination in Competitive Capitalism

meat prices may go down), or a change in price of other goods (a drop in the price of chickens)—all these factors, or just one of them, can cause the *entire* supply curve to shift. For example, in Figure 3-4, the movement from F to G reflects an increase in supply from level S to level S_1. Such shifts are called **changes in supply**.

What Do Supply Data and the Supply Curve Tell Us?

1. The number of steaks supplied per week rises as price rises and falls as price falls (the **law of supply**).

2. There is a price below which the firm will supply *nothing*. Reason: The firm that seeks to maximize profit likewise seeks to minimize losses. It will produce nothing if it cannot make a profit, or at least cover production expenses that cease if it ceases to produce.

3. Although, for a given firm with given physical facilities, the number of steaks supplied rises as the price rises, it rises slowly. The number of steaks finally reaches a maximum, because the efficiency of selling them decreases as sales keep rising.

The reason that the supply curve—unlike the demand curve—slopes *up* to the right is that the price of the product and the costs of production affect supply so strongly. The costs of production, in turn, depend on the degree of technology, on given prices of inputs, and on the firm's expectations for the future.

Since the ABC Meat Market is a competitive firm, it takes prices of resources as given and searches for the best technology with which to minimize its cost of producing. Whenever it adopts a new lower-cost technique, its entire supply curve shifts to the right, as in the movement from S to S_1 in Figure 3-4. Such a shift can also result from (1) a lowering of the firm's resource or input prices, (2) a lowering of the prices of other products, or (3) a change in the firm's expectations about the future.

What Causes Physical Efficiency to Decrease?

Let us assume for the time being that the efficiency of firms ultimately decreases; that is, their output per unit of input declines. Why, you may ask, does this happen, when a firm can hire all the resources it wishes at given prices? The reason is decreasing physical efficiency, which may come about for two reasons:

1. The use of some factors may not be susceptible of increase, and using more of other factors ultimately results in bottlenecks. (For example, automation can be used in the meat-packing industry only up to a certain point; then hand labor must be hired. But if you hire many more laborers and don't have enough refrigerated space to store the meat or enough customers to buy it, you find yourself overstocked and presently have idle workers to deal with.)

2. Even when all factors can be increased, productivity may still decrease because of problems beyond the control of management. (Drought strikes, meat-packing laborers go on strike, and so forth.)

For the retail meat industry, however, there is another factor that helps determine total supply: *the number of firms* in operation. In a competitive industry, there are no significant barriers to setting up new businesses or to going out of business. Expectations of profits and losses cause supply, therefore, to adjust quickly to changing market conditions, as reflected in prices.

Market Supply

We can chart supply the same way we chart demand. Figure 3-5 shows the process of adding up, or *aggregation*.

For simplicity, we have assumed that there are only two firms operating in the market. But the adding-up process is the same, even if there are thousands of firms. When steak is selling at $1.50, the ABC Meat Market will supply two steaks per week and the XYZ Meat Market will supply one. Total market supply at this price is three per week. At $2.00 per pound, ABC will supply four per week and XYZ three; total market supply at this price is seven per week.

The market supply curve takes its shape from the curves of the individual firms, so it slopes upward to the right. Remember that the number of firms helps to determine market supply. Naturally, more firms make a greater supply.

Before we go any further, let us sum up the distinctions between *movements along* demand and supply curves and *shifts in* them.

Difference Between Movements Along and Shifts in Curves

1. The only thing that can cause a *movement along* the demand curve for a product is a change in price of that product. Such movements are called *changes in quantity demanded*.

FIGURE 3-5 Market Supply of T-bone Steaks

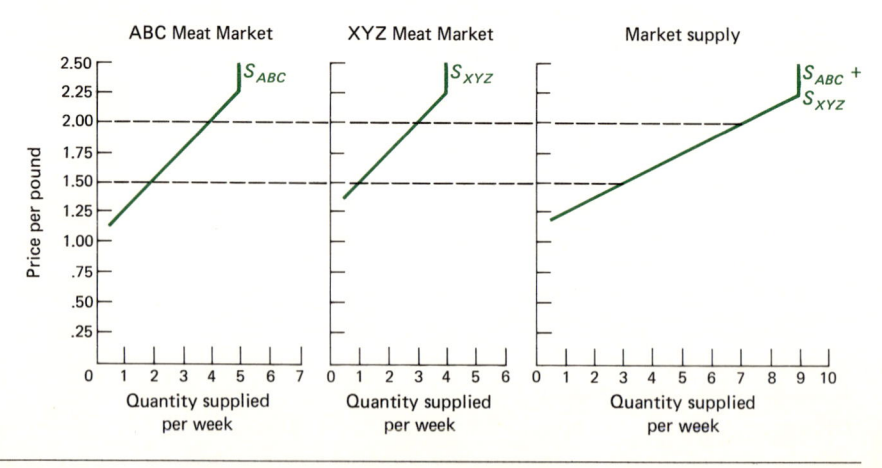

58   Supply and Demand: Price Determination in Competitive Capitalism

2. Factors that can cause a *change in demand* or *shift in* the demand curve for a product are things other than the price of that product: (a) changes in consumers' incomes, (b) changes in prices of other products, (c) changes in consumers' tastes, and (d) changes in consumers' expectations about future prices.

3. The only thing that can cause a *movement along* the supply curve for a product is a change in the price of that product. Such movements are called changes in *quantity supplied*.

4. Factors that can cause a *change in supply* or *shift in* the supply curve for a product are things other than the price of that product: (a) changes in techniques of production, (b) changes in prices of other products, (c) changes in prices of inputs or resources, and (d) changes in firms' expectations about future prices and market conditions.

5. Changes in the number of consumers can cause changes in market demand. Changes in the number of firms can cause changes in market supply.

COMPETITIVE PRICING

Now let's return to our original question: How is the price of T-bone steaks, or of any product, determined? The answer is that their price stabilizes at an equilibrium price, one that clears the market.

An **equilibrium price** is the price at which the quantity demanded is equal to the quantity supplied. It is the price that tends to prevail unless the factors (that is, supply and demand) operating in the market change.

Let's see how such an equilibrium price comes into being in a competitive market through the joint influences of supply and demand. Table 3-3, on page 60, shows price versus demand and supply for our minimarket, which—just to keep things simple—consists of only two consumers and two meat markets.

Table 3-3 shows that the equilibrium price—the price that prevails in this market—is $1.80 per pound. It is at this price that demand equals supply, or the market is cleared. At this price, there is no excess supply or excess demand. Because it is sometimes easier to understand relationships visually, Figure 3-6 shows these demand and supply schedules combined on the same graph.

As you can see, $1.80 is the equilibrium price—the price that clears this competitive market. This is so because any other price would create either scarcity or glut.

Suppose that for a while one of the meat markets cuts its price to $1.20 per pound. From Figure 3-6, on page 60, we can see that the consumers would like to buy nine steaks per week at that price, while the firms would supply only two. The difference—seven steaks—is **excess demand**; or, from the consumers' point of view, a shortage of steaks.

(Other examples of excess demand are long lines of drivers waiting for gas when a small gas station offers gas at cut-rate prices and the rush to get cheap balcony seats for a concert.)

Since the demand curve (D) reflects consumers' tastes, incomes, and the like, it indicates that the consumers are willing to pay more than $1.20 to obtain more than those two steaks they can buy at that price. As the consumers offer to pay more, the meat markets offer more steaks for sale. Only when steaks sell for $1.80 per pound is there no difference between the two sets of interests, supply and demand. Neither of the consumers is willing to pay more than $1.80 to buy the additional steaks that the meat markets would supply if the price were higher.

What's the matter with prices higher than $1.80? At a price of $2.40, the meat markets will gladly supply nine steaks per week. But at that price, one consumer will not buy *any* steaks, and the other consumer will buy only *one*. The difference—eight steaks—is **excess supply**. In order to sell steaks and clear the market, the meat markets lower their prices—moving along their supply curves—until the market is cleared at $1.80. (Other examples of excess supply are new cars left on the showroom floor at the end of a model year and new textbooks left on a bookstore's shelves after a new edition comes out.)

Equilibrium at a price of $1.80 lasts as long as the set of forces defining supply and demand holds. If supply changes, as in the shift to S_1 (more supplied at all prices), a new market-clearing price (or equilibrium price) comes into being, in this instance at $1.50, where $D = S_1$.

Note that *a change in supply cannot change demand, and a change in demand cannot change supply.* In a competitive market, demand and supply are independent of each other. Thus a change in the supply from

TABLE 3-3 Market Demand and Supply Schedules for T-bone Steaks

Price per pound	Demand per week		Supply per week
$2.50	0		9
2.40	1		9
2.10	3		7
1.80	5	= Equilibrium =	5
1.50	7		3
1.20	9		2
.90	11		1
.60	13		0

FIGURE 3-6 Market Demand and Supply: Equilibrium Pricing of T-bone Steaks

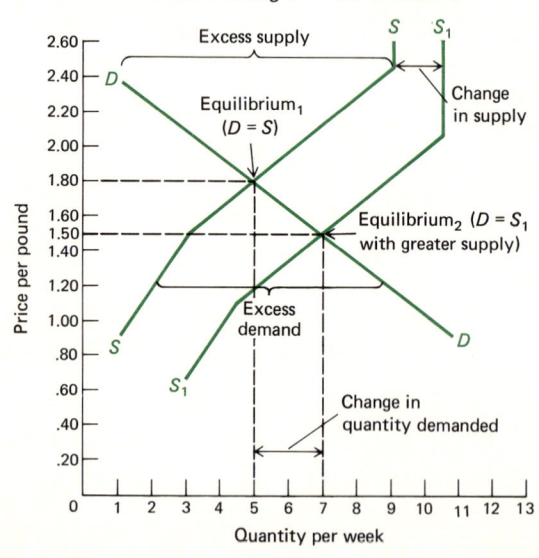

60 Supply and Demand: Price Determination in Competitive Capitalism

Competitive pricing: Putting supply and demand together (Herb Moyer)

S to S_1 results in a change in quantity demanded (see the bottom of Figure 3-6 between 5 and 7 on the horizontal axis).

It follows that (1) any change in supply or demand changes price, (2) any change in supply changes the quantity demanded, and (3) any change in demand changes the quantity supplied. The only exception occurs when equal and offsetting changes (either increases or decreases) of supply and demand occur simultaneously.

Conditions for Competitive Pricing

Let us summarize the conditions that are necessary for competitive pricing to exist.

1. *Completely flexible pricing.* If the government (or some other agency) had set the price of meat at $1.20, there would have been excess unsatisfied demand. Black markets would have developed—as they did for gasoline in the winter of 1974—to fill this unsatisfied demand at unregulated prices.

2. *Full information.* In order for prices to be bid up or down to equilibrium, buyers and sellers obviously need to be aware of their alternatives, such as other prices.

3. *Expectation of constant prices.* If consumers think that today's $1.80 price will come down to $1.50 tomorrow, they may not buy any steak

today. If producers think the same way, they may want to supply more steaks today than they would have otherwise.

4. *Free entry to and exit from markets*. Both buyers and sellers must be free to participate in the market or withdraw from it. In other words, there must be complete mobility of resources.

5. *Maximization of satisfaction and profits*. Buyers and sellers seek to maximize their satisfaction or profits, respectively, and always act to do so.

6. *Absence of conspiracies*. There must be no conspiracies between single buyers or sellers or between groups of buyers and sellers. Otherwise, prices might be pegged rather than being competitively flexible.

SUMMING UP

1. Studying the market system helps to answer three basic questions about the use of resources: (a) *what* goods are produced (composition), (b) *how* goods are produced (technique), and (c) *for whom* goods are produced (distribution).

2. To understand the market system, one needs to begin with conditions of *competition:* the market form in which a single person has no influence over the price at which she or he buys or sells.

3. Since each participant in a competitive market acts independently, *prices*—the signals for action in the market—are determined by unrelated movements of demand and supply.

4. There are two sides to every market: the demand side and the supply side. *Demand* is a set of relationships showing the quantities of a good that consumers will buy over a specific range of prices within a specific period of time.

5. One draws a demand curve for a good on the assumption of *ceteris paribus* (other things being equal). In other words, one assumes that the price, and only the price, of that good changes, not any of the other factors of demand.

6. We expect a demand schedule or demand curve to reflect the following facts.
    a. *Demand curves* slope downward to the right, which means that people buy more of a thing at low prices than at high prices (the law of demand).
    b. The strength of our taste for a good diminishes beyond some rate of consumption, as we use more and more of it in a given period of time.

7. The *law of demand* is based on (a) the income effect and (b) the substitution effect. The *income effect:* As the price of a good falls, the

consumer has more purchasing power and buys more of that good as a result. The *substitution effect:* As the price of a desirable good falls, it becomes relatively cheaper than those goods for which it is a substitute. Thus people buy more of it because it is cheaper.

8. There are exceptions to the normal case, such as *Veblen goods* (diamonds, caviar, sable coats), and, in poor countries, certain basic staple goods *(income-inferior goods)* such as beans and rice. When the price of these inferior goods falls, the purchasing power of consumers increases. Consumers eat less of their income-inferior goods than before and use their increased purchasing power to buy a more diversified diet.

9. For a given good, a *change in quantity demanded* is a movement along a demand curve. It can result only from a change in the price of the good. A *change in demand* is a shift of the demand curve, and can result from a change in any of the other factors affecting demand: income, tastes, and the prices of substitutes and complements.

10. Basic factors that can change demand are (a) consumers' income, (b) consumers' tastes and preferences, (c) prices of other products, (d) consumers' expectations for future market conditions and prices, and (e) number of consumers.

11. One can estimate the curve for market demand by adding individual curves, given that consumers buy independently of each other. Curves for market demand get their shapes from the demand curves of individuals, but measure larger quantities.

12. *Supply* is the set of relationships showing the quantities of a product that a firm will offer for sale at each possible price within a specified period of time.

13. Factors that can change supply are (a) changes in technology, (b) changes in production costs, (c) changes in prices of other goods, (d) changes in firms' expectations about future prices, and (e) changes in the number of firms.

14. A *supply curve* shows that (a) firms supply more of a given product at high prices than at low prices, and (b) there is a price below which firms supply nothing to the market.

15. Supply curves that slope upward to the right are based on the assumption that ultimately firms run into decreasing efficiency and increasing costs as they expand output, either because of fixed physical facilities or difficulty in managing a larger operation.

16. One can estimate the curve for market supply by adding supply curves of individual firms, assuming that each firm behaves independently of the others. Changes in the number of firms cause changes in market supply.

17. Competitive prices are *equilibrium prices.* That is, they are market-clearing prices. When there are equilibrium prices, demand and supply are equal and there is neither excess demand nor excess supply.

18. If prices are *above* equilibrium, there is *excess supply*—a market glut or excess. If prices are *below* equilibrium, there is *excess demand*—a market shortage. In either case, demand and supply are not in equilibrium.

19. Factors necessary to ensure competitive prices are (a) completely flexible prices, with neither *price ceilings* (a legal restriction on how high prices may be) nor *price floors* (a legal restriction on the limit below which prices may not move); (b) possession of full information by both buyers and sellers; (c) expectation of constant prices; (d) free entry into and exit from markets; (e) consistent effort of firms to maximize profits and of consumers to maximize satisfaction; and (f) no collusion between buyers and sellers; all must behave independently of each other.

QUESTIONS

1. Review the basic questions about use of resources, questions that are common to all societies. Be sure that you not only understand these questions but also realize why we need answers.

2. Define *competition*, as economists use the word. How does the economist's way of looking at competition differ from your familiar usage of the word?

3. What is *demand*? Does the economist's meaning of demand differ from your usual meaning? If so, what do you think accounts for the differences? What is the *ceteris paribus* assumption?

4. Why do demand curves usually slope downward to the right? What would it mean if one sloped *up* to the right? List the five basic factors that influence demand. Which of these factors, in addition to price, do you think will be most influential in determining the demand for (a) cars? (b) safety matches? Why?

5. Define the *income effect* and the *substitution effect*. For a small change in the price of a good, which of the two effects would you expect to be more important? What are inferior goods? Can you think of some possible examples beyond those given in the chapter?

6. What is the *law of demand*? How is it explained? What can cause a change in demand? A change in quantity demanded?

7. How does one derive curves for market demand? What assumption(s) does one use to do so?

8. What is the *supply curve*? How do competitive suppliers behave toward each other? Why do supply curves usually slope up to the right?

9. What factors determine supply? What can cause a change in supply? A change in quantity supplied?

10. How does one derive curves for market supply? What assumption(s) does one use to do so?

11. How is *price* determined in a competitive market? What does *equilibrium* mean, in relation to the operation of a market? What conditions must exist in a market for competitive prices to be established? Are they hard to establish? Do you know any markets in which these conditions exist, or are approximated?

12. Suppose that you are chief economist for an automobile industry council. You are asked to forecast industry sales for next year. You know that in the coming year personal income is expected to rise by 8 percent, that mass transit is going to be heavily subsidized by government, and that the population and its average age are expected to remain fairly constant. What influences will each of these factors have on your forecast?

SUGGESTED READINGS

Arrow, Kenneth J., and William M. Capron. "Dynamic Shortages and Price Rises: The Engineer Scientist Case." *Quarterly Journal of Economics and Business*, May 1959. Reprinted in *Economics: Readings in Analysis and Policy*, edited by Dennis R. Starleaf. Scott, Foresman, Glenview, Ill., 1969.

Heilbroner, Robert L. *The Making of Economic Society*. Prentice-Hall, Englewood Cliffs, N.J., 1962.

Heyne, Paul T. *The Economic Way of Thinking*. Science Research, Chicago, 1973.

Minahan, John. "Is Free Market a Dirty Word?" *Saturday Review*, July 12, 1975. Reprinted in *Readings in Economics*, 76/77. Dushkin, Guilford, Conn., 1976.

Mundell, Robert A. *Man and Economics*. New York: McGraw-Hill, 1968.

Spencer, Milton H. *Contemporary Economics*, 2d ed. Worth, New York, 1974. Chapter 4.

Application 3

Should We Let Supply and Demand Work? The Price of Gasoline

First Shortages, Then Price Hikes

The attachment of Americans to their automobiles (and to their boats, their power mowers, and so on) is well known. We have created an entire urban-suburban civilization around these machines, involving both our work and our recreational habits. Furthermore, our homes and offices depend for their comfort on electricity, and most electric-power plants burn oil. Our whole lifestyle is based on oil and its derivative, gasoline. So the price and availability of gasoline are sensitive subjects, important to all of us.

No sane person expects the producers to give gasoline away. But at the same time the public is confused and angry over the price fluctuations. Exactly how *is* the retail price of gasoline determined? Let's examine Figure A3-1, which gives us a simplified handhold on the subject.

For simplicity's sake, let's temporarily ignore some of the complexities in gasoline pricing, and assume the following:

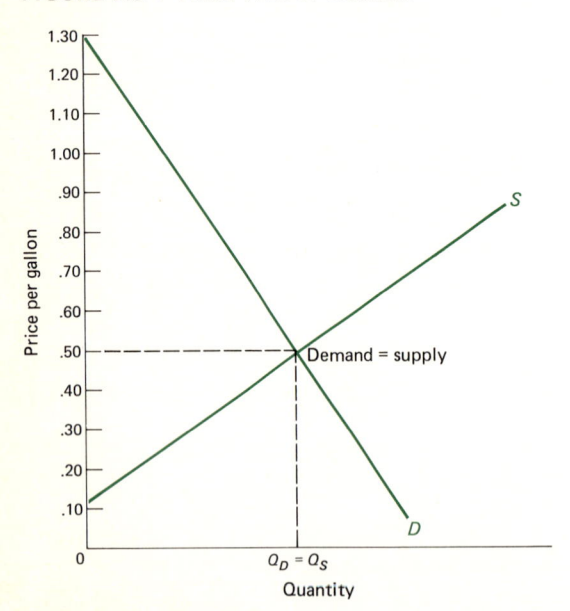

1. There is a single price for gasoline (no variations in price due to special mixtures, whose prices may vary from one market to another).

2. All the conditions necessary for competition discussed in Chapter 3 (full price information, and so on) are met.

We know from Chapter 3 that an *equilibrium* price is one that tends to eliminate excess supply or excess demand. In other words, it is a price that clears the market. In Figure A3-1, the equilibrium price (at which demand is equal to supply) is 50 cents per gallon. Changes in gasoline prices—such as the price hikes of the 1970s—must arise from changes in supply or demand, or in both. To understand why the price of gasoline rose, we must understand what happened to the demand for gas and the supply of gas.

The initial stimulus for these big price increases was the oil embargo imposed by the Arab nations in 1973, and the subsequent actions of the oil-exporting cartel (Organization of Petroleum Exporting Countries, **OPEC**). As you probably know, in the early seventies, the OPEC countries quintupled the price of their crude oil. Figure A3-2

FIGURE A3-1 Retail Price of Gasoline

FIGURE A3-2 Retail Price of Gasoline: OPEC Embargo

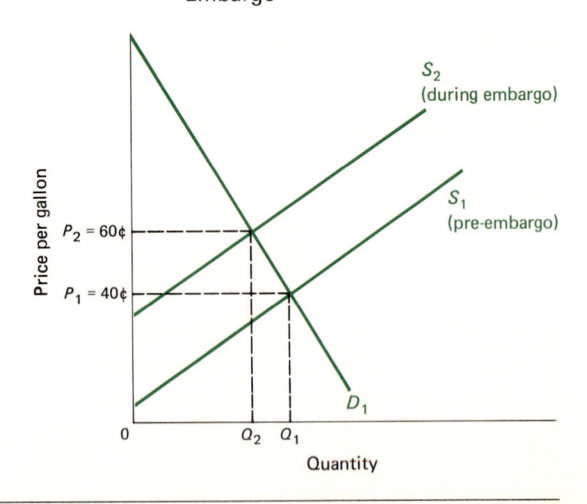

shows some of the effects of OPEC's actions on gasoline prices.

For the immediate pre-embargo period, supply is represented by S_1 and demand by D_1. The market was cleared at 40 cents per gallon (the equilibrium price). Gas stations were open long hours, seven days a week, and there were no waiting lines. There were even occasional gas-price wars, as wholesalers got rid of excess inventories.

Then the OPEC group instituted an oil embargo, and what happened? (Look again at Figure A3-2.) Since the United States had to import an increasing percentage of the crude oil that it refined into gasoline, the supply of gasoline dropped and the quantity demanded went down as well (from Q_1 to Q_2). Notice that it took a *50 percent* increase in the price of gasoline (from 40 cents to 60 cents a gallon), to clear the market and get rid of the lines at gas stations. The price went so high that people finally stopped buying so much.

Why did it take such a large price increase? Because consumers (including businesses) didn't reduce their purchases of gasoline very much as the price went up. This isn't surprising, since in our automobile- and truck-oriented society, there are no good substitutes for gasoline (although public transportation may someday help solve this problem). Another factor is that Americans spend a fairly small percentage of their incomes on gasoline. Even if gas goes up in price by 50 percent, it will not impoverish us or make us stop buying. It takes a *very large* increase in gasoline prices to cause us to cut back drastically on our buying of it. For the embargo period of 1973, when the United States had to do without imported Arab oil, economists estimated that the price necessary to clear the market would have to be somewhere between 60 cents and 80 cents per gallon. And the estimate was accurate.

What Can We Do?

Since the OPEC countries are in effect a **cartel**—a group of producers who behave like a monopoly—we must find ways to deal with them. In the 1970s, and well into the foreseeable future, we need to spend fewer dollars on monopolistically priced foreign oil. And it's not just money that's at stake. If the OPEC countries decide to cut off shipments of crude oil to us entirely, we may face another embargo-induced oil shortage. Clearly, every method we use to reduce our spending on foreign oil involves either supply or demand, or both. If only we could cut down on demand; our problem could be solved.

What are the ways to influence demand? Look at Figure A3-3, and note first that, before the OPEC oil embargo, Americans used a quantity of gasoline represented by Q_1 on the diagram.

Now suppose that we want to cut our gasoline consumption from this pre-embargo level of Q_1 to a post-embargo level of Q_3. We therefore have to restrict supply to Q_3, a level that will enable us to reduce foreign oil imports to an "acceptable" level, although it will not eliminate our need to import foreign oil entirely. However, if demand stays at the pre-embargo level (D_1) and if supply is only Q_3, it will take a price of 80 cents per gallon to clear the market. (Notice where those lines intersect.) Although this price will certainly get rid of queues at gas stations, ration the supply of gasoline, and perhaps induce greater exploration for petroleum and petroleum substitutes, it will hurt people with small incomes who have to commute to work in areas where public transportation is poor. In other words, gas at 80 cents a gallon would create a redistribution of income.

(One slightly optimistic note: High-priced gas discourages "frivolous" consumption—drag racing, teen-agers idly cruising up and down Main Street—and encourages people to use car pools, all of which would protect the environment from unnecessary gasoline fumes.)

What other alternatives do we have? One alternative would be to find good substitutes for

FIGURE A3-3 Retail Price of Gasoline: Changing Demand

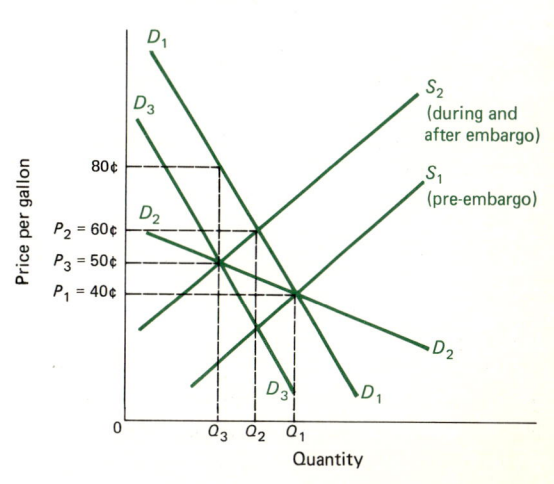

"Did you know our new car will accelerate to sixty miles in ten seconds?"

gasoline, such as a really good mass transit system in urban and suburban areas. Americans have very little taste for public transportation; nonetheless, with this alternative mode of transportation, people's demand for gasoline might become D_2 rather than D_1 (in other words, the curve would become more nearly horizontal). And note that with demand D_2 goes a more "socially acceptable" price of 50 cents a gallon. Gas at 50 cents a gallon will clear the market of Q_3 of gasoline. Also note that with D_2, there is a greater fall in the quantity of gasoline demanded, and therefore a greater fall in the demand for imported crude oil, than there is with D_1. But it may take years to create the substitutes reflected in the slope of D_2. In the meantime, the price of gas will probably move up along D_1 to 60 cents or even 80 cents a gallon. And in an attempt to remedy the situation, governments may tax away a large part of this increase and use the revenues to help create the substitutes.

A second means of adjusting to a smaller supply of gasoline (Q_3) without huge price increases is to decrease demand. Doing this requires changing our taste for using cars; decreasing our incomes (the recession of the mid-1970s has eased the situation); cutting the price of substitute goods (for example, mass transit); making wide use of car pools; putting a tax on cars with only one person in them; or raising the price of complementary goods (for example, cars). In addition—although it is unlikely—if we *believe* that gasoline prices will go down in the future, we will buy less gasoline today.

Suppose that for one or another of these reasons (or a combination of all of them), demand for gas shrinks from D_1 to D_3 (still, however, without there being good substitutes for gas). With demand smaller, Q_3, amount of gas, can be rationed in the marketplace with a market-clearing price of 50 cents per gallon—the same as with D_2 which, as you recall, reflects better substitutes for gas.

What About Supply?

In the long run, when gasoline refineries can expand, a large part of the solution to very high gasoline prices must be a bigger supply of gas. But for environmental and other reasons, it may not be good to have very low gas prices; this would only encourage an ever growing use of private cars, with the pollution and noise they bring in their wake. Still, we do have a society that now is, and will be for a long time, dependent on the automobile. To keep the price of gasoline within reach of most people for at least essential uses, we will have to increase supply. There are two main ways to do this.

1. *Increase the supply of other forms of energy*, for example, solar energy, nuclear energy, geothermal energy, and clean-burning devices to burn our vast coal reserves. This will free much of our crude oil for gasoline refining.

2. *Increase new discoveries of oil*, for example, the north slopes of Alaska and the offshore oil fields on the west and east coasts of the United States. (*A negative note:* In the case of offshore oil drilling there is controversy about environmental impact and the threat of oil spills.)

Whichever way we handle the situation, an increase in supply of crude oil and gasoline will keep the market-clearing price of a restricted supply (further restricted by a limitation on oil imports) below what it would otherwise be. Figure A3-3 indicates that if we had more oil, and if we burned more coal, this might increase the available (constrained) supply of gasoline from Q_3 to Q_2. And if demand were still D_1 (and consumers couldn't find any good substitutes), the market-clearing price of oil would be 60 cents rather than 80 cents a gallon, as it would be with D_1 and Q_3.

Strategies

So long as we rely on a free market system to ration gasoline by means of price, any strategy to deal with restricted imports has to involve changes in both demand and supply. Perhaps we should just let the price go to 80 cents (Figure A3-3) but give people rebates—maybe by allowing an income tax deduction for some maximum amount per year. At the same time, perhaps the government could put an excise tax on every gallon (to push the price to 80 cents) and with that tax money could finance research to produce new sources of energy and tap new oil fields. This strategy might eventually bring the price down to 60 cents or even 45 cents a gallon, especially if the public had new substitutes for the private car.

An alternative strategy is to set up a system of rationing and price controls. For example, suppose that the amount of gasoline the government allocates to private consumers is Q_3. The government can issue ration books (this is sometimes called **coupon economics**) and fix the price by law. It can decree that gas stations may charge 50 cents a gallon, which would be "fair" to the people who drive to work. Or perhaps it would let the price go as high as 80 cents, so that it could tax the increase and reinvest in the search for new energy sources.

In 1975, the Ford administration proposed a more nearly pure market solution. This proposal was to free from price controls all "new" oil produced in the United States. (A lot of "old" oil—that is, oil being pumped from wells that had been in existence formerly—had a controlled price far below the world market price for oil.) This proposal had a twofold purpose: (1) Letting oil companies charge a higher price for "new" oil would be an incentive to them to explore for oil and to drill new wells (increase supply). (2) The high price of gasoline would discourage people from consuming so much (reduce quantity demanded) and would also reduce dependence on imported oil.

In December 1975, the President and Congress compromised on a plan by which new oil was rolled back in price. However, over a period of two years, the prices of new and old oil would be permitted to move upward until they were level with prices of oil on the world market. Presumably this provided the stimulus to oil companies to explore for new oil and also to develop other energy resources as substitutes for oil, which would decrease the demand. By mid-1976, however, the percentage of imported oil reached a new high of 40 percent of total consumption. Domestic oil production fell through the first half of 1976. Finding a solution to the oil import problem appeared no closer.

SUMMING UP

1. The lifestyle of Americans depends heavily on the private automobile. Unfortunately, there are at present no good substitutes for buying gasoline.

2. *Equilibrium*, or market clearing, occurs when price equals supply equals demand (assuming that there is one competitively determined price for gasoline).

3. The oil embargo of 1973 cut down the U.S. supply of gasoline by reducing the amount of crude oil available to be refined. Then the *OPEC* countries, acting like a monopoly, caused world petroleum prices to quintuple.

4. A drop in the supply of gasoline in the United States results in a *very large* increase in price, because there are no good substitutes for gasoline. Consumers bid up the price in an effort to maintain their consumption pattern, that is, their lifestyle.

5. If the United States wants to reduce the number of dollars spent on foreign oil, there are three choices open: (a) reduce the demand for gasoline, (b) create better substitutes for gasoline, and (c) increase the supply of gasoline.

6. Once the government decides what level of oil imports is acceptable, it can allow the market price to ration that constrained supply. This will mean that the price of gasoline will go up by a large amount. If the government taxes away this price increase, it can use the revenues for research to find new substitutes for gasoline.

7. It may be unfair to solve the problem of tight gasoline supply solely through price rationing, since high gas prices hit the poor harder.

8. The best answer, though it may take years, is to decrease the *demand* for gasoline, so that a scantier supply of gasoline can be rationed out to those who need it, with smaller and more equitable price increases.

9. In the long run, we will have to increase supply, in order to overcome gasoline shortages. We can do this by (a) increasing our supplies of the usual forms of energy or finding new supplies or new forms of energy, and (b) discovering new sources of oil. Increased supplies of energy from either source will enable us to solve the gasoline-shortage problem with smaller price rises than would otherwise be obtained.

10. There are numerous strategies we could use to solve the gasoline problem. They involve either market or nonmarket (rationing and price controls) solutions.

QUESTIONS

1. Is it reasonable to suppose that the demand curve for gasoline slopes downward and the supply curve slopes upward (as in Figures A3-1 through A3-3)? Why?

2. From your own experience, is gasoline retailing competitive?

3. Looking ahead, do you think the factors affecting the supply of and demand for gasoline point to lower gasoline prices in the next:
   a. 2 years?
   b. 5 years?
   c. 15 years?

4. Would you be willing to let the price of gasoline go high enough to allocate a reduced supply of gasoline in the marketplace? Why, or why not?

5. If the OPEC cartel broke up, the price of foreign crude oil might become more competitive. What would happen to:
   a. the supply of gasoline in the United States?
   b. the demand for gasoline in the United States?

6. Will it be very hard to create good substitutes for gasoline in our society? Why, or why not?

7. Propose a strategy to solve our crude oil and gasoline problems.

SUGGESTED READINGS

Economic Impact of Petroleum Shortages. Hearings before the Subcommittee on International Economics, December 11, 12, and 13, 1973. Superintendent of Documents, G.P.O., Washington, D.C.

The Gasoline and Fuel Oil Shortage. Hearings before the Subcommittee on Consumer Economics, May 1 and 2; June 2, 1973. Superintendent of Documents, G.P.O, Washington, D.C.

Gramm, W. Phillip. "The Energy Crisis in Perspective." *Wall Street Journal,* November 30, 1973.

Grayson, C. Jackson, Jr. "Let's End Controls—Completely." *Wall Street Journal,* February 6, 1974.

International Economic Consequences of High-Priced Energy. Committee for Economic Development, September 1975.

Mead, Walter J. "Oil, Energy, and Environmental Concern." In *Economic Analysis of Pressing Social Problems,* by Llad Phillips and Harold Votey, Jr. Rand McNally, Chicago, Ill., 1974.

Components of an Economic Society: Households, Business Firms, Governments

What are the basic parts of our economy, and how are they interrelated? One useful view is that the economy is made up of three basic sections: (1) *households*, which provide all the factors of production and in return buy the output of the firms; (2) *business firms*, which employ these factors of production and produce goods and services; and (3) *governments*, which buy part of the output of firms, and take away some of the income of householders in the form of taxes. Governments also provide various forms of goods and services. These three sectors mesh in a system of flows of income and production called the *circular-flow model* of economic activity. In this chapter we shall study this circular-flow model and then describe the characteristics of each of the three sectors.

Two applications accompany this chapter. The first discusses the question of whether businesses are committed simply to competition and profits or whether they have a sense of social responsibility that transcends profits. The second concerns our neglected cities: with such a large percentage of our people living in cities, why is so little done to halt our cities' deterioration?

The Circular-Flow Model

The Simple Model

Let us begin by simplifying things, and assume for the moment that there are only two basic components of the economy: consumers and business firms. Consumers *own* all the factors of production; that is, the resources necessary for production to take place. Firms *hire* all the factors of production, produce the goods and services consumers use, and pay a return (income) to the factors.

Figure 4-1 illustrates this. Households provide factors of production to business firms. In return, business firms pay households income for the use of those factors of production. Labor, as a factor of production, receives its reward in the form of wages and salaries. Owners of land get theirs in the form of rent; owners of capital get interest; entrepreneurs get profits. Firms utilize the factors of production to produce goods and services for the use of the householders. Householders, with incomes obtained from firms' use of their factors of production, pay firms for goods and services. Firms now have incomes so they can pay the factors of production to produce more goods and services. And so the process continues.

The circular-flow model and the world of economic production have no beginning. You may start the analysis at any point. Only the amount of resources available (factors of production) limits the level of production—resources plus technology and efficiency of use of these resources, of course. Firms use these resources because householders use all the income they receive to buy the output firms produce by employing the resources.

The upper half of Figure 4-1, showing the flow of resources and the reverse flow of income, portrays the **factor markets**, in which the supply of and demand for factors of production interact to determine prices of factors. The bottom half, which shows flows of product output and reverse flows of payments for goods and services, portrays the product markets. In these, the supply of goods and services—and the demand for them—interact to determine prices of goods, as shown in Chapter 3.

The Complex Model

Figure 4-1 is a great oversimplification of our economic system. Let us now examine a more complex, more realistic circular-flow model.

Figure 4-1 assumes that households spend all their income on buying the goods and services firms produce. This is not realistic, because people do manage to save some of their income, and also pay some of their income to the government in the form of taxes, both of which reduce the demand for goods and services (see Figure 4-2). Since saving and paying taxes both mean *not* consuming, these two factors reduce households' demand for firms' output.

FIGURE 4-1 Simple Circular-Flow Model. The flow of resources, products, and income between firms and households is circular in nature.

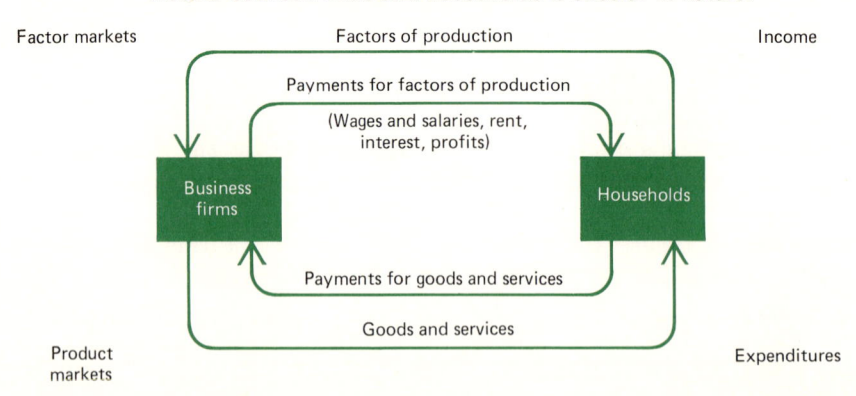

Figure 4-1 also assumes that all output goes to households in the form of goods and services. Again this is unrealistic. The complete model includes two other sources of demand for firms' output:

1. *Other firms.* When firms demand output from other firms, this is not counted as part of the flows of goods and services to households, but as capital goods that aid in the production of other goods and services.

2. *Governments.* Federal, state, and local governments demand output from firms.

In both complex and simple circular-flow models of the economy, the flows of income to households consist of wages, rent, interest, and profits. However, in the complex model, households spend their incomes not only on consumption, but also on savings and taxes. Governments enter the picture with spending for goods and services, and so do business firms themselves, with expenditures for investment. So the flow of funds is still circular.

The money that taxes siphon from households' incomes becomes part of the purchasing power governments use for their expenditures. In addition, financial institutions make available for investment the money they get from people's savings. This keeps the money flowing. (By *financial institutions*, we usually mean savings banks, commercial banks, and stock exchanges, though there are many other kinds.)

FIGURE 4-2 Complex Circular-Flow Model. Savings and taxes drain off households' purchasing power and thus reduce their demand for consumer goods. Investment and government expenditures increase the demand for firms' output. These additions are also part of the flow, in that taxes become part of the government's purchasing power. And financial institutions such as banks make savings available for investment.

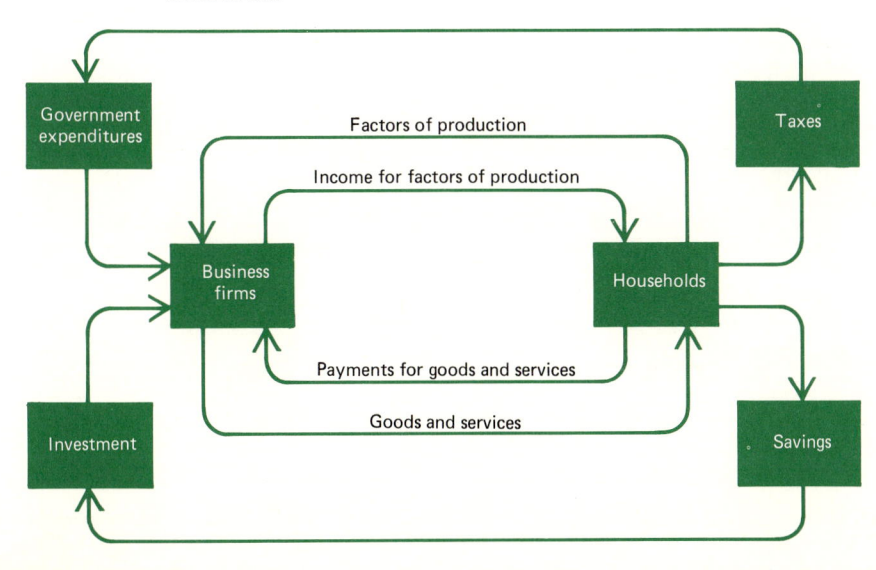

The Circular-Flow Model 73

It should be readily obvious to you that our economy is a great deal more complex than even the so-called complex model shows. Not only households, but also firms save. Firms also have to pay taxes to various governments, especially if the firms are incorporated and have, so to speak, a life of their own. Governments also provide goods and services to households (for example, public schools). Governments, furthermore, provide households with income. By this we don't mean just social security and welfare payments. Governments provide jobs; governments hire labor from households. And not only firms invest (demand capital from other firms); households also invest. The main form their investments take is home buying. (A house is considered an investment.) The list of activities that could be added to the model is endless. But the complex model gives us enough of a picture for us to continue our analysis.

What Does the Model Show?

The model tells us that there are three sources of demand for the output of firms: households, other business firms, and governments. There are, therefore, as many different levels of demand as there are combinations of spending patterns by these three parts of society.

This more complex system of economic flow doesn't necessarily result in a socially desirable level of demand. It is, of course, socially desirable to have full employment and a low rate of inflation. Yet households, because they have to set aside money for savings and for taxes, reduce their demand for consumer goods. Firms, by their investments, and governments, by buying output of business firms, may take up some of the slack—but not all. So you may have a decrease in demand for goods and services and, eventually, unemployment. (The circular flow decreases.) But if governments and business firms spend *more* than households have saved and have paid in taxes, then demand for products and services increases (the circular flow increases) and inflation may result. This is an oversimplification, but you get the general idea.

The rest of this chapter will deal with various aspects of the three sectors and show what determines their patterns of demand for goods and services.

HOUSEHOLDS

There are three basic questions about households: (1) Where do they get their income? (2) How do they use it? (3) What is their share of total income? Answers to these questions will give you an insight into the probable effects of the economic decisions of households on total output and income and on the level and composition of output.

The Sources of Income: Functional Distribution

When we are talking about sources of income, we speak of the distribution of income as a **functional distribution**. Households—in other words, people—receive their income from the wages and salaries they get from working; owners of land get theirs from rent; owners of capital get theirs from interest; businesses, both corporations and unincorporated firms, get theirs in the form of profits that are a result of their entrepreneurial activity. Economists look at these sources of income in terms of the functions they perform. It is convenient to view this functional distribution in relative terms, using percentage shares, as in Table 4-1.

Labor gets the largest portion of the money income, in the form of wages and salaries. Labor's share increased from 60 percent at the end of the 1920s to more than 70 percent at the beginning of the 1970s. Labor's increase is due mainly to the decline in the share that went to owners of unincorporated firms (proprietors' income), which fell by more than half during the same time span.

Corporate profits—which ran about 10 to 15 percent of total income during this period—vary according to the state of the economy. They go down in times of recession and go up when times are good. The share of income that comes from rent has been fairly steady (between 2 and 4 percent), while the share of income that comes from interest declined between 1929 and 1970 because of falling interest rates. However, in the 1970s the share of interest income went up to 6 percent and more because of the revival of high interest rates.

Many factors contributed to the changing ratios. Chief among them are changing market demand and supply for different resources, government's enlarged role in maintaining high levels of employment, strengthening of labor's power because of unions, growth in the number of corporations, and continued concentration of economic activity in corporate enterprise. You can see that both market and nonmarket forces play a role in determining the functional distribution of income.

TABLE 4-1 Percentage Functional Distribution of Income

	1929	1941	1950	1960	1974
Wages and salaries	60	62	69	71	75
Proprietors' income	17	16	15	10	6
Corporate profits	12	15	15	11	10
Rental income	6	3	4	4	2
Interest income	5	3	1	2	6

Source: U.S. Department of Commerce, *Statistical Abstract of the United States* and *Survey of Current Business Output,* 1974.

The Way Households Allocate Their Income

How do people spend their money? They usually spend almost 80 percent of it on personal consumption, of which about 15 percent (see Tables 4-2 and 4-3) is spent for consumer durables such as automobiles, furniture, and electrical equipment. The rest is divided evenly between nondurable goods (doughnuts, shoes) and services (movies, haircuts).

Householders pay about 15 percent of their income in taxes to the various levels of government, a figure that has grown in both absolute and relative terms from only 3 percent of their income in 1929. A substantial part of this increase is due to the increase in government expenditures for military goods and services. There have also been big increases in government social services: social security, Medicare, aid to education and housing, welfare and unemployment relief, highway construction, expansion of the park service—the list is a long one. (Almost 50 percent of the U.S. budget in 1975 was expenditures for human resources.) So we *are* getting something in return for our money.

The Way Personal Income Is Distributed

How is money distributed throughout the United States? Who has much, and who has little? Table 4-4, on page 78, gives us a general idea and shows the unequal nature of the distribution, even in the early 1970s. The highest-income people—those earning $25,000 a year and more—represented only 6 percent of families, but they received 16 percent of the U.S. income. Those with less than $5,000 a year (18 percent of families) received less than 5 percent of the income. You can see this inequality in another way when you look at the income ranking. The one-fifth, or 20 percent, of families with the lowest incomes received only 6 percent of the U.S. income, while the 20 percent of families with the highest incomes received 40 percent of the income.

When you convert the data on income distribution in Table 4-4 into a graph, you get a curve of the inequality of income. This curve has a special shape, which is called a **Lorenz curve** (Figure 4-3). It shows the difference between the actual distribution of income and a perfectly proportional distribution. By comparing the Lorenz curves for various

TABLE 4-2 Households' Allocation of Income, 1974

	Billions of dollars	Percent
Consumption	877	77
Savings	76.7	7
Taxes	170.7	16

Source: *Economic Report of the President*, 1975.

TABLE 4-3 Composition of Expenditures for Personal Consumption, 1974

	Billions of dollars	Percent
Durable goods	128	14
Nondurable goods	381	44
Services	368	42

Source: Ibid.

One household allocating part of its income (Herb Moyer)

countries, you can also compare the relative inequality in the distribution of income between one country and another. However, before you draw any conclusions, remember that the Lorenz curve shows money income only and not noncash production, such as food that farmers grow for their own tables. Therefore comparisons between countries, especially when noncash incomes are significant, may be misleading.

Since 1935, there has been some trend toward a more equal distribution of income in the United States, with the largest change between 1935 and 1945, mainly because of four factors: (1) The United States pulled out of the depression, and wartime gave rise to full employment, which increased workers' income quickly. (2) During the war, excess-profits taxes and a more progressive income tax reduced the

TABLE 4-4 Distribution of Family Income in the United States, 1971

	Percent of families in class	Percent of income received in class	Family income by rank	Percent of total income
Under $2,500	6	1	Lowest one-fifth	6
$2,500–$4,999	12	4	Second one-fifth	12
$5,000–$7,499	14	8	Third one-fifth	18
$7,500–$9,999	15	11	Fourth one-fifth	24
$10,000–$12,499	15	16	Highest one-fifth	40
$12,500–$14,999	12	14		
$15,000–$24,999	20	30		
$25,000 and up	6	16		

Source: U.S. Department of Commerce, *Statistical Abstract of the United States,* 1973.

after-tax income of the rich more than that of the poor. (3) Wartime labor scarcity increased opportunities to blacks and other minorities that had been discriminated against before. (4) Labor unions quadrupled their membership and increased the relative income of their members.

Then, between 1945 and 1955, the trend toward more equality in distribution of income continued, but slowed. (1) After the war, the labor unions continued to increase the relative incomes of their members, but met greater resistance in their efforts to do so. (2) Continued prosperity meant continued good jobs for minorities and women. There were also increased educational opportunities for minorities. (3) The GI bill enabled millions of men who would not have attended college to do so and to achieve higher levels of skill than they would have otherwise.

FIGURE 4-3 Lorenz Curve: Distribution of Family Income in the United States, 1971. The straight diagonal line shows what a perfectly proportional distribution of income would look like. The shaded area, which is the difference between the actual (unequal) and the perfectly proportional distribution, represents the inequality of income.

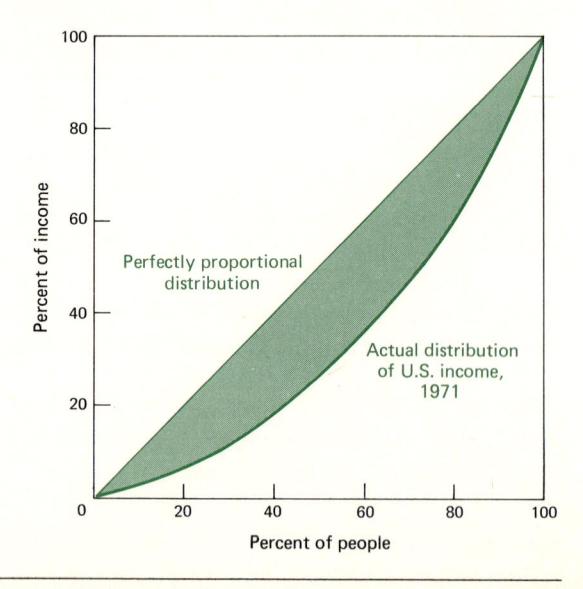

78 Components of an Economic Society: Households, Business Firms, Governments

These factors, however, were not felt as strongly as the factors that influenced the period from 1935 to 1945.

Since 1955, the distribution of income has remained relatively constant, because governments, at all levels, have imposed taxes that are less progressive in nature than in former years. Also the number of families that economists call "economically irrelevant" has been increasing. (When we say that certain workers are economically irrelevant, we mean they do not have the skills necessary for employment. Employers aren't looking for people with their skills. The economy, in other words, doesn't need them.) The increases in taxes and in the number of economically irrelevant workers have slowed the trend toward greater equality in income.

Economic Implications of Inequality in Income Distribution

Although the ethical implications of inequality in distribution of income are fascinating, we will restrict ourselves to the economic implications.

In underdeveloped countries, the main problem is to increase the economy's output so that all citizens can have a better standard of living. These countries need increased resources, especially capital, to shift the production-possibilities curve outward and increase economic growth. New capital can be made by increasing savings. Increasing savings withdraws resources from the production of consumer goods, thus making these resources available for investment, that is, producing capital. So to increase the formation of capital and to foster more rapid economic growth, a higher rate of savings is needed. The rich save a larger percentage of their income than the poor because the poor spend all their income just to keep alive or maintain a low standard of living. Thus a more *un*even distribution of income would increase the income of the rich and might increase savings. Therefore one might argue that an underdeveloped country, in order to increase savings and the rate of formation of new capital, ought to have a less equal income distribution than it already has.

On the other hand, in a developed economy, the main problem is how to maintain full employment and keep the large industrial system growing. To do this, you want consumers to demand all the goods and services that business firms can produce. Here one may reverse the argument of the preceding paragraph and say that a developed country ought to have *its* income more evenly distributed. That way, the rich would get a smaller slice of the pie. Savings would be less and consumer demand higher.

But we must keep at least two things in mind. First, this is a gross simplification; the problems of economic growth and full employment are much more complex than this brief sketch indicates. Second, economic *efficiency* (maximizing output with a given set of resources) is not the same thing as economic *equity* (what we think is right or wrong in a moral sense). The implications for distribution of income differ, depending on whether our goal is efficiency or equity and on what weight we give to each.

BUSINESS FIRMS

Today there are more than 10 million companies in the United States, from the corner grocery store to such corporate giants as AT&T. We can classify business firms primarily under three legal headings: (1) *Sole proprietorships*, (2) *partnerships*, and (3) *corporations*.

Sole Proprietorships

The commonest form of business organization is the **sole proprietorship**, an enterprise owned by one person, who is solely responsible for it. There are more than 9 million sole proprietorships in the United States, chiefly in agriculture, the retail trade, pharmacy, law, and medicine. They are usually small in scale and have an average life span of five to seven years. Although hundreds of thousands cease production each year, even larger numbers begin each year.

Advantages of a Sole Proprietorship
1. You can easily form a sole proprietorship; it doesn't take much cash. In many areas, just the act of beginning production is all that is necessary.

2. The sole proprietor is the only one to receive benefits when the firm succeeds, and is the only one reponsible for its activity, so there is a close correlation between effort expended and reward. Thus the incentives for efficiency are great.

Disadvantages of a Sole Proprietorship
1. The sole proprietorship has **unlimited liability**. This means that there is no differentiation between the assets of the business enterprise and the personal wealth of the proprietor. If the business incurs losses, the proprietor is responsible for them.

2. Sole proprietors must rely on themselves for all management skills, and since no one person can be a specialist in all managerial functions, the business may suffer. Inadequate management is the chief cause of failure in small, sole-proprietor businesses.

3. The sole proprietorship often runs out of capital, since the proprietor has to depend primarily on his or her own resources, and an individual's borrowing capacity is limited. (One person alone, for instance, has enough credit, or borrowing capacity, to borrow x dollars; two people

have $2x$; three people have $3x$; and so forth.) Sole proprietors also tend to have lower credit ratings than partnerships or corporations.

4. The sole proprietorship has *limited life,* in the sense that the lifetime of the business may be limited to the working lifetime of the proprietor.

Partnerships

A second form of business organization is the **partnership**, in which two or more individuals combine to operate a business enterprise. There are several kinds of partnerships, but the following is a general description.

Advantages of a Partnership
1. Because there are two or more people involved in the ownership, the partner-owned business has access to more capital. The enterprise can draw on the wealth and borrowing power of its several partners.

2. A business with more than one owner can count on specialized skills in management. One partner can be in charge of production; another of accounting; a third, of sales; and so on. Specialization of management functions strengthens a business greatly.

Disadvantages of a Partnership
1. A partnership, like a sole proprietorship, has unlimited liability. Each individual partner's personal wealth can be tapped to pay debts. Each partner is responsible not only for his or her own mistakes, but also for the mistakes of all the rest of the partners.

2. Partnerships have limited life, which fosters instability. Partnership agreements are automatically dissolved whenever a partner dies, or whenever one withdraws from the partnership because of a disagreement. The remaining partners may draw up a new partnership agreement, or they may not.

3. Partnerships have limited access to capital. Various devices that the corporation can use to raise financial capital are not available to the partnership.

Corporations

Corporations are legal entities that function separately from their owners. There are fewer corporations by far than there are sole proprietorships or partnerships, but corporations produce more, employ more people, and have more assets than all others combined.

Advantages of a Corporation
1. A corporation's owners have **limited liability**. This means that the people who own it—the stockholders—are not responsible for its debts. They can lose only the money they paid for their stock.

Obviously, the situation is not that simple. The owner-manager of a small corporation may very well have to pledge her or his own credit and take on a personal liability. For example, in order to raise additional funds, the manager may become personally liable by signing a personal note for a loan for the corporation. The discussion that follows, however, relates more to the larger corporation than the smaller.

2. Because a corporation is a legal entity, it can be sued (or it can sue) without the owners, the stockholders, becoming involved.

3. A corporation has **unlimited life**; it can continue to exist no matter who owns stock in it. Stockholders continually buy and sell their ownership instruments (shares of stock) with no effect on the company.

4. A corporation has access to greater amounts of money because of its ability to tap the market for financial capital, and has great flexibility in getting transfusions of capital because it can use a variety of financial instruments: bonds, preferred stock, and common stock. **Bonds** are instruments of debt; the corporation has to pay interest on them regularly, and counts this as a cost of production. Stocks, on the other hand, are equities or instruments of ownership, and the company is not required to pay dividends on them regularly. **Preferred stocks** are called preferred because the company has to pay dividends on them *before* it pays dividends to holders of **common stock**. Owners of preferred stock have no voting privileges, however, and usually there are limits on the amount of dividends the company can pay to them. Owners of common stock have full voting rights and no limitations on the amount of dividends that the company can pay them.

5. Because stockholders need not be managers of a corporation, and because the corporation can raise large amounts of financial capital, it can afford to hire efficient managers, capable of taking on very specialized management functions.

Disadvantages of a Corporation
1. Forming a corporation may take a long time and be very expensive, depending on the nature of the proposed firm. People involved in the formation of a new corporation have to follow state and federal laws, pay fees of incorporation, and pay lawyers' fees and other expenses.

2. A corporation has to pay taxes to both the state and federal governments (corporate income taxes, property taxes, and so on). This leads to **double taxation**, which means that the corporation pays taxes on the gross income it earns, and distributes parts of the remaining income as dividends to stockholders; then the stockholders have to pay income taxes on the dividends, since this money constitutes personal income.

3. State and federal governments pass laws that restrict the behavior of corporations. These restrictions do not apply to sole proprietorships or partnerships.

4. The larger the corporation, the more ownership gets separated from control, and the greater the possibility of conflict of interest between

Corporate stockholders having their say (Courtesy Arthur Lavine/Chase Manhattan Bank)

managers and owners. Large corporations may have thousands of stockholders. The largest corporations, such as AT&T, have millions. Stockholders who hold only a few shares have neither the time nor the incentive to take an active part in controlling the corporation by their votes.

When management sends out its annual report, containing a glowing description of what it has done for the stockholder this year, it includes a proxy card. This proxy card, if the stockholder signs and returns it, gives the company's management the right to vote his or her stock. If the corporation has paid the usual dividend, the stockholder generally mails the proxy card back. In this way management tends to become self-perpetuating and often may regard its stockholders as being, in a sense, the recipient of corporate welfare (after all, they get their regular dividend checks). Stockholders—busy people placated by regular payments of money—may become lethargic and uncritically accept the policies of management. Management may orient its policies first and foremost toward its own continued control of the corporation. In brief, we are implying that, in many large corporations, the stockholders may find it hard to control the management. If this occurs, the self-interest of these independent managers may conflict with the self-interest of the stockholders.

Big Business: Is It a Threat?

Americans have always worried about companies that get so big that they are able to dominate an industry, as evidenced by U.S. acceptance of the antimonopoly provisions of English Common Law and by the many antimonopoly or antitrust laws that Congress has passed since the Sherman Antitrust Act of 1890.

People have feared that large monopolistic firms would interfere in a competitive economy and even try to subvert the democratic political system, and that these firms would increase prices while reducing output, slow the rate of adoption of improved technology, and render the economic system more unstable and susceptible to business fluctuations. In addition, people have been afraid that firms of great size and wealth could encourage decisions by government that would be unduly favorable to them, and would ignore the public good.

Corporations are the dominant form of business organization, except in number. They comprise 13 percent of the number of firms, but produce 60 percent of total output. Table 4-5 shows that the four largest automobile corporations produced more than 90 percent of the output of the industry, not including imports, in 1967 alone. This was also true of the aluminum industry and the manufacture of electric light bulbs. In the computer industry one giant—IBM—dominated the many small firms that made up the rest of the industry. One must consider the degree of domination of an industry by a few firms and also by one super-giant firm.

Table 4-6 shows that in the United States in 1973 the hundred largest manufacturing corporations made about 50 percent of the profits, employed about 40 percent of workers, and made about 40 percent of the sales. Some of the big companies have more economic power than many national and state governments. For example, in 1972–1973, American Telephone and Telegraph had assets of more than $60 billion and revenues of more than $20 billion. General Motors had assets of more than $18 billion and sales of more than $30 billion.

Bigness does exist in various industries, and people fear it. At this point, however, you do not yet have the concepts and theories needed to deal with the questions "Is bigness bad or good?" and "Under what conditions would bigness be bad or good for the economy?" (We shall give considerable attention to these matters in Chapters 19, 20 and 21.) These questions are not easy to answer, but at this point we can say that bigness in a firm—in and of itself—is not necessarily "bad" economically. It depends on what the firm does with it and on the attitude of the majority of the population toward bigness.

Corporate giants cast shadows that go beyond national boundaries. **Multinational corporations** are international economic entities, which not only trade, but buy their raw materials and sell their finished products all over the world, and have production facilities in many countries. No one country can control the operations of these international firms. If unions in one country demand wage increases or a government in another country increases taxes, these multinational corporations can shift their production to plants in other countries. They are able to plan their manufacturing and marketing on a world scale.

In 1972 multinational corporations contributed about 15 percent of world production, about half of which was produced by U.S.-based multinational corporations. Japan and Western Europe also have their multinational firms (for example, Mitsubishi and Royal-Dutch Shell). But

TABLE 4-5 Concentration of Industrial Production in the Hands of a Few Large Companies

Industry	Percentage of output by four largest companies
Primary aluminum	100
Motor vehicles	92
Electric light bulbs	91
Cigarettes	81
Sewing machines	81
Steel ingots	64

Source: U.S. Bureau of the Census, 1967.

TABLE 4-6 Performance of the 500 and the 100 Largest Corporations, 1973

	Millions of sales, employees, and profits	Percentage of all U.S. corporations
For the 500 top corporations:		
Sales	$667,106	65
Employees	16	76
Profits	38,680	79
For the 100 top corporations:		
Sales	$419,583	41
Employees	8.7	41
Profits	26,335	52

Source: Fortune, May, 1974, 230–255.

the largest are American (for example, Exxon, ITT, GM), and many have 50 percent or more of their fixed assets outside the United States. These companies depend on getting a substantial share of their profits from foreign sources.

GOVERNMENTS

Governments—federal, state, and local—affect economic activities by four means: (1) expenditures, (2) taxation, (3) enactment of laws, and (4) regulatory agencies.

Expenditures: What Do They Spend All That Money On?

The expenditures of the federal government for all sorts of things, from guns to butter, stimulate output in the economy, both directly and indirectly. These expenditures stimulate output directly by demanding goods and services; they stimulate it indirectly by income transfers that do not require an immediate good or service in return, such as educational grants, social security, and interest on the national debt.

When you look at Table 4-7, you will immediately notice the figure for "Income security." Income security consists of social security and Medicare. Spending for these two programs had by 1974 climbed into first place, with 31 percent of total federal expenditures.

TABLE 4-7 Expenditures of the Federal Government, 1974

Item on which money is spent	Billions of dollars	Percent of total
National defense	78.6	28
Veterans' services	13.4	5
Interest on public debt	28.1	10
International affairs and finance	3.6	1
Space research and technology	4.1	2
Natural resources, environment, and energy	6.4	3
Income security	84.4	31
Health	22.0	9
Agricultural and rural development	2.2	1
Education and manpower	11.6	4
Commerce and transportation	13.1	5
All other	5.8	2
Total	273.3	100

Source: Economic Report of the President, 1975.

TABLE 4-8 Direct Expenditures of State and Local Governments, 1971–1972

	State			Local	
Item	Billions of dollars	Percent	Item	Billions of dollars	Percent
Education	17.2	27	Education	48.7	48
Highways	12.7	20	Police and Fire	7.7	7
Public welfare	12.2	20	Public welfare	8.9	9
Health	6.0	9	Highways	6.3	6
Natural resources	2.5	4	Health	7.0	7
Other	12.5	20	Other	27.4	23
Total	63.1	100	Total	106.0	100

Source: Bureau of the Census, *Government Finances in 1971–1972.*

Defense expenditures came second, with 28 percent. The four categories that are listed after defense expenditures are payments for obligations incurred in the past—obligations caused by national defense (veterans' services, interest on the national debt). Or they are expenses for keeping foreign allies strong or for space exploration, which are military in origin. When you add them all up, they amounted to 45 percent of total federal expenditures. But the federal budget has shifted, so that about the same proportion of it—44 percent—is spent on social programs.

Table 4-8 shows the way state and local governments generally spend their money. For states, the two major items in 1972 were education (27 percent) and construction and maintenance of highways (20 percent). These two added up to 47 percent of the states' budgets. For local governments, education expenditures ranked first, making up 48 percent of the total.

Taxation

Taxes drain off purchasing power that households (that is, people) could otherwise use to buy consumer goods. Thus taxation reduces consumer demand. Let us look briefly at the way taxation affects this demand.

Principles of Taxation

Who should pay for government services? And how much should they pay? There are two ways of looking at this problem: (1) benefits received, and (2) ability to pay.

Benefits Received. According to the **benefits-received principle**, people should pay taxes commensurate with the benefits they receive from government services. School taxes are an example: a family with two children in public schools should pay twice as much as a family with only one in public school, and a family with no children in public school should pay no school taxes.

"What did you do with all that money I gave you last year?"

This view conceives of government services as services that the taxpayer buys, much as she or he buys shoes or tomatoes in the market. It reverses the old adage that "you get what you pay for" to "you pay for what you get." The people who receive government services pay for them with taxes. By this reasoning, the more services you get, the more taxes you should pay.

Unfortunately, there are two flaws in the benefits-received principle. First, it is practically impossible in most cases to figure out a fair basis for taxes by this principle. For example, how could national security expenditures be distributed on the basis of benefits received? Suppose you refused to pay for fire protection (or couldn't afford to), and your house caught fire. Even the distribution of school taxes is not simple, because a person who never has children benefits from living in a society of better-educated citizens. Second, if one applied the benefits-received principle strictly, it would place heavy burdens on the poor and disadvantaged members of our society, who would be denied access to most government services because they could not pay for them. Government would then become incapable of dealing with the problems of poverty. The point is that the benefits-received principle may be more appropriate in some areas than others, and in some areas it may not be appropriate at all.

Notwithstanding these two drawbacks, the government has two major sources of tax revenue based substantially on benefits received:

1. *State sales taxes and federal excise taxes on gasoline.* These taxes are generally earmarked for construction and maintenance of highways; the more you use the highways, the more gasoline you must buy and the more taxes you must pay to maintain the highways.

2. *Payroll taxes.* These are put into various insurance funds, out of which social security, Medicare, and other benefit payments are made. As the social security program is expanded, the government increases these taxes to pay for the added benefits, and to compensate for inflation. (Although social security benefits do vary somewhat, according to variations in how much one has paid into the program, these differences are fairly limited and thus weaken this example.)

The Ability to Pay. The **ability-to-pay principle** of taxation assumes that those who have a larger income are capable of paying not only a larger tax, but also of paying a larger percentage of their income in taxes than those who have smaller incomes. According to this argument, when a person has a very low income, all of it goes to buy necessities just to keep the person alive. As the person's income increases, some of it can be devoted to nonnecessities. The higher a family's income, the more it can afford to spend on nonessentials and the larger percentage of its income it can pay in taxes, while still being able to buy essentials.

One tax based on the ability-to-pay concept is the graduated income tax. The taxpayer, after deducting for size of family and for certain expenditures (health-care expenses, interest payments, charity, and so on), pays a percentage of net income in taxes. The higher the net income, the higher the percentage. The only real flaw in this system is the difficulty of enacting tax laws that are equitable to all and of arranging the deductions in such a way that families are taxed at a comparable rate. For a long time there has been controversy about these deductions and about other rules relating to what is considered taxable income. Many people charge that tax loopholes benefit higher-income groups. One big loophole, which you have probably heard discussed, is the **capital gains tax**. It works this way: If you buy an asset and hold it for at least one year and sell it for a gain, only 25 percent of the difference, or capital gain (that is, the increase in value of the asset), is considered taxable income.

Types of Taxes

The **tax rate** is the percentage of income a person pays in taxes. We can classify taxes in relation to the tax rate and what happens to it as our income increases. From this point of view, taxes are either progressive, regressive, or proportional.

A **progressive tax** is one with a rate (that is, percentage of income) that increases as income increases. The best example of it is the federal income tax. As a person's taxable income gets bigger, the rate of taxation increases also.

A **regressive tax** is one with a rate (that is, percentage of income) that declines as income increases. A sales tax is an example: When you pay a sales tax on clothes, you pay it on the basis of how much you buy. The *rate* does not change as the amount you buy increases. However, the higher your income, the larger the percentage of income you put into saving, and the smaller the percentage of income you put into clothes. So the percentage of your income that the government takes for sales taxes declines as your income increases.

Here is how this works in figures. Suppose that the sales tax is 5 percent. Adams has an income of $100 a week and spends all of it on taxable items. Thus Adams spends 5 percent of income on sales tax. However, Bloggs makes $200 a week. Being richer, Bloggs saves $50 and spends only $150 on sales-taxable items. The sales tax Bloggs pays, as a percentage of income, is only $3\frac{3}{4}$ percent. *Note:* Some sales taxes have a stronger impact on low-income groups than others. A sales tax on bread would be much more regressive than a sales tax on swimming pools. In fact, if a sales tax is properly selective, it need not be regressive at all.

A **proportional tax** is one with a rate that remains the same as the taxpayer's income changes. Property taxes are an example: The tax rate per $100 valuation of a piece of property generally remains constant as the value of the property increases. As a family's income increases, the family tends to continue to spend the same proportion of its income on housing. Since the rate of taxes on property and the percentage of family income spent on housing are both constant, as income varies, the *percentage* of income devoted to property taxes tends to remain constant. Some states have proportional taxes on incomes. For example, Illinois has a flat $2\frac{1}{2}$ percent personal income tax.

Figure 4-4 shows that the progressive curve slopes upward, so that the tax rate increases (up the vertical axis) as the tax-base income increases (out the horizontal axis). The regressive curve slopes downward, so the tax rate decreases (down the vertical axis) as the tax-base income increases (out the horizontal axis). The proportional curve is horizontal, since the tax rate remains unchanged as the tax-base income increases (out the horizontal axis).

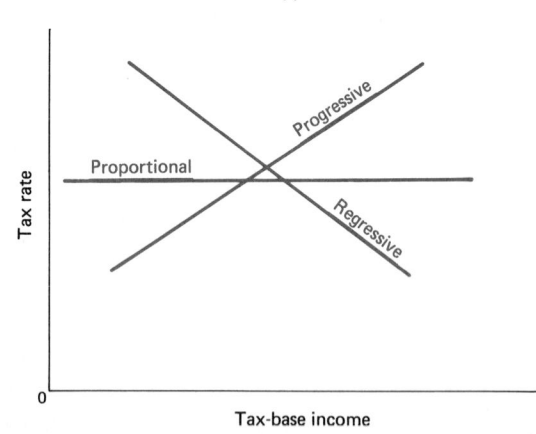

FIGURE 4-4 The Three Types of Taxes

Composition of Taxes

Table 4-9 shows where the federal government gets its taxes. As you would expect, personal income taxes are the most important source, bringing in 45 percent of the total in 1974. Payroll taxes, which mostly go to pay for social security and Medicare, are next, with 29 percent. These payroll taxes are regressive, since they apply to only the first $15,300 of income a person gets. Corporate income taxes come third, with 14 percent of the 1974 total.

Table 4-10 gives the same information about state and local governments. Note that state governments tend to get the biggest percentage of their tax money from sales taxes: 56 percent. Only about 21 percent of state money comes from personal income taxes. The local governments collect most of theirs from property taxes: 83 percent of the total.

Who Pays the Tax?

Usually you cannot shift the responsibility for paying your personal income taxes to another person. Most of us lack the economic power to pass on these taxes by making others pay higher rates for our service or products. Property taxes are, in effect, paid by those who use the property. For example, renters usually pay the property tax, indirectly, as

TABLE 4-9 Sources of Federal Taxes, 1974

Source	Billions of dollars	Percent
Personal income taxes	119.0	45
Payroll taxes	76.8	29
Corporate income taxes	38.6	14
Excise taxes	16.8	6
Estate and gift taxes	5.0	2
Other	8.7	4

Source: Economic Report of the President, 1975.

TABLE 4-10 Sources of State and Local Taxes, 1972

State Source	Billions of dollars	Percent	Local Source	Billions of dollars	Percent
Sales tax	33.3	56	Property tax	41.6	83
Personal income taxes	13.0	21	Sales tax	4.3	9
Corporate income taxes	4.4	8	Income taxes	2.2	4
Property taxes	1.3	2	Other	1.6	4
Other	7.9	13			
Total	59.9	100	Total	49.7	100

Source: Bureau of the Census, *Government Finances in 1971–1972.*

part of their rent unless their building has many vacancies, in which case the landlord may not be able to charge high enough rents to shift all the tax to the renters.

But what about corporate income taxes? Does the corporation pay them, or can they pass these taxes along to their customers through higher prices? If the corporation is operating in a field in which there is a lot of competition, the competition prevents it from passing the tax along to customers. If a corporation is in an industry in which there is little competition (for example, large firms that make a product for which there are few good substitutes), the firm may be able to shift the burden of the tax to the customer.

Is the tax structure as a whole—federal, state, and local—progressive or regressive? Federal income taxation, because of the large share coming from personal income taxes, is probably somewhat progressive. Tax loopholes (such as the exemption from taxes of the interest from tax-free municipal bonds and the low tax on capital gains) cancel some of the progressiveness of the personal income tax. State taxes, because of the predominance of sales taxes, are probably regressive, whereas local taxes are probably proportional, because of the predominance of property taxes. Data indicate that all taxes are proportional up to about $15,000 income and then become mildly progressive.

Government and the Rules of the Game

Governments—by enacting and enforcing various laws—set the rules for economic activity. To begin with, the Constitution itself sets some of the rules, and the Supreme Court has backed it up by its interpretations of the Constitution. Also there have been many statutes passed, plus countless laws relating to contracts. Virtually every business transaction involving a contract is limited by these laws. The many antitrust laws indicate how anxious Congress is to keep large corporations from exercising monopoly power. Bear in mind that labor unions—and the government itself—also have monopoly power.

Government and Regulation

To set limits for the nation's industries, many federal and state commissions regulate economic activities to varying degrees. For example, in every state, there are public utility commissions that set prices and make other guidelines for telephone, electricity, gas, water, and transportation services. Some argue that these utility commissions are politically biased. Perhaps so, but their function is to prevent the utility companies from taking advantage of the public through their power over prices.

To regulate economic activity between one state and another, the federal government has the following agencies:

1. *The Interstate Commerce Commission.* Established in 1886, responsible for overseeing rail, bus, and truck transportation; sets rate schedules, routes, and various conditions of competition.

2. *The Federal Trade Commission.* Established in 1914 to prevent and prohibit unfair competitive practices.

3. *The Food and Drug Administration.* Acts as watchdog against harmful or disease-carrying foods, cosmetics, and drugs; also checks the efficacy of drugs and the validity of drug advertising.

4. *The Civil Aeronautics Board.* Regulates air transportation and airports.

5. *The Federal Communications Commission.* Regulates TV and radio; grants, and revokes, licenses to broadcast.

6 *The Securities and Exchange Commisson.* Supervises the stock exchanges, the over-the-counter stock market, and the issuance of new securities; tries to prevent manipulation of stock prices; tries to ensure truthful and adequate information on stocks to stockholders, both present and potential.

7. *The Departments of Agriculture; Housing; Transportation; and Health, Education, and Welfare* have branches that perform overseeing and regulatory functions.

With all these agencies to protect the consumer and the business people, you'd think that the public would have a feeling of security. To the contrary, many people feel that in spite of this network of regulatory agencies, the consumer is often short-changed. Some people charge that many of the people serving on the commissions, in fact, favor the industries they're supposed to regulate, a case of the wolves guarding the sheep. This may be true, since many of them were executives in these very industries before they were appointed, and many of them, after their term of office, become executives in the same industries they have been regulating.

SUMMING UP

1. In the simple circular-flow model of the national economy, households provide firms with all the factors of production. Firms, in turn, pay to employ these resources, which they use to produce goods and services for the households. To complete the circle, households use the income from selling their resources to pay for the goods and services. Firms using the income from the sale of goods and services pay for still more factors of production to produce still more goods and services. And so on.

2. The more complex model of the national economy takes into account the fact that people do not spend all of their incomes. They save some

and pay some out as taxes. This reduces the public's demand for business firms' goods and services. The householder's savings go to financial institutions, which make them available for investments. The householder's tax dollars go to government, which uses them to buy goods and services, and thereby becomes industry's biggest customer. However, these flows of money from investment and from government to business firms, to buy industry's goods and services, are not always at a level that makes possible full employment and stable prices.

3. The concept of *functional distribution of income* has to do with the sources of income. In the 1970s, 75 percent of income in the United States came from wages and salaries; 10 percent was corporate profits; 6 percent was proprietor's income; 6 percent was interest income; and 2 percent was rental income.

4. Americans spend about 80 percent of their income on personal consumption and 15 percent on taxes; they save 7 percent. Of the amounts spent on consumption, they spend about 15 percent on durable goods, 44 percent on nondurable goods, and 42 percent on services.

5. The distribution of income in the United States is unequal. The 20 percent of families receiving the lowest incomes get only about 6 percent of the total U.S. income, while the 20 percent receiving the highest incomes get about 40 percent of it. When one diagrams the data on income distribution for a given period, one sees that the resulting curve is called a *Lorenz curve*.

6. The three main forms of business organization are the *sole proprietorship*, the *partnership*, and the *corporation*.

7. The advantages of a *sole proprietorship* are that (a) it is easy to form, and (b) there are high incentives to succeed. The disadvantages are that (a) its owner has *unlimited liability*, (b) it is difficult for a person working independently to specialize management functions, (c) access to capital is limited, and (d) it has limited life.

8. The advantages of a *partnership* are that (a) it has increased access to capital, and (b) it offers management more chances to specialize functions. The disadvantages are that (a) its owners have unlimited liability, (b) it has limited life, and (c) its access to capital is less than that of a corporation.

9. The advantages of a *corporation* are that (a) its owners have *limited liability*, (b) it constitutes a legal entity, (c) it has *unlimited life*, (d) it has greater access to capital than a sole proprietorship or a partnership, and (e) its management can specialize functions because of its larger size. The disadvantages are that (a) the process of forming a corporation takes a long time and is expensive, (b) corporate profits are double-taxed, (c) there are special laws directed at corporations, and (d) there is a danger of separation of ownership and control.

10. In many industries in the United States, a few very large firms

dominate the market. Some people charge that these monopoly-power firms prevent competition and bias political decision making.

11. The federal government spends nearly 50 percent of its money on defense or defense-related activities. States spend 47 percent of their money on education and highways. Local (city) governments spend 48 percent of theirs on education.

12. There are two main principles of taxation: (a) benefits received, and (b) ability to pay. According to the *benefits-received principle*, one should pay taxes on the basis of the amount of benefits one receives from government expenditures. According to the *ability-to-pay principle*, the tax rate should be higher for higher incomes.

13. A *tax rate*, which is the percentage of income one pays in taxes, can be either *progressive, regressive,* or *proportional*. When a tax is *progressive*, the tax rate increases as income increases (for example, the graduated federal income tax). When a tax is *regressive*, the tax rate decreases as income increases (for example, sales taxes). When a tax is *proportional*, the tax rate remains unchanged as income increases (for example, property taxes).

14. Personal income taxes are most important at the federal level, since they account for 45 percent of the total. Sales taxes are most important at the state level, bringing in 56 percent of the state's monies. Property taxes are most important at the local level, because they are the source of 83 percent of the total.

15. Generally speaking, taxes in the United States are proportional up to about the $15,000 income level, and then progressive, but only mildly so. This is because federal income taxes are only slightly progressive, whereas state sales taxes may be regressive, and local property taxes proportional.

16. Governments, by passing laws, set the rules for economic activity. Two important areas of law are those that deal with (a) contracts, and (b) antitrust legislation. Governments also affect economic activities through various regulatory commissions and agencies.

QUESTIONS

1. Using the complex circular-flow model, show how changes in (a) efforts to save, (b) efforts to invest, (c) payments of tax, and (d) spending by government all affect total output and employment. Show these changes in factors one at a time.

2. How has the functional distribution of income changed since 1929?

3. How would one compare a number of countries in terms of the level of equality in their respective distributions of income?

4. Choose a firm in each of four different industries and decide whether you would prefer to operate in that industry as a sole proprietorship, as a partnership, or as a corporation. Justify each of your decisions.

5. In general, which principle of taxation do you prefer: benefits received or ability to pay? Why?

6. Look at the taxes listed in Tables 4-9 and 4-10 and decide which are progressive, which regressive, and which proportional. Who ultimately pays each of the taxes?

7. "Economic activity is not determined by natural forces, but by the way governments define the rules of the game." Do you agree? Why?

8. With all the government regulatory commissions and agencies, the consumer is amply protected from improper business activity. Do you agree? Why?

9. You are the economic adviser for a federal commission studying taxes. You have been given the task of recommending comprehensive changes in the composition of taxes. What recommendations on tax changes would you make? Since any changes in the composition of taxes would shift the incidence of taxes (change the people who would be paying taxes), clearly state what changes in the incidence of taxes would occur. Justify these changes from an economic point of view; from a moral or ethical point of view.

SUGGESTED READINGS

Fortune Magazine, May 1975, lists the thousand largest manufacturing corporations, with information on their economic performance.

Green, Mark J., ed. *The Monopoly Makers: Ralph Nader's Study Group on Regulations and Competition.* Grossman, New York, 1973.

Heilbroner, Robert L., and Peter L. Bernstein. *Primer on Government Spending.* Random House, New York, 1971.

Josephson, Matthew. *The Money Lords.* Mentor, New York, 1972.

Kolko, Gabriel. *Wealth and Power in America.* Praeger, New York, 1962.

MacAvoy, Paul W., ed. *The Crisis of the Regulatory Commissions.* Norton, New York, 1970.

Turner, James S. *The Chemical Feast: Ralph Nader's Study Group Report on the Food and Drug Administration.* Grossman, New York, 1970.

Application 4

The Social Responsibility of Business: The Invisible Hand Versus the Good Corporate Citizen

The Effect of Competition on Business Morals

In Western Europe in the Middle Ages, the moral prescriptions of the church affected the economic behavior of merchants. The church held God over their heads. "The laborer is worthy of his hire" (Luke 10:7). "Thou shalt not steal" (Exodus 20:15). "Charity suffereth long, and is kind" (I Corinthians 13:4). The concepts of just price and just wages—plus the widespread idea that anyone who charged interest on money was guilty of usury—had the effect of limiting employers and merchants in their exploitation of workers and consumers or at least of making them feel guilty about doing it.

By the time Adam Smith wrote *The Wealth of Nations* in 1776, the dictates of the church that restrained economic abuses were replaced by the dictates of competition, which surprisingly enough exerted an even stronger effect, and in the same direction. Adam Smith's "Invisible Hand" was *competition*. According to Smith, businessmen were selfish and concerned only with their own personal gain. Greed ruled economic behavior, but competition restrained this greed, this desire to maximize one's own economic good, and channeled it into maximizing the public good. Not altogether, of course, but the effect of competition was noticeable, for the following reasons.

Each producer had such a small part of the total market that he or she could not control the price of a given product and thus gain an advantage over others. Each small producer seeking customers had to produce at the most efficient level, turn out the kinds of products and services the consumer wanted, and sell them at the lowest price commensurate with staying in business. The selfishness of these small producers was guided, as if by an Invisible Hand (competition), to maximize the welfare of society at large.

However, as Chapter 4 pointed out, today, although some industries do have to cope with fierce competition, many of the main industries in our economy are dominated by a few giant firms. So the tenets of the medieval church no longer exercise the force of law over the people, and monopoly power has weakened Adam Smith's Invisible Hand of competition.

How should corporate producers behave? Should they produce goods and services and price them with only the goal of maximizing their own profits, using every advantage their size and market dominance affords? Or should the corporation, like a good citizen, consider the social and economic needs of the society as a whole? In other words, what are the social responsibilities of business?

The Social Responsibility of Business

In the following paragraphs, we shall quote extensively from an article by economist Joel F. Henning—"Corporate Social Responsibility: Shell Game for the Seventies?" Henning asks, Whose responsibility is corporate social responsibility? "Is it that of corporate managers, or of shareholders, workers, other corporate constituencies, or some combination thereof? Or is affirmative government action required to determine the social obligations of private business?" He takes a dim view of the truthfulness of corporations' claims to social responsibility. Here are some of the points he makes.

1. Most expressions of social responsibility enrich only the media. Corporations spend hundreds of millions of dollars on institutional advertising, aimed at telling the public how socially concerned they are. For example, the public utilities, which are heavy spenders on advertising of this kind, have dismal records of exploiting the environment, being slow to hire minorities, and being inept in dealing with other issues facing our society. Then, too, programs that corporations have started with great fanfare have often fizzled out. The insurance industry, for instance, in the 1960s

"I figure someone has to hold the line."

pledged $2 billion to low-income urban housing, but it ended up mainly in commercial loans to business. In 1969 some of America's top corporations verbally supported the federal government's Operation Breakthrough, a plan to increase low-cost urban housing. But few projects were ever completed, and those few were in the suburbs. Henning comments: "The conclusion seems irresistible that the reputation of big business as social benefactor is self-made and unfulfilled."

2. The business community has no expertise in handling the present social crises of our society, since these crises cannot be solved by management and technology, fields in which business competence lies.

3. There is no accepted definition—even within the business community itself—of *what* the social responsibility of business really is.

4. Because of the large size of corporations, "business leaders are inevitably isolated from reality." If our top political figures, who must depend for their survival in office on political support from the people, have difficulty keeping in touch with reality, then it is understandable that corporate executives have an even more difficult time.

5. There is no practical way to judge corporate managers in the exercise of their social responsibility, since one cannot estimate the effectiveness of their dealing with social stresses by looking at their profit or loss statements.

6. During recessions, profits fall and some businesses suffer grave losses, intensifying our social problems at the very time the business community is least able to deal with them.

Henning winds up by saying:

> The conclusion remains that efforts to evoke a corporate conscience boil down to pleas for charity. And corporate charity is too tenuous a solution for our nation's pressing problems. We must demand from government that public needs be indentified and systematically satisfied.

Corporations are able to act like good citizens, and can so act without betraying their stockholders, but their own need for profits and expansion generally conflicts with their social consciences and takes precedence over social concerns. Business may or may not take socially responsible action, and the action may or may not be great enough or in the right direction. The social responsibility of business cannot substitute for well-conceived and well-executed government programs to alleviate economic problems. In fact, some of these programs may have to deal with the excessive power of big corporations themselves.

SUGGESTED READINGS

Berle, Adolf A., Jr., and Gardiner C. Means. *The Modern Corporation and Private Property*. Harcourt, Brace and World, New York, 1968.

Cohn, Jules. *The Conscience of the Corporation*. John Hopkins, Baltimore, 1971.

Hurst, James W. *The Legitimacy of the Business Corporation 1780–1970*. University Press of Virginia, Charlottesville, 1970.

Mason, Edward S., ed. *The Corporation in Modern Society*. Atheneum, New York, 1966.

Nader, Ralph, and Mark J. Green, eds. *Corporate Power in America*. Grossman, New York, 1973. Pages 151–170.

Application 5

The Cities: Our Society's Stepchildren?

Where Has All the Money Gone?

In February of 1975 the San Francisco school board, under pressure from the state to balance its budget, announced that it had somehow to reduce its expenditures for the year by $4 million. Therefore it announced that there was no longer enough money to support after-school sports, drama, and music programs. This meant, for one thing, the end of high school intramural and interschool athletic programs for the remainder of the year. The explosion of public fury following this announcement focused nationwide attention on San Francisco, because other school systems across the country had the same budget problems, caused by higher teachers' salaries, inflation, and cuts in state aid (resulting from a decline in enrollment in the inner-city schools). School boards in many cities were being forced to cut back staff, such as librarians, teachers' aides, and school psychologists.

San Francisco's school board, beleaguered by critics of its action, said that additional local revenues just could not be found; city property taxes had already been raised to their limit. The president of the local coaches' association argued that cutting after-school athletics would lead to an upsurge in juvenile delinquency and crime, and said, "The school board is trying to save $200,000, but it could be costing the city half a million dollars in vandalism."

A massive citizens' campaign to save the endangered programs resulted in $70,000 in private donations, which saved some of the cultural programs. In March a huge benefit rock concert took place in Kezar Stadium, featuring baseball's Willie Mays and singer Joan Baez, for the benefit of the Save Our School Sports Fund. This gave the school sports program a temporary stay of execution. But this was only an ad hoc solution; the problem remains.

In April of 1975 Abraham Beame, mayor of New York, announced that the Biggest City of Them All was bankrupt, and work had to come to a standstill on sixty-seven public building projects because the city could not meet its payrolls. Banks refused to lend more money to the city. After much political in-fighting and arguments with the state legislature, Beame succeeded in bringing about the formation of the Municipal Assistance Corporation (immediately nicknamed Big Mac), a group composed of representatives of banks and other financial institutions, and charged it with raising $3 billion in cash to help the city meet its borrowing obligations for the summer of 1975. Big Mac issued tax-exempt municipal bonds, some to mature in 1985 and some in 1990, but found that the market for them was not very good. Many bonds sold for as much as 10 percent less than their face value, reflecting the public's skepticism about the wisdom of investing in New York. Beame, a former accountant, in a desperate move to straighten out the city's books and restore public confidence, had the city council impose a wage freeze on city employees. He also laid off thousands of city employees, including police, firemen, teachers, and garbage collectors, which caused a wave of strikes among these workers and enraged the unions. The state government came to New York City's aid, to a limited extent. And so, reluctantly, did the federal government. Enough of the bonds were sold to meet the city's immediate emergency, but New York's long-range financial problem, like San Francisco's and Newark's and Chicago's and Boston's, remained unsolved.

What Cities Spend Their Money On

Pettingill and Uppal, in their book *Can Cities Survive?* point out that per capita spending by U.S. city governments from 1960 to 1972 increased by 181 percent, while per capita revenue increased only 164 percent. What caused the cities to have to spend so much more than before? And what are the sources of a city's revenue?

Expenditures increased in the 1960s in our cities for the following reasons:

1. There was a 50 percent rise in prices of goods and services.

2. City population increased by 2 percent during the 1960s which was a small expansion in numbers, but there was a large shift in the *composition* of population. Middle-class white, higher-tax-paying people fled to the suburbs, while the poor—especially minority group members—came to the big city. In broad areas of the cities, tax revenues fell. At the same time, expenditures rose enormously for such services as police, fire protection, and welfare programs.

3. Demand for better services also increased expenditures. People began to demand better schools, better police and fire protection, better health care for the poor and elderly, and better highways and streets. The demand for more and better welfare services has caused the cost of welfare to our cities to rise by more than 500 percent since 1960. (See Figure A5-1.)

4. The cities took over the burden of certain responsibilities formerly shouldered by nongovernment agencies, in the areas of education, transportation, hospital care, and housing. First, enrollments in parochial schools fell off, which meant an increase in the number of pupils in public schools. In addition, college students in many areas began to rely increasingly on community colleges financed by local governments, instead of going further afield and paying higher tuition to attend private colleges. Furthermore, cities have increasingly taken over city transit systems—and deficits incurred by public transportation systems have been increasing each year. Then too, there has been a rush to city hospitals as the cost of private hospitals has soared. Finally, cities have put up money in increasing amounts for public housing, to help the poorest segments of society.

FIGURE A5-1 Rise in Costs of Welfare to Cities, 1942–1972 (*Source of figures:* U.S. Bureau of the Census, *Statistical Abstract,* 1955, 1974.)

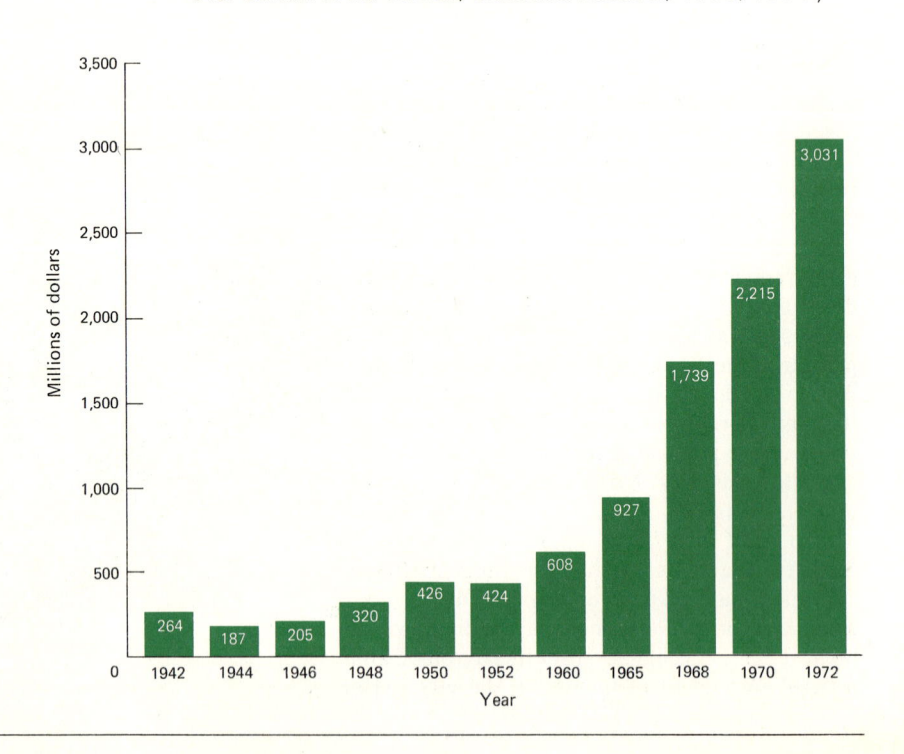

Year	Millions of dollars
1942	264
1944	187
1946	205
1948	320
1950	426
1952	424
1960	608
1965	927
1968	1,739
1970	2,215
1972	3,031

5. The productivity of city governments has not increased substantially over the years. Since the functions of urban government are primarily service-oriented, cities find it difficult to reduce their costs by increasing their productivity, by replacing human effort by machine effort.

6. In most of our major cities, strong unions have grown up. Teachers, police, firefighters, garbage collectors, and clerks—all have banded together. These unions have pushed hard, and often successfully, for higher wages. They have demanded raises at least high enough to compensate for inflation, and often high enough to increase their members' real incomes. They have been equally strong in resisting wage cuts and layoffs of employees.

Where Cities Get Their Money

With all this increase in expenditures, cities have been trying every source, looking everywhere for new ways to get more revenue.

1. Revenues from the general property tax, the traditional main source of revenues for cities, increased 192 percent between 1955 and 1972, but had fallen from 74 percent of the total urban tax revenue to 64 percent by 1972.

2. Cities had to find ways of raising revenues other than property taxes because small-property owners effectively resisted any further increases in property taxes. So city governments had to fall back on two unpopular taxes: city sales taxes and city income taxes. Revenue from these two forms of taxation went up by 337 percent between 1955 and 1972. People can get out of paying city sales taxes by driving outside the city to buy things (though with gasoline prices the way they are, that gets expensive too), and they can avoid high property taxes by moving to suburbs with lower taxes. But people find it difficult to avoid income taxes. It's hard to change jobs, even in the interests of escaping taxes.

3. A third marked change in cities' sources of revenue is the rapid growth of state and federal aid for cities. Between 1955 and 1972, these revenues from other governments increased by 695 percent. In 1955 they comprised 18 percent of total city revenue; by 1970 they had risen to 30 percent. (Of course, in the long run, this revenue still comes from the taxpayer, because state and federal governments get their revenues from taxes.)

Alternative Solutions to the Cities' Money Crises

In discussing the fiscal plight of American cities, Pettingill and Uppal suggest a number of ways cities might approach the problem of the growing gap between revenues and expenditures.

1. *Cities may raise more revenue from their own sources.* A major obstacle to this approach is public resistance to higher taxes. Both homeowners and businesses have shown increasing opposition to higher property taxes. Many American families—63 percent of them—now own their own homes and are sensitive to property taxes. Groups of homeowners and businesses have put political pressure on governments to prevent increases in property taxes. There is competition between one region and another for new industry and residents, which has led both businesses and households to move from high-tax areas to lower-tax areas. For example, even the New York Stock Exchange threatened to move out of New York if the city applied a proposed sales tax to stock purchases. (The city did apply the tax, but the Exchange did not move.) A city sales tax also sometimes forces buyers to the suburbs to escape the tax. But a person's ability to escape a city *income* tax is more restricted. You can't take your job with you if you flee to the suburbs. The tax has the additional advantage of taxing at the source those who earn their living in the city, even if they tried to escape taxation by living outside the city.

2. *Cities may seek increased state and federal aid.* Arguments in favor of this alternative run as follows. City governments generate benefits that affect an area that extends far beyond the city boundaries. Our population constantly moves around, and a child educated in one city may very well grow up and work in another, so that the education provided by one city is used in another. The migration of the rural poor lessens the need for government expenditures in the areas they leave and increases it in the areas to which they migrate. Hospitals service areas larger than the cities. Tourists and commuters use the facilities of the cities. The cities cannot tax federal and state property because of constitutional restrictions. Increased state and federal aid, therefore, can be justified as an offset to the reduced tax rolls of cities.

Furthermore, when people leave the high-tax-level cities for the suburbs, there is a reallocation of resources, part of which may be based not on market forces but on the "political accidents of differential tax burdens." All kinds of economic inefficiencies may result. As Pettingill and Uppal say, "It may increase the travel time of workers, extend the shipping distances for raw materials and finished products, and cause untimely replacement of old and still serviceable buildings by new ones." Transfer of funds from one government to another may reduce tax burdens and reduce this flight to areas in which taxes are lower.

3. *State and federal governments may take over services now performed and paid for by city governments.* Welfare programs, health care, and education are possible areas for such takeovers. But are these functions best controlled at the local level, or at the state or federal level by a centralized bureaucracy? The problem is by no means a simple one, and the arguments vary, depending on the specific function considered.

4. *Cities may join forces with their surrounding suburbs to form larger units.* This would broaden the tax base and make taxes more even. It would also reduce the flight from high-tax areas. Since both the central city and its suburbs are usually single economic units, merging of governments is a rational idea. However, regions that have low tax rates are reluctant to merge with nearby areas that have higher taxes. Also, people are against the impersonalization, the lack of a sense of individual participation that comes with larger governments.

5. *If all else fails and expenditures continue to exceed revenues, cities must cut expenditures.* It is rare today for city budgets to contain unnecessary expenditures. Therefore cuts in city expenditures are bound to mean reductions in the quantity and quality of services. What will be cut? Who will be hurt most? Will it be education and the children, or health services and the poor and the sick? Will the cuts be in police or fire protection, or in road maintenance or sewerage facilities? Or will the cities cut the salaries and numbers of their employees and make *them* pay the price of inadequate revenues? One economist has postulated that employees' unions have used their monopoly power to push wages and city costs up. He says that now that they must pay the price, he is hard put to weep overly much for them.

In an inflationary economy, no matter how much city hall tries to hold the line and prevent expenditures from rising, the city government still has to make these hard choices. Rising prices and set expenditures mean decreases in quantity and quality of services and/or decreases in employees' income.

Some Conclusions

In simplest terms, city administrations are faced with the classic problem of scarcity. City dwellers' desires for city services exceed the cities' ability to tax internally enough to pay for the services. Administrators are torn between conflicting political forces: those wanting increased services in various areas (differing groups competing for the scarce tax dollar), and those fighting increases in taxes (differing groups trying to make someone else pay the cost).

These are hard short-term political choices, but there is also a long-term aspect to administrators' decisions about expenditures and taxes. Suppose a city cuts its education budget. Will that eventually reduce the employability of its citizens and increase its future costs for welfare and police protection? Or suppose the city increases its property taxes. Will that increase the already pronounced exodus of middle-class families and businesses to the suburbs, and reduce the city's future tax base?

These are hard political and economic choices, but as long as there is a revenue gap, cities must make these choices.

We can see the problem more clearly if we use the concept of the production-possibilities curve (Figure A5-2). The curve labeled *PPC* shows what

FIGURE A5-2 A City's PP Curve

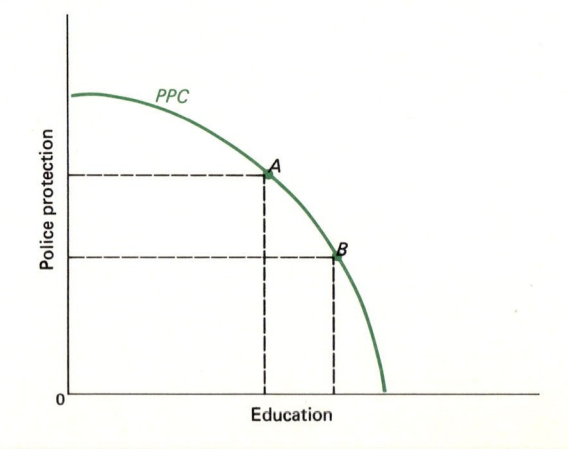

combination of services the city can give with the resources it now has. Suppose that the citizens want more of one kind of service, such as police protection. They must then give up some other service, such as education (a movement from point *B* to point *A*). The only way they can have more of both is to raise more revenue, which shifts the curve outward. This means more taxes. So to provide more taxes, people have to cut down on their consumption. However, what we see around us today is cities suffering declining sources of revenue, plus inflation at the same time. The combination of these factors is shifting their *PPCs inward*. The problem becomes how to cut back on services.

With New York City constantly on the brink of default and with other cities (Detroit, Cincinnati, Yonkers, and many others) showing evidence of similar fiscal troubles, the question arises: Will the federal government have to come to the aid of *all* U.S. cities in the future?

QUESTION

Imagine that you are the mayor of a city and you must deal with a revenue gap. Explore the causes of expenditures and sources of revenues and present your plan for doing away with the gap.

SUGGESTED READINGS

Birch, David L. *The Economic Future of City and Suburb*. CED, New York, 1970.

Olinsky, Saul. *Rules for Radicals*. Random House, New York, 1971.

Orofsky, Gilvert. *Harlem, the Making of a Ghetto*. Norton, New York, 1971.

Pettingill, Robert B., and Jogindar S. Uppal. *Can Cities Survive? The Fiscal Plight of American Cities*. St. Martin's, New York, 1974.

5
Measuring Economic Activity

In 1971 President Nixon unveiled the GNP clock in the lobby of the Bureau of the Census building. The machine had been preset, according to the predictions of statisticians, to tick off the value of output produced. When the President showed the clock to reporters, it was recording a one-trillion-dollar gross national product. It didn't seem to bother anyone that (1) the machine had been running for some time, waiting for the proper moment to be revealed, (2) actual GNP was a good bit less than the one trillion dollars predicted at the time, and (3) the one-trillion-dollar GNP was in part achieved by increased prices rather than by increased output.

But despite the gadgetry and the "slight" distortions of politicians, GNP and the concept of national economic accounting are important to a better understanding of the economy. Changes in the amount of the output of an economy can affect the material levels of existence of everyone within that economy. In this chapter we shall discuss these relevant concepts and measures of economic performance.

A most important question is: Even if the level of output in the economy increases, does it really mean that the individual member of the economy is better off? With all these urgings for increases in GNP, does such increase really improve material life? Application 6, which follows this chapter, will discuss that question. But first we need some basic understanding of the national economic accounts.

Background: Why Is National Economic Accounting Important?

Although most of these concepts were worked out before the war, economists introduced national economic accounts during World War II to meet the government's needs for wartime planning. Government

Nixon unveiling the GNP clock (UPI)

agencies had to have measures of economic performance in order to make the best allocation of output and to formulate policies that would keep the economy stable. A major problem for the United States was how to shift all those resources to fight the war and still minimize inflation. Data provided by the national economic accounts gave information about how much production could be used for consumption and how much income people would have for consumption. Now, knowing how much excess income people had, the government could estimate the size of government programs, taxes, savings, and government bond sales. The government needed to soak up consumers' excess income and reduce demand, so that prices could be kept down. The sale of government bonds was an important way to keep people from spending their incomes on consumer goods.

The national economic accounts—like a family's account books—give government policy makers the information necessary to formulate economic policy properly. This information is also important for business groups and consumers, who also have to make economic decisions. Do you buy your house now or next year? What you think the economy is going to do next year is important because—along with many other things—it not only affects your own income, but also the income of others, and *their* level of demand and prices. The totals of these accounts, especially when we compare one year with another, give us all indications as to whether the economy is changing, and if so, how.

The Expenditure and Income Approaches

People look at the national economic accounts from two points of view: (1) the **expenditure approach**, which concerns what kinds of goods and

"Remember when one billion was such a frightening figure?"

services people buy, or the kinds of expenditures they make and (2) the **income approach**, which concerns what kinds of income are generated by the output of the economy. To sum it up, the expenditure approach deals with kinds of output, while the income approach deals with kinds of income generated in the production of that output.

In effect the two approaches are two sides of the same coin, and the statistical results of each are equal. Suppose that the only output of an economy were one car, one machine to produce the car, and one schoolhouse. The expenditure approach to measuring economic performance would entail totaling the value of those three items of production. But the value of that output would be apportioned to the factors of production as income. The income approach would entail recording how much of that income is apportioned to each of the different factors of production. The two results—that obtained from the expenditure approach and that from the income approach—must be equal. The *value of what is produced is equal to the income distributed.* (See Table 5-1.)

The expenditure approach is concerned with what is produced. In Table 5-1, the total value is $18,000. The income approach is concerned with the income generated. The total income is $18,000. The two approaches lead to the same statistical results. In each case, the income generated must be equal to the value produced.

Gross National Product and Gross National Income

Gross National Product (GNP)

Gross national product measures the total dollar value of all final goods and services produced in a given period, in a given economy. Two elements of that definition need explaining.

1. When we say that only the value of **final goods and services** is included in the GNP, we avoid the possibility of counting output more than once in the GNP statistic. Most manufactured products use materials from several firms. These intermediate products become part of the final product, so the value of the final product also covers the cost of these intermediate products. To include the intermediate products separately would mean that we would be counting them twice, once when we included them separately and again when we listed the final product.

For example, intermediate products that go to make up our $3,000 car in Table 5-1 include $500 worth of steel and $100 worth of rubber, which the automobile producers buy and then incorporate into the car. When the manufacturer sells the car, the price must be high enough to cover the cost of all the intermediate products. Economists—to avoid counting a unit of output twice in the GNP—therefore list only the final value of the car, the price to the ultimate user.

This policy, however, creates a problem. Work in progress and inventory on hand at the end of the year represent output for that year, and should be included in the GNP for that year. At the same time, work that was in progress the year before and inventory that was produced the year before are also included in the final product, and they should not be included in the current year's output. Economists resolve this by subtracting from the GNP the inventory at the beginning of the year and adding to the GNP the inventory at the end of the year. Formally, this is accomplished by including in investment a net inventory figure (beginning inventory subtracted from ending inventory).

Let's look at our car again. At the beginning of the year, it was only partially completed and was worth about $1,000. That was output from last year, which should not be included in this year's GNP. But the car is completed this year, and sold to a consumer. Also, this year, more than

TABLE 5-1 Income and Expenditure Approaches

Income approach	Car	Expenditure approach Machine	Schoolhouse	Total
Labor	$1,000	$3,000	$ 6,000	$10,000
Interest	500	750	1,000	2,250
Rent	250	400	750	1,400
Profits	750	500	1,000	2,250
Depreciation	250	250	1,150	1,650
Indirect business taxes	250	100	100	450
	$3,000	$5,000	$10,000	$18,000

just that one car is produced. Half of the second car is made, say, $1,500 worth. That $1,500 in partially completed car should be counted as part of this year's output. Solution: Subtract the $1,000 work-in-progress car that was on hand at the beginning of the year (beginning inventory) from the $1,500 work-in-progress car that is on hand at the end of the year (ending inventory). Net inventory (part of investment) is +$500.

2. The GNP contains the total dollar value of goods and services for a specific time period only, usually one year. Only output for that year is included, and none from any prior period.

The three major groupings of expenditures on goods and services that are counted in the gross national product are (1) expenditures for private consumption, (2) expenditures for investment, and (3) expenditures for the government.

When we talk about expenditures for private consumption, we're actually talking about three kinds of expenditures: (1) When you buy a refrigerator or a car, you're buying **durable goods** (durable because it takes a long time to use them up). (2) When you buy food or clothes, you're buying **nondurable goods** (they are used up quickly). (3) When a barber cuts your hair or a waiter brings you a pizza, you're buying **services** (somebody does something for you). But remember that although the waiter who brings you that pizza is giving you a service, the pizza itself is a nondurable good.

Investment expenditures is really a simplified way of referring to **gross private domestic investment**. *Gross* means all investment output is counted, including investment that replaced depreciated and obsolete capital. *Private* means that only *non*government investment is counted. *Domestic* means that only investment made within the United States is counted. So, when General Motors builds a new plant for its Chevrolets in Michigan, this is included in investment because it represents output of U.S. resources. However, when GM builds another assembly plant for its Opel division in Japan, it is not part of our GNP. It may be owned by a company based in the United States, but the employment generated and production capacity created benefit the Japanese economy, not the U.S. economy. *Investment* is the act of creating capital, manufactured producer goods that aid in the production of other goods and services.

Gross investment is divided into (1) equipment and machinery, (2) business and residential construction, and (3) net changes in inventory. Remember that one subtracts beginning inventory from ending inventory. The balance is part of investment.

Government expenditures include only government purchases of goods and services. These are divided into three types: services, goods, and investment. *Services* include the salaries the government pays to its employees, such as soldiers and county agents. *Goods* are products used up in the operation of the government (paper, gasoline used in government cars, and so on). Government *investment*, like private investment, is the creation of capital or physical things that aid in the production of goods and services and exist for at least one year (typewriters, school

Volkswagens assembled in Wolfsburg, West Germany, are not part of our GNP. (Peter Menzel/Stock, Boston)

buildings, and so on). Of course, when we say government, we mean *all* levels of government: local, state, and federal.

GNP measures only the output of the economy, and therefore includes only those expenditures for goods and services (these are output of the economy) for the government. However, the government also spends money for things other than output that it demands, and these are not included in GNP. People receive these transfer payments without an immediate obligation to do something in return. The secretary taking dictation in the Department of Commerce provides a service (labor) for a paycheck. The secretary's salary *is* included in GNP. The family on welfare does not give goods or services in return for its check, nor does the jobless worker who receives unemployment compensation, nor does the wheat farmer from Kansas who receives agricultural subsidy payments. These government expenditures, since they do not involve concurrent production of either goods or services, are not included in GNP.

However, several adjustments still have to be made. Imports are included in these expenditures, and since imports were produced outside the United States, we must subtract them from GNP. Also, the United States produces goods that are not included in our expenditures for consumption, investment, and government: our exports. Since exports represent output of the U.S. economy, we must add them to GNP. The plus exports and minus imports can be shortened to $\pm$ net exports. In other words, we subtract imports from exports. If exports are larger, net exports are positive; and if imports are larger, net exports are negative.

For example, the United States imports Volkswagen Rabbits from Germany. They are part of our consumption, because Americans buy them. But the Rabbits are not part of our output. Therefore they must be subtracted from our GNP. On the other hand, we export wheat to Japan. It is not part of our consumption, because we do not consume it—the Japanese do. But it *is* part of our output and must be added to our GNP. In other words, we subtract the imports (Volkswagen Rabbits) and add the exports (wheat sold to Japan).

Table 5-2 contains a breakdown of the GNP for 1974. The formula for GNP is thus

$$\text{GNP} = C + G\ Inv + GX \pm NX.$$

Gross National Income (GNI)

Gross national income measures the total income at market prices generated in the production of all final goods and services during a given period, in a given economy. The term **at market prices** simply indicates that we compute the measure at the market level for goods and services and that this measure must cover all costs incurred through that market. You can keep this straight if you remember that GNP shows total output, while GNI shows how the income generated by that output is distributed. The two must be equal for the same time period.

Table 5-2 shows the breakdown for GNI in 1974. Naturally this summation includes the income earned by the factors of production (labor, capital, land, and entrepreneurship). Wages and salaries encompass all income earned by labor, including social security taxes paid by

TABLE 5-2 Gross National Product (GNP) and Gross National Income (GNI) for 1974 (billions of dollars)

Consumption (*C*)	877
Gross private domestic investments (*G Inv*)	209
Government expenditures (*GX*)	309
Net exports (*NX*)	2
Gross National Product (GNP) equals	1,397
GNP = *C* + *G Inv* + *GX* ± *NX*	
Wages and salaries (*W & S*)	856
Rents (*R*)	27
Interest (*I*)	62
Proprietors' income (*P Inc*)	93
Corporate profits (*CP*)	105
Capital consumption allowance or depreciation (*D*)	120
Indirect business taxes (*IBT*)	127
Miscellaneous	7
Gross National Income (GNI) equals	1,397
GNI = *W & S* + *R* + *I* + *P Inc* + *CP* + *D* + *IBT*	

Note: Gross national product is equal to gross national income.

employees and employers. **Wages and salaries** are the return to labor. **Rent** is the return to land; this figure includes an estimated rent for homes occupied by their owners. **Interest** is the return to capital. Only interest paid by private business is included; the interest on government debt and on consumer debt is not. **Proprietors' income** is the return to entrepreneurship in firms that are *not* incorporated. (Another term for proprietors' income is **profits of unincorporated businesses**.) **Corporate profits** are the return to entrepreneurship in firms that *are* incorporated.

Besides the five income items listed for GNI in Table 5-2, there are two costs that must be covered by the final value of the product, but cannot be apportioned to the factors of production. **Capital consumption allowance**, or **depreciation**, is a legitimate expense, since it measures the wearing out of capital each year, either through use or obsolescence. The other nonincome cost is **indirect business taxes**, or taxes on goods and services that are passed on to the consumer. Two main forms of these are excise and sales taxes. The firm pays excise taxes (for example, cigarette and liquor taxes) and passes them on to the consumer in the form of higher prices. These taxes are covered by the final value and must be listed separately in gross national income.

In brief, then, we see from Table 5-2 that the formula for gross national income is

$$GNI = W\&S + R + I + P\,Inc + CP + D + IBT.$$

Net National Product and Net National Income

Net National Product

GNP includes money spent, or output, to replace worn-out capital. Because economists find it useful to have a measure of output that does *not* include this depreciation, so that they can measure only net additions to total production, they use the expenditure approach to compute **net national product**, which is the net dollar value of all final goods and services produced during a given period. We speak of GNP as being "total value," indicating that depreciation *is* included, while we speak of NNP as being "net value," indicating that depreciation is *not* included.

Your car is not considered an investment, but part of consumption. (A salesperson's car would be an investment.) However, to give you an understanding of what is meant by depreciation, let us think about your car as an investment. After your new car is one year old, it is less valuable than when it was new. Its value has gone down for the following reasons: (1) It has been driven, and there is only just so much mileage one can get out of a car. Let us say that you can get 100,000 miles of driving out of the car. If you drove 20,000 miles the first year, the car is one-fifth used up. (2) The car is no longer new, styles have changed, and—most important—manufacturers have made improvements in cars since this one was made. This aspect of depreciation is called *obsolescence*. Just as a car, a consumer durable, decreases in value over time, investment goods—the capital people produce to aid in production, such as machines and factory buildings—depreciate by being used up and becoming obsolete, unless they have the most up-to-date improvements. One can say that depreciation is excluded from net national product because to count the value of capital used up in the process of current production would be to count something made in previous income periods.

Net National Income

By the same token, economists use the income approach to compute **net national income**, which is the net income (at market prices) generated in the production of all final goods and services during a given period. Once again, we speak of GNI as being total income, indicating that depreciation *is* included and we speak of NNI as being net income, indicating that depreciation is *not* included.

Table 5-3 contains a breakdown of NNP and NNI for 1974. For NNI, the only change from GNI (Table 5-2) is that depreciation is not included. For NNP, gross private domestic investment becomes net private domestic investment. The difference between gross and net is measured by the amount of depreciation, or capital consumption allowance. Net investment, therefore, measures only the additions to the capital stock of the economy. If the value of gross investment is greater than depreciation, then more capital is being created than is being lost through depreciation. Net investment is then **positive**, and the economy generally expands because its stock of capital is expanding. Depreciation may be greater than the value of gross investment. If so, net

TABLE 5-3 Net National Product (NNP) and Net National Income (NNI) for 1974 (billions of dollars)

Consumption (C)	877
Net private investment (N Inv)	89
Government expenditures (GX)	309
Net exports (NX)	2
Net national product (NNP) equals	1,277
NNP = C + N Inv + GX ± NX	
NNP = GNP − D	
Wages and salaries (W & S)	856
Rent (R)	27
Interest (I)	62
Proprietors' income (P Inc)	93
Corporate profits (CP)	105
Indirect business taxes (IBT)	127
Miscellaneous	7
Net national income (NNI) equals	1,277
NNI = W & S + R + I + P Inc + CP + IBT	
NNI = GNI − D	

Note: The difference between NNP/NNI and GNP/GNI is capital consumption allowances (depreciation).

investment is **negative**. In this case, the stock of capital is contracting because more capital is being lost than is currently produced. Capital stock, and thus the ability of the economy to produce, is contracting. This situation of a negative net investment has occurred during severe depressions (1930–1933) and during wars (World Wars I and II) when the need to produce war goods was greater than the need to produce investment. During the years 1917–1918, while the United States was fighting in World War I, total real output declined because the United States was at full employment when it entered the war. But during World War II, in 1942, 1943, and 1944, real output increased substantially (despite a negative net investment) because of the large amounts of unemployed labor and unused plant capacity remaining from the depression of the 1930s, and because employers used both labor and plant more intensively by the device of overtime.

National Income

The third major measure of the value of economic output is **national income**, which is a measure of income generated only by the factors of production. National income is net income at factor prices generated in the production of all final goods and services in a given time period. As before, *net income* means that depreciation is not included. **At factor prices** means prices obtained in the factor market for the factors of production, and therefore we are excluding indirect business taxes, which are paid as a part of market prices. For example, an excise tax is levied on cigarettes by the federal government and is collected not at the retail level, as with a sales tax, but at the manufacturing level. The market value for cigarettes for inclusion in GNP and NNP includes the excise tax. The income generated by the production of cigarettes at the factor market does not include the excise tax.

Table 5-4 shows the breakdown of national income for 1974. There is no comparable way to measure it using the expenditure approach.

TABLE 5-4 National Income for 1974 (billions of dollars)

Wages and salaries (W & S)	856
Rent (R)	27
Interest (I)	62
Proprietors' income (P Inc)	93
Corporate profits (CP)	105
National income (NI) equals	1,143
NI = W & S + R + I + P Inc + CP	
NI = NNI − IBT	

Note: National income includes only the income generated by the factors of production. The difference between net national income and national income is indirect business taxes.

Personal Income

Our first measure of economic performance was GNP-GNI, the second measure was NNP-NNI, and the third was NI. Our fourth measure of a nation's economic performance is **personal income**. Personal income consists of all income received by *people*, whether from production or by transfer payments. It is computed by deducting from national income those income flows that do not accrue to individuals, as distinct from corporations and governments, and by adding those income flows to people that are not included in national income.

First, to compute personal income (see Table 5-5), subtract that part of national income that does not accrue to people. Corporate profits consist of corporate taxes, the savings of corporations or retained earnings, and dividends. Dividends are distributed to the stockholders (people) and are retained in personal income. Corporate taxes and retained earnings (undistributed corporate profits) are not income to people and are subtracted from national income. Social security taxes are included in wages and salaries. These are transfer payments to the government and must also be subtracted from national income to derive personal income.

Second, add income people receive that is not included in national income. These are transfer payments *from* the government, such as unemployment compensation, welfare payments, social security payments, and interest on government debt. Although interest on government debt is not really a transfer payment, since it is a payment for the use of borrowed funds, we include it here by definition. (Remember that the accounts are definitional concepts, depending for their definition on the decisions of the authority responsible for computing the accounts.)

The computation can be condensed by deriving a figure for net transfer payments. Subtract the transfer payments *to* the government from the transfer payments *from* the government. If the latter is larger, it is a plus figure. If the former is larger, it is a negative figure.

Table 5-5 shows the breakdown of personal income for 1974. Once again, there is no comparable measure using the expenditure approach.

TABLE 5-5 Personal Income for 1974 (billions of dollars)

National income (*NI*)	1,143
Less corporate taxes (*CT*)	− 49
Less undistributed corporate profits (*UCP*)	− 23
Less transfer payments to the government (*TP* to *G*)	− 101
Plus transfer payments from the government (*TP* from *G*)	182
Equals personal income (PI)	1,152
PI = NI − CT − UCP ± NTP	

Note: One can compute *personal income* by subtracting from national income that part that is not income to people, and by adding incomes accruing to people that are not part of national income. In Table 5-5, *NTP* represents all transfer payments.

Personal Disposable Income

The fifth and last measure of economic performance is **personal disposable income**. This is the portion of people's incomes that they have control over; that is, they can control where and how this portion is spent. (See Table 5-6.) People do not have control over the part of their income paid to the government in taxes, such as personal income and property taxes. So personal *disposable* income is personal income less personal taxes.

One can also look at disposable income from the point of view of how people apportion it. They can either spend it (consumption), save it (personal savings), or use it to pay interest on consumption loans.

Personal disposable income is an important measure in the national economic accounts. It is, in effect, the measure of purchasing power of the consuming public. Changes in PDI result in changes in total consumer demand. Government economic policy must keep a close eye on this measure. How would tax changes affect it? How would changes in government expenditures affect it? The federal government made tax cuts for the 1974 and 1975 tax years precisely for the purpose of increasing personal disposable income to stimulate consumer demand.

Table 5-6 shows the breakdown of personal disposable income for 1974. Table 5-7, on page 116, summarizes the formulas for the national economic accounts.

Circular Flow: Another View

The use of a tabular step-by-step procedure to present the national economic accounts is a useful exercise. However, as we learned from Chapter 4 and the circular-flow model, the economy is a system of flows of income and production. Our understanding of the national economic

TABLE 5-6 Personal Disposable Income for 1974 (billions of dollars)

Personal income (*PI*)	1,152
Less personal taxes (*PT*)	−171
Equals personal disposable income (PDI)	981
PDI = PI − *PT*	
or	
Consumption (*C*)	877
Personal savings (*PS*)	77
Interest on consumer loans (*ICL*)	27
Equals personal disposable income (PDI)	981
PDI = C + PS + ICL	

Note: One can compute *personal disposable income* by subtracting personal taxes from personal income, or by adding consumption, personal savings, and interest on consumer loans.

TABLE 5-7 Summary of the National Economic Accounts

1. GNP = C + G Inv + GX ± NX
   GNI = W & S + R + I + P Inc + CP + D + IBT
2. NNP = C + N Inv + GX ± NX
       = GNP − D
   NNI = W & S + R + I + P Inc + CP + IBT
       = GNI − D
3. NI = W & S + R + I + P Inc + CP
       = NNI − IBT
4. PI = NI − CT − UCP ± NTP
5. PDI = PI − PT
       = C + PS + ICL

Note: This summary of the formulas for the National Economic Accounts uses the notations contained in Tables 5-2 through 5-6. If you have any problem in interpreting the notation, refer to the appropriate table.

---

accounts should be improved if we consider the accounts from a flow viewpoint. Figure 5-1 is such a flow presentation.

Output and income flow from gross national product through the other four accounts to disposable income. Siphoned off from each account are savings of businesses and government receipts of taxes. Reverse flows of demand for consumption, investment, and government expenditures relate back from net receipts by people, businesses, and government.

Final-Value and Value-Added Methods

We have been defining the various national accounts and what goes to make them up. But how does one compute the values for gross national product? By two methods: the final-value method and the value-added method.

1. *The **final-value method***. The sum of prices to the ultimate users of goods and services produced. These final values include all values added at substages of production. To avoid double counting, one does not list intermediate products.

2. *The **value-added method***. Commodities go through many stages of production. As an unfinished product moves from one firm to another, it is changed in form, or location, or is stored. Each of these functions adds value. The sum of these additions to value equals the final value of the product.

Let us examine Table 5-8 (page 118) where we have used a desk as an example. *Stage 1:* Lumbermen cut down a tree and transport it to the sawmill. By the time the tree arrives at the sawmill, it is worth more than when it stood in the forest. Value has been added to it—say, $2.50—because of the expenditure of labor, land, capital, and entrepreneurship. *Stage 2:* The sawmill cuts the tree into lumber. Again, value is added—say, $2.00—and again it is equal to the cost of the factors of production used at that stage. At each succeeding stage (the furniture factory and the retailer) the expenditure of resources means that value is being added. The furniture factory takes $4.50 worth of materials, applies resources, and sells the resulting product for $10.00. Value added was $5.50. The values added at each stage are equal to the final value, or the price to the ultimate user.

Table 5-9 (page 118) shows how this value-added method of computation works. The left-hand side shows how the income produced by the added value was distributed during production by the furniture factory, Atlas Furniture Company. Labor (one factor of production) received wages plus social security taxes, or $865,000. Land ownership received rent, or $250,000. Corporate profits earned were $150,000. However, the factors of production are not the only contributors to value added. De-

FIGURE 5-1 The Flow of the National Economic Accounts, 1974. As income is circulated to the three sectors of the economy—the people (or households), businesses, and government—there are also reverse flows of demand for the output of the economy. These flows stress the interdependency of the various parts of the economy with each other and with the whole.

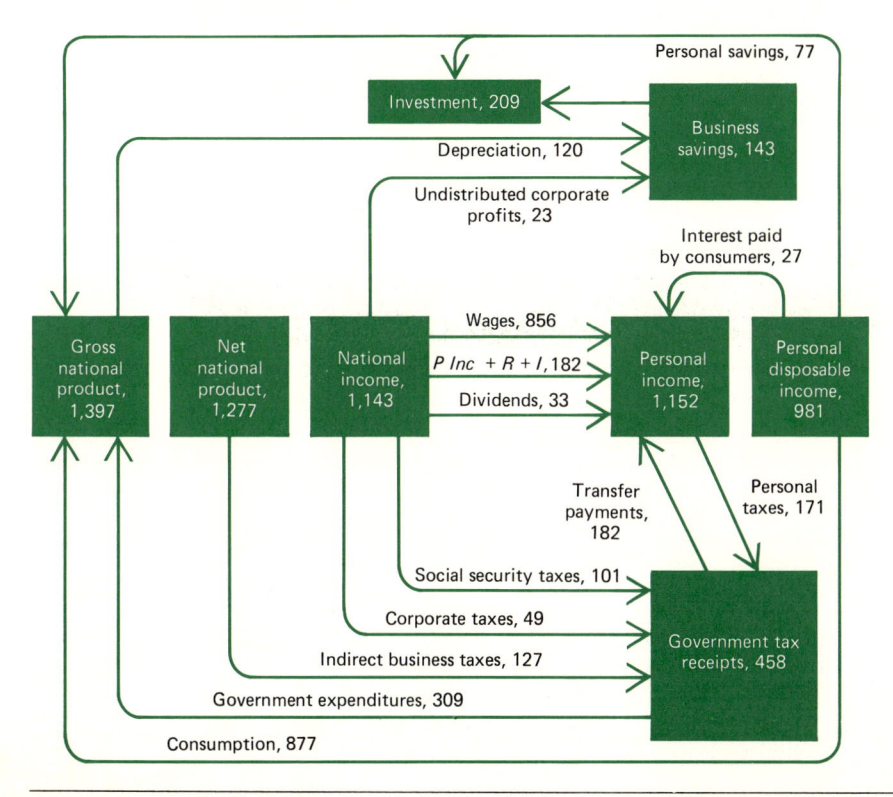

Final-Value and Value-Added Methods

preciation and business taxes also contribute, $300,000 and $150,000 respectively, because the company has to count these costs into the expense of making furniture.

The right-hand side of Table 5-9 shows how the production of furniture now embodying the value added at that stage was distributed. Two companies, the Smith Company and the Jones Company, bought furniture to sell at retail; together, they paid $1,400,000. Various firms bought office furniture directly from the Atlas Furniture Company for their own use: $400,000. This becomes part of gross investment. The government bought $600,000 worth and Atlas exported $250,000 worth. Because ending inventory was less than beginning inventory, the total production figure must be reduced by that difference (−$100,000). Last, and most important, not all the value was created at this stage of production (the fashioning of wood into furniture). The raw materials bought by the firm acquired their value at prior stages of production. Value added, according to both the final-value method and the value-added method, was thus $1,915,000.

The British (and several other European countries) are using a *value-added tax* to raise tax money. Since 1973 there has been a 10

TABLE 5-8 Stages of Production of a Desk

Stages	Value of product sold	Value added
1. Lumbering	$ 2.50	$ 2.50
2. Sawmill	4.50	2.00
3. Furniture factory	10.00	5.50
4. Retailer (the final value)	20.00	10.00
Final value		$20.00

Note: The value added does not include values from prior stages. When one adds all the values at each stage, the total equals the final value.

TABLE 5-9 The Atlas Furniture Company, Statement of Value Added

Income generated by valued added		Sources of value added	
Wages	$ 850,000	Net sales to U.S. government	$ 600,000
Social security taxes	15,000	To Smith Company	600,000
Rent	250,000	To Jones Company	800,000
Interest	200,000	To business firms	400,000
Depreciation	300,000	To exports	250,000
Taxes other than corporate income taxes	150,000	Inventory increase or decrease	
Corporate profits	150,000	Inventory decreased	−100,000
Income generated by valued added	$1,915,000	Value of production	$2,550,000
		Cost of raw material	−635,000
		Value added	$1,915,000

percent tax applied to value added at each stage of production on most manufactured articles. The British call it the VAT. The French have a similar tax, which they call a **turnover tax**. Thus far the United States does not have a value-added tax, but who can tell how long we will be without one?

Current, Constant, and Per Capita GNP

In the early 1960s Senator Barry Goldwater, a Republican, and Secretary of Labor Arthur Goldberg, a Democrat, debated on educational TV. Each used extensive statistics concerning the national economic accounts. With these statistics, each of the speakers proved that the only time American people were well off was when his own party was in power. Who was lying, the statistics or the statistician? In a sense, neither, because the debaters were using different measures, sometimes including, sometimes excluding the effects of the prices on GNP. It would have been "fairer" if they had made clear to the onlookers what measures they were using. When statistics are being bandied about, a healthy skepticism is needed, especially concerning whether prices are or are not included. As Disraeli said, "There are three kinds of lies: lies, damn lies, and statistics."

Gross national product may change because of changes in (1) prices and (2) level of real output. But only the changes in real output (that is, in number of products produced) affect material well-being. To obtain GNP data for comparative purposes, therefore, you must do away with price changes. Here's how you do it.

Statistics on GNP before the data are adjusted for price changes are called **money**, or **current**, **GNP**, which is the output of a given year valued in the prices of that year. (In 1940 you could buy a brand-new Oldsmobile for less than $1,000. But at that time many people were paid only $25 a week, and the best hamburger was 25 cents a pound.)

Real, or **constant**, **GNP** is the output of a given year adjusted for price changes. (A brand-new Oldsmobile today might cost $4,000 to $9,000, depending on which model you buy and how many extras are included and the price of hamburger has more than quadrupled.) Converting money to real GNP involves the use of a **price index**, which is a measure of changes in the price level.

There are various kinds of price indexes, depending on what you're measuring. Two well-known indexes are (1) the **consumer price index**, compiled and published by the Bureau of Labor Statistics, which measures price changes for a certain marketbasket of goods purchased by a family of four in an urban area, and (2) the **wholesale price index**, which measures changes in wholesale prices. In addition, the national income division of the Commerce Department has developed an index called (3) the **general price index** (or more formally the **GNP implicit price deflator**), by which you can convert current to constant GNP.

Now let's see how this works. Pick a specific year as the base year, and consider it as 100; then compare the prices that prevailed in all other years to the prices that prevailed during the base year. Let's say that in year 2, prices increased by 20 percent over the base year. Okay, the price index for year 2 is 120. Let's say that in year 3, prices were 10 percent lower on the average than prices in the base year. Then the price index for year 3 is 90. By the same token, a price index of 132 means that prices in general have increased by 32 percent over the base year. A price index of 84 would mean that prices had declined by 16 percent from the base year.

To convert money GNP to real GNP, divide money GNP by the price index and multiply by 100. For example, if you take 1970 as the base year (in other words, 1970 = 100), and if the price index today is 130, to find the real or constant GNP for the year, you divide this year's money GNP by 130 and multiply by 100. That gives you this year's GNP in terms of 1970 dollars; in other words, *real GNP*.

Real GNP does not account for changes in population, so when you divide real GNP by population, you have **per capita real GNP**. This is the best-known statistic for comparing a nation's relative material well-being at one time with its material well-being at another time, as we saw in Application 2.

Table 5-10 gives a sampling of real GNP, with the accompanying price index. The year 1958 is the base year for this particular set of statistics. Therefore its price index is 100; money GNP in 1958 is equal to real GNP. You can see that the ratio of money GNP to the price index for that year multiplied by 100, equals real GNP.

Look at the way prices dropped between 1929 and 1933 during the Great Depression. From 1933 onward, prices rose.

If the price index is less than 100, this means that prices are lower than for the base year. So when you convert money GNP to constant

TABLE 5-10 U.S. Current GNP, Price Index, and Constant or Real GNP for Selected Years (billions of dollars; 1958 = 100)

Year	Money GNP	Price Index	Real GNP
1929	103.1	50.64	203.6
1933	55.6	39.29	141.5
1940	99.7	43.87	227.3
1945	211.9	59.66	355.2
1950	284.8	80.16	355.3
1958	447.3	100.00	447.3
1960	503.7	103.29	487.7
1965	684.9	110.86	617.8
1970	974.1	135.29	720.0
1974	1,396.7	170.11	821.1

Source: Economic Report of the President, 1974.

GNP, the amount increases. This is known as **inflating current GNP** to obtain a real figure that compensates for lower prices. When the price index is greater than 100, it indicates that prices are higher than the base year, so money GNP is greater than constant. The conversion is known as **deflating current GNP** to account for increases in price.

Output Excluded from GNP

Recall what we said earlier about the national economic accounts being *definitional* concepts. The people responsible for computing the accounts define what will be considered output; they do not include all output. By definition, they exclude the following kinds of output from the national income accounts.

1. *Services by homemakers.* If one had to buy these services on the market—children's nurse, house cleaner, cook, chauffeur, companion—the cost would be prohibitive. The Chase Manhattan Bank of New York estimated in 1973 that the services of the average homemaker, if bought in the open market, would cost $257.53 a week. Economists exlude these services when they are figuring the national accounts because homemakers don't get paid in money.

2. *Illegal goods and services.* These illegal activities involve production, supply, demand, and a price in a market. Economists exclude them, however, because it is impossible to estimate their monetary value. You can't ask the local pushers how much heroin they sold last year, or the owners of gambling joints what their takings were. (Imagine a mayor analyzing the way GNP had increased in the city because drug sales had increased 10 percent.)

3. *Labor of children in the household.* If your daughter or son mows the lawn, it doesn't add to the GNP. But if he or she mows the *neighbors'* lawn and is paid $2.00, economists count it in.

4. *The labor in do-it-yourself projects.* When you buy wood and brackets to build bookshelves in your living room, economists include the materials you bought in GNP. But the labor it takes you to build them doesn't count.

5. *Volunteer help to nonprofit organizations.* For example, the Red Cross has a paid staff; their wages *are* counted. But if you donate your services—even though you work very hard for long hours, this volunteer help isn't counted in the GNP.

Economic Transactions Excluded from GNP

Just as economists exclude certain types of production, they also exclude the following types of economic transactions:

1. *The buying and selling of intermediate products.* This is excluded

because intermediate products are included in the final value of the products. This exclusion prevents counting them twice.

2. *The buying and selling of used items* such as cars and homes. This is excluded because the production of these items took place and was included in a prior time period. Their resale now constitutes only a change in ownership, not an increase in production of goods and services.

3. *The buying and selling of financial securities such as bonds and stocks.* This is excluded because production has not taken place, only the transfer of ownership of debt.

SUMMING UP

1. The national economic accounts are measures of economic activity. They are definitional concepts, and in each country the economists who compute the accounts define what is to be included and what excluded.

2. The *expenditure approach* to economic accounts analyzes the kinds of output the economy produces. The *income approach* looks at the kinds of income generated by the economy's output.

3. There are five main kinds of yardsticks used to measure national economic accounts. The first consists of *gross national product*, computed by the expenditure approach, and *gross national income*, computed by the income approach.

4. *Gross national product* is the total value *at market prices* of all *final goods and services* produced during a given period. GNP is made up of consumption, *gross private domestic investment, government expenditures,* and net exports.

5. *Gross national income* is the total income at market prices generated in the production of all final goods and services produced during a given period. GNI is made up of *wages and salaries, rents, interest, proprietors' income, corporate profits, capital consumption allowances,* and *indirect business taxes.*

6. The second measure of economic performance consists of *net national product,* computed via the expenditure approach, and *net national income,* computed via the income approach. Both exclude capital consumption allowances.

7. *Net national product* is the net value of all final goods and services produced in a given period. NNP is made up of consumption, net private domestic investment, government expenditures, and net exports.

8. *Net national income* is the net income at market prices generated by the production of all final goods and services produced in a given period.

NNI is made up of wages and salaries, rent, interest, proprietors' income, corporate profits, and indirect business taxes.

9. The third measure of a nation's economic accounts is *national income*, which is the net income *at factor prices* generated in the production of all final goods and services in a given period. NI is made up of wages and salaries, rent, interest, proprietors' income, and corporate profits.

10. The fourth measure is *personal income*, which is all income received by private citizens. PI is made up of national income, less corporate taxes, less retained earnings, plus or minus net transfer payments.

11. The fifth measure, *personal disposable income*, is the income that people can dispose of. PDI is made up of personal income less personal taxes, or consumption, personal savings, and interest on consumer loans.

12. Economists use two methods, the *final-value method* and the *value-added method*, to compute the values of the gross national product. When they use the final-value method, they add all the prices paid by the ultimate consumers of all goods and services produced. When they use the value-added method (the second method), they first compute the value added at each stage of production, and second, total all the values added.

13. *Money*, or *current, GNP* for a given year is GNP valued in the prices of that year. *Real*, or *constant, GNP* is the output of a given year adjusted for changes in prices. One computes *real*, or *constant, GNP* by dividing money GNP by the *price index* and multiplying by 100. However, the best single measure of comparative well-being is *per capita real GNP*, which one finds by dividing the real or constant GNP by the total population.

14. The following output is excluded from gross national product: (a) services by homemakers, (b) illegal goods and services, (c) labor of children in the household, (d) labor on do-it-yourself projects, and (e) volunteer help to nonprofit organizations.

15. The following transactions are excluded from gross national product: (a) the buying and selling of intermediate products, (b) the buying and selling of used items, and (c) the buying and selling of financial securities.

QUESTIONS

1. Economists in the Soviet Union do not include services as output when they are computing national income accounts. If you were doing it, would you include services as part of the national income accounts?

2. From the following data for a hypothetical nation, compute:
   a. gross national product.
   b. net national product.
   c. national income.
   d. personal income.
   e. personal disposable income.

	Billions of dollars
Consumption	300
Gross private domestic investment	150
Government expenditures	200
Imports	35
Exports	30
Capital consumption allowances (depreciation)	50
Indirect business taxes	25
Social security taxes	20
Transfer payments from the government	35
Corporate taxes	20
Retained earnings	10
Personal taxes	100

3. Gross national product is equal to gross national income, and net national product is equal to net national income. Why?

4. Of the two methods of computing the national economic accounts, the final-value method and the value-added method, which do you think is easier to use? Why?

5. If you were listening to a politician quote national income statistics, what information would you need to adequately understand the statistics?

6. Compute real GNP of a hypothetical nation from the following data.

Year	Money GNP	Price index
1929	103.1	50.6
1940	99.7	43.9
1950	284.8	80.2
1960	503.7	103.3
1970	974.1	135.3

7. The national economic accounts are definitional concepts and do not include all output or economic transactions. What kinds of output and transactions are excluded from the national economic accounts? Why?

SUGGESTED READINGS

Economic Report of the President, 1975. G.P.O., Washington, D.C., 1975.

Ruggles, Nancy D. *The Design of Economic Accounts*. Columbia, New York, 1970.

Sirkin, Gerald. *Introduction to Macroeconomic Theory*. Irwin, Homewood, Ill., 1974. Chapter 1.

United Nations Statistical Office. *Basic Principles of the System of Balances of the National Economy*. United Nations, New York, 1971.

Application 6

Is GNP Growth a Measure of Human Well-being?

There is a temptation to use various concepts of the national economic accounts as measures of material well-being. Many people, economists among them, view increases in per capita real GNP as proof that everyone is better off. Up until ten years ago, most people went along with this idea. But since then, critics have started questioning not only the use of real GNP growth as a measure of human welfare, but also the morality of economic growth itself. You may well ask, "Am I *really* better off as GNP increases?" If the nation increases the annual output of cars and color television sets, will we all be happier for it?

The attack on the use of GNP as a measure of human well-being is threefold. First, since GNP doesn't include *all* output and costs, it is not an accurate measure of output contributing to well-being. Second, there is a large amount of counted output that does not contribute to material well-being, and may even detract from it by wasting resources. Third, the very process of increasing GNP may decrease well-being.

What GNP Does Not Include

In Chapter 5, when we discussed national economic accounting, we noted that not all output is included in GNP. Remember that the labor of homemakers, illegal production, labor on do-it-yourself projects, labor by children in the household, and volunteer labor are all excluded from GNP. But when comparing the change in output from one year to the next, one tends to think that these exclusions don't really matter.

The women's liberation movement has been striving to obtain concrete recognition for work in the home by placing dollar values on household chores. However, the amount of housework as a percentage of GNP does not change much from one year to the next. Although the value of household services is estimated at about 25 percent of GNP, the distortion in GNP that results when some people hire housekeepers (included in GNP) or some people marry their housekeepers (causing a decrease in GNP) is too slight to count.

As for illegal production, such as gambling, prostitution, and dope peddling, who is going to convince anybody that this sort of thing adds to the well-being of the public or that the level of it changes very much from one year to the next?

As for the other excluded items—do-it-yourself work, children's work in the household, and volunteer work—no one can measure them accurately enough to give statistics, so they are excluded in the measurement of GNP.

In addition, GNP statistics fail to take into account many costs outside the realm of the marketplace itself, such as pollution. The air, the rivers, the oceans, and the land are all free dumping grounds for the wastes that are by-products of the production and consumption of goods. This pollution, however, does cost society something, because pollution affects the aesthetic quality of the environment, causes physical discomfort, threatens health, disrupts the food chain, and unbalances the atmosphere. For example, in the United States we pollute the air with more than 200 million tons of aerial garbage each year, even though we know dirty air is a major factor in such diseases as emphysema, bronchitis, and lung cancer, and contributes to colds, pneumonia, and asthma. If air pollution continues at this rate, we may soon have air pollution so bad that it destroys buildings, as it has in Venice.

The cost of all this pollution is not paid by either the producers or consumers of the products that create the pollution, but by those who are hurt by the pollution. Since this kind of cost is not reflected in GNP or in the cost of the specific products, we cannot make completely intelligent choices in the marketplace about what to produce and how much to produce. If the costs of pollution were reflected in the price of the products we buy, the composition of our output would probably be quite different from what it is now.

The problems of estimating the costs of pollution are hard to overcome. As we'll see in Application 17, however, one can theoretically subtract the cost of pollution from the final value of the product. It would be much like subtracting depreciation from gross investment to get net investment. After one had subtracted the external costs from the final value, one would have "net economic product," a phrase coined by economist Paul Samuelson.

If you measured the net economic value of production in these terms, some products would add less to the country's well-being than their value. In fact, some kinds of output might even detract from the country's well-being. How much do people benefit from the output of a chemical plant in Cincinnati after you deduct the destructive effects of the millions of gallons of waste the plant pours annually into the Ohio River? What is the contribution to public well-being of a new car after you deduct the car's pollution of the air with hydrocarbons and carbon monoxide? It is true that the chemicals farmers use substantially increase the per-acre yields of crops, but these chemical pesticides, weed killers, and fertilizers do not go away after they have done their work. The rains wash them down through the soil and into the water table, thence into the rivers and our drinking water, and into oceans, where they often disrupt the food chain. Fish and birds eat smaller creatures that have eaten pesticides, for example, and these poisons build up in the bodies of the fish and birds. Livestock eat feed containing the chemicals, so that every hamburger we eat contains traces of DDT and weed killer. Some people have even become unwilling to feed their children milk and liver because they are afraid of the hidden DDT content.

What Does Contribute to Well-being?

One can also attack GNP as a measure of well-being by challenging the contributions to social welfare of large parts of the output included in GNP figures. Does the flood of advertising to which we are all exposed make us healthier, happier, or wiser? We haven't space here to go into the pros and cons of advertising. (We'll look at some of those in Chapter 21.) There seems little doubt, however, that a lot of the money spent on advertising is wasted, as far as material improvement is concerned. Advertising that does not give information on which to base an economic decision or that actually gives wrong information does not benefit the consumer. Neither does money spent on advertising aimed at competition that is not based on price. For example, the advertising war between Procter and Gamble and Lever Brothers in the mid-1960s did not increase the public's well-being, but it did increase soap costs and boosted the GNP by more than $40 million.

And then there are defense expenditures. In his book *The Depleted Society*, Seymour Melman concedes that defense expenditures do contribute to the country's well-being, since they increase individual and national security. However, he feels that the amounts of these expenditures are much larger than necessary for reasonable security. Expenditures that make it possible for U.S. military forces to kill each human being on earth a hundred times over certainly do not increase security or well-being.

The forms of output that increase GNP but not human well-being—and certainly you can add many more to the few mentioned here—use up resources of the economy that could have been used to produce other things that do add to material well-being. In other words, the opportunity costs of these "wasted" resources are the goods we could have produced by using the resources in other ways. **Opportunity cost** measures the cost to society of wasted resources.

Is Growth Evil?

One school of thought challenges the present rate of economic growth (the idea of a constantly increasing GNP) itself. Followers of this school feel that increases in GNP not only fail to increase present material well-being, but also decrease future well-being. They equate increases in output with increases in pollution and argue that our present-day technology is increasing the amount of pollution per unit of output. They maintain that the technology now in use, especially in the chemical and agricultural industries, is causing a great deal of pollution, and they feel that if we continue to increase pollution at the present rates, we shall be responsible for disastrous future consequences, perhaps threatening human survival.

Robert Heilbroner, in an article called "Growth and Survival," seems to take this view. Heilbroner is not so much concerned about the exhaustion of the earth's natural resources by continued growth as he is about the exponential growth of pollutants. He says that "the exponential curves of growth, human and industrial, will sooner or later overtake the finite capabilities of the biosphere, bringing dreadful declines in population and in the quality of life." Growth itself is not the enemy, he says, but pollution. Heilbroner's recommended solution is public (government) control over family size and consumption habits and over the volume and composition of industrial and agricultural output.

Exponents of no growth also charge that because of our continued emphasis on growth and on increases in GNP, we are depleting the earth's supply of nonreproducible resources, such as fossil fuels and minerals. (*Fossil fuels* are those formed from fossils, such as coal and oil.) We may have a high standard of living now, but our grandchildren, and their children, may live in a world that is poverty-stricken, because of the depletion of natural resources.

Many economists take issue with these pessimistic views. Our space here is too limited to permit us to survey the large amount of literature on the economics of pollution. We'll look more closely at the subject in Application 17. However, we do not believe that growth per se causes pollution. The problem lies in the way production and consumption take place. We believe that industry can control pollution by various devices and incorporate the cost of controlling it into the market price of the products. Or there could be government regulation of the matter. How to eliminate pollution or even *how much* of it to eliminate (the question of opportunity cost enters in) are the questions. But it is highly probable that we *can* control pollution and still maintain growth. In fact, we need continued growth to be able to produce the devices necessary to control pollution.

To the claim of the no-growth school that we are using up nonreproducible resources, one could make at least two responses:

1. The normal workings of the market will slow down industry's use of scarce resources and encourage the shift to more plentiful ones, and will also encourage technological innovation that will lead to new resources. Figure A6-1 shows the situation. As resources become scarcer, normal supply S decreases to S_1. That is, the supply curve shifts up to the left. Prices increase and quantity used shrinks. The higher price causes users of the scarce resource (let's say it is oil) to use a more plentiful resource (coal). It also forces them to develop new resources (atomic energy).

FIGURE A6-1 Shift in Supply of a Scarce Resource

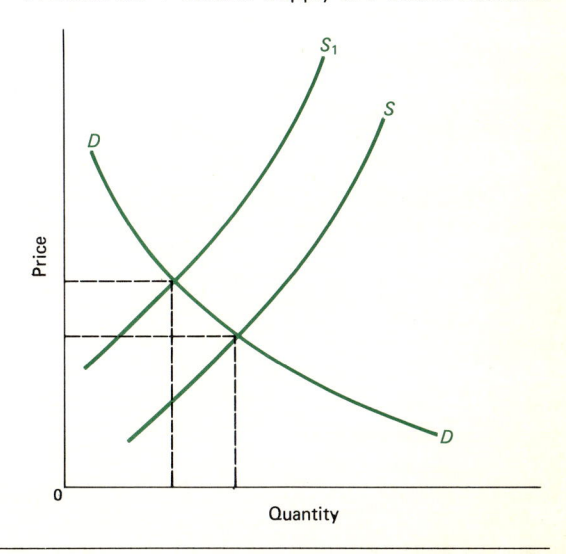

2. Technology has developed during the past 250 years at an unbelievable pace. Scientists and engineers have brought forth many new resources. There is no reason to believe that this process will stop. Something not considered a resource today may become one tomorrow. On the other hand, today's resource may be old-fashioned and even useless tomorrow, because of tehnological change.

Again, let us emphasize that we are not trying to examine all the pros and cons of these economic positions. We just want you to be aware of some of the viewpoints, because these arguments force us to stop and think. Can society control pollution? Can science solve the problem of the scarcity of resources? The problems are serious ones, but they do not justify the dire predictions set forth in the Club of Rome's 1972 book *The Limits to Growth,* which declared that we are all guilty of ruining the earth and making it uninhabitable for future generations.

Alternatives to Using GNP as a Yardstick

If we can't use GNP to measure material well-being, what alternatives do we have? Someone from the National Bureau of Economic Research wants to introduce a system that would classify almost everything as some kind of asset: tangible assets (machines, factories), intangible assets (education), environmental assets (rivers, natural resources), and sociopolitical-environmental assets (a democratic form of government). Economists say that this system is useful and possible, at least in principle, but that categorizing all these assets and computing their value would be very difficult.

In the Johnson, Nixon, and Ford administrations, efforts to improve social statistics achieved little, though we don't know how hard the statisticians tried. The director of the Johnson administration's study (entitled *Toward a Social Report*) admitted that "the act of measuring the output of public programs is in its infancy."

Some economists propose that we treat damage to nonmarket assets, physical as well as aesthetic, in the same way we treat the depreciation of capital assets of a business. (But how does one measure such damage?) Others say that we ought to pinpoint all those activities included in the GNP that are particularly injurious to the quality of the environment. Again, the main obstacle is the enormous problem of concept and measurement. What is the cost of hearing loss to a child raised next door to an airport? What is the cost of cancerous lungs to a person who works in a factory that makes polyvinyl chloride? How much is a dead Lake Erie worth? What dollar value does one attach to a reduced life span caused by smog? What price does one set on the lost beauty of a sewage-glutted river?

A Possible Conclusion

Arthur Okun, chairman of President Johnson's Council of Economic Advisers, in an article in *Survey of Current Business,* maintained that not only were the national economic accounts not measures of material well-being, but should not be so considered.

> What you can and do measure is the output resulting from market-oriented activity. The key to market-oriented activity is the presence of price tags—the essential ingredient in an objective standard of measurement.... But if you were to be seduced by your critics into inventing price tags that neither exist nor can be reasonably approximated for things that money can buy, you would have sacrificed the objective yardstick.

Okun made the following plea to those computing the accounts:

> I know you will not ignore the GNP. I urge that you not try to "fix" it—to convert GNP into a purported measure of social welfare. You are doing your job so well that people are asking you to take on a different and bigger job. Resist at all costs, for you can't do that job; indeed, nobody can. Producing a summary measure of social welfare is a job for a philosopher-king, and there is no room for a philosopher-king in the federal government.

SUMMING UP

1. Arguments that GNP does not accurately measure people's well-being are as follows:
   a. GNP does not include all the output and costs of our society. Housework, illegal production, labor on do-it-yourself projects, volunteer labor, and labor of children in the household are all excluded. GNP also fails to take into account the costs of pollution caused by production and consumption.
   b. Some output included in GNP does not contribute to material well-being: for example, a great deal of advertising and many defense expenditures.
   c. Economic growth itself intensifies pollution and depletes the world's supply of nonreproducible resources.

2. Alternative measures of well-being founder on the problem of assigning values to nonmarket costs and benefits.

QUESTION

Name five types of production that are counted as part of GNP, and analyze the costs and benefits of each. Would increases in their output increase our material well-being?

SUGGESTED READINGS

Andrews, Frederick. "Measuring Society." *Current*, March 1972.

Cole, H. S. D., et al., eds. *Models of Doom*. Universe, New York, 1973.

Heilbroner, Robert L. "Growth and Survival." *Foreign Affairs*, January 1972.

Meadows, Donella H., et al. *The Limits to Growth*. Universe, New York, 1972.

Mesarovic, Mihajlo, and Edward Pestel. *Mankind at the Turning Point*. Dutton, New York, 1974.

Okun, Arthur. "Should GNP Measure Social Welfare?" *Survey of Current Business*, July 1971.

Possell, Peter, and Leonard Ross. *The Retreat from Riches*. Viking, New York, 1972.

6

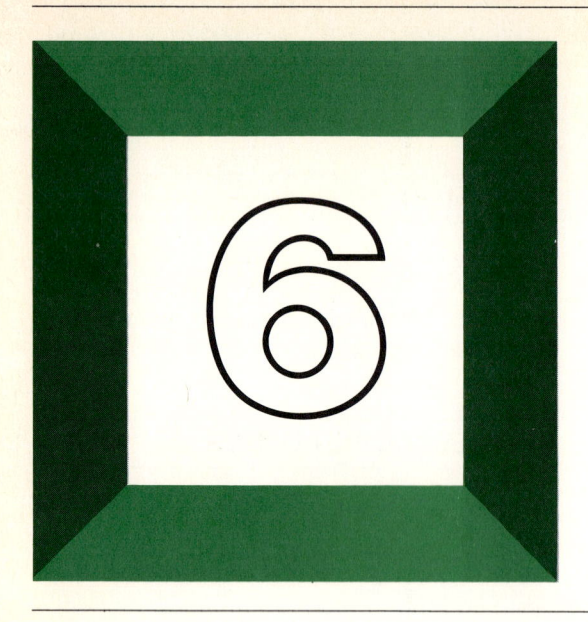

Business Fluctuations

During the Great Depression of the 1930s, President Roosevelt said that one-fourth of America's people were "ill-fed, ill-clothed, and ill-housed." At that time one-fourth of the U.S. labor force was totally unemployed, and another one-fourth was only partially employed, that is, worked less than a full week. Even as late as January 1942, when we were already at war, more than 10 percent of the U.S. labor force was still unemployed.

Thirty years or so later, in 1974, newspapers reported that some old people were eating dog food to stay alive, as inflation of more than 12 percent per year eroded their fixed incomes. At the same time, unemployment in general was approaching 9 percent, or even higher in some sections of the country. The rate was double for adult blacks and triple for teen-age blacks.

The history of the United States is marked by these recurrent periods of unemployment and depression, followed by recovery, prosperity, and inflation. However, the long-term tendency has been toward economic growth of about 3 percent per year. The chief problem of economic policy still remains: In our affluent society, how can employment and prices be stabilized in the face of changes in business activity? The first section of this chapter explores the nature of business fluctuations, the second discusses employment, and the third discusses the effects of changes in prices.

It's easy to guess who pays the cost of unemployment: the unemployed, and the employers with idle equipment. But who pays the cost of inflation? In Application 7, we will analyze this question.

Fluctuations: Characteristics and Clues

Kinds of Business Fluctuations
Economists can identify four kinds of fluctuations in the economy.

1. The **secular trend** is the expansion or contraction of an economy over very long periods of time, fifty to a hundred years. Within these long-run trends, shorter fluctuations occur. These are called business cycles.

2. **Business cycles** are variations in general economic activity; that is, fluctuations in output, income, employment, and prices. They happen over and over again, but not necessarily in any regular or periodic way, and take place over a period of six to eight years. These business cycles will be the main topic of this chapter. Within these business cycles, regular seasonal fluctuations occur.

3. **Seasonal variations** are fluctuations that occur regularly within each year. For example, employment in agriculture increases in the summer as harvest time approaches, and retail sales increase just before Christmas and Easter. To judge the significance of these seasonal increases or decreases in economic activity, you must compare them to the levels of activity at the same time in other years. In other words, to analyze various other influences on business activity, you must make allowances for seasonal activity and "filter out" the seasonal effects.

4. **Random variations** are irregular variations that one can't account or plan for, since they don't follow any regular pattern. Examples of random variation are the depressed agricultural output caused by the drought of 1936; the steel strike of 1959; and the stock market panic when President Kennedy was assassinated.

Phases of a Business Cycle

In the beginning of the **contraction phase** of a business cycle, the level of economic activity begins to fall. (See Figure 6-1.) Output and employment start to sag, and investment and consumption start to shrink. Prices tend to creep downward. As the contraction continues, unemployment may become high, investment and consumption low and sluggish. A great deal of plant capacity sits idle, and price drops may be very noticeable. Profits fall.

In the **expansion phase**, unemployment begins to diminish and unused plant capacity begins to be put into operation again, while income, output, and consumption rise. At this stage, prices may stay relatively

FIGURE 6-1 The Phases of a Business Cycle

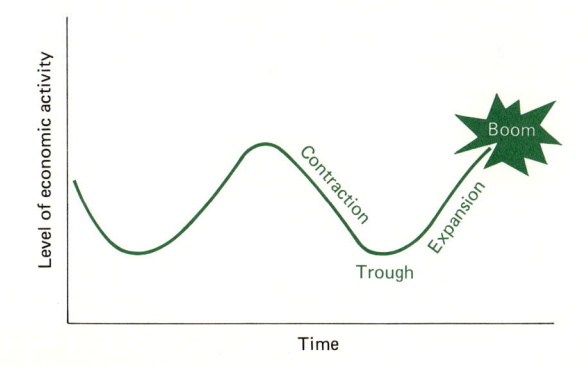

stable. As the expansion continues, the nation approaches full employment and full utilization of capacity. Investment and consumption rise, and because of high levels of demand, so do prices. Profits rise.

Do Business Cycles Follow a Regular Pattern?
The very word *cycles*, the concept of phases, and diagrams such as Figure 6-1 seem to imply regularity or uniformity. However, history shows that although business cycles do recur, there is little or no regularity or uniformity to them. Because of this lack of uniformity, many economists say that the terms *business fluctuation* or *economic instability* are more appropriate than *business cycle*.

For example, in Figure 6-2, there is no uniformity in the length of them from one peak to another. It took nine years for the United States to go from the peak in 1960 to the next peak in 1969, but only two years to go from the peak in 1953 to the next peak in 1955. And there is no uniformity in the contraction phases, either. In the Great Depression,

FIGURE 6-2 American Business Cycles. The midline indicates the long-term trend; the solid line indicates wholesale price levels; the shaded area indicates levels of business activity. (*Source:* Reproduced by permission of the Cleveland Trust Company.)

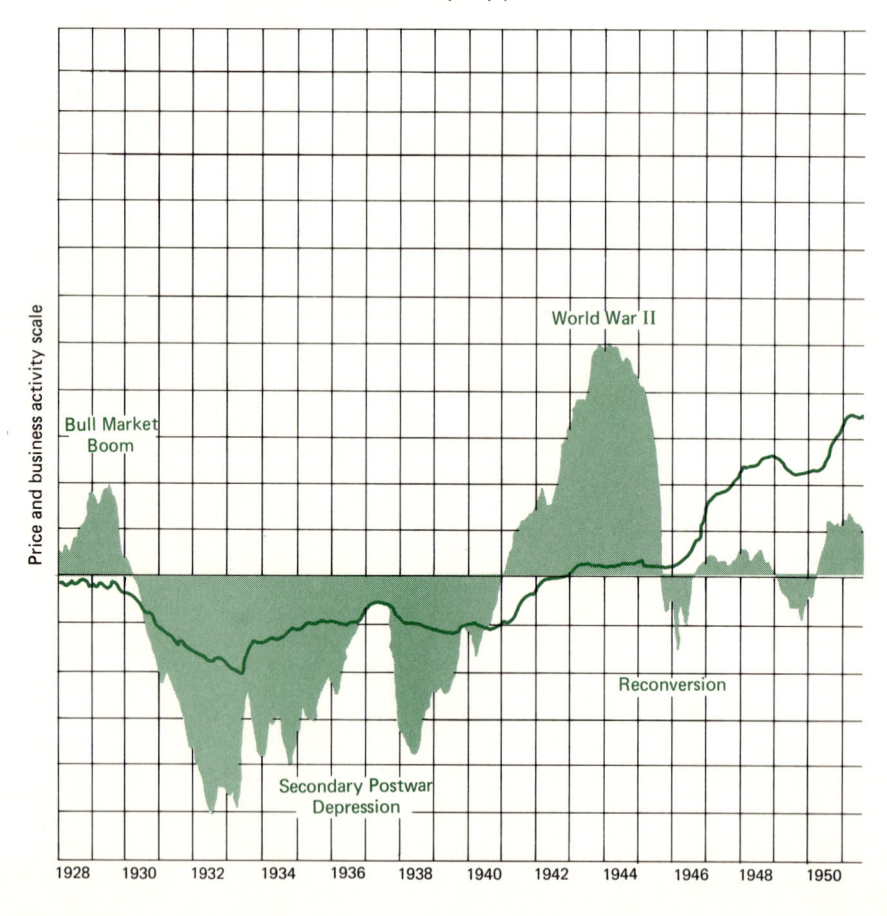

132   Business Fluctuations

the contraction phase lasted from 1929 to 1933, about three and a half years. In the recession of 1949, the contraction phase was about one year. Similarly, there is no uniformity in the expansion phases. You can also see that there has been no uniformity in the *intensity* of the various phases of the business cycles.

Durable- Versus Nondurable-Goods Industries
Not only do the cycles differ from one to another, but also each cycle differs in the way it affects various kinds of economic activity. The biggest differences are those in price and output in industries that produce durable goods and industries that produce nondurable goods. Over the whole cycle, in the durable-goods industries, output varies widely. Prices vary much less. In the nondurable-goods industries, prices vary, but output tends to be more stable.

In the durable-goods industries (heavy equipment and machines, major appliances, new buildings), the main effect of declining demand during the recession and depression phases is reduced output and employment. In the nondurable-goods industries (food, clothing, furniture), the main impact of declining demand is on prices. To learn why this variation occurs, let's think about the differences between durable

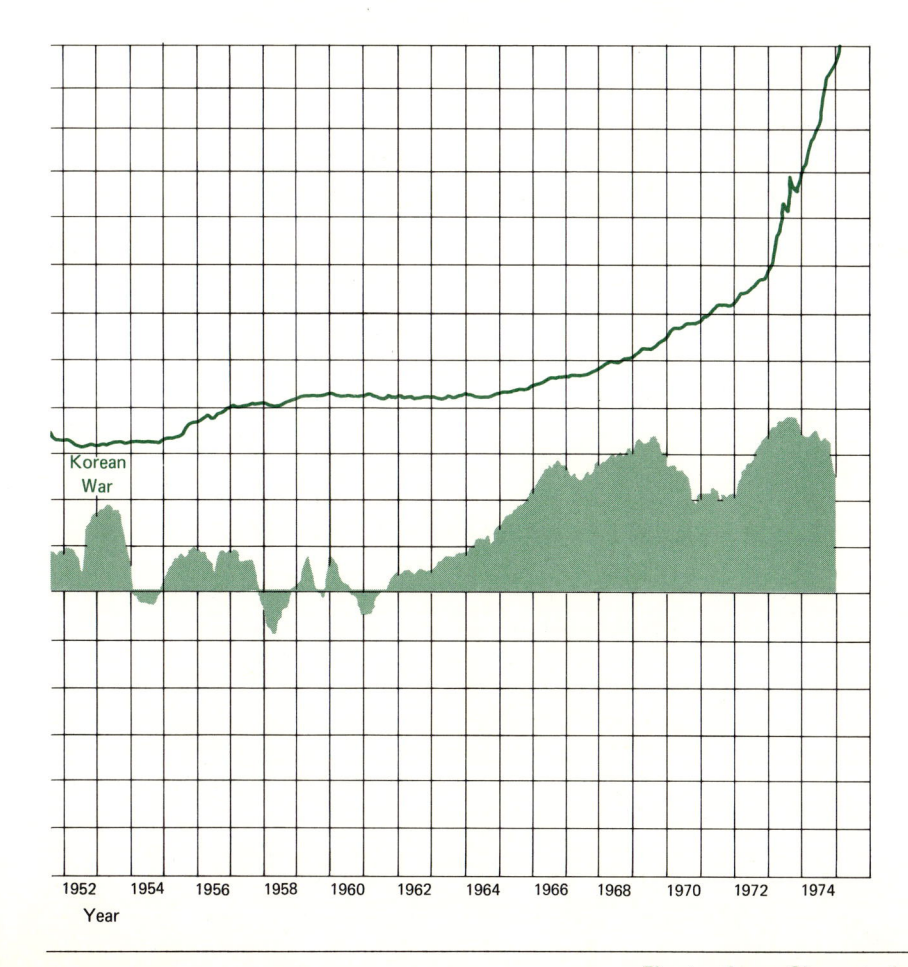

Fluctuations: Characteristics and Clues

and nondurable goods, and the differences between these industries in the nature of competition.

1. People can postpone buying new durable goods for a long time. When times are bad, the consumer repairs the old car or washing machine rather than buying a new one. A manufacturer faced with falling demand and dwindling profits repairs the machines on hand rather than buying new ones. And, with plenty of idle plant space going begging, the manufacturer sees no point in building a new plant or a new wing on the old one.

2. The industries that make consumer and producer durables (cars, steel, electrical equipment) are highly concentrated industries, with just a few large companies and less competition than in other industries. Various forms of monopoly power are manifest, so the big firms tend to protect their prices. They react to decreases in demand by cutting back on the quantity they produce.

During a recession, when decreased consumer buying is combined with decreased production by the large durable-goods companies, supply decreases. Prices may also go down, but at a slow rate. In the recession of 1958 and the one in 1969 and 1970, prices rose rather than fell. The likely reason is that the concentrated durable-goods industries prevented their own prices from falling, and even increased them in order to maintain profits.

3. People can't postpone buying nondurable goods (food, clothing, furniture) because there is a recession. Thus the demand for the output of these industries is more stable. But it still falls off in a recession.

4. In the nondurable-goods industries, there are many small companies and more competition. These firms can't stabilize prices by cutting supply, and because they lack power, their prices fluctuate more with the business cycle.

Leading Economic Indicators
The general level of economic activity moves with the business cycle. However, there are exceptions. In 1974, real or constant GNP fell by about 5 percent. Inflation increased at a two-digit rate and business profits in some industries were high, yet unemployment increased. In the recession phase, the general level of activity goes down. With the recovery phase, it goes up. Changes in output and price vary in degree as well as timing in different kinds of activity. Some kinds of economic activity, called **leading indicators**, lead the business cycle by decreasing or increasing before the rest do.

The department of commerce has put together a list of eleven of these key indicators. They are (1) average work week, (2) percentage of companies reporting slower deliveries, (3) change in prices of so-called sensitive materials, (4) number of new businesses formed, (5) number of building permits issued, (6) stock prices, (7) new orders for consumer goods, (8) new orders for plant and equipment, (9) the nation's money supply, (10) change in total liquid assets, and (11) the layoff rate. Economic forecasters use these leading indicators to predict cyclical changes. Most economists wait for a trend to show up in the index of leading indicators. When the indicators move in the same direction for three months in a row, most economists agree that the economy is going to move in that direction.

There are other small signals of economic change. For example, in October of 1975 the general manager of Chevrolet, noting that truck sales were up 34 percent over October of 1974, said, "Trucks are always a weather vane for business. People buy them to make money with them." However, a recent Federal Reserve study said that stock market prices outperformed all other indicators as a predictor of business conditions over the last seventy-five years.

Unemployment

Full employment is a main goal of any country's national economic policy. But **full employment** doesn't mean that every person in the nation has a job. The term refers to the labor force in general, which, by definition, includes anyone in the United States age sixteen or over who has a job or is actively seeking one. Full employment doesn't even mean that all the labor force is employed. Allowances are made for people who are temporarily between jobs or are in the process of changing jobs.

Kinds of Unemployment
You may think that unemployment is unemployment, and that's that. But economists have identified three different *kinds* of unemployment.

Frictional Unemployment. Frictionally unemployed people are those who are unemployed for a while as they move from one job to another. There are imperfections in the labor market that cause **frictional unemployment**:

1. Labor immobility of one kind or another, such as inability to commute or relocate.

2. Workers' inadequate knowledge of the job market.

3. The impossibility of instantly matching job-hunting people with job vacancies.

The amount of frictional unemployment depends on the degree of these imperfections. When everybody in the labor force is employed except for people who are frictionally unemployed, we say that full employment exists.

Unemployment Due to Lack of Demand. During recession and depression phases of a business cycle, the demand of the public for goods and services may not be enough for achieving full employment. Although frictional unemployment is a fact of life in all phases of a business cycle, unemployment due to lack of demand is a direct result of the "down" phase of a business cycle. Consequently, a government, to get rid of this kind of unemployment, has to try to achieve economic stability and reduce business fluctuations.

Structural Unemployment. Changes in the structure of the economy are what cause **structural unemployment**. These changes in structure may come about because of changes in technology or because of changes in the composition of output, which lead to shifts in the pattern of demand for labor. Such structural changes affect both skilled and unskilled workers. In the 1950s and early 1960s, the shift from coal to oil for heating homes left massive unemployment in the anthracite coal mines in eastern Pennsylvania. In Minnesota many workers became jobless when iron ore deposits in the Mesabi Range were exhausted. On the West Coast, in the late 1960s, large numbers of engineers who worked in the aerospace industries lost their jobs because of the government's cutback in its aerospace program when the Vietnam War caused reallocation of defense expenditures. All these events are examples of structural unemployment.

Problems That Accompany Unemployment

The worst aspect of structural unemployment involves unskilled workers, many of whom are members of minority groups (blacks, Chicanos, Puerto Ricans). Since World War II, with the advent of computers and countless technologically sophisticated gadgets, the demand for unskilled labor, as a percentage of total demand for labor, has dropped greatly, even though the percentage of unskilled laborers in the labor force has remained constant. Many jobs for the unskilled have disappeared entirely. One tragedy of the last thirty years is that our educational system seems incapable of giving students the skills they need to make them employable. The needs of minority groups, in particular, are not met.

"Merry Christmas, Staff!"

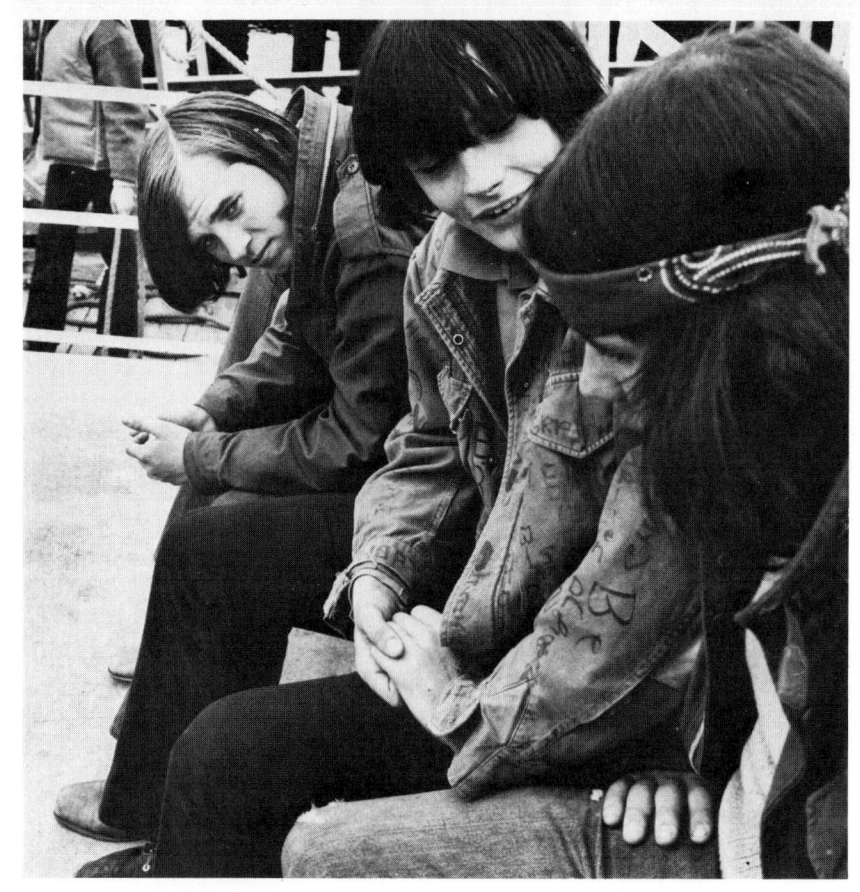

Teen-agers suffer especially from the discouraged-worker effect. (Julie O'Neil/Stock, Boston)

Unemployment due to lack of demand is a serious problem. However, if we can just maintain greater stability in the business cycle, we seem to have the tools to control it. Structural unemployment, though, is much more difficult to control. We must give the hard-core unemployed the new skills they need to survive in today's economy. Job-training programs in the last ten years have, for the most part, failed. Minimum-wage laws, originally introduced to help unskilled workers and young people entering the job market for the first time, may actually be hurting them. These laws have caused wages to rise beyond the productive ability of the unskilled worker and the teen-ager. Some people argue that a reduction in these minimum-wages—at least for certain categories of workers—would increase employment among teen-agers.

We should also mention the discouraged-worker effect. Workers who have been rendered unemployed by so-called structural changes eventually give up seeking work and just drop out of the labor force. Teen-agers especially suffer from this discouragement. They never find jobs in the first place, and in time disappear from the labor force and from our GNP statistics, as if they had become invisible.

The continuous unemployment rate among blacks, Chicanos, and Puerto Ricans, which is twice, and among youth three times, the national average, indicates the magnitude of our failure to deal with structural unemployment among those who are unskilled and discriminated against.

Economic Costs of Unemployment: The GNP Gap
The costs of unemployment to society are both economic and psychological. Obviously we can measure the economic costs in terms of goods and services the unemployed could have produced if they had had jobs. One economist, Sherman Maisel, in a book called *Fluctuations, Growth, and Forecasting*, estimates that unemployment in the depression of the 1930s cost the economy $650 billion in foregone product (using 1957 prices as a basis). This was more than enough to pay for World War II, to provide every family in the United States with a new home and two cars, or to give all who can use it a college education.

Tom Wicker, in an article in the *New York Times* in July of 1975, estimated that every 1 percent of unemployment adds $16 billion annually to the federal budget: $14 billion in lost tax revenue and $2 billion in government payments for unemployment and other benefits.

We can also measure economic costs of unemployment as the difference between actual GNP achieved and potential GNP, or the GNP that could have been obtained with full employment. Figure 6-3 shows actual and potential GNP (assuming 4 percent unemployment). The difference between the two is called the GNP gap.

The GNP gap, the amount of output sacrificed when the economy does not fully use its existing resources, was marked between 1957 and 1965. Between 1965 and 1968, unemployment fell below 4 percent and actual GNP exceeded the 4 percent potential. This GNP surplus occurred because of the 1965 tax cut, plus high government expenditures for the war on poverty and the escalation in Vietnam. This period of full employment was brief, and the gap reappeared by the end of 1969. You can see that it is extremely difficult to utilize the labor force fully and hold unemployment down to the 4 percent level.

Psychological and Social Costs of Unemployment
In a society basically still ruled by the work ethic, to be out of work—especially to be unemployed for a long time—causes people acute mental suffering. An extreme example, which appeared in the newspapers in the late 1960s, is the case of the engineer in the San Francisco Bay area who, after being unemployed for a long time, committed suicide. He left a note, saying that he did what his country wanted; he became a good engineer and he worked hard. Now nobody wanted him anymore.

In addition to mental anguish, prolonged unemployment causes insecurities about one's self-worth. It creates family strain that goes beyond economic privation. In the past, and even more so today, prolonged unemployment has placed the individual psychologically, as well as economically, beyond the pale of normal society.

High levels of unemployment also put social and political stress on society at large, especially when high rates of unemployment exist among minorities. Entire minority groups—blacks, Chicanos, and Puerto Ricans—become conscious that their unemployment problems are particularly serious. In a very real sense, they become pitted against more affluent groups. To paraphrase Abraham Lincoln, a society that is half affluent, half deprived, cannot long endure, or, at least, cannot expect to have social tranquility.

Prices and the Problem of Inflation

During various phases of a business cycle, the level of employment changes. Thus a nation must not only maintain economic growth but also try to maintain full employment. Another problem is inflation. During various phases of a business cycle, the level of prices changes. Since World War II, prices have primarily been rising. This, as we all know, is inflation.

As prices of goods and services increase, the amount of them that a dollar will buy naturally decreases. Thus inflation causes a decrease in

FIGURE 6-3 The GNP Gap. The straight line represents potential GNP; the jagged line is actual performance of the economy; the distance between the lines as you read GNP for any given year is the GNP gap. (*Source: Business Conditions Digest,* June 1975, 61.)

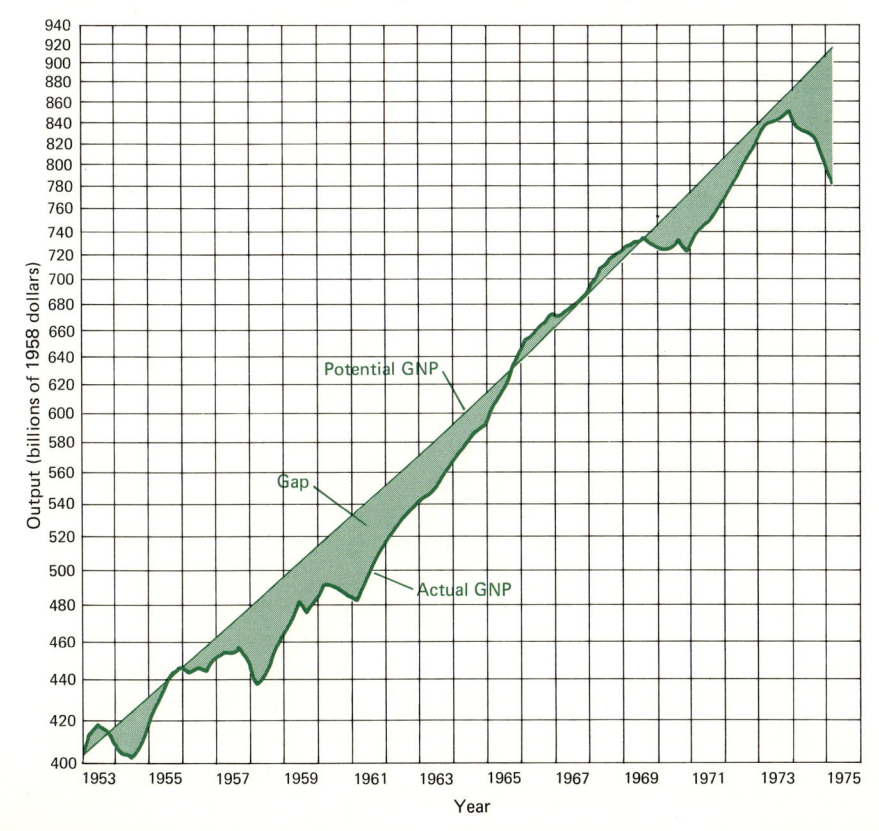

FIGURE 6-4 Rates of Unemployment and Inflation, 1953–1975 (*Source: Business Conditions Digest,* June 1975, 22 and 56.)

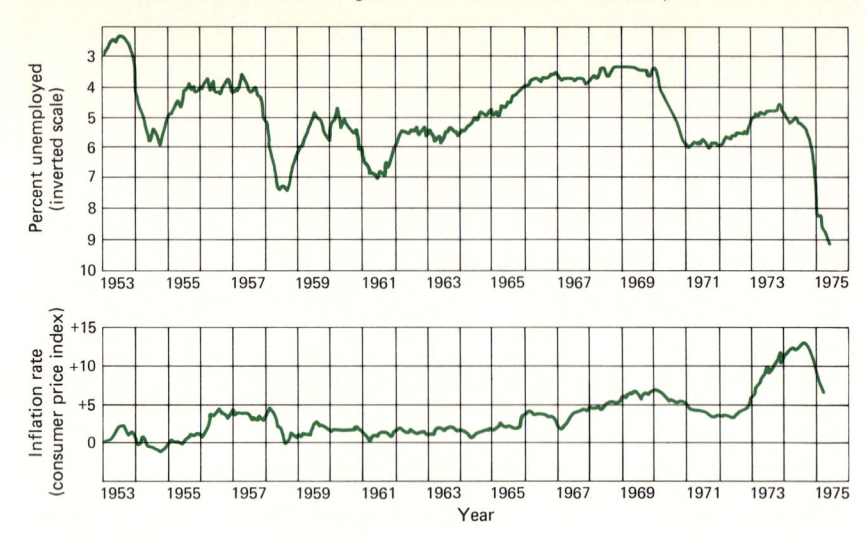

the purchasing power of the dollar. Figure 6-4 shows the rates of unemployment and inflation in the United States between 1953 and 1975.

Kinds of Inflation

There are three kinds of inflation, which economists classify according to their source or cause.

1. *Demand-pull inflation.* Remember that in our discussion of supply and demand, we said that when demand increases (for a given supply of a good), the price of that good will increase. The same sort of phenomenon occurs for the entire economy. When the economy is at full employment, output, over a short period of time, cannot increase because there are no resources (especially labor) available to increase it. When demand for goods and services increases, there are not enough productive facilities to increase output in order to meet this increased demand. Consequently, markets ration out their goods or services, causing increased prices and eventually forcing decreases in the quantity the public demands. Thus the economy brings back into line the quantity of a good or service demanded, according to the economy's ability to supply.

Let's look at an example of a demand-pull situation: In 1966 President Johnson escalated the war in Vietnam by increasing our troops there to more than 500,000 men. To maintain these troops in combat half a world away, the U.S. government had to buy billions of dollars worth of equipment and supplies. The government had also sharply increased its expenditures on antipoverty programs, and there had been tax cuts in 1964 and 1965. As a result of this combination of events, the economy had reached full employment. Unemployment had dropped below 4 percent. Thus the economy was able to meet the increased

One response to inflation: A community food co-op. Without fancy equipment or paid workers, prices can be less. (Jeff Albertson/Stock, Boston)

demand for armaments only by drawing resources away from the production of other commodities. It did this by increasing the prices of resources used to make nonmilitary goods. Then prices of resources used to make armaments increased, which increased the price of the finished products. At the same time, the supply of resources to other markets declined, decreasing supply and increasing prices. That is what we mean when we say that the marked inflation of 1967–1969 was primarily due to demand-pull inflation.

In brief, then, demand-pull inflation occurs when an economy's demand exceeds the ability of that economy to supply at existing prices. Too many dollars are chasing too few goods. The effect is to force prices up.

2. *Cost-push inflation.* When the suppliers of resources increase their prices faster than their productive efficiency increases, cost-push inflation occurs. When resource costs go up faster than increases in productivity, a company's production costs per unit increase. These increased production costs mean that the firm, in order to maintain profits, has to increase prices.

The usual example people give of cost-push inflation is this: When unions force industry to give workers wage increases and the workers do not produce correspondingly more output, cost-push inflation occurs. Suppose that workers in the carpet industry increased their productivity 3 percent and the union obtained wage increases of 4 percent. You can see that the carpet manufacturer's labor costs per yard of carpet go up. (Increased productivity reduces labor costs per unit by 3 percent, while wage increases raise cost per unit 4 percent; net cost increase is 1 percent.) Right after the war (between 1945 and 1949), labor unions

Kinds of Inflation 141

staged a real drive to increase wages. They argued that wage rates had stayed at about the same level during the war, while both productivity and company profits had risen dramatically.

The labor unions naturally wanted workers' wages to catch up. On the whole, industry leaders did not fight this move to increase wage rates, because a strong demand-pull inflation was already under way because of depression and war-postponed consumption. It was easy to pass the wage hikes on to the consumer in the form of higher prices.

In the 1970s, the whole world experienced a singularly agonizing case of cost-push inflation. At the beginning of the 1970s, the world's major oil-producing and oil-exporting countries formed an association: OPEC. Among them, the OPEC countries control the bulk of the world's oil. And between 1971 and 1974, they quintupled the price of their crude oil. The industrialized world is heavily dependent on oil. It is primarily oil that keeps the wheels of industry turning, that generates electricity for our power plants, that gets most of us to work. Therefore the OPEC countries' increases in oil prices quickly increased costs of production generally and set off a worldwide inflation and economic crisis.

3. *Administered-price inflation.* This might also be called *profit-push inflation,* or *sellers' inflation.* Monopolistic firms have considerable influence over supply and therefore over price. Companies big enough to influence price decide on a pricing policy. Setting prices becomes one of the firm's administrative functions.

Such companies may decide that it is easier to increase their profits by just increasing prices rather than by increasing their efficiency and lowering their costs. During periods of prosperity, when demand is at a high level, these firms can easily exercise their power to increase prices, and price increases from such a source are hard to detect. During a period of recession, when demand is falling, these firms may again decide to increase prices in order to maintain their profits. They have a certain target rate of return on their investment that they seem to try to maintain by raising prices.

However, during these periods of falling demand one can most readily spot administered-price increases. In the recessions of 1958 and of 1970–1971; and in the recession that began in 1974, prices of certain goods rose, while employment and real GNP fell. As you can see, one can trace much of the inflation during recession back to the fact that monopolistic corporations increase their prices even though demand is falling, because they want to keep on earning high profits.

Remember, though, that administered-price inflation takes place during both rising and falling phases of the business cycle, so we are never entirely safe from this kind of danger.

Both cost-push and administered-price inflation exist whenever there is not enough competition to keep prices under control. For example, in cost-push inflation, the people who supply the resources have enough monopoly control over the supply of their resources to give them economic power to force prices up. (Remember that this resource may be labor itself.) In administered-price inflation, the reason certain firms have so much power over prices is that they control, to an extent, the supply of finished products for which there are no good substitutes. Cost-push and administered-price inflation can interact, causing prices to spiral upward.

What Effect Do Price Changes Have?
When prices go up or down, this movement has a financial effect on all of us. It affects the economy in three ways: (1) by redistributing real income, (2) by redistributing real wealth, and (3) by changing the level of output.

1. *Redistribution of real income.* First, we should make a distinction between *money* and *real* income. **Money income** is the number of dollars a person receives in income, or the number of dollars in the paycheck, for most people. **Real income** is what can be bought with money income. You can see that your real income can change when there is either (a) a change in your money income, or (b) a change in the general level of prices and the purchasing power of the dollar. In the following discussion, we shall assume that the total pie (the level of output) remains constant; that is, that the total level of output is unaffected by changes in prices.

In terms of income, there are two broad classes of people: people whose incomes are fixed, or semifixed, and those whose incomes are variable. When there is inflation, the people with fixed or semifixed incomes suffer because their money income does not increase as fast as prices do; their real income therefore declines. People with fixed incomes are usually nonunion workers, those living on welfare or pen-

"You've no idea what's happened to prices—you'll have to pull a really big job the first thing when you get out!"

sions, and those with income based on interest; that is, the widows and orphans, the elderly and the poor, and the unorganized.

The money incomes of people with varied incomes, though, often increase faster than prices go up, for example, the incomes of the people whose earnings come from the profits of a business. Some elements of cost for the business may tend not to increase as fast as prices. In industries where this occurs, profit margins increase. In general (although there are exceptions), the money incomes of those who obtain their incomes from profits tend to increase faster than prices increase.

Organized labor generally has enough clout to increase wages at least as fast as prices rise, and often more so, so organized labor usually can enjoy increased real income—at least for a time. This is particularly true when unions make their contracts for short periods.

During a **deflation**, when prices fall, those with fixed incomes temporarily enjoy increases in their real income, because a dollar buys a little more. This does not apply to unorganized labor, because unorganized labor does not have enough economic power to prevent wage cuts. ("Times are hard. You lot will just have to take less per hour.")

What happens to people with variable incomes during a deflation? Those with income from profits tend to suffer losses in real income. Suppose you are living on the income from stock you own in one company. The company has to lower its prices because of the deflation. But the company still has to pay for resources (labor and materials), and the costs of these resources lag behind the fall in prices. Thus the margin of profit gets narrower and narrower, and presently the company is unable to pay dividends to its stockholders.

As for organized labor in a deflation, it has the economic power to keep employers from cutting back wages, in spite of falling prices.

2. *Redistribution of real wealth.* In terms of real wealth, there are three categories: debtors (who borrow money), creditors (who lend it), and savers (who save it).

During an inflation, debtors benefit. But creditors and savers lose real wealth; that is, their wealth does not buy as much as it used to. Suppose you are the debtor. Let's say you borrowed $100 from your brother a year ago, and suppose that there has been a 10 percent inflation during the year. Prices in general were 10 percent lower a year ago, and thus purchasing power of each dollar was 10 percent higher. If you repay the loan today, you're 10 percent richer, assuming that you didn't pay interest. But your brother, the creditor, is 10 percent poorer. He lent you the money when prices were lower and purchasing power higher. If he spends that $100 today, he'll get 10 percent less for it than he would have a year ago.

Now suppose that your brother had saved that $100 instead of lending it to you. Unless he earned interest on it, he would still have lost 10 percent, because a year ago when he saved the money, its purchasing power was 10 percent higher than it is today. (The creditor and saver would not be hurt by inflation if the rate of interest increased enough to compensate for the inflation and to pay them back for the risk, for the loss of liquidity, for the fact that they could not use the money themselves, and for all the other sacrifices people make in order to earn interest on their money.)

During a deflation, just the reverse holds true: Creditors and savers benefit, and debtors lose real wealth. Creditors lent money when prices were higher and each dollar was worth less, but they are paid back when prices are lower and thus the dollar's purchasing power is greater. Savers, too, are better off. They saved money when prices were higher and each dollar bought less. But now that prices have come down, their savings have higher purchasing power. Debtors, on the other hand, are hurt, because they borrowed money when prices were higher and purchasing power lower, but now they have to pay it back when prices are lower and dollars have greater purchasing power.

3. *Changed level of output due to changed prices.* We have been assuming that the economy's output was unchanged as prices changed and that as prices changed, some groups gained at the expense of others. What happens if the total output changes? Relative redistribution of wealth still takes place, but its adverse effects on some groups may be lessened; or sometimes the adverse effects are accentuated. Let us see why.

A strong inflation can lead to recession and unemployment for a number of reasons: (a) Since all prices do not increase at the same rate, a sharp inflation may quickly cause structural distortions. Some firms' costs rise faster than they can raise prices of their output, so their profits are reduced. They may even take losses. They reduce their output, they lay off workers, and they may even go bankrupt. (b) Rapidly rising prices confuse both producers and consumers, so that people hesitate to make decisions. This causes a decrease in demand for output. (c) Consumers may revolt against rising prices and refuse to buy. This again causes decrease in demand. (d) People who are hurt by the redistributive effect of higher prices have to cut back on their buying, again decreasing the demand for output. The lucky ones who actually benefit from higher prices may step up *their* buying, but their increased demand may not compensate for the decreased demand on the part of those who are caught in the squeeze of higher prices.

The net effect of all this is a decrease in total demand for the economy's output, which means that output falls off and so does employment. The result is *recession*.

We have been discussing sharp increases in prices. But moderate increases in price can actually be beneficial to output, for the following reasons: (1) When inflation is slight, business and industries can see in advance that the costs of their resources (labor and materials) are going to go up by a certain amount next year, so they can raise their own prices slightly and thus counter the structural effects of varying rates of price changes. (2) The prices of products may increase faster than the prices of resources, so that the profits of business and industry increase. When business people are making high profits, they are more inclined to invest. Thus more jobs open up, employment rates rise, and the rate of economic growth increases.

However, if a moderate inflation continues for a long time, it becomes what is called **creeping inflation**. And this may become a threat to the economy, for three reasons: (1) Creeping inflation can accelerate until it becomes a severe inflation, with all its potential for causing recession. (2) Creeping inflation can generate a wage-price spiral, resulting in serious inflation. Unions demand wage increases to compensate for past inflation and often add an extra margin for anticipated future inflation. During a prosperous period, business people are reluctant to face a strike, so they agree to grant the unions their wage hikes, which in turn increase the costs of production. Businesses pass these higher costs on to consumers through higher prices, which often reflect an extra profit margin for the firms. (3) In due course, creeping inflation results in redistribution of wealth and puts serious economic strain on disadvantaged groups. The result is *recession*.

A moderate deflation, bringing about a gradual fall in prices, may also contribute to increases in output. Deflations, however, are quite rare, especially since World War II. During the prosperous part of the 1920s (1922 to 1929), prices sloped gently downward because of increases in productivity without corresponding increases in workers' wages. (The unions had a hard time surviving during the 1920s.) The general population enjoyed increases in their real income as prices fell. At the same time, businesses had larger profits, since productivity increased faster than prices fell. Both factors kept the demand for consumer and capital goods high.

But deflation, too, can create problems. When the decrease in prices is very rapid, it tends to reduce the level of output. The following sequence occurs: (1) Retail prices fall faster than prices of *factor inputs* (the resources an industry uses to manufacture things). This squeezes out profits and introduces losses. (2) Since prices do not fall uniformly, the structure of prices becomes distorted. Some firms have their profits wiped out entirely. (3) Business people, when faced with falling prices, become very pessimistic and tend to withhold further investment. All these conditions lead to decreases in output. The result is *recession*.

Employment and Prices

To prevent the economy from continually plunging down and climbing up, governments try to initiate policies of stabilization, aimed at maintaining full employment and stable prices. It is difficult to attain both objects at the same time, since they are often contradictory.

Figure 6-5 shows that as output increases, more people get jobs, so unemployment is reduced and prices remain stable. At this stage there is still some unused space and unemployed labor that industry can use without raising its prices. However, as output reaches point A, industry can achieve further increases in output only by raising its prices. Although point A is reached before there is full employment of all labor, certain categories of skilled labor and other resources may be in short supply. Beyond point A, the ever expanding output creates an ever greater demand for resources, which means that the prices of these resources will increase still further and inevitably the general level of prices will also rise. At point *B* (full employment), any further effort to increase output will result in continued demand-pull inflation; prices increase but real output cannot. In other words, demand-pull inflation occurs before the economy reaches full employment because some forms of labor and resources are in shorter supply than others. More expensive resources force up the prices of products before full employment is achieved.

From this we can see that there is a tradeoff between employment and prices. Beyond some point of resource use, if you want to reduce unemployment you have to accept some increases in prices. We can diagram this tradeoff between employment and prices. The resulting curve, called a **Phillips curve**, looks like the one in Figure 6-6.

When we examine Figure 6-6, which covers the period from World War II to 1967, we see a Phillips curve representing a relationship that many considered politically acceptable: unemployment at 4 to 4.5 percent, inflation at 4 to 5 percent. If the government then had tried to force the unemployment rate below 4.5 percent prices would have increased too much. The point of this Phillips curve is that, before 1967, the tradeoff between inflation and unemployment was a politically acceptable one.

FIGURE 6-5 Prices and Employment. As output increases, industry starts using resources that were formerly unemployed, and prices remain stable. At point *A*, some resources start to be in short supply; this forces prices up. At point *B*, there is full employment. Further increases in demand only result in still higher prices.

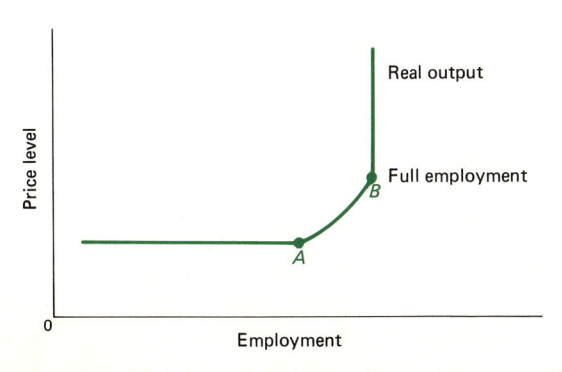

FIGURE 6-6 A Phillips Curve. The horizontal axis is the percentage of unemployment; the vertical axis, the percentage rate of inflation. The Phillips curve shows the relationship between the two. Note the shift in the Phillips curve since 1967, necessitating two curves.

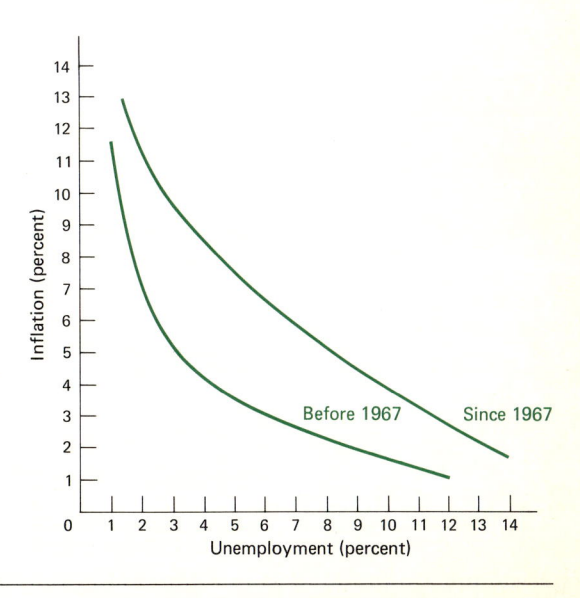

Employment and Prices

Now look at what has been happening to the Phillips curve since 1967: a steep shift upward with the tradeoff between unemployment and rising prices at a much higher level. During the recession of 1970–1971, unemployment of about 6 percent was coupled with an inflation rate of about 7 percent, making the government's policy of economic stabilization much harder to carry out. In the recession of 1974–1975, the tradeoff was even less acceptable. In 1974 unemployment reached 9 percent, while inflation exceeded 12 percent.

Whenever the government tries to reduce unemployment, it has to stimulate output, which increases demand, which in turn increases prices. On the other hand, whenever the government tries to reduce inflation, it has to somehow or other reduce demand, which reduces output, which in turn increases unemployment. When the tradeoff between inflation and unemployment is politically unacceptable, any effort the government makes to reduce unemployment just increases an already politically unacceptable level of inflation; and vice versa.

This increase in the tradeoff level can be attributed to a number of causes: (1) Structural unemployment may have increased substantially, since the proportion of teen-agers and women in the labor force has risen, and the proportion of unskilled workers has increased, as well as the proportion of those with obsolete skills. Structural unemployment is relatively unresponsive, even to government efforts to stimulate total demand. (2) Large companies and labor unions have increased their monopoly power over prices. Regardless of the unemployment situation, these monopolies are perhaps taking a larger share of incomes than they used to. (3) The inflationary impact of foreigners on the domestic economy has increased. For example, no government policy of domestic stabilization could possibly keep international oil prices from rising. (4) Certain government policies have reduced the mobility of certain resources, particularly human resources. For example, the fear of losing unemployment benefits discourages unemployed workers from leaving areas in which there is surplus labor. Residence requirements for welfare and food stamps may also keep people from moving to a new community.

SUMMING UP

1. There are four kinds of economic fluctuations: (a) the *secular trend*, which is the expansion or contraction of the economy over very long periods of time; (b) *business cycles*, which are repetitive but not regular variations in general economic activity; (c) *seasonal variations*, which happen regularly at the same time each year; and (d) *random variations*, which have no regular pattern or recurring cause.

2. The two phases of the business cycle are (a) the *contraction phase*, when unemployment and unused capacity are high and investment and

consumption are low; and (b) the *expansion phase*, when investment, consumption, and employment are high and prices may be rising.

3. In business cycles, there is no regularity in the length of the cycle or any of its phases, nor is there regularity in the intensity of activity. Many consider the term *business fluctuation* more descriptive than *business cycle*.

4. Prices in durable-goods industries tend to be more stable over a given business cycle than prices in nondurable-goods industries. (a) During a contraction in economic activity, people postpone buying new durable goods such as automobiles and washing machines; they tend to repair and keep using them. But they must continue to buy nondurable goods, such as food and clothing. (b) Nondurable-goods industries are more competitive than durable-goods industries; thus individual firms cannot limit the drop in their own prices.

5. *Leading economic indicators* are measures of economic activity that point the way to coming increases or decreases in economic activity shortly before there is an actual rise or fall. Economists use these leading indicators (stock-market prices, building permits, average work week, and so on) as tools with which to forecast economic activity.

6. There are three kinds of unemployment: (a) *Frictional unemployment* includes people who are unemployed only for short periods of time as they move from one job to another. (b) *Unemployment due to lack of demand* occurs when there is not enough total demand for industry's output for full employment to be attained. (c) *Structural unemployment* is due to structural changes in the economy, which take place because of changes in technology and the composition of output, with resulting changes in the pattern of demand for labor.

7. The *GNP gap* reveals the economic costs of unemployment by showing the difference between potential and actual gross national product. The cost of unemployment in economic terms may be high, but the individual psychological and social costs, plus social and political tensions, may be even higher.

8. There are three kinds of inflation: (a) *demand-pull inflation*, in which total demand for an economy's output exceeds the ability of the economy to supply at existing prices, and prices rise to ration the scarce supply; (b) *cost-push inflation*, in which suppliers of resources increase their prices faster than workers increase their productivity, which pushes cost of production up, forcing companies to increase their prices; (c) *administered-price inflation*, in which firms, exercising monopoly power, increase prices to either augment or maintain profits.

9. Cost-push inflation and administered-price inflation exist because of the dearth of competition in certain industries and can interact to cause an upward spiraling of prices.

10. During periods of inflation, redistribution of *real income* occurs, because those with fixed or semifixed incomes cannot increase their

money income to compensate for rising prices. Those with variable incomes can usually increase their real incomes, since their money incomes go up faster than prices do. The reverse occurs during a period of *deflation*, when prices fall.

11. There is also redistribution of real wealth during a period of inflation, as debtors benefit from inflation because they borrow high-purchasing-power dollars and pay back low-purchasing-power dollars. Creditors and savers lose in an inflation because they lend (or save) high-purchasing-power dollars and are paid back low-purchasing-power dollars. The opposite occurs during a deflation, when prices are falling.

12. A strong inflation can lead to recession, as cost distortions put pressure on some firms, confuse both producers and consumers, and weaken the consumer's willingness and ability to buy. Moderate inflation may increase output and income by stimulating investment. *Creeping inflation* (or moderate inflation over a fairly long period) may eventually have bad effects on the economy.

13. A government cannot readily achieve both full employment and stable prices at the same time, especially in a noncompetitive economy. As the economy increases its output, some resources run out before full employment is attained. The prices of these resources will increase, and prices in general will increase, before full employment is reached.

14. A diagram of the tradeoff between more employment and higher prices is called a *Phillips curve*. The Phillips curve for the pre-1967 period had politically acceptable levels of tradeoff between unemployment and inflation. But since 1967 the Phillips curve has shifted upward, and the levels of tradeoff between unemployment and rising prices have become much higher.

15. This shift in the Phillips curve has made the government's economic stabilization policy more difficult and complex. The tradeoff that exists now between unemployment and inflation is politically unacceptable. Any effort to rectify one seems only to worsen the already politically unacceptable level of the other.

16. The shift in the Phillips curve is probably due to (a) increased amounts of structural unemployment; (b) increased amounts of cost-push and, especially, administered-price inflation; (c) increased impact of international inflationary forces that are beyond the control of the government's domestic stabilization policy; and (d) reduced mobility of workers.

QUESTIONS

1. Some economists have said that the term *business cycle* is not accurate, and they advocate using such terms as *business fluctuation* or

economic instability. What is the basis of their objection? Do you agree with them?

2. Define the following terms:
   a. Secular trend
   b. Concentrated industries
   c. Leading indicators
   d. Frictional unemployment
   e. Structural unemployment
   f. The GNP gap
   g. Demand-pull inflation
   h. Cost-push inflation
   i. Administered-price inflation

3. Compared to clothing prices, washing machine prices tend to be stable, although there are wide variations in production over a given business cycle. Why is that so?

4. Unemployment due to the public's lack of demand for industry's output fluctuates as business activity fluctuates, while structural unemployment may not. Why is this so?

5. How does the existence of monopoly power affect the level of prices?

6. How does the level of prices affect the distribution of real income? the distribution of real wealth?

7. In a market economy, it is difficult to have full employment and stable prices at the same time. Why?

8. The Phillips curve seems to have shifted upward in recent years. What implications does this have for an economic policy that will stabilize the economy? Why did this shift occur?

9. You are a member of the President's Council of Economic Advisers in 1974. You have just told the President that the country cannot have full employment and stable prices at the same time. Furthermore, inflation in 1974 is 12 percent and unemployment is just over 9 percent. The President charges you to advise him which should be decreased: inflation or unemployment. Which would you counter with government policy: inflation or unemployment? Give *economic* justification for the one you've chosen. Since some groups are hurt by inflation and others by unemployment, your decision hurts some and helps others. Give ethical and moral justification for your decision.

SUGGESTED READINGS

Chandler, Lester V. *America's Greatest Depression, 1929–1941*. Harper & Row, New York, 1972.

Economic Report of the President. G.P.O., Washington, D.C., published annually.

Gordon, Robert A. *Economic Instability and Growth: The American Record.* Harper & Row, New York, 1974.

Lekachman, Robert. *Inflation: The Permanent Problem of Boom and Bust.* Random House, New York, 1973.

Maisel, Sherman J. *Fluctuations, Growth, and Forecasting.* Wiley, New York, 1957.

Terkel, Studs. *Hard Times.* Avon, New York, 1971.

U.S. Department of Commerce. *Survey of Current Business.* G.P.O., Washington, D.C. Especially the January issues.

Application 7 *Who Is Hurt by Inflation?*

The Story of One Inflation

In Chapter 6 we said that inflation causes a redistribution of real income and real wealth. Now let's zero in on *one* inflation and analyze how the 12 percent inflation in the United States in 1974 hurt various groups within the economy. When we were analyzing the effect of inflation in Chapter 6, we assumed that total output remained constant during an inflation. During the inflation of 1974, however, the economy was simultaneously going through a recession. Real GNP declined more than 5 percent, and unemployment increased to more than 8 percent. Real disposable income, the most comprehensive measure of purchasing power, fell by 4.3 percent. Obviously those people who lost their jobs suffered the most. Not only did their money income fall because they had to rely on unemployment compensation and welfare, but also this shrunken income was further eroded by the 12 percent inflation.

The elderly and the poor (and many of the elderly are also poor) were the hardest hit. Elderly people spend about 80 percent of their income on food, housing, transportation, and medical care, the very items that increased most rapidly in price. All of these rose, on an average, by *more* than 12 percent. So it is likely that the inflation took more purchasing power away from the elderly than the 12 percent it took from the average family.

Although social security benefits increased by 11 percent from September 1972 to July 1974, the consumer price index rose by 18 percent. During the rest of 1974 the gap widened. Elderly people derive more of their income from private pensions than from social security, and most of these private plans do not have cost-of-living adjustments. Furthermore, the elderly cannot supplement their declining real income by finding full-time or part-time jobs, and most of the wealth of elderly people is in fixed-yield assets (interest on government bonds).

But you don't have to be elderly to be poor, and all the poor suffered greatly from the inflation in 1974. When prices rose in 1974, the increase was the same for the lower-, middle-, and upper-income groups. However, when we compare the impact of inflation on the poor from 1971 to 1974 with the impact on higher-income groups, we find that prices increased by 27.7 percent for the poor and only 24.4 percent for upper-income groups, an extra 3.3 percent for the poor. The reason prices increased more rapidly for the poor is that the poor spend a greater proportion of their income than the rich do on the goods with the fastest-rising prices, especially food. A much larger portion of the expenditures of the poor than of the rich are for food. And from 1971 through 1974, prices of food rose considerably more than prices in general. During periods of rapid inflation, people on public assistance suffer because of the time lags between price increases and aid increases. For example, adjustment for price changes in the food stamp program are made every six months. The family getting food stamps did not receive adjustments for the inflation of the second half of 1974 until July of 1975.

Taxes and Inflation

In 1974 the low- and middle-income taxpayer suffered more than wealthier taxpayers because of the effect of inflation on taxes. In 1974 low-income groups had a 13.8 percent increase in social security taxes and a 31 percent increase in personal income taxes. Middle-income groups fared almost as badly. Their social security taxes went up 21.6 percent and their personal income taxes 26.5 percent. These increases occurred because social security tax rates changed and because the money incomes of many people rose, putting them in a higher tax bracket. Tax brackets are narrower at the low end of the income ladder, and therefore even small increases in income will push a family into a higher tax bracket. Income-tax exemptions also tend to make the effects of inflation more severe for the poor than for the rich. To a poor person who relies heavily on standard deductions in computing after-tax income, the standard deduction from taxable income is fixed, and inflation causes the standard deduction to be worth less.

Well-off people are more likely to use itemized deductions. As inflation increases, they can partially offset the cost of inflation by claiming increased deductions, which lower the amount of taxes they owe. Also, in the upper-income brackets income spreads are much wider. This means that it takes a larger jump in income to shift a rich family into the next higher tax bracket. In this way 1974 inflation made the tax system less progressive by putting more of the burden of taxes on the lower- and middle-income groups. This compounded the damaging effects of inflation on these groups.

Does Anyone Come Out Ahead?

Workers in industry also felt the impact of inflation. From mid-1972 to mid-1974, the purchasing power of their weekly paychecks dropped by 5 percent, establishing a trend that was reversed only late in 1975. Only in the primary metals, tobacco, and mining industries did the purchasing power of people's weekly paychecks increase.

Declining real income hit the middle and upper-middle classes, too. Over this same two-year period (1972 to 1974), the average real income of lawyers fell 4.4 percent (average salary, $23,500), and of engineers, 4.8 percent (average salary, $18,500).

Savers and lenders also lose heavily to inflation. The 5 percent interest a bank may pay to savers is not enough to offset a 12 percent inflation, such as that in 1974. Although savers and

TABLE A7-1 A Summary of Data on the 1974 Inflation/Recession

	Percentages
All of 1974	
Inflation rate	12
Decline in real GNP	5
Unemployment	8
Decline in real disposable income	4.3
Rise in social security taxes	
For low-income groups	13.8
For middle-income groups	21.6
Rise in personal income taxes	
For low-income groups	31
For middle-income groups	26.5
September 1972–July 1974	
Increase in social security benefits	11
Increase in consumer price index	18
Fall in average real income of lawyers	4.4
Fall in average real income of engineers	4.8
Fall in purchasing power of workers' weekly paychecks	5
1971–1974	
Price increases for upper-income groups	24.4
Price increases for the poor	27.7
First 6 months of 1974	
Taxable profits increased	23

lenders are better off than they would have been if they had put the money under the mattress and not received any interest at all, the inflation canceled out all their interest and even eroded part of their principal. An article by Lewis Beman, appearing in *Fortune* in November 1974, estimated that households had "$856 million more in bank accounts, savings and loan associations, and government bonds than they owed in home mortgages and consumer loans." Since the wealthy tend to keep their investments in assets more responsive to inflation than savings accounts and government bonds, the cost of the rate of inflation's exceeding the rate of interest on savings is borne mainly by the middle class.

While real wages are falling, what is happening to profits? In the first six months of 1974, taxable profits increased by 23 percent, primarily as a direct result of inflation. Business firms that had bought materials the year before took advantage of the general increase in prices to raise the prices of items to be sold in the current year and thus made a profit. Even when operating profits (that is, profits obtained from producing alone) decrease markedly, corporations can still continue to make profits as they benefit from the inflation.

The only one who really gains from inflation is the net debtor. As prices continue to go up, the purchasing power of the money the debtor pays back continues to go down. Beman's article points out that "the biggest net debtor at the end of 1972 was the government sector ... which owed a total of $400 billion; corporations ... were almost $360 billion in the red."

Table A7-1 summarizes the data on the 1974 inflation/recession. Note that the time period differs for different statistics, and be careful to apply the correct time period to each statistic.

SUMMING UP

The two-digit inflation of 1974 was accompanied by recession and by more than 8 percent unemployment. This made it the worst of all possible worlds. It is hard to find anyone who benefited from this inflation, but it is apparent that, as usual, the poor, the unemployed, and the elderly bore the brunt of it.

There are, of course, many nonincome, in-kind resources available to the poor. But the time lag between inflationary price rises and adjustments in such welfare programs as food stamps and rent subsidies added to the inflationary pressures on the poor.

This time, the middle class bore a good share of the costs, too. The rich not only have extra monetary resources so they can withstand inflation/recession, but they also have the flexibility to avoid many of its costs.

QUESTION

1. What classes of people (with respect to income and assets) are in the most unfavorable position when there is an inflation such as the one in 1974? the most favorable position? Why?

SUGGESTED READINGS

Beman, Lewis. "Inflation: Winners Are Hard to Find." *Fortune*, November 1974.

"Who's Helped or Hurt by Inflation?" *U.S. News and World Report,* March 3, 1969.

7
Income and Employment: The Beginnings

I have called this book the *General Theory of Employment, Interest, and Money*, placing the emphasis on the prefix *general*. The object of such a title is to contrast the character of my arguments and conclusions with those of the *classical* theory of the subject, upon which I was brought up and which dominates the economic thought, both practical and theoretical, of the governing and academic classes of this generation, as it has for a hundred years past. I shall argue that the postulates of the classical theory are applicable to a special case only and not to the general case, the situation which it assumes being a limiting point of the possible positions of equilibrium. Moreover, the characteristics of the special case assumed by the classical theory happen not to be those of the economic society in which we actually live, with the result that its teaching is misleading and disastrous if we attempt to apply it to the fact of experience.

Thus wrote John Maynard Keynes (rhymes with *gains*) in 1936, beginning the book that shook up the school of economics that had been dominant for over a hundred years. This book launched the Keynesian revolution in economics. Because of Keynes, many governments ultimately changed their policies. World leaders changed their minds about how various forces interact to determine the equilibrium level of income and employment and about how to control that level. It was, in short, a yeasty book.

As Chapter 6 showed, the central problem of any economy is to control the destructive forces of unemployment and inflation. The Keynesian model has become the most widely accepted economic theory by which people hope to understand, and ultimately solve, these urgent problems. Keynesian theory is not a cure-all, but it has many strengths.

In this chapter we will examine the foundations of the Keynesian model. Building on these foundations, in Chapters 8 and 9 we will construct the Keynesian model in stages. We want you to learn from these three chapters the basic facts of the modern theory of income and employment. This theory exercises great power over your money and your standard of living, and even the laws that govern you.

THE NEOCLASSICAL THEORY

Before Keynes wrote *The General Theory of Employment, Interest, and Money* in 1936, most economists belonged to the school of **neoclassical economics**, so-called to distinguish it from classical economics, a theory supported by economists who wrote prior to 1872. Many aspects of neoclassical economics are still accepted by most economists today. However, in this chapter we are analyzing only the neoclassical theory of income and employment. Keynes made basic changes in that theory. But many economists maintain the Keynes's changes lay within the general framework of neoclassical theory, and they continue to call Keynes a neoclassical economist.

Before 1936 neoclassical economists said that a market-oriented economy had enough built-in self-corrective mechanisms that if left to its own devices, its income would move to that level at which its labor force would be fully employed. They also claimed that if unemployment occurred (1) it would be due to temporary overproduction and would be quickly corrected by market forces, or (2) it would be due either to interference by the government or to insufficient degrees of competition, or (3) it would be due to the unwillingness of workers to adjust their wage demands to market forces.

Three theories led economists to this conclusion that income would of its own accord move toward the level at which full employment exists:

1. Say's law.

2. The abstinence theory of interest.

3. The theory of wage and price flexibility.

Say's Law

Jean Baptiste Say (1767–1832) was a French historian writing around 1800. Economists know him mainly for **Say's law**: *Supply creates its own demand.* We can best illustrate Say's law by the simple circular-flow model (Figure 7-1). Recall its basic premise that households provide all the resources—labor, land, capital, and entrepreneurship—to firms, and firms pay households for these resources. Using these resources, firms produce goods for consumption by households. In turn, households pay for these goods and services with the income they get from selling their resources to firms.

In terms of the simple circular-flow model, "Supply creates its own demand" means that firms, while they are in the process of turning out all the goods and services that constitute supply, are at the same time acting as the sources of the income that housholds need to buy the firms' output. The level of that income is stabilized at the point of full employment because when firms employ all the labor available, households receive enough income to buy all the firms' output produced by that labor.

Say's law is stunning in its simplicity. Unfortunately, it does not hold up in real life.

FIGURE 7-1 Say's Law and the Simple Circular-Flow Model

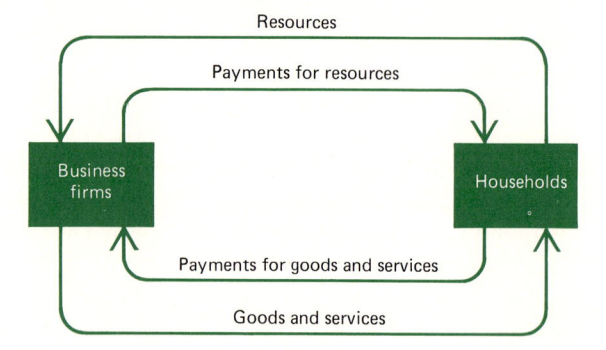

FIGURE 7-2 The Complex Circular-Flow Model

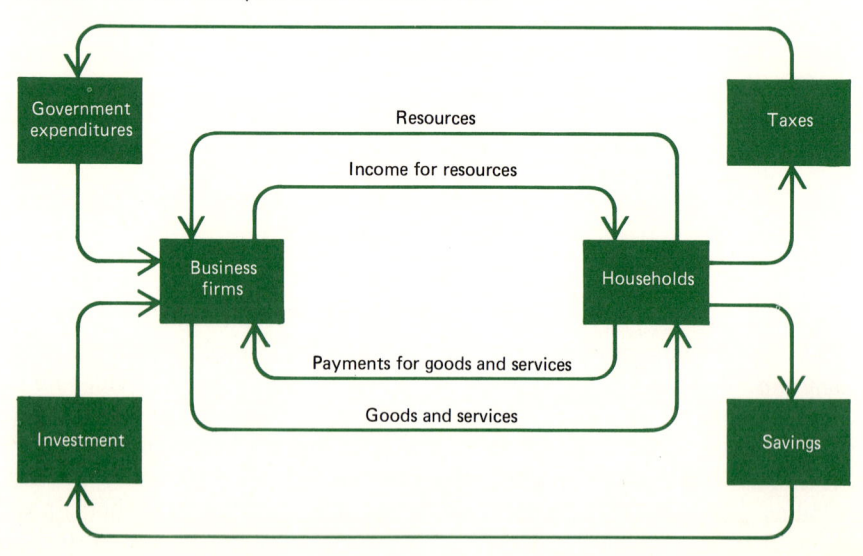

158 Income and Employment: The Beginnings

The Abstinence Theory of Interest

Neoclassical economists readily agreed that the simple circular-flow model illustrating Say's Law was not adequate for an industrialized twentieth-century economy. However, they maintained that even a more complex circular-flow model (Figure 7-2) showed that income, left to itself, would move toward the level at which full employment would exist.

This is the neoclassical reasoning: Households must use some of their money for savings and taxes, which means that savings and taxes siphon off some income that they would otherwise spend on consumption. Firms get most of their support—that is, demand for their output—from households. But firms *also* derive support from two other sources: government expenditures and investment. Economists of the neoclassical school used to maintain that these four factors—taxes, savings, government expenditures, and investment—could be linked so as not to disturb the basic theory that income would adjust itself at the level at which full employment existed.

When people worried that these taxes and government expenditures would have a disturbing effect on this finely balanced model, the neoclassicists had an answer: Just see to it that government expenditures and taxes are *equal*, and keep them both at the lowest possible levels. They'll balance each other off, and this will keep the effects of government fiscal activity to a minimum.

What about savings and investment? Would *they* balance each other off? Or would they create an imbalance and perhaps cause instability and nudge income to a level that would mean less than full employment?

The neoclassical economists said that savings and investment would be coordinated through the medium of the interest rate. They explained this link by using the **abstinence theory of interest**. People prefer to consume goods and services now, rather than later, because present consumption yields greater satisfaction than future consumption. If people are to be made to save—that is, to abstain from consumption—they must be given a reward. This reward is called *interest*. Given interest, the consumer is willing to abstain from present consumption, in other words, save. Then in the future the consumer will be able to consume more because he or she will have more money (savings plus interest) with which to do so. The higher the interest rate (the reward for saving), the larger the quantity saved. Thus, the abstinence theory of interest provides the link between savings and investment.

The amount of money saved determines the *supply of loanable funds*. As Figure 7-3 shows, the curve for the supply of loanable funds slopes up to the right because the higher the interest rate, the larger the quantity saved. Therefore, the abstinence theory of interest explains why the supply of loanable funds slopes up to the right.

The decisions of businesses to expand their productive capacity by building new plants and equipment are what determine the demand for loanable funds. A person will make an investment when the return realized from that investment is at least equal to the cost of the interest on the money borrowed to make it. In other words, people make investments that have a rate of return equal to or greater than the interest rate. Neoclassical economists said that the rate of return on an investment was determined by its productivity and thus in the long run by the state of the economy's technology. The demand curve for loanable funds in Figure 7-3 slopes down to the right because falling interest rates make possible greater amounts of investment. One could say that the interest rate is like rent paid on money. More investment is profitable at a 6 percent interest rate than at a 10 percent one, because the 6 percent rate also includes all investment that has a rate of return between 6 and 10 percent.

Thus the interest rate links investment and savings. And the intersection between the supply of loanable funds (amount of money saved at different levels of interest) and the demand for loanable funds (amount of money invested at different rates of return) determines the equilibrium interest rate. The interest rate causes the savings that people wish to withhold from the demand for consumption to become equal to the investment that businessmen wish to add to the demand for consumption. The equality always becomes evident; demand always uses up the supply. The level of employment of resources still determines the level of income. The level of income still moves to full employment.

FIGURE 7-3 Supply of and Demand for Loanable Funds. The supply of loanable funds (S) slopes up to the the right because the higher the interest rate, the more people wish to save. The demand for loanable funds (D) slopes down to the right because the lower the interest rate, the more investment there is that yields a rate of return equal to or greater than the interest rate.

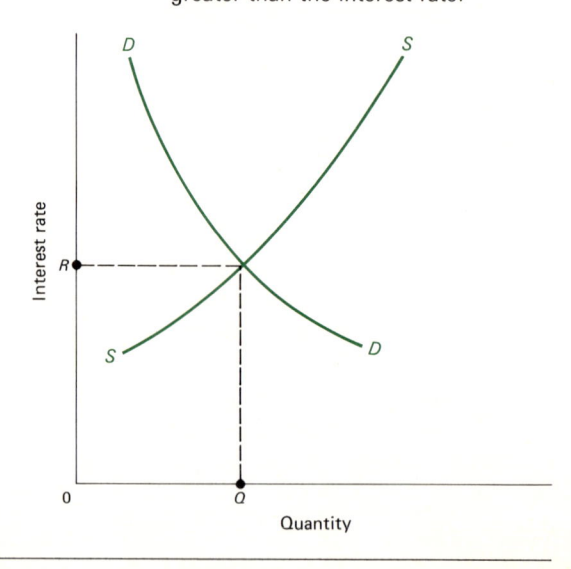

Wage-Price Flexibility

Neoclassical economists recognized that there can be temporary overproduction in certain areas, because of either errors in estimating consumer demand or a failure of the interest rate to bring what people are willing to save into line with what businesses are willing to invest. Fluctuations in the market prices of labor and of products, however, quickly wipe out these temporary states of overproduction. As overproduction develops, workers lose their jobs and start to compete with workers who are still employed. This has the effect of reducing wages. As wages fall, competition between firms forces prices down. Declining wages and declining prices together eliminate overproduction.

Elimination of overproduction is brought about by two effects of falling wages plus falling prices: (1) Total demand by workers is maintained, even though the money volume of spending declines, because prices of products fall in the same proportion as wages. Competition forces down wages, but also forces down prices. The neoclassicists assume that, because of competition, the decline in prices will be proportional to the decline in wages. The worker is no worse off, in effect, when wages fall 10 percent if prices also fall 10 percent. (2) The fall in prices causes those with savings to demand more goods, which eliminates excess supply. As prices fall, people with savings have greater purchasing power. Their savings can buy more at the new lower prices. Feeling richer, savers buy more, and save less. This increase in savers' consumption, as prices in general fall, is called the **Pigou effect**, after its neoclassical originator.

To review: if the nation's budget is balanced (and balanced at a low level) so that government does not affect the market, and if there is enough competition in both the labor market and the product market, then the level of the nation's income automatically adjusts itself to the point at which there is full employment.

In the early 1930s the British government, in the throes of the Great Depression, sought answers from various neoclassical economists. Surely these economists could work some magical cure that would revive the economy so that the level of income would rise to the point of full employment. Obviously the mechanism that ordinarily achieved this state of affairs was not working. Something was interfering with it.

Government fiscal activity was the culprit, said the neoclassicists. Let the government balance its budget and reduce its expenditures as much as possible, they ordered. So the British government in the early 1930s obediently slashed its expenditures and raised its taxes. That will do for a start, said the neoclassical economists, but in addition, because wage-price flexibility is not working, you must counter the influence of labor unions by forcing down wages; when the cost of wages falls, prices will fall too, and demand will then increase.

John Maynard Keynes, pondering the situation from his chair at Cambridge University, disagreed with these recommendations. He believed they would worsen rather than help the depression. Keynes's ideas had been anticipated by his fellow economists, and many of them were being discussed by his contemporaries. However, it was Keynes who finally put these ideas together.

THE KEYNESIAN CRITIQUE

Keynes, who died in 1946, has been rightly called the most influential economist of the twentieth century. His book *The General Theory of Employment, Interest, and Money,* published in 1936, refuted the income-determination theory, that held that the level of income would automatically move toward a position in which there was full employment. His *General Theory* largely replaced neoclassical income theory. Lyndon Johnson was a Keynesian; Richard Nixon said, "We are all Keynesians," as did economist Milton Friedman. Today most economists are Keynesians, in that they at least accept his ideas and use his tools of analysis, though they may add various refinements of their own.

What About Say's Law?

Keynes said that Say's law did not apply to modern industrial society. In Say's eighteenth-century French world, production was small-scale and craft-oriented. People worked with simple machines, mostly made of wood. It did not take huge amounts of capital to repair them or replace them. Investment was therefore modest, and so was the need for savings. Households and firms (as viewed in the simple circular-flow model) were correspondingly small. Cottage industry abounded, and very often products were made to order. However, Say's law was an oversimplification even in his own day, because much of the French economy, and even more of the British, was taken over by larger-scale industries, as the Industrial Revolution accelerated during the latter part of the eighteenth century.

Neoclassical economists replied that they recognized the oversimplification of Say's law and came up with the complex circular-flow model, which made adjustments for the more complex world.

The Abstinence Theory of Interest: Not True

Essential to the neoclassical theory of income was the *abstinence theory of interest,* which linked the desired level of savings (remember that saving always means decreased consumption) to the desired level of investment (which always means increased demand) through the interest rate. With government expenditures and taxes balanced, at the lowest possible levels, the neoclassical idea of the economic world seemed to be fairly valid.

Cottage industry in Say's world: Knitting stockings on wooden machines (The Bettmann Archive, Inc.)

But Keynes questioned the neoclassical theory that desired or planned savings and desired or planned investment are always linked. He invalidated the abstinence theory of interest, as follows:

1. *Savers and investors are different groups and are differently motivated.* Business groups make all the investment decisions and base them on comparative costs and on returns on investment. Profitability is the main reason for investment. Households are the savers. They outsave businesses, even though large corporations do save great amounts in the form of undistributed profits. But in a wealthy society, households also save great amounts. Their motivation for saving, however, naturally differs from that of the business investors. But the simple fact of these differences in motivation is not important. The important point is: Why should the interest rate link savings and investment?

2. *The interest rate does not determine the level of savings.* People who save are going to save regardless of the level of the interest rate, and their motives vary. Some save because of custom or morality. Some save to provide security in old age; some to pay for a large purchase, such as a house or automobile. Some save to provide a fund for emergencies; some save to send their children to college. In sum, people's motivations for saving are varied and are not substantially influenced by the level of the interest rate. Therefore, a certain rate of interest is not necessarily required to make people save. Many people would probably set aside money each month even if no interest rate existed.

3. Not only did Keynes break the tie between planned investment and savings, by showing that the interest rate did not determine the amount of savings, but he also weakened the tie between investment and the interest rate. He said that businesses, in computing the probable returns on their investments, had to estimate future business conditions. Therefore, if you want to analyze why businesses invest, you must take into account their expectations of future conditions. This inclusion of expectations—a psychological factor that the neoclassical economist failed to give any weight to—weakened the relationship between planned investment and the level of interest rates.

So economists were left without the comforting mechanism of the interest rate that coordinated savings and investment at full employment. Without this, the economy could experience declining demand and unemployment, or increasing demand with resulting rises in employment, and possibly inflation. Let us see why.

Look at Figure 7-2 again. If planned savings are greater than planned investment, consumer demand for the firms' output of consumer goods shrinks, and investment demand does not take up all the slack. So total demand falls, and along with it, output, income, and employment fall.

Now suppose the reverse occurs. Suppose that savings are less than planned investment. This means that savings do not cause consumer demand for the output of firms to decrease as much as investment causes the firms' output to increase. As total demand increases, so does output, income, and employment. Eventually, when full employment exists, further increases in demand only generate increases in prices.

Lack of Wage-Price Flexibility

What did Keynes have to say about the neoclassical economists' reliance on wage and price flexibility to correct any excess supply that might lead to unemployment? Remember that the neoclassicists said that a temporary oversupply of goods would cause unemployment, which would cause workers to compete harder for jobs, and that this would push wages down, which in turn would force prices down. Proportionate declines in wages and prices would leave real income unchanged, and thus real levels of demand for goods. People with savings would increase their level of consumption, and this would stimulate demand, and so on. Keynes said there were three factors that weakened this tidy theory:

1. The flexibility of wages and prices is not great enough to generate these movements. Many corporations have so much monopoly power in commodity markets that they can keep prices of commodities from moving downward. Many labor unions also exercise monopoly power in factor markets in the same way; the unions are able to keep wages from moving downward. To Keynes's arguments, one can add that since 1936, governments have interfered more and more in the workings of the market, rendering it more inflexible. This has been true especially in the areas of minimum-wage laws and price-support systems for agriculture.

2. Even if wages and prices were both to decline, it is unlikely that real spending for goods and services would remain unchanged. After all, prices and wages never fall uniformly. Therefore, some groups would be hurt and some helped. And the two groups would never offset each other. Furthermore, the burden of debt of workers would siphon away a large percentage of their incomes, thus cutting down on their spending. Finally, people are psychologically conditioned to plan their spending on the basis of money in hand rather than real income.

3. Even if one could overcome the obstacles generated by both factor 1 and factor 2, in order for the economy to expand very much as a result of increased real savings brought about by a decline in prices, there would have to be sharp drops in prices, and prices would have to stay low for a long time. There are easier ways to stimulate demand during periods of excess supply.

To summarize: (1) Wage-price flexibility does not exist in sufficient amounts. (2) If it did, real spending would drop anyway. (3) Even leaving aside factor 1 and factor 2, there are easier ways to eliminate a generalized excess supply in the economy.

THE KEYNESIAN CONCLUSIONS

Neoclassical economists were mistaken when they said that income would automatically move toward a level that would ensure full employment. Of course, the national level of income may arrive at a position at which there is full employment and relatively stable prices, but there are no mechanisms that ensure this. Therefore, it is more likely that the level of income will be either at a position at which there is unemployment or at which there is inflation. Both states are bad. So let's ask ourselves, what factors determine the level of income?

It is the level of **effective demand**, the total demand for commodities and services, that determines an economy's level of income. A business will produce only if it can expect profits. It can sell its goods only if there is demand for the product. In this case, what's true for one business is true for the entire economy: Output, and therefore income, will match effective demand. Increase income and employment will follow suit. Reduce income and employment will suffer. But remember that *there are no automatic market mechanisms that can force effective demand to the level at which there is full employment.*

This being so, the implication of Keynes's theory is that to achieve full employment, the government must manipulate effective demand. Not since the days of **mercantilism**, from the sixteenth through the eighteenth centuries, has economic theory made it the responsibility of the government to maintain economic welfare. That is why some economists have called Keynes a modern-day mercantilist.

Incidentally, when we talk about the level of income here, we mean the **equilibrium income**. Recall that in Chapter 3, which was about demand and supply, *equilibrium price* was the price resulting from the working out of the central tendency of the market. Here too, equilibrium means central tendency. If all the factors are constant, equilibrium income is the central tendency. It is the income we have after all the forces in the model have worked themselves out. It is a stable income, so long as the various factors in the model do *not* change.

There are five factors that determine the level of effective demand:

1. Intended consumption.

2. Intended savings.

3. Intended investment.

4. Government expenditures.

5. Taxes.

Three of these—consumption, investment, and government expenditures—make up effective demand. Increases in these items increase demand; decreases in any of them reduce demand. Savings and taxes siphon off the purchasing power of people and prevent them from using this money to satisfy their consumption demands.

Because these five factors determine demand, they also determine income and employment. So let's analyze the nature of the first three—consumption, savings, and investment—and show how they relate to changes in the level of income. Then, in Chapter 8, we will first take a simple nongovernment model and show how these factors determine an equilibrium level of income; then we will make the model more complex by adding in government expenditures and then taxes.

The Consumption Function

You are already familiar with the idea of a function or curve. In the analysis of demand and supply, you saw that demand is not a relationship between a specific price and a specific quantity of a good or service, but between various quantities at various prices. When you draw a diagram of the demand schedule, it becomes a demand curve, which shows the functional relationships between prices and quantities demanded. The same thing is true for the **consumption function**. It is not a specific quantity consumed by people at some given income level; it is a schedule, showing the relationships between levels of income and quantities consumed during a given period of time. A diagram of this schedule shows the functional relationship between income levels and quantities consumed.

The *consumption schedule*—or *function*—relates quantities consumed to levels of income. One must understand it in order to identify all the factors that influence the level of employment and income. Therefore, one must relate the various factors involved to income. So we shall deal not only with the consumption function—with how much people *consume* at different levels of income. We shall also deal with the **savings function**, the amount people *save* at different levels of income during a given period of time, and with the **investment function**, the amount people *invest* at different levels of income during a given period of time.

Let's build our income model in steps, just as we did our supply-and-demand model. First we show consumption schedules for individuals; then we add individual schedules to get an economy-wide consumption schedule. We diagram this and have a consumption function or curve for the whole economy. Again, as before, we assume that income is the only thing that changes. All other factors affecting the quantity of goods and services that people consume are fixed.

One could construct a consumption schedule for an individual in much the same way as one constructs a demand schedule for an individual. Ask each individual how much she or he would spend on consumption at each level of income and how much he or she would save. Table 7-1 shows consumption schedules for three individuals, A, B, and C. Note

TABLE 7-1 Consumption Schedules for Individuals

A		B		C	
Income	Consumption	Income	Consumption	Income	Consumption
$ 2,000	$ 3,500	$ 2,000	$ 3,000	$ 2,000	$ 3,000
4,000	5,000	4,000	4,000	4,000	4,800
8,000	8,000	8,000	6,000	8,000	8,400
12,000	11,000	12,000	8,000	12,000	12,000
16,000	14,000	16,000	10,000	16,000	15,600
20,000	17,000	20,000	12,000	20,000	19,200
24,000	20,000	24,000	14,000	24,000	22,800
28,000	23,000	28,000	16,000	28,000	26,400

TABLE 7-2 Consumption and Savings Schedule

Income (billions of dollars)	Consumption (billions of dollars)	Savings (billions of dollars)
210	240	−30
240	260	−20
270	280	−10
300	300	0
330	320	10
360	340	20
390	360	30
420	380	40
450	400	50

The Consumption Function

that each differs from the other. However, each shows that quantity consumed increases with income—but *not as rapidly as income increases*. When one adds the consumption schedules and the income schedules of all the individuals, one obtains an economy-wide consumption schedule.

Table 7-2 is an example of a consumption schedule for an entire economy. It shows that at low levels of income, people live beyond their means by consuming more than income (income levels 210, 240, and 270). At income level 300, consumption just equals income and savings are zero. Above income level 300, consumption is less than income, so the economy can save money. Figure 7-4 is a diagram of the data in Table 7-2.

To bring our analysis into focus, we have drawn, in Figure 7-4, a line from the origin upward, at an angle of 45 degrees. We shall call that line the 45° line.

Note that $0A = AB = BC = C0$. In other words, any point on the 45° line is equal to whatever is measured on the vertical axis.

There is argument about the exact shape of the consumption function. However, for our purposes, we make the simplifying assumption that the consumption function is a straight line, slopes up to the right, and crosses the 45° line. Where the consumption function crosses the 45° line (at 300), quantity consumed is equal to income. Whenever the economy drops below income level 300, consumption is greater than income. For example, at level 210, consumption is 240, which leaves the economy 30 in the hole, because at that point the consumption function lies above the 45° line. When that happens, economists have a word for it: **dissavings** —the opposite of savings. Dissavings means that more is being consumed than is being produced within the economy.

On the other hand, if the income level is above 300, consumption for the economy is less than income, and the consumption function lies below the 45° line. The distance from the consumption function to the 45° line measures savings.

FIGURE 7-4 The Relationship Between Income and Consumption. The distance from the income axis to the 45° line is the same as the distance from the 45° line to the consumption axis. Each point on the 45° line shows where income (the distance right on the axis) is equal to consumption (the distance up to the 45° line). Where the consumption function C_f crosses the 45° line, consumption is equal to income.

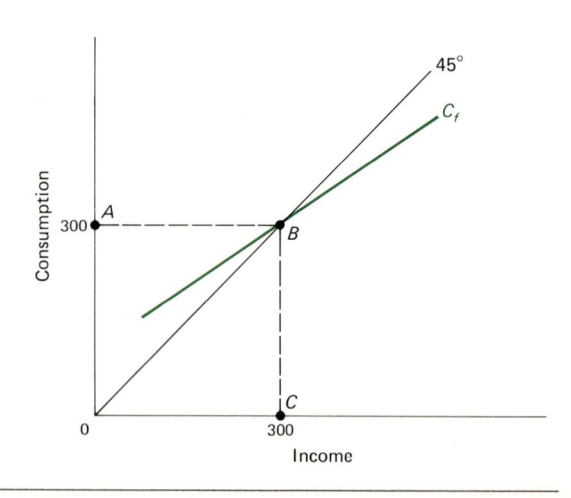

To sum up, if the economy's C_f is *below* the 45° line (income levels over 300), positive savings take place. If the C_f lies *above* the 45° line (income less than 300), negative savings, or dissavings, take place.

Everyone knows how easy it is for private citizens to consume more than their income and wind up dissaving. They perhaps start out by drawing on their savings, until the savings are gone; then they borrow or perhaps apply for public assistance. In a fairly similar way, an entire economy can consume more than it produces, and experience overall dissavings. An economy can draw on its accumulated savings, its capital stock, by the mere fact that it does not produce enough capital to replace worn-out and obsolete capital; its net investment becomes negative, and it comes face to face with dissavings. The economy can borrow from other countries, which means that foreigners' money gets invested in one's own country. Or it can obtain foreign aid, in the form of gifts or international charity. The last two options, borrowing or accepting charity, mean that more is imported than is exported. In other words, the economy is consuming more than it is producing.

The depression of the 1930s was so severe that in the United States and several other countries net investment was negative and consumption exceeded income. So the United States had dissavings. Israel, several times during its brief existence, has been forced into dissavings by the necessity of maintaining a strong military stance and the need to absorb a constant flood of new immigrants. Israel has financed its excess of consumption over income in part by international borrowing, but primarily by gifts from the world Jewish community.

The Savings Function

Out of any given income, people either consume or save. So once you know the consumption schedule (see Table 7-2) or the consumption function (Figure 7-4), you can find the savings schedule and savings function, since savings is the act of *not* consuming. In brief:

$$\text{income} = \text{consumption} + \text{savings}.$$

In Table 7-2, the third column, the savings schedule, is the difference between income and consumption.

Figure 7-5, on page 170, expresses this savings function graphically. However, you could have used the consumption function in Figure 7-5 to derive the savings function. The distance from the consumption function to the 45° line represents savings, either positive (incomes above 300) or negative (incomes below 300). If you measured off those distances on the income axis, with negative savings (dissavings) lying below the income axis, you would also have a savings function.

A Change in Consumption and Savings

When we were talking about demand and supply in Chapter 3, we stressed the distinction between a change in *quantity demanded* and a change in *demand*. The same distinction applies to other functions. A change in quantity consumed or quantity saved is a movement along a specific C_f (consumption function) or S_f (savings function) caused by a change in income. When a *non*income factor changes, it changes the entire schedule of consumption and savings and results in a shift of these functions. This constitutes a change in consumption and in savings.

Figure 7-6 shows a *change in quantity consumed* as a movement along C_1 from A to B because of a change in income. A *change in consumption* itself is a shift from C_1 to another consumption function, C_2, because of a change in one of the five *non*income factors.

The following are five kinds of *non*income factors that can shift the consumption and savings functions:

1. *Changes in social customs, mores, or attitudes toward savings.* Everyone knows about the Protestant ethic: hard work, thrift, rational investment. Use it up, wear it out, make it do, or do without. A penny saved is a penny earned. The stronger people's feelings about thrift, the higher the savings function. Today's young people seem to be less concerned with personal savings, since institutional programs, such as pension funds and insurance programs, have reduced the need for individual saving.

2. *Changes in assets of consumers.* There are three ways of looking at people's asset positions: (a) What are their liquid assets? (b) What is their debt level? (c) What is their stock of goods (especially durable goods)?

FIGURE 7-5 The Savings Function. One can plot the savings function (S_f) from Table 7-2 or derive it from the consumption function (C_f). The distance from C_f to the 45° line measures savings. These distances should be marked off from the income axis to the savings function.

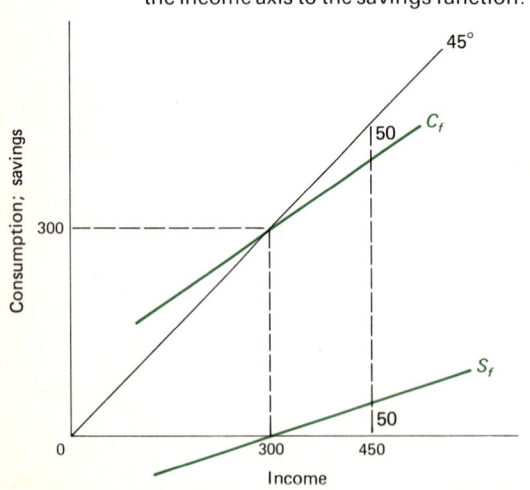

FIGURE 7-6 Change in Consumption and Change in Quantity Consumed

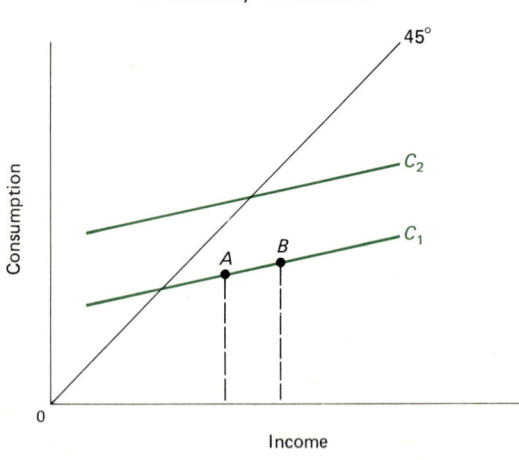

First, **liquid assets** are assets in the form of money or something that can be quickly converted into money, such as savings accounts and government bonds. People like to have some assets in liquid form for several reasons, mainly, being prepared for an emergency. Once people have accumulated comfortable amounts of liquid assets, they can use their incomes for consumption. Second, paying off debt reduces income available for consumption over a period of time. When people accumulate debt quickly, this temporarily increases their consumption. However, when people are paying off debt, they consume less, of necessity.

Since the level of debt affects consumption, the terms of consumer debts are important factors in determining consumption. What is the interest rate? How long a time will it take for repayment? These and other conditions of consumer loans encourage (or discourage) consumers from borrowing, and thus affect their level of consumption.

When you accumulate durable goods (cars, refrigerators, and so on), your consumption in the immediate future usually drops off sharply. If today you go on a spree and buy a washer, dryer, and color-television set, you will probably not need new ones for several years, and this will surely lower your spending rate.

3. *Changes in expectations about future earnings.* If people expect that their earnings will increase in the future, and if they feel secure, they are inclined to consume more now than they would if things were otherwise. Young couples just starting a family borrow heavily to establish a home, expecting that their income will increase over the years. However, if there is a recession and they start to feel insecure about their jobs, or if inflation is cutting into their real income, people cut present consumption and increase their savings, to hedge against future want.

4. *Changes in taxes.* When taxes go up, the amount people have to spend on daily consumable items naturally becomes smaller, no matter what their income is. Households pay part of their taxes out of income that they would otherwise spend for consumption, and part out of income that they would save. The effect of taxes is to decrease both consumption (taxes shift the C_f down) and savings (taxes shift the S_f down).

5. *Changes in the distribution of income; changes in demographic (population) factors.* Changes in the way income is distributed have a strong effect on the consumption function. Poor people have to consume a much larger proportion of their incomes than the rich people do. Therefore, if something happens to redistribute the wealth so that the poor get a larger portion of it, the consumption function will shift upward and slope upward at the same time. Changes in the age of the population also affect the position of the consumption function. The larger the percentage of people in age groups that are not income earning, the more people there are who are consuming without working to finance that consumption (for instance, children and the elderly). The baby boom that lasted from 1945 through 1955 has been a strong element in keeping consumption high. But the large drop in the birthrate over the last decade is going to reduce aggregate consumption in the future.

The interest rate is the cost of investment. (Mike Mazzaschi/Stock, Boston)

The five factors listed above can be divided into two broad categories: objective (or economic) factors and psychological factors. We consider changes in assets of consumers, changes in taxes, and changes in distribution of income and demographic factors to be objective or economic factors. We consider the psychological factors to be changes in social customs, mores, or attitudes toward savings, and changes in expectations about future earnings.

The Intended Investment Function

There are two kinds of investment: *autonomous* and *induced*. **Autonomous investment** is *not* affected by changes in people's incomes and consumption. It is affected by factors outside the model. In other words, the level of autonomous investment is independent of the factors within the model. **Induced investment**, on the other hand, is induced or generated by changes within the model—specifically by changes in income and consumption. For example, if the level of income increases, the quantity consumed also increases. This increases the need for plant and equipment (that is, for capacity) to produce the increased quantity of consumer goods demanded. This increased investment needed to expand capacity to take care of increased consumption is *induced* investment. For purposes of our model here, we shall assume that induced investment is zero and that we are dealing only with autonomous investment. Later, when we have completed our model, we shall add induced investment.

New business investment for a corporation (Herb Moyer)

What Determines Autonomous Investment?

Businesses keep on investing—that is, creating capital—just as long as they expect that the returns from an investment are going to be at least equal to the cost of that investment. There are two factors that determine how much they invest. These factors are: (1) the cost of investing and (2) the expected rate of return.

1. *The interest rate.* When you invest your money in something, such as a machine or a building, and you put down some cash and borrow the rest, the cost of investing is not the price of the machine or building. You get this purchase price back by the device of *depreciation,* which is a legitimate cost of producing the product. Depreciation is built into the final price of any product. The *cost* of the investment is the interest that you must pay on the money you borrow to buy the something *or* the interest you forgo by using your funds instead of lending them out. In other words, if you had not bought that something, you would have had an *opportunity* to lend your cash to somebody else and have interest payments flowing back to you.

2. **Marginal efficiency of capital.** The marginal efficiency of capital is the expected rate of return on capital. In other words, it is the stream of income that businesses expect to get over the life of the capital relative to its price. Two main things, plus a number of smaller factors, determine the marginal efficiency of capital:
    a. *Productivity of capital.* The more productive the capital, the greater the profit one can expect to get back from an investment. The productivity of capital changes with the development of new

The Intended Investment Function

machines that reduce the costs of labor or capital, or with the development of a new process, a new product, or new markets. So it can be said that any growth in productivity means greater potential profits to investors.
b. *Expectations.* Since the marginal efficiency of capital deals with future returns, it is bound to be influenced by the future economic activity investors expect. This introduces a psychological and potentially irrational element. A President may have a heart attack, a new kind of plane may crash, or meteorologists may predict a severe winter—and people in business may overreact. They may become more pessimistic, or more optimistic, than economic conditions warrant, and their attitudes may change almost overnight.
c. *Other factors.* Some of the other factors that affect the marginal efficiency of capital are the price of capital itself (for example, the sale price of a machine); the risks connected with the investment; taxation (especially when the taxes are directly tied to the investment); and in the case of house construction, population growth and migration.

How Much Investment Will People Make?
Figure 7-7 shows how to go about figuring how much autonomous investment is likely to be made. The *MEC* (marginal efficiency of capital) curve shows the quantity of investment likely to yield an expected rate of return equal to, or greater than, the interest rate. The *MEC* curve slopes down to the right. This is so because as the interest rate falls, larger amounts of investment (capital instruments) will yield an expected return equal to or greater than the interest rate.

Instability of Investment
In good times and bad, over the years consumption and savings have shown amazing stability. Investment, on the other hand, has varied greatly, as Figure 7-8 shows. You can understand this pattern of investment if you just stop to think of the instability of the factors that determine the quantity invested. Interest rates fluctuate widely. The influences on people's expectations about the future are both rational and irrational. The flow of technological innovations is not even, so that industry improves its production techniques in fits and starts. Furthermore, the government itself may inject instability into the investment scene through changes in its economic policies and through loss of public confidence due to scandals.

However, since World War II, a number of changes have tended to increase the stability of investment. For one thing, the Employment Act of 1946 committed the government to economic stabilization. This gave business people greater confidence than they formerly had and reduced the likelihood of short-term variations in investment. Corporate retained earnings increased, so that corporations have not had to depend so heavily on the capital markets for investment funds. However, investment is still the most unstable component in the model.

How Does Investment Fit into Our Model?

We have made a number of assumptions: (1) We have assumed that the consumption function is a straight line that slopes up to the right. This means that as people's incomes increase, they spend more on consumer goods, but they spend lower *percentages* of their incomes on these goods. (2) We are including in our category of intended investment only autonomous investment. (To review, *autonomous* investment is investment that is not affected by people's levels of income.)

Now look at Figure 7-9 on page 176, which takes two different approaches to the matter of intended investment as it relates to the equilibrium level of income. (Note that *II* in Figure 7-9 stands for "intended investment," *not* roman numeral two!) Remember that the equilibrium level of income is the stable level of income that will not change unless one of the factors in the model changes.

One approach—called the **savings-equals-intended-investment approach**—is the bottom of the diagram. This shows the relation of savings (which *reduces* consumer demand) to investment (which *adds to* consumer demand). Note that the intended-investment function that intersects the savings function is parallel to the income axis. Since the

FIGURE 7-7 Factors That Determine Autonomous Investment. The *MEC* curve shows the quantity of investment at various interest rates. Investments must yield a rate of return equal to or greater than the interest rate. To find out how much investment is likely to take place, one must know the rate of interest that an investor is going to have to pay in order to borrow the money to make the investment.

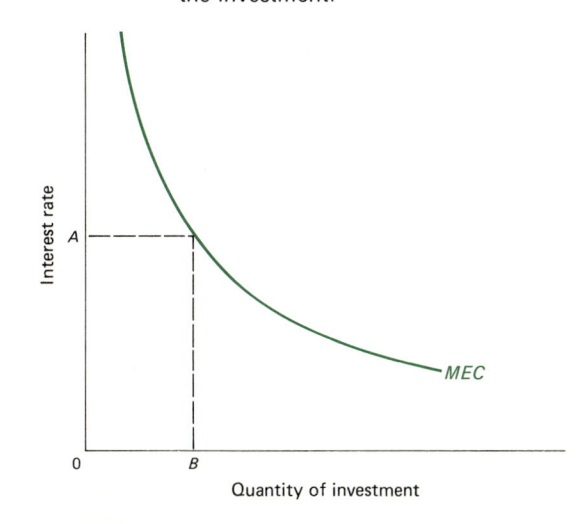

FIGURE 7-8 Consumption and Investment, 1929–1970. Variations in investment are much greater than variations in consumption, since people have to go on consuming things like food, fuel, clothing, and housing. (Source: *Economic Report of the President*, 1973; U.S. Department of Commerce, *Business Conditions Digest*, March 1973).

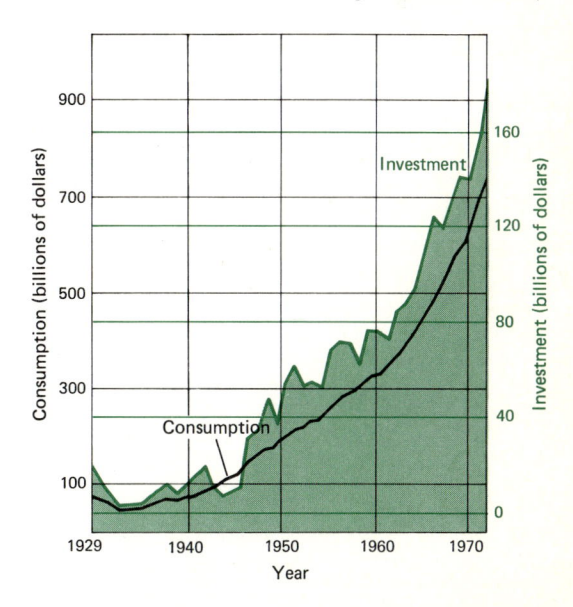

FIGURE 7-9 Equilibrium Income: Relation Between Consumption (C_f), Savings (S_f), and Intended Investment (II). The bottom of the diagram shows intended investment in relation to savings. To find equilibrium income (E), one assumes that savings equals intended investment. Or one can add intended investment to the consumption function, so that aggregate demand equals aggregate supply. Both approaches give the same equilibrium income (E).

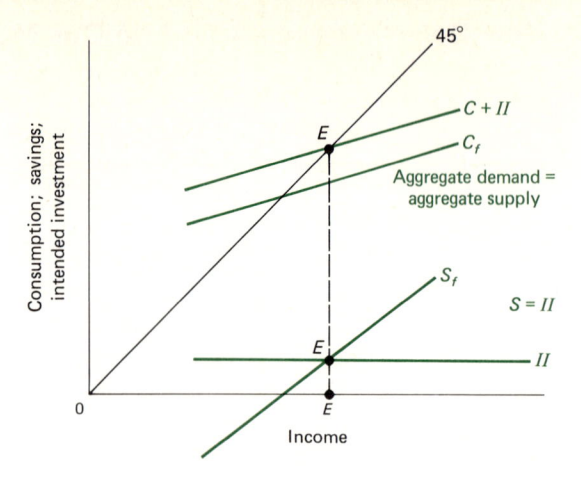

vertical distance from the income axis to the II function measures intended investment, and since it must be the same at all levels of income if it is to be consistent with the fact that investment is not affected by income, the two lines are parallel.

The second approach—called the **aggregate-demand-equals-aggregate-supply approach**—adds the intended-investment function to the consumption function. Putting the II function here points up the relation of aggregate demand to aggregate supply. (Both these approaches will be discussed further in Chapter 8.) Note again that $C + II$ is parallel to the consumption function (C_f). The vertical distance from C_f to $C + II$ measures intended investment. Since intended investment must be the same at all levels of income if it is to be consistent with the fact that autonomous investment is not affected by income, the two lines are parallel.

SUMMING UP

1. *Neoclassical economics* theorized that in a market-oriented economy the level of income would automatically move to a position at which there would be full employment. Three theories supported this conclusion: (a) Say's law, (b) the abstinence theory of interest, and (c) the theory of wage and price flexibility.

2. *Say's law* states that supply creates its own demand. In terms of the simple circular-flow model, owners of resources receive incomes generated by producing supply and use those incomes to buy the total supply of goods and services that the economy produces.

3. In terms of the complex circular-flow model, the neoclassicists said that taxes and government expenditures need not have disturbing effects if both factors were kept equal and balanced at as low a level as

possible. The way to get rid of the disturbing effects of savings and investment is through the rate of interest, as analyzed in the abstinence theory of interest.

4. The *abstinence theory of interest* states that people would rather consume now than save now and consume later. Therefore, people need a reward—interest on savings—to make them save. The higher the reward, the larger the quantity saved. Thus, the curve showing quantities of loanable funds saved slopes up to the right when measured against the interest rate.

5. How much people invest depends on the rate of return, which in turn depends on the productivity of technology. Thus, the curve showing the quantities of loanable funds demanded at various interest rates slopes down to the right. More investment yields returns equal to (or greater than) the interest rate at a lower interest rate than at higher interest rates.

6. The equilibrium interest rate is the rate at which the *supply* of loanable funds is equal to the *demand* for loanable funds. Therefore, the interest rate is the stabilizer that causes the amount of savings people wish to accrue (decreasing demand) to equal the amount of investment people wish to make (increasing demand).

7. If industry produces a temporary surplus, this surplus is quickly eliminated, because industry lays off workers, and the unemployed then compete for jobs, so wages fall. Also, as firms compete to sell off excess goods, prices fall. However, the worker's real income, and in general real demand, do not fall, since wages and prices fall proportionately. Because lower prices mean that the purchasing power of each dollar is greater, people with savings feel richer and thus increase the quantity of goods and services they demand (the *Pigou effect*).

8. John M. Keynes, in his 1936 book, *The General Theory of Employment, Interest, and Money,* rejected the neoclassical conclusion that income always tends toward a position at which there is full employment.

9. Keynes said that Say's law was a gross oversimplification not only of the twentieth-century industrial world but also of Say's own eighteenth-century French world.

10. Keynes felt that the abstinence theory of interest was not valid because the interest rate does not correlate intended savings with intended investment, for these reasons: (a) The people who save are different from the people who invest and have different motivations. (b) The interest rate does not determine the level of savings, since the reasons why people save are largely unrelated to the level of the interest rate. (c) Business groups' expectations of the future are not strongly affected by the interest rate. Expectations are largely a psychological factor. Yet they have a strong influence on the rate of investment. These criticisms by Keynes weakened the traditional belief in the relationship between investment and the interest rate.

11. Since the investment rate does not correlate savings and investment, desired savings can exceed desired investment. This reduces demand, and, eventually, income. On the other hand, desired savings can be *less* than desired investment. People can spend too freely. This increases demand and income.

12. Keynes attacked the remaining support of the neoclassical income theory—wage and price flexibility—by making the following observations: (a) Wages and prices are not flexible enough because there is not enough competition. (b) Even if wages and prices were to be flexible enough, real spending would drop anyway. (c) Leaving a and b out of the picture, there are easier ways to get rid of a general excess supply of goods and services in the economy.

13. Keynes concludes: (a) There is no market mechanism to make the actual level of income coincide with the preferred level of income at full employment. The actual level may exist at full employment, at less-than-full employment, or at full employment with inflation. (b) The level of income is determined by the level of *effective demand*, in other words, by the total spending in the economy.

14. Five factors determine the level of effective demand: intended consumption, intended investment, government expenditures (these three add to effective demand), intended savings, and taxes (these two detract from effective demand).

15. The *consumption function* shows the functional relationship between quantities consumed and various levels of income. One assumes two things: (a) that all *non*income factors affecting the quantity consumed are fixed, and (b) that the consumption function is a straight line that crosses the 45° line (consumption is equal to income at that point) and slopes upward.

16. One can derive the *savings function* from the consumption function, since income is equal to consumption plus savings. Therefore, the difference between consumption and income is savings. The savings function is a straight line that crosses the horizontal axis and slopes upward. The distance from the savings function to the horizontal axis is equal to the distance from the consumption function to the 45° line.

17. A change in the quantity consumed or saved is due to a change in income, which causes a movement along the curve of the consumption or savings function. A change in both consumption and savings is due to a change in a *non*income factor, which causes the whole consumption and savings functions to shift.

18. Nonincome factors that may cause a change in consumption and savings are (a) changes in social customs, mores, or attitudes toward savings, (b) changes in assets of consumers (both quantity and composition), (c) changes in expectations about future earnings, (d) changes in taxes, and (e) changes in distribution of income and changes in demography (the distribution and density of population).

19. There are two kinds of investment: autonomous and induced. *Autonomous investment* is influenced only by factors other than income and consumption. *Induced investment* is determined by changes in income and in quantity consumed. To keep our model simple, we assume here that induced investment is zero.

20. People make that amount of investment for which they can expect a rate of return equal to or greater than the cost of the investment. The cost of an investment is equal to the interest paid for the funds needed to finance it. The expected rate of return is the *marginal efficiency of capital*, and it is determined primarily by increases in productivity and by expectations of future economic activity.

21. Of the three components that increase effective demand, investment is the most variable. The reason is that there are fluctuations in the three main factors determining the volume of investment: interest rates, expectations of the future, and the flow of technological improvements.

22. If one is making a diagram of the relation between consumption, savings, and intended investment, one can put the intended-investment function above the horizontal axis, and it will intersect the savings function. This emphasizes the relation of savings (which reduce the demand for consumption) to investment (which adds to it). This is called the *savings-equals-intended-investment approach*.

23. Alternatively, one can add the intended-investment function to the consumption function; this is called aggregate demand. This function emphasizes the effect of total demand on income and is called the *aggregate-demand-equals-aggregate-supply approach*.

QUESTIONS

1. Explain how a neoclassical economist would defend the conclusion that the level of income always tends to move toward a point at which there is full employment. Include the role of Say's law, the abstinence theory of interest, and wage-price flexibility.

2. How did Keynes refute the neoclassical conclusion about income and employment, especially as it referred to the three foundations of neoclassical theory: Say's law, the abstinence theory of interest, and wage-price flexibility?

3. What was Keynes's conclusion about the relationship between income and full employment? How is the level of income determined, according to Keynes?

4. What are the five factors that determine effective demand? How do changes in each of the five affect effective demand?

5. Which of the following factors change the quantity people consume or save, and in what direction? Why?
   a. An increase in the holding of consumer durables.
   b. A decrease in taxes.
   c. An increased desire for security in old age.
   d. An increase in income.
   e. A decrease in the amount of money that people hold.

6. Distinguish between autonomous and induced investment.

7. Does autonomous investment increase or decrease when the following things happen? Why?
   a. The interest rate increases.
   b. A new breakthrough in science opens up new areas of technological innovation for industry.
   c. The stock market collapses and the general feeling is one of pessimism.

SUGGESTED READINGS

Ackley, Gardner. *Macroeconomic Theory.* Macmillan, New York, 1961. Chapters 5–12.

Cochrane, James L. *Macroeconomics Before Keynes.* Scott, Foresman, Glenview, Ill., 1970.

Cochrane, James L.; Samuel Gubens; and B. F. Kiker. *Macroeconomics: Analysis and Policy.* Scott, Foresman, Glenview, Ill., 1974. Chapters 3 and 4.

Dillard, Dudley. *The Economics of John Maynard Keynes.* Prentice-Hall, Englewood Cliffs, N.J., 1948.

Farrell, Michael J. "The New Theories of the Consumption Function." *Economic Journal,* 69 (December 1959), 678–696.

Robinson, Joan. *Economic Philosophy.* Aldine-Atherton, Chicago, 1962. Chapters 2 and 3.

8. Income and Employment Without Government

Before we go any further, let's review the conclusions drawn from Chapter 7.

1. The neoclassical theory that income will automatically move to a position at which there is full employment does not hold true. The abstinence theory of interest is also wrong, in that the interest rate does not link savings to investment. Also, the flexibility of wages and prices is not great enough to correct an oversupply of an economy's goods and services.

2. The factor that determines an economy's level of income and employment is the volume of effective demand in the economy.

3. This level set by the total volume of spending is not necessarily the best level for employment and prices. Our system may not be capable of automatically bringing about full employment and an acceptable level of prices, because of the problems cited above, in conclusion 1. That is why the United States often has unemployment and/or inflation.

4. Five factors determine the level of effective demand (and thus of income): consumption, savings, investment, government expenditures, and taxes.

Note: The market system in the United States creates a level of income that ordinarily does not seem to lend itself to full employment and low prices. The economy, if left to its own devices, may—and in fact often *does*—embody unacceptable amounts of unemployment and/or inflation. It seems that the U.S. system of private capitalism may simply have a tendency toward less than full employment and/or higher than desired price levels.

181

In Application 8, we will explore this question of the inherent instability of the capitalist economy of the United States, by looking at the history of business cycles since 1920.

Now we will again build a simple model to enable us to approach a hard subject. Let's say that government expenditures and taxes are both zero. This leaves us with only three factors to deal with: consumption, savings, and investment. Now let's see what happens.

THE SIMPLE MODEL

Savings Equals Intended Investment

Figure 8-1 shows the intended investment function *(II)* parallel to the horizontal axis and intersecting the savings function (S_f). This placement, which emphasizes the relation of investment to savings, is called the **savings-equals-intended-investment approach**. It shows the relation of savings, which diverts people's money away from their demand for goods and services, to investment, which supplements or adds to consumption demand. For example, you save money for a down payment on a house, by denying yourself many things you would like to have. Then,

FIGURE 8-1 Simple Model: Savings Equals Intended Investment. Equilibrium income is that amount of income at which savings equals investment: income *A* (360). Income levels above it (*B* = 420) yield involuntary (unplanned) additions to inventory (*DE* = 20). Income levels below it (*G* = 330) yield involuntary decreases in inventory (*HI* = 10).

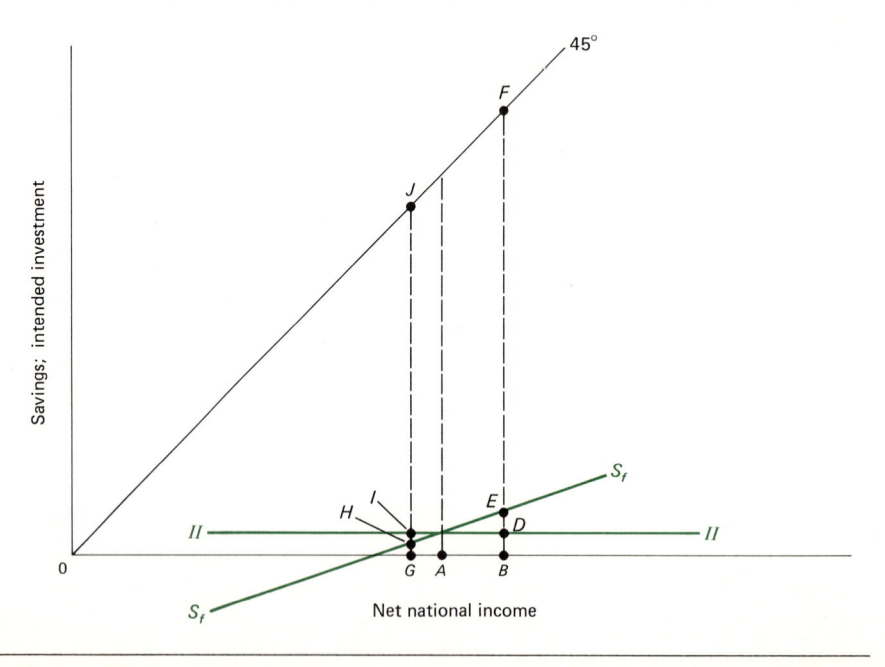

182   Income and Employment Without Government

when you buy the house, you invest, by paying out the capital you have created to buy the house. You increase demand for output from many firms—output needed to build the house.

What is the equilibrium level of income? And what does it take to maintain it? Chapter 7 defined equilibrium income, but let's review it. Remember that Chapter 3 defined equilibrium *price* as the central tendency of the market, a price that didn't change as long as supply and demand didn't change. Furthermore, any price other than the equilibrium price automatically triggers forces that push the price toward the equilibrium point. In the same way, the equilibrium level of *income* is the central tendency of the market. That level of income will not change so long as the factors in the model (consumption, savings, and investment) do not change. Any other level of income would be unstable and would trigger economic forces that push the level of income toward equilibrium.

Now look at Table 8-1. The data are based on Table 7-2, except that we have added data on intended investment. Note that investment is constant at 20, because we include only autonomous investment, which does not change when income changes. In the savings-equals-intended-investment approach, the equilibrium level of income is 360 (the same as income A in Figure 8-1).

When an economy's consumption, savings, and investment are as shown in Figure 8-1 and Table 8-1, the equilibrium level of income is the level at which savings equals investment (income level A in Figure 8-1 and 360 in Table 8-1). To prove this, one must first show that the economy cannot maintain levels above A (or 360) and then show that it similarly cannot maintain income levels below A (360).

From here on, we will cite Figure 8-1 only, and after each reference to Figure 8-1, there will be numbers in parentheses that refer to corresponding points in Table 8-1. If you follow the discussion on both the diagram and the table, you will understand the explanation better.

Now bear in mind that businesses produce most of their goods and services with the intention of selling them to consumers. However, they

TABLE 8-1 Savings Equals Intended Investment
(billions of dollars)

Income	Consumption	Savings	Intended investment
210	240	−30	20
240	260	−20	20
270	280	−10	20
300	300	0	20
330	320	10	20
360	340	20	20
390	360	30	20
420	380	40	20
450	400	50	20

do set aside a portion of their output for investment. Let's say that at income B (420), which is above the equilibrium level, businesses produce BD (20) for investment (BD is the distance from the horizontal axis to the intended investment function, II). This leaves DF (400) remaining for the public to consume.

But the public has its own ideas. Let's say that people plan to save BE (40), which is the distance from point B to the savings function (S_f). So people spend only EF (380). This leaves a gap here, because businesses produce DF (400) for consumption, and people consume only EF (380). Business firms are left with the remainder, DE (20), as unsold output, which must be added to their inventory. This is called **unplanned** or **involuntary additions to inventory** (because inventories are defined as business investment).

Business firms which have this unwanted inventory stashed in their warehouses or on the shelves of their stores must reduce orders to the companies that supply them with raw materials. Manufacturers cut production, which reduces their income, so they must lay off workers. Gradually the economy takes a turn downward, moving from income level B (420) back toward the equilibrium income level A (360), continuing until the economy reaches income A (360). This happens because at any level above A (360), what businesses produce for consumption is greater than what consumers wish to consume. Note that the savings function lies above the intended investment function. Business firms are forced to hold these unwanted additions in their inventories. They react by reducing inventories—and income.

Now, at any level below the equilibrium income, which for our purposes is G (330), businesses produce GI (20) for investment, which is more than the amount people save, GH (10). They also produce IJ (310) for consumption, which is less than what the public wants to consume, HJ (320). Now people are consuming more than businesses produce for consumption. When they do this, they reduce business inventories. Thus there are **unplanned** or **involuntary reductions in inventories** equal to HI (10).

When businesses find that their inventories are slipping below what they want them to be, they order more from their suppliers, to replenish the inventories. Manufacturers then increase output, which increases their income, so they hire more workers. The economy moves from income level G (330) toward the equilibrium level of income A (360). Any lower income would result in unplanned decreases in inventories.

Income level A (360) is an equilibrium level because, at that level, what businesses plan to produce for investment is equal to what the public plans to save, and what businesses plan to produce for consumption is equal to what the public plans to consume. The plans of businesses mesh with the plans of the public.

In this state of balance, businesses have neither *involuntary accumulation* of inventories (in which businesses produce *more* than people consume, and the savings function lies above the intended investment function) nor *involuntary reduction* in inventories (in which businesses

An extreme result of involuntary accumulation of inventory (Peter Southwick/Stock, Boston)

produce *less* than people consume, and the savings function lies below the intended investment function). What they plan in the way of inventory is what they get.

To summarize: At equilibrium income, people's savings equal business firms' intended investment. At income levels *above* equilibrium, businesses want to invest *less* than what people want to save. As a result, consumers demand less than what businesses produce for consumption. (Bear in mind that businesses *must* produce at a certain level of output just to maintain a given level of income.) So when cost-conscious citizens, intent on saving money, buy fewer consumer goods and services than businesses offer for sale, company executives watch gloomily as their warehouses fill with unwanted inventory. They must somehow dispose of this inventory. First they reduce orders to the manufacturers; then they may offer the goods for sale at lower prices. For example, in the first three months of 1975, the GNP fell at a rate equivalent to an annual rate of 10.4 percent. It was the fifth consecutive quarter of decline. The economists' explanation was that businesses had to stand still temporarily while they sold off their huge inventories. It was the biggest sell-off of inventories in history: $18 billion worth! In a case like this, business output falls, and so does business income.

Savings Equals Intended Investment

At income levels *below* the equilibrium, the reverse occurs. Businesses want to invest *more* than the amount people want to save. As a result, consumers are willing to buy more than businesses have for sale. So inventories fall to such a point that businesses increase their volume of new orders. Business output increases, and so does business income.

Ex-ante and Ex-post Investment

By now you can see that there is a strong relationship between savings and investment. The key aspect of this relationship is that *savings reduce demand* (by lowering the level of people's consumption), while *investment adds to demand* (that is, adds investment demand to consumer demand for the output of business). In order to arrive at an equilibrium level of income, savings and investment must balance off at a level that both businesses and consumers want. The demand of businesses for investment has to equal the demand of consumers for a given amount of savings. When these two factors are not equal—when the balance is out of kilter—businesses take steps to remedy the situation, by changing their incomes and their number of employees.

It is this important relation of savings to investment that calls attention to the distinction between ex-ante and ex-post investment.

Ex-ante investment is the amount of investment that businesses plan to make.

Ex-post investment is the amount of investment that they actually do make.

(A device to help you remember: *ante* is like the first part of "anticipate," and *post* is like "past.")

To get a clear idea of this relation, look again at Figure 8-1 and Table 8-1. We are going to use the same letters and numbers we used before. (Again, after the letters from Figure 8-1, we will include the corresponding figures from Table 8-1, in parentheses.)

In Figure 8-1, at income level *B* (420), ex-ante or planned investment is equal to *BD* (20), while ex-post or actual investment is equal to *BE* (40). This is because unplanned accumulations to inventory *DE* (20) are added to ex-ante (planned) inventories, and inventories are considered investment. This means that businesses are in an uncomfortable position. Their actual investment is twice what they planned.

At income level *G* (330), businesses are again in a bad spot, because their ex-ante (planned) investment is *GI* (20), while their ex-post (actual) investment is *GH* (10)—only half of what they planned. This is because unplanned reductions in inventory *HI* (10) are deducted from ex-ante (planned) inventories.

In both cases, business firms' ex-post (actual) investment is equal to consumers' ex-post (actual) savings. This equality is due either to unplanned additions to inventories or to unplanned subtractions from them. One has to take into account the fact that *inventories—whether planned or unplanned—are part of investment*.

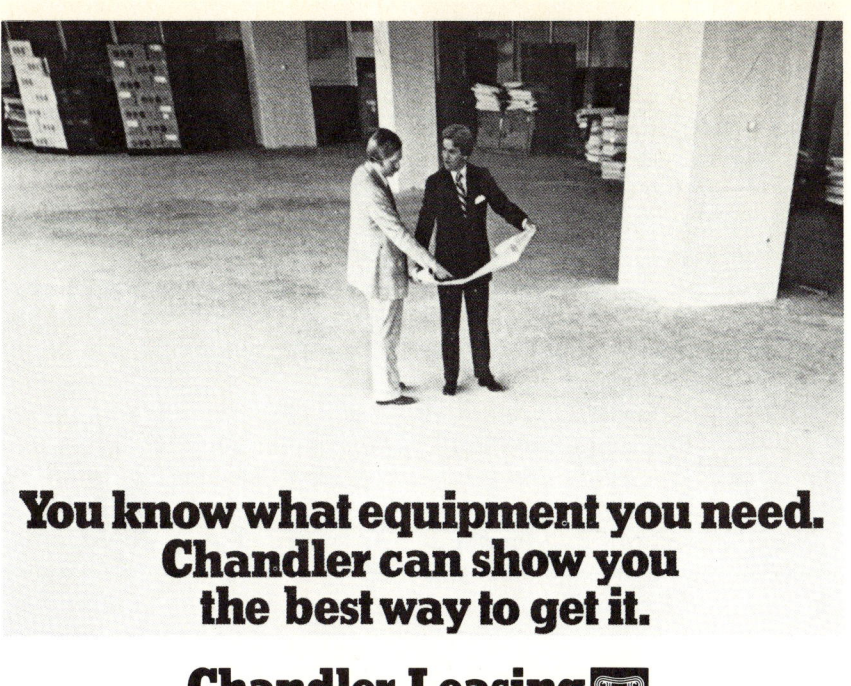

You know what equipment you need. Chandler can show you the best way to get it.

Chandler Leasing
A Heller Financial Services Company

An appeal to businesses that are planning investment (Courtesy Chandler Leasing and Walter E. Heller & Co.)

However, an economy does not achieve equilibrium income simply because it arrives at a point at which actual investment equals actual savings. Unplanned (involuntary) changes in inventory cause businesses to either reduce or increase their orders to manufacturers. These changes in orders naturally cause the level of output to either rise or fall, and with it, the level of income and employment. Each factor affects each other factor. Only at the equilibrium level does ex-ante (planned) investment by business equal ex-post (actual) savings by consumers. At that point, all expectations are met. There are neither increases or decreases in planned inventory. The level of income is in equilibrium.

Aggregate Demand Equals Aggregate Supply

Now let's approach the subject of the equilibrium level of income from another angle: Suppose we look at aggregate demand and aggregate supply (Figure 8-2). In this simple model, aggregate (in other words, total) demand is composed of (1) consumption demand plus (2) investment demand, which is represented by the line $C + II$ in Figure 8-2; the letters stand for "consumption plus intended investment." (Remember that to simplify things we are leaving government out of the picture. There are no government expenditures and no taxes.)

In our analysis of the national economic accounts (Chapter 5), we concluded that the income generated in an economy is equal to the value of the economy's output. So in Figure 8-2, we could say that the 45° line that represents income also represents output. In effect, then, we are assuming that the vertical distance from the horizontal axis to the 45° line—the aggregate supply function—is the output that businesses think they can sell at that level of income. ("Small cars are moving pretty well. Let's make twenty thousand Dustrats, and see how they sell.")

Figure 8-2 shows that, at income A, aggregate demand equals aggregate supply. This is the equilibrium level of income. To establish this, one has to show that any other level of income would *not* be an equilibrium.

Look at Figure 8-2. Again we will use Table 8-1's figures in parentheses. Note that, at any income above the equilibrium level, aggregrate supply (the 45° line) is greater than aggregate demand $(C + II)$. In other words, businesses plan to supply more than consumers plan to demand. In Figure 8-2, at income B (420) aggregate supply is BF (420), while aggregate demand is only BK (400, or $C + II$). Supply exceeds demand by KF (20), which reflects unplanned additions to inventory. ("How can we ever unload two thousand tons of chicken feathers when

FIGURE 8-2 Simple model: Aggregate Demand Equals Aggregate Supply. At income A (360), equilibrium income is at the level at which aggregate demand $(C + II)$ equals aggregate supply (45° line). At income B (420), aggregate supply exceeds aggregate demand, and excess inventories KF (20) pile up. At income G (330), aggregate demand exceeds aggregate supply, and there is an inventory deficit of JL (10).

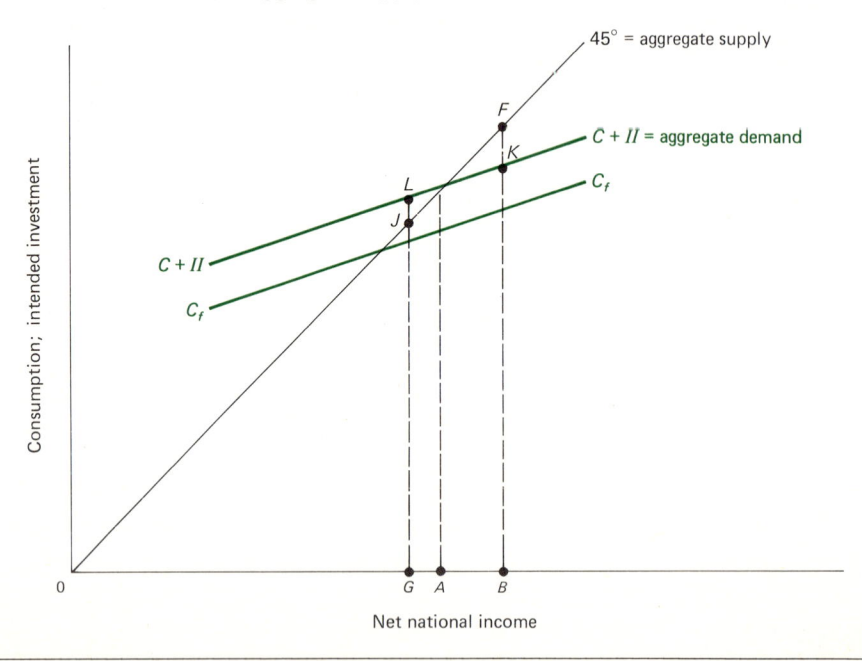

188   Income and Employment Without Government

we've ordered more than people want to buy? Cancel our order for more.") Output, income, and employment—go down. Income shrinks in the direction of *A* (360), the equilibrium level.

At any income below the equilibrium level, aggregate demand *(C + II)* is greater than aggregate supply (the 45° line). Consumers demand more than businesses can supply, and inventories gradually dwindle away. ("Hey, listen to this! Insomnia Motels have increased their order by ten thousand chicken-feather pillows. Phone around and see if you can locate ten thousand yards of heavy striped ticking for pillow covers.") Output, income, and employment go up. At income *G* (330) in Figure 8-2, aggregate demand is *GL* (340) *(C + II)*, while aggregate supply is only *GJ* (330). Demand exceeds supply by *JL* (10), which reflects unexpected reductions in businesses' inventories. When this happens, income expands in the direction of *A* (360), the equilibrium level.

So you see, our economy really *must* seek equilibrium. Any unsettlement on either side of *A* sends the income level tilting back toward that equilibrium.

Now note that Figure 8-3 includes both intended investment *(II)* and savings *(S_f)*. Thus we can compare the savings-equals-intended-investment and the aggregate-supply-equals-aggregate-demand approaches. Both wind up with the same equilibrium level of income: *A* (360).

FIGURE 8-3 Simple Model: Aggregate Demand Equals Aggregate Supply, Plus Savings Equals Intended Investment. When both approaches are included in the same diagram, the same equilibrium level of income applies to both: *A* (360).

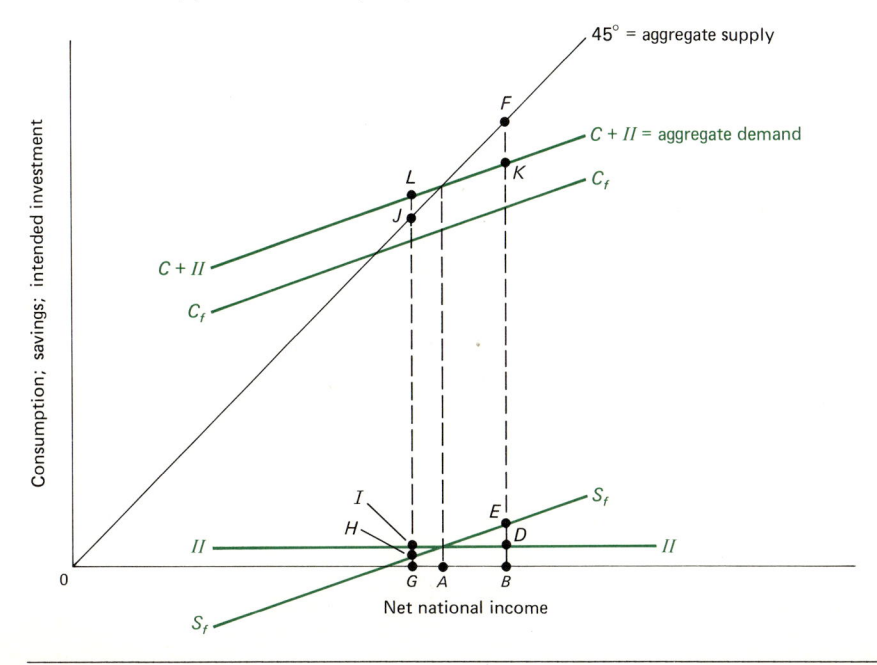

Aggregate Demand Equals Aggregate Supply

THE MULTIPLIER

Average and Marginal Propensities to Consume and Save

At this point let's inject a modest amount of mathematics to help you understand a few new concepts: (1) the *average* propensities to consume and save, (2) the *marginal* propensities to consume and save.

The **average propensity to consume** is the percentage of a given income that people tend to consume (or spend for consumer goods). The formula is

$$APC = \frac{C}{Y}.$$

where Y is the level of income and C is consumption. The **average propensity to save** is the percentage of a given income that people tend to save. The formula is

$$APS = \frac{S}{Y}$$

where S is savings. Since income equals consumption plus savings, the average propensity to consume plus the average propensity to save equals 1, or in other words, 100 percent of income.

The **marginal propensity to consume** is the percentage of any *change* in income that people tend to spend on consumer items. The formula is

$$MPC = \frac{\Delta C}{\Delta Y}$$

where ΔC means the *change* in consumption and ΔY means the *change* in income. (The triangle symbol is the Greek letter delta. It means a change in some quantity.) The **marginal propensity to save** is the percentage of any *change* in income that people tend to save. The formula is:

$$MPS = \frac{\Delta S}{\Delta Y}.$$

Again, the marginal propensity to consume plus the marginal propensity to save equals 1, or in other words, 100 percent of the increase in income.

Remember that $APC + APS = 1$ and $MPC + MPS = 1$.

The key thing to remember here is that the *average* propensities to consume and save have to do with the *percentage* people consume and save out of a specific level of income, while the *marginal* propensities to consume and save have to do with the percentages people consume and save out of *changes* in income.

For example, suppose that the level of income in the economy is $400 billion and the level of consumption is $300 billion. Then the *aver-*

age propensity to consume is

$$\frac{C}{Y} \quad \text{or} \quad \frac{300}{400} \quad \text{or} \quad \frac{3}{4} \quad \text{or} \quad .75.$$

Savings equal $100 billion ($Y - C = S$). The *average* propensity to save is

$$\frac{S}{Y} \quad \text{or} \quad \frac{100}{400} \quad \text{or} \quad \frac{1}{4} \quad \text{or} \quad .25.$$

Now suppose that the level of income in the economy increases by $50 billion, the level of consumption increases by $40 billion, and the level of savings increases by $10 billion. Then the *marginal* propensity to consume is

$$\frac{\Delta C}{\Delta Y} \quad \text{or} \quad \frac{40}{50} \quad \text{or} \quad \frac{4}{5} \quad \text{or} \quad .80.$$

The *marginal* propensity to save is

$$\frac{\Delta S}{\Delta Y} \quad \text{or} \quad \frac{10}{50} \quad \text{or} \quad \frac{1}{5} \quad \text{or} \quad .20.$$

For a picture of the marginal propensity to consume, see Figure 8-4, which shows a section of the consumption function. Income increases from 150 to 200 (shown by arrows from *A* to *B*). Consumption increases from 175 to 200, shown by arrows from *B* to *E*. Income increases by 50 and consumption by 25. The MPC equals

$$\frac{25}{50} \quad \text{or} \quad \frac{1}{2} \quad \text{or} \quad .50.$$

FIGURE 8-4 The Marginal Propensity to Consume (MPC)

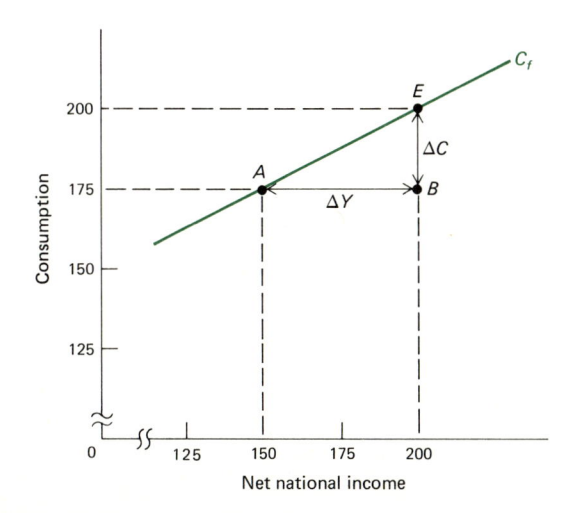

Average and Marginal Propensities to Consume and Save

TABLE 8-2 The Average and Marginal Propensities to Consume and Save

Income	Consumption	Savings	APC	APS	MPC	MPS	II_1	II_2
210	240	−30	1.14	−.14	.67	.33	20	30
240	260	−20	1.08	−.08	.67	.33	20	30
270	280	−10	1.04	−.04	.67	.33	20	30
300	300	0	1	0	.67	.33	20	30
330	320	10	.97	.03	.67	.33	20	30
360	340	20	.94	.06	.67	.33	20	30
390	360	30	.92	.08	.67	.33	20	30
420	380	40	.90	.10	.67	.33	20	30
450	400	50	.89	.11	.67	.33	20	30

Now look at Table 8-2. We arrived at these figures by taking the data on income, consumption, and savings from Table 8-1 and computing the marginal propensities to consume and save. Try this yourself to see how it works.

How Changes in Aggregate Demand Affect Changes in Income

Whenever aggregate demand shifts—as evidenced by a shift in investment or a shift in consumption, or both—it is a sure sign that the equilibrium level of income has also changed, because the additional money people are spending or investing must be coming from *somewhere*.

Figure 8-5 shows a case of aggregate demand (the sum of consumption plus investment) shifting up by 10, from AD_1 to AD_2. Perhaps

FIGURE 8-5 The Multiplier Effect. Aggregate demand shifts up from AD_1 to AD_2, an initial increase of 10, which increases equilibrium income B to C, an increase of 30. An initial change in aggregate demand changes equilibrium income by an amount larger than the initial change in aggregate demand. Since the change in income is a *multiple* of the initial change in aggregate demand, this is called the *multiplier effect*.

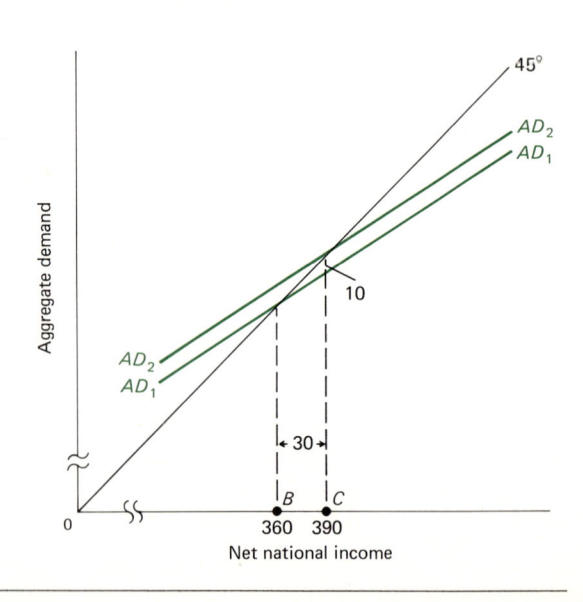

Income and Employment Without Government

this shift is due to an increase in autonomous investment or to an upward shift in the consumption function. Whatever the reason for it, this upward shift causes the equilibrium level of income to rise from B to C, or an increase of 30. Note that this figure of 30 is three times as big as 10, which is the upward shift in aggregate demand.

The point we are trying to make is that income always changes by *more* than the initial shift in aggregate demand. This phenomenon is called the **multiplier effect**, because the amount of change in the equilibrium level of income is a multiple of the initial amount of change in aggregate demand. To define a multiplier, think backward, like this:

The change in income due to a given initial change in aggregate demand is a multiple of that change in demand. This multiple is called the multiplier.

There are two important points to keep in mind: (1) In order for a new level of income to be permanent, the initial upward shift of aggregate demand must be permanent. (2) The amount of increase in income is related to the amount of the initial upward shift of aggregate demand. As income increases, there is a movement up AD_2, so that in the end AD_2 is equal to income C.

In Figure 8-5, in which income changes by 30 and aggregate demand initially changes by 10, the multiplier is 3.

Why a Multiple?

The reason why income changes by a multiple of the initial change in aggregate demand is that people's marginal propensity to *consume* is greater than zero. Or, put another way, their marginal propensity to *save* is less than 1. In other words, the marginal propensities to consume and save are the keys to the multiplier concept. Table 8-3 explains why this is so. It shows that the public will spend two-thirds of any increase in income on consumer goods and services.

TABLE 8-3 How the Multiplier Effect Works, Given That the Marginal Propensity to Consume (MPC) Equals $\frac{2}{3}$

	Initial amount of capital
Autonomous investment	$1,000,000
Second round of spending	666,666
Third round of spending	444,444
Fourth round of spending	296,296
Fifth round of spending	197,530
Sixth round of spending	—
Seventh round of spending	—
Eighth round of spending	—
Total income generated	$3,000,000

Suppose a savings bank invests $1 million in a new bank building. Even before construction starts, many people begin to earn incomes from this project, so aggregate demand increases. Workers, manufacturers, and many suppliers of goods and services start to benefit. Given that these people have an MPC of $\frac{2}{3}$, they will spend two-thirds of this new income and save one-third. This generates more new income, so a second round of spending begins. The people in round two, in their turn, also spend two-thirds of what they get and save one-third. This income generation continues, and on each round of spending, people spend two-thirds and save one-third. So during each round, one-third becomes savings. Finally all the original $1 million *winds up as savings*. But the total increase in income that has been generated by all this spending is $3 million or three times the bank's original investment. The multiplier here is, of course, 3.

The Multiplier Formula

There is a simple and useful formula for computing the multiplier *(M)*. You would do well to memorize the **multiplier formula**:

$$M = \frac{1}{1\text{-MPC}} \quad \text{or, since } 1 - \text{MPC} = \text{MPS}, \quad M = \frac{1}{\text{MPS}}.$$

The multiplier is the reciprocal of the marginal propensity to save. For those of you who know a little mathematics, here is how the formula works when MPC equals $\frac{2}{3}$:

$$M = \frac{1}{1\text{-MPC}}, \quad M = \frac{1}{1\text{-}2/3}, \quad M = \frac{1}{1/3}, \quad M = 1 \times \frac{3}{1}, \quad M = 3.$$

Remember that in order for this increase in income to be permanent, the increase in autonomous investment must remain at the new higher level. This means that more new investment has to be made to replace the $1 million that originally came from the bank.

Instantaneous Multipliers Versus Periodic Multipliers

You may have the impression that the multiplier process takes place very quickly. That is, strictly speaking, not true. However, the concept of the **instantaneous multiplier** (a multiplier effect that takes place instantaneously) is useful to us at this stage, so we will use it for the time being, unless we say we are using another concept.

However, you must recognize that the process of generating and regenerating demand, output, and income takes *time*. Those people and businesses in Table 8-3 who received income as a result of the savings bank's initial investment of $1 million had to have *time* to make the necessary decisions about spending their new incomes ("Should we pay Junior's college bills, or buy a new Dustrat?"). And then they had to have time to act on these decisions ("Goodbye, Junior, and don't forget to give this check to the bursar."). And when the money filtered down to the people in round 2, they also had to have time to make decisions and to spend their new incomes. (Though they had less money to make decisions about, because the people in round 1 had saved one-third of theirs.)

So you can see that it would be much more realistic to visualize a **periodic multiplier**, a multiplier effect that takes place over several periods of time, as the money from the original investment passes down the line, from one round of expenditures to the next. It is true that an economy feels the biggest impact of a multiplier within the first few time periods (usually about eighteen months) after the initial investment, but the long-range effects of a multiplier are spread over several time periods. These long-range effects create difficulties for the people who are trying to formulate government economic policy. A government policy maker who is trying to figure out how much money the government should pump into the economy in order to stimulate demand must be aware of previous changes in demand and their continuing impact on the economy's income.

THE ACCELERATOR PRINCIPLE

In Chapter 7, when we discussed the two kinds of investment (autonomous and induced), we assumed that induced investment was zero, in order to simplify our model. We left out induced investment. Now we are going to look at it.

Whenever the equilibrium level of income increases, people consume more goods and services, and this increase in consumption brings on, or induces, new investment. If you look at Figure 8-5, you see a higher income level (c) that would intersect the consumption curve just as before, but higher up; in other words, at a point indicating a greater quantity consumed. The level of quantity demanded is higher. This increase in quantity consumed means that industry has to have an increased capacity to produce goods and services, and this in turn requires larger amounts of investment. That is what we mean by *induced* investment. Additional investment naturally follows increased consumption. Table 8-4, on the next page, shows this chain of events, using the shoe industry as an example.

Let us say that you are a shoe magnate, and you own a factory that makes shoes. Each of your 100 shoe-making machines produces 1,000 pairs of shoes a year, and has a life span of 10 years. In period 1 (imagine that each period equals one year), your 100 machines are equally divided as to age, so you act as you usually do, and order 10 new machines to replace 10 that wore out. In period 2, however, the demand for shoes picks up by 1 percent, so you order an additional machine that year: 10

for replacement and 1 for expansion (that 1 machine is induced investment). You want to take advantage of that demand for 1,000 extra pairs of shoes, since you naturally want all the business you can get.

In period 3, the demand for shoes increases by 2 percent (more than the 1 percent increase in period 2). Now you need 103 machines to meet demand. So you order 12 new machines: 10 for replacement and 2 for expansion (those 2 machines represent induced investment). In period 4, demand increases at an increasing rate: 3 percent. Now you need 106 machines. You order 13 new ones—still 10 for replacement, plus 3 for expansion. Induced investment continues to increase. In period 5, although demand continues to increase, the rate of increase remains the same: 3 percent. You now need 109 machines. You order 13 new ones: 10 for replacement and 3 for expansion. Note that this year your induced investment did not increase. In period 6, demand still increases, but at a lower rate, only 2 percent. Now you need 111 machines, but you order only 12 new ones: 10 for replacement and only 2 for expansion. Your induced investment has decreased.

This example shows that your demand for extra new machines (your induced investment) does not depend on the absolute level of demand for shoes. It depends on the *percentage increase in demand* for shoes. If you're going to increase your induced investment and keep expanding your plant's capacity to produce shoes, you must be able to see that there is an increasing rate of increase in demand for shoes. If the percentage increase in demand falls off, you are going to cut back your induced investment. And this also has a multiplier effect on the economy's income—only in a downward direction.

This cause-and-effect situation is called the **accelerator principle** You can see that a small increase (1 percent) in the amount of consumer demand causes a much larger increase in induced investment. And this, in turn, has its multiplier effect on income. Higher incomes bring about an increase in demand for consumer goods and services, which has an accelerator effect on the economy.

However, this same accelerator factor introduces a strong unstable element into the growth of an economy's income. The reason is that

TABLE 8-4 Induced Investment and the Accelerator Principle in the Shoe Industry

Time period	Percentage increase in demand for shoes	Number of pairs of shoes demanded	Total number of shoe machines	Demand for new machines
1		100,000	100	10
2	1	101,000	101	11
3	2	103,020	103	12
4	3	106,110	106	13
5	3	109,293	109	13
6	2	111,479	111	12
7	0	111,479	111	10

FIGURE 8-6 Induced Investment

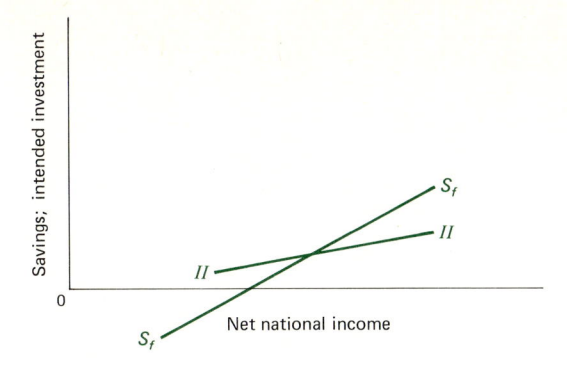

[Graph: vertical axis labeled "Savings; intended investment", horizontal axis labeled "Net national income". Two lines labeled S_f and II crossing.]

whenever there is a decrease in the rate of growth of consumers' demands, the acceleration starts to go in the opposite direction—down. The accelerator becomes a negative one, and this causes declines in income.

Economists often use this interaction between the multiplier and the accelerator to explain business cycles, which we discussed in Chapter 6. As an economy climbs up out of a recession, the increases in consumer demand bring the positive accelerator into play. This causes a rapid upswing in the economy. Gradually, though, the rate of growth embodied in that upswing slows down. Then the negative accelerator takes over and begins to pull the economy down.

Also, the accelerator does not work in the earliest phases of recovery from a recession, because there is still a lot of unused capacity (that is, idle machines and empty plant space). Until that idle capacity is used up, one hardly notices that times are getting better. Only when an economy's recovery has reached the stage at which all machines and plant space are fully utilized, does it begin to feel the effects of the accelerator.

In Figure 8-6, you see that when the accelerator is positive (that is, when induced investment is rising and both income and consumption are also rising), the curve depicting intended investment (II) slopes upward. The opposite occurs when the accelerator is negative; then the II curve slopes downward.

Bear in mind that *the multiplier relates autonomous investment* (plus any other change in aggregate demand) *to changes in income,* whereas *the accelerator relates induced investment to changes in income.*

The Paradox of Thrift

During a recession, when income is falling and the newspapers are full of stories about rising unemployment, people begin to feel insecure and uncertain about their futures. Perhaps they retrench and reduce their

FIGURE 8-7 The Paradox of Thrift

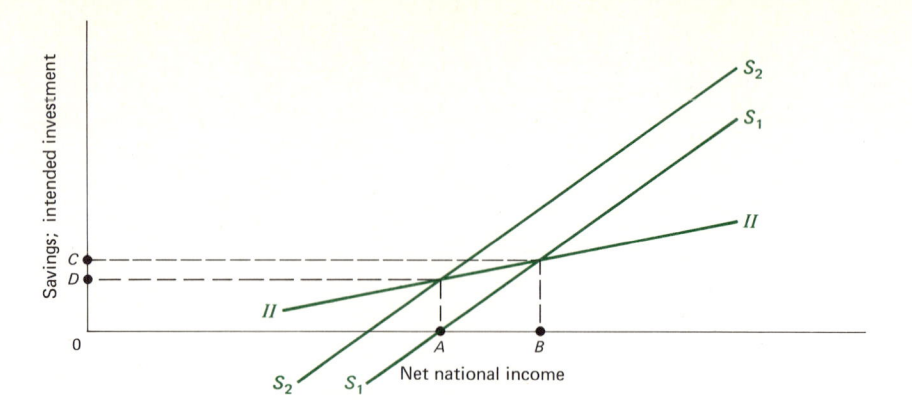

consumption, so that they can save more. ("How about raising vegetables in that space behind the garage?") They may sleep more peacefully, knowing that their savings account is fatter. But if *everyone* does the same thing, if everyone cuts back and scrimps and saves, it may be disastrous for the economy. Eventually what happens is not an increase in savings, but a *decrease* in the quantity actually saved. This effect is known as the **paradox of thrift**.

Figure 8-7 shows this peculiar reverse effect. Suppose there is a recession, with its accompanying fall in aggregate demand and income and its usual dismal increase in unemployment. The people who still have jobs nervously begin to cut back their spending so that they can save more. The line marked S_1 is the initial level of savings, before the recession. Income then stands at B, and quantity saved at C.

What happens when people begin to save more? Just the opposite of what you would expect. When everybody's savings increase, the savings function shifts upward to level S_2. Intended investment is now equal to savings only at income A. This indicates that income has fallen from B to A, and that the actual quantity people are saving has decreased to D.

The moral of all this is that when an entire economy tightens its belt, consumer demand falls and income decreases. The quantity actually saved decreases too.

Therefore, paradoxically, during a recession if everybody is trying hard to save more, the *amount* of savings becomes less.

SUMMING UP

1. When one builds a model of a society, omitting the factors of government and taxes and using only consumption, savings, and investment, the equilibrium level of income is the level at which savings equal

intended investment. At income levels above equilibrium, people consume less than businesses produce for consumption. Businesses must endure *unplanned* or *involuntary additions to inventories*, which means that they then have to cut their orders to manufacturers. The results are reductions in output, employment, and income.

2. At income levels below equilibrium, people consume more than businesses produce for consumption. Businesses experience *unplanned* or *involuntary reductions in inventories*, which cause them to increase their orders to manufacturers. The results are increased output, employment, and income.

3. *Ex-ante investment* is investment that is desired or planned. *Ex-post investment* is investment that actually takes place. Ex-post (actual) investment always equals savings, because involuntary additions to or subtractions from inventories cause these two factors to be equal. An equilibrium income occurs only when ex-ante and ex-post investment and ex-ante and ex-post savings are all equal. At that point, all expectations or plans of businesses and the public are satisfied.

4. In our simple, *non*government model, aggregate *demand* is consumption plus intended investment, and aggregate *supply* is the 45° line in our diagram. An economy reaches equilibrium income when aggregate supply and aggregate demand are equal. When the income level is above equilibrium, aggregate supply is greater than aggregate demand, and unplanned increases in business inventory push the level of income back toward equilibrium. At income levels below equilibrium, aggregate demand is greater than aggregate supply, and unplanned decreases in business inventory push the level of income up toward equilibrium.

5. The two approaches—(a) savings equal intended investment, and (b) aggregate demand equals aggregate supply—produce the same result: the same level of income.

6. The *average propensity to consume* is the percentage of a specific level of income that people tend to consume:

$$\text{APC} = \frac{C}{Y}.$$

The *average propensity to save* is the percentage of a specific level of income that people tend to save:

$$\text{APS} = \frac{S}{Y}.$$

The *marginal propensity to consume* is the percentage of any *change* in income that people tend to spend on consumption:

$$\text{MPC} = \frac{\Delta C}{\Delta Y}.$$

The *marginal propensity to save* is the percentage of any *change* in income that people tend to save:

$$\text{MPS} = \frac{\Delta S}{\Delta Y}.$$

7. When aggregate demand shifts, income changes. However, a given change in aggregate demand causes income to change by an amount larger than the initial change in demand, an effect called the *multiplier effect*. The degree to which the change in income is greater than the initial change in aggregate demand is called the *multiplier*.

8. The multiplier effect is due to the fact that the marginal propensity to consume is greater than zero. When people have an increase in income, from whatever source, they do not save all of it. They spend part of it, which generates demand for more goods, thus creating more income.

9. The *multiplier formula* is

$$M = \frac{1}{1-\text{MPC}}, \quad \text{or} \quad M = \frac{1}{\text{MPS}}.$$

The multiplier is the reciprocal of the marginal propensity to save.

10. *Induced investment* is investment brought on by increases in income, which cause people to consume a greater quantity of goods and services. In turn, this increases the demand for more capacity (capital) to produce the greater quantity of goods and services.

11. By means of the *accelerator principle*, one can analyze the ups and downs of induced investment over time. An increase in the rate of growth of consumer demand causes a much larger increase in the demand for additional capacity. However, any decrease in the rate of growth of consumer demand causes a much larger decrease in the demand for additional capacity.

12. The accelerator principle introduces an element of economic instability, in that, after an economy reaches full capacity during a recovery, increases in the rate of growth of consumer demand generate large increases in induced investment. This causes income to expand rapidly. At some point, the rate of growth in consumer demand begins to slow down, and a negative accelerator (due to declining induced investment) pulls the level of income and the economy down.

13. Induced investment causes the intended investment (II) function to slope upward, so that economies with higher levels of income make larger quantities of investment. (We are assuming a positive accelerator here.)

14. The *paradox of thrift* is that during a recession, when the savings function shifts upward because everyone wishes to save more, income falls because of a fall in aggregate demand. This causes the quantity saved to decline.

QUESTIONS

1. Draw relevant diagrams and explain how one arrives at the equilibrium level of income for the following models:
   a. Nongovernment model with savings-equals-intended-investment approach.
   b. Nongovernment model with aggregate-demand-equals-aggregate-supply approach.

2. Assume that the MPC = $\frac{2}{3}$ and the APC = $\frac{2}{3}$.
   a. Suppose that the equilibrium level of income equals 300. What are the equilibrium levels of consumption, investment, and savings? Assume that government expenditures and taxes are both zero.
   b. Suppose that for the situation in part a, investment increases by 10. What are the new equilibrium levels of income, consumption, savings, and investment? Explain your answers.

3. Show how one may use a multiplier-accelerator model to explain business cycles.

4. During a recession, would it be in an individual's self-interest to increase her or his savings? Would it be in the interest of the whole economy if everybody increased savings during the recession? Why?

5. One economist said, "Savings always equals investment, whether the economy is at equilibrium or not." What makes that condition true? If an economy is not at equilibrium, what will occur to bring it toward the equilibrium point?

SUGGESTED READINGS

Ackley, Gardner. *Macroeconomic Theory*. Macmillan, New York, 1961. Chapters 13–15.

Canterbery, E. Ray. *Economics on a New Frontier*. Wadsworth, Belmont, Calif., 1969.

Cochrane, James L.; S. Gubins; and B. F. Kiker, *Macroeconomics: Analysis and Policy*. Scott, Foresman, Glenview, Ill., 1974. Chapters 5 and 6.

Dernburg, Thomas. "Income and Employment Theory." In *International Encyclopedia of the Social Sciences*. Macmillan-Free Press, New York, 1969, Volume 7, 122–131.

Dillard, Dudley. *The Economics of John Maynard Keynes*. Prentice-Hall, Englewood Cliffs, N.J., 1948.

Heller, Walter. *New Dimensions of Political Economy*. Harvard, Cambridge, Mass., 1966.

Okun, Arthur M. *The Political Economy of Prosperity*. Norton, New York, 1970.

Application 8

The U.S. Economy: Ups and Downs

In Chapters 7 and 8 we talked about the Keynesian system of income determination in a private-enterprise, market-oriented economy. We saw that the multiplier effect and the accelerator principle lead to expansion and contraction, but that there are no automatic mechanisms that can *ensure* stability. Theoretically, capitalism has no inherent stability, that is, no built-in stabilizers to see to it that everyone has a job. Let's look into this and discuss economic stability in our economy. We shall explore, in brief, the history of business fluctuations in the United States since 1920, in order to gain a better insight into the factors that cause business cycles.

The Depression of 1921

The 1921 depression was short, a little more than a year, but very severe. Money GNP fell from $91.6 billion to $70 billion, a drop of nearly 24 percent. Prices fell by more than 12 percent, and unemployment increased by more than four million people (to about 12 percent of the labor force).

The most significant characteristic of the 1921 depression was its sharp drop in prices. Prices of agricultural products fell even more steeply than prices of manufactured goods, leaving the agricultural sector in a precarious profit position throughout the 1920s. The steeper decline in prices of what farmers sold (relative to what they bought) narrowed their profit margins. Yet farmers had to accept these low agricultural prices and use the money to pay off the large mortgages they had taken when they expanded production during and just after World War I.

The Prosperity of the 1920s

From 1922 to 1929, the economy expanded rapidly from a low of $70 billion in money GNP in 1921 to a high of $104.4 billion in 1929. This expansion was marred by two mild recessions, one in 1924 and the other in 1927. Even so, there was less than 5 percent unemployment. Prices declined somewhat between 1921 and 1929, from a price index of 52.8 in 1921 to an index of 51.3 in 1929. (1967 is used as a base year. In other words, in 1967 the index was 100.)

The two main props of the prosperity of the 1920s were (1) the expansion of the construction industry and (2) the increase in output of a number of "new" industries, especially the automotive industry. Both residential and business construction expanded through 1926, but then residential construction began to fall off. Further expansion in business construction, however, maintained the increases into 1927, at which time they began to decline.

This development of new industries in the 1920s was a main cause of high effective demand. Radios, electric power, chemicals, telephones, motion pictures, durable consumer appliances, and cars—especially cars—contributed to the boom. Although most of these industries were not new in the 1920s, they grew up in the 1920s. **Primary demand** (that is, demand by those who had never owned certain goods before) was large. Automobile production went from 2.2 million per year in 1920 to 5.5 million by 1929—more than double in nine years.

The direct effect of this expansion was that people began to demand these new products in increasing numbers. ("I'd give anything to have a refrigerator. You never have to empty the drip pan, and you don't have to stay home to let the ice man in.") The indirect effect on maintaining demand was even greater. Car makers had to have vast quantities of raw materials and semifinished parts. Their needs stimulated booms in the steel, rubber, glass, textile, and petroleum industries and created a new service industry: the gasoline station. Governments (mainly local and state) had to build $10 billion worth of roads for these new machines. But most important were the capital investments that auto makers had to make for plant and equipment to expand their production capacity. Although the impact on total demand by the other "new" industries was not as great as the automobile's impact, it was substantial and also had both direct and indirect effects.

Another factor that contributed to the expansion of the 1920s was an increase in profit

The Roaring Twenties: On the road to depression (Culver Pictures, Inc.)

margins, which encouraged people to invest more. Productivity went up sharply, while the number of people with jobs in manufacturing stayed fairly constant and prices actually fell slightly. The result was higher profits.

There are three ways in which gains due to increases in productivity can be spread around: (1) Manufacturers can distribute these gains in the form of higher real wages. But in the 1920s the union movement was relatively weak, so the unions did not put much pressure on the companies to share this new productivity with the workers. (2) Manufacturers can pass along these gains to the consumer in the form of lower prices. Although prices did fall in the 1920s, they did not fall very much. (3) The gains may go to the business community in the form of higher profits, as both wages and prices remain constant, and as costs go down because of increased productivity. This is primarily what happened in the 1920s.

Despite the general prosperity, there were some weak spots in the economy. The agricultural sector was semidepressed because of (1) overexpansion by farmers during the war years, (2) a profit squeeze due to the fact that during the 1921 depression prices of what farmers sold fell faster than prices of what they bought, and (3) the high mortgages farmers had accumulated during the war years. Another casualty was the coal industry, which suffered from chronic overproduction and underemployment because of the overexpansion during the war. The textile industry, especially in New England, also suffered unemployment because (1) textile mills shifted to the South and (2) demand was stagnant.

A problem that soon became more serious than the rest was developing over the international means of payments. After World War I, the German government owed huge sums of money (reparations) to the Allies. The U.S. treasury encouraged private individuals and institutions to lend more to the German government, so that Germany might pay war reparations to England, France, and Italy—so that in turn these countries could pay to the United States the money they borrowed during World War I. This was a very circular process and in the long run dangerous to the economy. (We shall say more about this later.)

The Depression of 1929–1933

In 1929 the U.S. economy—and for that matter, the world economy—entered the worst depression in history. Money GNP in the United States fell from about $104 billion in 1929 to about $56 billion by 1933. Unemployment increased to the worst level ever: 25 percent of the labor force was unemployed and another 25 percent was partially employed. Prices dropped by about 24 percent. Oddly enough, the very factors that led to the prosperity of the 1920s laid the foundations for the depression.

The large primary demand for automobiles (demand by those who had never had cars before), and for the products of the other new industries, was beginning to drop off by 1929. There was a time lag before the onset of **secondary (replacement) demand** (demand for commodities to replace worn-out consumer goods), which was needed to prop up demand to the levels of 1929.

To see this, look at Figure A8-1, which is an idealized version of the life cycle of the automotive industry. During Stage I (1895–1920), people invented the automobile and worked to improve it. This stage is referred to as *the perfection of the innovation*. Note that the rate of growth of demand is relatively slow. In Stage II (1920–1929) the perfected innovation enters the primary market, and it catches on quickly. In Stage III (beginning in 1929) primary demand has become saturated. While the shift to replacement demand is going on, excess capacity develops. Output falls from its 1929 high.

As the demand for the products of the new industries fell, a negative accelerator effect appeared, and there was a fall in induced investment, both in the new industries themselves and in those industries that had been stimulated by them. By June of 1929, there was excess capacity, so people decreased their investing. Manufacturing output declined.

FIGURE A8-1 Growth Curve for the Automotive Industry

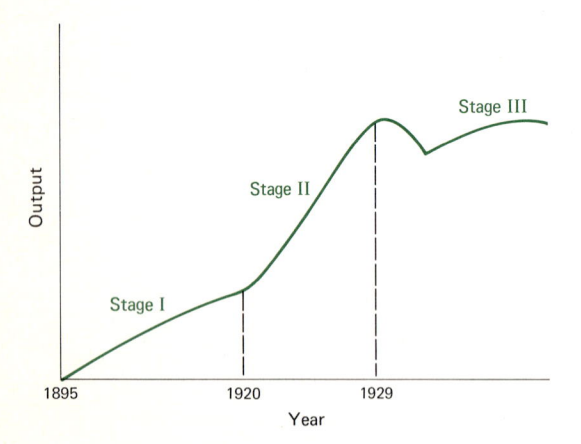

The construction industry, the second major stimulator of the 1920s economy, had been hit by excess capacity and falling output as early as the middle of 1927. By the end of 1929, it had collapsed.

One thing that weakened the ability of working people to buy the output of industry during the decade was the increasing profit margins of businesses. The fact that the wage share of income fell reduced the ability of large numbers of people to buy.

To put it in Keynesian terms: As demand fell toward the end of 1929, investment fell also. The large savings caused by the widening of the profit margins reduced consumption demand. Aggregate demand fell, and so did income.

Agriculture, textiles, and coal mining were already in trouble. The depression in 1929 made their bad situations worse. At the same time, the decline in both the construction industry and the new industries (especially automobiles) resulted in large amounts of excess capacity, a sure trigger to economic contraction. There were also additional aggravating factors that helped push an already weak economy over the brink to disaster.

For a year the stock market had been going up. Prices of stocks rose beyond any reasonable relationship to potential earnings. In October of 1929 the market simply collapsed. The main function of a stock exchange is to make it easy for people to acquire money capital they need for investment purposes. This function was lost. (Investment banks help corporations to float new stock issues so they can get investment capital. The existence of the stock market makes it easier for them to do so.) Another key function of the stock market is to mirror the psychological view of investors. During the year before the crash, it mirrored such optimism that no one noted the signs of decline. After the crash, pessimism ruled. Many people felt there was no hope.

From 1929 to 1933, the U.S. banking system also came close to complete collapse. Before the crash, banks had made some risky loans. They made large loans to people who gave them stocks to hold as security. When the stock market crashed, it crashed so quickly that banks were left holding large amounts of corporate stock—a huge capital loss. In addition, banks owned large numbers of mortgages. When mortgage holders could no longer make their monthly payments and real estate values plummeted, the banks were left holding innumerable chunks of illiquid property. All these factors eroded their asset position, and banks began to fail. People panicked. Long queues of frantic people lined up outside banks, waiting to withdraw deposits. This caused even secure banks to fail. By 1933, when Roosevelt took office, the banking system was in a desperate position.

Furthermore, between 1929 and 1933, the supply of money shrank from $26.4 billion to 18.8 billion. This sharply reduced the volume of spending in the 1930s. As a result, prices fell by about 24 percent.

As the U.S. banking system deteriorated, so did international trade, and quickly, too. The shift from government ownership to private ownership of war debts meant that private means of international payments became linked to reparations and war-debt payments. When the market collapsed in 1929, the structure of repayment of war debts crumbled also, bringing down the private system of international payments. A further blow to international trade came in 1931, when the United States started a round of retaliatory tariff increases that further reduced imports and put a damper on world production. These and other factors so weakened international banking that most of the leading industrial states—including Austria, Germany, England, and the United States—abandoned the gold standard (for a while).

Weak Recovery: 1933–1937

Franklin Delano Roosevelt was a charismatic leader. But he was also a man of moods and contradictions. In July of 1932, when he was campaigning for the presidency, he said in a radio speech, "Any government, like any family, can for a year spend a little more than it earns. But you and I know that a continuance of that habit means the poorhouse."

And then he was elected. In 1933, when he became president, Roosevelt set about building a fire under the economy by increasing government expenditures. This government spending had the effect of creating what were, for that time, large deficits. Congress also passed a series of laws aimed at correcting weaknesses in the economy.

The national debt jumped from $19.5 billion in 1932 to $36.5 billion by 1937, a jump of $17 billion in five years. This stimulated an increase in GNP of $35 billion between 1933 and 1937. Private investment remained low, however. (In 1929 net private domestic investment was $8.3 billion. By 1933 it had dropped to *minus* $5.6 billion, and in 1937 it was still only $4.6 billion.) Therefore, America's initial recovery from the Great Depression was brought about primarily by deficit spending on the part of the government.

The Recession of 1937–1938

President Roosevelt, concerned about the increasing federal deficits, decided that private investment should shoulder more of the task of coping with the continued depression. So in 1937 the federal government reduced deficit expenditures. Private investment, however, failed to take up the slack and continue the expansion. As a result, output declined and unemployment increased from about 14 percent to 18 percent. For the first time in the history of U.S. business cycles, a second recession came along before the economy had recovered from the first. In 1938, the government went back to its policy of increasing government expenditures. Under the stimulus of increased federal debt, the economy again began its slow expansion.

The Early Forties and World War II

During 1940 and 1941, as the United States increased its military expenditures and its exports to its allies, who were already at war, the recovery began to quicken. Observers could see the multiplier and accelerator effects of this increased output in the form of increases in both consumption and investment.

When the United States entered the war, on December 7, 1941, the economy went all out in the war effort. However, because there was so much unemployment left over from the depression of the 1930s (unemployment was still at 10 percent in 1941), the economy did not reach full employment until the beginning of the third quarter of 1942. Until then, there had been sharp increases in output of military goods, consumer goods, and investment goods. Once full employment was achieved, the economy, which was now on the production-possibility curve, had to cut back on the production of investment and consumer goods in order to continue to increase output of goods needed by the military.

Since there was full employment and plenty

of overtime work, people had higher personal incomes. Yet the nation's need for more and more military goods reduced the availability of consumer goods, so demand pressed on supply. The government prevented excess demand by imposing higher taxes and price controls, and even more important, by encouraging people to save and to buy government bonds. Perhaps one of the most potent fighters against inflation was Kate Smith singing "God Bless America" in a tear-jerking performance that sold millions of war bonds.

Thus large amounts of personal savings—plus price and wage controls and rationing—kept inflation within reasonable bounds. In the four war years from 1941 to 1945, the consumer price index increased only from 44.1 to 53.9.

The Postwar Boom: 1945–1948

At the end of the war, there was a slight dip in the economy as the United States shifted from war production to civilian production. Then, despite many people's fears that there would be a repeat of the 1930s, the economy began to expand rapidly. Even though the government cut back its military spending by more than $55 billion, the demand for consumer goods, investment, and export goods created a boom.

Because of the depression and then the war, both business investment demand and consumer demand had been kept low for fifteen years. After the war ended, businesses rushed to invest in plant and equipment, because of depreciation, obsolescence, and the need to reconvert to peacetime production. And because residential construction had been in the doldrums since 1928, there was a serious shortage of housing. All through the depression and war years, people had postponed buying new durable goods, such as cars and refrigerators—the so-called consumer durables. Now that the war was over, everybody rushed to buy them. As late as the summer of 1947, people who wanted refrigerators had to put their names on numbered waiting lists and wait for delivery anywhere from six weeks to three months. The same wait was required for cars.

Where did everybody get all this money to spend? It came from a number of sources, much of it from the profits and retained earnings of corporations. Also people's large savings—in both bank accounts and war bonds—was supplemented by a hefty tax cut in 1946. In addition, the government made large transfer payments to veterans. It gave them separation pay as they got out of the service, plus certain military bonuses, and twenty dollars per week for fifty-two weeks (creating the so-called "52-20 Club"). On top of all this, there was a sharp jump in consumer debt. High levels of employment and income obviously only added more fuel to the fire.

Americans were not alone in their headlong rush to achieve the good life, to gratify demands they had postponed for so long. They were joined by the rest of the world. Exports rose to new highs as a war-ravaged world turned to the United States for consumer goods and for investment to rebuild the world's economy. The U.S. government did a lot to help. Through the foreign-aid system known as the Marshall Plan, the United States provided more than $8 billion to finance exports to countries in need.

Unfortunately, under the impact of all this demand, inflation developed. Between 1945 and 1948, the consumer price index rose from about 54 to 72 (1967 is still the base year). Although much of this increase was due to demand-pull inflation, cost-push inflation also played a part. During this postwar period there were many strikes, as labor unions, in an effort to catch up after the wartime freeze on wages, sought large wage increases.

The Recession of 1949

In late 1948 the economy had its first postwar recession, a short, mild downturn caused primarily by excess inventory that businesses accumulated as output temporarily outstripped demand. Money GNP dropped by about $1 billion, while real GNP increased by $0.5 billion. Unemployment went from 3.8 percent (1948) to 5.9 percent (1949). However, by the beginning of 1950, the economy began to recover.

The Korean War and the Expansion of 1950–1953

In June of 1950, war broke out in Korea, and the recovery from the 1949 slump accelerated and became another boom. Consumers, fearing another round of inflation and also fearing that the government would again put on controls, increased their purchases. As the Cold War became hotter, the government increased its military expenditures, both to fight the war and to increase U.S. military strength in general. Real GNP rose from about $256 billion in 1949 to about $365 billion in 1953. Prices, however, followed suit. The consumer price index rose from 71.4 in 1949 to 80.1 in 1953 (using 1967 as a base). Predictably, unemployment fell from 5.9 percent in 1949 to 2.9 percent in 1953, or to just about half.

The Recession of 1954

When the Korean War ended, consumers stopped buying so much, and so did the government; inventories piled up. In 1954 along came a recession. This too was mild and short, however, because the government took prompt fiscal and monetary steps to ease the situation. A tax cut plus an easy money policy softened the downturn.

The Expansion of 1955–1957

In 1955 a boom in residential construction and in demand for consumer durable goods, especially cars, caused U.S. national output to expand quickly. (Auto production reached heights in 1955 not duplicated until the mid-1960s.) But in 1956 and 1957, the market for consumer durables, saturated by the sales of 1955, again sagged. However, the economy held steady because of increases in producer durable goods and in nonresidential construction. Real GNP increased from about $365 billion in 1954 to $441 billion in 1957. Inflation surged again too: the consumer price index increased from 80.5 in 1954 to 84.3 in 1957 (1967 = 100). Although the unemployment rate dropped below 5 percent, it held stubbornly at 4.3 percent, in spite of the expansion.

Economic policy makers, remembering the unemployment of the 1930s, had for a long time feared unemployment more than all other evils. Now, however, faced with the persistent increase in inflation between 1946 and 1957 (except for pauses during the recessions of 1949 and 1954), economists changed the focus of their worries. They began to show an almost pathological concern with inflation.

The Recession of 1958

By the end of 1957 the investment boom slacked off. Demand for consumer durables was still at a low point after the saturation of the 1955 boom. And the government further restricted demand, both by cutting its expenditures and by following what many people considered a too tight money policy. The result was the most severe recession to come along since the war. Real GNP fell by more than $5 billion, and unemployment rose to 6.8 percent. For the first time, inflation accompanied the fall in output, and the consumer price index rose from 84.3 in 1957 to 86.6 in 1958 (with 1967 = 100 as the base).

Weak Recovery: The Recession of 1960–1961

Although the recession of 1958 was severe, it was short—less than one year. Business recovered, consumer demand picked up, and so did government demand, so that 1959 saw a renewed expansion. However, this recovery was not strong enough, and the economy went through another recession in 1960 and 1961, a mild one this time. Some people claimed that the steel strike of 1959 was the main cause of this recession.

The Expansion of the 1960s: 1962–1969

Between 1962 and 1969 the economy expanded without interruption—the longest expansion in U.S. history. Yet, early in the sixties Presidents Kennedy and Johnson were both concerned about the slowness of growth, the high unemployment rates (between 5 and 6 percent between 1962 and 1964), and the now unavoidable problem of chronic poverty. (One good thing was that price increases were slight. The consumer price index rose only from 89.6 in 1961 to 92.9 in 1964.)

The government used deliberate economic policy to combat these problems. To attack chronic poverty, there was Johnson's "War on Poverty." The government stepped up its expenditures, which gave some stimulation to the economy. The real stimuli, however, were the Johnson tax cuts in 1964 and 1965. The 1964 tax cut alone amounted to $11 billion, which had a marked effect on the economy: Unemployment fell from 5.2 percent in 1964 to 4.5 percent in 1965. As the tax cut worked its magic, the economy moved toward full employment.

The 1965 escalation in Vietnam compounded our problems, as defense expenditures increased

Light Ahead

ever, both unions and corporations took advantage of the full-employment situation. Unions increased their wage demands. Corporations granted the wage increases and passed the higher production cost on to the consumer in the form of higher prices. Therefore, part of the blame for the inflation can be placed on a cost-push situation. Another share of the blame goes to administered-price inflation, because corporations took advantage of high demand to increase their profits by further increasing prices.

Inflation and Unemployment: The Recession of 1970–1971

Toward the end of the sixties there was such a high rate of inflation that in 1969 the government, in alarm, adopted some restrictive policies. The effect was only to increase unemployment. The fact that prices kept going up and up in 1968 and 1969 probably also cut back demand, as real income and wealth were redistributed. In addition, more and more small firms were caught in profit squeezes, as the prices of what they bought rose faster than the prices of what they sold.

Unemployment crept upward, from 3.5 percent to 4.9 percent in 1970 to 5.9 percent in 1971. Real GNP fell by $2.6 billion in 1970. The consumer price index rose from 109.8 in 1969 to 116.3 in 1970 and 121.3 in 1971. It was a repetition of 1958. The economy suffered from the worst of conditions, *stagflation:* high unemployment and high inflation.

from $50 billion in 1965 to $80 billion by 1968. Government—all levels of government—increased spending during this period, pouring out money, especially on schools and highways. After all, the babies born during the baby boom of 1945–1952 were now growing up and needed these things. Then, too, people's demand for consumer goods continued to be enormous, which caused a spurt in the growth of the GNP. Unemployment fell to 3.5 percent by 1969.

There was, however, substantial inflation. The Consumer Price Index rose from 92.9 in 1964 to 109.8 in 1969—17 points in only five years—in large measure caused by the overheating of the economy; that is, by demand-pull inflation. How-

The New Nixon Economic Policy: 1971–1973

In 1971, although the economy was beginning to recover and GNP was expanding, prices were still rising. The balance of payments was getting worse and worse, and unemployment was still high. Existing fiscal and monetary policy could not deal with all these problems at the same time. So in August of 1971 President Nixon took several steps, announcing fiscal programs designed to increase demand and employment, a ninety-day wage and price freeze, and the first of a number of "phases" to control prices. Also, to help the balance of payments, Nixon floated the dollar in international exchange markets. All this took everybody by surprise. A few weeks before, Nixon had said that he did not believe in controls and that he would never devalue the American dollar.

In 1972 price increases were noticeably less, and so was unemployment. Our balance of payments improved, and GNP increased sharply. As a result, in Phase II and Phase III, Nixon loosened price controls. (See Application 9, which deals with wage and price controls.) But in 1973 prices went up again, by about 8 percent, and the dollar depreciated by 12 percent on the international market. So one might say that Nixon's medicine worked, but not for long.

Inflation and Unemployment Again: 1974

In 1974 unemployment rose rapidly, to more than 8 percent. Inflation passed 12 percent, for the year, and real GNP fell by more than 9 percent. How do you control inflation and unemployment at the same time? Improving one makes the other worse.

Four things contributed to the inflation:

1. At the end of the October 1973 Arab-Israeli war, the Organization of Petroleum Exporting Countries (OPEC) boycotted the industrialized countries. In addition, they more than quadrupled the price of crude oil. (Many people believe that the boycott and the rise in oil prices were contrived by the international oil companies.)

2. In 1973–1974, agricultural prices rose rapidly for the following reasons:
   a. The United States sold a billion dollars' worth of wheat to the Russians.
   b. The anchovy crop off the coast of Peru was poor.
   c. Demand for U.S. agricultural exports increased in 1974 (because of the 1973 depreciation of the dollar).
   d. The Department of Agriculture had enforced restrictive policies over the preceding ten years. (For a more complete explanation, see Application 18.)

3. In an effort to maintain profits, those corporations that had enough monopoly power to vary prices responded to falling demand and rising costs by increasing their prices.

4. The Federal Reserve Bank increased the supply of money rapidly in 1973. Then, in mid-1974, it slammed on the brakes by driving interest rates up over 12 percent.

Unemployment went up fast in 1974; Detroit's auto industry was particularly hard hit. The oil shortage (whether contrived or not) and the rise in gasoline prices caused both a decrease in demand for cars and a shift to smaller, more efficient cars. Two-digit inflation also decreased real demand, for the following reasons: Inflation redistributes real income and causes the profits of smaller competitive firms to fall, as the prices of things they buy go up faster than the prices of things they sell. Furthermore, inflation in food prices causes people to stop buying consumer durables and to buy only necessities. When real incomes go down, this puts the damper on total demand. As unemployment goes up, people who still have jobs begin to feel insecure and retrench by increasing their savings and reducing their debts.

In the mid-1970s, the central problem is how an economy can combat at the same time high unemployment, falling or very slowly growing real GNP, and significant inflation. Simply using fiscal and monetary policy to expand the economy, to reduce unemployment, and to contract the economy in order to control inflation is not feasible. Will the government have to resort, continually or intermittently, to wage-price controls? Only time will tell.

Is American capitalism inherently unstable? You can see from this short record of the past fifty years that the U.S. economy is subject to ups and downs in levels of output, employment, and prices. Only lately have people realized that all possible combinations of these three can exist at the same time.

The U.S. economy can have terrible drops in prices, income, and employment (the recessions and depressions prior to 1945). The United States can have stable or near-stable prices, low unemployment, and expanding output (as in the 1920s and the first half of the 1960s). It can have expansions accompanied by substantial inflation (1945–1948, 1950–1953, 1955–1957, 1965–1969, 1972–1973). Finally, recession, with falling real incomes and high unemployment, can occur at the same time as sharp increases in prices (1958, 1970–1971, and 1974 to late 1975).

SUMMING UP

TABLE A8-1 History of Business Cycles

Year	Description	Current GNP (billions of dollars)	Percentage of unemployment	Consumer price index (1967 = 100)
1921	Depression; severe, but short, contraction.	70	12	52.8
1922 to 1929	Prosperity of the 1920s, with only two short, mild recessions. Based on expansion of the construction industry and especially on the growth of certain "new" industries: most important, the auto industry.	74.3 104.4	4.0 3.2	50.5 51.3
1929 to 1933	The Great Depression, directly caused by slump of demand in the construction industry and the new industries. Made worse by the stock market crash of 1929, the near collapse of the U.S. banking system, the sharp decrease in the supply of money, and a sharp contraction in international trade.	104.4 55.6	3.2 24.9	51.3 38.8
1933 to 1937	Deliberate, but inadequate, deficit spending by the Roosevelt administration. A slow, weak recovery.	55.6 90.4	24.9 14.3	38.8 43.3
1937 to 1938	In 1937, Roosevelt cut government expenditures, but private investment did not take up the slack. For the first time the economy suffered a recession before it had recovered from a prior contraction.	90.4	14.3 18	43.3
1939 to 1945	Huge military expenditures both in the United States and in Europe before and after U.S. entry into World War II. Rapidly expanding GNP. Until the labor force was fully employed in late 1942, there were expansions in military, consumer and investment output. After full employment, output for investment and consumption shrank while military production expanded. Higher taxes, personal savings, and price controls with rationing restrained inflation.	90.5 211.9	17.2 1.9	41.6 53.9
1945 to 1948	Postwar boom, fueled by demand for consumer goods and investment, deferred for fifteen years. Supplemented by increased exports to feed and help rebuild war-torn countries. Domestic investment and consumption demand were financed by savings from the war, tax cuts, government transfers to discharged servicemen, and consumer debt. Substantial inflation.	211.9 257.6	1.9 3.8	53.9 72.1

Year	Description	Current GNP (billions of dollars)	Percentage of unemployment	Consumer price index (1967 = 100)
1949	First postwar recession, caused primarily by excess inventory, as output temporarily outstripped demand.	256.5	5.9	71.4
1950 to 1953	The Korean War expansion, fueled by the Cold War and increases in military expenditures for Korea, as well as by anticipatory buying of consumer goods. Continued inflation.	284.8 364.6	5.3 2.9	72.1 80.1
1954	Post–Korean War recession, caused by decreases in consumption and cuts in government military expenditures. Kept mild by appropriate fiscal and monetary policy.	364.8	5.6	80.5
1955 to 1957	Boom, sparked by high levels of demand in 1955 for consumer durables and houses; maintained through 1957 by high levels of demand for producer durable goods. Continued serious inflation.	398 441.1	4.4 4.3	80.2 84.3
1958	The most severe of the postwar recessions, caused by a drop in government expenditures and investments, plus low demand for consumer goods. First recession in history to exhibit marked inflation along with rising unemployment.	447.3	6.8	86.6
1959 to 1961	Recovery in 1959, but not a strong one, followed by a mild recession in 1960–1961. Some people say the steel strike of 1959 was the main cause.	483.7 520.1	5.5 6.7	87.3 89.6
1962 to 1965 to 1969	Continued expansion from 1962 through 1969. In early 1960s growth was slow and unemployment high, while prices went up only slightly. The tax cut of 1964 increased output, but the Vietnam escalation of 1965 increased government expenditures and overheated the economy. Unemployment fell; inflation increased.	560.3 684.9 929.1	5.6 4.5 3.5	90.6 94.5 109.8
1970 to 1971	Inflation at end of 1960s set the stage for recession of 1970–1971. Government efforts to decrease inflation cut back demand and income. Consumers held back buying as inflation redistributed real income and wealth. Small competitive firms suffered profit squeezes. As unemployment increased, there was substantital inflation.	976.4 1,155.1	4.9 5.9	116.3 121.3

Year	Description	Current GNP (billions of dollars)	Percentage of unemployment	Consumer price index (1967 = 100)
1972 to 1973	Price and wage controls began in August 1971 when President Nixon—to expand employment, control inflation, and reduce deficit in the balance of payments—used expansionary fiscal policy, floated the dollar on the international exchange, and froze wages and prices for ninety days. Nixon's policies were only temporarily successful. In 1973 prices increased by 8 percent and the dollar depreciated by 12 percent in exchange markets.	1,155.2 1,289.1	5.6 4.9	125.3 133.1
1974	Worst recession since the 1930s began in 1974. Inflation of over 12 percent; unemployment more than 8 percent by the end of 1974. Real GNP fell by more than 9 percent. Number one policy problem today is how to combat unemployment and inflation at the same time.	1,397	5.6	147.7

QUESTIONS

1. What factors that contributed to the expansion of the 1920s laid the foundations for the Great Depression of the 1930s?

2. What were the major factors contributing to economic expansion during the 1960s? What problems did they create?

3. Trace the origins of the recession-inflation of 1974. What economic policy do you think would have been appropriate to handle the situation? Explain your reasoning.

SUGGESTED READINGS

Cagan, Philip, et al. *Economic Policy and Inflation in the Sixties.* American Enterprise Institute for Public Policy Research, Washington, D.C.; 1972.

Gordon, Robert A. *Economic Instability and Growth: The American Record.* Harper & Row, New York, 1974.

Mitchell, Broadus. *The Depression Decade.* Rinehart, New York, 1947.

Soule, George. *Prosperity Decade 1917–1929.* Harper Torchbooks, New York, 1947.

9

Completing the Model: Adding Government and Fiscal Policy

Before Keynes, the neoclassical economists' creed was "Let government affect the economy as little as possible. Balance the budget. A competitive market economy will correct itself." After Keynes, economists changed their tune to "The government must involve itself with the economy, because the economy is not self-correcting. The level of income is rarely the socially preferred one. The economy must be managed!"

To the simple model of Chapter 8 we will now add the *government sector* (taxes and government expenditures) to see what happens when the government becomes involved. How can a government change an economy's level of income?

In the recession that began in 1974, both prices *and* unemployment rose at the same time. People coined the word *stagflation* to describe the unusual state of affairs. "Perhaps," they said, "our model can't provide solutions for the problems of the economy. Perhaps we need something more." (In Application 9, we shall look at wage and price controls.)

Adding Government Expenditures to the Simple Model

We can add government expenditures to our model in the same way we added intended investment to it: by seeing them in relation to (1) the savings function, and (2) the consumption function.

How do government expenditures affect savings and consumption? Recall our discussion in Chapter 8 of determining the equilibrium level of income. We spoke of the two approaches to the subject: the savings-equals-intended-investment approach, and the aggregate-demand-equals-aggregate-supply approach. When we consider government expenditures in relation to the *savings* function, they become part of the savings-equals-intended-investment approach. But considered in

Government expenditures on a large scale: U.S. Navy supply depot at Guam (Courtesy U.S. Navy)

relation to the *consumption* function, government expenditures become part of the aggregate-demand-equals-aggregate-supply approach.

One Approach: Savings Equals Intended Investment Plus Government Expenditures

Figure 9-1 shows the savings-equals-intended-investment approach of Chapter 8 with government expenditures added. Savings, you recall, has a depressing effect on demand for output. But government expenditures, along with investment, add to consumer demand for the total output of firms. So government expenditures increase the demand for output. The point of equilibrium is now the point at which savings equals intended investment *plus government expenditures*. (Remember that without the existence of taxes, all these expenditures must be financed by borrowing.)

In Figure 9-1, the $II + GX$ (intended investment plus government expenditures) function is parallel to the II function, and also parallel to the horizontal axis. We are assuming here that government expenditures are determined only by political factors and are not affected by the level of income of the economy. This is, of course, not a realistic assumption, but the real factors involved *are* largely political, and this assumption is useful for simplifying our model. If you understand this simple model, you can experiment with your own assumptions about how government expenditures vary with the level of national income.

To repeat, with government expenditures included, a nation's equilibrium income is the income at which *savings equals intended investment plus government expenditures*. This is income A in Figure 9-1, and 390 in Table 9-1. (*Note:* Our discussion will rely mainly on Figure 9-1, but you can also follow it in Table 9-1, on page 216. As in Chapter 8, we have inserted number values after the letter symbols from Figure 9-1.)

Let's assume a level of income that is above A (390)—say, the high income level of B (450). Businesses produce for investment BD (20), for government demand DE (10), and the rest for consumption EG (420). The public, however, cautiously insists on saving BF (50) and consumes only FG (400). So business is producing more for consumption (EG = 420) than the public is consuming (FG = 400), creating involuntary (unplanned) additions to inventory, in the amount of EF (20). Businesses cut orders to manufacturers, and try to decrease the unwanted stockpile of goods. Manufacturers suffer dwindling output and income, so they lay off workers. Income moves to the equilibrium level A (390).

At any income below this, say at H (360), businesses produce for investment HI (20), for government demand IJ (10), and for consumption JK (330). The public saves HI (20), and consumes the remainder, IK (340). This means that businesses are producing less for consumption (JK = 330) than the public demands (IK = 340). The results are involuntary (unplanned) reductions in inventory, equal to IJ (10). Businesses increase their orders to manufacturers. Manufacturers increase their output, have a welcome surge of income, and hire more workers. Income again moves toward A (390), the equilibrium level.

FIGURE 9-1 Savings Equals Intended Investment Plus Government Expenditures. The simple model of Chapter 8 with the addition of government expenditures *(GX)* above intended investment *(II)*, so that *GX* is the distance between *II* and *II + GX*. The equilibrium level of income is now A, where S_f equals *II + GX*.

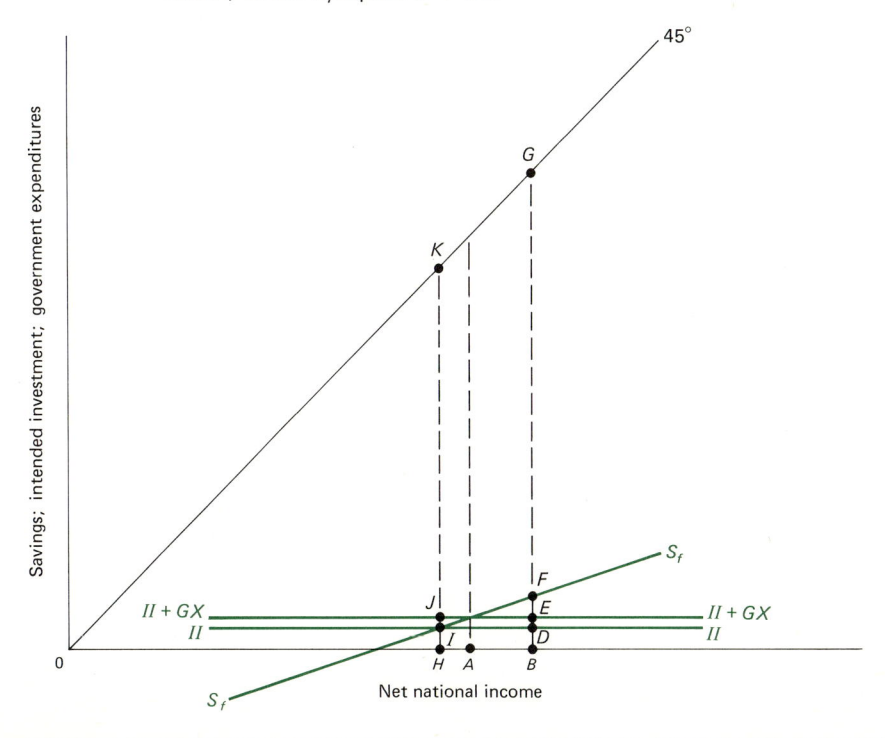

Adding Government Expenditures to the Simple Model

TABLE 9-1 Government Expenditures Added to the Data in Table 8-1

Income	Consumption	Savings (S)	Intended investment (II)	Government expenditures (GX)
210	240	−30	20	10
240	260	−20	20	10
270	280	−10	20	10
300	300	0	20	10
330	320	10	20	10
360	340	20	20	10
390	360	30	20	10
420	380	40	20	10
450	400	50	20	10

Note: The equilibrium level of income (S = II + GX) is 390 and is equal to A in Figure 9-1. Income B in Figure 9-1 equals 450, and income H equals 360.

FIGURE 9-2 Aggregate Demand (C + II + GX) Equals Aggregate Supply. The simple model of Chapter 8 with the addition of government expenditures. Aggregate demand becomes consumption plus intended investment plus government expenditures (C + II + GX). Equilibrium income is again at the level at which aggregate demand equals aggregate supply (45° line).

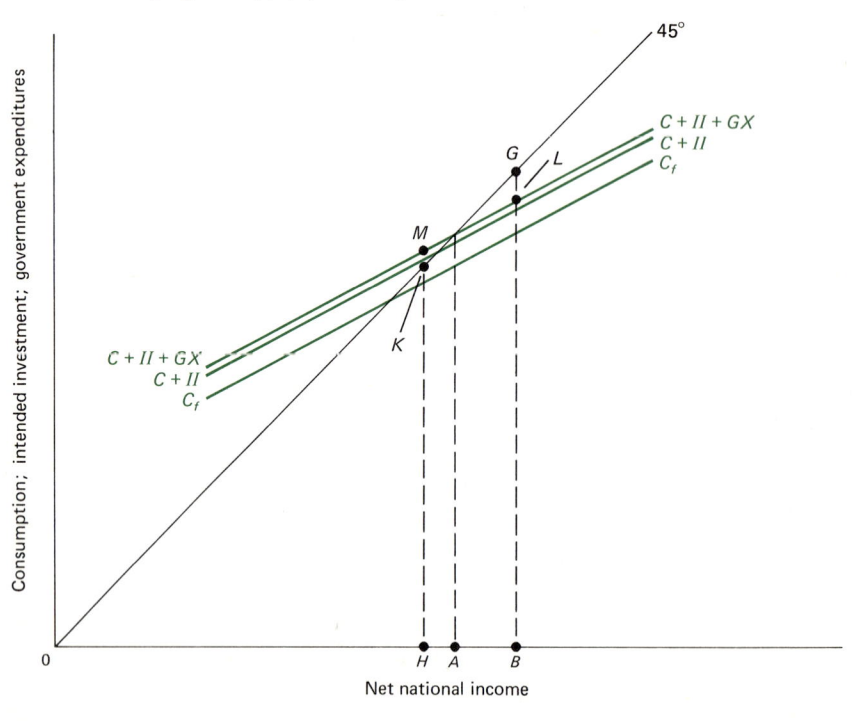

216 Completing the Model: Adding Government and Fiscal Policy

It is only at the equilibrium level of income that production for investment plus government expenditures equals savings, and that the amount produced for consumption equals the amount consumed. At that level, there are neither involuntary increases nor involuntary decreases in inventory. Income stays at a particular equilibrium level, however, only as long as the various functions in the model are fixed.

Another Approach: Aggregate Demand Equals Aggregate Supply
Now let's consider government expenditures and the consumption function, and how they fit into the aggregate-demand-equals-aggregate-supply approach to equilibrium income.

Figure 9-2 shows government expenditures added to consumption plus intended investment: $C + II + GX$, which all now adds up to aggregate demand. (Aggregate supply is still the 45° line.) The equilibrium level of income is A (390), where aggregate demand and aggregate supply are equal. When income is B (450), *above* the equilibrium level, demand is less than supply. Businesses produce more than the public demands and inventories begin to pile up, so businesses cut their orders to suppliers. The results are losses in income, drops in output, rises in unemployment. The level of income moves down toward A (390)—the magic number.

When income is H (360), *below* the equilibrium level, demand exceeds supply. Businesses produce less than the public demands, and inventories melt away, so businesses rush new orders to suppliers. The results are gains in income and in output and rises in employment. Income moves up, toward the equilibrium level A (390).

In Chapter 8, the equilibrium income was 360, because consumption (340) plus investment (20) was equal to aggregate supply at income level 360. In Chapter 9, aggregate demand increases by 10 (government expenditures), and because of the multiplier the equilibrium level of income increases by 30, to 390.

Now we combine Figure 9-1 with Figure 9-2 to get Figure 9-3 (page 218). You can see that *both* approaches—savings equals intended investment, and aggregate demand equals aggregate supply—generate the *same equilibrium level of income, A* (390).

Adding Taxes to the Simple Model

Consumption, investment, and government expenditures together make up aggregate demand. Savings *reduce* aggregate demand (because savings decrease consumption).

Now let's add taxes to our model. Taxes affect two components of the model: consumption and savings. You pay taxes out of income that you would have chosen to spend on consumption, or perhaps to use partly for savings.

FIGURE 9-3 Savings Equals Intended Investment Plus Aggregate Demand Equals Aggregate Supply

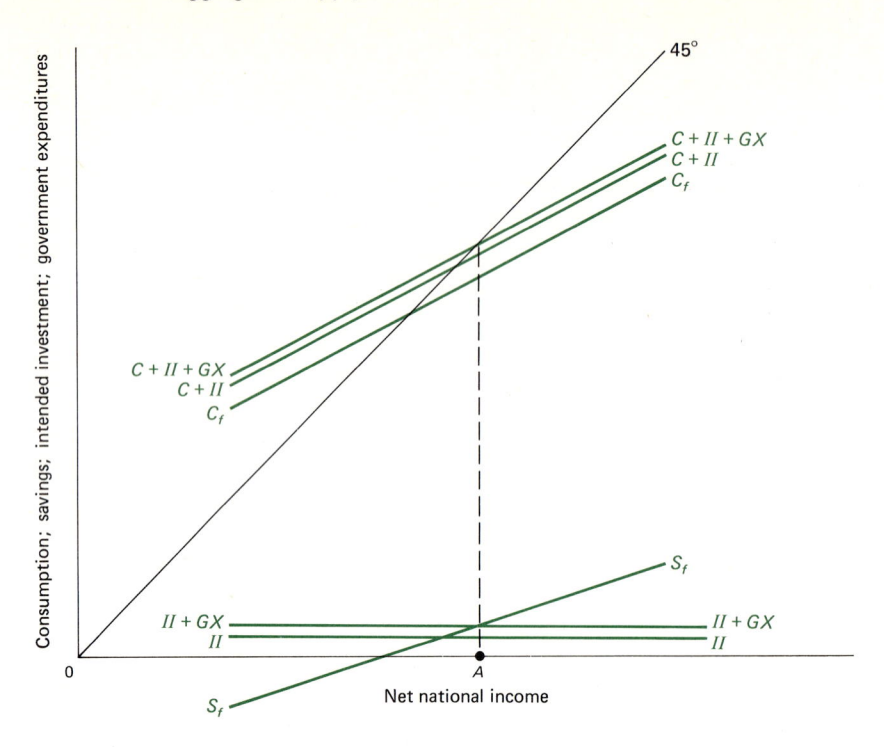

Suppose that there were no taxes. How much of your tax money would you have spent on consumption and how much would you have saved? That would depend on your marginal propensities to consume and to save (see Chapter 8). Since taxes change our disposable income, this means that the MPC concept applies. Suppose taxes are levied at $30 billion (see Table 9-2). This would cause disposable income to shrink by $30 billion, and it would affect people at all levels of income. If our marginal propensity to consume were two-thirds (as it is in Table 9-2), our consumption function would shift downward by two-thirds of $30 billion, or by $20 billion. At the same time, since our marginal propensity to save is one-third, our savings function would shift downward by $10 billion. Figures 9-4, 9-5, and 9-6, plus Table 9-2, show what happens when taxes are included in the model.

Note that including taxes shifts both consumption and savings functions down proportionately, so that the new functions are parallel to the old. We are assuming that all the taxes are proportional taxes. (To review the definition of proportional taxes, see Chapter 4.) If taxes are proportional, there is no change in the distribution of income or in the marginal propensity to consume and to save; thus C_f and C_{at} are parallel in the figures, as are S_f and S_{at}.

218   Completing the Model: Adding Government and Fiscal Policy

TABLE 9-2 The Complete Model of a Nation's Economy, Including Government Expenditures and Taxes

Income	Consumption before taxes	Consumption after taxes	Savings before taxes	Savings after taxes	II	GX	Taxes
210	240	220	−30	−40	20	10	30
240	260	240	−20	−30	20	10	30
270	280	260	−10	−20	20	10	30
300	300	280	0	−10	20	10	30
330	320	300	10	0	20	10	30
360	340	320	20	10	20	10	30
390	360	340	30	20	20	10	30
420	380	360	40	30	20	10	30
450	400	380	50	40	20	10	30

One Approach: Savings Plus Taxes Equals Intended Investment Plus Government Expenditures

You can see in Figure 9-4, on the next page, that introducing taxes into the model causes the savings function S_f to shift downward. Taxes are measured by the vertical distance from savings after taxes (S_{at}) to taxes plus savings after taxes $(T + S_{at})$.

Now that we have added taxes and government expenditures to the model, the savings-equals-intended-investment approach becomes the *taxes*-plus-savings-equals-intended-investment-plus-government-expenditures approach. Now two main factors reduce consumption demand: taxes and savings. That elusive equilibrium level of income is now the level at which these two main factors—savings and taxes—are offset by two supplemental elements of demand: intended investment and government expenditures.

The process can be expressed algebraically:

$$C + S + T = \text{aggregate supply (income)},$$

$$C + II + GX = \text{aggregate demand (for products)}.$$

In an equilibrium situation:

$$C + S + T = C + II + GX.$$

When you subtract C from both sides:

$$S + T = II + GX \text{ (A in Figure 9-4, or 330 in Table 9-2).}$$

Those who prefer graphic illustrations may look at Figure 9-4. The equilibrium level of income is A (330 in Table 9-2).

How does it happen that equilibrium income is only 330 now that we have added the effects of taxes? In Figure 9-1 and Table 9-1 the equilibrium level was 390. But that was when we were counting only government expenditures. Add taxes, and the level goes down by 60 points, to 330. Why? Income B (390) is now *above* the equilibrium. At

FIGURE 9-4 Another addition to the Simple Model: Savings Plus Taxes Equals Intended Investment Plus Government Expenditures. When taxes are included, the savings function drops to S_{at} (savings after taxes). $S = II + GX$ becomes $S + T = II + GX$. Equilibrium income is now A.

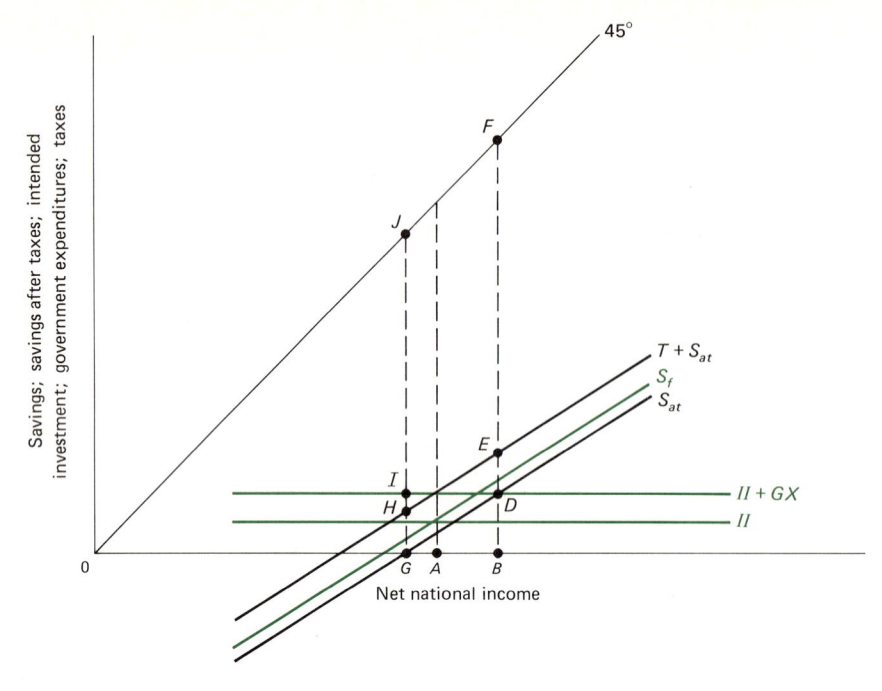

that level businesses produce BD (30) for investment and the government, and the rest (DF, or 360) for consumption. The public wishes to consume only EF (340) and use the rest (BE, or 50) for savings and taxes. This lowers the quantity of goods that businesses sell. Inventories pile up (DE, or 20), so firms cut their orders to suppliers. Manufacturers cut output, lay off workers, and lose money. The national level of income drifts downward, toward A (330).

The reverse happens at income level G (300), because that's *below* the equilibrium level. So businesses produce only IJ (270) for consumption, plus GI (30) for investment and the government. But the public consumes HJ (280), and uses the rest (GH or 20) for savings and taxes. So they're consuming more than business is producing, with the usual results: unplanned reduction of inventories (HI, or 10). Businesses increase their orders, manufacturers increase their output, hire more workers, and earn more money. The national level of income drifts upward, toward A (330).

Another Approach: Aggregate Demand Equals Aggregate Supply

Now let's try a different approach—aggregate demand equals aggregate supply—and see if the same formula for equilibrium income holds, now that we have added taxes to the picture. People pay part of their taxes

220 Completing the Model: Adding Government and Fiscal Policy

with money they would have spent on consumption and part out of money that they would otherwise have saved. In Figure 9-5, consumption shifts down from C_f to C_{at}. As it does so, aggregate demand also shifts down, to $C_{at} + II + GX$. This means that equilibrium income is again at the level at which aggregate demand equals aggregate supply—income level A (330).

At income B (390), aggregate demand (BK, or 370) is less than aggregate supply (BF, or 390). The excess supply of KF (20) causes business firms to cut orders to manufacturers, who in turn cut output, lose income, and then must lay off workers. National income drifts downward, toward A (330), as it did when we used the approach of savings plus taxes equals investment plus government expenditures.

At income G, or 300, aggregate demand GL (310) is greater than aggregate supply GJ (300). This excess demand JL (10) causes businesses to increase orders to manufacturers, who in turn increase output, income, and number of workers. National income drifts upward, toward the equilibrium level A (330).

By now the process should be clear. In Figure 9-6, on the next page, the same equilibrium level of income is reached by approaching the problem from the standpoint of savings plus taxes equal investment plus government expenditures, or by approaching it from the standpoint of aggregate demand equals aggregate supply.

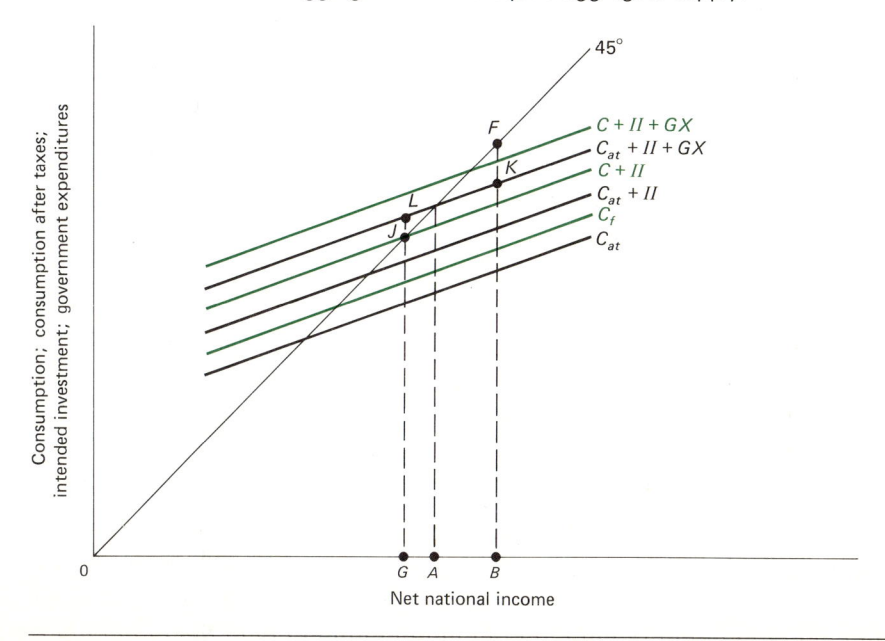

FIGURE 9-5 The Effect of Taxes on the Nation's Economy: Aggregate Demand Equals Aggregate Supply. When taxes are included, the consumption function drops to C_{at} (consumption after taxes), bringing aggregate demand down to $C_{at} + II + GX$. Equilibrium income is now A, at which level aggregate demand equals aggregate supply.

Adding Taxes to the Simple Model

FIGURE 9-6 The Effect of Taxes on the Nation's Economy: $S + T = II + GX$, and Aggregate Demand Equals Aggregate Supply. One obtains the same equilibrium level of income whether one uses savings plus taxes equals intended investment plus government expenditures, or aggregate demand equals aggregate supply.

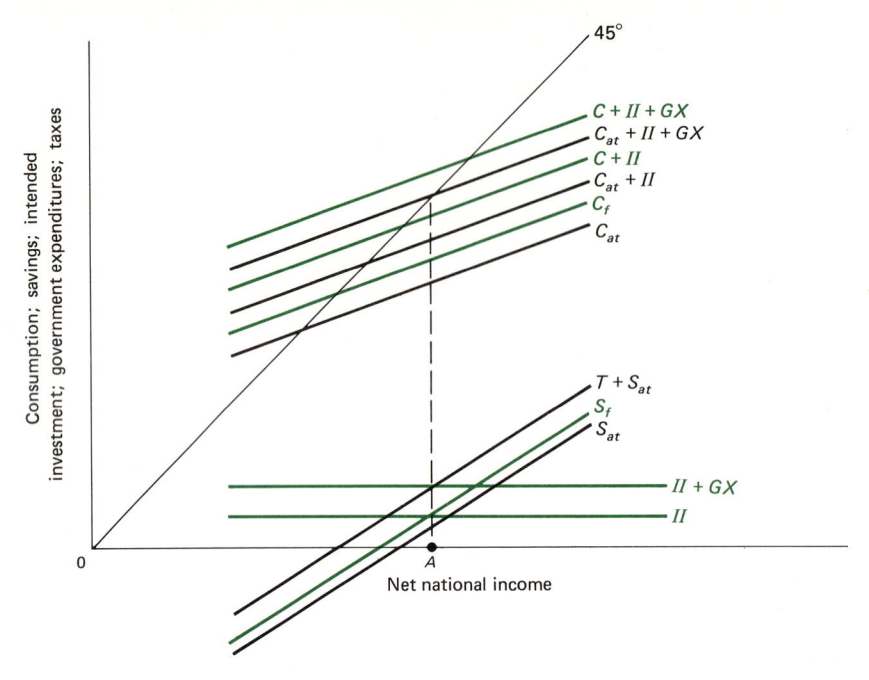

Deflationary and Inflationary Gaps

John Maynard Keynes came to the conclusion that a nation does not always achieve a full-employment equilibrium level of income. A country could be at an equilibrium level of income and still have unemployment. *Or* it could have full employment. *Or* it could have inflation. There were no automatic market mechanisms that could bring income to any one level that might be socially preferred.

The Deflationary Gap
Look at Figure 9-7. Suppose that there is full employment at B, but that the equilibrium level of income is only A. It is obvious there is a large amount of unemployment. To do away with this unemployment, income would have to increase by AB. However, it is apparent that the economy could not maintain an income of B. The reason is that at point B, aggregate supply would exceed aggregate demand by DE, and inventory changes would then cause income to drop back to A. An increase in demand of DE would be needed in order to achieve full employment. This gap, DE, is called the **deflationary gap**. To get rid of it and to push income up to the level B, aggregate demand would have to shift to E.

How could this be achieved? There are several ways: by increasing consumption, by increasing investment, or by increasing government expenditures. It can also be done by reducing taxes and savings. (In the recessionary year of 1975, and continuing in 1976, the Ford administration increased government expenditures and also gave tax refunds to induce people to consume more.)

The Inflationary Gap
Figure 9-8, on the next page, shows another situation, in which equilibrium income is again A, but this time the level at which there is full employment is F. If you look at that aggregate-demand curve, you will see that the economy cannot maintain the F level, because of excess demand. This excess demand will cause money incomes to go up to A. But there was already full employment at F. Manufacturers cannot hire more workers (there are none to hire), so they cannot increase output. How would you go about moving money income from F to A? If you increase prices, the result is inflation. This excess demand (GH in Figure 9-8) is called the **inflationary gap**. To keep prices from increasing, you would have to decrease aggregate demand: lower consumption, cut down investment, or cut down government expenditures. (In the inflationary year of 1967, the Johnson administration raised taxes, by means of a 10 percent tax surcharge, in order to induce people to consume less.)

In brief, the *de*flationary gap is the deficit in demand that leads to unemployment, and the *in*flationary gap is the excess of demand that leads to inflation.

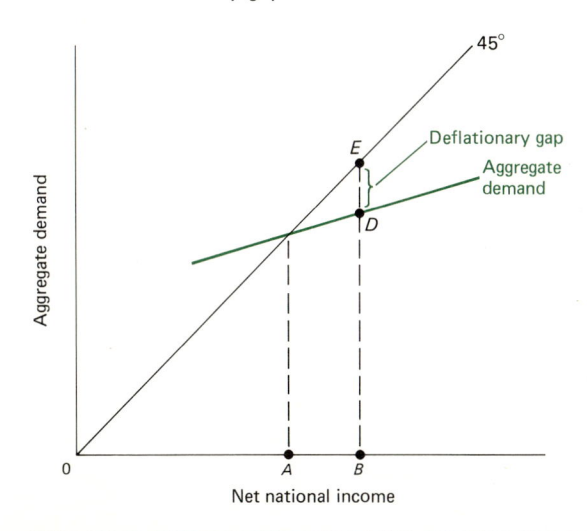

FIGURE 9-7 A Deflationary Gap. Although equilibrium income is A, the income that will achieve full employment is B. The deficit between actual demand and demand necessary to obtain full employment is DE, called the *deflationary gap*.

FIGURE 9-8 An Inflationary Gap. Although equilibrium income is *A*, the income that will achieve full employment (and relatively stable prices) is *F*. The excess demand, which causes inflation, is *GH*, called the *inflationary gap*.

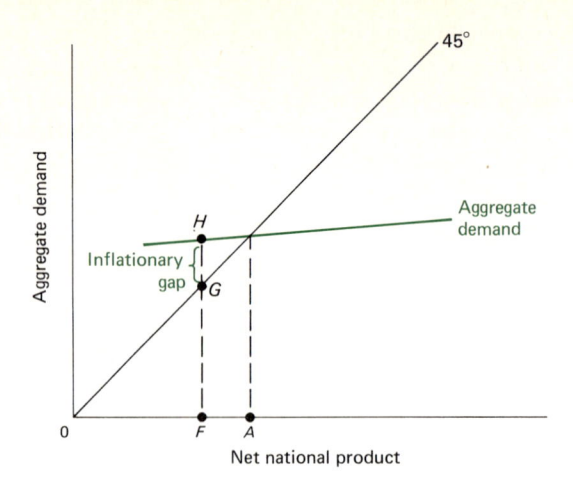

The Balanced-Budget Multiplier

The government sector includes (1) government expenditures and (2) taxes. Suppose the government decides it must increase its *expenditures* by $10 billion this year. It also decides to increase *taxes* by $10 billion at the same time. When both *GX* and *T* increase by the same amount, the equilibrium level of income also increases by the same amount. When both decrease by the same amount, what happens? The opposite is true. When a government makes a balanced-budget decrease in taxes and in expenditures, equilibrium income falls by the amount of the decrease. The **balanced-budget multiplier** is 1.

We can explain this best through an example. Suppose that government expenditures and taxes both increase by 10 and that the marginal propensity to consume is three-fourths, or .75. An increase in government expenditures of 10 means that aggregate demand goes up by 10. Now comes the difficult part. When *taxes* go up by 10, only 75 percent of that increase (remember that MPC = .75) has a depressing effect on consumption. It is assumed that people take the extra 25 percent of the tax increase out of their savings. In other words, consumption drops by 75 percent of 10, or 7.5. So government expenditures add 10 to aggregate demand, but taxes reduce aggregate demand by 7.5. The net effect on aggregate demand is thus an increase of only 2.5. Yet we have just said that equilibrium income will rise by 10. This happens because 2.5 is one-fourth of 10, so when the MPC is .75, the multiplier is 4. If you multiply 2.5 by 4, you get 10. It looks like this:

$$M = \frac{1}{1-\text{MPC}} = \frac{1}{.25} = 4 \times 2.5 = 10.$$

(Remember that the multiplier applies to changes in aggregate demand and that the balanced-budget multiplier applies to equal and same-direction changes in taxes and government expenditures.) With aggre-

Completing the Model: Adding Government and Fiscal Policy

gate demand increased by 2.5 and with a multiplier of 4, total income increases by 10. In brief, when the government makes a balanced-budget increase of 10 (that means increasing both expenditures and taxes by 10), the equilibrium level of income also increases by 10. No matter what the marginal propensity to consume, the results are the same. You can test this by choosing a different MPC and using the same $10 for government spending and taxes.

The existence of the balanced-budget multiplier emphasizes the fact that changes in the federal budget affect the level of income even when the changes are of a balanced-budget nature.

Fiscal Policy

In the days before Keynes, the neoclassical economists favored little government involvement in business affairs, a balanced national budget, and a government that ran itself as cheaply as possible. This meant a bare minimum of local public services. These tenets were based on the idea that when a market economy developed problems, it would automatically adjust itself so that the problems disappeared.

But today everyone knows that there is no such happy ending. A market economy does not have enough self-corrective mechanisms to move income toward some preferred level. Therefore, when equilibrium income rises above or falls below the preferred level, the cry for help goes out to the government: "Devise policies that will force the economy toward the preferred level of income."

The makers of government economic policy have three approaches they can use to try to make the situation better:

1. **Fiscal policy.** Raise or lower government expenditures and taxes.

2. **Monetary policy.** Vary the supply of money and the rate of interest.

3. **Incomes policy.** Fix wages, prices, and profits.

The rest of this chapter will explore the various aspects of fiscal policy. We will have to wait to discuss monetary policy until we have analyzed money itself, and have seen how it can be increased or decreased. Only after the discussion of monetary policy will we analyze incomes policy. We will end with a discussion of the various ways government tries to maintain full employment and still keep prices at some generally satisfactory level.

Discretionary Fiscal Policy

Although there are factors in an economy that do tend to "automatically" offset economic instability, these stabilizers are not powerful enough to prevent business fluctuations, variations in employment, and the constant changes of prices. Nor are these stabilizers completely automatic. Federal policy makers must still formulate economic policies—and be able to change them quickly—in order to deal with the

"I don't care what your economics professor told you in college —we're not going to base *our* fiscal policy on deficit financing."

constantly changing problems of economic stablilization. When we say **discretionary fiscal policy**, we mean a fiscal policy that has to be watched and changed, at the discretion of those who are doing the watching, on a day-to-day, month-to-month, year-to-year basis to cope with changing economic conditions.

Functional Finance

Functional finance (or, as some call it, compensatory fiscal policy) aims at compensating for changes in aggregate demand in an economy's private sector by varying the pubic sector: government expenditures and taxes. When there is a recession, with increased unemployment and a deflationary gap, fiscal policy should aim at eliminating this gap by increasing aggregate demand. When there is a business boom, with increased prices and an inflationary gap, fiscal policy should aim at eliminating the gap by decreasing aggregate demand. Only the government has the power to achieve such goals.

How Functional-Finance Economists Handle Recession

Suppose you are a follower of the functional-finance school of thought and your country is in the midst of a recession, with income falling, unemployment rising, and a wide deflationary gap. You want to increase aggregate demand. How do you handle the situation? One direct way is to increase government expenditures, since government expenditures are a large component of aggregate demand. Then you could cut taxes, which would shift the consumption function upward, again increasing aggregate demand. The decrease in taxes also increases investment.

How Are Deficits Financed?

Increasing government expenditures and decreasing taxes makes sense, but this policy has one big drawback. It creates a deficit in the federal budget; that is, expenditures are larger than income from taxes. The government can cover, or pay for, a deficit in three ways:

1. *A government can simply print currency to pay for the deficit.* It has been done several times. The Continental Congress printed currency during the American Revolution. Both the North and the South printed large amounts of currency during the Civil War. In 1922–1923, the Weimar Republic in Germany printed currency to cover World War I reparation payments. However, printing currency to cover deficits is considered highly risky because of its inflationary impact on an economy. (The hyperinflation in Germany in 1922–1924 under the Weimar Republic is a frightening example of chaos caused by printing money to cover government deficits. Inflation was so bad that a wheelbarrow full of marks was needed to buy a loaf of bread.)

2. *The government can issue interest-bearing debt instruments (bonds and notes) for sale to private individuals and nonbanking corporations.* The U.S. government did this with Liberty Bonds during World War I and War Bonds during World War II. When people buy government bonds, their purchasing power is siphoned off. They cannot consume as much or invest as much, so these government bonds tend to counteract the expansionary effects of the deficit. This was indeed the government's purpose in selling war bonds to individuals. The public saw the purchase of war bonds as a gesture to help pay for the war. Actually, the most useful aspect of these bonds was that they drained away purchasing power and thus decreased inflationary pressures.

3. *The government can issue bonds and aim their sale at banks.* The Federal Reserve helps banks keep their reserves high by buying government bonds from the banks, thus increasing their reserves. There are still enough loanable funds to loan to the public for consumption and investment and to loan to the government. This third method—selling government bonds to banks—is the one that results in the greatest degree of expansion for a given deficit.

Covering the national deficit during World War I: A Liberty Bond ad (The Bettmann Archive, Inc.)

Note that in both the second and third methods of deficit financing, the government, through the sale of these bonds, is tapping private savings.

How Functional-Finance Economists Handle Inflation

Suppose you are a follower of the functional-finance school of thought and your country is in the midst of an inflation, with rising prices, excess demand, and a nasty inflationary gap. You want to decrease aggregate demand. How do you handle the situation? One direct way is to cut government expenditures. You could also increase taxes, thereby reducing consumption and probably investment. Decreasing government expenditures and increasing taxes makes sense, but this policy has one problem. It creates a budget surplus, which simply means that the government is taking in more money from taxes than it is spending.

The government can use this surplus in three possible ways:

1. *The government can use the surplus to pay off the national debt owed to individuals and nonbanking institutions.* However, this increases the purchasing power of these groups, and tends to increase consumption and/or funds for investment.

2. *The government can use the surplus to pay off the national debt owed to banks.* However, this increases the banks' liquid assets and can increase the supply of funds that they have to loan to the public for consumption and investment borrowing.

3. *The government may deposit the surplus in Treasury vaults or in Federal Reserve Banks, to be used to cover future budget deficits.* The first two possibilities generate expansive forces that tend partially to counteract the contracting or shrinking effect of the original budget surplus. The third possibility removes the surplus funds from circulation and keeps them from counteracting the effects of initial efforts to decrease aggregate demand.

Notice that we have shown little concern in this discussion with the effect of these policies on the size of the national debt. Our concern here is the expanding and contracting effects achieved by following these policies of functional finance. How do these policies affect the level of aggregate demand? How do they affect employment and prices? We have not mentioned how deeply the government must go into debt to implement these policies. In Chapter 10 we will finally discuss the problem of the national debt—a subject that requires an entire chapter.

Government Expenditures

Some people, marveling at the simplicity of functional finance, have advocated that government expenditures be the primary device used to compensate for variations in private spending. They argue as follows: (1) Government expenditures have a greater impact on the economy because each government dollar spent increases aggregate demand, while only part of a change in taxes affects aggregate demand. (2) When the government spends money, taxpayers get more than a simple increase in aggregate demand. They get highways, schools, and hospitals; bureaucrats and bombers; and many other goods and services.

There are a number of problems associated with using government expenditures to counter variations in private spending. The most difficult is *timing*. How can the government time its expenditures in such a way that they offset the fluctuations in the private sector? Economic forecasting is far from being an exact science. For one thing, a group of economists cannot analyze the nation's economy and come up with a unanimous opinion. Then, too, statistical information about the economy is often inadequate because it takes so long to collect such information and process it. Forecasters generally have to work with economic statistics that are one to three months old.

Once a recession has hit and the economic forecasters in Washington realize it, the government hurries to oil the economy with expenditures. But it takes *time* to design a program of expenditures, more time to get Congress to approve the program, then still more time to set up the administrative machinery and to begin the project. Often, the recession may already be over and the country may be in the midst of an inflation before these projects are really under way. Now, in the new inflationary period, how can the government immediately cut off expenditures? Can it leave highways ending in the middle of nowhere or schools and hospitals half completed?

Since the timing of government expenditures to offset business fluctuations is such a thorny problem, some people advocate that the government use transfer payments to manipulate the economy. At least a government can shuffle these payments around in a hurry. *Transfer payments* are monies the government spends on such causes as social security, pensions to disabled persons, welfare, veterans' benefits, subsidies to businesses, and so forth. The important difference between transfer payments and other forms of government expenditures is that the government does not receive anything in return for its money at the time it makes transfer payments. When the government buys a forest or pays wages to a soldier, it receives trees or the services of the soldier, and by extension the public receives them too. But when these transfer payments go out to millions of people, they do not produce any goods or services that add to the national product. The recipients spend the money for their living expenses and thus create only demand.

Those who view as too slow the attempts of government economists to stimulate the economy by functional-finance methods say that government should manipulate transfer payments. That is, when a recession develops, the government should stimulate the economy quickly by increasing welfare, social security, school lunch programs, farm subsidies, and the like. It sounds feasible, doesn't it?

But there is a catch. What happens when an inflation comes along? Can Congress be heartless enough to reduce transfer payments at the very time that rising prices are so cruelly affecting many of those who receive these payments? This would mean that the poor and helpless, who benefit from many of the transfer programs, would have to bear the brunt of the anti-inflationary measures, and they are the people least able to afford it. Remember the public outcry that arose when the Nixon administration discontinued the Job Corps program, which trained high school dropouts in various useful skills? What Congress wants to take milk away from babies? Would any senator or representative be willing even to introduce such a bill?

Clearly, it is easier for the government to introduce expenditures than to cut them out. Relying on expenditures to counteract economic instability encourages growth of a larger and larger government. Furthermore, special interest groups, such as farmers and defense contractors, rush forward each time there is a rumor of a cut and try to protect their own areas of government expenditure. Thus government expenditures carry within them a hidden trigger that may touch off inflation. Therefore, should government expenditures simply be set at levels needed to carry out useful projects? Or should they be determined primarily by variations in the nation's economic activity?

"Which way to the confessional?"

Taxes

Because of these flaws that government economists find in a system of using expenditures to counter business cycles, some people feel that Congress ought to set government spending at whatever level is right to take care of society's needs and then use variations in *taxes* to speed up or slow down the economy.

But this approach also has its problems. During a recession, the government can certainly aim its expenditures directly at those people who need help. But if the government cuts taxes, it is not directly helping the people without jobs. It is only helping them indirectly, by stimulating consumer demand. The government is increasing taxpayers' income and, thus, the money they have for investment. All this eventually should create new jobs. But the structurally unemployed are not helped even *indirectly* by a cut in taxes. (Remember that structural unemployment means unemployment due to changes in technology and/or in the composition of demand.)

Furthermore, people take money for taxes only partly out of money they would otherwise have used for consumption, so it is only this part that affects aggregate demand. Therefore, larger variations are needed in taxes than would be needed in government expenditures to achieve the same relative effect. When the marginal propensity to consume is .75, a $12.25 billion decrease in taxes would be needed to create a $10 billion initial increase in aggregate demand, in order to increase income by $40 billion. But only a $10 billion increase in government expenditure would generate the needed multiplier effect to increase income by the desired $40 billion.

Of course, there are other aspects to this argument. For example, who is going to decide what the billions will be spent on? If the government cuts taxes, then private individuals and firms will make most of the spending decisions. If the government increases expenditures, the spending decisions are made publicly, by lawmakers and cabinet members. Who *should* make the decisions? That is not entirely an economic question, but one you will have to answer for yourself. Your perspective on it will, we hope, be broader as a result of taking a course in economics.

Just as special-interest groups affect the level and composition of expenditures, they also affect the composition, incidence, and level of taxation. Whenever taxes are to be changed, lobbyists for special interests descend upon Washington. Obviously, groups that are politically strong obtain tax concessions. And, more often than not, political strength is associated with wealth. Over the last two decades, the federal tax structure has become less and less progressive.

Balanced Budget

We discussed earlier the effect of the balanced-budget multiplier being 1. If the government increases both expenditures and taxes by the same amount, the equilibrium level of income increases by the same amount. In the case of a balanced decrease in the budget, the reverse applies. People who are concerned about the level of the national debt favor using a fiscal policy whereby the government would make balanced-budget changes sufficient to change aggregate demand as needed. Such a course of action would not affect the level of the national debt.

There are two problems associated with this idea. First, to achieve stability, the government would have to vary both taxes and expenditures by larger amounts. For example, assume that the MPC is .75 and that in order to achieve full employment national income must increase by $40 billion. The multiplier is 4. If the government increased expenditures only, it would have to increase them by $10 billion. If the government decreased taxes only, it would have to decrease them by $12.25 billion. If the government followed a balanced-budget policy, it would have to increase both expenditures and taxes by $40 billion.

Second, if the government followed a balanced-budget policy, it would have to increase taxes along with government expenditures, even during a recession. And a recession is a very hard time, politically or economically, to squeeze more taxes out of people.

There is one other problem connected with using government expenditures to stabilize an economy: the size of the government. The federal government keeps getting bigger and bigger. For example, in the years between 1950 and 1971, the federal payroll quadrupled and the number of employees rose from 2.1 million to 2.9 million.

Faults in the Keynesian System

People have been arguing about the Keynesian system ever since 1936, when his *General Theory* was first published. One does not need to hear all sides of this debate to understand Keynes's economic theory. However, there have been changes in the structure of the economy itself that have reduced the relevance of the Keynesian model. Let's look at some.

Writing in 1936, Keynes assumed that there was a close correlation between employment and the level of income. If the level of income increased, employment would also; the reverse would happen when income declined. Keynes felt that unemployment (except for frictional unemployment) was due to the fact that an economy did not have enough aggregate demand to achieve the desired level of income. But in Chapter 6, when we talked about business fluctuations, we said that a third variety of unemployment had made itself felt since World War II: structural unemployment. In structural unemployment, changes in technology and patterns of demand render groups of workers with certain kinds of skills irrelevant or unneeded. Since these skills are no longer needed, increasing effective demand does not help create jobs for structurally unemployed people. This is one problem Keynes did not take into account.

A second weakness involves the Keynesian model's utility as a tool for analyzing inflation. One can use the model to analyze the effects of demand-pull inflation, since the inflationary gap is essentially demand-pull inflation. (Demand exceeds supply and forces prices up, and this has the effect of rationing the short supply.) However, to cite Chapter 6 again, we mentioned two other kinds of inflation: cost-push inflation and administered-price inflation. These inflationary forces stem from the exercise of monopoly power either by the suppliers of resources or by manufacturing firms. The monopolists may increase prices not only during periods when the level of demand is high, but also during times when demand is falling. Keynes did not take into account these last two kinds of inflation.

A Crisis in Policy?

Today people in the United States know that the Phillips curve has shifted (refer again to Chapter 6), and they face the question of whether there is a politically acceptable tradeoff between unemployment and inflation. Further, they know that changes in aggregate demand have little impact on structural unemployment, or on cost-push and administered-price inflation. In light of this, people may legitimately question whether fiscal policy is at all effective in today's economic world.

In the mid-1970s, both inflation and unemployment were at unacceptably high levels. If the government ran a deficit in order to reduce unemployment, inflationary pressures would increase. If the government had budget surpluses and used them to reduce inflation, unemployment would increase. Is fiscal policy now irrelevant? John Kenneth Galbraith, and other economists who are calling for changes in economic structure, feel that in some ways it is and call for an incomes policy. That is, Galbraith wants to supplement monetary and fiscal policies with control of wages and prices.

On the other hand, in the early 1950s Professor Milton Friedman of the University of Chicago, winner of the 1976 Nobel Prize in economics, launched his "monetarist counterrevolution" against the Keynesian system. However, before you can understand the monetarist criticisms of Keynes, you must understand money and our monetary system. Therefore, in Application 11, at the end of our section on money (Chapters 11, 12, and 13), we will explore the monetarist critique.

SUMMING UP

1. When one includes government expenditures in the simple model, and diagrams the GX curve so that it intersects savings, the equilibrium level of income is where savings equals intended investment plus government expenditures. At incomes *above* the equilibrium level, businesses produce more for consumption than the public consumes, and therefore have involuntary additions to inventories. At incomes *below* the equilibrium level, businesses produce less for consumption than the public consumes, and therefore have involuntary reductions in inventory.

2. When one includes government expenditures in the simple model, aggregate demand becomes consumption plus investment plus government expenditures. The equilibrium level of income is still the point at which aggregate demand equals aggregate supply (the 45° line). At incomes above that, businesses supply more goods and services than the public demands, and thus have unplanned additions to inventory. Therefore, income moves down toward equilibrium. At incomes below the equilibrium level, aggregate demand is greater than supply, and businesses have unplanned reductions in inventory. Thus, income also moves up, toward equilibrium.

3. People pay their taxes in part from money they would have spent on consumption and in part from income they would have saved. So taxes

shift both the consumption function and the savings function downward. How great the shift is depends on the marginal propensities to consume and to save.

4. When one includes taxes in the simple model, the equilibrium level of income becomes the level at which taxes plus savings equals intended investment plus government expenditures. At incomes above the equilibrium level, businesses produce less for investment and for the government than people save and pay out in taxes, so that businesses produce more than the public consumes. Thus, businesses have involuntary accumulation of inventories, and income moves toward the equilibrium level. The reverse occurs at incomes below the equilibrium level.

5. For equilibrium to exist, aggregate demand must still equal aggregate supply, even after taxes and government expenditures are added. Now, however, taxes push down the C_f, and thus the rest of aggregate demand. At incomes above the equilibrium level, aggregate supply exceeds aggregate demand. This excess supply causes income to fall. When incomes are below the equilibrium level, the reverse occurs.

6. When an economy does not have enough demand to achieve an income that engenders full employment, this deficiency in demand creates a *deflationary gap*. When an economy has full employment, an excess of demand creates an *inflationary gap*.

7. When there is a balanced-budget change (a change in which government expenditures and taxes move in the same direction and by the same amount), the equilibrium level of income changes by the same amount and in the same direction. The *balanced-budget multiplier* is equal to 1. Income changes because any change in expenditures affects aggregate demand by the full amount, while a change in taxes affects *only* aggregate demand by that portion the public takes away from consumption to pay taxes. The public dips into savings to pay part of the tax increase.

8. *Discretionary fiscal policy* involves the conscious manipulation of government expenditures and taxes to move aggregate demand toward a preferred level of employment and prices as needed to cope with changing economic conditions.

9. *Functional finance*, or compensatory fiscal policy, is a policy by which the government compensates for changes in aggregate demand in the private sector. To stimulate employment during a recession, the government should increase expenditures and decrease taxes. This strategy will lead to a budget deficit. To curb price increases during an inflation, the government should cut expenditures and increase taxes. This strategy will lead to a budget surplus.

10. The *advantages* of a government's varying its expenditures instead of varying taxes are as follows: (a) All of a government's expenditures stimulate aggregate demand, while only part of its taxes do. (b) The public gets goods and services in return for the government's expenditures. (c) The government can aim its expenditures directly at those in

need; tax cuts aid the needy only indirectly, by stimulating general demand.

11. The *disadvantages* of a government's varying expenditures instead of varying taxes are as follows: (a) It is hard to mesh government expenditures with the vagaries of business fluctuations. (b) It is politically very uncomfortable to cut off government programs once they have begun. Restricting variations in expenditures to variations in *transfer payments* (welfare, for example) means that the public does not receive any goods or services in return for the government expenditures. Another difficulty is that when the government cuts down on transfer payments during inflation, it is the underprivileged who bear the brunt of the anti-inflationary measures.

12. Relying on the balanced-budget multiplier to increase or decrease aggregate demand without changing the size of the national debt creates problems for these reasons: (a) To achieve the desired objective, the government must vary both expenditures and taxes by larger amounts than is necessary when it varies them and leaves the budget *un*balanced. (b) The political and practical problems of varying expenditures and taxes.

13. The Keynesian model of income and employment has become less relevant of late because of the increased importance of (a) structural unemployment, which does not respond readily to changes in aggregate demand, and (b) cost-push and administered-price inflation, which tend not to respond readily to declines in aggregate demand.

14. With the recession that began in 1974, a crisis in policy emerged. Both inflation and unemployment climbed to politically unacceptable levels. The policy of *functional finance* (compensatory fiscal policy) can reduce inflation only by increasing unemployment, or it can reduce unemployment by increasing inflation. It cannot handle both at the same time.

15. Galbraith and the structural school call for an incomes policy (wage and price controls to supplement fiscal and monetary policy). Friedman and the monetarists have other recommendations.

QUESTIONS

1. Draw the relevant diagrams and explain how one obtains the equilibrium level of income in the following situations:
   a. Savings equals intended investment plus government expenditures:
   b. Without taxes, aggregate demand equals aggregate supply.
   c. Savings plus taxes equals intended investment plus government expenditures.

    d. In the complete model of an economic society, aggregate demand equals aggregate supply.

2. Assume that the MPC = $\frac{2}{3}$, the APC = $\frac{2}{3}$, and the equilibrium level of income is 300.
    a. Government expenditures increase by 10. What is the new equilibrium level of income, consumption, savings, investment, and government expenditures? Explain your answers.
    b. Assume that taxes increase by 10, in addition to the increase in government expenditures in part a. What is the new equilibrium level of income, consumption, savings, investment, government expenditures, and taxes? Explain your answers.

3. Parts a and b of question 2 depict a balanced-budget increase; you should show an increase in income of 10 by the end of part b. Use a different MPC, and recompute a and b. With different MPCs, is the balanced-budget multiplier still 1?

4. How can one use a multiplier-accelerator model to explain business cycles?

5. How can one get rid of a deflationary gap? an inflationary gap?

6. If one wishes to stimulate aggregate demand by increasing government expenditures, the form in which the government makes these expenditures makes no difference. A dollar of expenditures is a dollar of expenditures! Do you agree? Explain (and be complete).

7. At the beginning of the 1970s, economists in increasing numbers became concerned about the "crisis in economic policy." What were they concerned about?

8. You are a member of the Joint Economic Committee of the Congress. The committee must formulate a plan for implementing functional finance during a recession with significant amounts of unemployment. They must decide whether to increase government expenditures for goods and services, or to increase transfer payments, or to decrease taxes, or some combination thereof. What would you recommend? Since the plan the committee adopts would benefit some people more than others, what *economic* justifications can you give for your choice over any alternative? What *moral* justification can you give for your choice over any alternative?

SUGGESTED READINGS

Dillard, Dudley. *The Economics of John Maynard Keynes*. Prentice-Hall, New York, 1948.

Economic Report of the President. G.P.O., Washington, D.C., published annually.

Hansen, Alvin. *A Guide to Keynes.* McGraw-Hill, New York, 1953.

Lekachman, Robert. *Inflation.* Vintage Books, New York, 1973.

Lekachman, Robert, ed. *Keynes's General Theory: Report After Three Decades.* St. Martin's, New York, 1964.

Robinson, Joan. *Economic Philosophy.* Aldine-Atherton, Chicago, 1962. Chapter 4.

Robinson, Joan. "The Second Crisis of Economic Theory." *Papers and Proceedings of the American Economic Association,* 1971.

Stein, Herbert. "Fiscal Policy." In *International Encyclopedia of the Social Sciences.* Macmillan-Free Press, New York, 1968. Volume 5, 460–471.

Tobin, James. "Inflation and Unemployment." *American Economic Review,* March 1972.

10

Automatic Stabilizers and the National Debt

John Maynard Keynes's theory of income and employment made it clear that there are no mechanisms in our present market-oriented economies that are capable of automatically adjusting income to the full-employment level. Equilibrium income may be at a level that permits unemployment or at a level that permits inflation. In order to achieve a preferred position (full employment plus price increases that are slight enough to be acceptable), a government must use discretionary, or deliberate, policy and vary it to compensate for deficiencies in aggregate demand.

Some people—notably the Keynesians—tended not to worry much about the effect of this discretionary fiscal policy on the national debt. They did not ignore what was happening to the size of the national debt, but they were more concerned with reaching a desired level of employment and prices. On the other hand, there were mechanisms built into the structure of the American economy that tended to counteract automatically, to some degree, variations in employment and prices.

In this chapter we shall first discuss these automatic stabilizers that moderate recessions and check inflations. Then we will discuss the national debt.

AUTOMATIC STABILIZERS

Prior to World War II there were some business slumps that were relatively mild. However, occasionally the economy suffered severe depressions: 1907, 1921, 1929, and 1937. Until 1974-1975, U.S. recessions had been mild ones since World War II: 1949, 1954, 1958, 1960, 1969-1970. One explanation for the mildness of the contractions after the war, in comparison with many of those before it, is the postwar appearance of a number of new stabilizing characteristics in the economy. People refer to them as automatic stabilizers.

Automatic stabilizers are structures in an economy that tend to lessen a recession. They also tend to lessen an inflation, but they have not proved strong enough to prevent business fluctuations. These stabilizers are not varied by deliberate manipulation, as are changes resulting from the government's discretionary policy, and they were not created by the government to function as stabilizers.

The inflation-recession of 1974–1975, the worst since the 1930s, presented a special problem. The existence of both recession and inflation at the same time brought into question whether automatic stabilizers are able to function under such conditions.

In the following section we shall discuss the functioning of the stabilizers until the 1974–1975 recession. Then we shall discuss the way they function during an inflation-recession.

The Employment Act of 1946

At the end of World War II, many people worried that the severe unemployment of the 1930s would reappear. So Congress passed the Employment Act of 1946.

1. This act made the federal government responsible for promoting employment and consumer purchasing power. The act formally made the government responsible for policies for economic stabilization.

2. The act created a Council of Economic Advisers to advise the President on stabilization and other economic problems. It also required the President to make an economic report each year, which is published under the title of *The Economic Report of the President*.

3. The act decreed that Congress was to participate in formulating economic policy. To this end, the act established a joint congressional committee, called the Joint Economic Committee.

A Longer Horizon

When the Employment Act of 1946 became law and the business community realized that from now on the government was going to accept the responsibility for stabilizing the economy, businesses began to act with greater confidence. They were free from the fear of another Great Depression. This new freedom encouraged businesses to plan further into the future. That is, they could plan their investments for longer periods of time.

This longer *horizon* (or planning period) itself stabilized aggregate demand. Businesses felt that when times got bad, they could count on the contractions being short. So they did not shy away from new planned investments. From 1946 to 1974, the United States had a relatively more stable climate for investment. That by itself was a boon to the business community, since investment is the most variable component of aggregate demand.

Increased Size of Government Expenditures

Prior to the Great Depression of the 1930s, the share of aggregate demand attributable to government expenditures was no more than 10 percent. Today this share has risen to between 25 and 30 percent. In other words, the federal government—plus state and local governments—buys at least one-fourth of the nation's goods and services. This growth introduces a large stable element into aggregate demand, because government expenditures are not readily influenced by variations in national income.

However, despite the overall stabilizing effect of large government demand, variations in the *composition* of this demand can seriously affect local areas. For example, during and after the 1966 Johnson build-up in Vietnam, the military shifted its emphasis to more conventional weapons. This reduced the demand for engineers in the aerospace industry. Massachusetts alone lost 125,000 jobs. The closing of military installations after Vietnam created pockets of hardship throughout the nation, as did the canceling of certain projects, like the SST (supersonic transport plane), which affected Seattle and other areas.

Progressive Taxes

The post–World War II period has seen the rise of a number of structural features that have tended automatically to vary the tax rate and government expenditures in the way recommended by functional-finance economists.

The rate at which incomes are taxed is graduated. Therefore, income taxes are progressive. These taxes do have a stabilizing effect, even though they were not specifically designed to act as stabilizers. For example, during a recession, money incomes fall. Many people move into lower tax brackets. Thus, the absolute amount the government collects in taxes declines, and also a lower general tax rate applies. During an inflation, the reverse occurs. Money incomes rise. Many people move into higher income brackets, where higher tax rates apply.

As you can see, a progressive tax structure means lower tax rates during a recession, and higher ones during an inflation. At both extremes, tax collections nudge the level of disposable income in a direction that counteracts recession or inflation.

Expenditures That Stabilize

Certain forms of federal expenditure also change in a contracyclical manner; that is, they increase during a recession and decrease during an

"I hope you'll bear in mind this is for a government that has everything."

inflation, like unemployment compensation, for example. Social security payments also increase during a recession because, as jobs get scarce, more eligible people apply for social security. During an inflation, as the job picture gets brighter, the trend reverses, and people postpone retirement. Welfare payments rise more rapidly during a recession (jobs are scarce) than during an inflation (jobs are plentiful). Agricultural subsidies increase during a recession, as farm profits are falling. But subsidies fall during an inflation, when farm profits are rising.

Stabilizers Versus Today's Dilemma

Since 1969 the U.S. economy has experienced high inflation and unemployment at the same time. There is not only a crisis in fiscal policy, but there is also a weakening of the strength and functioning of the automatic stabilizers.

High inflation, when coupled with weak demand and high unemployment, tends to confuse investors, because it introduces instability. ("Should we go ahead and build the new plant? If we wait another five years, it'll cost us double. But the way business looks, we might go under in another five years.") Some economists argue that this confusion among investors has been a factor contributing to the low levels of investment in recent years. The investment doldrums has slowed economic growth and increased unemployment. At the same time low levels of investment have kept the supply of goods low, because they have kept the amount of new plant capacity at a low level.

The falling incomes of the unemployed have counteracted the rising incomes due to inflation. This has neutralized the stabilizing effect of progressive taxes.

What are the automatic stabilizers supposed to do in such situations? What discretionary fiscal policies would work? Policy makers simply do not know how to easily decrease both inflation and unemployment at the same time, no matter what discretionary policies or automatic stabilizers they invoke.

The Full-Employment Budget

We have presented two factors that determine the balance of the federal budget. The first one—discretionary fiscal policy—was discussed in Chapter 9. Functional finance is the keynote of this policy, by which the government deliberately creates a deficit to combat recessions (unemployment) and a surplus to combat inflation (rising prices). The second factor involves automatic stabilizers. During a recession, tax receipts fall and government expenditures tend to rise, generating a deficit. During an inflation the reverse occurs, which tips the scale toward a budget surplus.

Because of these two factors—discretionary, or deliberate, fiscal policy and automatic stabilizers—it is hard to measure the impact of budget policy. It cannot be done by simply looking at projected budget balances, or even actual balances. In 1958, President Eisenhower projected a near-balanced budget. But this balance meant cutting back federal expenditures. Unfortunately, there were, at the same time, decreases in private investment. So the country entered the recession of 1958, and the actual deficit in the federal budget was $12 billion. Sometimes the error is in the other direction: in 1972, the projected deficit was $33.9 billion, while the actual deficit was only $15.9 billion. The economy had expanded more rapidly than anticipated, which increased tax receipts.

Comparing projected and actual budget balances is not very informative. One cannot see the impact of the federal budget on the economy because that impact depends on the state of the economy. For this reason, economists developed the concept of the **full-employment budget**. Instead of balancing government expenditures against actual tax receipts, the full-employment budget balances government expenditures against the level of tax receipts that *would* exist if the economy were at full employment.

For example, the 1972 full-employment balance was a $7.7 billion deficit, while the 1973 full-employment balance was a $5.8 billion surplus. This indicates that the level of expenditures in 1972 was more expansionary than in 1973. The full-employment deficit of 1972 (during a period of close-to-full employment) had an inflationary effect. The 1973 full-employment surplus had a contracting effect.

The economist's ideal of full employment (Cary Wolinsky/Stock, Boston)

THE NATIONAL DEBT

In our discussion of functional finance, we mentioned the national debt only briefly. We did not discuss its size or how fast it is growing. Then we were mainly concerned with how to maintain economic stability and how to minimize the economic and social costs of unemployment and inflation. We have been assuming that when the government increased the national debt, it was for a worthwhile purpose. This may be, but we must recognize the fact that many people are worried about the national debt. Some of their concerns stem from their misconceptions about various aspects of that debt. Let's look at some facts about it. Table 10-1 lists the figures for the national debt from 1929 to 1974 and Figure 10-1 presents them in graphical form, on page 246.

The Size of the Debt

Back in 1929, the federal debt was about $16 billion. In 1974 it was $493 billion—a rise of more than 2,980 percent in forty-five years (see Table 10-1). To understand what this increase means, you have to bear in mind a number of points:

1. Most of the increases have occurred during wars, to pay for the huge expenditures by the military. Table 10-1 shows that the expenditures during World War II (1940 to 1946) increased the debt by about $200 billion. That alone accounts for almost half the total debt in 1974. After a slight fall between 1946 and 1950, the debt rose sharply again during the Korean War (1950 to 1954). From 1964 to 1972, during the Vietnam War, debt went up by more than $100 billion. (The United States spent an estimated $3 billion a month in Vietnam, more than $30 billion a year.)

2. To assess the significance of the national debt, one must compare it with other measures of economic activity. To do so makes the size of the figures less frightening. For example, columns 2 and 4 of Table 10-1 show the size of the debt and the size of interest payments. But now look at columns 5 and 6. The debt, as a percentage of GNP, and the interest payments, as a percentage of GNP, have both fallen since 1946. Look at that 124 percent debt figure for 1946. Note that it was down to 35 percent by 1974.

The figures for interest payments as a percentage of GNP fell, too, until the period between 1964 and 1974, when they rose to 2.2 percent of GNP. There was a reason for this rise. The government was trying to

TABLE 10-1 National Debt, GNP, and Interest (in current dollars)

1 Year	2 National debt (billions)	3 GNP (billions)	4 Interest payments (billions)	5 National debt as percentage of GNP (2 ÷ 3)	6 Interest as percentage of GNP (4 ÷ 3)	7 Per capita national debt	8 Current per capita disposable income
1929	16.3	103.1	0.7	16	0.7	134	
1940	50.9	99.7	1.1	51	1.1	382	573
1946	259.5	208.5	4.2	124	2.0	1,827	1,100
1950	256.7	284.8	4.5	90	1.6	1,689	1,364
1954	278.8	364.8	5.0	76	1.4	1,404	1,600
1960	290.4	503.7	7.1	58	1.4	1,604	1,937
1964	318.7	632.4	8.3	50	1.3	1,651	2,280
1970	389.2	976.5	18.3	40	1.9	1,895	3,376
1974	493	1,397	31.3	35	2.2	2,324	4,621

Source: *Federal Reserve Bulletin,* April 1975; U.S. Department of Commerce, *Survey of Current Business,* April 1975.

FIGURE 10-1 Graphical Representation of National Debt and GNP from Table 10-1

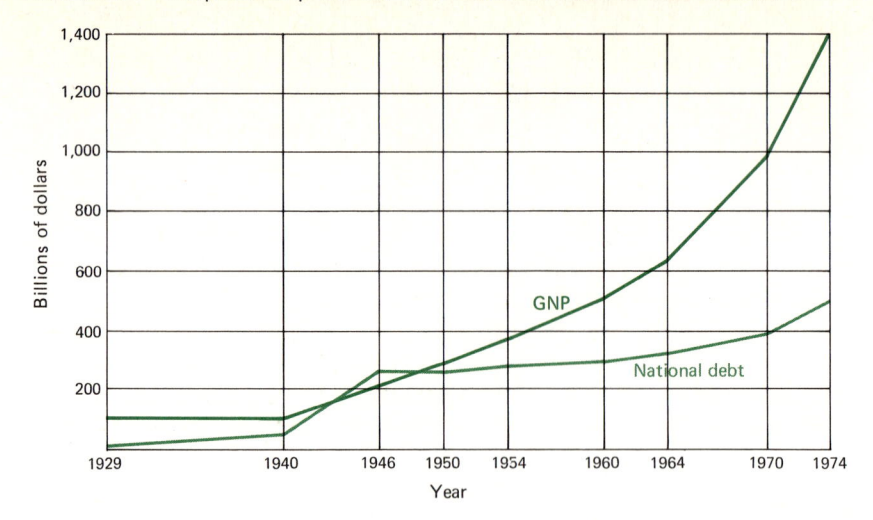

put the brakes on the post-1966 Vietnam inflation, so it increased the interest rates. When interest rates go up, the government has to pay more too.

3. Another figure that fell between 1946 and 1960 was per capita national debt (column 7 in Table 10-1). After 1960 it rose again. But it did not go up as fast as per capita disposable income (column 8), so the burden of the debt on the public actually decreased.

All this goes to show that increases in the national debt show up whenever our country is involved in a war. Also, although the dollar level of national debt keeps growing and growing, when one compares it with the overall level of economic activity (GNP), the actual amount does not seem so unmanageable. Everything is relative.

Qualitative Significance

There is a big difference between government debt and individual debt. When you borrow money, you increase your purchasing power in the present. You can buy that car or piano you want. The pinch comes in the future, when you must use part of each month's paycheck to repay the loan. For the next thirty-six months you will be in debt to the bank. This will inevitably reduce your future purchasing power and cut down the number of things you will buy. Thus, one effect of borrowing by an individual is to reduce that person's purchasing power over a period of time. Some people get so deeply in debt that their incomes cannot cover repayment and they become insolvent.

Debt owed by the government is different. Federal borrowing *transfers* purchasing power from one group to another—from those who buy government bonds to those who receive the income from govern-

There is a big difference between government debt and individual debt: Debtor's prison in seventeenth-century England (The Bettmann Archive, Inc.)

ment expenditures. The country's purchasing power continues at the same level. When the government eventually pays off the bonds, this again transfers purchasing power from one group to another—from taxpayers, whose taxes go to pay the debt, to the bond holders.

When the government pays interest on the national debt, the same thing happens. The citizens pay their taxes, which go to pay the interest. The people to whom the government owes the debt receive the interest payments. The net result is no change in total purchasing power.

If the national debt were to be evenly distributed among the entire population, according to the amount of taxes each person paid, each citizen would own a little of the debt. The government would owe a little to you, a little to me. When you paid your taxes, you would know that your tax money would return to you in the form of interest payments. Your right hand would pay your left.

Qualitative Significance 247

However, the national debt is *not* evenly distributed, and so income is redistributed from some groups to others. This does have some effect, but it is quite different from what most people worry about when they think of the national debt.

Most people view the national debt the same way they view the debt of private individuals. Thus, they believe that increasing the national debt today simply shifts the burden of paying it off to future generations.

But government debt is not like private debt. A good way to illustrate the difference is to consider the question: Who pays for wars financed by government debt?

Who Pays for Wars?

This question gets to the heart of the matter. The generation that lives through the war pays for it. Future generations only have problems of income redistribution. (One group pays the taxes; another group receives interest on the debt.) The generation that fights the war must shift its resources from consumer goods and services to the production of military supplies. The consumption and investment people forgo in the process is part of the economic cost of the war. This is the case regardless of whether taxes are enough to pay for the war or whether the government must borrow additional money to pay for it.

One big cost of war to future generations is a decrease in investment capability. When the shift to military production results in a decrease in investment, future generations are left with smaller amounts of capital. This reduces their ability to produce in the future. Wars siphon off resources that might otherwise have been invested in capital to produce consumer goods and government programs to improve the quality of life for all citizens.

To summarize: The cost of a war to the economy at large is not affected by the method of financing the war. The government can obtain the money by raising taxes or by going further into debt. It is what the people give up to produce the military goods that is the real cost. And this cost is borne by the current generation. However, because investment is curtailed while the war is going on, future generations suffer the inestimable cost of decreased capital resources.

Some Problems

Although our generalization that the national debt is mostly a problem of income distribution is basically valid, there are other ramifications. Let's look at some of them.

1. As long as the government owes the national debt to residents of the United States, it remains just a matter of income distribution, of one hand paying the other. However, what happens when nonresidents

(foreigners) buy the bonds that comprise our national debt? To pay interest on any debt held by foreigners, the United States must let production flow out of the economy to earn the foreign exchange to pay the nonresidents. This naturally reduces the level of production for domestic use. This problem was of little importance for the United States between 1946 and the early 1970s, since only about 5 percent of our national debt was held by foreigners. But when the oil crisis occurred, the OPEC countries began to hold everybody's debt, including ours. Now almost 11 percent of our debt is held by foreigners.

2. The fact that the national debt is essentially a question of income distribution does not eliminate it as a problem. The people who get most of the interest payments are the higher-income groups, who have spare money to lend. Thus, the income-distribution effect of debt, like that of taxes, seems to be to transfer money from the poor to the rich. (As we mentioned in Chapter 4, the U.S. tax structure is only moderately progressive. There are income-tax loopholes and regressive payroll taxes. And corporations have a habit of shifting their tax burden to the shoulders of consumers.)

All questions of fairness aside, redistributing income from the poor to the rich tends to increase savings, because people can save only if they have money left over to do so. Savings reduce consumption, reduce the marginal propensity to consume, and reduce the size of the multiplier. However, there is one good thing. Since interest payments are so small a percentage of the total GNP, it is unlikely that there is very much impact from this income redistribution.

A broader approach to the national debt takes into account more than who pays the taxes that pay the interest and who receives that interest. The broader approach includes who receives the benefit of the tax monies, who is helped by the money that created the debt. When one takes this broader approach, the question of who really benefits most from government activity becomes very complex.

3. Some people charge that a large national debt nudges the economy toward inflation. Here are some of the reasons they give:
   a. The government takes the easy way out when it finances its programs by increasing the debt instead of increasing taxes. As a result, people fail to scrutinize government programs as hard as they ought. They do not try to find cheaper alternative programs. The results are government waste and higher demand, which bring on inflation. A pay-as-you-go program would make taxpayers more careful.

   These government expenditures take the choice of what is to be produced away from private decision makers and give it to public or government policy makers. The fact that the government can keep going deeper into debt increases the ability of these government policy makers to decide what is going to be produced. The government takes purchasing power (money) away from private individuals and uses it for whatever the *government* decides is necessary. The private sector does not get to make the choice.

b. The highly **liquid** (meaning easy to convert to money) nature of government bonds makes people feel rich. It encourages them to spend more on consumption. In a fully employed economy, this increased spending is inflationary.
c. Because government debt is highly liquid, it can, if it is large, feed inflationary spending by consumers and investors. Instead of reducing consumption in the midst of an inflation, people may sell their share of the government debt (that is, their government bonds). After World War II, there was an orgy of consumption, largely financed by people who sold off the government bonds they had bought during the war. Therefore, there was an inflation between 1945 and 1949.

Bear in mind that although large amounts of privately held government debt can push the economy toward inflation in a fully employed economy, the opposite happens when there is a large amount of unemployment. Then, if a great deal of government debt is in private hands, it provides a spending cushion against contractions in economic activity.

4. The management of a huge government debt is difficult. Each month, if not each week, as part of the debt matures, it is necessary to refinance billions of dollars' worth of government securities. The amounts are so large that they may affect the money markets and cause the nation's interest rate to rise. The government, in its financing of the national debt, may destablilize the economy it is trying to stabilize.

Financing the national debt may distort the economy by a "crowding out" effect. For example, the financing of the huge 1975 deficit undoubtedly forced some private individuals and firms out of the financial capital market. This may have distorted the economy by reducing the rate of capital formation and growth, and possibly even depressing the economy. After all, the economy ordinarily raises about $200 billion from the financial capital markets. Imagine the reactions of these markets when they were asked to absorb an additional $80 billion to cover the government's deficit. It is unlikely that this could be accomplished without crowding someone out.

Conclusions

Whatever problems a large national debt spawns are insignificant compared with the necessities it pays for. Fiscal policy is predicated on the idea that the government may run a deficit during a recession in order to increase aggregate demand and reduce unemployment. During an inflation the government can generate surpluses to balance off the deficit. In other words, the national debt is a stabilizer. We must be ready to increase it or decrease it to facilitate the stabilizing actions of fiscal policy. The cost of the debt to the general economy is slight compared with the benefits gained from a device that helps minimize unemployment and curb inflation.

SUMMING UP

1. Business fluctuations after World War II (1945) were much milder than before the war, in part because of certain new characteristics in the U.S. economy that tended to create greater stability. These are called *automatic stabilizers*.

2. The automatic stabilizers contributed to economic stability in the following ways: (a) The Employment Act of 1946 committed the federal government to work toward maximum employment and stable prices. (b) The government's assumption of responsibility for economic stabilization gave businesses the confidence to plan their investments for longer periods of time in the future. They extended their economic horizons, which created greater investment stability. (c) Government expenditures, which are not readily influenced by business fluctuations, increased from 9 percent of GNP in 1929 to from 25 to 30 percent of GNP in the 1970s. This buying by the government created a larger and more stable element in aggregate demand. (d) Progressive income taxes caused an automatic increase in tax rates during inflation (as incomes went up) and an automatic cut in tax rates during a recession (as incomes declined). (e) Certain forms of government expenditure (unemployment compensation, social security, welfare, and agricultural subsidies), which rise during recessions and fall during inflations, counteracted business fluctuations.

3. The high rates of inflation and unemployment that have shaken our economy since 1974 have possibly weakened these automatic stabilizers and upset their functioning. Inflation and unemployment confuse investment decisions and cause progressive income taxes to lose their stabilizing functions, as inflation raises some incomes while unemployment lowers others.

4. The best concept to use in measuring the impact of the federal budget on the economy is the *full-employment budget*. According to this concept, actual government expenditures are compared with theoretical tax receipts that the government would have received if the economy had been at full employment.

5. Between 1929 and 1974 (forty-five years) the federal debt rose from $16 billion to $493 billion. Of this, $322 billion piled up during World War II, the Korean War, and the Vietnam War.

6. The national debt, when considered as a percentage of GNP, is not as impressive as one might think. The debt fell from 124 percent of GNP in 1946 to 35 percent of GNP in 1974. Interest payments fell from 2 percent of GNP in 1946 to a low of 1.3 percent of GNP in 1964 and rose again to 2.2 percent of GNP in 1974. The increase was due primarily to increases in the interest rate between 1964 and 1974. Per capita national debt fell between 1946 and 1960, and although it has since risen, it has not risen as fast as per capita disposable income. One can conclude that the national debt as a burden on the public has decreased since World War II.

7. The greatest effect of the national debt is in income redistribution. Money is transferred from taxpayers to the government, which uses the money to pay the interest on the debt. The people who receive the interest on the debt are the holders of government bonds.

8. Whether a government uses increased taxes or higher debt to finance war, the generation that lives through the war pays for it. (The reason is that wars consume resources that, otherwise, people would consume. These resources are used to supply the military machine.) However, there is one exception: When wars siphon away resources, future generations have less capital to work with and therefore can produce less output.

9. Some problems arising from a large federal debt include the following: (a) If foreigners hold the national debt, we must sell the output of our economy to other countries to earn the foreign exchange to pay interest to the foreigners. This decreases production for domestic use. Fortunately foreigners hold only small amounts of our debt. (b) The income-redistribution effect of the national debt transfers income from the poor to the rich, which somewhat decreases the marginal propensity to consume. (c) A large national debt may nudge the economy toward inflation in a fully employed economy, but during a recession it may provide a spending cushion against business slumps. (d) A large national debt is very hard to manage because the need to refinance large amounts may upset the money market and push up interest rates, and because the government's fiscal-stabilizing policy may collide with its policy of debt management.

QUESTIONS

1. The automatic stabilizers are not strong enough to prevent business fluctuations. How do you think they could be strengthened? What new ones might be invented?

2. Are private and public debts the same? If not, in what ways do they differ?

3. Under what conditions would you start to worry about the size of the national debt?

4. Should General Motors pay off all its bonds as quickly as possible and maintain a balanced budget? Does the same reasoning apply to the federal debt?

5. You are the economic adviser to the President and you need to help him formulate a position on discretionary fiscal policy and automatic stabilizers. It is 1974; inflation is 12 percent and unemployment is 9 percent. What strategy will you recommend to the President? Are you going to emphasize discretionary fiscal policy or automatic stabilizers?

How and why? Remember that policy recommendations are rarely cost free. Most often, policies benefit some and not others. In your recommendations be sure you establish the positions' *economic* justifications. Also be sure you establish your *moral* or *ethical* justifications.

SUGGESTED READINGS

Bowen, William G.; Richard G. Davis; and David H. Kopf. "The Public Debt: A Burden on Future Generations?" *American Economic Review*, September 1960, pp. 701–706.

Economic Report of the President. G.P.O., Washington, D.C., published annually.

Heller, Walter W. *New Dimensions of Political Economy.* Norton, New York, 1967.

Okun, Arthur. *The Political Economy of Prosperity.* Norton, New York, 1969.

Scherer, Joseph, and James A. Papke, eds. *Public Finance and Fiscal Policy.* Houghton Mifflin, Boston, 1966.

Application 9

Wage and Price Controls: Effective Tools or Market Distortions?

In Chapter 9 we talked about functional finance and how fiscal policy could be used to control inflation and recession; that is, to compensate for variations in nongovernment demand. However, we also pointed out that the Keynesian model, which is the theoretical basis for functional finance, can deal only with inflations caused by having more demand than supply, *not* with inflations caused by monopolies (cost-push and administered-price inflations). A fiscal policy of higher taxes and lower government expenditures can eliminate inflationary gaps by reducing aggregate demand. A different fiscal policy (lower taxes and higher government expenditures) is capable of closing a deflationary gap and doing away with unemployment by increasing aggregate demand. In other words, fiscal policy can cut down on inflation by contracting demand and cut down on unemployment by expanding it—but one fiscal policy cannot deal with both inflation *and* unemployment at the same time.

Let's look at a real-world example from the 1970s. By the end of 1974, unemployment had risen to more than 8 percent, real GNP had dropped by 9 percent during the year, and at the same time the rate of inflation for the year had been more than 12 percent. (Table A9-1 gives an overall picture.) Functional finance could not solve the unemployment and inflation problems at the same time. A number of economists maintained that the only way to deal with an inflation—especially cost-push and administered-price inflation accompanied by high employment—was to introduce an **incomes policy**.

When a government has an incomes policy, it tries to control wages and prices so as to maintain people's real income. The government can do this in two ways: through **wage and price guidelines**, which are essentially voluntary, and through **wage and price controls**, which are mandated by law.

TABLE A9-1 Wholesale Price Index and Consumer Price Index, 1929–1974 (1967 = 100)

Year	WPI All commodities	CPI All items
1929	49.1	
1933	34.0	
1939	39.8	41.6
1940	40.5	42.0
1941	45.1	44.1
1942	50.9	48.8
1943	53.3	51.8
1944	53.6	52.7
1945	54.6	53.9
1946	62.3	58.5
1947	76.5	66.9
1948	82.8	72.1
1949	78.7	71.4
1950	81.8	72.1
1951	91.1	77.8
1952	88.6	79.5
1953	87.4	80.1
1954	87.6	80.5
1955	87.8	80.2
1956	90.7	81.4
1957	93.3	84.3
1958	94.6	86.6
1959	94.8	87.3
1960	94.9	88.7
1961	94.5	89.6
1962	94.8	90.6
1963	94.5	91.7
1964	94.7	92.9
1965	96.6	94.5
1966	99.8	97.2
1967	100.0	100.0
1968	102.5	104.2
1969	106.5	109.8
1970	110.4	116.3
1971	113.9	121.3
1972	119.1	125.3
1973	134.7	133.1
1974	160.1	147.7

Note: Be aware of the large jump between 1973 and 1974.

Wage and Price Guidelines: Please Cooperate

As early as the Truman administration, the President had tried to persuade unions and businesses to show restraint in wage and price increases. It was not until the Kennedy years, however, that the administration set forth wage-price guidelines for unions and corporations.

In 1961, Kennedy issued the following wage and price guidelines: Wage increases should not exceed productivity increases for the economy as a whole, and prices should not increase more than increases in costs. At that time, the general level of productivity was increasing at the rate of 3.2 percent per year. This meant that industries whose productivity increased by 3.2 percent would have stable prices (increases in productivity would exactly offset increases in wages). But those whose productivity increased less than 3.2 percent would have to grant wage increases greater than their productivity increase. Their costs would go up, and thus they would have to raise their prices. In industries where productivity increased to more than 3.2 percent, relative labor costs would decline, and so they could cut prices.

Presidents ever since Kennedy have threatened to take reprisals against violators of these guidelines by varying tariffs, by boycotting or not buying from the offenders, by antitrust suits, and by selling government-stockpiled material to force the violator to compete in the marketplace against the government. But the greatest weapon the President has against violators is persuasion, or what has become known as **jawboning**. However, except for a few temporary victories, such as the 1962 confrontation between Kennedy and the president of U.S. Steel over the rise in the price of steel, guidelines and jawboning have been fairly ineffectual in controlling overall movements of wages and prices.

Wage and Price Controls: Obey the Law

In August 1971, President Nixon went beyond just setting guidelines for wages and prices. In an effort to control inflation, he froze wages, prices, and rents for ninety days. That is, he fixed them and then set up a system of controls backed by specific punishments for violators. Nixon went through various phases, from Phase I to Phase IV, so that these wage and price controls varied. They were finally abandoned in 1974.

Disadvantages of Controls

1. *Noncompliance.* The main problem with controls (except perhaps in a police state) is, How do you get the public to accept them? During World War II, people accepted wage, price, and rent controls because Americans almost unanimously supported the war. A few people cheated, but most did not. These controls held price increases down to 14 percent from November 1941 to August 1945, almost four years, which is only 3.5 percent inflation per year.

Various other countries have used similar controls during peacetime. Success always depends on whether the government can persuade the general public to accept the idea. In 1964–1965, the Israeli government, in order to reduce the deficit in its balance of payments, established wage and price controls. Labor was in short supply, and broad sectors of the labor force wanted higher wages. A series of wildcat strikes (not approved by union leaders) and sick call-ins kept increasing wages, and thus thwarted the government's efforts at control. The result was increased inflation, difficulties with international payments, and, in 1966, recession.

France had a similar reaction to controls in 1968. The student strike in Paris spread to many groups of workers and triggered such a great number of wildcat strikes (again union leaders were opposed) that French controls could no longer work. The resulting inflation eventually led to a 14 percent devaluation of the franc.

Also, in England in 1973, the miners in the nationalized coal mines refused to accept the government's offers of wage increases, and struck. The struggle dragged on for weeks, as factories had to shut down for lack of heat or electricity and homes and offices were cold and dark. Finally the government backed down, the miners won a slightly higher wage, and the whole country was hit by yet another wave of inflation.

Noncompliance is not necessarily as dramatic as these examples. Black markets may spring up as people lose patience and become willing to pay a higher, noncontrolled price to get what they want. And some businesses, tired of controlled prices and small profits, are willing to provide goods for these illegal markets. Mass purchases from black markets bypass the legal businesses selling under controlled prices and eventually render the controls ineffective.

2. *The inefficiency of allocation of resources.* Noncompliance by the public can defeat wage and price controls in the long run. However, another factor threatens their utility. The inefficiency in the allocation of resources that follows in the wake of controls can create disequilibrium in the economy. Most economists agree that the best feature of a market-oriented economy is that free (competitive) markets, via the mechanism of varying prices, make continual adjustment in the allocation of resources among a host of products.

If the supply of a given good increases, the price of it goes down. This leads to public demand for a greater quantity of it, to absorb the increased supply. If the demand for a given product decreases, the price of it goes down, which causes the makers of it to cut back on the quantity supplied. Then the resources used for that product can be reallocated to some other, more wanted product. It is all as logical and clear-cut as a football game. Prices need to be able to move freely in response to changing conditions of supply and demand.

If the government sets up wage and price controls, the markets no longer interact to create prices. Conscious human (committee) decisions now determine prices. Not only do most economists feel that committees cannot do as good a job as the market in deciding on prices and allocation of resources, but they also realize that wage and price controls are intended to interfere with the market and produce lower prices than the market does. Look, for example, at Figure A9-1.

Some people say that in the long run it is always the economy itself that has to compensate for these price distortions. If prices are lower than equilibrium, shortages (excess demand) develop, and the short supply must be rationed. Black markets develop. The same thing applies to the market for labor; labor is as much a commodity as steel or copper.

When a government imposes controls, one result that is perhaps as important as the creation of shortages is the bad effect on the quality of products. Firms cut corners. As they lower their costs in an attempt to compensate for the restrictions on price increases, output suffers. Lower quality, inferior standards, and less service result. Hence, one can hardly doubt that controls raise the *real* prices of many products as a result of these kinds of adjustments by business firms.

When President Nixon removed wage and price controls in early 1974, inflation took a sharp upturn. But economists say that the double-digit inflation of 1974 was partially caused by the market's readjusting to the shortages brought about by the former controls on wages and prices. In other words, even though the controls were no longer in effect, their presence was felt, for they left shortages in their wake that fueled inflation.

One interesting example of the effects of controls and their removal was the beef shortage of 1973. During the first half of 1973, beef prices were controlled. Then early in August President Nixon announced that beef would be decontrolled on September 12. Immediately, beef dealers, expecting that prices would go up after decontrol, began to withhold beef cattle from the market. Because of the controls that were still in effect, the prices of beef could not rise in response to the restriction in supply. Instead there were widespread shortages of beef.

3. *The high administrative and social costs.* Let's consider the enormous economic and social costs of substituting laws and administrators for the action of the free market in determining wages and prices. For example, during World War II wage and price controls were imposed. By the end of the war there were 70,000 paid employees of the Wage and Price Administration, plus almost 350,000 volunteer price-control workers. Then there were additional administrative expenses, such as the cost of the five *billion* ration coupons that had to be handled each *month* by the banks (this was in the last months of 1944, as the war neared its end).

FIGURE A9-1 Without controls, the price would be P, where supply and demand are equal and the market is cleared. With controls, the price would be below equilibrium, say at P_1, and an excess demand (deficit in supply) would result, amounting to BC.

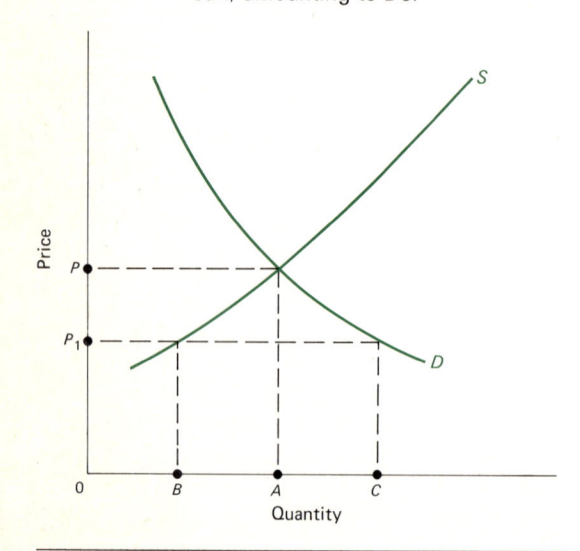

FIGURE A9-2 Under competitive conditions, supply S_1 would apply, and price quantity would be P_1 and Q_1, respectively. If monopoly power existed, supply would be S_m, price would be higher (P_m), and quantity less (Q_m). If controls were to be introduced, price could be set at P_1, thus duplicating the competitive, more efficient situation.

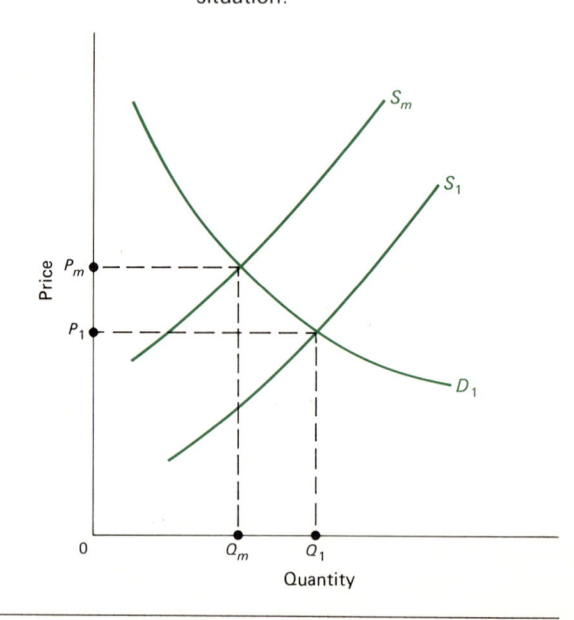

"We've decided to absorb increased costs ourselves, Jackson, rather than pass them on to the customer — you're fired!"

Suppose there were no wage and price controls to interfere with the market (Figure A9-1). Then equilibrium price and quantity would be P and A, respectively. But in order to lower the price, the government fixes price at P_1. Quantity supplied immediately drops, and there develops an excess demand of BC (B is the quantity supplied under price control, while C is quantity demanded; BC is the difference). In order to counter that excess demand, the government has to ration the short supply.

A country that sets up a wide system of controls also has to sacrifice a good many economic freedoms. Controls interfere with the relationships between workers and jobs, firms and prices, and costs and profits. If the government runs into a lot of opposition from the public, and if a strong black market develops, the state has to use its police power to enforce the wage and price controls.

When Controls Work
In spite of all the problems we have pointed out (the difficulty in getting the public to comply, the inefficiency in allocation of resources, the high administrative and social costs of controls) incomes policies *have* worked at various times in the past. During World War II, wage, price, and rent controls held increases in wholesale prices to only 14 percent for a span of almost four years. Whether President Nixon's controls, introduced in August 1971 (Phase I), worked well is a matter of considerable controversy. Some people point out that during Phase I there was virtually no increase in consumer prices and during Phase II there was only a 3.4 percent price increase over a seventeen-month period. So there are differing views of the situation. Milton Friedman and some other economists maintain that the inflation was under control *before* Nixon's wage-price freeze, and that the freeze was therefore unnecessary. Furthermore, they maintain—quite rightly—that the consumer price index does not take into account shortages or decreases in quality. Nor can one ignore the effect on the 1974 inflation of the removal of price controls. Were Nixon's wage and price controls successful? The debate continues.

Some economists maintain that even during the period of Johnson's wage guidelines in the 1960s, when simple jawboning was the principal control, prices were held down.

Provided that the general population approves of the importance of controls (as it did during World War II), an incomes policy can indeed work. Also, controls may be effective as a device to break the cycle of inflationary expectations of producers and consumers (as Nixon's Phases I and II did). But can controls come to our rescue during a period of high unemployment and inflationary pressures that are outside the control of the free market (the recession of 1974–1975 and the OPEC's high oil prices)?

Now what if the market is not free? What if this inflation is caused by monopoly power (cost-push and administered-price inflation)? In that case, even without any controls, the market will not operate efficiently anyway.

Pause for a minute and look at Figure A9-2. Let's say that a government decides to let competitive pressures determine price. Price is P_1.

However, suppose that monopoly power enters the picture. Then supply can be restricted to S_m and the price raised to P_m. The quantity exchanged goes from O_1 to O_m. If the government puts in price controls, it can force the price back down to P_1 again and increase the allocative efficiency of the market.

In other words, when firms with monopoly power use that power in such a way that the allocative functioning of the market is distorted, an incomes policy may very well counteract this distortion. However, suppose that a significant factor in the inflation is monopoly power. Then policies aimed at fighting inflation by making adjustments in the market will not work anyway. The government can control these monopoly forces only indirectly.

As for economic freedom, the concept is understandable only within the context of a competitive market system. The Invisible Hand of business maximizes the public good only if competition exists. If an inflation is being caused by monopoly power, then economic freedom (if indeed we can call it that) is being exercised mainly by the powerful at the expense of the weak. If the government does not take direct action to control the economically powerful (those with monopoly power), an incomes policy may be the only way in the short run to protect the majority of society, who are economically weak, from the economically powerful.

SUMMING UP

1. When a government uses the functional-finance approach to fiscal policy, it can counteract inflation *or* it can counteract unemployment, but not both at the same time. Furthermore, use of such a policy cannot overcome inflation that is caused by the exercise of monopoly power (cost-push and administered-price inflation).

2. To conquer these inadequacies of fiscal policy, some economists call for an *incomes policy;* that is, *wage and price controls.*

3. There are three main criticisms of wage and price controls: (a) It is difficult to get everyone to comply. (b) Controls lead to inefficiencies in allocation of resources. (c) The administrative and social costs of controls may be very high.

4. There are three arguments in favor of wage and price controls: (a) Controls have worked at times, especially when the public has approved of the reasons for instituting them and when they have succeeded in breaking a cycle of inflationary expectations. (b) Controls can lower high prices and increase the allocative efficiency of a market when an inflation is caused by the exercise of monopoly power. (c) Controls may be the only way to protect the economically weak majority from the economically powerful minority when an inflation is caused by those with monopoly power, and the "economic freedom" of the many is being taken away by the monopoly power of the few.

QUESTIONS

1. What are the most favorable conditions under which a government can use wage and price controls?

2. Under what conditions is it hardest for a government to use wage and price controls?

3. If you had been running things during the 1974–1975 recession, would you have used wage and price controls? If so, how would you have gone about it, and why? If not, why not?

SUGGESTED READINGS

McCracken, Paul W. "Two Years and Four Phases Later." *Wall Street Journal,* August 13, 1973.

Miller, Roger L., and Rayburn M. Williams, *The New Economics of Richard Nixon.* Canfield Press, San Francisco, Calif., 1972.

Pohlman, Jerry E. *Economics of Wage and Price Controls,* Grid, Columbus, Ohio, 1972.

Weber, Arnold R. *In Pursuit of Price Stability.* Brookings Institution, Washington, D.C., 1973.

11

Money in the Modern Economy

Money is an important part of economics. Yet the factors of production, the resources essential to producing things (land, labor, capital, entrepreneurship) do not contain money. Money is not directly a part of the process of production. How does money contribute to turning out automobiles or typewriters or haircuts?

There are some questions we must answer in this chapter and in Chapter 12: What is money? What are its functions? How is it increased or decreased, and how is this process controlled? How does the banking system work? How does money affect the level of economic activity and prices? Most important, how can the government influence the supply of money in order to bring about a desired level of income and employment?

A Barter System of Exchange

People can produce goods and services without the existence of money; where there is no money, goods must be exchanged for other goods. When this happens, the system of exchange is called **barter**.

For example, Farmer Nielson needs a hundred bushels of wheat and a pair of shoes, size eleven. He looks around his farm to see what he can barter and decides that his 250-pound pig is surely worth a hundred bushels of wheat and a pair of size-eleven shoes. He takes his pig to his nearest neighbor, Farmer Gomez, a wheat farmer, and offers to barter the pig for the wheat and the shoes. Farmer Gomez agrees that it's a fair exchange, but although he has the wheat, he doesn't have the size-eleven shoes. So Farmer Nielson goes down the road to Camilla McGrath. Her father died recently and left a closet full of size-eleven shoes, but she has no wheat. Her brother on the next farm also has some of their late father's size-eleven shoes, and he has plenty of wheat, but

One version of a barter system (Herb Moyer)

he doesn't want the pig. Farmer Nielson will probably make his trade eventually, but it may cost him a lot of time and effort.

The central requirement of the barter system is what is called a **double coincidence of demand**, or of wants. Not only must Farmer Nielson want what the other person has, but also the other person in the exchange must want what Nielson has. Establishing mutuality of needs is usually time consuming and therefore inefficient. How much easier it would be for Nielson to take the pig to the butcher in town, sell it for money, buy the wheat from the miller, and then drop by the shoemaker's and pick up a pair of size-eleven shoes.

A Money System of Exchange

The more complex economies become, the greater the necessity to replace barter with a system of *money exchange*. As a society specializes its labor and other resources, it must also specialize the means by which exchanges are made.

Your instructor is not only a teacher, not only a college teacher, but, even more specialized than that, an economics instructor, producing a service called education. How should he or she be paid? In a society without money, would one student barter potatoes, another mow the instructor's lawn, or another clean the classroom? Although barter was used in the early days of our country, it is too cumbersome today. The existence of money makes possible efficiency, a smooth flow of goods and resources, and a more highly developed economy.

But what is money? What is the essential ingredient that makes a thing money?

A thing becomes **money** when people accept that thing in exchange for goods and services in general. *Money is money because people say it is money* and accept it in exchange for almost anything else. Governments may decree that something be accepted as payment for all debts, public or private. Although this *encourages* acceptance of that thing as a medium of exchange, it does not guarantee it. In the past, money consisted of gold and silver or paper backed by gold and silver. You could exchange a paper five-dollar bill for a five-dollar gold piece. This increased its acceptability as money. Today if you take a five-dollar bill to a Federal Reserve Bank, you will get in return only a new five-dollar bill. And yet you can still exchange it for goods and services.

In the long run, it is just the *acceptance* of the thing called money in exchange for goods and services that makes it money.

The Functions of Money

There are four functions that money performs:

1. Money acts as a **medium of exchange**. The central ingredient of money is its acceptability by others. When money is exchanged for goods and services, it is functioning as a medium of exchange.

2. Money is a **standard of value or unit of account**. Money serves as a measure by which a value can be set on goods and services. In a barter economy, if Farmer Nielson wanted to know the value of his pig, he compared it with the value of other goods. The pig might be worth a hundred bushels of oats and the extraction of an aching tooth, and so on.

In a money economy, the pig's value is set in terms of the monetary unit of the country. The monetary unit of the United States is the dollar, so here the pig is valued in dollars. Although other nations have differing standard units (pounds, francs, and so on), in each country money functions as a standard of value or unit of account and makes it possible for people to place a value on goods and services.

3. Money acts as a **store of value**. In a barter economy, how can Farmer Nielson *save?* He can do so only by storing goods. He can stash away wheat or preserve the products of the pig (bacon, ham, sausages), or he can accumulate larger numbers of things. But it costs a lot to store these things, and such products can deteriorate over a period of time. It would be simpler if Nielson could sell his output and save the accumulated *money.* (Money occupies little space; it doesn't rot or breed weevils. It just sits there.)

But money *does* fluctuate in value, because of increases or decreases in prices. Inflation reduces the purchasing power of money and therefore reduces its value. Deflation causes the reverse to happen. This variation reduces the efficiency of money as a store of value.

Currency going into circulation (J. P. Laffont/Sygma)

4. **Money is a means of deferred payment.** Money facilitates lending and the repayment of loans. In a barter economy, borrowing is a most cumbersome affair. Suppose that Nielson's land is next to the river, and one year the river floods and destroys his wheat crop. He goes to Farmer Gomez, who lives in the unaffected uplands, and borrows wheat so he can plant a new crop. But because of the flood, wheat is now relatively scarce—that is, in short supply—with a high relative exchange value. The

following year the weather is fine, and there is a bumper crop. Nielson, with plenty of wheat today, pays Gomez back for the wheat he borrowed last year. But with this year's abundance of wheat, the scarcity value of wheat has declined markedly, compared with last year, and wheat has a low relative exchange value.

It is more efficient to base credit on a general medium of exchange: money. One expects money and its scarcity value (in simple language, its purchasing power) to be less subject than barter items to variations outside people's control.

However, the value of money—its purchasing power—does vary as prices vary, and this reduces the usefulness of money. There have been times in history when the supply of money increased so rapidly that it led to monetary disaster. During the American Revolution, for example, the Continental Congress issued so much currency with no backing that the people lost confidence in it. The purchasing power of that money dropped so low that the expression "not worth a Continental" became popular.

Characteristics of a "Good" Money

Many things have performed the function of money. During the American Revolution, in Massachusetts wheat served as money, and in Virginia tobacco was legally defined as money. American Indians used strings of colored beads called wampum as money; some African tribes have used cattle and cowry shells, and some groups in the South Sea Islands have used large stones. Even human slaves have functioned as money in some parts of the world. Gold, silver, and copper, however, are the materials that most commonly serve as money.

What characteristics should one look for in a good money? (1) It should be portable, or easy to carry. (2) It should be easy to recognize, but hard to counterfeit or duplicate illegally. (3) It should be easily subdivided, to allow for small as well as large purchases. (4) The cost of storing it, that is, physically storing it in a safe place, should be low. (5) It should be durable, and not wear out or rot quickly. (6) The relative supply should not vary so greatly that large variations in relative scarcity value occur, since purchasing power changes as prices vary.

The Supply of Money

The **supply of money** in the United States is defined as follows:

Money consists of all demand deposits in commercial banks plus currency and coin in circulation.

Demand deposits are what you know as **checking accounts**. They are called demand deposits because you can withdraw these deposits "on demand," by presenting a check.

A **check** is merely an order to a bank from the holder of a demand deposit to transfer some money from the deposit and pay it to someone else. The deposit is the money, not the check. If there is no deposit, the check is worthless.

Table 11-1 indicates that about 75 percent of our money supply is in the form of demand deposits. However, the economic importance of "checkbook money" is even greater than that, since about 90 percent (by value) of all economic transactions are accomplished by means of demand deposits.

The keepers of demand deposits are **commercial banks**. In fact, commercial banks are, by legal definition, the institutions that hold demand deposits. Since demand deposits comprise the bulk of the U.S. money supply, commercial banks hold most of the supply of money in the United States.

The second largest component of our money supply is **currency in circulation**, which means currency that is in use rather than in the vaults of banks or of the Federal Reserve. Currency is the paper money in the U.S. economy. It is issued by the Federal Reserve, not by the U.S. Treasury.

Coins are the smallest part of the supply of money, but a very vital part of it. These metal tokens are minted by the Treasury and issued through the Federal Reserve Banks.

Today both currency and coin are called **fiat money**. Their value as monetary instruments is greater than their value as commodities. The five-dollar bill as a monetary instrument is worth five dollars in goods and services. As a *commodity* (waste paper or perhaps a wall decoration) it is worth very little. The twenty-five-cent coin, if it were melted down and sold as metal, would be worth far less than twenty-five cents. Currency and coin are also defined as **legal tender**, which is any money the law says must be accepted as payment for all debt, public (owed to or owed by the government), or private (owed by one individual to another).

Each of the three different kinds of money—demand deposits, currency, and coin—has its own advantages and disadvantages. The convenience of paying for things through the medium of checks that transfer

TABLE 11-1 The United States' Supply of Money (as of February 1974)

Kind of money	Amount (billions of dollars)	Percent of total
Demand deposits	200.4	77
Currency	50.2	19
Coins	7.3	4
Total	257.9	100

Source: *Federal Reserve Bulletin*, February 1974.

"I'm holding onto my cash. I think money is going to come back."

demand deposits is fairly obvious. One does not have to carry large sums in currency. Most people use demand deposits most of the time to pay for all larger bills or expenses.

However, checks have two disadvantages: (1) Not everyone is willing to accept a check in economic exchange. The fear of fraud or of inadequate funds in the check payer's demand deposits, plus the trouble of collecting on bad checks, reduces the acceptability of checks as money. (2) For small purchases, a check ordering a transfer of a demand deposit is a very inefficient form of money. Imagine a child in a candy store puling out a checkbook to pay for a two-cent purchase. Coins and currency are better in such cases.

Money Is Debt

Demand deposits are liabilities of commercial banks. Currency is a liability of the Federal Reserve banks. Both are non-interest-bearing debt. In effect, the supply of money is the monetization of certain forms of debt. The commercial bank that holds your demand deposit promises to pay you in money the amount of your account when you demand it. If you go into the bank and demand the deposit, the bank will give you currency. But what is currency? A ten-dollar bill says on the face of it that it is a Federal Reserve Note. The Federal Reserve promises to pay you ten dollars for it. Like the demand deposit, the ten-dollar bill is a promise to pay. But if you go to the Federal Reserve bank and demand payment, you will receive only a new bill or change for the old one.

Since government will not exchange anything tangible for currency, like gold or silver, what is currency good for? What are demand deposits good for? Their worth lies in the fact that people are willing to exchange goods and services for them. Thus, by definition, they are money. The value of money is not the gold or silver that backs it up (there is today no gold or silver backing the U.S. supply of money), but the goods and services that the money can buy. That value depends on the *prices* of the goods and services to be bought. The lower the prices, the more a given amount of money can buy, and thus the higher the value of money.

Savings Accounts, Near Money, and Credit Cards

Savings accounts are called **time deposits**, because technically the savings bank can require that the depositor give the bank thirty days' notice before withdrawing the funds, although this is rarely done. For different purposes, economists use different definitions of the money supply. By our definition, savings accounts are excluded from the supply of money. So to keep our analyses simple, we will leave savings accounts out of the money supply.

Savings accounts are not generally considered money. You cannot take your savings account book into a supermarket and use it to buy a Thanksgiving turkey. You must convert your savings account into money (demand deposits, currency, or coin) before you can spend it. When you make a deposit in a savings institution, you transfer money—a demand deposit (if you are depositing a check) or currency (if you are using cash)—from you, the depositor, to the savings institution. To spend the savings deposit, you have to reverse the procedure.

Savings deposits, however, are the most important kind of **near money**. Near money is any asset that can be quickly and easily converted into money with little risk of loss. Another major form of near money is government securities, such as treasury bills and federal bonds. A person or economy that has lots of near money is in a *highly liquid* situation. In other words, the person or economy has a great many assets that can be quickly converted into money.

When an economy has a large amount of near money (that is, is in a highly liquid state), the average and marginal propensity to consume tends to increase. If the economy is already in an inflationary gap, high liquidity may worsen the inflation. However, if the economy is in a recession, with a deflationary gap, high liquidity may soften or cushion the contraction.

What about credit cards? Are they substitutes for money? The credit card is only a quick and convenient way to *borrow* money. At the end of the month, the borrower gets a statement of purchases made with the credit card during the month and must pay in *money* for what was charged. All a credit card does is reduce the inconvenience and risk of carrying around a large amount of money. It is not a substitute for

Credit cards: Substitutes for money? (Mike Mazzaschi/Stock, Boston)

money. But credit cards do enable people to increase their purchasing power temporarily. This can affect total demand, and thus the level of income, employment, and prices. Furthermore, the public's ability to vary purchasing power temporarily by using credit cards can make it harder for the government to carry out a stabilization policy.

The Origins of Commercial Banking: Goldsmith Banking

The origins of today's commercial bank were the goldsmiths of seventeenth-century England.

In the early 1600s in England, the safest places to store valuables were the vaults and safes of the goldsmiths of London, who made useful items out of gold. Wealthy people put their gold and silver in these vaults for safekeeping; the goldsmiths charged a fee for this watchdog service. At first, the goldsmiths had to return the same gold and silver that people had entrusted to their care. However, after a while, people said the goldsmith did not have to return the piece of gold that was deposited, just an amount of gold of equivalent value. This relaxing of the rules began a series of developments that eventually led to the modern commercial bank.

The depositor—the person who left gold with the goldsmith—received a document stating the value of the gold deposited. (This document was equivalent to your bankbook, which shows how much you have deposited.) When Lady Upton-Chase found that she needed money or wanted to buy something, she could take this document and transfer ownership of all (or any part) of the gold to a third party. She would write, "I order you, the goldsmith, to pay to the third party so-and-so much of the gold on deposit."

Thus the modern check was born. Since the goldsmiths were internationally known, these endorsements of deposits to another person were widely accepted as a means of payment. Thus, they functioned as money. Deposits of gold at goldsmiths eventually became today's demand deposits. But the story does not end there.

The goldsmith became known as a person with money to lend, and people who needed money began borrowing from the goldsmith. At first goldsmiths lent their own gold. In time, they realized that people who stored gold with them would not want that gold back for a while. There was always a certain amount of stored gold in their vaults, so they began to lend some of it. After a while the borrowers, instead of taking the gold, accepted documents stating that they had gold on deposit with the goldsmith. The borrowers would *endorse* these documents of deposit (write checks) over to those people they wished to make payments to.

The goldsmiths were soon creating documents of deposits in amounts much larger than the amounts of gold they actually had in their vaults. Since these documents attesting to deposits were accepted as payment, they functioned as money. Thus the goldsmiths, by making loans and creating deposits (attested to by documents), were creating and increasing the supply of money.

The goldsmiths, however, had to be prepared to give gold back when people presented these documents transferring deposits (checks). Not all of these documents were presented at the same time, fortunately. Thus, the goldsmiths were able to keep a reasonable supply of gold—enough to meet these demands—on hand at all times. This was the origin of fractional reserves, that is, the need to have on hand an amount of gold smaller than the total amount of deposits, to meet possible demands for withdrawal of deposits in gold.

So one sees in seventeenth-century English banking the *origins* of our modern commercial banking system: (1) deposits that can be withdrawn on demand; (2) the check as a means of transferring these deposits and the functioning of these deposits as money; (3) the practice of lending money by creating a deposit and increasing the supply of money; and (4) the need to keep reserves of gold in amounts that are fractions of total deposits, which make possible the lending and creation of new deposits, and thus a larger supply of money.

Chapter 12 will show how commercial banks today are like the goldsmiths of long ago: By their lending activities, the banks increase and decrease the amount of demand deposits, thus the money supply.

The Future of Money, or Can the Computer Replace Currency and Coin?

The kinds of money used today are demand deposits and currency and coin. Will they always be the money used? Imagine the next step in the development of money. The following may sound like fiction, but the technology needed to accomplish it exists.

Imagine an economy without currency and coin, and also without checks as you know them. Imagine a great central computer. In its memory banks are entered all expenditures and all receipts of money. All receipts of income are fed directly into the computer and added to each individual's account. No more depositing of paychecks, no more lugging around dirty, germ-covered currency and coin.

Everyone has an account. Everyone has her or his own card, perhaps keyed to the thumbprint. Every place that sells things, every place at which people make payments has terminals connected to the computer. When you buy something, you take your card, slip it into the terminal, and it types out the deduction to be made from your account at the computer.

No more bad checks. If you overdraw your account, lights will instantly flash, and a recorded voice from the computer terminal will say, "You're overdrawn." No more hours spent figuring your bank balance. You can obtain it on request from the computer. No more hiding income from the Internal Revenue Service. The computer knows all. Big Daddy will indeed have become a machine.

The Economy and the Supply of Money

How do changes in the supply of money affect the level of economic activity? Two major factors are (1) the absolute size of the supply of money and (2) the rapidity with which the supply of money changes hands in a given period of time.

For example, there are three people in the economy: Farmer Nielson, Harvey Pulaski the shoemaker, and Florrie Jackson the baker. The supply of money in the economy is $20. Florrie Jackson buys $20 worth of sausages from Farmer Nielson. Therefore, Farmer Nielson exchanges $20 worth of output for $20 in money. Farmer Nielson buys $20 worth of shoes from Harvey Pulaski, and again exchanges $20 in output for $20 in money. Finally, Harvey Pulaski buys $20 worth of bread from Florrie Jackson, and there is a further exchange of $20 in output for the same $20 in money. Although the supply of money is only $20, this $20 has changed hands three times, and the total output supported through this process is $60. Figure 11-1 shows the circular-flow diagram.

Figure 11-1 The Circular Flow of Money and Output

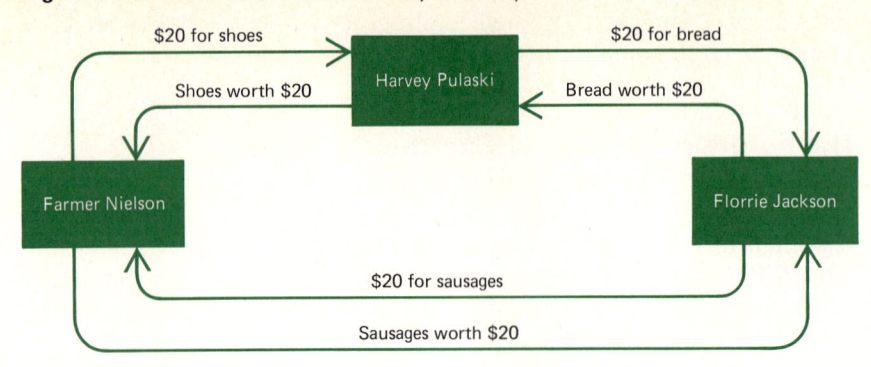

The Equation of Exchange

One can express the circular-flow process in Figure 11-1 in the form of an equation, called the **equation of exchange**:

$$MV = PQ.$$

M stands for the supply of money and V is the **velocity of exchange**, or the number of times the supply of money changes hands in a given period. One might call MV the *effective supply of money*. Also, if P is the average price level of the goods sold, and Q is transactions in physical terms and can be restricted to include only the output of net final goods and services, then PQ (the money value of that output) is *net national product* (remember national income accounting in Chapter 5).

$$MV = PQ = \text{NNP}.$$

Let's make an equation from our example: M, the supply of money, is $20; V, the velocity of exchange, is 3 (since the money changed hands 3 times); and Q, physical output, is the sausages, shoes, and bread. It can be seen that MV equals PQ, since $20 \times 3 = 20 \times 3$.

So the equation of exchange works perfectly in this extremely simple model. Although the gigantic economy of the United States, with its 215 million people and its multitude of transactions and output, is vastly more complex, it operates the same way.

(We have considered PQ as being NNP and velocity V as being essentially the velocity of income. Now we can define Q as including *all* economic transactions. We can say that Q includes the buying and selling of intermediary products, financial instruments, and even used items. When one defines transactions Q that way, velocity V is much higher. One can call it the velocity of transactions. Here, in order to keep our analysis simple, we shall consider only the velocity of income.)

The Velocity of Exchange, V

You now see that the dollar value of output PQ is determined by changes in the supply of money, and also by changes in the velocity of exchange

270   Money in the Modern Economy

TABLE 11-2 The Velocity of Exchange

	M (billions of dollars)	NNP (billions of dollars)	V
1950	116	266	2.3
1955	135	367	2.7
1960	142	460	3.3
1965	168	625	3.7
1970	215	887	4.1
1973	270	1,179	4.3

Source: *Economic Report of the President, 1974,* G.P.O., Washington, D.C.

(the number of times the money supply M changes hands). The supply of money is controlled by the monetary authority responsible for doing so. (In the United States, it is the Federal Reserve.) The velocity of exchange cannot be controlled. It depends on the structure of the financial system and on the actions of the public. One can easily measure velocity by dividing the net national product by the supply of money. Table 11-2 shows the velocity of exchange between 1950 and 1973.

Note in Table 11-2 that money is moving faster and faster. There has been a long-term increase in the velocity of exchange, from 2.3 to 4.3. So, although NNP has grown faster than the supply of money, the increase in velocity of money has offset this differential. The velocity of exchange has risen over the years because the public is able to use the supply of money more and more efficiently—for three reasons: (1) Financial institutions and financial markets have been growing both more complex and more available to the public. The increased use of savings accounts, stocks and bonds, government securities, and various forms of private short-term commercial credit has moved money more rapidly from one use to another. (2) The public has greatly increased its use of credit cards, which has cut down its need to hold money. (3) The public has increased its use of institutions such as banks and other financial structures, which has reduced its need to hold money for longer periods of time.

One must be wary about accepting this long-run increase in velocity without qualification. The dates used in Table 11-2 are mostly good years; the table does not show the contraction of velocity during recessions. When people see hard times ahead, they tend to retrench and hold onto their money longer. Businesses and consumers seek the safety of greater liquidity, that is, larger holdings of money itself—cash.

Output, Prices, and *M* (for Money)

To examine the way changes in the supply of money affect output of goods and services and their prices, we must make a simplifying assumption: We will assume that V (the velocity of exchange) is constant.

Given the equation of exchange, $MV = PQ$, when M (the supply of money) increases and V (the velocity of exchange) is constant, then PQ (the value of output) must increase. The important question is: Will P (prices) increase, or will Q (output) increase? The clue to the answer lies in the discussion of business fluctuations in Chapter 6. There we pointed out that during a recession, when there is high unemployment and excess capacity in factories, output can increase without much increase in prices. Therefore, if the United States has a recession, and the supply of money *(M)* increases, prices *(P)* will remain relatively stable and output *(Q)* will increase. We also said in Chapter 6 that as an economy approaches full employment, some resources will be in shorter supply than others, and prices will begin to increase. Therefore, as money *(M)* increases and the economy approaches full employment, prices *(P)* begin to rise, along with output *(Q)*. Obviously, when the economy is at *full* employment, any increase in the supply of *(M)* will only result in an increase in prices *(P)*. Output *(Q)* cannot increase any further, because all resources are fully employed.

If an economy wants to increase output and employment, it must increase its supply of money. On the other hand, if it wants to decrease inflation, it must decrease its supply of money.

But remember, we are assuming that the velocity of exchange *(V)* is constant. When V changes, it either reinforces or counteracts the effects of changes in the supply of money.

The Demand for Money: An Alternative

There is another way of looking at the way the supply of money affects output and prices. For many reasons, people need to hold part of their assets in the form of money. People do not receive income at the same time that they have to pay for the goods and services they buy. For example, professors are paid once a month. Although they pay the usual recurring bills on the first of the month, they must keep some money on hand to buy food, gasoline, haircuts, and so forth, for the rest of the month. This is called holding money for **transaction purposes**. People also need to hold money for emergencies: The car breaks down, the water heater springs a leak, or someone gets sick. This is called holding money for **precautionary purposes**. In addition, people hold money to take advantage of economic opportunities. Stock prices may be low, or there may be a sale on coats. One needs money on hand to take advantage of these opportunities. This is called holding money for **speculative purposes**.

Whatever the reason, people want to hold certain amounts of money. How much they hold depends on their incomes, the amounts and kinds of assets they have accumulated (durable goods, liquid assets, and so on), and their personal lifestyles. If the supply of money increases, people find themselves holding more cash than they wish, and they may invest all or part of it, or they may spend all or part of it on more consumer goods and services. Therefore, when money increases, both investment and consumption demand increase.

Suppose the supply of money decreases. Then people have less cash on hand than they want, so they have to either decrease their consumption (an uncomfortable solution) or convert other assets into cash. That is why investment and consumption demand both fluctuate with the supply of money.

Because people want to hold a certain amount of their assets in the form of money, they react when what they actually hold is not what they want to hold. If they have more assets in the form of money than they want when the supply of money increases, they increase their investments. They also buy more consumer goods. This expands the economy. Income increases, which has the effect of increasing the amount of money that people wish to hold. This process continues until what people wish to hold becomes equal to the increased supply of money. When the supply of money decreases, the reverse occurs.

Thus the two monetary approaches (the equation of exchange and the demand to hold money) lead to the same conclusions. An increase in the supply of money increases effective demand and expands the economy. A decrease in the supply of money decreases effective demand and contracts the economy.

SUMMING UP

1. When people use the *barter* system, they exchange goods for goods and do not use money. The most serious flaw in the barter system is the need for *double coincidence of demand*. That is, the person you wish to trade with must have what you want, and also want what you have.

2. When people use a *money exchange* system, they exchange goods for money and then money for goods. This is a much more efficient way to carry out the four functions money performs: (a) It is a *medium of exchange*. (b) It is a *standard of value or unit of account*. (c) It is a *store of value*. (d) It is a *means of deferred payment*.

3. The characteristics of a good money are the following: (a) It is portable, or easily carried. (b) It is easily recognized, but hard to counterfeit or duplicate. (c) It is easily subdivided. (d) It costs little to store. (e) It is durable. (f) The supply of it is relatively stable.

4. The *supply of money* in the United States is defined as all *demand deposits* and all currency and coin in circulation. About 75 percent of the supply of money is in the form of demand deposits *(checking accounts)*. *Commercial banks* are banks that can hold the demand deposits of others. *Currency* is issued by the Federal Reserve, while *coins* are minted and issued by the Treasury. *Fiat money* is any money that has

greater value as a monetary instrument than as a commodity. *Legal tender* is any money that the government says is to be accepted for all debts, public and private.

5. *Demand deposits* are debts (liabilities) of commercial banks. *Currency* is a debt (liability) of the Federal Reserve.

6. *Near money* is any asset that can be quickly and easily converted into money with little risk of loss. The two most important forms are savings accounts and federal government securities.

7. Goldsmith banking in seventeenth-century England established the basic structures of modern commercial banking.

8. One can use the *equation of exchange*, $MV = PQ$, to describe how changes in the supply of money affect economic activity. In this equation, M is the supply of money, V is the velocity of exchange, P is the price level, and Q is actual output.

9. Assuming *velocity of exchange (V)* to be constant, when the supply of money *(M)* increases, *PQ* increases. If there is unemployment and unused plant capacity as M increases, output *(Q)* increases and price *(P)* is relatively stable. As the economy approaches full employment, price *(P)* begins to increase while M is still increasing, and when the economy reaches full employment, only prices increase.

10. An alternative approach to how changes in the money supply affect economic activity examines why people hold money. They hold it for purposes of *transactions, precaution,* and *speculation*. The amounts they want to hold depend on their incomes, the quantities and kinds of assets they have, and their lifestyles.

11. When the supply of money increases, people have more money on hand than they want, and they try to convert it to other assets (invest it) or they spend it on more consumption. If the supply of money decreases, people have less money on hand than they want, and they try to increase their cash on hand by cutting back on their consumption or by reducing their investments (or both).

QUESTIONS

1. What are the four basic functions of money? How does rapid inflation affect the performance of these functions?

2. "Money is the root of all evil." Why don't we do away with it?

3. Money in the United States takes three forms: demand deposits, currency, and coins. What determines the form used for a particular purpose?

4. Suppose that our government suddenly printed up enough money to give everyone a new fifty-dollar bill. What would happen to output and prices? State clearly the assumptions you are making about employment and velocity of exchange.

5. Define the following terms:
   a. Double coincidence of demand
   b. The supply of money
   c. Near money
   d. Fiat money
   e. Commercial bank

6. What characteristics of goldsmith banking make it like the present commercial banking system?

7. What are the characteristics of a good money? Pick three commodities, and analyze their favorable and unfavorable characteristics as a good money.

8. "Money is money because people say it's money." Do you agree? Why?

9. What effect do credit cards have on the supply of money?

SUGGESTED READINGS

Chandler, Lester V. *The Economics of Money and Banking*, 6th ed. Harper & Row, New York, 1973.

Cochran, John A. *Money, Banking and the Economy*, 3d ed. Macmillan, New York, 1975. Chapters 13, 17.

Friedman, Milton. "Quantity Theory of Money." *The International Encyclopedia of the Social Sciences*, Vol. 10. Free Press, New York, 1968. Pp. 432–446.

Nadler, Paul S. *Commercial Banking in the Economy*. Random House, New York, 1973.

12

Commercial Banking and the Creation of Money

In Chapter 11 we discussed the functions, the characteristics, and a little of the history of money. We mentioned that the bulk of the money supply is in the form of demand deposits, which are held by commercial banks. So in analyzing how the supply of money is increased or decreased, and how it is controlled, we must look again at commercial banking.

The Simple Economy: Four Assumptions About a Simple Model

The U.S. banking system is so complex that the best way to approach it is to set up a simple model. We will call it the Simple Economy and make four assumptions about its banking system to enable us to analyze the process of increasing and decreasing the supply of money in simple terms. Then we will drop these assumptions, one by one, so that the analysis will gradually become more complex and realistic. Finally, we will examine that giant jigsaw puzzle, the U.S. banking system.

Here are the four simplifying assumptions:

1. There is only one bank in the Simple Economy's banking system. That bank, the First National Bank, is a monopoly bank. In other words, the First National Bank is the Simple Economy's banking system.

2. The government has no control over the First National Bank, so there are no regulations that restrict its banking activities.

3. There is no paper currency or coin. The Simple Economy's entire money supply consists of the demand deposits (checking accounts) in the First National Bank.

4. There is no international trade. This last assumption is the only one

The grass roots of banking: The teller's cage (Courtesy Management Accounting)

we will not drop later in the discussion. If we were to take international trade into account, we would make our discussion of banking transactions unnecessarily complex at this stage.

First we will analyze the process of increasing and decreasing the supply of money in the simplest model. Then we will drop assumption 3 and show what effects currency and coin have on the money supply. Then we will drop assumption 2 and show what happens when the government regulates the supply of money. Finally we will drop the assumption that there is only one bank and analyze the functioning of a multibank system with many separately incorporated banks. At that point we will analyze the U.S. banking system in relation to the supply of money.

Table 12-1 The First National Bank's Balance Sheet

Assets		Liabilities and net worth	
Loans	$1,000,000	Demand deposits	$1,000,000
Buildings and equipment	500,000	Net worth	500,000

Now let's consider the First National Bank, an established and ongoing commercial bank (Table 12-1 shows its balance sheet), with *liabilities* of $1 million, all in demand deposits. In other words, the First National owes its depositors $1 million. It also has $500,000 in *net worth*, which represents the equity or ownership of the stockholders in the bank. Last, it has $1.5 million in assets, $1 million in the form of loans. The First National has loaned that $1 million to the citizens of the Simple Economy. The other $500,000 in assets is in the form of the bank's buildings and equipment. Remember that for the First National's books to balance, the bank's assets and liabilities plus net worth have to be equal, just as they must in any company's accounting balance sheet.

The following short tables will show only *changes* in the balance sheet. This will help us focus on the effects of banking transactions on the supply of money. Note that there is only $1 million in money in the Simple Economy, and remember that all of the Simple Economy's money is in the form of demand deposits (no currency and no coin).

Money Creation in the Simple Model

Joe Bloggs, one of Simple Economy's more ambitious citizens, has made a discovery which he hopes will make him rich. He has invented mottled-gray bubble gum that will blend into sidewalks. He goes to see Elvira Snodgrass, president of the First National Bank, to tell her of his discovery. "Wonderful!" says Snodgrass. "No more of those unsightly pink blobs on our sidewalks. You'll make a pile out of this invention, son!"

When Bloggs asks to borrow $10,000 to set up a bubble-gum factory, Snodgrass approves the loan. Table 12-2 shows what happens then.

First, Bloggs signs a promissory note, stating that he will pay the bank $10,000 in six months' time. To the bank, this promissory note is an

Table 12-2 The Effect of a Loan on the First National Bank's Balance Sheet

Assets		Liabilities	
Loans	+$10,000	Demand deposits	+$10,000

asset, since Joe Bloggs now owes the First National Bank $10,000. The category "Loans" increases by $10,000. But now the First National must pay Bloggs that money he has borrowed. It does this by increasing his demand deposits at the bank by $10,000; by this act, it increases the supply of money in the Simple Economy by $10,000.

"But," you may say, "where did the First National Bank get the $10,000 to give Joe Bloggs?" The answer is simple. The bank created that demand deposit by simply writing on Bloggs's account, "plus $10,000." *The bank creates demand deposits to pay for the loans that it makes.* It cannot just take the demand deposit from somebody else's account, because what would *that* person do if he or she wanted to use that demand deposit? Nor can the bank take it from accounts in its own name, because that would mean that the bank owed money to itself, which is an absurdity. The point we are trying to make is that commercial banks create demand deposits when they make loans.

With that $10,000 demand deposit, Bloggs first hires a contractor to build his factory and pays the contractor $2,500. He makes this payment by writing a check on his account. So Bloggs's account goes down by $2,500 and the account of the contractor goes up by $2,500. There is no change in the Simple Economy's supply of money, for accounts are only transferred. Bloggs then buys machinery for $2,500, and writes another check to pay for it. Again his account shrinks by $2,500, while the machinery seller's demand deposits increase by $2,500. Again, there is no change in the supply of money, only transfers of demand deposits. When Bloggs buys raw materials for $2,500, the same thing happens. And it happens again when he hires workers and starts producing bubble gum.

In effect then, as Bloggs spends his demand deposit, his account is slowly transferred to those to whom he makes payments by writing checks. The supply of money changes hands as the demand deposit at the bank is transferred. (Isn't this like your own experience with commercial banks?)

Now Bloggs starts selling bubble gum to retail stores, which the store owners pay for by writing checks drawn on their own demand deposits. Bloggs deposits those checks, so his account increases while the accounts of the store owners decrease. Still no change in the *supply* of money. Joe makes profits, and eventually his demand deposits increase to $10,000.

Now Bloggs can pay off his promissory note to the bank. He goes to the office of President Snodgrass and writes a check for $10,000. Snodgrass writes "Paid" on the promissory note and deducts the amount from Blogg's account. (In effect, Bloggs has received and paid off an interest-free loan. To keep our analysis simple, we have avoided the subject of interest on loans.)

Table 12-3 shows the transactions on the books of the First National Bank. Note that the account called "Loans" decreases by $10,000 as Bloggs pays off the note. The First National Bank's demand deposits are also decreased by $10,000 as the bank deducts the check from Bloggs's

TABLE 12-3 Decrease in the Supply of Money

Assets		Liabilities	
Loans	−$10,000	Demand deposits	−$10,000

demand deposits. The Simple Economy's supply of money actually decreases by $10,000, for Blogg's check to the bank decreases only his own demand deposit and is not transferred to any other account.

What has this analysis showed us? (1) When a commercial bank (First National Bank) makes a loan, and creates a demand deposit in order to make the loan, the supply of money is *increased*. (2) When a loan is paid off by means of a check that decreases demand deposits, the supply of money is *decreased*.

Enter Currency and Coin

We are about to drop assumption 3 because there are two basic weaknesses in this simple model: (1) For small purchases, it is very inefficient to write checks transferring demand deposits; one needs paper currency and coin. (2) The existence of currency and coin provides an automatic check on the ability of the First National Bank to expand the supply of money.

The first weakness (no currency or coin) is apparent. When a supply of money consists only of demand deposits, all transactions, no matter how small, have to be made by checks and transferring demand deposits. The child next door buying a peppermint at the candy store must write out a check for two cents. When you buy a newspaper, you must write a check for twenty-five cents. The cost of handling checks for these small amounts is greater than the value of the transactions. Therefore, one important function of currency and coin is to provide a more efficient form of money for small-value transactions.

The second weakness is that in this simple model without currency or coin, the bank (by lending) can expand the supply of money without limit. When we introduce currency and coin, you will see that they provide an automatic check on the ability of the bank to expand loans and thus to expand the supply of money.

We said in Chapter 11 that people in the United States find it most comfortable to hold about 25 percent of the supply of money in the form of currency and coin. (This percentage varies somewhat from place to place and from one month to another.) We will assume that the Simple Economy people are like Americans. They also want to hold 25 percent of the supply of money in the form of currency and coin. And we will also assume that this percentage does not vary.

TABLE 12-4 The Effect of the Government's $1 Million Deposit of Currency and Coin on the Balance Sheet of the First National Bank

Assets		Liabilities	
Cash in vault	+ $1,000,000	Demand deposits	+ $1,000,000

Let's introduce currency and coin into the economy. The Simple Economy's government wants to spend $1 million more than it receives in taxes. To cover this deficit, it issues $1 million in currency and coin. (In Chapter 11 we said that currency and coin are really government debt.) What happens when the government deposits the currency in the First National Bank? Table 12-4 shows the effect on the First National's balance sheet.

The bank now has an asset of $1 million called "Cash in vault," and also a liability of $1 million, which is the demand deposit held by the government that represents the deposit of currency. The Simple Economy's supply of money has increased by $1 million, the demand deposit owned by the government. Remember that the actual cash in the First National Bank's vault is not yet part of the supply of money, because it is not yet in circulation.

The government spends the $1 million for various goods and services, like roads, bombers, and education. This spending transfers the demand deposit from the government to the individuals who sell these goods to the government. Remember, though, that people want 25 percent of their supply of money in the form of currency and coin. Therefore, they withdraw from their demand deposits $250,000 in cash.

Table 12-5 shows the results. Only $750,000 remains in the vault in cash, and demand deposits are only $750,000. The supply of money, however, is still $1 million consisting of $750,000 in demand deposits and $250,000 in currency and coin in circulation, in people's pockets.

Now the First National Bank has assets in a form that does not earn it any income (the $750,000 cash in its vault). The bank's officers want to put those assets to work earning income. So they lend out $1 million, which, as you already know, creates demand deposits of $1 million.

TABLE 12-5 The Effect on the First National Bank of a Withdrawal by Depositors of $250,000 in Cash from Their Demand Deposits

Assets		Liabilities	
Cash in vault	$750,000	Demand deposits	$750,000

Enter Currency and Coin

TABLE 12-6 The Effect of the First National Bank's Balance Sheet of a Second Withdrawal of $250,000 by Depositors

Assets		Liabilities	
Cash in vault	$ 500,000	Demand deposits	$1,500,000
Loans	1,000,000		

Remember that the bank can lend more money than the amount of cash it holds in its vault because the depositors want to keep only 25 percent of the supply of money in the form of currency and coin.

Now the demand deposits are $1 million fatter. What happens? Well, the people still want to keep 25 percent of the country's money in the form of currency and coin, so they withdraw *another* $250,000 in cash. Table 12-6 shows the net results. "Cash in vault" is down to $500,000 and the total of demand deposits is $1.5 million. The supply of money is now $2 million—$1.5 million in demand deposits and $500,000 in currency and coin in circulation.

The First National Bank still has assets in a form that does not earn them any income (the $500,000 "Cash in vault"). The bank's officers want to put the assets to work, so they extend *more* loans. Let's say they loan $2 million, and thereby create demand deposits of an additional $2 million. The citizens of the Simple Economy still wish to keep 25 percent of their money in the form of currency and coin. To do this they withdraw $500,000 in cash, reducing demand deposits by a like amount.

Table 12-7 shows the net results. The First National Bank's vault no longer has any cash at all. Loans and discounts are $3 million and demand deposits are $3 million. The country's supply of money is now $4 million; that is, $3 million in demand deposits and $1 million in currency and coin in circulation. If the bank extends still more loans, and thereby creates still more demand deposits, the depositors, to get the 25 percent of the total money supply in currency and coin that they want, will demand more currency than the bank has.

In effect, *the amount of currency and coin in the vaults of the bank places a limit on the amount that the bank can lend.* Since the people want to hold 25 percent of the money supply in the form of currency and coin, the country's total supply of money is limited to four times the amount of currency and coin available, or one dollar in cash for every

TABLE 12-7 The First National Bank's Balance Sheet When It Increases Loans to $3 Million

Assets		Liabilities	
Cash in vault	0	Demand deposits	$3,000,000
Loans	$3,000,000		

Enter the Federal Reserve (Courtesy Federal Reserve System)

three dollars in demand deposits. In order to increase its lending, and thus the supply of money (demand deposits), the First National Bank would have to get more currency and coin from the government.

To summarize, currency and coin perform two functions: (1) For purchases that have small value, they are a more efficient form of money than demand deposits. (2) They provide an automatic check on the ability of the bank to make loans, create demand deposits, and increase the supply of money.

Enter the Government

Let us now drop our second assumption—that there is no government regulation. The Simple Economy's government creates a Federal Reserve Bank for the purpose of controlling lending by the First National Bank. The government requires that the First National Bank keep assets in the form of reserves equal to a specific percentage of its demand deposits, and gives the Federal Reserve Bank the power to increase or decrease these reserves. (Bear in mind that the Federal Reserve is only a banker's bank. It does not engage in banking activities involving the public.)

Reserve Requirements

Remember that a bank's reserves are not demand deposits, but some form of assets that the banking authority defines as reserves. The U.S. government defines **reserves** as all deposits by banks in the Federal Reserve, plus currency and coin held in the vaults of commercial banks.

Let's say that the Simple Economy's Federal Reserve Bank defines reserves as the U.S. Federal Reserve does. This means that the First National Bank may count as reserves all First National Bank deposits at the Federal Reserve Bank, plus all currency and coin the First National Bank holds. The law says that the First National Bank must keep a minimum quantity of reserves equal to a certain percentage of its demand deposits. This percentage is called the **required reserve ratio**. For example, suppose that the required reserve ratio is 20 percent and that the First National Bank has $1 million in demand deposits. According to law, the First National Bank must have $200,000 in reserves (20 percent of $1 million) or $200,000 in deposits at the Federal Reserve Bank, and/or in currency and coin.

Table 12-8 shows that the First National Bank has $1 million in reserves and also $1 million in demand deposits. Since there is only a 20 percent required reserve ratio, to comply with the law, the First National Bank is required to hold only $200,000 of those reserves. The other $800,000 of its reserves are not required, and are called **excess reserves**. A bank's required reserves plus its excess reserves equal its *total reserves*.

Now consider the excess reserves of the First National Bank—assets it is not required to have and that are not earning income for it. What can the First National Bank do to remedy this? Table 12-9 shows the First National Bank's accounts after it lends out $1 million, which in turn creates (or increases demand deposits by) $1 million (the payment of the loan). The First National Bank's total reserves are still $1 million, because there has been no change in deposits at the Federal Reserve Bank and no change in currency and coin. All that the First National Bank has done is to create a loan, and therefore to create a demand deposit. However, demand deposits are now $2 million, and the amount of reserves that are required (which must be 20 percent of demand deposits) increases to $400,000. Excess reserves decrease, to $600,000, since some of those excess reserves now become part of required reserves.

TABLE 12-8 Reserves Versus Demand Deposits for the First National Bank

Assets		Liabilities	
Required reserves	$ 200,000	Demand deposits	$1,000,000
Excess reserves	800,000		
Total reserves	$1,000,000		

TABLE 12-9 The First National Bank's Accounts After It Lends $1 Million (thus increasing demand deposits by $1 million)

Assets		Liabilities	
Required reserves	$ 400,000	Demand deposits	$2,000,000
Excess reserves	600,000		
Total reserves	$1,000,000		
Loans	$1,000,000		

The First National Bank still has $600,000 worth of non-income-earning assets (the remaining excess reserves of $600,000). Table 12-10 shows that the bank's officers finally increase their loans by $3 million, which increases demand deposits by the same amount, to $5 million. Nothing has happened to the First National Bank's total reserves because there has been no change in either its deposits at the Federal Reserve or its holdings of currency and coin. However, required reserves (20 percent of demand deposits) now equal total reserves, and there are no excess reserves left in the bank. So the First National Bank cannot lend another penny to anyone.

Each time a bank extends loans and creates demand deposits, its required reserves must increase by 20 percent of the increase in demand deposits. Since the act of lending and creating demand deposits does not affect total reserves, this increase in required reserves must come out of excess reserves. Now the First National Bank has reached the position (see Table 12-10) of zero excess reserves. It cannot lend any more money, because, if it tried to, the law would require it to hold more reserves than it has, and it would be violating the banking laws. The bank must have excess reserves before it can lend more and increase its demand deposits further. These excess reserves can then quickly become required reserves to comply with the law that specifies 20 percent required reserves.

In comparing Tables 12-8, 12-9, and 12-10, one can see that $800,000 in excess reserves enables the bank to create five times that amount in demand deposits. Because the required reserve ratio is 20 percent, the

TABLE 12-10 The First National Bank's Accounts After It Lends $3 Million More and Reduces Its Excess Reserves to Zero

Assets		Liabilities	
Required reserves	$1,000,000	Demand deposits	$5,000,000
Excess reserves	0		
Total reserves	$1,000,000		
Loans	$4,000,000		

First National Bank can expand the supply of money by five times its excess reserves. This means that it needs only one dollar of reserves for every five dollars of demand deposits. This is the bank's **fractional reserve requirement**. If the required reserve ratio were to be increased by 50 percent, the bank would need one dollar of reserves to create two dollars of demand deposits. If the required reserves were to be increased still further, to 100 percent, the bank would have to hold one dollar for every dollar it loaned. In other words, required reserves and demand deposits would have to be equal.

Enter Many Other Banks

Now remember the first assumption that the First National Bank is the only commercial bank in Simple Economy. It is a *monopoly* bank; it is, in fact, the entire commercial banking system. A monopoly bank can lend money and create demand deposits (money) that are a multiple of its excess reserves. The First National Bank can do this because depositors cannot write checks and deposit them in other banks. There *are* no other banks.

The behavior of an individual commercial bank in a multibank system differs from that of a monopoly bank with respect to its excess reserves, lending, and creation of demand deposits.

Now we will drop the assumption that there is only one bank, a monopoly bank, in the economy. Let's assume that there are more than 13,000 separately incorporated, privately owned, commercial banks, and that the economy being discussed is the U.S. economy. Now we can begin to analyze the U.S. banking system.

The Federal Reserve and Clearing Checks

In the United States, there are *twelve* Federal Reserve Banks, each of which serves one large district. And a Federal Reserve Bank performs an important function not previously discussed: It serves as a national clearinghouse for checks. Now what does that mean?

In our system, with its many commercial banks, you can write a check on your account in one bank and have it deposited in an account in another bank. How do banks collect or receive payment for such checks from other banks? They do it through the Federal Reserve (Fed) collection process.

Table 12-11 shows what changes take place in this collection process. You write a check for $1,000 on a demand deposit in the Bank of America in California, and this check is deposited in the First National Bank of Boston. The demand deposits in the First National Bank of Boston are increased by $1,000. To collect its money, the First National Bank sends the check to the Federal Reserve, which increases the First National Bank's deposits with the Fed. In other words, the reserves of the First National Bank increase by $1,000. Meanwhile, back at the

TABLE 12-11 The Effect of One Check on the Federal Reserve and Two of Its Member Banks

Bank of America		Federal Reserve	First National Bank of Boston	
Assets	Liabilities	Deposits	Assets	Liabilities
Reserves −$1,000	Demand deposits −$1,000	First National Bank of Boston +$1,000 Bank of America −$1,000	Reserves +$1,000	Demand deposits +$1,000

Bank of America, the situation is the opposite. The Federal Reserve reduces the Bank of America's deposits with the Fed by $1,000. In other words, the reserves of the Bank of America decrease by $1,000. The Federal Reserve then sends the canceled check to the Bank of America, which reduces *your* demand deposits by $1,000.

In brief, in a multibank system, when a check is drawn on an account in Alpha Bank and deposited in Bravo Bank, there is a transfer of both demand deposits and reserves (deposits at the Federal Reserve). The Federal Reserve acts as the third party, the go-between.

Lending by Individual Banks: A Little Goes a Long Way

Now we are going to deal with a number of independent banks in the Federal Reserve System. Let's call our four representative banks Alpha, Bravo, Charlie, and Delta.

An individual bank in a multibank system can lose both demand deposits and reserves overnight to other banks, through a flow of checks. Therefore, Alpha Bank—an individual bank in a multibank system—cannot lend money and create demand deposits that are a multiple of its excess reserves. Alpha Bank, following a conservative rule, lends an amount *equal only to its own excess reserves*. If it lends more, it runs the risk of losing (through a flow of checks) so much of its reserves that it cannot meet the law's reserve requirements.

Table 12-12 shows the changes in the relevant accounts for Alpha Bank as it applies this rule. Part a shows that Alpha Bank, before it lends $800,000, has $1 million of established demand deposits. On the basis of its past experience, Alpha Bank estimates that these deposits will remain within the bank. Alpha Bank also has $1 million in reserves, of which $200,000 are required and $800,000 are excess, since the required reserve ratio is 20 percent.

Part b of Table 12-12 shows Alpha Bank lending only an amount equal to its excess reserves. Suppose, however, that the worst occurs (part c) and that all these new demand deposits flow out as checks to *other* banks, for example, to Bravo Bank.

TABLE 12-12

(a) Alpha Bank before it lends $800,000	
Assets	Liabilities
Required reserves $200,000	Demand deposits $1,000,000
Excess reserves $800,000	
Total reserves $1,000,000	

(b) Alpha Bank after it lends $800,000	
Assets	Liabilities
Reserves $1,000,000	Demand deposits $1,800,000
Loans $800,000	

(c) Alpha Bank after checks have cleared	
Assets	Liabilities
Reserves $200,000	Demand deposits $1,000,000
Loans $800,000	

(d) Bravo Bank after receiving checks	
Assets	Liabilities
Reserves $800,000	Demand deposits $800,000

Bravo Bank now has an increase in demand deposits of $800,000 (part d). It sends these checks to the Federal Reserve, which promptly increases Bravo's deposits there by $800,000 and at the same time reduces Alpha's deposits there by $800,000. The Federal Reserve then sends the canceled checks to Alpha Bank, which duly notes the fact that its demand deposits have shrunk by $800,000.

Part c shows us, however, that even though Alpha Bank has lost $800,000 in reserves and demand deposits, it can still meet its obligations. It still has its required reserves ($200,000 in reserves is adequate because the bank has $1 million in demand deposits and the required reserve ratio is 20 percent).

In Table 12-13, part a shows that Bravo Bank now has excess reserves of $640,000. Part b shows Bravo lending up to its limit of $640,000, thereby creating demand deposits of $640,000.

Now suppose the worst happens (part c). All the checks drawn on Bravo Bank's newly created demand deposits flow to Charlie Bank. Charlie Bank now has an increase in its demand deposits of $640,000. Charlie sends these checks to the Federal Reserve, which increases Charlie Bank's deposits with the Federal Reserve (and its own reserves) by $640,000 (part d). At the same time, the Fed deducts $640,000 from Bravo Bank's deposits at the Fed (and lowers Bravo's reserves by that amount). When Bravo gets these canceled checks back, it records the information that it has $640,000 less in demand deposits.

Table 12-13

<table>
<tr><th colspan="2" align="center">(a) Bravo Bank before
it lends $640,000</th><th colspan="2" align="center">(b) Bravo Bank after
it lends $640,000</th></tr>
<tr><th>Assets</th><th>Liabilities</th><th>Assets</th><th>Liabilities</th></tr>
<tr><td>Required reserves
$160,000
Excess reserves
$640,000
Total reserves
$800,000</td><td>Demand deposits
$800,000</td><td>Reserves
$800,000

Loans
$640,000</td><td>Demand deposits
$1,440,000</td></tr>
<tr><th colspan="2" align="center">(c) Bravo Bank after
checks have cleared</th><th colspan="2" align="center">(d) Charlie Bank after
receiving checks</th></tr>
<tr><th>Assets</th><th>Liabilities</th><th>Assets</th><th>Liabilities</th></tr>
<tr><td>Reserves
$160,000

Loans
$640,000</td><td>Demand deposits
$800,000</td><td>Reserves
$640,000</td><td>Demand deposits
$640,000</td></tr>
</table>

Bravo Bank has followed the rule and lent only as much as it held in excess reserves. Even though it has lost the newly created demand deposits and equivalent reserves, it can still satisfy the legal reserve requirement.

We could continue to analyze this process at great length. At each round of lending, the excess reserves diminish (as excess reserves are reclassified as required reserves), so that excess reserves decrease as they move through the banking system. Note that each bank can lend only to the limit of its excess reserves, creating demand deposits (money) to pay for the loans. However, as excess reserves filter through all the banks, the whole banking system makes loans and creates demand deposits that are a multiple of the original excess reserves in Alpha Bank.

Table 12-14 shows what happens. Alpha Bank created $800,000 in demand deposits. This money, by means of checks, was transferred to Bravo Bank. Bravo Bank took this $800,000 and created $640,000 in demand deposits. If we had continued our analysis, you would have seen that Charlie Bank then created $512,000 in demand deposits. And when that money got over to Delta Bank, Delta Bank created $409,600. As the money went further and further, the other banks in the system created $1,638,400. Because the required reserve ratio is 20 percent, the whole banking system could create $4 million in new demand deposits, even though each bank made loans and generated new demand deposits only

TABLE 12-14 Demand Deposits Created

Bank	Amount
Alpha Bank	$ 800,000
Bravo Bank	640,000
Charlie Bank	512,000
Delta Bank	409,600
Rest of the banks	1,638,400
	$4,000,000

up to the amount of its excess reserves. If each bank lends an amount equal to its excess reserves and uses only demand deposits to pay out money for the loans, the formula for the deposit multiplier is:

$$DM = \frac{1}{R},$$

where R is the required reserve ratio. In our example above, R is 20 percent. The deposit multiplier equals

$$\frac{1}{.20} \quad \text{or} \quad 5.$$

But There Are Leakages

We have seen that it is technically possible, with a 20 percent required reserve ratio, for banks to have a maximum potential of creating new demand deposits five times the original excess reserves. However, the full multiple creation of demand deposits rarely takes place. There are what are called **leakages** in the process, which reduce the ability of the commercial banks to expand demand deposits.

1. Suppose that people who borrow from the bank withdraw currency and coin from their demand deposits. This has the effect of withdrawing reserves from the banking system, thus reducing the amount of demand deposits that can be created. For example, suppose that when Alpha Bank lends out the original $800,000, one of the borrowers demands $100,000 in currency as payment, instead of a demand deposit. So, instead of $800,000 in checks being transferred from Alpha Bank to Bravo Bank, only $700,000 in checks is transferred. Reserves (deposits at the Federal Reserve) shifted from Alpha to Bravo are $700,000 (not $800,000). Bravo's excess reserves are thus $560,000, not $640,000. Bravo Bank cannot make as many new loans or create as large demand deposits, and this effect is passed on through the rest of the system. The $100,000 taken as currency in payment of loans at Alpha Bank reduces the original excess reserves in the banking system, and thus the total of new loans and demand deposits.

Banks often encourage loans by individual consumers as well as by businesses. (Courtesy The Boston Five)

2. We have assumed so far that each independent bank lends up to the limit of its excess reserves, that it lends every penny it can, provided it can maintain enough reserves to meet the legal minimum. In practice, bankers are often much more conservative and want to keep a cushion or extra reserve in case checks are drawn against them in amounts greater than the amounts of the new demand deposits. What if some depositors write checks against Alpha Bank's original deposits and this money flows into other banks? If Alpha has not kept some of its excess reserves on hand, it will not be able to meet these unexpected transfers of demand deposits and reserves. However, if banks do lend out amounts less than their excess reserves, then the amount of the demand deposits created in the system is much less.

But There Are Leakages   291

3. The fact that the banking system has excess reserves (the ability to make loans) does not mean that there are always good opportunities to lend. During a business slump, bankers may fear that some potential borrowers will not be able to repay loans. So when times are bad, bankers may not lend up to the maximum. Also, at times there may not be much demand for loans even when interest rates are low.

When we take these leakages into consideration, the formula for the deposit multiplier becomes more complex:

$$DM = \frac{1}{R+E+C},$$

where R is the required reserve ratio, E is excess reserves *not* used by the banking system, and C is the currency withdrawn by those receiving loans.

A Final Word About Excess Reserves

In our analysis of the way money is created under government regulation, we have pointed out the crucial role of excess reserves. Without excess reserves, banks cannot extend loans and create demand deposits. Therefore, control over the amounts of reserves in the banking system means control over the amount of lending that is done, and, by extension, control over the supply of money itself.

In the United States, the key institution in this control is the Federal Reserve Bank. Only the Federal Reserve has the power to increase or decrease the required amount of excess reserves in the banking system.

SUMMING UP

1. Our analysis of the banking system of the imaginary Simple Economy is based on four assumptions: (a) There is only one bank in the system, the First National Bank. (b) There are no government regulations. (c) There is no currency or coin. The economy's supply of money is limited to the amount of demand deposits in the First National Bank. (d) There is no international trade.

2. The First National Bank increases the supply of money by extending loans, which are paid to the borrower by creating new demand deposits. The borrowers pay off the loans by checks drawn on their demand deposits. This decreases the supply of money in the economy.

3. The Simple Economy banking system, limited by our four assumptions, has the following weaknesses: (a) For purchases of small value,

demand deposits are a very inefficient form of money. (b) The First National Bank's ability to expand the supply of money through lending is unlimited. But we can counter these weaknesses by dropping our third assumption and introducing currency and coin.

4. People like to hold a certain percentage of a nation's money in the form of currency and coin. The amount of currency and coin can provide an automatic check on a bank's ability to extend loans and increase demand deposits. As the bank lends out money, it creates more demand deposits, and demand deposits are money. Then people withdraw more currency and coin from the bank in order to maintain that desired percentage of the money supply in the form of currency and coin. When the bank no longer has any currency and coin left in its vaults, it can no longer lend, and create demand deposits.

5. Varying the quantity of currency and coin is not an efficient way to regulate the total money supply. A more efficient system is to (a) establish a central bank, such as the Federal Reserve System, (b) require commercial banks to keep assets in the form of reserves equal to a certain percentage of demand deposits, and (c) empower the central bank (the Federal Reserve in the case of the United States) to vary the amount of reserves. In the U.S. banking system, *reserves* are defined as deposits of commercial banks at the Federal Reserve plus cash in the vaults of the commercial banks.

6. In a one-bank (monopoly) system, loaning money creates demand deposits, but does not affect total reserves. However, in a system that has a government-imposed *required reserve ratio*, an increase in demand deposits raises the figure for required reserves. Banks must then count their *excess reserves* as part of their required reserves. When all its reserves come under the heading of "required," a commercial bank cannot extend loans, because it has no more excess reserves that it can reclassify as required reserves when demand deposits increase.

7. Because the required-reserve ratio is less than 100 percent—that is, it is *fractional*—commercial banks can create demand deposits that are a multiple of their reserves.

8. In our simple model of the banking system in the Simple Economy, the monopoly bank need not be concerned about a flow of checks and reserves to other banks because there is only one bank in the system. Therefore, a monopoly bank can expand the supply of money (create demand deposits) by lending out money equal to a multiple of its reserves. The size of the multiplier depends on the size of the required reserve ratio.

9. When we drop the assumption that there is only one bank and assume that there are 13,000 banks, with the Federal Reserve controlling all of them, we are approximating a model of the U.S. banking system. The Federal Reserve acts as a national clearinghouse for checks. When Alpha Bank receives a check from Bravo Bank, Alpha sends it to the

Federal Reserve. The Federal Reserve increases Alpha's deposits (reserves) with the Federal Reserve and reduces Bravo's deposits (reserves) with the Fed. When Bravo Bank receives the check, it reduces the demand-deposit account on which it is drawn.

10. When checks flow from one bank to another, both reserves and demand deposits are transferred. To avoid letting its reserves fall below the required level, an individual bank in a multibank system makes loans (and thus creates demand deposits) only up to the level of its excess reserves. But as these excess reserves gradually filter through the banking system, the banking system creates demand deposits (money) that are a multiple of the original excess reserves.

11. In the real world, the banking system does not increase the supply of money by the full multiple of its excess reserves because of the following *leakage* effects: (a) Some borrowers want currency instead of demand deposits in payment for their loans, which has the effect of withdrawing reserves from the banking system, thus reducing the amount of demand deposits that can be created. (b) Some banks will not lend up to the limit of their excess reserves because they fear that an unexpected flow of checks to another bank might drain off reserves not only from their new demand deposits, but also from old demand deposits. (c) If there is a business slump, some banks will not lend money up to the limit of their excess reserves, because they fear that some loans will not be repaid. Sometimes, too, there is not enough demand for loans, even when interest rates are low.

QUESTIONS

1. What effects do the following transactions have on the demand deposits and reserves of Alpha Bank? Of the whole commercial banking system? Why? (The required reserve ratio is 20 percent.)
   a. Ernie Jones withdraws $100 from his demand deposit account in Alpha Bank.
   b. Susan Smith borrows $500 from Alpha Bank, but puts the proceeds into Bravo Bank.
   c. Betty Cohen deposits $200 in her account at Alpha Bank by a check drawn on someone else's account at Alpha Bank.
   d. Susan Smith pays off her loan at Alpha Bank by a check drawn on her account at Alpha Bank.

2. What effects do these four transactions have on the supply of money? Why?

3. Why must a commercial bank maintain a certain level of reserves under the U.S. banking system? What are excess reserves, and what is their significance?

4. In a commercial banking system, how is the supply of money increased and decreased?

5. In a multibank system, an individual bank makes loans only up to the level of its excess reserves, while the whole commercial banking system can lend out money that is a multiple of the original bank's excess reserves. Why is there this difference?

6. What leakages can prevent a commercial banking system from lending at the full multiple of its original excess reserves?

SUGGESTED READINGS

Barger, Albert E. *The Money Supply Process.* Wadsworth, Belmont, Calif., 1971

Chandler, Lester V. *The Economics of Money and Banking,* 6th ed. Harper & Row, New York, 1973. Chapters 6 and 7.

Klein, John J. *Money and the Economy,* 2d ed. Harcourt Brace Jovanovich, New York, 1974. Chapters 5–7.

U.S. Congress, House Subcommittee on Domestic Finance, Committee on Banking and Currency. *A Primer on Money.* 88th Congress, 2nd session, August 5, 1964.

Application 10   *First Steps in Banking*

The following selection from *Punch*, the British humor magazine, requires no introduction.

Q. What are banks for?
A. To make money.
Q. For the customers?
A. For the banks.
Q. Why doesn't bank advertising mention this?
A. It would not be in good taste. But it is mentioned by implication in references to Reserves of £249,000,000 or thereabouts. That is the money they have made.
Q. Out of the customers?
A. I suppose so.
Q. They also mention Assets of £500,000,000 or thereabouts. Have they made that too?
A. Not exactly. That is the money they use to make money.
Q. I see. And they keep it in a safe somewhere?

Application 10   295

A. Not at all. They lend it to customers.
Q. Then they haven't got it?
A. No.
Q. Then how is it Assets?
A. They maintain that it would be if they got it back.
Q. But they must have some money in a safe somewhere?
A. Yes, usually £500,000,000 or thereabouts. This is called Liabilities.
Q. But if they've got it, how can they be liable for it?
A. Because it isn't theirs.
Q. Then why do they have it?
A. It has been lent to them by customers.
Q. You mean customers lend banks money?
A. In effect. They put money into their accounts, so it is really lent to the banks.
Q. And what do the banks do with it?
A. Lend it to other customers.
Q. But you said that money they lent to other people was Assets?
A. Yes.
Q. Then Assets and Liabilities must be the same thing?
A. You can't really say that.
Q. But you've just said it. If I put £100 into my account the bank is liable to have to pay it back, so it's Liabilities. But they go and lend it to someone else, and he is liable to have to pay it back, so it's Assets. It's the same £100, isn't it?
A. Yes. But ...
Q. Then it cancels out. It means, doesn't it, that banks haven't really any money at all?
A. Theoretically....
Q. Never mind theoretically. And if they haven't any money where do they get their Reserves of £249,000,000 or thereabouts?
A. I told you. That is the money they have made.
Q. How?
A. Well, when they lend your £100 to someone they charge him interest.
Q. How much?
A. It depends on the Bank Rate. Say five and a half per cent. That's their profit.
Q. Why isn't it my profit? Isn't it my money?
A. It's the theory of banking practice that ...
Q. When I lend them my £100 why don't I charge them interest?
A. You do.
Q. You don't say. How much?
A. It depends on the Bank Rate. Say half a per cent.
Q. Grasping of me, rather?
A. But that's only if you're not going to draw the money out again.
Q. But of course, I'm going to draw it out again. If I hadn't wanted to draw it out again I could have buried it in the garden, couldn't I?
A. They wouldn't like you to draw it out again.
Q. Why not? If I keep it there you say it's a Liability. Wouldn't they be glad if I reduced their Liabilities by removing it?
A. No. Because if you remove it they can't lend it to anyone else.
Q. But if I wanted to remove it they'd have to let me?
A. Certainly.
Q. But suppose they've already lent it to another customer?
A. Then they'll let you have someone else's money.
Q. But suppose he wants his too ... and they've let me have it?
A. You're being purposely obtuse.
Q. I think I'm being acute. What if everyone wanted their money at once?
A. It's the theory of banking practice that they never would.
Q. So what banks bank on is not having to meet their commitments?
A. I wouldn't say that.
Q. Naturally. Well, if there's nothing else you think you can tell me ...?
A. Quite so. Now you can go off and open a banking account.
Q. Just one last question.
A. Of course.
Q. Wouldn't I do better to go off and open a bank?

13

The Fed Again: Monetary Policy and the Role of a Central Bank

Money affects the economy in so many vital ways that no government can allow the process of increasing or decreasing the supply of money to go unregulated. Regulation is important because one can influence the level of employment and prices, by varying the supply of money.

In the United States, the institution that regulates the lending activities of commercial banks, and thus the supply of money, is the Federal Reserve. In this chapter we shall examine the structure of the Fed and how it controls the amount of lending and the supply of money.

Following this chapter there are two applications. Application 11 explores the argument between the monetarists and the Keynesians over the role of the supply of money in government policy making. How important is money? Application 12 discusses the multiplicity of independent authorities that formulate and execute government policy on economic stabilization. Does the United States have too many?

The Structure of the Federal Reserve

Where do *banks* go when they want to go to the bank? They go to a Federal Reserve Bank, which is a banker's bank.

When Congress passed the Federal Reserve Act of 1914, it did not create just one bank. It divided the country into twelve Federal Reserve Districts, with a Federal Reserve Bank in each. Figure 13-1 shows the twelve districts and the location of the twelve Federal Reserve Banks. For example, the first Federal Reserve District takes in all of New England. Its Federal Reserve Bank is in Boston. The twelfth district consists of seven western states plus Alaska and Hawaii. Its bank is in San Francisco.

All **national banks** (commercial banks chartered by the federal government) are required to be members of the Federal Reserve Sys-

Figure 13-1 Boundaries of Federal Reserve Districts and Their Branch Territories (*Source: Federal Reserve Bulletin.* Reproduced by permission of the Board of Governors of the Federal Reserve System.)

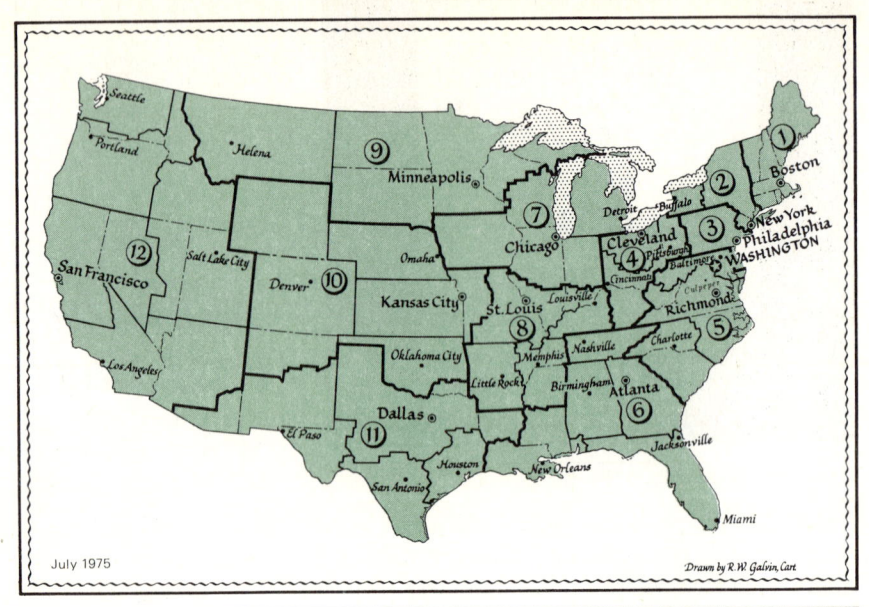

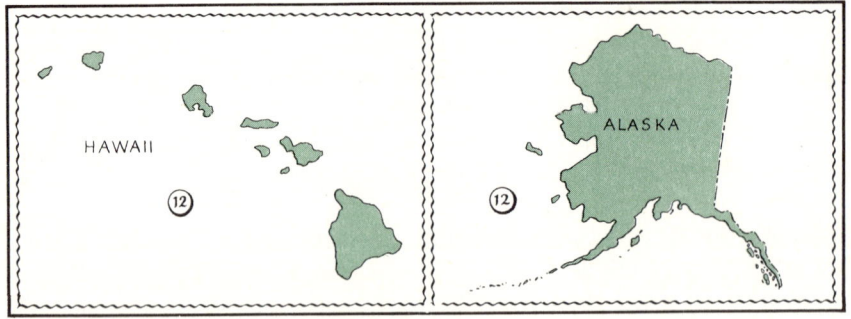

— Boundaries of Federal Reserve Districts   — Boundaries of Federal Reserve Branch Territories
★ Board of Governors of the Federal Reserve System
⊙ Federal Reserve Bank cities   • Federal Reserve Branch cities
• Federal Reserve Bank facilities

tem. **State banks** (commercial banks chartered by the various state governments) can join it if they wish. Slightly fewer than half of U.S. commercial banks are members of the Federal Reserve System. They comprise the larger commercial banks in the United States, and control more than 70 percent of U.S. banking assets.

Each Federal Reserve Bank is technically owned by the commercial member banks in its district. On becoming a member, each commercial bank must buy stock in its local Federal Reserve Bank, the amount depending on the size of its capital surplus. It receives a fixed 6 percent annual dividend on these shares.

The main policy-making body of the Federal Reserve is the board of governors, in Washington, D.C. There are seven governors, who are appointed for terms of fourteen years by the President, with the advice and consent of the Senate. Like the Supreme Court, the Board of Governors of the Federal Reserve is substantially independent of the executive branch of government. Only rarely has a President had the chance to appoint a majority of the board of governors, since a President ordinarily appoints a new member only once every two years. Therefore, a President who wanted to play God with the nation's money supply would not be able to do so unless all seven members of the Board of Governors of the Federal Reserve died or resigned at the same time. A nice built-in safety valve, isn't it?

There are two main committees that help the board of governors formulate policy:

1. *The Federal Open Market Committee* controls decision making about the most important weapon the Fed has in controlling excess reserves, lending, and the supply of money: open market operations, which we will say more about later. In addition to the seven governors, the committee consists of certain others appointed by the board, who do the day-by-day work.

2. *The Federal Advisory Council* consists of twelve people, one from each of the twelve boards of directors of the Federal Reserve Banks. They advise the governors about problems in the various districts of the system.

Each of the twelve Federal Reserve Banks has a nine-member board of directors. Three are appointed by the board of governors in Washington, to represent the national interest. Three are elected by the member commercial banks—one from the large banks, one from the medium-size banks, and one from the small banks; they represent banking interests in the particular district. These six appoint the remaining three, who represent the general economic community. (A congressional report in August 1976, however, charged that only big business interests were represented.)

So we see a mixture of both private and public elements in the Federal Reserve System. The national board of governors, with its two main support committees and its three appointed members on each board of directors of the twelve Federal Reserve Banks, is the public element. The ownership of the twelve district Federal Reserve Banks by the commercial banks in that district, plus the fact that the commercial banks appoint three members to the board of directors of their district Federal Reserve Bank, is the private element.

General Powers of the Federal Reserve

In Chapter 12 we pointed out that commercial banks must have excess reserves in order to make loans and create demand deposits, and that as a bank increases its demand deposits, it must transfer or reclassify excess reserves as required reserves. Also, in a multibank system, the individual commercial bank needs a safe margin of excess reserves in case its customers decide to write an unexpectedly large number of checks, thereby transferring demand deposits and reserves to other banks.

The device we used in Chapter 12 to explain the central bank was a hypothetical economy, Simple Economy, with one central bank that had the power to vary the amount of excess reserves held by commercial banks. This power is called the **general power** because it enables a central bank to increase or decrease the excess reserves that a commercial bank must have in order to make any kind of loan.

The U.S. Federal Reserve has three powers over excess reserves: open-market operations, the discount rate, and the required reserve ratio.

Open-Market Operations

What is for sale in the open market? Debt instruments that are short term (maturing in ninety days to one year), highly liquid (easily sold for a cash return), and relatively free of risk. Examples are *prime commercial paper* (promissory notes of large secure corporations), *banker's acceptances* (short-term debt of banks), and *Treasury bills* (short-term debt of the federal government).

In the open market, the Federal Reserve is an important customer. It buys and sells already issued federal government debt (primarily Treasury bills), which has the effect of increasing or decreasing excess reserves in the commercial banking system. This effect makes open-market operations the most important of the Fed's three weapons. The added advantage of this weapon is that it can be applied selectively. Remember that in open-market operations, the bonds are not bought directly from the government.

1. *Increasing reserves.* To increase a commercial bank's excess reserves, the Federal Reserve buys government-debt securities in the open market, as shown in Figure 13-2.

Let's say that a certain commercial bank, Alpha Bank, has custom-

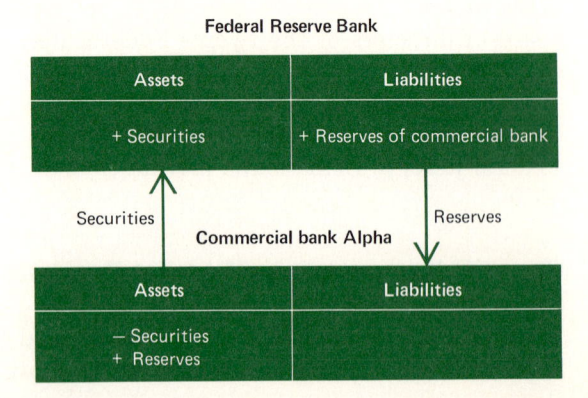

Figure 13-2 Changes in Assets and Liabilities of both the Federal Reserve Bank and the Commercial Bank When the Commercial Bank Sells Government Securities to the Federal Reserve

ers begging for loans, but Alpha does not have enough excess reserves to lend any more money or to create any more demand deposits. Along comes the Fed and buys some assets—government securities—from Alpha Bank. To pay for these assets, the Fed increases Alpha Bank's deposits with the Federal Reserve. This means that the Fed is taking on a liability. Alpha Bank is exchanging its government securities for a deposit at the Federal Reserve Bank. So Alpha's total reserves increase, and thus its excess reserves also increase.

But what happens when the Federal Reserve buys government securities from *non*commercial banking institutions or from private individuals? (See Figure 13-3.) Along comes an ordinary citizen, Joe Reed. The Fed buys a government security from him and gives him a check in return. Reed deposits the check in his account at his commercial bank, Alpha Bank. Alpha sends the check to the Federal Reserve, which increases Alpha's deposit with the Fed. That is, it increases Alpha Bank's reserves. The Federal Reserve has an increase in its assets (the government security it bought from Joe Reed) and an equal increase in its liabilities (the deposits of the commercial bank at the Fed). Joe Reed's total assets are unchanged. The decrease in his holdings of government securities is exactly equal to the increase in his demand deposits. The effect of all this on Alpha Bank is an increase in assets (its reserves increase because its deposits with the Federal Reserve increase), and an increase in liabilities (Reed's demand deposit account). Thus Alpha Bank's total reserves have increased and, therefore, so have its excess reserves.

Figure 13-3 Changes in Assets and Liabilities of the Federal Reserve Bank, Plain Citizen Joe Reed, and Commercial Bank Alpha When the Federal Reserve Bank Buys Government Securities from a Private Citizen

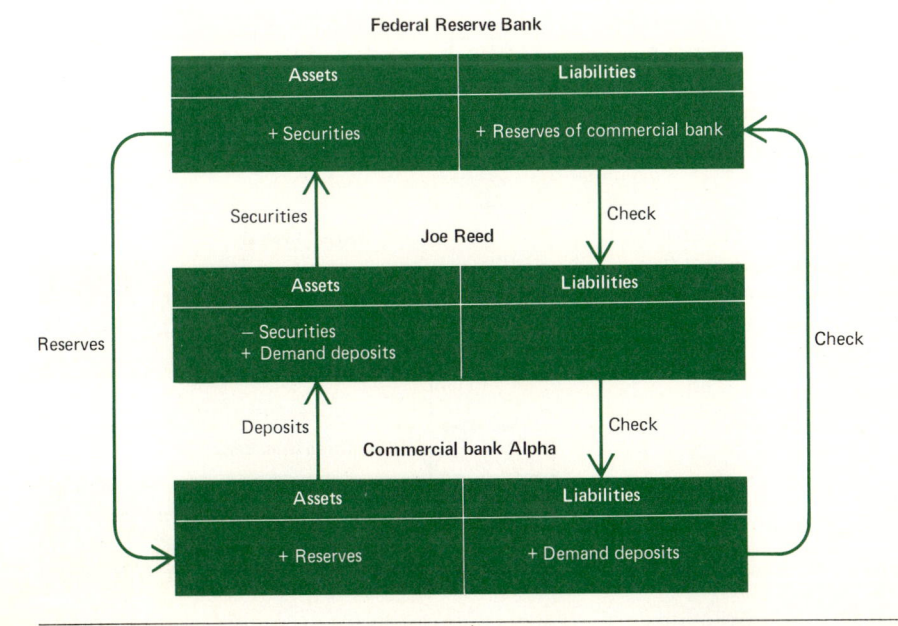

Federal Reserve Bank

Assets	Liabilities
+ Securities	+ Reserves of commercial bank

Joe Reed

Assets	Liabilities
− Securities + Demand deposits	

Commercial bank Alpha

Assets	Liabilities
+ Reserves	+ Demand deposits

General Powers of the Federal Reserve 301

2. *Decreasing reserves.* To decrease a commercial bank's excess reserves, and also to decrease its total reserves, the Federal Reserve sells government securities. Figure 13-4 shows how this works.

First, the Federal Reserve sells the government security to a commercial bank (Bravo Bank). When Bravo Bank buys a government security from the Fed, it pays for it by accepting a reduction in its deposits with the Federal Reserve. The Fed's assets decrease (by the amount of the securities sold to Bravo Bank). Its liabilities also decrease, because Bravo Bank's deposits with the Fed decrease. This means that Bravo Bank's total reserves decline. Therefore, Bravo Bank's excess reserves decline.

How does it affect excess reserves and the supply of money when the Federal Reserve sells government securities to *non*commercial banking institutions, or to private individuals? Figure 13-5 shows what happens.

Here is Maria Deluca, citizen, who buys a government security from the Fed and gives a check in return. The Fed collects on the check by reducing the deposits with the Fed of Charlie Bank, the commercial bank that holds Deluca's demand deposits. The Fed sends Deluca's check to Charlie Bank, which reduces the amount of demand deposits in her account. The Fed's assets decrease by the amount of the securities sold to Deluca. There is an offsetting decrease in the Fed's liabilities (Charlie Bank's deposits with the Federal Reserve). The total assets of Maria Deluca are unchanged. Her holdings of government securities increase and her demand deposits decrease by equal amounts. Charlie Bank's assets decrease (its reserves—that is, its deposits at the Federal Reserve—are less) and there is an equal decrease in its liabilities (the demand deposits of Maria Deluca).

Therefore, when the Federal Reserve sells government securities, the effect is to reduce total reserves, and thus to reduce excess reserves of the whole commercial banking system. Because of this decrease in the excess reserves of commercial banks, their lending ability decreases, and so does their power to increase demand deposits (the supply of money).

Figure 13-4 What Happens to Assets and Liabilities of the Federal Reserve Bank and Commercial Bank Bravo When the Fed Sells Government Securities to Commercial Bank Bravo

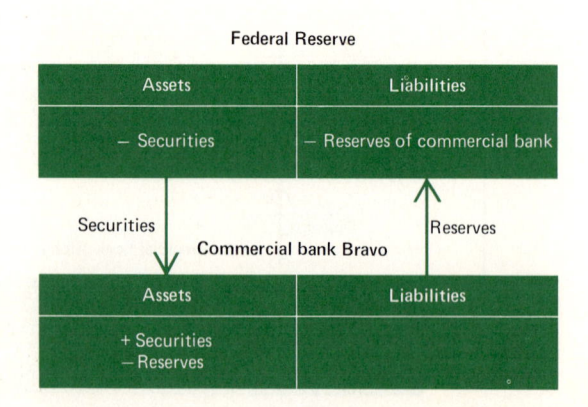

Federal Reserve	
Assets	Liabilities
− Securities	− Reserves of commercial bank

Commercial bank Bravo	
Assets	Liabilities
+ Securities − Reserves	

The Discount Rate

The Federal Reserve Bank, as we have said, is a banker's bank to its commercial bank members: It holds deposits for them and helps collect or clear checks between commercial banks. The Fed also makes loans to member commercial banks by buying either their promissory notes or by buying from the banks IOUs of nonbanking corporations or individuals defined as acceptable by the Fed. When the Fed buys such promissory notes, it deposits the proceeds in the commercial bank's Federal Reserve account, increasing the bank's total reserves, and thus increasing its excess reserves.

The commercial banks do not get all these services free. The Federal Reserve Bank charges interest for making these loans. It is called a *discount* rather than interest, because the Fed collects the interest charge when it makes the loan.

For example, a commercial bank, Delta Bank, sells the Fed a $1,000 promissory note that matures in three months. The **discount rate** (interest rate) is 8 percent per year, or a 2 percent discount for the three-month period. Delta Bank actually receives from the Fed only $980, or $1,000 less 2 percent. Delta's deposits at the Federal Reserve increase by $980. In other words, Delta pays the Fed $20 for the privilege of using $1,000 for three months.

If the Federal Reserve wants to encourage commercial banks to increase their reserves this way (that is, to increase their deposits with the Fed), it can reduce the cost of borrowing by *lowering the discount rate*. If the Fed wants to discourage commercial banks from increasing

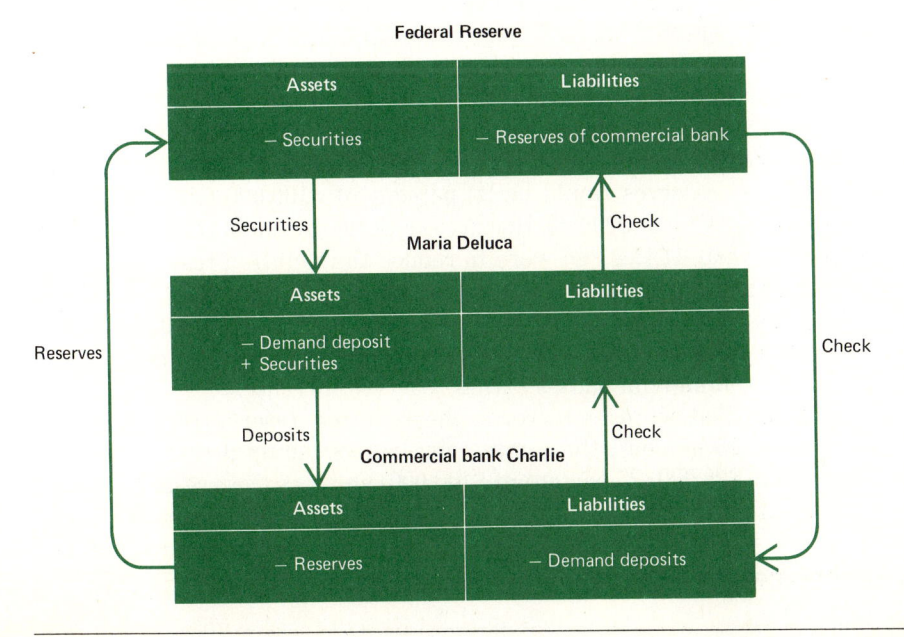

Figure 13-5 What Happens to Assets and Liabilities of the Federal Reserve Bank, Maria Deluca, and Commercial Bank Charlie When the Fed Sells Government Securities to a Private Citizen

reserves this way, it can increase the cost of borrowing by *increasing* the discount rate.

Note: The Federal Reserve cannot reduce the reserves of commercial banks by this device. It can only use the discount rate to *encourage* or *discourage* the increasing of reserves by commercial banks. In addition, the Federal Reserve in recent years has restricted its lending through discounting to situations in which commercial banks are in temporary need of reserves.

Note: There is a difference between discount-rate policy and discount policy. *Discount-rate policy* has to do with variations in the discount rate and their effects. The *discount policy* has to do with when discounts come into effect, and what kind. As a means of power over excess reserves, the Fed's ability to manipulate the discount rate is not as important as its operations in the open market.

However, through the responses of the commercial banks the Federal Reserve discount rate controls interest rates on loans of all sorts: mortgage loans, car loans, and so forth. When the Fed raises its discount rate, this is the sequence of repercussions in the economy: (1) Everybody knows the higher rate is a signal that the Fed is tightening credit. (2) The higher rate discourages commercial banks from increasing their reserves, and thus keeps them from making as many loans. (3) The higher discount rate pushes up all other interest rates.

The Required Reserve Ratio

When a commercial bank makes a loan, as you know, the essential ingredient is excess reserves. The bank cannot loan more money and create more demand deposits once it reaches the bottom of its excess-reserve barrel, because it might risk dropping below the required reserve ratio. The final weapon by which the Fed can affect the banking system is that it can change the *required reserve ratio*.

Varying the required reserve ratio does not change the total reserves of a commercial bank, just the proportion of total reserves that the bank must have on hand, that are *required*. Therefore, it changes the proportion that is counted as excess.

For example, a commercial bank has $100,000 in demand deposits and $25,000 in total reserves. If the required reserve ratio is 20 percent, its required reserves would be 20 percent of $100,000 (the amount of demand deposits) or $20,000. Its excess reserves would be $5,000 ($25,000 minus $20,000). If the Fed were to reduce the required reserve ratio to 10 percent, the commercial bank's required reserves would be $10,000 (10 percent of $100,000) and its excess reserves would be $15,000 ($25,000 minus $10,000). In other words, if the Fed lowers the required reserve ratio, the commercial bank's excess reserves increase.

If the Fed were to increase the required reserve ratio from 20 percent to 25 percent, the commercial bank's required reserves would increase to $25,000 (25 percent of $100,000) and its excess reserves would decrease to zero ($25,000 total reserves minus $25,000 required reserves). In other words, if the Fed increases the required reserve ratio, the commercial bank's excess reserves decrease.

Clearly, the Fed's ability to vary the required reserve ratio is a very powerful weapon, since it means that the Fed can readily change the excess reserves of the whole commercial banking system. The problem is that it is *too* powerful to be used often. Small percentage changes in the reserve ratio can have enormous effects on the reserve position of commercial banks. That is why the Fed varies its activity on the open market on an ongoing basis, giving the economy the **fine tuning** it needs to carry out its monetary policy and only rarely and cautiously tampers with the reserve ratio. Changes in the reserve ratio most often signify major shifts in Federal Reserve policy.

A Review: How the Fed Nudges the Banking System

If the Federal Reserve wishes to *increase* the excess reserves of commercial banks to enable them to increase loans and create more demand deposits (the supply of money), it can do the following: (1) *buy* government securities on the open market, (2) *lower* the discount rate, or (3) *lower* the required reserve ratio.

If the Federal Reserve wishes to *decrease* banks' excess reserves, to reduce commercial banks' ability to make loans and create more demand deposits, it can do the following: (1) *sell* government securities on the open market, (2) *raise* the discount rate, or (3) *raise* the required reserve ratio.

Specific Powers of the Federal Reserve

No sooner had Congress passed the Federal Reserve Act of 1914, which brought the Federal Reserve Bank into existence, than people came forth with ideas to improve it. So, over the years Congress has passed amendments giving the Federal Reserve additional powers, especially in the areas of lending and credit. Powers added to the Fed over specific areas of lending are called **specific powers**.

Margin Requirements on Stocks

The **margin requirement** is the percentage of cash required as a down payment on the purchase of a share of stock. The Bank Act of 1933 gave the Federal Reserve power to set the *margin* that buyers of stock in the various stock exchanges must pay when they buy corporate stock. The purpose of the margin is to control speculation on the stock market. To many, after the disaster of the stock-market crash in 1929, it seemed like locking the barn door after the horse is stolen.

If the Federal Reserve wants to reduce speculation on the stock exchange, it can increase the margin requirement. Let's say that the Federal Reserve increases the margin from 50 percent to 75 percent. This means that a person buying stock must pay cash equal to 75 percent of the value of the stock and can borrow only 25 percent of its purchase price. It works in reverse too. For example, in 1974, the stock market fell drastically from the high 900s to below 600. (These figures are from the **Dow Jones Industrial Index**, which measures changes in the prices of stock on the New York Stock Exchange.) To stimulate demand for securities, the Federal Reserve dropped margin requirements to 50 percent. The market began to climb.

The Federal Reserve's responsibility for watchdogging speculation in the stock market does not clash with its responsibilities for controlling excess reserves. Variations in stock-market margin requirements do not affect the total or excess reserves of commercial banks.

Regulations X and W

Beginning in World War II, Congress gave the Federal Reserve the power to regulate consumer and real estate loans. **Regulation X** concerned loans on consumer goods, while **Regulation W** involved real estate loans. These regulations made the Federal Reserve responsible for determining the minimum down payment on a loan and the maximum length of time in which a loan could be repaid.

If the Federal Reserve wanted these loans to *decrease*, it *increased* the minimum down payment and *reduced* the length of time in which the loan could be repaid. This made it harder for people to scrape up the cash down payment and harder to make the monthly payments. If the Fed wanted to encourage loans on consumer goods and real estate, it did the opposite.

These regulations were only used during World War II and the Korean War; they expired in the late 1960s. Some economists feel that these regulations should be permanent and should be frequently used by the Federal Reserve for combating unemployment and inflation. They feel that the Fed's use of these regulations would counter the inadequacies and the uneven impact of traditional monetary policy. We will discuss the shortcomings of monetary policy at the end of this chapter.

Regulation Q

Regulation Q empowers the Federal Reserve to set the maximum interest rates that commercial banks may pay on savings accounts (time deposits) and on demand deposits. The Fed forbids banks to pay interest on demand deposits and states the maximum interest rates payable on savings accounts.

The importance of Regulation Q lies in its effect on the availability of mortgage money. Most people cannot buy a house if they cannot get a mortgage. So the construction industry is highly sensitive to changes in availability of mortgage money. Therefore, Regulation Q enables the Federal Reserve to influence the rate of home building.

Regulation Q works this way: It applies only to commercial banks—not to savings and loan associations. Yet savings and loan associations are prime sources of funds for mortgages. Suppose the Fed wants to increase the amount of money available for mortgages. It uses Regulation Q to keep interest rates on savings accounts at commercial banks relatively low (in comparison with rates at savings and loan associations). So people with savings take their money out of commercial banks and deposit it in savings and loan associations. The result is that the savings and loan associations have a lot more money available to lend to home buyers, which stimulates residential construction. If the economy is expanding at too high a rate and the Federal Reserve wants to put the brakes on construction, it uses Regulation Q again, to channel funds in the *opposite* direction, back to the commercial banks.

However, commercial banks have complained about this disparity between the interest rates on savings account in banks and in savings and loan associations. Commercial banks charge that the Federal Reserve's use of Regulation Q is unfair because it limits their ability to attract long-term savings accounts and hold them.

Moral Suasion

The Federal Reserve has one more invisible weapon in its arsenal of controls over lending and the supply of money—**moral suasion**, that is, persuasion. The Federal Reserve has various subtle ways of letting commercial banks know that what they are doing is undesirable. You may wonder whether in our system, based on privately owned corporations engaging in economic activity for a profit, banks will stop doing something just because the Federal Reserve tells them to. Remember, however, that the Fed can always back up its moral suasion with more persuasive kinds of action.

Functions of the Federal Reserve

The Federal Reserve performs several functions. We have already mentioned many of these, but let's review them.

The Fed Regulates the Supply of Money

Through its control over commercial banks' excess reserves, the Federal Reserve regulates the supply of money. By means of its operations in the open market, and its variations in the discount rate and in the required reserve ratio, the Federal Reserve may increase or decrease the banks' excess reserves. Commercial banks must have excess reserves in order to make loans and create new demand deposits, which are the main form of money.

The Fed Acts as a National Clearinghouse for Checks

When a commercial bank receives a check written against an account in another bank, it gets paid by sending the check to the Federal Reserve Bank. The Federal Reserve Bank, when it receives the check, increases the deposits with the Federal Reserve of the bank sending the check and reduces the deposits of the bank on which the check is drawn. The Federal Reserve Bank then sends the check to the bank on which it is drawn. *That* bank reduces the amount of demand deposits in the account of the person who wrote the check.

The Fed Issues Paper Currency

The Federal Reserve issues all the paper money in circulation. The Federal Reserve does not use the issuance of currency as a device to control the overall supply of money, but it must make certain that there

The demand for currency increases during the Christmas season. (Bob Gomel/ TIME-LIFE Picture Agency © Time Inc.)

is enough currency around to meet the economy's needs. For instance, the need for currency varies from season to season.

Before Christmas, people want to hold cash to buy Christmas presents so demand for paper currency increases. As people withdraw currency from their demand-deposit accounts, commercial banks run low on cash in their vaults. The banks therefore order more currency from the Federal Reserve, which fills their currency order and reduces their deposits with the Fed by an equal amount. In this way the Fed increases the supply of currency in the economy each Christmas season.

After Christmas, business falls off and people become uneasy about holding more currency than they actually need, so they deposit the excess in their demand-deposit accounts. The commercial banks now have more cash in their vaults than they want, so they send the excess back to the Federal Reserve, which stashes away the cash and increases the banks' deposits with the Fed. In this way the Fed withdraws currency from circulation. This nice elasticity in the supply of currency helps take care of seasonal changes in the volume of business.

The Fed Regulates and Examines Member Banks
Congress has given the Federal Reserve the power to regulate many of the activities of member commercial banks. To check whether these banks are obeying the rules, the Fed periodically examines their books. Not much escapes the Fed's notice, which helps to keep the member banks honest and in good fiscal condition.

A foreign central bank: The Bank of England in London (William Raftery)

The Fed Acts as a Banker's Bank
When commercial banks want to go to the bank, they go to the Federal Reserve, which loans them money by accepting—at a discount, to be sure—their short-term debt instruments. The Federal Reserve also holds deposits of member banks, deposits that form part of the member banks' total reserves.

The Fed Is a Fiscal Agent and Bank for the U.S. Treasury
The U.S. Treasury itself keeps deposits at the Federal Reserve and writes checks on them. Furthermore, the Federal Reserve handles the national debt for the government. When the Treasury issues the federal debt, the Federal Reserve sells the debt instruments and collects the proceeds for the Treasury. When this debt *matures* (is due for payment), the Federal Reserve pays what is owed out of the Treasury's account.

The Fed Is a Fiscal Agent for Foreign Central Banks and Treasuries
A number of foreign central banks and treasuries use the Federal Reserve as their bank in the United States. The Federal Reserve treats them as impartially as it does its own member banks or the U.S. Treasury. It loans money, buys and sells debt intruments, and in general acts as their fiscal agent.

Functions of the Federal Reserve

Monetary Policy

Monetary policy is what causes the Federal Reserve to manipulate the money supply and the interest rate to achieve economic goals. The most important goal is to reach acceptable levels of unemployment and inflation. Therefore, in order to analyze monetary policy, one needs to know how changes in the money supply and the interest rates influence employment and prices.

Varying the Supply of Money

In Chapter 11 you looked at the effects of changes in the money supply on employment and prices. You learned that increases in the supply of money expand effective demand, while contractions reduce it. Therefore, to counter unemployment, a nation's monetary policy should be to expand the money supply. On the other hand, to counter inflation, a nation's monetary policy should be to cut back the money supply.

Varying Interest Rates

What happens to an economy when interest rates vary? When interest rates go up, people do not want to borrow as much to buy consumer goods, because the cost of borrowing money is so high. And businesses do not want to buy as much new plant and equipment, for the same reason. So investment decreases. (Remember that investments need to have an expected rate of return equal to or greater than the interest rate.) Also, when interest rates go up, government expenditures at the state and local levels that are financed by borrowing tend to go down. State and local governments must be concerned about their taxpayers moving to other locales, with lower tax rates. So state and local governments are more sensitive than the federal government about raising taxes to pay increased interest costs on borrowed money. (You knew, didn't you, that state and local governments have to borrow heavily in order to see themselves through the fiscal year?)

All in all, raising interest rates decreases aggregate demand by decreasing consumption based on consumer borrowing, on investment, and on debt-financed expenditures by state and local governments.

What happens when interest rates go down? Just the reverse of what happens when they go up. People more readily borrow money to buy consumer goods, because credit is cheaper. Businesses increase their investment spending, because there are more investments that yield a return equal to or greater than the cost of the interest. And state and local governments increase their deficit-financed expenditures, too, because the price of money is low.

Some Recommendations on Monetary Policy

During a recession, when there is a lot of unemployment, monetary policy should aim at expanding aggregate demand by increasing the supply of money and decreasing the interest rate. During an inflation, monetary policy should aim at decreasing aggregate demand and dis-

TABLE 13-1 The Federal Reserve's Monetary Policy

What should the Fed do about unemployment?	What should the Fed do about inflation?
Increase excess reserves	*Decrease excess reserves*
Buy government securities	Sell government securities
Lower the discount rate	Raise the discount rate
Lower the required reserve ratio	Raise the required reserve ratio

couraging price increases by reducing the supply of money and increasing the interest rate. Table 13-1 outlines the methods the Federal Reserve can use to combat unemployment or inflation.

What to Do When Recession Hits

Suppose there is a recession. Aggregate demand is very low, unemployment is very high; nobody is buying much, and people are just holding their money. What can be done? The monetary policies that increase the supply of money also lower the interest rate and combat unemployment.

During a period of high unemployment, the Federal Reserve should follow policies that increase excess reserves. In the discussion of the Fed, you learned how this can be done. The Federal Reserve should do one or more of the following:

1. *Buy government securities on the open market.* The proceeds are used to increase the deposits of commercial banks with the Federal Reserve; that is, the commercial banks' total and excess reserves rise, so that they can lend out more money.

2. *Lower the discount rate.* This encourages commercial banks to discount acceptable short-term debt and increase their total and excess reserves.

3. *Lower the required reserve ratio.* This does not change commercial banks' total reserves, but it does lower the percentage of reserves that are required, and thus it creates more excess reserves.

What to Do When Inflation Hits

Suppose there is an inflation. Aggregate demand is high, and prices are rising fast. What can be done? During a period of rising prices, the Federal Reserve should follow policies that decrease the supply of money and increase interest rates. From the discussion of the Fed, you know how this can be done. The Federal Reserve should do one or more of the following:

1. *Sell government securities on the open market.* This has the effect of reducing the commercial banks' deposits at the Federal Reserve, which means that the banks' excess reserves go down by a like amount, and they have fewer loanable funds.

2. *Raise the discount rate.* This makes it more expensive for commercial banks to borrow from the Federal Reserve, and, therefore, discourages

commercial banks from increasing their reserves by means of short-term debt.

3. *Raise the required reserve ratio.* This leaves commercial banks' total reserves untouched, but makes them hold a higher percentage of their total reserves as required reserves, which leaves a smaller percentage of excess reserves.

Remember that each of these general powers has different effects. Open-market operations can increase excess reserves or decrease them, and are also more selective than the other powers. For day-to-day fine tuning of monetary policy, the Federal Reserve uses mainly open-market operations. Varying the discount rate cannot decrease excess reserves, but it does have a strong immediate impact on interest rates. It causes the interest rates for various kinds of debt instruments (mortgages, personal loans) to fluctuate readily. Varying the required reserve ratio is too strong and unselective a weapon for the Federal Reserve to use often. The use of this weapon generally signals a major change in Federal Reserve policy.

Weaknesses of Monetary Policy

The monetary policy we have outlined above does not contain all the solutions to economic problems. Here are five weaknesses in it:

1. During a serious recession or a depression, monetary policy may be quite ineffective. Commercial banks may already have all the excess reserves they need. (a) As business goes into a slump, people may shy away from borrowing, to such an extent that more loans are paid off than are made. So the banks' excess reserves increase without the help of the Federal Reserve. (b) With the economic outlook so gloomy, banks are often unwilling to run the risk of lending. So no matter what the Fed does to increase excess reserves, banks refuse to increase loans and the supply of money. (This is what the commercial banks did during the Great Depression of the 1930s.) (c) The banks may have money they are willing to lend, but people are just not borrowing. During a mild recession, however, monetary policy aimed at increasing excess reserves may work well, as it did in the recession of 1954. That recession was caused by the decline of defense expenditures at the end of the Korean War. At that time people's confidence in the economy was strong. There was a tax cut; and an easy-money policy increased excess reserves, thus stimulating bank lending, increasing the supply of money, and reducing interest rates.

2. Monetary policy may curb inflation, provided that it is a demand-pull inflation. The Federal Reserve can dry up excess reserves so much that the banks cannot make loans. Then people cannot get money to buy things with. However, if the inflation is caused by factors *not* susceptible to control by the lowering of aggregate demand (cost-push and administered-price inflation), monetary policy may not be the cure. For

example, the inflation of 1973–1974 was caused in part by the raising of oil prices by the OPEC (Organization of Petroleum Exporting Countries) and the rise in agricultural prices. The Federal Reserve tried to use monetary policy to decrease prices. But its **tight-money policy**, that is, charging very high interest rates on the money it lent, only led to commercial banks raising *their* interest rates to 12 percent. A liquidity crisis (that is, a shortage of assets that could be easily converted into money) in the banking system was predicted. The Fed was forced to back off from its tight-money policy before the double-digit inflation could be contained. (*Double-digit inflation* means inflation at any rate higher than 9 percent per year.)

3. When an economy runs into high inflation and high unemployment at the same time, a tight-money policy aimed at controlling inflation just worsens the already high unemployment. For example, in the inflation-recession of 1974–1975, the United States had two-digit inflation plus 9 percent unemployment. People spoke of this as *stagflation*. In such a situation, if the Federal Reserve tries to reduce inflation, it increases unemployment, and vice versa. What choice should the Federal Reserve make? They all look bad.

Once inflation has begun, it is very hard to turn off—for many reasons. Two important reasons are that (1) people expect inflation to continue and act to anticipate it, and that (2) cost-of-living escalators are built into many labor contracts and into many forms of government expenditures. Once there is high inflation—if the nation's chief concern is reducing inflation—it then may be necessary for the United States to endure considerable unemployment, for a long time, in order to reduce the rate of price increases.

4. During inflation, a tight-money policy of lowering demand by raising interest rates does not affect the economy *evenly*. It hits some groups harder than others. For instance, in the construction industry, high interest rates cause the demand for new houses to plummet. Each time there has been a period of tight-money policy and high interest rates, the construction industry has experienced serious cutbacks, with consequent layoffs of workers.

Commercial banks, as their excess reserves dwindle, do not lend their reduced supply of money evenly. They play favorites. Safe customers get loans, but risky ones do not. The more risky firms (generally smaller-scale, newer firms) not only face higher interest rates, but also have difficulty getting loans. Larger corporations do not have this problem. They are isolated from the tight-money situation because, when *they* want money, they can dip into their own retained earnings and depreciation funds.

And let's not forget the plight of the consumer. When the Fed raises interest rates in order to fight inflation, it also raises the price of borrowing for the public, who are already hurt by high prices. A tight-money policy causes the low person on the totem pole—the borrowing consumer—to pay a major share of the cost of fighting inflation.

5. As the Federal Reserve increases the money supply during a recession and decreases it during an inflation, changes in the velocity of exchange, V, may partially counteract these trends. During a recession, the velocity of exchange may decrease, which reduces the impact of an increased supply of money. Pessimistic consumers and businesses try to hold on to their money. During an inflation, the velocity of exchange, V, may increase, which reduces the impact of a decreased supply of money. Optimistic consumers and businesses, expecting that prices will go up still higher, continue to buy at an ever greater rate.

The recent growth of **nonbanking lending institutions** that are beyond the control of the Federal Reserve has increased the speed with which people's savings are transferred to borrowers. During inflation, these institutions increase their interest rates, and this hastens the transfers of money, so that the velocity of exchange increases. Some critics say that in order for monetary policy to become more effective, these non-banking institutions (non-financial intermediaries) have to be brought under the control of the Fed.

Monetarism

Monetarism is an approach to economic policy in which the supply of money plays the dominant role. Milton Friedman, the economist who founded the monetarist school, maintains that both fiscal policy and monetary policy based on Keynesian analysis are wrong. He and his followers charge that the Keynesians underestimate the effects of the supply of money on the economy. Friedman says that people have a stable and predictable demand for money, a demand related to the size of the economy, and that, therefore, the supply of money and its relationship to national income should be the key to government policy, both fiscal and monetary. To control unemployment and inflation, the monetarists say, the government should follow a policy of increasing the supply of money at a proper and constant rate.

This monetarist attack on Keynesian fiscal and monetary policy deserves full treatment. So in Application 11, which follows this chapter, we will explore this controversy.

SUMMING UP

1. The Federal Reserve System (the Fed) is organized as follows: (a) There are twelve Federal Reserve Banks in twelve districts. (b) All *national* commercial banks must be members of the system, while *state banks* may join if they wish. (c) Each member bank must buy some stock in its particular district Federal Reserve Bank. (d) A seven-member board of governors in Washington controls the system. Its members are appointed by the President, with the advice and consent of the Senate,

for terms of fourteen years. (e) The Open Market Committee and the Federal Advisory Council are the two main committees under the board of governors. (f) Each Federal Reserve Bank has nine people on its board of directors: three appointed by the board of governors, three elected by the member banks, and three from the local community.

2. The so-called "general powers" of the Federal Reserve entitle it to control the excess reserves of its member banks by the following devices: (a) *Open-market operations*. To increase its member banks' excess reserves, the Fed buys government securities in the open market; it buys them from the commercial banks and pays for them by increasing the banks' deposits with the Federal Reserve. To reduce its member banks' excess reserves, the Fed sells government securities in the open market to the commercial banks and deducts the amount of the sale from the banks' deposits (reserves). (b) *Varying the discount rate*. When the Fed wants to encourage an increase in excess reserves, it lowers the *discount rate*, so that money becomes cheaper for the commercial banks to borrow. The banks therefore borrow more, which increases their deposits with the Fed and increases their excess reserves. When the Fed wants to discourage the discounting, it increases the discount rate. (c) *Varying the required reserve ratio*. The Fed can lower or raise the percentage of a bank's total reserves that are considered "required" which in turn raises or lowers the reserves that are counted as "excess."

3. The Federal Reserve has *specific powers* over certain aspects of lending. (a) The Fed sets the *margin requirement* for stock purchases. The *margin* is the percentage of cash required as a down payment on a purchase of corporate stock. The balance may be borrowed. (b) The Fed had the power to regulate consumer and real estate loans. *Regulations X* and *W* are no longer in force. Regulation X applied to loans on consumer goods; regulation W, to loans on real estate. These regulations empowered the Fed to set the minimum down payment and maximum time for repayment of loans. (c) *Regulation Q* empowers the Fed to set the maximum interest rates that commercial banks may pay their customers on deposits (savings and demand).

4. The functions of the Federal Reserve are the following: (a) It regulates the supply of money. (b) It acts as a national clearinghouse for checks. (c) It issues all paper currency. (d) It regulates and examines member banks. (e) It acts as a banker's bank. (f) It acts as a fiscal agent and bank for the U.S. Treasury. (g) It acts as a fiscal agent for certain foreign central banks and treasuries.

5. *Monetary policy* involves manipulating the supply of money and the interest rates so as to achieve low unemployment and only slight price increases. The Board of Governors of the Federal Reserve is the group responsible for administering monetary policy.

6. To overcome unemployment, one should increase the supply of money and decrease the interest rate in order to increase aggregate demand. To increase excess reserves, and thereby increase the money

supply, the Fed should: (a) buy government securities on the open market, (b) lower the discount rate, or (c) lower the required reserve ratio.

7. To overcome inflation, one should decrease the supply of money and increase the interest rate in order to decrease aggregate demand. To decrease excess reserves, and thereby decrease the money supply, the Fed should (a) sell government securities on the open market, (b) raise the discount rate, (c) raise the required reserve ratio.

8. The weaknesses of this monetary policy are the following: (a) During a severe recession, the policy may not work. People are afraid to invest, so they pay off loans and shy away from further borrowing, so that banks' excess reserves increase without Fed interference. (b) During an inflation, monetary policy may be ineffective in dealing with kinds of inflation that are not susceptible to the lowering of aggregate demand (cost-push and administered-price inflation). (c) Monetary policy becomes ineffectual when inflation accompanies high unemployment. (d) A *tight-money policy* hurts some groups more than others: for example, the construction industry; small-scale, new firms; the individual consumer borrowing to buy a home, car, or appliance. (e) Changes in the velocity of exchange may partially offset the Fed's monetary policy.

9. Milton Friedman and other economists of the monetarist school of thought reject fiscal and monetary policy aimed at stabilizing aggregate demand. They believe that a constant and proper level of increase in the supply of money is the key to containing both inflation and unemployment.

QUESTIONS

1. Some people say that the Federal Reserve System is a combination of the government sector and the private sector. Identify both the government and the private elements in the structure of the Federal Reserve System.

2. Given that the required reserve ratio is 20 percent, describe the way the following transactions would affect the following accounts: Required Reserves, Excess Reserves, Total Reserves, and Supply of Money.
    a. A commercial bank *buys* $10,000 in government securities from the Federal Reserve Bank.
    b. A commercial bank *sells* $10,000 in government securities to the Federal Reserve Bank.
    c. A commercial bank discounts a $1,000 note at 8 percent for 90 days at the Federal Reserve.
    d. The Federal Reserve raises the required reserve ratio to 25 percent.
    e. The Federal Reserve lowers the required reserve ratio to 15 percent.

3. What are the general powers of the Federal Reserve? How do they work? Why are they called general powers?

4. What would you advise the board of governors of the Fed to do in case of an inflation? of a recession? What would you have advised them to do in the 1974–1975 economic situation?

5. When the Federal Reserve practices a policy of tight money in order to combat inflation, who pays the cost? Give reasons.

6. How does a cost-push inflation complicate monetary policy?

7. You have just been appointed to the Board of Governors of the Federal Reserve System. The chairman has asked you to review monetary policy and present your recommendations on:
   a. Federal Reserve policy to counter inflation or unemployment.
   b. the groups in the economy that obtain advantages or disadvantages from your recommendations.
   c. the economic justification for your recommendations.
   d. the ethical justification for your recommendations.
   e. how you would deal with significant amounts of inflation and unemployment at the same time.

SUGGESTED READINGS

Board of Governors of the Federal Reserve System. *The Federal Reserve System: Purposes and Functions,* 6th ed. G.P.O., Washington, D.C., 1974, Chapters 1 and 4.

Chandler, Lester V. *The Economics of Money and Banking,* 6th ed. Harper & Row, New York, 1973. Chapters 22–28.

Federal Reserve Bank. *Federal Reserve Structure and the Development of Monetary Policy, 1915–1935.* 92nd U.S. Congress, First Session, 1971. G.P.O., Washington, D.C., 1971.

Federal Reserve Bank. *Monthly Bulletins and Annual Report of the Board of Governors,* published monthly and annually.

Federal Reserve Bank of Chicago. *Modern Money Mechanics.* Chicago, 1971.

Friedman, Milton. *Capitalism and Freedom.* University of Chicago Press, Chicago, 1962. Chapter 3.

Application 11

Does Money Really Matter? Monetarists Versus Keynesians

The most serious challenge to Keynesian theories of economics—especially to the monetary and fiscal policies discussed in Chapters 9 and 13—has come from the University of Chicago's Professor Milton Friedman and the monetarist school of economics. These economists say that monetary policy is more important than fiscal policy, and that in order to stabilize an economy, a steady rate of growth in the supply of money must be ensured. The monetarists do not simply say that money matters. They go further, and say that money matters more than anything else.

The Monetarist Position

The basic tenet of the monetarists is that the biggest single factor in determining real income, money income, and the level of prices is the *rate of growth of the money supply*. They contend that people want to keep a fixed percentage of their assets in the form of money, a percentage that depends on their real incomes, their standards of consumption, and the composition of their other assets. As you know from Chapter 11, if the supply of money increases too quickly, people find themselves holding more money than they wish to hold. They try to re-establish the old equilibrium, by demanding more nonconsumption assets, such as land, machinery, stocks, and bonds; and/or more consumer goods—either of which causes the economy to expand. If the supply of money shrinks, the reverse happens, and the economy contracts.

This variation in the supply of money also affects prices. Beyond some point, as the economy expands, demand-pull inflation sets in. Conversely, as the supply of money and the economy contract, excess capacity and excess inventory drive prices down.

The monetarists recommend that the Federal Reserve concentrate only on maintaining a steady increase in the money supply, at about 4 to 5 percent per year. This, they say, would force the economy into a stable growth with low inflation.

The 5 percent growth in the money supply would provide enough expansion to accommodate the 3 percent increase in productivity that some economists feel is ideal. It would also provide enough flexibility to reinforce sectors of the economy that have less capacity than others, so that inflation would be mild.

Friedman challenges the assumption that by means of continuous **fine tuning** of fiscal policy and monetary policy, one can cause the economy to grow with relative stability. He says that changes in fiscal policy are ineffective and that the monetary policy of changing the interest rate also accomplishes little, since it is the *percentage rate of change in the supply of money* that is most closely correlated with changes in levels of income and employment. Furthermore, because nobody can accurately predict future business trends, it is dangerous to use changes in the rate of growth of the money supply for fine-tuning purposes.

Thus the monetarists make simple and direct recommendations for government economic policy: Let the monetary authority (the Federal Reserve) increase the supply of money at a fixed rate of 4 to 5 percent per year and the economy will adjust itself. Although this will not eliminate all economic instability, it will avoid extreme variations. As Friedman notes, "We do not know enough to avoid minor fluctuations. The attempt to do more than we can will itself be a disturbance that may increase rather than reduce instability."

Monetary policy has at times seemed to complicate stabilization rather than solve the problems of economic fluctuations. After World War II the Federal Reserve used its open-market operations to peg the price of government securities, and neglected the postwar inflation. In 1957 the Fed enforced such a tight policy, in an attempt to fight inflation, that it contributed to the 1958 recession. Often just before or during an inflation, the Fed has increased the supply of money by greater amounts than the 5 percent recommended by Friedman. This has fed the inflation; 1973 is a good example.

The Keynesian Defense

Walter Heller, former chairman of the Council of Economic Advisers (under Presidents Kennedy and Johnson, from 1961 to 1964), defends the policy implications of the Keynesian model. He says, "Summing up the key operational issues, they are: Should money be king? Is fiscal policy worth its salt? Should flexible man yield to rigid rules?"

A flaw in the monetarists' theory is the implied assumption that velocity of exchange remains constant. (The monetarists say that V is constant in the short run, but not in the long run.) As you saw in Chapter 11, V does not remain constant. Not only has velocity of exchange increased in the past few years, but it varies greatly over short-run periods. These variations indicate the economy's responses to variations in many factors, including fiscal policy (taxes and government expenditures). Variation in the supply of money is not the main stimulus that brings about changes in money income and real income. It is only one of a number of factors, including variations in fiscal policy and interest rates, that cause such changes. Critics of monetarism claim that the rigid link that the monetarists would forge between money and economic activity just does not exist.

The monetarists' demand for a rigid monetary rule opens up several areas of debate. What money are they talking about? Is it to be just demand deposits plus all currency and coin in circulation? Or does it also include various forms of near money? If near money is excluded, don't variations in these highly liquid assets affect the situation?

The monetarists want to include near money in the supply of money, while the neo-Keynesians do not include it. This explains some of the conflict in policy recommendations.

Also, how much time elapses between an increase in the supply of money (however one defines it) and the effect of that increase in the form of improved economic activity? The data that Friedman presents show great variability in time lags.

If there is any validity to the Phillips curve (remember Chapter 6), and if there is some trade-off between inflation and unemployment, what clues does one get from the monetarists that can be used to decide at what level the tradeoff should be with this fixed growth in the money supply? If the Federal Reserve should increase the money supply at a certain fixed annual rate, this would force into the open certain changes in the economy. There would be fluctuations in the interest rate that would be too large for comfort.

Friedman's followers rely on the workings of a flexible system of markets to translate changes in the supply of money into changes in prices and output. But doesn't this hark back to the utopian world of the neoclassicists, with their reliance on flexible markets? Isn't there evidence that markets today are too inflexible (noncompetitive) to have the capability of translating changes in the supply of money into hoped-for changes in price and output? The recent disastrous price increases of OPEC are enough to make us doubt the markets' power to do so.

A Conclusion

Milton Friedman and the monetarist school of economists have affected the thinking of many in the profession. People have begun to pay a lot more attention to the role of the money supply and monetary policy. These factors have assumed greater importance in government economic policy. Nearly everyone agrees that money does matter. However, most economists are unwilling to concede that money is the only—or even the primary—thing that matters. Nor are they willing completely to abandon fine tuning of the economy. Many continue to espouse correcting for ups and downs in economic activity by making continuous adjustments in fiscal and monetary policy—a little of this and a dash of that—and prefer this on-the-spot approach to the measured-recipe method of following the rigid monetary rule and adding 5 percent to the money supply each year.

SUMMING UP

1. The monetarists claim that the rate of growth of the money supply is the primary factor that influences the level of economic activity (employment and prices), and that deliberate (discretionary) monetary policy that does not change the money supply has scant effect on economic activity. This, plus the fact that no one can accurately predict future business affairs, makes fine tuning of the economy inadequate and dangerous. Mone-

tarists therefore advocate a simple monetary rule: Let the government increase the supply of money by a fixed rate of 4 to 5 percent per year.

2. The Keynesians point to the following weaknesses in the monetarist position: (a) The velocity of exchange is not constant, either in the short or long run. Therefore, there is no rigid link between the economy and the supply of money. (b) The monetarists leave a number of questions unanswered: What do they define as being money? What about variations in time between changes in the supply of money and changes in the economy? What about the substantial inflexibility (caused by monopolists) in the structure of prices that prevents the economy from responding in a hoped-for way to changes in the supply of money?

3. Economists in general do not accept the monetarists' conclusions that it is money and only money that is of primary importance, nor would they willingly give up the fine tuning of the economy.

QUESTIONS

1. What are the basic elements of the monetarists' position? Do they seem justified? Why?

2. What are the basic elements of the Keynesians' rebuttal of the monetarists? Do they seem justified? Why?

3. What is your position on the role of money in stabilizing the economy?

SUGGESTED READINGS

Friedman, Milton, and Walter Heller. *Monetary Versus Fiscal Policy.* Norton, New York, 1969.

Maisel, Sherman J. *Managing the Dollar.* Norton, New York, 1973.

Application 12

Fiscal Policy, Monetary Policy, and Debt Management: Too Many Cooks?

The Economy: Many Hands Make Heavy Work

The past few chapters have dealt with fiscal policy, monetary policy, and the national debt. So you now have some insight into the way the federal government formulates and executes its economic stabilization policies.

To adjust fiscal policy, one must adjust government expenditures and taxes—which involves the House of Representatives, the Senate, and the President.

To do anything about monetary policy, one must change the supply of money and the interest rates—which is the exclusive job of the Board of Governors of the Federal Reserve. The board of governors does not have to take orders from anyone, not even the President and the Congress. They just do their thing as they see it.

Then there's the national debt, which nobody can really do anything about, since it is left over from past fiscal policies. All one can do is take care of it, pay off bits of it as they mature or fall due, and then refund it—that is, issue new debt instruments and sell them—in order to finance ever larger amounts of debt. Who actually carries out these chores? The U.S. Treasury. Can the management of this gigantic debt create problems in fiscal and monetary policy, and thus in economic stabilization? You bet it can!

Many institutions stick their fingers into the government's economic stabilization policies. Can there be disagreements about what's the right policy? Can one agency embark on one course and another on a contradictory course? Can the actions of one agency offset the actions of others? In other words, are there too many cooks?

An analogy can be drawn between too many cooks spoiling the broth and too many government branches spoiling the economy: The President and Congress plan the menu (fiscal policy), the Board of Governors of the Federal Reserve puts the food on the table (monetary policy), and the Treasury Department later deals with the dirty dishes (the national debt).

Fiscal Policy

The President sets fiscal policy, but it's Congress that decides about expenditures and taxes, and enacts laws to carry out these decisions. The President can try to control this process by persuasion, and by using the veto. But the two may clash, especially when the President is not from the same political party as the majority of Congress.

In 1975 Congress often disagreed with the White House, not only over fiscal policy but also over energy policy. For example, Congress tried to establish its own energy policy so that it could prevent President Ford from carrying out *his* energy policy, which was to reduce the U.S. consumption of oil by slapping a larger import tax on oil and thus raising the price of gasoline. Congress had its way when it came to the tax cut, though. To move the economy out of its doldrums, the President recommended a tax cut. Congress proceeded to pass legislation giving people a much larger tax cut than President Ford had suggested, and giving people in the lower-income groups a much bigger boost.

You can see that disagreements between Congress and the President over direction and magnitude of economic programs can cause a real logjam in fiscal policy.

Monetary Policy

How much actual money is there going to be in circulation? That decision is up to the Board of Governors of the Federal Reserve System, whose members, you recall, are appointed by the President (with the approval of the Senate) for a fourteen-year term and cannot be removed from office except by impeachment. This makes them independent of direct control by the President or the Congress. So the governors do not have to run for office, they don't have to kowtow to any authority, and they are answerable only to themselves.

Naturally the board doesn't always see eye to eye with the President. For example, in 1966–1967, at the height of the Vietnam escalation, the Federal Reserve moved to tighten credit, in order to counteract rising inflation brought on by the large expenditures of the war in Vietnam. This looked like an open admission that the operations in Vietnam were hurting the United States by pushing the economy into a dangerous inflation. President Johnson, stung by this implied judgment, boasted that the American economy could produce "both guns and butter." But the Fed was right. Its contraction of the money supply successfully—but only momentarily—cooled a rapidly overheating economy, without much rise in unemployment.

In 1968 Johnson admitted that there was a mounting problem of inflation and persuaded Congress, after considerable delay, to put through a tax increase (a 10 percent tax surcharge). The Fed, apparently fearing that the tax increase would restrict the economy too much, loosened credit and increased the supply of money. This action definitely contradicted the actions of the President and Congress.

On the other hand, sometimes fiscal policy and monetary policy have meshed very well. Take the recession of 1954. When the Korean War ended, toward the close of 1953, defense expenditures went down by about $10 billion a year, a large budget cut. This should have decreased GNP by several times that amount, because of the multiplier. By all rights, the United States should have had a severe recession. Instead, President Eisenhower and Congress used their power over fiscal policy to cut taxes, and the Federal Reserve used its power over monetary policy to expand credit. This one-two punch softened the impact on

"Say, I think I see where we went off. Isn't eight times seven fifty-six?"

the GNP of that $10 billion cut in defense expenditures to less than $10 billion, so that the resulting recession was mild and relatively short.

Debt Management

The U.S. Treasury is responsible for managing the national debt. If the actual total of the debt were small, refunding it (that is, floating new loans to pay for it) would be no problem and reissuing the debt would have little impact on the money market or on interest rates. And if the annual deficit in the budget were small, the Treasury wouldn't make any waves when it went about raising the extra money to cover the deficit.

But today both the size of the national debt and the size of the annual budget deficits are so enormous that one cannot help worrying about their impact on the money supply and on interest rates. To counter high unemployment, the Fed's monetary policy in 1975 was to try to lower interest rates. Fiscal policy, as set forth by President Ford and Congress, was to give everybody a tax rebate in order to stimulate the economy and get those jobless people back to work again—a good idea, except that it increased the deficit in the federal budget. The deficit for fiscal 1975 alone was more than $45 billion, while the estimates for fiscal 1976 are running at $80 to $100 billion.

Where is all that money coming from? A lot of it must be siphoned away from private use to cover these deficits. The results are predictable. The interest rate will rise again, thus counteracting the administration's own antiunemployment tactics.

And when the Fed increases the supply of money to cover the Treasury's need for funds, as it undoubtedly will, this input of new money will probably set off another round of inflation. And so it goes.

Even if the Fed and the Treasury do cooperate with each other, managing the national debt in the late seventies will be tricky, and costly. By costly, we mean inflationary. And what happens if the Fed and the Treasury don't cooperate with each other?

The point of what we're saying is that several groups have power to control our economy: The House of Representatives, the Senate, the President, the Board of Governors of the Federal Reserve, and the Treasury Department. What would happen if they didn't agree; or if they worked at cross purposes? Chances are that things would get messy.

QUESTION

Make up as many scenarios as you can, each portraying a different set of possible conflicts between the government agencies that formulate and administer fiscal policy, monetary policy, and management of the national debt.

14

Expansion and Growth

Until now, we have dealt with macroeconomic and microeconomic principles that are primarily *static*. That is, they are like a snapshot of a situation at a point in time, rather than like a motion picture showing the situation changing with the passage of time. Static principles of economics, such as supply and demand and national income determination, have helped us analyze problems as diverse as how to keep the price of gasoline from rising too much, and whether wage-price controls are effective tools against inflation or just distort the market.

We are about to explore some problems that—at least in some of their aspects—require a **dynamic framework**, one that explains how things change over a period of time. We will examine, for example, the growth record of the U.S. economy and its prospects for the future. In this chapter we will discuss several theoretical explanations of economic growth, and in Applications 13 and 14, we will present the following related problems: (1) Can we have growth without massive defense spending? (2) Do we have to choose between more growth and a clean environment?

Let's begin by making a distinction between expansion and growth. We'll use **expansion** to refer to the extensive process by which the output of an economy grows as it uses more and more resources. **Growth** refers to the intensive process by which productivity, output per hour of labor (or income per capita), increases.

Sources of Expansion

An economy can achieve expansion by using more resources. First, it might achieve expansion because of an increase in the *supply* of total resources (land, labor, and capital). Let's look at each of those resources to see how—and how much—each might contribute to expansion.

Land represents all the natural resources of a nation, not only the surface soil but the subsoil minerals, the timber, and the water. It is tempting to think of all resources as being fixed: so many acres of land, so many acre-feet of water, tons of minerals, and so forth. Although it is useful to know (or estimate) the economy's resources at a particular time, you should realize that they can change as time and technology change the ways of producing things and the things that can be produced.

Consider the case of offshore oil, under the continental shelf: A few years ago no one was even sure it was there. After geologic surveys confirmed its existence, it was still only a potential resource that might be tapped someday. Now, technology, has made a difference. With new oil-drilling technology, and with high world oil prices, offshore oil has become a resource, something available to use.

Another example of technology creating a resource occurred in iron mining. In the Mesabi iron range, the richest iron ore was mined and the second-grade ore, called *taconite*, was thrown aside because it was too expensive to refine. Now, with new technology, the mining companies are working the Mesabi range again, this time getting iron from the taconite. The price of iron makes it economical, definitely worth the trouble.

We should note here that technology and changes in technology affect not only expansion, through making resources out of previously unusable potential resources. They also, as you shall see shortly, increase the productivity of resources that are employed and, thereby, are a major source of growth.

Labor represents the human resources of a society. In a sense, labor is the most basic of all resources. Without labor, nothing happens. The whole process of expansion and growth depends on human motivations, work, aspirations, and skills. An increase in population or an increase in participation in the labor force (for example, women during and since World War II) increases a society's total output (that is, it creates expansion).

Capital is the physical result of investment. Capital consists of the plant and equipment and tools with which people work. There is also human capital. Capital's productivity rises with specialization, and specialization is limited by the size of the market. In a small town in a largely rural (perhaps low-income) area of the United States, there's not much specialization of either labor or capital. If you get sick, you go to the town doctor, who is almost certainly a general practitioner. If you have a leaky roof, you go to the town's general handyman, a jack-of-all-trades. If your car's engine is idling badly, you take it to the town mechanic, no matter whether the car is a Chevy or a Datsun.

Now, what happens if you live in a city and have the same problems? If your medical problem is a skin rash, you go directly to a dermatologist or you are referred to one. If you have a roof leak, you call in a firm of roof specialists. If you have car trouble, you probably find a garage that specializes in that particular make of car.

Whether in small town or city, the kind and amount of capital that people have to work with has a lot to do with their productivity. The more capital, and the more sophisticated the capital available to workers, the greater their output.

The difference in these two situations is due to *different market sizes*. The small (poor) town has few consumers and relatively little aggregate demand. The city has many consumers and a lot more aggregate demand. In the city there are enough people with enough purchasing power to warrant the investment that results in specialized tools, machines, and plant facilities. Without this capital, jobs for those in the (increasing) labor force will not be created and the society will not be able to use its (potential) natural resources.

Increasing Efficiency and Growth

There is a link between efficiency and growth. As more and more resources are used in production, growth may occur because the cost per unit of output goes down and efficiency therefore increases. As the economy uses existing plants, or builds more plants, and as it employs more people and uses more land (natural resources), output may increase more rapidly than input. In other words, a 5 percent increase in the use of inputs may generate more than a 5 percent increase in output. Let's examine the reasons for this.

According to Adam Smith and other classical economists, *specialization* is a major reason for such increases in output. As we said in Chapter 2, in an economy whose market size is growing, there is more and more specialized use of labor and capital, which leads to more and more output. In fact, large market size, as we mentioned a bit earlier, is necessary if specialization is to exist in a community.

Technological change, the growth in knowledge or advances in techniques that result in more productive capital goods and more efficient organization, is perhaps the main thing that holds out hope for future growth. If all our prospects for growth depended on specialization, the future might prove as gloomy as the classical economists (Adam Smith, David Ricardo, Karl Marx, and others) predicted. Their dismal view prevailed through much of our industrial history. To see why, examine Figure 14-1, on the next page.

Let's suppose that the economy shown in Figure 14-1 has met various preconditions for growth: attitudes favorable to growth, financial institutions to receive and channel savings into productive investments, a government to establish and enforce commercial rules, people drawn into the market system—all the things we have discussed in previous chapters. Suppose also that it has at least one industry that has a high growth potential whose effects seem likely to spread throughout the economy.

What will happen first as the economy starts to grow and expand? In the early years, its productivity and per capita income may rise

Figure 14-1 Growth Paths of an Economy

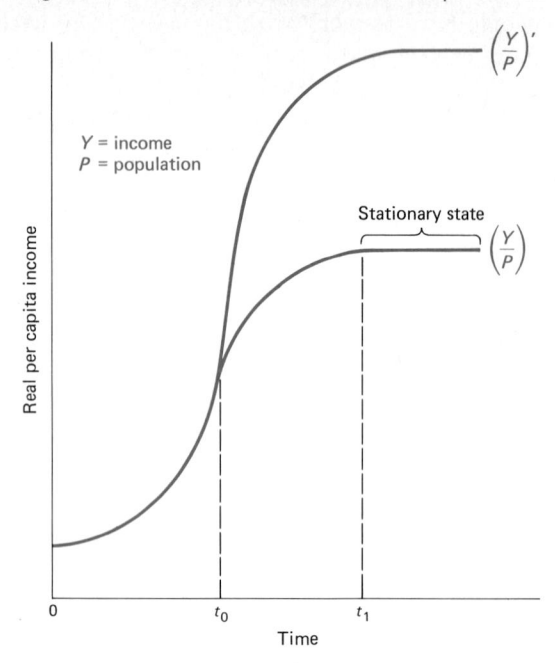

rapidly. The part of the growth path (Y/P) from zero up to time t_0 represents this period. As the size of its market gets larger (as reflected in its growing per capita income), it begins to enjoy all the efficiencies of increased specialization. The slope—rate of change—of (Y/P) increases, indicating that real per capita income is growing faster and faster.

Then, after time t_0, the slope of (Y/P) becomes less steep, which means that if the economy remains on this growth path (even at full employment), growth will be slower. (As time passes, the increments in growth will get smaller and smaller.) This implies that there are barriers or resistances to rapid growth. What are they? Why can't the economy simply keep on growing at the same rate?

Decreasing Efficiency and Growth

Let's answer the question of why there is a slowdown in the growth rate:

1. In the short term, some resources may be relatively fixed in usage. For example, the Atlas Company makes stereo sets, for which plant and equipment are the fixed inputs. Now it naturally takes longer to put new plant and equipment into use than it does to vary the use of other inputs (labor, land, and materials). So if Atlas wants to make more stereos, and if it starts using more labor and land without increasing its use of capital (plant and equipment), then its productivity (output of stereos per unit of additional input) will in the long run decline. Why? Basically, because of overcrowding. With a fixed number of machines

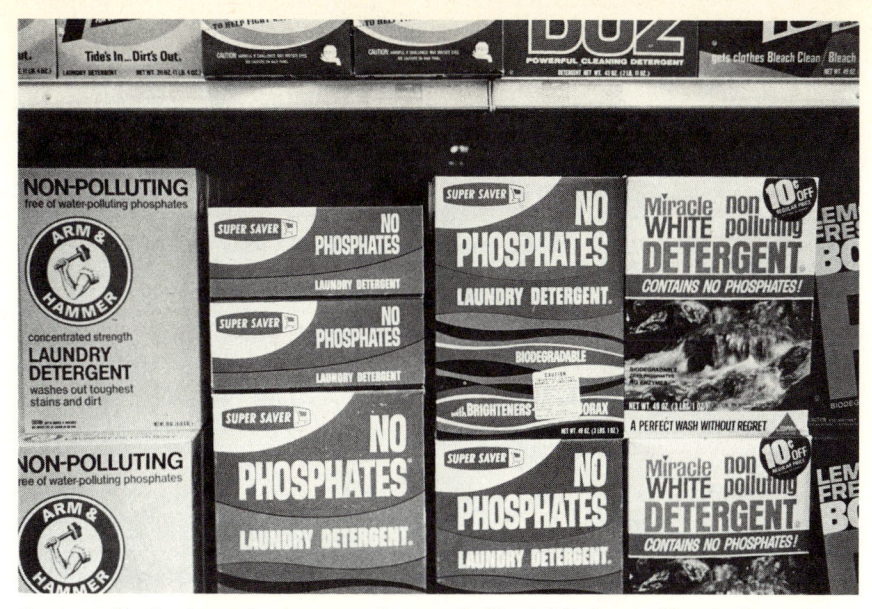

Coping with the hazards of economic growth (Daniel S. Brody/Stock, Boston)

and a fixed amount of plant space, workers may start having to wait to use machines. They may finally get in each other's way and disrupt the specialized routines of the plant. (In Chapter 16 we will discuss this effect under the *law of variable proportions*.)

2. As an economy begins to suffer diminishing efficiency, the rate at which per capita income grows slacks off. At some point (t_0 in Figure 14-1), diminishing efficiency (due to the slowness of increase in plant and equipment) begins to more than offset the increased amount of efficiency resulting from specialization. The slope of the (Y/P) curve becomes less and less steep. When it reaches zero (past t_1), the society is in a **stationary state**. Real per capita income is at a maximum and will not grow further until something in the economy changes.

The Classical View

The classical economists (Adam Smith et al.) who talked about the stationary state disagreed about how high the upper limit to (Y/P) might be. Smith was among the most optimistic. Unlike others, Smith refused to look upon technology as containing a fixed number of choices. Some classical economists gloomily predicted that a society would use techniques that added less and less to productivity as time went on and that it would finally run out of new technological choices. They felt that this gradual disappearance of new technology—combined with the need to produce more and more food for a growing population on a fixed supply of land—would ultimately produce the stationary state at a fairly low

"Now will you have the vasectomy?"

level of real per capita income. But Smith had slightly more optimistic hopes for the future. He believed that population growth might be held in check because as people become accustomed to more goods and services, they might develop a taste for goods rather than children.

The most pessimistic of the classicists was the English economist, Thomas R. Malthus. Parson Malthus (he was a preacher) originated what has become known as the **Malthusian specter**. His grim view of the future derived from two influences: the supply of people and the supply of food to maintain them. Malthus argued that the supply of people (the population) will increase at a geometric rate (1, 2, 4, 8, 16, and so on), that is, double each generation, or every twenty-five years. On the other hand, the food supply will increase only at an arithmetic rate (1, 2, 3, 4, 5, and so on). Finally, widespread starvation will result unless people are able to restrict the population. According to Malthus, there will be wars, plagues, and famines that ultimately will bring population into line with the means of sustaining people.

Has the Malthusian Nightmare Already Started?

We said in Chapter 2 that one-fourth of the world's population lives in high-income countries. For this lucky minority, the ominous predictions of the classical economists have obviously not come to pass. For the other three-fourths, however, the scenario, especially Malthus's version, has real meaning. Everyone reads about starvation, plague, famine, and war in such countries as Bangladesh and the Sahel. The photographs from those areas are heart-rending. Real per capita income in such countries is extremely low. For example, in India, each year population growth presses ever harder on the means of sustaining India's 600 million people. In spite of the green revolution (that is, the growth in agicultural productivity), India often needs foreign relief in the form of massive shipments of grain and other foodstuffs to prevent widespread starvation. For such countries, the low-level stationary state is a grim reality.

But what about that one-fourth of the world's people who live in Europe, North America, Australia, and Japan? Why have they escaped? Look again at Figure 14-1, and let's use the United States as an example. The United States has experienced, at least over the last 150 years, a continuous shifting of Y/P, our growth path. Each time, before the economy has actually reached a point of declining growth (such as t_0), it has moved onto a higher growth path, such as $(Y/P)'$. A series of such shifts has kept the U.S. economy from entering a stationary state. A study of our industrial history suggests that there are two major reasons for this: technological change and population increase.

Technological Change

A large part of U.S. productivity and increase in real income is due to the fact that U.S. industry has constantly changed the techniques by which it produces things. There is an old story about the clerk in the U.S. Patent Office who resigned, in the early nineteenth century, because he was sure that most of the important inventions had already been made. But Americans as a rule are optimistic about the future and count on technological change to increase their incomes and their productivity. To a great extent, their optimism is justified. Except for cyclical variations in investment in new forms of technology (such as the depression of the 1930s), U.S. industry has kept pushing ahead, using new methods as fast as people invent them. Beginning with the cotton gin in the late eighteenth century and continuing through the glamorous devices made possible by the aerospace technology of the 1960s and 1970s, U.S. industry has employed better and better machinery and tools, which have raised the productivity of American laborers. The United States has also made larger and larger investments in people themselves, spending billions on such things as education, health programs, parks, and slum clearance—all of which have helped raise the productivity of the American worker.

Population Increase

In 1930 there were 123 million Americans. In 1975 there were 213 million—almost double! This increase in population has been favorable to growth in the United States. Until people began to question the idea in recent years (more about that in Application 14), Americans believed that growth in numbers would make them better off in the long run, which naturally influenced their willingness to have children. During the nineteenth century, when we were an agricultural society, large

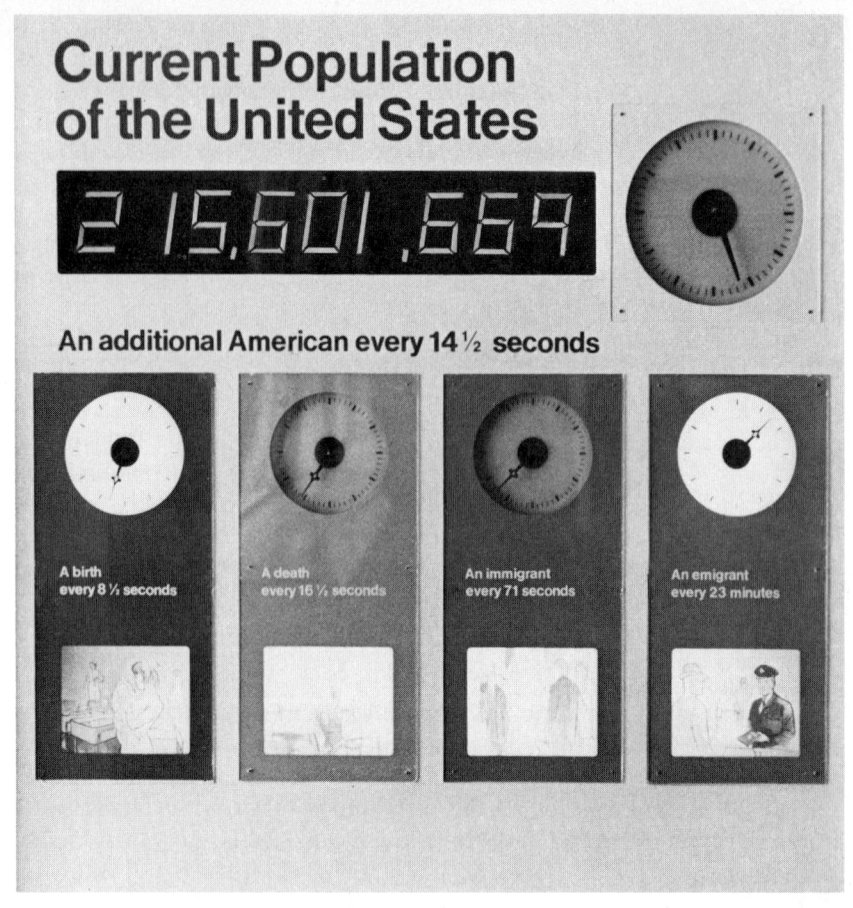

Population board at Boston's Museum of Science (Philip Jon Bailey)

families were like money in the bank. Children started working on the farms at an early age and were active producers.

Likewise, when the United States was becoming an urban industrial society, in the late nineteenth and early twentieth centuries, large families (together with waves of immigrants) were a good thing because they produced the labor force needed to build and operate mass-production factories.

But now that the United States is a mature industrial, or post-industrial, society, large families are no longer an *economic* asset. Children are consumers, not producers. So now, in the second half of the twentieth century, Americans are trying to halt the population explosion. Birth-control information is free in most states, and the advent of the Pill, plus the passing of laws to legalize abortion (it is now legal in all states to terminate a pregnancy during the first three months) have combined to reduce the number of births from 27.7 live births per thousand in 1920 to 15 live births per thousand in 1975—a drop of 45 percent in fifty-five years. Americans appear to be fast moving toward zero population growth.

Instead of trying to expand its labor force, the United States is trying to expand its capital. This means that industry produces things through techniques that are ever more **capital-intensive** (using relatively more capital than labor or land) rather than through techniques that are **labor-intensive** (using relatively more labor than capital or land). As this is done generally, **capital deepening** occurs, that is, relatively more and more capital is used (raising the capital-to-labor ratio for the economy).

By contrast, **capital broadening** occurs when capital instruments (tools, plant, and the like) grow at the same rate that labor grows.

There is a lesson to be learned from U.S. economic history: The Malthusian nightmare need not come true at all. Technological change can rapidly increase a nation's ability to produce food. Population increase need not be a drag on industrial growth. In fact, an educated populace *can* slow the population growth to zero.

But whether the experience of the United States (and other industrial nations) will be repeated in other nations as they attempt to industrialize, or whether the grim Malthusian scenario will indeed come to pass for most of the world's poorer countries, remains to be seen.

Full-Employment Growth

Up to now we have viewed economic growth in terms of increase in productivity. Clearly, the increase in productivity does determine the upper limit, the potential for growth of a nation. Actual performance, however, may be a lot less than this potential. As we pointed out in Chapters 6 through 9, the economy does not have to operate at a full-employment level in order to achieve growth.

To make clear what determines full employment and full-employment GNP, we'll introduce the concept of the **aggregate production function**, which is the relationship between output and employment in a given economy at a specific time. Figure 14-2, on the next page, shows such a relationship. Note that Figure 14-2 tells us that full employment corresponds to 100 million employed and $1.5 trillion in output. It does not tell us whether all 100 million people will actually find jobs or whether the economy really will produce that 1,500 billion (or 1.5 trillion) in output. Rather, it tells what *can* be produced if all people in the labor force are employed.

Let's review what determines the actual level of output and employment. Figure 14-3, on the next page, summarizes these factors. The equilibrium level of employment is at E, which is $1.3 trillion ($1,300 billion) while full employment *(FE)* is at $1.5 trillion. There is thus a $200 billion gap between *actual* employment and output and *full* employment and output. (With 30 million unemployed, according to Figure 14-2, the level of employment is 70 million at $1.3 trillion output.)

Only an increase in aggregate demand (total spending or $C + I + GX$) will fill this gap. The size of the increase depends on the income and employment multiplier. The multiplier's size depends on people's marginal propensities to consume and save and on the amounts of people's incomes that go to taxes. (To review this model, reread Chapter 9.)

But one never knows for sure that, at any given time, an employment gap *will* be filled. As you learned in Application 8, the United States has a mixed record where employment is concerned. The United States has a long history of growth (at a compound rate of 2.1 percent over the last hundred years), but the curve is jagged because of ups and downs in the level of employment. The United States has rarely had negative growth (except in depression years such as 1930, 1931, 1932, and in the mid-1970s), but it has also rarely reached full employment.

What has this meant in terms of the growth path for the U.S. economy? Look at Figure 14-4, in which

$$\left(\frac{Y}{P}\right)_{fe}$$

represents the growth of real per capita income at full employment. The curve in Figure 14-4, labeled

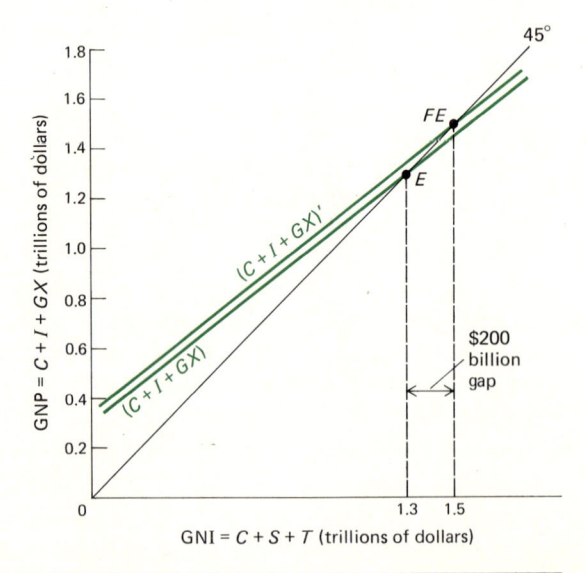

$$\left(\frac{Y}{P}\right)_{ufe},$$

represents the less-than-full-employment growth of an economy. Gaps in the growth, such as AB, (at time t_1) are derived from gaps in output

Figure 14-2 Aggregate Production Function *(APF)*

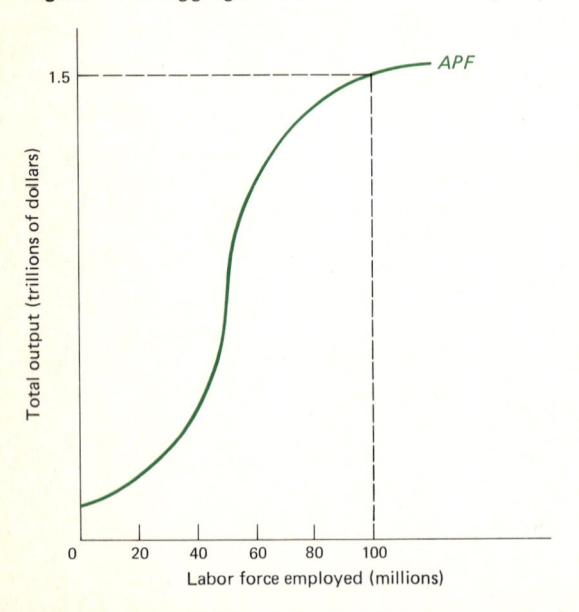

Figure 14-3 Equilibrium Employment and Output. E = equilibrium level of employment and output; FE = full employment; C = consumption; I = investment; GX = government expenditures; T = taxes, GNI = gross national income, S = savings, and GNP = gross national product

Expansion and Growth

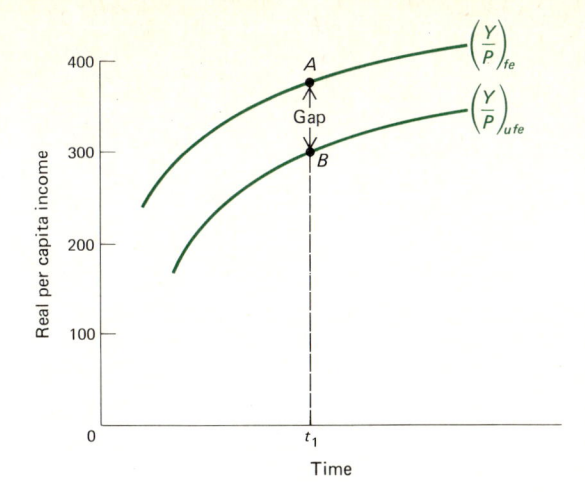

Figure 14-4 Full-Employment and Less-Than-Full-Employment Growth

and employment, such as those in Figure 14-3. If you divide the $200 billion gap shown in (static) Figure 14-3 by the population at that time, you get AB, the difference between actual per capita income and full-employment per capita income. The per capita gap represents a *loss* to each member of the society. This loss is permanent, since it can never be offset later in real terms, by more than full employment. You can't go back today and earn money you didn't earn five years ago because you were out of a job.

Growth at Full Capacity: How Fast Should It Be?

To this point, we have considered only the effects of *investment* on employment (the I in $C + I + GX$). Net investment creates new plant and equipment, and therefore more productivity capacity. This means that GNP must grow from year to year to ensure that the additional capacity will be utilized.

Let's examine the rate at which an economy must grow in order to avoid idle capacity and the falling off of investment that will surely follow. Bear in mind that we are not retracing earlier steps. The effects of idle laborers are not the same as the effects of idle plants. In some ways, if the human suffering of the unemployed is left out of the picture, idle plants are an even more serious economic problem than idle laborers, because jobs can be created only when there is enough plant and equipment to employ people productively. In an industrial economy, even the simplest jobs require some tools or equipment. An increase in the labor force increases our productive capacity (full-employment GNP), whereas increased autonomous and induced investments increase both productive capacity *and* GNP through their multiplier-accelerator effects.

In discussing the relation between investment and growth in GNP, we shall ignore government investment, because here we are trying to find out how *private* investment must behave in order to avoid idle capacity. (Also, government investment does not depend on GNP growth.)

So, leaving government out of the picture, equilibrium GNP is the level of GNP at which savings equals investment ($S = I$). Since growth is a long-run process, one first needs to know how private savings behave in the long run. In the past, savings have always seemed to rise proportionally with income. In other words, the average propensity to save (APS) has been constant. Since income equals consumption plus savings, the average propensity to consume (APC) has also tended to be constant.

You remember from our analysis of the multiplier-accelerator (Chapter 9) that, for a growing economy, each year's increase in GNP must be greater than last year's. Also, each year's increase in investment must be greater than last year's. Both GNP and investment must therefore grow each year by increasing *absolute* amounts. Let's use an arithmetic example.

Assume that the equilibrium GNP (*EGNP*) in period t_0 is $1.4 trillion, and that it took $240 billion of private investment (*I*) to make the GNP attain that equilibrium. Now suppose that this investment (I = $240 billion) gave rise to $80 billion of new capacity. This means that each dollar of investment creates one-third of a dollar of new capacity. Assume that the multiplier is 2. With a multiplier of 2, to use the $80 billion of new capacity in period t_1, the economy will need $40 billion of new investment. Let's suppose that private investment comes up with that much.

Now investment in t_0 equals $280 billion (240 + 40). How much will investment have to be in t_1 if the economy is going to keep on using its full capacity? The $40 billion of new investment in t_0 gave rise to this new productive capacity: $40 billion $\times \frac{1}{3}$ = $13.33 billion. So, if the economy is to use all that capacity, investment in t_2 must rise over that in t_0 by $53.33 billion ($240 billion + $40 billion + $53.33 billion = $333.33 billion total investment in t_2).

This example illustrates that (in the absence of government investment) *private investment is the key to full capacity GNP growth*. It also shows that if the economy is to maintain full-capacity use of plant and equipment, private investment must increase by larger absolute amounts each year.

Full Employment Versus Full Capacity

Is it possible to have a full-employment growth rate that exceeds the full-capacity growth rate? As a matter of fact, this does happen in the underdeveloped nations. If a society saves and (productively) invests relatively little, it will have little *capacity*. Even if it uses all its capacity, it may fall far short of employing its entire labor force. Unemployment and underemployment result.

Even in an industrial nation such as the United States, it is possible for the full-employment rate to be greater than the full-capacity rate. Indeed, some economists feel that this is one of the problems in the U.S. economy in the 1970s. Paul McCracken, former chairman of the Council of Economic Advisers, said in 1973 that the employment rate *could* be higher in the United States, but that U.S. industry does not have the additional plant and equipment needed. Although other factors contributed to high U.S. unemployment rates in the 1970s, the lagging growth of new plant and equipment was an important ingredient.

Capital Formation: The United States and Other Nations

You have seen that capital investment and the capacity resulting from it are necessary to create jobs. Some economists say that the United States is not saving and investing enough to create that capacity. It is true that the United States does not save and invest nearly as large a percentage of its GNP as some other industrial countries. (U.S. savings rates are half those of Japan and significantly less than those of some of the Western European nations, excluding Great Britain).

Yet you have also seen that the United States has enjoyed a compound growth rate in its national product of 2.1 percent for more than a hundred years. Apart from cyclical periods of high unemployment such as the 1930s, the U.S. employment record has compared favorably with that of other nations. Why, then, is the United States having trouble creating industrial jobs? It is not because of a decline in the percentage of investment going into fixed investment as opposed to inventory (about 10.9 percent of GNP went into fixed investment in 1973). This percentage has been fairly constant for many years. Some economists believe a major problem is that the United States is diverting a large part of its investment into uses that do not create capacity. Environmental protection is usually cited as the main use of this sort. A billion dollars' worth of investment in "scrubbers" to clean a plant's pollution from the air or its effluents from the water creates no new capacity, or very little. While it may have as much *static* effect on aggregate demand ($C + I + GX$) and employment, it does not create the additional capacity for subsequent *dynamic* periods that will ensure future jobs and a decline in the level of unemployment.

What can be done about this problem? Paul McCracken says three things: First, Americans must recognize the tradeoff between investing in a cleaner environment and creating more capacity and jobs (they should make an informed choice about what they want). Second, when they have recognized the tradeoff, they must establish the optimum balance among improving the environment, creating jobs, and maintaining the supply of goods. (Presumably, this balance would be somewhere between the extremes of stopping or sharply reducing growth and stopping or sharply reducing the cleanup of air and water). Third, Americans could enlarge the percentage of the GNP that goes into capital formation. This would mean higher corporate profits to provide investment funds, or the incentives to induce firms to secure these funds in the financial capital markets.

SUMMING UP

1. In order to be able to analyze many economic problems, one needs a *dynamic* rather than a *static* framework, that is, a structure that shows change through time.

2. *Expansion*, a process by which total output increases, comes about through the use of more resources, land, labor, and capital. *Growth* is a process by which productivity, output per hour of labor (or income per capita), increases and becomes more complex.

3. According to Adam Smith and other classical economists, growth takes place because of the increased productivity that accompanies specialization in the uses of resources. This specialization is limited by the size of the market. As the market grows, more and more specialization takes place. But because of limited supplies of land and, ultimately, diminishing efficiences, an economy's growth will diminish beyond some point and will ultimately reach a *stationary state*.

4. The stationary state may be high or low in terms of real per capita income. Smith envisioned it as becoming high, since with the development of better technology, people might prefer more goods to more children. Malthus thought it was likely to be low, since population increase would outstrip the food supply, and famine, plagues, and the like would result.

5. The classical scenario (the Malthusian version in some cases) has come true in many poor countries, whose growth has been very slow, or nonexistent, and whose investment in education has been slight.

6. The industrial nations have escaped the stationary state, for two reasons: (a) Technological change has shifted their growth paths upward and overcome the long-term tendencies toward stagnation. (b) As growth has occurred, the rate of growth of their populations has tapered off.

7. Even a growing economy's growth is not necessarily accompanied by full employment. Therefore, a society's *actual growth path*—the change in its real per capita income as time goes by—may be less than its full-employment potential.

8. The *aggregate production function* is the relationship between total output and the labor force employed. It tells us how much output an economy produces at various levels of employment.

9. *Aggregate demand*, the total spending of a society on consumption, investment, and government, is what determines levels of employment. When this level is inadequate, less than full employment results.

10. The United States has a long record of growth; over the last hundred years, its output has increased at a compound annual rate of 2.1 percent. But it has had long periods of less than full employment, and therefore its growth path has been below the full-employment level. Thus, the United States has lost a great deal of per capita income.

11. Investment creates not only jobs but also more production capacity. The effect of idle workers is different from the effect of idle machines. Creating jobs requires plants and machines that are the fruits of investment.

12. Leaving government investment out of the picture, equilibrium GNP is that level of GNP at which $S = I$. In the long run, the rates of savings (and investment) and consumption in relation to income have been constant.

13. The full-capacity rate of growth may be below the full-employment rate. This sometimes happens in societies that have inadequate amounts of savings and productive investment. Indeed, some economists believe that it may account for part of our problem in the United States in the 1970s.

14. In the 1970s, the United States appeared to be putting a smaller part of investment into fixed things (plants, new processes) that increase capacity. While nonfixed (primarily environmental) investments create jobs, they do not create additional ability to produce and more long-term demand for labor. According to Paul McCracken, Americans can do three things about this: (a) recognize the tradeoff between an improved environment and more jobs from more plant capacity, (b) find the optimum balance between growth and cleaner air and water, and (c) consider devoting more of the GNP to investment.

QUESTIONS

1. What do we mean by full-employment growth? What do we mean by full-capacity growth?

2. Why is a dynamic framework more useful than a static one for analyzing growth relationships and problems?

3. Which do you think is more important: full-capacity growth or full-employment growth? Does it make a difference whether you refer to the long run or the short run? What is the relationship between full-employment growth and full-capacity growth?

4. Is expansion or growth more important to improving the material well-being of people? Why?

5. If you were asked to recommend ways to increase the amount of savings and investment in the United States, what would you propose?

6. Do you think the United States should devote more of its gross national product to investment? Why?

SUGGESTED READINGS

Adelman, Irma. *Theories of Economic Development.* Stanford University Press, Stanford, Calif., 1961 (for those who know some mathematics).

McCracken, Paul W. "The Need for More Plant Capacity." *Wall Street Journal,* October 17, 1973.

Ridker, Ronald G. "To Grow or Not to Grow: That's Not the Relevant Question." *Science,* 1973. Reprinted in *Readings in Economics, 76/77.* Dushkin, Guilford, Conn., 1976.

Slichter, Sumner H. *Economic Growth in the United States.* Free Press, New York, 1966.

Stahl, Sheldon W. "On Economic Growth." *Monthly Review, Federal Reserve Bank of Kansas City,* February 1975.

Application 13

Can We Have Growth Without Massive Military Spending?

Do Wars Keep the Economy Healthy?

Must the American economy have heavy injections of government spending for war and defense in order to achieve full-employment, full-capacity growth? Opinions vary greatly. Let's look at two contrasting views.

Writing about the period since World War II, Douglas Dowd, an economist critical of many aspects of the American economy, says, "The key to this process of sustained growth—i.e., the absence of even a serious recession, let alone a depression—is to be found in the record of federal purchases, and in that category, the key factor is purchases geared to the military." Dowd says that between 1946 and 1971, 80 percent of the $1.4 trillion of federal expenditures was in some way connected with defense. This, he argues, is the primary reason for the stability and growth of our post–World War II economy.

Other observers claim that the connection between defense spending and the growth of the American economy is not at all clear. It is true, they say, that defense spending has helped to create jobs and stimulate consumption and investment spending, and that massive war expenditures beginning in 1941 had a lot to do with reducing unemployment from 14.6 percent in 1940 to 1.2 percent in 1944. It is also true that unemployment reached its lowest postwar point (2.9 percent) in 1953 when Korean War expenditures were at their peak. Yet the unemployment rate swung up and down widely between 1946 and 1970, and defense spending was probably only one of several factors affecting employment and growth.

To put these two positions in perspective, see Table A13-1. From the mid-1940s to the end of the 1960s, unemployment varied from 2.9 percent to 6.8 percent of the civilian labor force. The high points in unemployment (1949–1950, 1958–1963) reflect downturns in the economy. Notice, however, that they do not correspond to downturns in military spending either in absolute terms or in terms of a percentage of GNP. (Military spending includes military purchases and military salaries, but not interest on the national debt associated with deficits attributable to war or defense spending.) The low points in unemployment (1946–1948, 1951–1953, 1955–1957, 1965–1969) also reflect upturns in the economy, not upturns in defense spending. These conclusions generally follow even if one introduces a time lag of a year or so between changes in defense spending and changes in the rate of unemployment.

The single exception appears to be 1953–1954, when the percentage of the GNP consumed by national defense fell from 13.5 percent to 11.3 percent (in absolute terms, it fell by about $8 billion) and unemployment rose from 2.9 percent to 5.6 percent. Even if the income (and employment) multiplier was large, say 2 or 3, a decline of $8 billion in defense spending in 1954 should not by itself have produced a near doubling of unemployment. In fact, GNP rose in 1954, and it appears that a rise in people's spending for personal consumption, together with a rise in net exports, more than offset the decline in defense spending. The rise in unemployment was probably largely due to industry's having to make a transition from producing military to producing civilian goods.

On the basis of these data and the relationship between defense spending and employment, we can say two things with a fair amount of confidence:

1. The United States has apparently not used *variations* in defense spending as a strategic weapon to combat unemployment.

2. Military spending constitutes a large, relatively stable portion of GNP (aggregate demand).

If there had been no military spending in the United States since 1946, unemployment would have been much higher. The same thing could be said, however, about *other* federal expenditures. As Arthur Okun, a former chairman of the Council of Economic Advisers in the Johnson administration, put it, "Ever since Keynes, economists had recognized that the federal government could stimulate economic activity by increasing the injection of federal expenditures into the income stream or by reducing the withdrawal of federal tax receipts." If any net increase in GX or decrease in T in the $C + I + GX = C + S + T$ equilibrium is stimulative, then there is nothing unique about defense spending. Lord Keynes himself expressed it well in 1936, when he wrote about societies that lower unemployment by engaging in government spending:

> Ancient Egypt was doubly fortunate, and doubtless owed to this its fabled wealth, in that it possessed *two* activities, namely, pyramid-building as well as the search for precious metals, the fruits of which, since they could not serve the needs of man by being consumed, did not stale with abundance. The middle ages built cathedrals and sang dirges. Two pyramids, two masses for the dead, are twice as good as one.

In other words, the government might have spent the same amount of money on developing the world's best system of mass transit or on some income-maintenance scheme to supplement the earnings of the nation's poorest citizens, and achieved the same effect on the economy.

What About Reaching Potential?

In the 1960s, the government began to shy away from using fiscal policy (both expenditures and tax cuts) as a "fireman's tool" to cure unemployment fires already burning. The emphasis turned instead toward stimulating the economy, toward using its productive potential (only 4 percent unemployment). People believed that, in the long run, and especially if the economy could move toward full capacity as well as full employment, this would bring forth the continued investment needed to increase productivity and create new jobs as well. The primary device used was the massive federal tax cut of 1964; the government reduced income tax withholding rates and offered an investment tax credit to business firms.

To see how close the United States has come to reaching its potential GNP, examine Figure A13-1. (If your memory of GNP gaps is vague, review Chapter 6.) Since 1955, the performance has been uneven. In the late 1950s, the gap between actual and potential GNP widened. Yet during this period, defense spending was growing, though slowly, and it remained nearly constant as a percentage of GNP. Beginning in the early 1960s, the United States moved toward reaching its potential GNP, with the pace quick-

TABLE A13-1 The Federal Government's Purchases of Goods and Services for the Military and Their Relation to GNP, 1945-1969

Year	Amount of military spending (billions of dollars)	Percentage of GNP	Unemployment as a percentage of civilian labor force
1945	75.9	35.5	1.9
1946	18.8	8.9	3.9
1947	11.4	4.9	3.9
1948	11.6	4.5	3.8
1949	13.6	5.3	5.9
1950	14.3	5.0	5.3
1951	33.9	10.3	3.3
1952	46.4	13.4	8.1
1953	49.3	13.5	2.9
1954	41.2	11.3	5.6
1955	39.1	9.8	4.4
1956	40.4	9.6	4.2
1957	44.4	10.0	4.3
1958	44.8	10.1	6.8
1959	46.2	9.6	5.5
1960	45.7	9.1	5.6
1961	49.0	9.4	6.7
1962	53.6	9.6	5.6
1963	55.2	9.5	5.7
1964	55.4	8.9	5.2
1965	55.6	8.4	4.5
1966	60.6	8.1	3.8
1967	72.4	9.2	3.8
1968	79.0	9.3	3.6
1969	79.2	8.5	3.5

Source: James L. Clayton, "The Economic Impact of the Cold War," *Impact of the War in Southeast Asia on the U.S. Economy*, U.S. Senate Foreign Relations Committee, G.P.O., Washington, D.C., 1970.

Figure A13-1 Actual and Potential Gross National Product. GNP in 1972 dollars, annual rate. (*Source:* Joint Economic Committee, Congress of the United States, *Joint Economic Report,* 1973.)

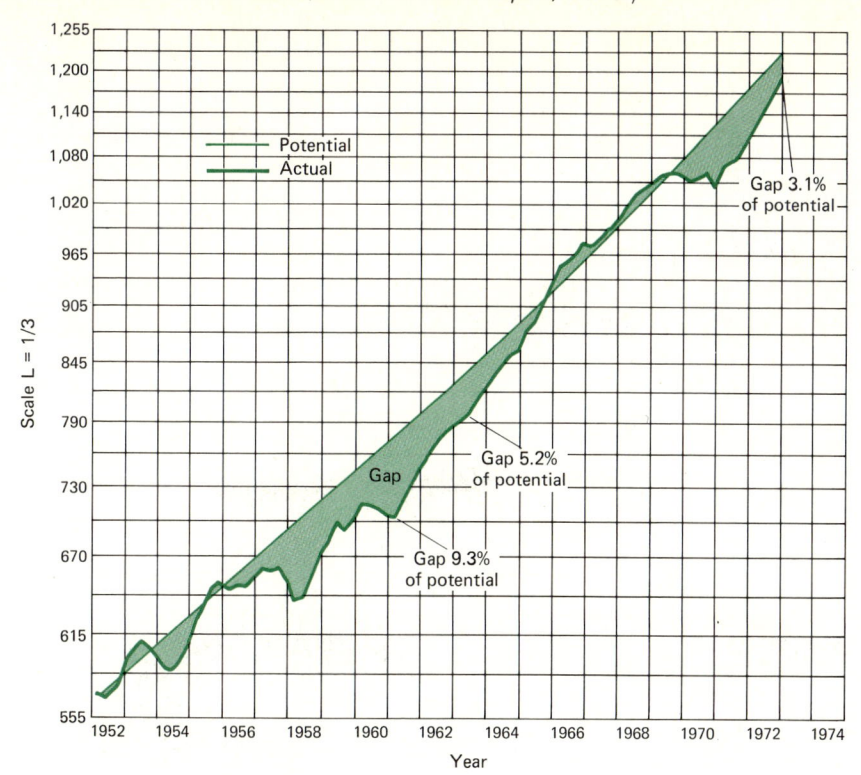

ening after the tax cut of 1964. By 1966, the economy was running just about at or slightly above potential, and continued to do so through 1969. Note in Table A13-1 that in this period there was no significant change in the percentage of GNP spent on defense.

So you can see that the following occurred: (1) Defense spending from 1951 to 1970 was a stable component of government spending and therefore provided a floor under aggregate demand, income, and employment. (2) Movement toward full-potential growth in the sixties was caused by fiscal (tax) policy, not change in defense spending.

Defense Spending: Does It Encourage or Retard Technological Change?

Some economists argue that large defense expenditures actually reduce our full capacity rate of growth. They feel that research and development skills and resources which are put to military uses do little to increase the nation's industrial capacity. As a result, the United States gives up larger increases in capacity that could be used to help solve not only employment problems but also income-distribution problems, such as problems of the cities, of racial minorities, and of poverty.

There is another way of looking at this. A good many people feel that the government's expenditures for defense (and space exploration) have helped increase our full capacity growth through fostering technological change (in communications equipment and in many other things).

Who is right? It's hard to say; both viewpoints may be right. The unanswered question is: What is the net effect, the relation between what the economy gives up in technological change in the private sector versus what is gained? One cannot estimate this at present.

kinds of stimulants must be applied. But while the government is stimulating growth, it must at the same time control inflation. This may well be one of the most important problems facing the United States in the years to come.

QUESTION

Suppose that you are chairman of a special task force on employment. The President of the United States calls you in and says that he is going to propose an extraordinary increase of $20 billion in federal spending in order to create one million new jobs. He can't decide, though, whether to increase the spending of the Defense Department (which maintains that it needs a new manned bomber system) or the Department of Health, Education, and Welfare (which wants to expand educational benefits, medical care benefits, and other such programs). The President wants to know whether there will be different economic effects from the two types with expenditures of equal size. What would you tell the President?

"All right, suppose we abolish war, and the entire world is at peace—then what?"

What About the 1970s?

In the 1970s the American economy came upon progressively harder times, both in terms of full employment and full capacity. Between 1973 and mid-1975, unemployment climbed to about 9 percent. Many industries, especially those making durable consumer goods such as automobiles, were operating far below capacity. Figure A13-1 shows that in 1973 the gap closed slightly, to 3.1 percent of potential. The rapid inflation and high unemployment of 1974 and 1975 doubtless increased it again. Under these conditions, investment was not creating new capacity quickly enough to absorb a rapidly growing labor force.

What does this portend for the future? Defense spending in the 1970s certainly did not fill employment and capacity gaps. The end of major military commitments in Southeast Asia reduced the U.S. need for defense spending. If growth is to remain a major objective of U.S. policy, other

SUGGESTED READINGS

Clayton, James L. *The Economic Impact of the Cold War.* Harcourt, Brace & World, New York, 1970.

Dowd, Douglas F. *The Twisted Dream.* Winthrop, Cambridge, Mass., 1974.

"Impact of the War in Southeast Asia on the U.S. Economy." *Hearings Before the Committee on Foreign Relations, United States Senate,* G.P.O., Washington, D.C., 1970.

Keynes, John Maynard. *The General Theory of Employment, Interest and Money.* Harcourt, Brace & World, New York, 1936.

Melman, Seymour, ed. *The War Economy of the United States.* St. Martin's, New York, 1971.

Okun, Arthur M. *The Political Economy of Prosperity.* Norton, New York, 1970.

Stevens, Robert Warren. *Vain Hopes, Grim Realities: the Economic Consequences of the Vietnam War.* F. Watts (New Viewpoints), New York, 1976.

Application 14

More Growth Versus a Clean Environment

More than a century has passed since the era of the "dismal science" and its grim Malthusian predictions. Optimism about the material future of human beings has grown. Improved technology and better organization, plus growing supplies of resources (including labor), have caused more and more countries to follow Britain and the United States toward ever higher levels of real income and better standards of living. Evidently the economists' assumption about growing output chasing rising aspirations was correct.

In the 1970s, however, the optimists began to qualify their optimism. (As Don Marquis said, "An optimist is a guy who has never had much experience.") Economists and noneconomists alike challenged this view of unlimited growth and its benefits—particularly with respect to the quality of the environment. Let's examine the nature of these disputes.

The Economists' View

Economists in general will not concede that pollution of the environment is the result of economic growth *per se*. Many also believe that the market system can offer solutions to the problems of pollution. In addition, many economists believe that continued growth is necessary, not as an end in itself, but as a means of solving a Pandora's box full of economic problems. Walter Heller (chairman of the council of Economic Advisers during the Kennedy and Johnson administrations) summarized these views as follows:

> In the starkest terms, the ecologist confronts us with an environmental imperative that requires an end to economic growth—or a sharp curtailment of it—as the price of biological survival. In contrast, the economist counters with a socioeconomic imperative that requires the continuation of growth as the price of social survival.... Like it or not, economic growth seems destined to continue.

Heller goes on to say the following: (1) Ecologists disagree with economists about whether real growth (improvement in the quality of life) has occurred, considering negative externalities. (2) Ecologists envision absolute bans and absolute limits to growth; economists envision marginal tradeoffs and cost-benefit relations. (3) Ecologists want to rely on government to solve ecological problems; economists would rely on the price system to create solutions. Walter Heller says that growth could be checked, but that this "would throw the fragile ecology of our economic system so out of kilter as to threaten its breakdown."

Most economists would probably agree with Heller that it is the *pattern* of growth of the U.S. economy, not growth itself, that has created environmental pollution. Heller makes the point that scares about the environment (based on the view that resources are static) occur periodically. He also says that our attempts to solve problems such as poverty, discrimination, and pollution have so mortgaged future GNP growth that there is no choice left; the economy *has* to grow.

Economists generally agree that good environmental quality is a scarce commodity. Most of them say that the market system does not adequately incorporate externalities, such as pollution of the nation's water supply by industry, into its pricing system. However, this problem cannot be solved by limiting growth or by eliminating it.

Let's examine the problem of water. The world is running out of clean water, yet our need for it is growing with each passing year. Industries use millions of gallons of it hourly—for quenching steel ingots, for washing paper pulp, for cooling nuclear power plants, for cleaning newly slaughtered animals being readied for market, for washing away the chemicals from textile mills, and for thousands of other uses. The *effluent*—that is, the used water that flows out of factories—is usually dumped into nearby rivers or streams. The water itself is not used up in this process. Rather, we have to clean it so that we can use it again, for bathing, swimming, cooking, and drinking.

To solve this problem, we could do two things: (1) *set minimum standards for industrial effluents* (though this would circumvent the market, and create large bureaucratic costs), and (2) *tax industrial effluents* (this would make firms—and ultimately consumers—internalize the costs of pollution).

How Population Enters the Picture

Both economists and ecologists point out that the problems of economic growth are inextricably tied in with the problems of population growth. However, as industrialization and urbanization take place, population growth tends to level off—even to decline. Families that live in urban, industrial societies acquire education and realize that children are consumers, not producers. Also, since a pollution-free environment is a "luxury" good, demand for it rises with income. As the economy continues to grow, people may be expected to demand more of this luxury (income superior) good and substitute it for the relatively less desirable (income inferior) good, in other words, more children.

It is mainly ecologists who present the antigrowth view, but some economists join in. Fundamentally, the arguments are founded on the belief that it is nature that imposes the limits to growth. As the distinguished historian Arnold Toynbee put it:

> More and more people are coming to realize that the growth of material wealth, which the British industrial revolution set going, and which the modern British-made ideology has presented as being mankind's proper paramount objective, cannot in truth be the "wave of the future." Nature is going to compel posterity to revert to a stable state on the material plane and to turn to the realm of the spirit for satisfying man's hunger for infinity.

Economist Kenneth Boulding has argued that we must move from viewing the economy as an open system, with unlimited resources and growth (the "cowboy economy"), to a "spaceship earth" closed economy (the "spaceman economy"). Boulding says that in the latter system, consumption and production that use up finite (nonreproducible) resources is not "good." Society must distinguish between reproducible and nonreproducible resources.

As Ecologists See It

Others, such as Herman Daly, argue that "growthmania"—the insistence that growth is the solution to economic problems—has outlived its usefulness. This view is reinforced by certain famous computer studies (the 1971 Club of Rome study is the most famous one) that predict disaster unless present growth trends are reversed. Daly and others argue not only for **zero economic growth (ZEG)**, *no* increase in GNP, but also **zero population growth (ZPG)**, no increase in population. To alleviate any hardships that this reversal of industrial history causes, they want to see constant controls on physical wealth and distribution of income.

Ecologists reject the market solution, which would entail forcing industries to internalize the externalities. Two observers, Richard England and Barry Bluestone, maintain that this would require *total recycling* of wastes, with an accompanying "astronomical cost."

As Economists See It

Economists in favor of ZEG have argued that using selective means, such as tax cuts, to stimulate consumer spending is *not* necessary to maintain full employment. They say that a guaranteed annual income can maintain a full-employment level of spending just as well, and accomplish many of the same objectives.

In rebuttal, economists who oppose ZEG generally (1) attack the idea (which is implicit in the computer models) that the supply of resources is static—that the world will soon run out of oil, coal, and other essentials; (2) argue that leaving resources unused so that future generations may use them may not be as important as the capital and technology that would result from using them in the present; (3) feel that the ZEG and ZPG groups underestimate the ability of the price system to ensure efficient use of resources, to cause substitutes to be developed, and to force industry (when required to) to internalize the externalities that may have been ignored in the past.

Who is right? What is the wave of the future? Higher levels of real income, or ZEG and ZPG? With population growth in the United States down to fifteen live births per thousand of population annually, it looks as though Americans are casting their votes on the side of ZPG, at least.

SUMMING UP

1. Until recently, twentieth-century economists, unlike their nineteenth-century forerunners, generally held an optimistic view of economic growth and its potential for solving economic problems. In the 1970s, growth is becoming the villain responsible for using up our planet's resources.

2. Certainly it is not economic growth alone that is responsible for polluting the environment. In fact, many economists believe that economic growth and the free market can solve the problems of environment in the future.

3. Walter Heller says that economic growth seems destined to continue and that (a) economists and ecologists disagree over whether the quality of life has improved in recent years; (b) ecologists see absolute limits to growth and to resources, while economists do not; and (c) ecologists want government to solve environmental problems, while economists rely heavily on the market system.

4. The market system does not incorporate externalities, such as pollution of the nation's water supply by industry, into its pricing system. The solutions to this might be (a) to set minimum standards for industrial effluents, or (b) to tax industrial effluents so that producers (and ultimately consumers) would have to pay the full social costs of polluting the water.

5. Economic growth is inextricably intertwined with population growth. However, population growth declines with economic growth, since children in an urban, industrial society are nonproducers and people begin to prefer environmental improvement to more children.

6. Arnold Toynbee argued that growth is not the wave of the future, but that natural forces will force the world's people to revert to a stable state, that is, no growth.

7. Some economists and ecologists decry "growthmania" and argue for both *zero economic growth* and *zero population growth*. They feel that obtaining these would necessitate government controls over physical wealth and distribution of income.

8. Ecologists reject the idea of the free market offering the solution to environmental pollution, on the grounds that the cost of total recycling of wastes would be astronomical.

9. Economists in favor of ZEG say that a guaranteed annual income (with its income redistribution effect) is a good substitute for economic growth. A guaranteed annual income, they say, would sustain consumption demand and thereby keep employment at an acceptable level.

10. In rebutting the gloomy arguments of the ecologists, economists who oppose ZEG (a) attack the view that resources are static, (b) maintain that it is better to leave capital and technology to posterity than to leave unused resources to posterity, (c) feel that proponents of ZEG and ZPG underestimate the ability of the price system to change patterns of resource use and to induce people to use substitutes for nonreproducible resources.

QUESTIONS

1. What is the relationship between economic growth and the solutions to such ills as poverty, discrimination, and the welfare situation?

2. Is pollution of the environment *necessarily* the result of economic growth? If not, what else might it result from?

3. How may the market system—either with or without additional government control—develop solutions to problems of pollution.

4. What does Boulding mean by the "spaceship earth" concept?

5. State what you think of the arguments for and against ZPG.

SUGGESTED READINGS

Barkley, Paul W., and David W. Seckler. *Economic Growth and Environmental Decay: The Solution Becomes the Problem.* Harcourt Brace Jovanovich, New York, 1972.

Boulding, Kenneth E. "The Economics of the Coming Spaceship Earth." In *Environmental Quality in a Growing Economy.* Johns Hopkins, Baltimore, 1966.

Daly, Herman E. "The Steady-State Economy: Toward a Political Economy of Biophysical Equilibrium and Moral Growth." In *Toward a Steady-State Economy,* edited by Herman E. Daly. Freeman, San Francisco, 1973.

Deacon, Robert. "Environmental Quality: A View from the Marketplace." In *Economic Analysis of Pressing Social Problems,* by Llad Phillips and Harold Votey. Rand McNally, Chicago, 1974.

Easterlin, Richard A. "Population." In *Contemporary Economic Issues,* edited by Neil W. Chamberlain. Irwin, Homewood, Ill., 1973.

The Editor. "2074." *Challenge,* May/June 1974. Reprinted in *Readings in Economics, 76/77.* Dushkin, Guilford, Conn., 1976.

Forrester, Jay. W. *World Dynamics.* Wright-Allen, Cambridge, Mass., 1971.

Heilbroner, Robert, *Business Civilization in Decline.* Norton, New York, 1976.

Heilbroner, Robert L. "Growth and Survival." *Foreign Affairs,* 50 (October 1972).

Heilbroner, Robert L. "The Human Prospect." *Skeptic: The Forum for Contemporary History,* Special Issue No. 2, 1974. Reprinted in *Readings in Economics, 76/77.* Dushkin, Guilford, Conn., 1976.

Heller, Walter W. "Economic Growth and Ecology, an Economist's View." In *Economics, Mainstream, Reading and Radical Critiques,* 2nd ed., edited by David Mermelstein. Random House, New York, 1973.

Hoskins, W. Lee. "An Economic Solution to Pollution." *Business Review,* September 1970.

Humphrey, Thomas M. "The Dismal Science Revisited." Federal Reserve Board of Richmond, September 1970.

Johnson, Warren. "The Guaranteed Income as an Environmental Measure." In *Economic Growth vs. the Environment,* edited by Warren Johnson and John Hordesty, Wadsworth, Belmont, Calif, 1971.

Kaysen, Carl. "The Computer that Printed Out W*O*L*F." *Foreign Affairs,* 50 (July 1972).

Meadows, D. H. et al. *The Limits to Growth.* Universe Books, New York, 1972.

Pale, Edwin L., Jr. "The Economics of Pollution." *New York Times*, April 19, 1970.

Toynbee, Arnold. *The Observer*, London, June 11, 1972.

Votey, Harold. "Population Pressure and the Quality of Life." In *Economic Analysis of Pressing Social Problems*, by Llad Phillips and Harold Votey. Rand McNally, Chicago, 1974.

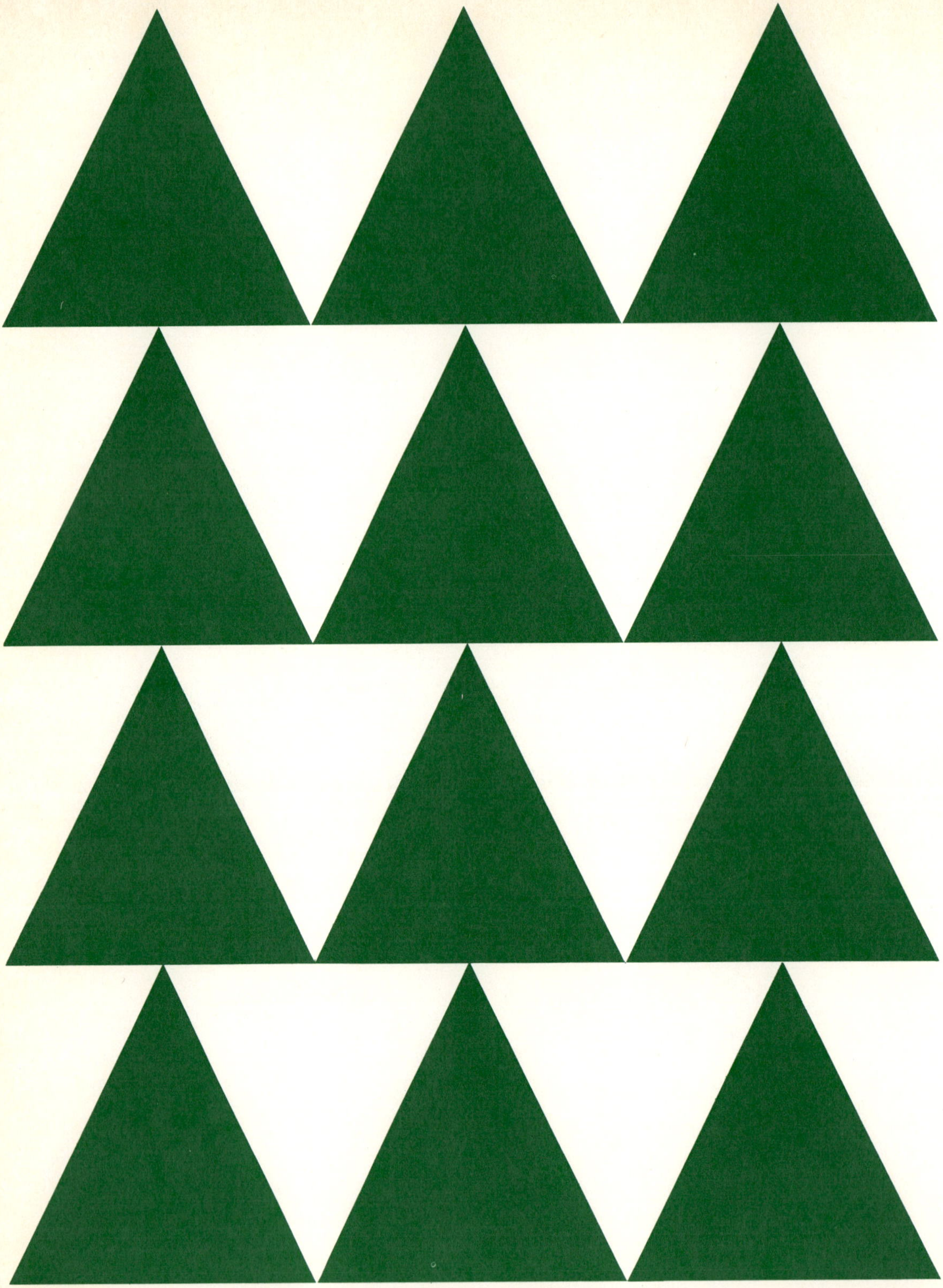

PART TWO

Microeconomics

Part Two deals with microeconomics, *how markets work to allocate resources and distribute income. We mentioned this subject in Part One, when we discussed scarcity, supply and demand, and the parts of our economic society. Then, however, we were building toward an understanding of* macro *economic forces and problems.*

We will now closely examine the market system, setting forth the theoretical foundations on which demand and supply are based, and making some assumptions about how consumers and producers behave. Then we will discuss what private and social costs are, and when they may differ.

The core of any study of microeconomics is a range of models of markets, based on the competitiveness—or lack of it—in the behavior of firms in those markets. The models we will examine will range from pure competition to pure monopoly. We will discuss the setting of prices, the determination of how much is produced, and the relative efficiency of various markets in producing goods and satisfying consumers. Our final topic will be the side of the market that supplies resources to the firms producing goods and services. And we will discuss wages, interest, rent, and profits.

15

The Demand Side of the Market

In Chapter 3, as a preface to the study of aggregate demand, we discussed demand and the shape of a demand curve. Before you study Part Two, review Chapter 3. To help you review, here is a brief summary.

What Is Demand?

To an economist, **demand** is a set of relations representing the quantities of a good (a commodity or service) that consumers will buy over a given range of prices in a given period of time.

The demand schedule, in other words, reflects the way consumers react when faced with variations in the price of a good. Explanations or models of demand—like all models—depend on certain assumptions: (1) Consumers know about, and can choose freely among, alternatives. (2) Consumers seek the maximum satisfaction from the goods they can buy with their limited incomes. (3) Things other than a good's price that might affect consumers' spending for that good—such as people's incomes and tastes, their expectations about future prices, the prices of other goods, and the number of consumers—are assumed *not* to vary during the given time period.

With these assumptions in mind, look at Figure 15-1, on page 352, which is a hypothetical demand curve for hamburgers. The demand curve (*D*) shows the relationship between prices of hamburgers in a given week and the quantity one person will buy at each possible price. Note that the person will not buy any hamburgers if their price goes as high as 70 cents each, and will buy an increasing number as their price falls. If the price goes to 20 cents apiece, that person will buy ten per week. The important thing to remember is that there is a relationship between price and quantity demanded, a relationship that is called the **law of demand**. This law states that price and quantity demanded are

Bargain-basement sale: As prices fall, quantities demanded increase. (Ellis Herwig/Stock, Boston)

inversely related. (An increase in price results in a decrease in quantity demanded; a decrease in price results in an increase in quantity demanded.)

We will explain this negative relationship, this downward-sloping demand curve, in two ways: (1) in terms of income and substitution effects, and (2) in terms of a theory of demand, called **utility theory**, the theory that people buy goods based on the satisfaction they expect to derive from those goods.

Income and Substitution Effects

Look at Figure 15-1. Price (vertical axis), the independent variable, is the factor that changes. Quantity sold (horizontal axis) is the dependent variable and responds to changes in price. Now suppose that the price of a hamburger falls from 50 cents (point A) to 45 cents (point B). According to the law of demand, this 5-cent decrease in price should result in an increase in the quantity demanded. In other words, the negative ΔP (recall that the Greek letter delta, or Δ, means a change) should result in a positive ΔQ from 4 to 5.

The ΔQ (the greater number of hamburgers bought) is, first, the result of the **income effect**, the change in quantity demanded caused by a change in consumer purchasing power resulting from a change in the price of a good. With the same money income, a person can now buy more hamburgers (and/or other things, such as Cokes, french fries, or fried chicken), so that person is in effect richer than before. Since, by assumption, hamburgers are a desirable good, part of the positive change in quantity is attributable to this income effect, the strength of which depends on what percentage of income an individual spends on hamburgers. If that individual hardly ever buys one, a price drop for hamburgers has little or no effect on his or her purchasing power. Whatever the strength of the effect, however, the income effect usually acts in a direction opposite to the direction of a price change. (If hamburger prices increase, the income effect will be a negative one.)

Second, the ΔQ is also the result of a **substitution effect**, the tendency to buy more of a cheaper good and substitute it for more expensive goods. In this case, the person can substitute the now relatively cheaper hamburgers for fried chicken, pizza, and other foods (we are assuming that the prices of these other foods have not changed). Since there are almost always some substitutes on the market, the substitution effect tends to confirm the law of demand. Taken together, the two effects—income and substitution—ordinarily cause the demand curve to have a negative slope.

The above market scenario is not the one that always takes place. Although this scene is repeated in the majority of instances, it is not universal. Let's look at some exceptions:

1. Consumers sometimes value a good just *because* it is expensive, and because people with high social status consume it. If, for instance, Beluga caviar or imported perfumes sold for a dollar a quart, people might not believe they were worth much. These goods could after all be bought

Figure 15-1 Hypothetical Demand Curve for Hamburgers

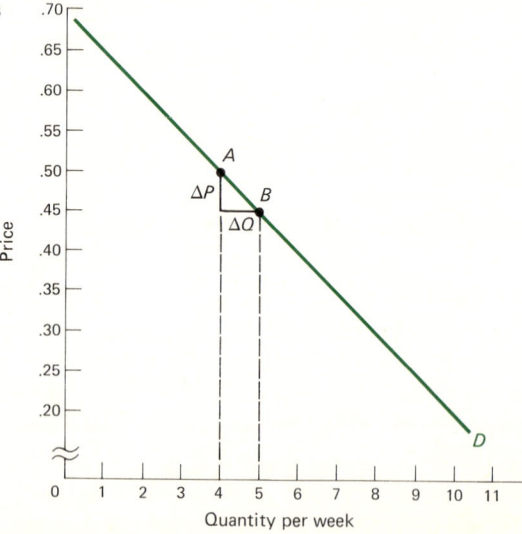

352   The Demand Side of the Market

Catering to the substitution effect (Harry Wilks/Stock, Boston)

by the masses. Such goods, which people buy more of at higher than at lower prices, are called **Veblen goods**, after Thorstein Veblen (1857–1929), an American economist who wrote a stinging analysis of the motives behind the consumption habits of rich people. (Veblen's *The Theory of the Leisure Class* caused a sensation when it was published in 1899.) The demand curve for a Veblen good slopes up to the right.

2. Sometimes people have to spend a large part of their income on certain cheap goods simply because they have low incomes that permit them few choices. For example, basic food staples such as rice in Asia, or corn or wheat or potatoes in other parts of the world (including poor areas of the United States). If the price of one of these staples falls, its consumers have more purchasing power and the income effect becomes potentially more important than the substitution effect. If the price of rice falls in India, the income effect may move in the same direction as price, because people may spend less on rice and spend their newly freed purchasing power on milk, meat, and other high-protein foods. Conversely, when rice goes up in price, because people have to spend more on rice, they have to do without the diversified diet. Goods with an income effect that moves in the same direction as price and outweighs the substitution effect—that is, goods that people buy less of as their price falls—are called **Giffen goods**, after Sir Robert Giffen, a nineteenth-century English economist. Such goods constitute a special case of so-called *income-inferior goods*, with an income effect that always moves in the same direction as price, but that is usually outweighed by the substitution effect.

Income and Substitution Effects

Utility: Another Way to Explain Demand

Whenever you buy something, you make a choice. In a well-ordered market system, there are many alternative choices. How do you make such choices? Why, for example, do you choose to deny yourself and put part of your paycheck in a savings account rather than spend it all on goods and services? Why do you choose to eat a hamburger rather than a pizza?

The answers lie in the market conditions, in the way the consumer makes choices, and in the consumer's objective. Let's make the following assumptions about these factors:

1. *Consumers buy competitively.* You, as an individual consumer, have no influence over the market price at which you buy things. There are no quantity discounts, no consumer co-ops. If toothpaste costs a dollar a tube, you pay a dollar. You pay prices as "given."

2. *Consumers have limited money incomes and full information* (at least price information) about the choices available.

3. *Consumers are rational;* they can make choices in a way that moves them toward their objective.

4. *Consumers want to maximize their total utility or satisfaction* within the limit of their money incomes.

These four assumptions are the basis for the study of **consumer choice**. **Utility theory**, one part of that study, attempts to explain consumer choice on the basis of the *utility*—or subjectively measured satisfaction—that one may derive from consuming any particular combinations of goods. We shall assume that utility can be measured in terms of *utils*, or units of satisfaction.

Most consumers in most situations do buy as competitors. You can haggle over the price you pay for a car. You can join a co-op. You can even get a quantity discount (10 percent off on that *case* of beer), but these are the exceptions.

Everyone knows that consumers have limited money incomes; everyone must live within a budget. Also, most consumers can read the newspaper, and thus have easy access to price information, even if they do not always understand the technical features of things they buy.

What about rationality? *Rationality,* as we use the word, simply means that what consumers do and how they do it is consistent with achieving the maximum utility (satisfaction) from their choices. The key word *utility* means satisfaction, not usefulness. A new recording by a great new rock group may give you a lot of utility, but have little usefulness, since it will not mow your lawn or cook your food or bring you the evening news.

Diminishing Satisfaction

What happens as a consumer (who conforms to our four assumptions) makes choices? There is always a behavioral margin, a tendency for a consumer to buy one more (or less) unit of a good or service as its price changes, to the point at which all income is spent. The additional satisfaction derived from the last unit of a good purchased is called the **marginal utility** of that good.

What happens to marginal utility as you buy successive units of a certain good (in a given period of time)? Going back to hamburgers: Beyond some point (say a second hamburger at one meal), you get less and less satisfaction from each additional hamburger. The principle that operates here is called the **law of diminishing marginal utility**. Why must price fall to get you to buy more (increase the quantity you demand)? Because additional satisfaction (marginal utility) diminishes as you obtain more units of the same good in a given period of time.

Maximization of Utility

In order to maximize utility—in other words, achieve the greatest possible satisfaction—the consumer must make judgments about the marginal utility of each additional dollar spent on the goods. Let's assume that you are a consumer who buys only two goods: hamburgers (h) and pizza (p). To get the maximum obtainable utility while living within your income, you will buy a combination of the two goods that satisfies the following equilibrium conditions:

1. $\dfrac{MU_h}{P_h} = \dfrac{MU_p}{P_p}$.

2. $P_h H + P_p P =$ income.

The capital H stands for *number* of hamburgers bought, and the capital P stands for *number* of pizzas bought.

Condition 1 tells you that you must make the marginal utility of a hamburger (MU_h) divided by its price (P_h) equal to the marginal utility of a pizza (MU_p) divided by its price (P_p). Why is this so? Suppose that it was not so. Suppose that you considered the marginal utility of a dollar spent on hamburgers to be greater than the marginal utility of a dollar spent on pizza ($MU_h > MU_p$). (The > means "is greater than.") What will you do to maximize utility? You will spend less money on pizza and more on hamburgers. As you give up pizza, you lose its MU (which will increase as you have less of it) and gain the MU of hamburgers (which will decrease as you consume more of them). You will be in equilibrium only when the MU/P, or marginal utility per dollar (price), is the same for both goods.

Condition 2 simply shows that you spend *all* your income on hamburger ($P_h H$) (remember that H is the number of hamburgers bought) and on pizza (P being the number of pizzas bought). In other words, you must live within your income. The second condition is really an income or a **budget restraint**.

Of course, this two-good example is unrealistic. No one lives on just two goods; not even Robinson Crusoe did. We are just using this as a model. However, one can readily extend the principle of maximization of utility to any number of goods. The conclusion remains the same: In equilibrium, the consumer will make the marginal utility (MU) of a dollar spent on one good equal to the MU of a dollar spent on any other good. Our first equilibrium condition becomes

$$\frac{MU_h}{P_h} = \frac{MU_p}{P_p} = \frac{MU_n}{P_n},$$

where n represents the nth or last good.

An Arithmetic Illustration

Let's assign some numbers to MU and P for an arithmetic illustration.

Joe Bloggs, an impoverished student, has $4.50 to spend on lunch this week. On Monday he goes to the cafeteria in the student union and finds that this week pizza is $1.00 and hamburgers are 50 cents. After griping about prices getting higher, he calculates that the first pizza he eats this week will give him 50 utils (50 utils per dollar), and that his first hamburger will give him 30 utils, or 60 utils per dollar (because he can get two for a dollar). Remember, though, that if he bought a second hamburger, its marginal utility would be less than that of the first.

First, he buys a hamburger, and then continues to make the same kind of choice every noontime for the rest of this week. But now that he's already had a hamburger for lunch this week, a second hamburger lunch (on Tuesday) doesn't taste quite as good. Its MU falls to 25 (or its MU/P to 50). But that's what the MU/P of a first pizza is! So now he's indifferent; that is, at this point, he'd just as soon buy one as the other. But on Wednesday and Thursday (his third and fourth choice days this week), he'll buy a pizza one day and a hamburger the other, in some order (maybe he'll toss a coin).

Table 15-1 shows how Bloggs maximized utility in his choice of luncheon menus. By Friday, not only are Bloggs's taste buds dulled, but he has also reached his budget restraint. In equilibrium, then, he will buy three pizzas and three hamburgers this week, and

$$\frac{MU_h}{P_h} = \frac{MU_p}{P_p}.$$

TABLE 15-1 Maximizing Utility: Hamburgers Versus Pizza

| | Hamburgers (50 cents) | | | | | Pizza ($1.00) | | | |
A	B	C	D	E	A	B	C	D	E
1	$ .50	30	60	1st	1	$1	50	50	2nd
2	1.00	25	50	2nd	2	2	45	45	3rd
3	1.50	20	40	4th	3	3	40	40	4th
4	2.00	15	30	6th	4	4	35	35	5th
5	2.50	10	20	7th	5	5	30	30	6th

Column A = number of hamburgers or pizzas bought.
Column B = dollars spent on hamburgers or pizza.
Column C = marginal utility per dollar spent on hamburgers or pizza (MU_h or MU_p).
Column D = order in which consumer makes choices $\frac{MU_h}{P_h}$ or $\frac{MU_p}{P_p}$.
Column E = choice.

The Demand Side of the Market

Deriving a Demand Curve

Now let's examine the demand curve, the essential topic in this section. Suppose we want to know what Joe Bloggs's demand curve for hamburgers looks like (Figure 15-2). We know one point on that curve (hypothetical point A). When hamburgers are selling for 50 cents apiece, Joe will buy three per week. But the manager of the cafeteria, in an effort to pull in more business, runs a big sale on hamburgers and drops the price to 25 cents apiece. The price of pizzas stays the same ($1.00). If you recalculate the MU_h/P_h for the 25-cent price, the figures are much higher (120, 100, 80, 60, 40). Bloggs is going to buy a lot more hamburgers, seven, to be exact. At this point he will make the new MU_h/P_h equal to MU_p/P_p. (He'll spend all his money and will be in equilibrium.) Thus seven hamburgers per week at 25 cents each constitutes another point on Joe's demand curve (hypothetical point B). Connecting points such as A and B, we obtain curve D_h shown in Figure 15-2. This is Bloggs's demand curve for hamburgers.

Why does the curve slope the way D_h does? Because of *diminishing marginal utility*. If the *MU* of hamburgers had not fallen as Bloggs ate more of them per week, this curve would not slope downward. This is an important point to remember. It is also important to remember that it is the *marginal* utility of a good rather than its *total* utility that determines the demand for it, and that determines the prices people are willing to pay for it.

The so-called **paradox of value** is that people are willing to pay a very high price for diamonds, but only a low price for water. Yet the total utility of water is much greater than that of diamonds. People must have water to sustain their lives, and everybody can get along without diamonds. The marginal utility of diamonds, however, is much higher. So people are willing to pay more for another diamond than they are for the last unit of water consumed.

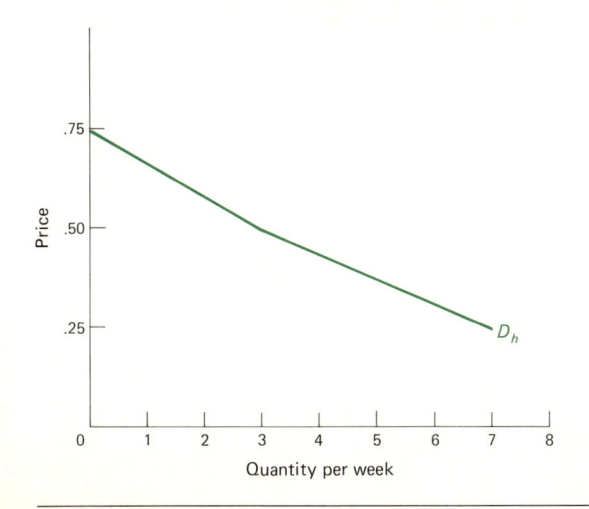

Figure 15-2 Joe Bloggs's Demand for Hamburgers

Market Demand

In Chapter 3 you learned that market demand is the sum of the demand curves of all consumers in the market. At each possible price, one adds the quantities demanded by all consumers (assuming no interdependence among buyers). When these points are plotted, they form a demand curve such as that in Figure 15-3.

Market demand, D_m, in Figure 15-3 slopes down to the right, just as Bloggs's demand curve in Figure 15-2 did. The reason is the same in both cases: *diminishing marginal utility*, as people consume more of a certain good in a given period of time.

Elasticity: Responsiveness of Quantity Demanded to Changes in Price

The answers to many questions about our market system depend on how much, or how little, consumers respond, by means of the quantity they demand, to changes in the price of a given product. Will a tariff on imported oil cause oil companies to cut back sharply on imports of crude oil and gasoline? If toothpaste goes up to five dollars a tube, will people still buy it? Will Detroit break out of its sales doldrums by cutting prices? The answers depend mostly on the extent to which consumers respond to price changes.

Figure 15-3 Market Demand for Hamburgers

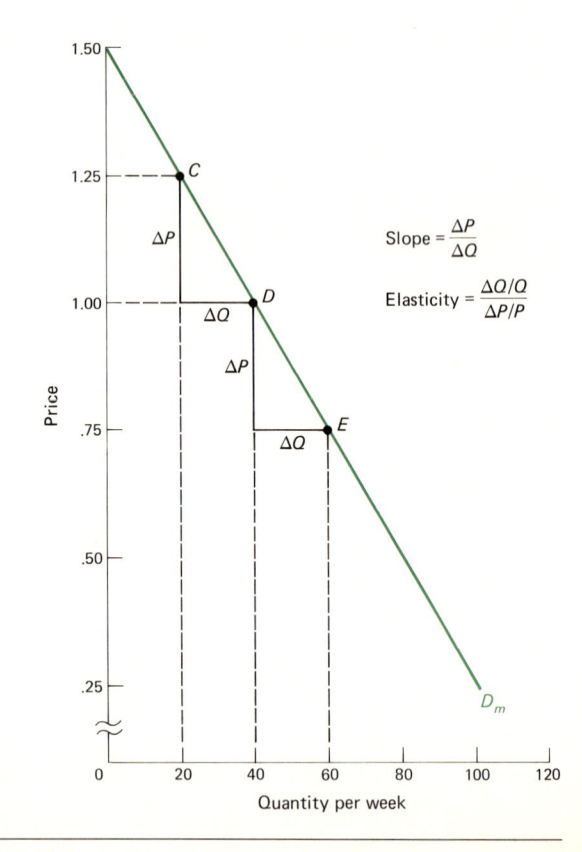

$$\text{Slope} = \frac{\Delta P}{\Delta Q}$$

$$\text{Elasticity} = \frac{\Delta Q/Q}{\Delta P/P}$$

358   The Demand Side of the Market

The *measure* of the response, the change in quantity demanded as a result of a small change in price, is called the **price elasticity of demand** Demand elasticity may be of three types:

1. **Price elastic** (quantity demanded changes at a faster rate than price)

2. **Price inelastic** (quantity demanded changes at a slower rate than price)

3. **Unit elastic** (quantity demanded changes at the same rate as price)

Elasticity of demand (E_d) is not the same as the slope of the demand curve. If it were, one could not compare one product with another with respect to the way quantity demanded responds to changes in price. The units of measurement of quantity and price are very different, depending on whether one is discussing weekly demand for cars or weekly demand for hamburgers. Therefore, to get a **pure number**—one that is independent of the units of measurement of price and quantity—we define elasticity as

$$E_d = \frac{\Delta Q/Q}{\Delta P/P} = \frac{\text{percentage change in quantity demanded/quantity}}{\text{percentage change in price/price}}.$$

The Δ (Greek delta) represents a change; Q is the quantity demanded; and P is the price.

How do we compute the price elasticity of demand? Suppose you want to know the *market* price elasticity of demand for hamburgers when the price drops from $1.25 to $1.00 in Figure 15-3. You cannot rely on the slope of D_m because it would not give a number to compare with the price elasticity of demand for other goods. In other words, you need a pure number, a number that is independent of its units of measurement. Imagine comparing the elasticity of demand for wheat and automobiles without one. You would be comparing a change from a price of a few dollars per bushel with a change from a price of several thousands of dollars per car. Also the $\Delta Q/\Delta P$ relation differs depending on whether one measures from $1.25 to $1.00 or from $1.00 to $1.25.

The usual way to solve this problem of differing results if one is moving up rather than down the curve is to take the *average rate of change* of quantity with respect to price, divided by the average of the prices in question. For example, let's calculate the average rate at which quantity demanded (Q) changes as price (P) changes when the price of hamburgers goes from $1.25 to $1.00 (Figure 15-3).

The formula for calculating the average elasticity of demand E_d (called the **midpoint formula**) is as follows, where Q_1 equals old quantity, Q_2 equals new quantity, P_1 equals old price, and P_2 equals new price:

$$E_d = -\frac{\Delta Q/Q}{\Delta P/P} = -\frac{[Q_2 - Q_1]/[(Q_1 + Q_2)/2]}{[P_2 - P_1]/[(P_1 + P_2)/2]}$$

$$= \frac{\text{change in quantity/quantity}}{\text{change in price/price}}.$$

Since the twos cancel out, you are left with the average change in quantity demanded and the average change in price.

You can now take the data in Figure 15-3 and calculate the E_d for hamburgers that cost between $1.25 and $1.00.

1. $\dfrac{Q_2 - Q_1}{Q_1 + Q_2} = \dfrac{40 - 20}{20 + 40} = \dfrac{20}{60} = .33$.

2. $\dfrac{P_2 - P_1}{P_1 + P_2} = \dfrac{1.00 - 1.25}{1.25 + 1.00} = \dfrac{-.25}{2.25} = -.11$.

3. $E_d = \dfrac{.33}{-.11} = -3 \text{ or } 3$.

Note that elasticity comes out as a negative number, since you are dividing a positive ratio by a negative ratio. Since the negative sign has no economic significance, however, you can ignore it.

The price elasticity of demand between $1.25 and $1.00 is 3. In other words, demand is very price elastic; $\Delta Q/Q$, the rate at which the *quantity* of hamburgers sold changed, was three times as great as $\Delta P/P$, the rate at which the *price* of hamburgers changed.

If you calculate the elasticity of demand between $1.00 and 75 cents, you will discover that it is different from that between $1.25 and $1.00, even though the price drops by the same amount. Although there are constant elasticity-of-demand curves, they are rare. Normally the price elasticity of demand changes continuously, even along a straight-line demand curve.

Differing Elasticities of Demand

The best way to understand this is through a graph (see Figure 15-4). In our example, demand was price elastic ($E_d > 1$), which is shown in Figure 15-4 (d). *Price elastic* means that quantity demanded changes more rapidly than price. There are two other possibilities for demand/price elasticity.

1. Demand may be *price inelastic* ($E_d < 1$), as shown in Figure 15-4(b). (The < means "is less than.") *Price inelastic* means that quantity demanded changes less rapidly than price. In our example, a 10 percent decrease in hamburger prices might have resulted in only a 5 percent increase in quantity demanded. Keep in mind a special qualification about Figures 15-4(b) and (d). Almost any straight-line demand curve has varying elasticities throughout its length. Some parts of Figure 15-4(b), therefore, exhibit greater elasticity than some parts of Figure 15-4(a). The two curves are shown here merely to illustrate the general configuration of elasticity and inelasticity, not to reflect particular points on either curve.

2. Demand may be *unit elastic* ($E_d = 1$), as shown in Figure 15-4(c), with respect to price. This means that quantity demanded changes at the same rate as price. In the example, if a 10 percent reduction in the price of hamburgers brought about a 10 percent increase in the quantity demanded, demand elasticity would have been unitary.

In addition to these ranges of price elasticity, there are two unusual straight-line cases.

1. *Perfect inelasticity*, Figure 15-4(a), is the demand condition in which $E_d = 0$. In other words, for the given range of prices, quantity demanded does not change at all as price changes. (If eyeglasses go to $500 a pair, a myopic person will still keep buying them. If insulin goes up in price, the diabetic will continue to buy it.)

2. *Infinite or perfect elasticity*, Figure 15-4(e), is the demand condition in which $E_d \to \infty$. (The ∞ symbol means "infinity.") For the given range of quantities, price of the good is constant, and the public will buy any quantity of it at the going price.

The demand curve in part a is perfectly inelastic; E_d is zero. This means that consumers will buy Q_0 of this product, no matter what the

Figure 15-4 Differing Elasticities of Demand

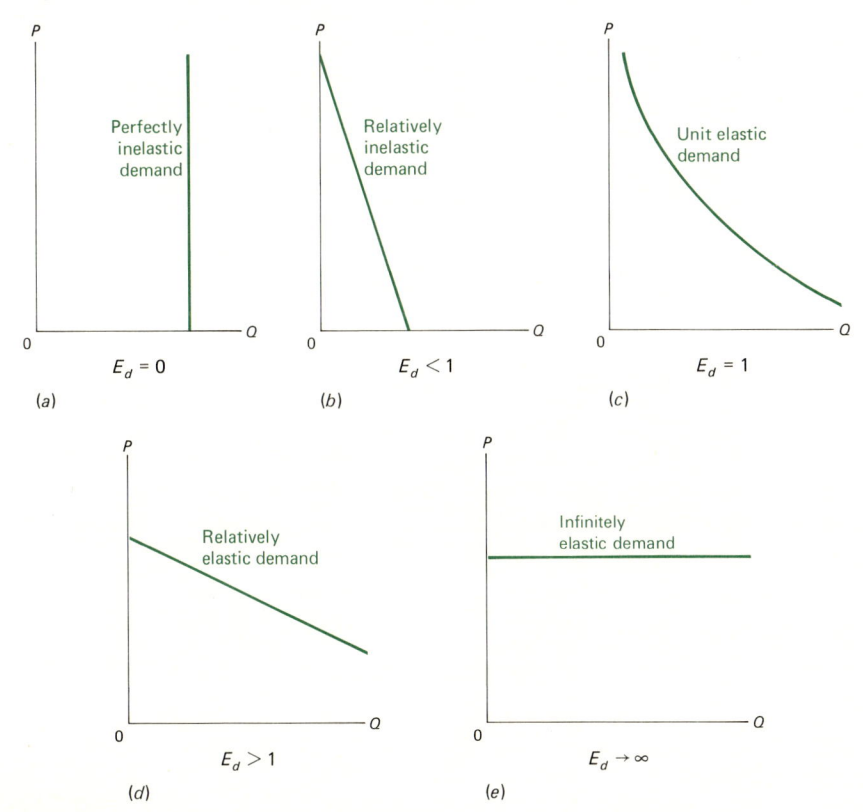

price (at least for the given range of prices). The demand curve in Figure 15-4(e) is infinitely elastic; E_d approaches infinity. This means that consumers will buy any quantity as long as its price remains P_1, and presumably nothing at any higher price.

Demand curves ordinarily do not look like either Figures 15-4(a) or (e). Each is a limit: one the upper, the other the lower. To explain why, we will present the factors that determine price elasticity of demand:

1. *Substitutability.* The demand curve in Figure 15-4(a) implies that there may be no good substitutes for the item (for example, gasoline to run one's car). Consumers are willing to buy a certain quantity at any given price. On the other hand, Figure 15-4(e) implies virtually perfect substitution; any price above P_1 will eliminate demand. (If toothpaste goes to five dollars a tube, you may decide to brush your teeth with baking soda.)

Real-world elasticities are ordinarily between the two extremes of Figures 15-4(a) and (e). For example, as a general rule, there are good substitutes for toothpaste. There are, on the other hand, no good substitutes for gasoline as an automobile fuel.

2. *Proportion of income spent on the good* (budget restraint). If the price of cars goes up 10 percent, people *must* cut back on the number of cars they buy because their purchasing power (assuming no change in income) compels them to. Thus the E_d tends to be high for cars and other goods on which people spend a large part of their income. If the price of hamburgers goes up 10 percent, people *need not* drastically cut down the number they buy, because their purchasing power is not greatly reduced.

3. *Postponability.* Consumers buy some goods now because they cannot postpone buying them. Food and medical care fall in this category; their price elasticity of demand is thus low. But people can postpone purchases of other goods, such as consumer durables (cars, TVs, refrigerators, washing machines, and so forth). Demand for them is quite price elastic. In the mid-1970s, as the price of new cars rose, many people chose to repair older cars, so the E_d for new cars has been quite high.

4. *Complementarity.* The price elasticity of demand for a good may be linked to its use in conjunction with other goods. In recent years, the popularity of automobile air conditioners has increased. Their price has declined with mass production. In turn, this appears to have decreased the price elasticity of demand for automobiles themselves.

In the next few chapters we are going to see some important applications of the concept of price elasticity of demand, especially in Application 18, on U.S. farm problems.

SUMMING UP

1. *Demand* is a set of relations representing the quantities of a good (a

commodity or service) that consumers will buy over a given range of prices in a given period of time.

2. The assumptions on which demand theory rests are (a) that consumers know about, and can choose freely among, alternatives; (b) that consumers seek the maximum satisfaction from the goods they can buy with their limited incomes; (c) that consumers are rational; and (d) that factors other than prices, which might affect demand, do not vary.

3. One can explain the *law of demand*, that demand curves slope downward, or that price and quantity are inversely related in two ways: (a) in terms of income and substitution effects, and (b) in terms of *utility theory*.

4. The *income effect* is the change in quantity demanded caused by a change in the consumer's purchasing power resulting from a price change. A decrease in price increases the consumer's purchasing power and an increase in price decreases it. In either case, *for desirable goods*, the income effect causes price and quantity to be inversely related.

5. The *substitution effect* is the consumer's tendency (when the price of a good changes) to buy more of a cheaper good and substitute it for a more expensive good. The substitution effect also causes price and quantity to be inversely related. The combination of the two effects—income and substitution—almost always causes the demand curve to slope downward.

6. Goods that are exceptions and do not have a downward-sloping demand curve are *Veblen goods* (goods for which people prefer to pay higher prices) and very inferior goods called *Giffen goods* (goods that people buy less of as their prices fall because consumers can now afford other, more desirable goods).

7. *Utility theory* holds that people choose certain goods and combinations of goods because this certain choice gives them more satisfaction than other combinations. The key assumption of utility theory is that people not only evaluate the utility (satisfaction) of different goods, but whenever they spend their incomes, they rationally choose the combinations that maximize their utility or satisfaction.

8. In utility theory, one assumes that the satisfaction the consumer gets from the last unit consumed—the *marginal utility*—of the good will ultimately diminish. This is called the *law of diminishing marginal utility*.

9. For a consumer to be in equilibrium (that is, to maximize her or his utility), two conditions are necessary:

$$\frac{MU_a}{P_a} = \frac{MU_b}{P_b}$$ (marginal utility per dollar must be equal for all goods bought).

$$P_a A + P_b B = Y$$ (all income must be spent).

10. One can extend the conditions for maximization of utility to any

number of goods. A downward-sloping demand curve, no matter what quantity of goods is involved, depends directly on the assumption of diminishing marginal utility.

11. The *paradox of value* is that the price people are willing to pay for a good is determined by its *marginal* utility rather than its *total* utility. Thus, people pay much higher prices for diamonds than for water.

12. The sum of all the individual demand curves is the market demand curve. Since the individual curves slope downward (because of diminishing marginal utility), so does the market demand curve.

13. One may calculate price elasticities of demand E_d by means of the *midpoint formula*:

$$E_d = -\frac{\Delta Q/Q}{\Delta P/P} = \frac{[Q_2 - Q_1]/[(Q_1 + Q_2)/2]}{[P_2 - P_1]/[(P_1 + P_2)/2]}.$$

14. The *price elasticity of demand* (E_d) measures the response of consumers to a change in price of a good by measuring the rate of change in the quantity of the good that consumers demand. Demand may be *price elastic*:

$$E_d > 1 \qquad \frac{\Delta Q}{Q} > \frac{\Delta P}{P}$$

price inelastic:

$$E_d < 1 \qquad \frac{\Delta Q}{Q} < \frac{\Delta P}{P}$$

or *unit elastic*:

$$E_d = 1 \qquad \frac{\Delta Q}{Q} = \frac{\Delta P}{P}.$$

15. Demand may also be at the extreme limits of demand elasticity: (a) *perfect inelasticity* ($E_d = 0$), in which quantity demanded does not change at all as price changes, and (b) *infinite elasticity* ($E_d \to \infty$), in which the public buys any quantity at the going price.

16. The factors that determine price elasticity of demand are (a) substitutability, (b) proportion of income spent on the good, (c) postponability, and (d) complementarity.

17. Price elasticities of demand are very important when it comes to analyzing various economic problems, such as farmers' incomes and monopolistically priced oil imports.

QUESTIONS

1. What factors do you think are most important in determining your demand for (a) cars, (b) toothpaste, (c) beer, (d) trips to Europe? Do you

suppose that these same factors are also most important for consumers in general with regard to these goods? What factors do you think are most influential in determining the price elasticity of your demand for these goods?

2. What are income and substitution effects? Which of these effects usually has the greater influence on the shape of the demand curve? Why?

3. What is the law of demand? This law—like all social principles—is not universal. Under what conditions do you think it does *not* hold true?

4. What are the assumptions of the utility theory of demand? Are they realistic? If not, why make such assumptions?

5. Consider the following demand schedule.

Price	Quantity demanded
$1.00	100
1.50	75
2.00	50
2.50	30

   a. Calculate the price elasticity of demand for price increases from $1.00 to $1.50; $1.50 to $2.00; $2.00 to $2.50.
   b. Indicate for which prices (if any) demand is price elastic; price inelastic; unit elastic.

SUGGESTED READINGS

"Detroit's Dilemma on Prices." *Business Week*, January 20, 1975.

North, Douglass C., and Roger Leroy Miller. "The Economics of Abortion Repeal." In *The Economics of Public Issues*. Harper & Row, New York, 1973.

Radford, R. A. "The Economic Organization of a P.O.W. Camp." *Economica*, November 1945. Reprinted in John R. McLean and Ronald A. Wykstra, *Readings in Introductory Economics*. Harper & Row, New York, 1971.

Solmon, Lewis C. *Economics*, 2d ed. Addison-Wesley, Reading, Mass., 1976. Chapter 27.

Application 15

Will Redistributing Income Make People Happier?

> What distinguishes men from pigs is not that they are more happy, but that they can control their environment.
>
> W. A. Lewis

The above title is somewhat deceiving. It may make you think that we are going to deal with the relation between the distribution of income and the happiness of human beings. Actually, economists do not know any more than other people do about what makes people happy. Does having more money make people happier? Or was Groucho Marx right in his cynical comment, "Money can't buy friends, but it sure can buy you a better class of enemies"?

The Distribution of Satisfaction

What economists can do is talk about utility or satisfaction, and make assumptions about whether (and at what rate) it changes as people have more income. Two things are self-evident: (1) The utility or satisfaction derived from having more income to spend (or save) is not necessarily the same as the happiness derived from that income. (2) Economists have no "utilmeters" on which to record people's satisfaction. Therefore, the law of diminishing marginal utility of income is only an *assumed* (unproved) relationship. (For example, Elvira Snodgrass is earning $500 a week and gets a $10-a-week raise. Randolph Hertz is earning $100 a week and also gets a $10-a-week raise. According to the principle of diminishing marginal utility of income, Snodgrass's satisfaction is increased only slightly. Hertz, however, is overjoyed.)

The little deception in the wording of the title was not designed to mislead you, but to draw your attention to this limitation of economics. We also wanted to lead into a discussion of the important relationship between the distribution of income and the total utility (or satisfaction) of various income groups.

The Distribution of Income

What has happened in the last thirty or so years to the distribution of income in the United States? Table A15-1 shows that there was relatively little change in the 1960s. There has actually been little change since 1947. Other data collected by the federal government (as published in the *Statistical Abstract of the United States*) show that between 1935 and 1947 the distribution of income became less unequal in the United States. You know from Chapter 15 that if you assume a **diminishing marginal utility of income**, then redistributing income so that less of it goes to upper-income groups and more to middle- and lower-income groups *increases* a nation's utility. (The loss in utility by those at the top is more than offset by the gain in utility by those at the bottom, assuming that all people have the same total utility of income functions.)

Now what if you do not accept the idea of diminishing marginal utility of income? Suppose you believe that the marginal utility of income is constant, that each bit added to your income adds the same amount to your satisfaction no matter what your income is. In that case, you could not use utility as an argument in favor of redistributing income. However, you could cite utility to "justify" the fact that the percentage shares of income did not change very much from 1947 to 1971.

Suppose you assumed **increasing marginal utility of income** (people get more and more satisfaction from each increment in their incomes). You could then use utility as an argument for redistributing income in favor of *upper*-income groups. The percentage of wealth belonging to upper-income groups decreased between 1935 and 1947. In addition, the percentage belonging to the wealthiest 5 percent decreased in the 1960s (as shown in Table A15-1). This redistribution of income must have led to an overall decrease in utility, if you assume an increasing marginal utility of income.

Governments and Income Distribution

Governments have an enormous effect on the distribution of income, and thus on total satisfaction or utility of the populace. The strength of this effect depends not only on what governments extract from people in the way of taxes, but also on what people receive in the form of transfer payments (unemployment compensation, subsidies to farmers, social security, and the like), as well as services they receive from governments (police and fire protection, job training, public schooling, food stamps, and the like). If you add all three elements, you can see that in the past forty years government in the United States *has* redistributed income. For example, in 1950 households earning more than $7,500 per year received 26 percent of total U.S. income *before* taxes, transfer payments, and government services were considered, but only 19 percent of income *after* these three items were included. At the same time, those earning less than $1,000 received 1.4 percent of income before one took into account the three adjustment factors, but 4 percent after. You can see that the government, like Robin Hood, takes from the rich and gives to the poor.

So whether you believe that government redistribution of income has increased Americans' utility or welfare depends on whether you believe in increasing or in decreasing marginal utility of income. Most economists assume a decreasing marginal utility of income. Therefore, they feel that the government's redistribution of income has indeed increased total utility.

Note: Although people have used arguments based on diminishing marginal utility to back up many government money-collecting devices, such as the progressive income tax, this is only one of several reasons given for redistributing income. Other arguments have ranged from moral reasons (a highly unequal distribution of income is "wrong") to the multiplier effect. (More people spend more money when the poor get a larger percentage of national income because the poor spend a larger proportion of their incomes than the rich do.) Arguments against income redistribution have not rested solely on grounds of utility, but have included the argument that people need income incentives to save (or accumulate capital) and, if the government steps in and redistributes income, it takes away these incentives.

The models and assumptions gained from a study of economics do not lead to any final truths about the "best" distribution of wealth. The distribution of income in a society affects many aspects of both economic and noneconomic performance. What we have pointed out here is that the utility or welfare of the people is one aspect—and an important one.

TABLE A15-1 Percentage Share of Aggregate Income Received by Each One-fifth of Families and Unrelated Individuals (selected years)

Income rank	1971	1969	1967	1965	1963	1961	1947
Total families, percentage	100.0	100.0	100.0	100.0	100.0	100.0	100.0
Lowest one-fifth	5.5	5.6	5.4	5.3	5.1	4.8	5.0
Second one-fifth	11.9	12.3	12.2	12.1	12.0	11.7	11.8
Third one-fifth	17.4	17.6	17.5	17.7	17.6	17.4	17.0
Fourth one-fifth	23.7	23.5	23.7	23.7	23.9	23.6	23.1
Highest one-fifth	41.6	41.0	41.2	41.3	41.4	42.6	43.0
Highest 5 percent	14.6	14.0	15.3	15.8	16.0	17.1	17.2

Source: The 1973 Economic Report of the President, Hearings Before the Joint Economic Committee of the United States, G.P.O., Washington, D.C., 1973.

QUESTIONS

1. What assumption would you make about the marginal utility of income? Why?

2. For what reasons other than the marginal utility of income could you argue for or against redistributing income?

3. Considering both the utilitarian and nonutilitarian aspects of the question, do you believe that income in the United States should be redistributed? Why? What effects would such a redistribution be likely to have on American welfare, growth, price stability, and employment?

SUGGESTED READINGS

Easterlin, Richard A., "Does Money Buy Happiness?" *Public Interest*, Winter 1973. Reprinted in *Readings in Economics*, 76/77, Dushkin, Guilford, Conn., 1976.

Ginsburg, Helen, ed., *Poverty, Economics and Society*. Boston: Little, Brown, 1972. See particularly A. C. Pigou, "Transferring Income from the Rich to the Poor," pp. 108-112; Milton Friedman, "Liberalism and Egalitarianism," pp. 282-283; and R. H. Tawney, "Equality and Liberty," pp. 283-284.

Gordon, David M., ed. "Government Impact on the Distribution of Income." In *Problems in Political Economy: An Urban Perspective*, Section 4, pp. 268-321. D. C. Heath, Lexington, Mass., 1971.

Joint Economic Committee of the United States. *The Distribution of Personal Income*. G.P.O., Washington, D.C., 1965.

North, Douglass C., and Roger Leroy Miller. "The Economics of Income Distribution and Government Programs." In *The Economics of Public Issues*. Harper & Row, New York, 1973.

16

The Supply Side Of The Market

In Chapter 15, we examined in detail the theory behind demand. Now we will do the same for supply. We are going to repeat some of the material on supply and demand from Chapter 3, which in Chapter 15 we suggested you reread.

What Is Supply?

To an economist, **supply** is a set of relations between the various prices for a firm's product in a given period of time and the quantities that a firm (or industry) will offer for sale at those prices.

We shall concentrate on one firm, the Better Burger Company, and to simplify our analysis we shall assume that it has no control over the price at which it can sell its product. It takes price as given and sells as much as it finds profitable at the given price. It is, in other words, a quantity adjuster, not a price setter. What determines how much it will produce? Basically, the *costs* of production. Underlying any firm's supply schedule is a schedule of costs.

What Determines Economic Costs?

Two factors will determine the cost to the Better Burger Co. of making and selling a thousand hamburgers: (1) The *prices* it pays for resources (cooks, waiters and waitresses, buildings, land, finance capital, beef and buns, and the like), and (2) The *productivity* of those resources. For the time being, let's assume that prices of both product and resources are competitively determined and therefore lie outside the control of the Better Burger Co. In the next few chapters, when we introduce non-competitive markets, we will drop these assumptions. For now, we will

Supply involves quantities offered for sale. (Philip Jon Bailey)

present the technological conditions of supply to show how the productivity of resources determines costs and, through costs, supply.

Remember from Chapter 2 that, to society, costs mean **opportunity costs**, or what firms have to give up in order to produce a chosen good. These costs include both money costs and nonmoney costs. Nonmoney costs, often called *psychic costs*, are important in determining how people behave economically. Suppose the Better Burger Co. takes great pride in, and derives great satisfaction from, producing a superior hamburger. The entrepreneur who heads Better Burger Co., Bertha Berson, likes making top-notch hamburgers so much that any other job, to induce her to leave the hamburger industry, would have to offer an income great enough to make her overcome her distaste for other businesses.

You saw the effects of opportunity costs when you studied the production-possibilities curve. Since there are alternative uses of resources, Better Burger Co. (or any other firm) must compete for the use of resources. It must bid resources away from other uses, and the prices it pays to do so, times the amounts used, are its *economic costs*. Whether the Better Burger Co. can obtain these resources depends on their productivity when used by the Better Burger Co. compared with their productivity when used by another firm (to produce the same product or a different one).

Explicit and Implicit Costs

Firms must buy or contract in the marketplace for most of the resources they use. The costs of these resources are **explicit costs**. The costs of resources a firm already owns are **implicit costs**.

For example, Bertha Berson, the owner of Better Burger Co., has to hire a lot of resources: a manager, cooks, people to wait on table, a building, and so forth. She hires most of these in the market; she pays wages, rent, and interest to get them. These are her *explicit costs*.

Suppose, though, that she happens to already own a choice commercial lot and that she also has good managerial skills. She decides to build the hamburger stand on her own lot and manage it herself. Is there a cost? There is, because both the land she owns and the labor she puts into the venture could have been used to produce something else. She might have leased the lot to another firm; she might have found a job elsewhere. To determine Bertha Berson's economic costs, one has to add these two implicit costs to the explicit costs.

In order for her to stay in business very long, she must use resources at least as efficiently (productively) as they could be used elsewhere. In order for society in general to conduct its economic affairs most efficiently, *all* firms must use resources as productively as the resources would be used in alternative ways. Thus, firms must cover their opportunity costs, including the implicit costs of using self-owned resources.

Profit

Profit is a part of costs. **Profit** is a return or payment to the entrepreneur, the person who organizes a business venture, who pulls the necessary resources together and makes it a going business. Any market system requires people with this skill in order to operate efficiently, and firms must bid for such a skill. Therefore Better Burger Co., in order to succeed, must be able to pay for leadership. Profit is thus an implicit cost to the business. A payment to the entrepreneur just equal to the cost of hiring her or him away from other employment is a **normal profit**. Profits in excess of this (profits larger than necessary to bid for an entrepreneur's services) are called **economic** or pure **profits**. Some economists think of normal profits as being earned and economic profits as being *un*earned, in the sense that they are not necessary in order for a firm to secure entrepreneurial talents and are therefore not costs of production.

Now let's see what will happen to productivity and cost as a firm adjusts its rate of output. What will happen to Better Burger Co.'s productivity (hamburgers per hour of labor) as its output changes?

Four Kinds of Time Periods

When firms decide to produce more or less of a product, they run into problems of flexibility. If the Soviet Union wants to buy two million bushels of American wheat after U.S. farmers have already harvested their wheat crop, the farmers cannot make any adjustment in output. The Better Burger Co., however, has greater flexibility. If there is a rush on the Company's burgers on Wednesday, because of a convention in town, by Thursday morning the company can triple output to meet the increased demand.

Economists distinguish between different production (supply) time periods on the basis of this flexibility—this freedom (or lack of it) which a firm and industry have in adjusting output.

Market Period

A firm's **market period** is the period *after its output is already produced*. By definition, the firm can no longer adjust the level of production; supply is fixed. For the Better Burger Co., the market period is no great problem, since it takes only minutes to grind additional meat and produce more hamburgers. For wheat farmers, however, the market period is a matter of months; for tree farmers it may be several years. Economists are more interested in periods in which changes in output can take place than they are in the market period, the least flexible of firms' production periods. After all, once production takes place, resources cannot be reallocated, and questions of efficiency for that period are meaningless to society.

Short-Run Period

The **short-run period**, in which the firm has enough flexibility to vary its use of resources (inputs), is a very important period, during which the firm uses certain *fixed* inputs (for example, plant capacity) that it cannot add to or take away from. It can, however, alter the use of *variable* inputs (usually labor). The short run is the period of actual production.

For example, Better Burger Co. starts with one hamburger shop, certain machinery and equipment, a given number of tables and employees, and neon signs in the shape of steers. If hamburger sales boom, in the short run, Better Burger Co. can hire more cooks and order more beef and buns, and another carload of ketchup. But what happens to productivity and supply as more of these variable inputs are used with that same fixed plant? If entrepreneur Berson believes that hamburger sales will continue to rise in the foreseeable future, she may plan to expand her shop or build more shops herself or perhaps start a franchising operation. This leads into the next period.

Long-Run Period

The **long-run period** is a planning period, in which a firm can vary *all* the resources it uses, including size of plant and amount of equipment. This is not a time of actual production. Rather, it is a time during which the firm can examine all the alternatives that modern technology makes available and choose which route to take. Once the firm makes its choice and carries out its plans, it is in the short-run period; it has its plant and equipment set up and can produce things. The only limitation on the firm's choice in the long run is technological availability. For example, Better Burger Co. hires technicians, architects, and engineers who tell Bertha Berson that, given the present technology, there are twenty choices as to size of plant and ways to produce and sell hamburgers. Berson can decide within these limits about plant capacity and amount of automation. ("Microwave ovens, yes. Disposable plates, no.")

Historical Period

In the **historical period**, one can drop even the limitations of technology.

Although no firm can utilize the historical period, from society's standpoint studying the historical period, being able to see the effects of changing technology on productivity, is very important. For example, visualize the hamburger business fifty years ago. Think what has happened since then to the technology of production and distribution. From small mom-and-pop hamburger stands, the hamburger industry has advanced to massive franchise operations, with single franchises selling thousands of dollars' worth of hamburgers per week. Automation of food preparation and even cooking has been developed. Then visualize complex industries such as steel and automobiles. Think of the technological changes that have affected their productivity and supply.

Note: Do not try to sort out these production periods in terms of clock or calender time. That is not the point. A firm is in three periods—market, short run, and long run—simultaneously. It markets its products, varies the output of its present plant, and makes plans for the future all at the same time. The amount of calendar time involved in these periods differs enormously from one industry to another. It is very short for hamburger stands, but very long for U.S. Steel. The point here is the analytical distinction between the periods. Now let's see what happens to costs and productivity in each period.

Costs and Supply in the Market Period

Since a firm cannot vary the resources it uses in production during the market period, there are no **variable costs** (costs associated with changes in output) at that time. All costs during the market period fall into the category of **fixed costs** (costs that do not vary with output). Of course, there are costs associated with marketing itself, but these are not production costs (costs incurred in producing the product). For example, Better Burger Co.'s variable costs might consist of wages paid to cooks, purchases of an extra ton of beef, and so forth. Its nonproduction fixed costs might be interest costs on money borrowed from banks, mortgage payments, and insurance.

During the market period, just as all costs are fixed, so is total output fixed. The die is already cast, and the firm has a limited amount of product to sell. Supply, therefore, is a vertical line from the output axis (Figure 16-1 on the next page). Q_0 represents the total output already produced. During the market period, there may be variations in demand, and the firm may decide to market more or less of the product, and it can vary the price it charges. Resources, however, cannot be bid into or away from this industry during the market period.

Costs and Supply in the Short-Run Period

As we mentioned before, this is a very important period. In the short-run period, firms produce all their goods and services, and employ all people and other resources. What happens to output as firms employ more variable resources along with those that are fixed? In answering this question, we must rely on an important assumption, the law of variable proportions.

The Law of Variable Proportions

The **law of variable proportions** (often called the *law of diminishing returns*) states that as a firm uses successive equal units of a variable input in conjunction with a fixed input, additions to output (marginal output) derived from the variable input begin to diminish, beyond some point.

Let's translate that into hamburgers: The Better Burger Co. circulates an advertisement saying that if you come into the restaurant, you will be served a hamburger within five minutes after you sit down, or you'll be given a hamburger free of charge. Business picks up. But the company has only ten grills, a hundred cubic feet of refrigerator space, a hundred booths, and various other limitations on plant and equipment. Now suppose that the firm hires more cooks to handle the growing trade. Initially, marginal productivity—the additional hamburgers turned out per hour by the additional cooks—may rise, as the firm employs the grills and other equipment more efficiently and fully, and reaps the advantages of specialization. Beyond some point, though, the cooks begin to get in each other's way. This causes the number of additional hamburgers they turned out per hour to decline. Table 16-1 gives a numerical illustration.

At first, marginal productivity rises, as the second and third cooks add more to output than the first. The fourth cook, however, adds less to output than the second and third, though more than the first. Diminish-

FIGURE 16-1 Supply in the Market Period. Costs and output during the market period are fixed.

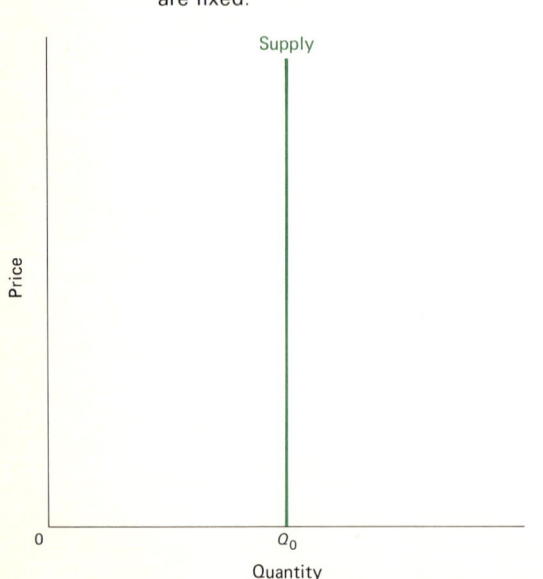

FIGURE 16-2 Short-Run Total Costs

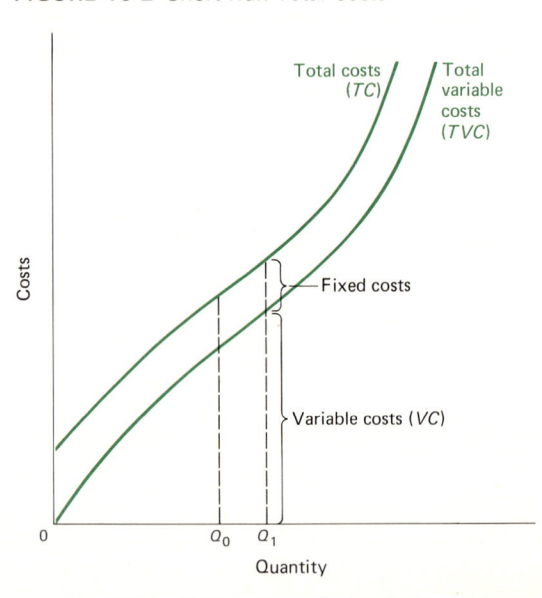

374 The Supply Side of the Market

ing marginal productivity has set in. The diminished productivity continues as the firm adds the fifth and sixth cooks. At this point, marginal productivity is approaching zero (the sixth cook only cooks five hamburgers per hour).

Examples of diminishing returns to the variable input abound. Agriculture provides a particularly clear one. Suppose an Iowa corn farmer has a certain amount of land, five hundred acres. The corn has been planted. Land is the fixed input (along with the other resources already employed to plant the crop). Now, the farmer can decide how many times to cultivate the field. Let's suppose that if the farmer does not cultivate at all, the yield will be thirty bushels per acre. If the farmer cultivates once, the yield may rise to forty bushels. Twice, and the yield rises to forty-eight bushels per acre. Three times, to fifty-three bushels per acre. A fourth cultivation may add nothing to the yield per acre.

Although the law of variable proportions is difficult to demonstrate in practice, its logic is perhaps clearest in agriculture. If there were never diminishing returns, each additional use of a variable resource on a given piece of land would yield either equal or greater increases in output. Therefore, all the world's food (corn or wheat or rice or whatever) could be raised on one plot of land. Thus, one can demonstrate the validity of the law by means of a logical absurdity.

Short-Run Supply
The law of diminishing returns has a great effect on short-run supply for a firm that buys its inputs competitively (that is, at market-given prices).

We have assumed that the firm's total variable costs (TVC)—costs resulting from increasing output—will not change because of higher prices for wages and other inputs, but *will* change with the changing marginal productivity of the variable inputs. Also, the firm's total fixed costs (TFC) do not change as output changes.

Figure 16-2 gives the picture of the firm's total costs. As output grows up to Q_0, variable cost grows, but at a decreasing rate (the slope of total costs (TC) decreases or gets flatter). This corresponds to increasing

TABLE 16-1 The Law of Variable Proportions or Diminishing Returns (numbers are hypothetical)

Inputs, the variable resource (extra cooks)	Total physical product (hamburgers per hour)	Additional or marginal physical product (hamburgers per hour)
0	0	
1st	12	12
2nd	30	18
3rd	50	20
4th	65	15
5th	75	10
6th	80	5

marginal productivity (hiring the third cook in Table 16-1). Beyond Q_0, the slope of TC increases, reflecting diminishing returns or diminishing marginal productivity (the fourth, fifth, and sixth cooks). Note that at every rate of output (such as Q_1) the distance between VC (variable costs) and TC is constant and equal to the (constant) fixed cost. Thus total cost equals total variable cost plus total fixed cost.

One can derive a firm's unit or average costs from its total costs (TC). There are three average costs (Q stands for quantity produced):

$$\text{Average fixed cost} = AFC = \frac{TFC}{Q},$$

$$\text{Average variable cost} = AVC = \frac{TVC}{Q},$$

$$\text{Average total cost} = ATC = AFC + AVC = \frac{TC}{Q}.$$

Figure 16-3 shows what happens to these costs as output increases. Averaged fixed cost *(AFC)* gets smaller and smaller as output increases. (*TFC* gets divided by larger and larger numbers). It will never be zero. But, as production grows, *AFC* will be a less and less important part of total cost. For example, you buy a machine for $100 and use it to produce Bleeps. If you only make two of them, your fixed cost for each Bleep is $50. But if you take the plunge and make a hundred of them, your fixed cost for each Bleep is only $1.

Average variable cost declines as long as the average productivity of the variable input is growing. In Table 16-1, *AVC* went down to the point at which the firm hired three extra cooks. (You can calculate average productivity in Table 16-1 by dividing total product by the number of variable inputs.) When average variable product is at its greatest, *AVC* is at a minimum (see Figure 16-3). Average total cost naturally depends on both kinds of costs: fixed and variable. As output grows, *AFC* gets smaller and smaller, and *ATC* therefore becomes more and more determined by *AVC* (*AVC* approaches *ATC*).

Marginal cost, which is the cost of producing an additional unit of output, is critically important in analyzing the supply of a firm. Marginal cost (given constant resource prices) depends entirely on marginal productivity. That is, it depends on the productivity of the input hired to produce an additional unit of output.

The supply curve—what the firm will produce in response to various possible prices—depends on marginal cost, which in turn depends on marginal productivity. If you examine Figure 16-4, you will see that the short-run supply curve slopes up to the right. The cause of this (given constant resource prices) is rising marginal cost, which, in turn, depends on diminishing returns or diminishing marginal productivity. As marginal productivity decreases (as each additional unit of variable resource produces less and less additional output), marginal cost rises. As marginal cost rises, the firm must receive higher prices for its products in order to make it worthwhile to produce a greater quantity to sell. Consider the increase in output from Q_0 to Q_1 in Figure 16-4. When the firm runs into diminishing returns (diminishing marginal productivity), its marginal costs (the cost of supplying $Q_1 - Q_0$) rise, and it must obtain a higher price to induce it to produce additional output.

Long-Run Supply

In the long run, when all inputs are variable and the only limitation is the available technology, what will the firm's supply curve look like? Since supply depends on costs, let's look at long-run costs and then move on to the supply curve itself.

In the long run, all costs are variable ones. Figure 16-5 shows what these costs look like (still assuming constant resource prices). Total cost increases in the long-run period as output, *and plant size*, grows. There are three possible rates of such increase.

1. The rate of growth of total cost *(TC)* may slow down so that the slope of *TC* gradually becomes less steep. This means that the cost of each unit produced gradually becomes smaller as the firm expands and increases its output. (In Figure 16-5, this happens as far as output rate Q_0.) When a firm does this, it is achieving what economists call **economies of scale** (when the cost of each unit produced falls as output increases with larger plant size).

A real-world example of economies of scale is the case of electronic watches. Consider the data in Table 16-2.

FIGURE 16-3 Average and Marginal Cost Curves

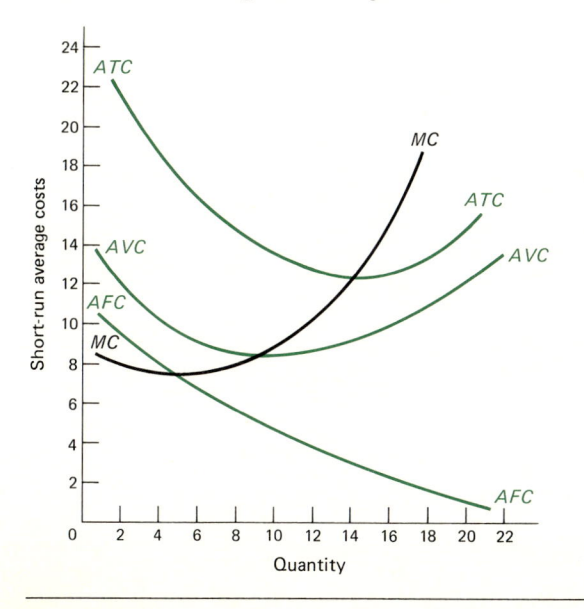

FIGURE 16-4 Short-Run Supply Curve

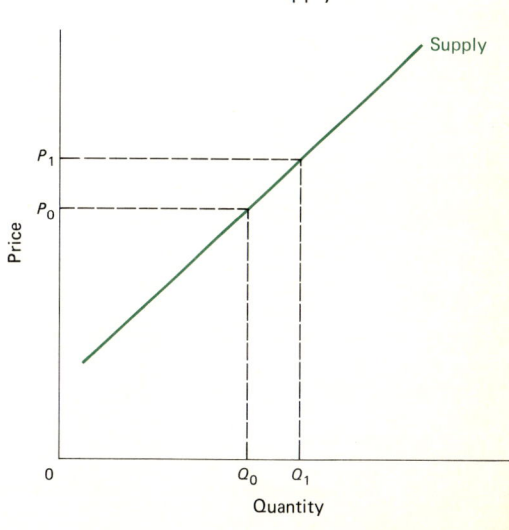

TABLE 16-2 Driving Down the Cost of Electronic Watches

	1972 10,000-unit production run	1975 100,000-unit production run
Quartz crystal	$ 3.00	$ 1.50
Circuit (C/MOS)	10.00	2.50
Watch case	4.00	2.00
Liquid crystal display	3.00	1.00
Other hardware	7.50	2.00
Labor	5.00	1.00
Battery	.80	.50
Total manufacturing cost	$33.30	$10.50

Source: Business Week, April 22, 1972.

Notice that in 1972 it cost $33.30 apiece to produce electronic watches when they were produced in 10,000-unit runs (more than half the cost was composed of circuitry and hardware). By 1975, with newer technology, such as integrated circuits from Texas Instruments, and with a larger production run (larger scale), the cost of producing each watch had fallen to $10.50.

2. Total cost may just keep on rising in a constant rate; the slope of TC is then constant. (In Figure 16-5, the part of TC from Q_0 to Q_1 reflects this.) In this situation there are *zero economies of scale* with constant unit cost (or constant returns to scale).

3. The rate of growth of total cost may speed up, so that the slope of TC gradually gets steeper. This means that the cost of each unit produced gradually increases. (In Figure 16-5, this is true for output rates greater than Q_1.) When a firm has this to contend with, it is facing what economists call **diseconomies of scale**.

FIGURE 16-5 Long-Run Total Costs

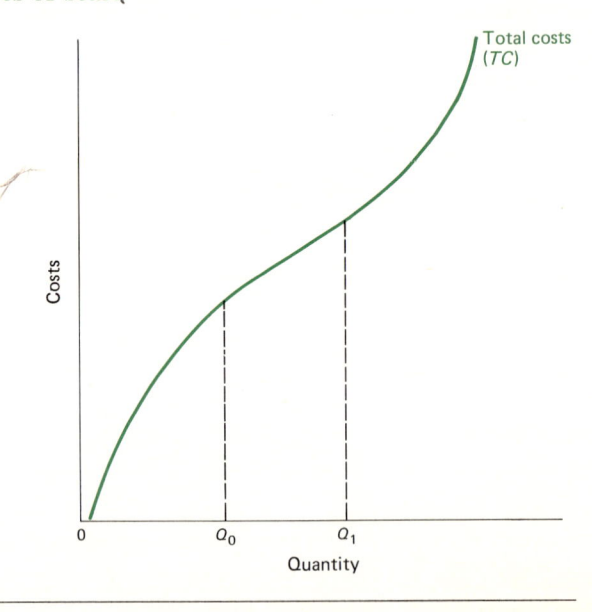

These three concepts—economies of scale, zero economies of scale, and diseconomies of scale—affect everyone through prices and have a heavy impact on long-run supply. Figure 16-6 gives the general picture. Long-run average total cost (ATC) is a U-shaped curve, an envelope, which encloses all short-run choices about plant size that are possible with present technology. These short-run choices are reflected in the $SATC$s from 1 to 11. Each of the $SATC$s represents a particular size of plant and equipment capable of producing various rates of output at different average costs. The larger plants reflect more efficient technological choices (the economies of mass production). Finally, the $SATC$s rise and reflect inefficiency and the problems of management. Suppose you are trying to decide what size plant to build to produce a particular good. You hire engineers, who tell you that there are eleven possible sizes of plant that you could choose: $SATC$s from 1 to 11. For simplicity's sake, long-run ATC is drawn as a smooth curve.

Again, economies of scale take place until the firm is producing quantity Q_0. Economists say that these economies derive from (1) specialization and division of labor, (2) improvements in management, (3) complete utilization of the productive process and its by-products, and (4) more efficient machines and equipment. For a combination of these reasons, the firm's average cost per unit continues to fall, up to Q_0.

Between Q_0 and Q_1, there are neither economies nor diseconomies of scale. One size of plant is as efficient as another. Average cost is constant, and there are zero economies of scale.

FIGURE 16-6 Long-Run Average Costs

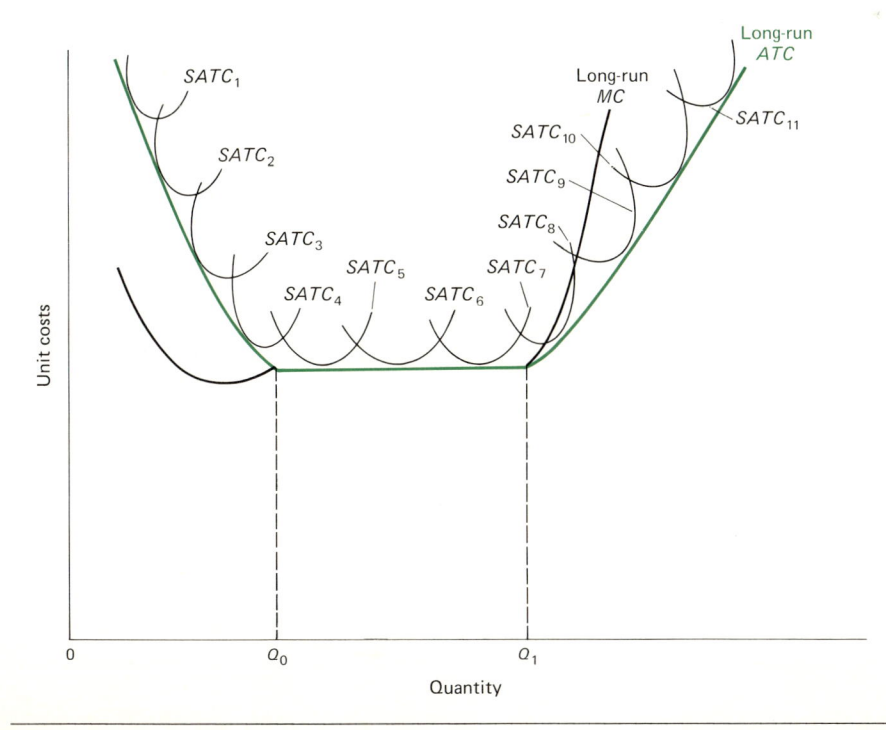

Costs and Supply in the Short-Run Period

After output gets beyond Q_1, diseconomies of scale begin to be evident. The main one concerns management. Consider the problem of communication, which is the key to management. As a firm grows, its channels of communication multiply. Suppose the firm has two managerial people; it needs two channels of communication. Then, if it adds a third managerial person or department, the number of communications channels rises to six. This exponential rise leads to the problem of **discommunication**, or, in other words, the problems that a large organization encounters in achieving effective decision making.

Thus, a firm's long-run supply can reflect any or all three of these conditions: economies, zero economies, or diseconomies of scale. Figure 16-7 compares the supply curves of these states.

Because the costs of a firm that is experiencing *economies of scale* are decreasing, the firm will supply more output at lower prices than at higher prices. At the same time, its rates of output are greater than before, and so is its plant size. Supply curve S_0 shows this. When the firm experiences *zero economies* (no diseconomies) *of scale* (curve S_1), it has constant average cost and will supply varying amounts of output at a constant price. When the firm has *diseconomies of scale*, its average (and marginal) cost rises, and it will supply more only if it can get higher prices for its output. The upward-sloping supply curve S_2 in Figure 16-7 illustrates this.

As you shall see in the next few chapters, economies of scale are especially important when it comes to analyzing the effectiveness of antitrust laws and public regulation of monopolistic industries.

FIGURE 16-7 Long-Run Supply Curves

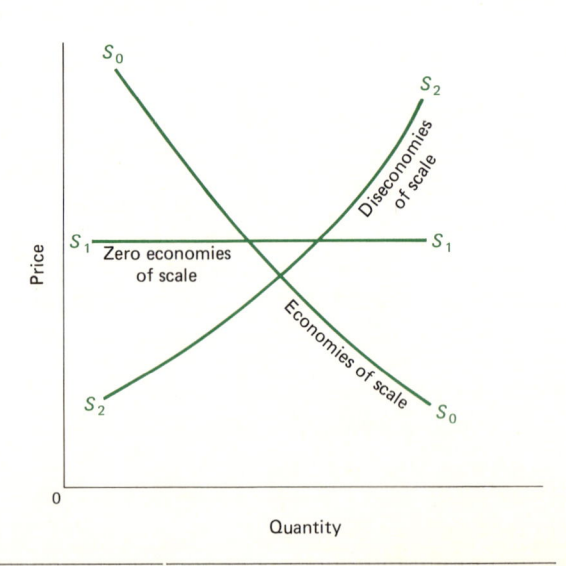

Supply on the industry-wide level: Transporting goods to the consumer (Ellis Herwig/Stock, Boston)

Supply Curves for a Whole Industry

To find out what the supply curve for a whole industry looks like, one adds the supply curves of individual firms in the industry for a given period.

In the real world, cost conditions for an entire industry may differ from those of the firms that make up the industry. Here we have assumed that all costs relating to economies (or diseconomies) of scale reflect **internal economies of scale**, or those connected with individual firms. There may also be **external economies of scale**, or those brought about by variations in the output of the whole industry or by actions that cannot be controlled by individual firms.

For example, in the hamburger industry, Better Burger Co. can increase its output by hiring more workers at the going wage. If all hamburger firms in the same area hire more people, though, the wages they all must pay their workers will rise. The higher wage will increase the marginal cost of all firms and shift the industry's supply curve to the left. (We will discuss these industry cost complications later.)

For the present, let's say that a simple supply curve for an industry derives its shape from the technological conditions of firms (diminishing returns, economies, zero economies, or diseconomies of scale) as they expand or contract their output.

Elasticity of Supply

Elasticity of supply, like elasticity of demand, is important when analyzing markets. For example, if the U.S. government lifts all controls from the price of domestically produced crude oil, by how much will oil companies increase the quantities of oil they supply? And if the government were to remove the supports from farm products, what effect would this have on our supply of food? These questions involve the **price elasticity of supply**, or the rate at which quantity supplied changes as price changes.

Elasticity of supply can be estimated by the same formula used to estimate elasticity of demand in Chapter 15. If Q equals quantity supplied and P equals price, the formula for elasticity of supply E_s is

$$E_s = \frac{\Delta Q/Q}{\Delta P/P} = \frac{\text{change in quantity/quantity}}{\text{change in price/price}} = -\frac{[Q_2 - Q_1]/[(Q_1 + Q_2)/2]}{[P_2 - P_1]/[(P_1 + P_2)/2]}.$$

We will have to go into further detail later about elasticity of supply. But for now, let's apply it to the production periods we have just discussed. E_s may be (1) elastic, (2) unit elastic, or (3) inelastic.

If firms make no change in the quantity they supply as the price of the product changes, supply is perfectly inelastic (this represents supply in the market period or very short-run period).

If firms increase the quantity they supply at a slower rate than the price of the product increases, supply is price inelastic (as in the case of diminishing returns in the short-run period).

If firms increase the quantity they supply more rapidly than the price of the product increases, supply is price elastic (up to the point of infinite elasticity, as in the decreasing-cost case in the long run).

Time is the most important factor in determining the elasticity of supply. Elasticity of supply usually increases as the time increases that is available for producers to make adjustments, by bringing in more resources, or by selling off plant and equipment. If you think of the very long-run or historical period, you see that *technological change* is a factor that has greatly increased the elasticity of supply of the economy as a whole, as well as of firms and industries.

Some Final Words About Supply

As we shall see in Chapters 18, 19, 20, and 21, there are complications in identifying supply in particular markets that differ on the basis of their competitiveness. Under conditions of pure competition, the firm's supply curve is the same as its marginal cost curve. In other kinds of markets, between pure competition and pure monopoly, this is not the case. For this reason, it is difficult to talk precisely about supply in many market situations. Instead, economists concentrate on cost.

SUMMING UP

1. *Supply* is a set of relations between the various quantities of a product that a firm will supply to the market and the prices that may exist within a given period of time.

2. Supply depends on two factors: (a) the prices a firm pays for resources, and (b) the productivity of those resources. Assuming that a firm has no control over the prices of its resources, its supply depends entirely on productivity or technological conditions.

3. To society, costs mean *opportunity costs*, or what you have to give up in order to produce X rather than Y. A single firm must therefore use resources productively in order to hire them to its own uses rather than have other industries bid higher and employ them in other ways. In using resources, a firm may incur either *explicit costs* (the direct expense of using resources it buys), or *implicit costs* (the alternative costs of using self-owned resources). The total costs of production include both kinds of costs.

4. *Profit* is a payment to the entrepreneur who assembles resources and creates a going firm. A *normal profit* is a payment just large enough to hire the entrepreneur away from other employment. An *economic or pure profit* is any profit in excess of normal profit.

5. There are four kinds of production periods: a market period, a short-run period, a long-run period, and a historical period. In the *market period*, supply is given, because output has already been produced, so there can be no change in use of resources at this stage. In the *short-run period*, firms can make changes in output by varying some inputs while others remain fixed. The *long-run period* is a planning period, in which the firm can vary all inputs, within the limits of a given set of technological choices. The *historical period* is useful in that one can see how technology has changed and analyze the effects of these changes on supply.

6. In the short-run period, the *law of variable proportions* (sometimes called *diminishing returns*) comes into play. Economists state it this way: As a firm uses successive equal units of a variable input in conjunction with a fixed input, additions to output (marginal output) begin to diminish, beyond some point. The effect of this law is that costs ultimately rise in the short run and that the short-run supply curve of a firm slopes upward. This is true in spite of any initial increase in marginal productivity as output expands.

7. Total short-run cost is the sum of total fixed and total variable cost. Average total cost is the sum of average fixed and average variable cost. *Marginal cost* is the cost of producing one additional unit of output. Marginal cost determines the shape of the firm's short-run supply curve.

8. In the long-run period, all costs are variable. As output grows and total cost increases, there are three possibilities: (a) If cost rises more slowly than output, there are *economies of scale*. (b) If cost rises at the same rate as output, there are *zero economies of scale*. (c) If cost rises more rapidly than output, there are *diseconomies of scale*. Economies of scale result from (a) specialization of labor, (b) improved management, (c) improved utilization of productive processes, and (d) improved efficiency of machines and equipment. Diseconomies of scale arise primarily from *discommunication*, or problems that managements of large firms face in trying to communicate.

9. A long-run average-total-cost curve includes all short-run cost curves. So that it will take in all cost possibilities, it is drawn as a U-shaped curve. When there are economies of scale, the long-run supply curve slopes downward, which indicates that as a firm increases its output, it can lower its prices. Where there are zero economies of scale, long-run supply is a straight line at a given price. Where there are diseconomies of scale, the long-run supply curve slopes upward, which indicates that the firm will supply more output only if prices rise.

10. One can obtain the supply curve for a whole industry by adding the supply curves of all the individual firms in the industry. This industry supply curve takes its shape from the technological conditions that the firms in the industry must deal with.

11. *Price elasticity of supply* measures the rate at which quantity supplied changes as price changes. Supply may be (a) price elastic, (b) unit elastic, or (c) price inelastic.

12. Time is the most important factor affecting the elasticity of supply of firms. As the time that firms take to make adjustments in input and output lengthens, elasticity tends to increase.

13. For a purely competitive firm, the supply curve is the same as the marginal cost curve. This is only true of competitive markets. Economists in analyzing noncompetitive markets, therefore, concentrate on the costs of firms.

QUESTIONS

1. If you were running a business, what would the *supply* of your firm mean to you? Does this have the same meaning as "supply" did when we discussed it in Chapter 16?

2. It is necessary, for the sake of social efficiency, that firms bid for resources and pay them their opportunity cost. Why is this so?

3. It's quite possible that there are many people in business who do not consider their *implicit* costs. If so, what effect do you think this is likely to have on the nation's economic efficiency?

4. Why is *normal profit* necessary if a market system is to operate efficiently? What about *economic profits*? Are they necessary too? (Give a thoughtful answer here.)

5. Why would one be unable to associate particular amounts of calendar time with the concepts of market period, short-run period, long-run period, and historical period?

6. List as many reasons as you can why the *law of variable proportions* is likely to take effect in the short run in the operation of a business.

7. Suppose that a firm that is expanding its output has a very large total fixed cost. What will happen to its average total cost as it expands output? Can you think of any firms or industries in which this is likely to happen?

8. Why does marginal cost have such a strong influence on the supply response of a firm?

9. Can you think of any firms (or industries) in which long-run average cost is likely to (a) fall? (b) remain constant? (c) rise as output increases?

10. Why is elasticity of supply important when it comes to analyzing the operation of a market system? Think back over the last half century: What factor do you suppose has most influenced the elasticity of supply of the aluminum, automobile, and petroleum industries?

SUGGESTED READINGS

Dean, Joel. "Opportunity Versus Outlay Costs." Reprinted in *Readings in Introductory Economics*, by John R. McKean and Ronald A. Wykstra. Harper & Row, New York, 1971.

"Electronic Watches for the Mass Market." *Business Week*, April 22, 1972.

Enthoven, Alain C. "Economic Analysis in the Department of Defense." *American Economic Review*, LIII (May 1963). Reprinted in *Economics: Readings in Analysis and Policy*, edited by Dennis R. Starleaf. Scott, Foresman, Glenview, Ill., 1969.

Heyne, Paul T. "Opportunity Cost and the Supply of Goods." In *The Economic Way of Thinking*. Science Research Associates, Chicago, 1976.

Mundell, Robert A. "The Market and Equilibrium." In *Man and Economics*. McGraw-Hill, New York, 1968.

North, Douglass C., and Roger Leroy Miller. "The Economics of Abortion Repeal." In *The Economics of Public Issues*. Harper & Row, New York, 1973.

Application 16

Markets for Illegal Goods

There is an old adage, *What the public demands, the market will provide*. In other words, if people know about a good, have a taste for it, and have the income to indulge that taste, entrepreneurs will supply it. They will do so at any price equal to or above their cost of producing and distributing it. This applies not only to goods that are legal, such as cars, groceries, and shoes, but to those that are illegal, such as marijuana, gambling, and prostitutes.

Let's examine the sale of illegal goods. How are the prices of illegal goods determined? What would happen to their prices if they were legalized? We shall examine only the *economic* aspects of illegal market operations. There are, of course, other aspects—moral, political, and medical.

Each time an illegal good is sold, an economic crime is committed. Table A16-1 shows that so-called economic crimes include crimes against the person and against property. They also include arson and vandalism, driving under the influence of alcohol, and tax frauds. But the biggest category of economic crimes is illegal goods and services. According to these estimates, sales of illegal goods and services amounted to about $8.1 billion, or approximately 54 percent of the total economic impact of crime. More than 85 percent of this involved gambling (illegal gambling, not the legalized gambling of Las Vegas).

Now remember that data on the GNP do not include sales of illegal goods and services. Therefore, the sales of these illegal things caused the GNP to be understated by about $8 billion. We say *about* $8 billion, because if these transactions had been legal, their prices would probably have been very different. (We will discuss that in a moment.)

We have not used such old data from choice. Surprisingly, the United States has not made figures available on the economic impact of crime since the publication of these data from 1965. These data do give us some idea of the economic cost of crime. However, the data for 1975, if there were any available, would undoubtedly show much higher totals, because the frequency of most kinds of economic crimes has increased since 1965. This increase, plus the inflation of the last decade, would make the totals much larger.

The composition of crime has almost certainly changed as well. Abortion during the early stages of pregnancy is no longer illegal. Other factors, however, have increased. White-collar crime, for example, or theft by employees, has risen dramatically since 1970. So has vandalism. And the percentage of crimes against property as part of the total economic cost of crime has surely increased, since the number of property crimes has increased more rapidly than the number of other kinds of crime.

TABLE A16-1 Economic Impact of Crime, 1965

	Millions of dollars	
Crime against the person		815
Homicide*	750	
Rape*	65	
Crimes against property		3,932
Robbery, burglary, larceny, auto theft*	600	
Unreported commercial theft	1,400	
Embezzlement	200	
Fraud	1,350	
Forgery	82	
Arson and vandalism		300
Other crimes		2,036
Driving under the influence	1,816	
Tax fraud	100	
Abortion	120	
Illegal goods and services		8,075
Narcotics	350	
Loan sharking	350	
Prostitution	225	
Alcohol	150	
Gambling	7,000	
Total		14,858

* FBI index crimes.

Source: The President's Commission on Law Enforcement, *Task Force Report,* Chapter 3.

Pricing Illegal Goods

Whether or not to legalize marijuana is a widely discussed issue in the United States and there is a great deal of precedent for this kind of national discussion. During World War I, prohibitionists agitated to make the production, distribution, sale, and even the possession of intoxicating liquors illegal, and they succeeded. The nation adopted a constitutional amendment, and Congress passed supporting legislation—the Volstead Act—which became law in 1921. Prohibition has been called "the noble experiment." The people who voted it into law genuinely believed it would do away with alcoholism and other tragic and violent situations caused by the abuse of alcohol. (It took another constitutional amendment, in the early thirties, to repeal Prohibition.)

An amusing sidelight to Prohibition is that it made an exception of wine that was manufactured for sacramental purposes. After the act became law, the consumption of sacramental wine rose dramatically. Economists Douglass C. North and Roger Leroy Miller, with tongue in cheek, wonder whether Prohibition induced Americans to become more religious.

Prohibition led to (1) reduced supplies of liquor, (2) higher prices for alcoholic beverages, and (3) illegal markets (speakeasies, bathtub gin, and so on) to cater to the tastes of people for the product they could no longer buy legally.

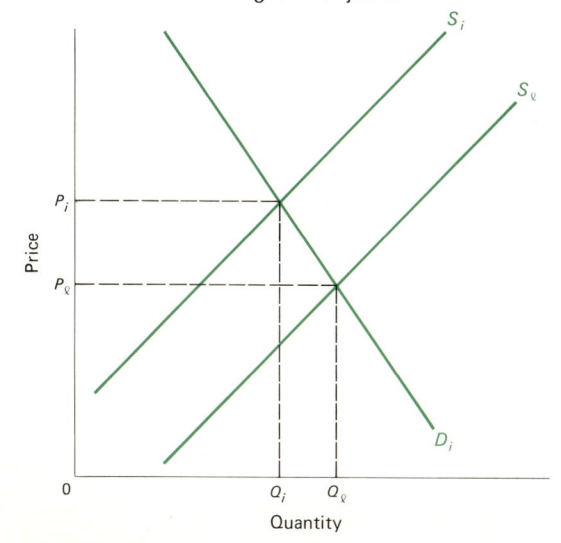

What causes results like these? Since Prohibition is no longer a burning issue, let's examine a more contemporary example, marijuana, and reverse the process. Suppose the manufacture, distribution, consumption, and possession of marijuana were legalized. What would be the *economic* effects? Look at Figure A16-1, in which D_i is the demand for illegal marijuana and S_i its illegal supply. The illegal price is P_i, and Q_i joints of pot are sold. Supply S_i for the illicit dealer is determined by the costs of production, including the risks of arrest and imprisonment. In a legal business one can buy insurance against risks, but the marijuana dealer cannot, unless the police can be bribed to look the other way. In any case, risk is an added cost of business.

Information costs, too, are higher. The dealer cannot advertise in newspapers or on TV, and so is denied an efficient mechanism to transmit information to potential consumers.

Effect of Illegality on Demand

What about illegal demand? Presumably some would-be consumers are scared off by the risks of arrest and punishment. On the other hand, there may be some for whom the thrills of furtive purchases and consumption offer positive utility. It is difficult to say what effect illegality has on demand.

It is also hard to say what effect legality would have on demand if marijuana were to be legalized. In 1975, a study among twenty-three-year-olds at the Institute for Social Research in Ann Arbor, Michigan, concluded that if marijuana were legalized, 15 percent of the subjects would use it more often, 11 percent were uncertain, and 74 percent would be unaffected. The study concluded, "Ironically, the older age groups may be most affected by any changes in the marijuana laws, since most young people already seem to have made their choice."

For these reasons, let's suppose that legalization per se would not cause people to substitute marijuana for other drugs, such as alcohol, and thus legalization would not change demand. We do not know what the income elasticity of demand for marijuana is. However, based on the ISR study, we shall assume that the price elasticity of demand for marijuana is fairly small (as reflected in the overall shape of D_i, which has varying elasticities along its entire length).

FIGURE A16-1 Pricing of Marijuana

The risky business of advertising an illegal good (John Dominis/TIME-LIFE Picture Agency © Time Inc.)

Effect of Illegality on Supply

Supply would almost certainly be increased by legalization, because (1) costs of risks would be lowered (no payoffs), (2) average information costs would fall (there could be advertising, brand names, FDA inspection, and so on), (3) larger, more efficient "firms" (the legitimate drug industry) would appear in the market and take advantage of the economies of scale available at all stages of production, from harvesting to retailing. For these reasons, supply shifts from S_i, to S_l. The quantity of marijuana consumed increases from Q_i to Q_l (a relatively small increase, if the Institute for Social Research is right). The lower price would probably mainly benefit the relatively low-income consumer who may have been excluded from the market at P_i or who had less reliable information about quality than that available to more affluent consumers (who probably had a large number of alternative suppliers).

Is this an argument for legalizing marijuana? No, we are simply setting forth what economic results one could expect if it *were* legalized. As we said before, there are ethical, moral, and medical aspects to the question, as well as economic ones (as there are for all illegal goods).

SUMMING UP

1. Illegal markets supply illegal commodities and services as long as consumers have the knowledge, tastes, and incomes to demand them, and as long as "firms" can cover their costs (including normal profit).

2. Each sale of illegal goods involves an economic crime. More than half of all the economic impact of crime involves illegal goods and services. The largest percentage of earnings from illegal transactions is from gambling.

3. Making goods and services illegal (if income is spent on them) reduces the GNP because illegal transactions are not included in calculations of national product.

4. Prohibition of alcoholic beverages in the early twenties was the first national experiment in banning "undesirable" goods. It resulted in (a) reduced supplies of liquor, (b) higher prices for alcoholic beverages, and (c) illegal markets.

5. In the case of marijuana, illegality causes higher risks and information costs, and thus smaller supply. For any given level of demand, the price of illegal marijuana tends to be higher than that of legal marijuana.

6. According to a recent study, if marijuana were legalized, the quantity of it that would be demanded would probably increase very little. Any increase would probably derive from use by people in older age groups.

7. Legalization would probably cause the supply of marijuana to increase significantly. Risks and information costs would probably fall, as legitimate drug firms entered the market to take advantage of economies of scale in production and distribution.

8. Legalization of marijuana would probably result in a significant reduction in its price. But whether it (or other illegal goods) should be legalized is not only an economic question; it is also an ethical, moral, and medical question.

QUESTIONS

1. What things determine the price elasticity of demand for an illegal good such as marijuana?

2. Why do you suppose the major change in demand for legalized marijuana might come from older people?

3. Evaluate the following statement: "The way to eliminate economic crime is to allow people to buy legally anything they have the income and taste for."

4. What things determine the price elasticity of supply of an illegal good?

SUGGESTED READINGS

Brecher, Edward M. "Marijuana: the Health Questions." *Consumer Reports*, March 1975.

Institute for Social Research. "Drug Use Still High Among American Youths, Latest Findings from Longitudinal Study Show." *ISR Newsletter*, Ann Arbor, Mich., Summer 1975.

North, Douglass C., and Roger Leroy Miller. "The Economics of Abortion Repeal." "The Economics of Euphoria." "The Economics of Prostitution." In *The Economics of Public Issues*, 2d. ed. Harper & Row, New York, 1973.

Phillips, Llad. "The War on Crime: Prevention or Control." In *Economic Analysis of Pressing Social Problems* by Llad Phillips and Harold Votey, Jr., Rand McNally, Chicago, 1974.

Pogue, Thomas F. *An Econometric Analysis of Inter-City Differences in Crime Rates*. Bureau of Business and Economic Research, University of Iowa, Iowa City, 1973.

17

Private Versus Public Costs and Benefits: Are They Always the Same?

In Chapters 15 and 16 we took a close look at the theoretical foundations of demand and supply. By putting supply and demand together in a theory that explains how prices are determined in competitive markets, we will be able to explain the quantities of output a competitive society tends to produce under varying conditions. We will also explore the relationship between the *private* costs and benefits of using resources to produce and exchange goods (the relations established in the market system) and the *public* or social costs and benefits (the costs and benefits to society). Application 16 explored one case in which private and social costs and benefits might differ, the question of legalizing and fully costing marijuana. Application 17 will explore another, the problem of cleaning up the air.

Equilibrium Price

There is an old saying that you can make an economist out of a parrot by teaching it to say: "Prices are determined by supply and demand." As you saw in Chapter 3, this statement is true of prices under *competitive market conditions*, that is, when buyers and sellers act independently of each other and no buyer or seller has any influence over market price. At the same time, the statement leaves much to be explained, so the parrot would still have a lot to learn.

We shall now examine the interrelation of supply and demand. Give this section close attention, for it will give you a foundation for what follows.

Figure 17-1 shows how supply and demand, in a competitive market, interact to establish prices. Let's say the product is kitchen clocks. Demand slopes down to the right, for the reasons discussed in Chapter 16. What price tends to result?

At first glance, it appears that there are many possible prices, any one of which may prevail. Suppliers, looking at their own (private) costs and benefits, offer more and more clocks for sale, provided that the price is above P_4. Below that price, it does not pay them to supply *any* clocks, for reasons that we will examine in Chapter 18. Likewise, consumers, examining their own (private) benefits and costs, demand more and more clocks at prices below P_3. The price that tends to be established is an **equilibrium price**.

An equilibrium price is a price that the independent influences of supply and demand tend to create, and that makes supply and demand equal.

The equilibrium condition is that demand and supply be equal. In Figure 17-1, this happens when clocks are at price P_0, where demand and supply intersect. So P_0 is the equilibrium price, because at prices above P_0, there is excess supply; firms offer more clocks for sale than consumers are willing and able to buy. For example, at price P_1, firms supply P_1B, whereas consumers buy only P_1A. The difference, AB, is excess supply. In order to clear this market, firms (assuming that they do not want to keep AB), must offer their clocks for sale at lower prices. First, one firm must cut its price, then another. The bidding of price downward continues until the price of clocks reaches P_0, at which point firms are supplying precisely the number of clocks consumers will buy.

At prices below P_0, the reverse process (bidding upward of price) occurs. At price P_2, for example, there is excess demand for clocks. Consumers offer to buy P_2D, while firms offer to sell only P_2C. The

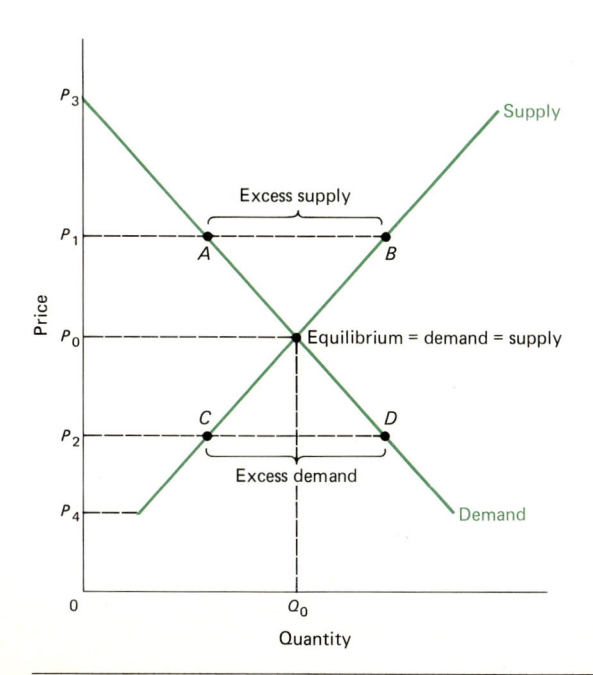

FIGURE 17-1 Equilibrium Pricing Under Competitive Market Conditions

difference, CD, represents excess demand; in order to satisfy their demand, some consumers bid up the price. The upward pressure on price stops at P_0, for here there is no excess demand. At this (unique) price, there are as many clocks available as consumers are willing and able to buy.

Private Equilibrium

Output rate Q_0 in Figure 17-1 is **private equilibrium**. It establishes a relation between buyers' privately, and noncollusively, determined benefits and sellers' privately determined costs (including the profit necessary for entrepreneurship).

It is true that this equilibrium depends on the assumption of pure competition and that in the real world a lot of *non*competitive situations exist. (The telephone company is an example.) And when noncompetitive forces do determine supply or demand, private equilibrium usually leads to less efficiency and less consumer utility than would be the case in a competitive market situation. In the noncompetitive situation, market forces do not work to produce as much output as consumers want to buy, given their incomes and tastes, nor do market forces compel companies to operate as efficiently as technology permits.

As you will see in the next four chapters, where there is no competition, either firms produce less or consumers pay higher prices (or both). Although the absence of competition has caused many people to prod the government to change the results of market decisions, even in noncompetitive private markets decisions do get made, resources do get allocated, and the market system does, in essence, ration what is produced. (Telephones are cheap enough so that most people can afford to have a phone. But long-distance calls are expensive enough to keep the number of calls within reasonable limits.) Figure 17-1 implies all of this in market equilibrium points such as P_0 Q_0.

The question is, in terms of price and output, are the private equilibrium results of the market system consistent with the social or public costs and benefits of using resources?

Social Equilibrium

Unfortunately, the decisions made in private markets, even legal ones, are not always socially desirable. For example, the price of gasoline, though higher than it used to be, is still too low to reflect the social costs of using gasoline: pollution, car-strangled cities, the high rate of traffic deaths, and other public problems that private cars create. Similarly, the prices of cigarettes and liquor are too low to reflect the public costs of medical care, research on lung cancer and liver disease, alcoholism, and public protection associated with the private use (or misuse) of these goods. In effect, then, since the prices of cigarettes and liquor do not reflect their full social costs, the public consumes too much of them.

"Up another twenty cents a fifth! How do you expect people to survive?"

We must distinguish between a private cost or benefit and a public one. Just as there is a **marginal private cost or benefit** from producing and consuming more or less of a good, there is a **marginal social cost or benefit**, which is the added cost or benefit to society of producing and consuming more or less of a good. The *differences* between privately expressed (market) costs and benefits and publicly expressed (nonmarket) costs and benefits are called **externalities**, or *spillover costs and benefits* (**spillovers** for short). When you add private costs and externalities, you get **social costs**. If there are no cost externalities, private and social costs are the same, and public costs are simply the sum of all private costs.

Spillover Effects

Figure 17-2 illustrates these spillover effects. Let's use good X as an example. It could be an urban freeway that enables trucks to haul goods to market, or it could be a conveniently located river into which manufacturers dump their plant wastes. In Figure 17-2 demand is the marginal private benefit (or utility) of consuming various amounts of good X, and MC_1 is the marginal private cost to the consumer (for simplicity, we shall assume that MC_1 is constant). Equating the marginal private cost with the marginal private benefit, the consumer demands B of good X. However, MC_2 shows the "true" or social costs of producing and using X; we will assume that MC_2 is also constant. At the actual rate of private consumption B, there is a spillover (externality) measured by the vertical distance CD. This spillover represents a social disequilibrium that society must bear (cleaning up the polluted river, adding another lane to the freeway, and so on).

A Tax to Create Public Equilibrium

The public equilibrium in Figure 17-2 is at A output, whereas the private equilibrium is at B. The difference (AB) represents a public disequilibrium. Suppose that the public takes action to correct the disequilibrium (for example, to reduce the number of private cars driven by a single occupant). One way to do this is through a tax, a high enough tax to make private and social cost equal (CD in Figure 17-2). At the higher cost, reflecting the tax, consumption will be reduced to the socially optimal level of A.

The social equilibrium in Figure 17-2 is, as we have said, the point at which the public demands A, for here the marginal social cost equals the marginal private (and assumed public) benefit. For simplicity, we have assumed here that there is no difference between the two. Suppose that the marginal social benefit (MSB) were greater than the marginal private benefit (MPB); this would be a positive benefit externality. In such a case, public demand would be to the right of private demand in the

FIGURE 17-2 Spillover Effects

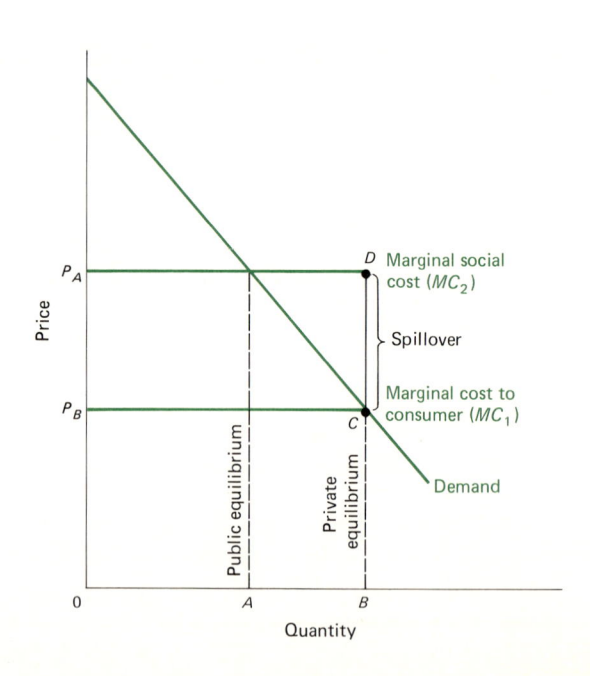

diagram, and social equilibrium would be the point at which $MSB = MC_2$. The new equilibrium point for consumption of the good would be greater than A (or the point at which $MSB = MPB = MC_2$).

If the benefit externality were negative (that is, if the public as a whole demanded less of the good at all prices than private individuals acting singly), then public demand would be to the left of the demand curve in Figure 17-1, and the social equilibrium point would be at a consumption rate less than A.

For example, planting trees in a parkway along a suburban street may yield externalities in terms of shade, beauty, and a pleasant play area for children. Here, however, benefits cannot be **internalized**, recognized and acted on privately in the form of demand by individual homeowners for trees; a great many people are so thoughtless of their surroundings or so lacking in appreciation of beauty that they could not be persuaded to spend money on trees to beautify their street. So society, that is, the city government, must provide these trees.

On the other hand, suppose that a single homeowner decides to raise chickens and coyotes to sell. Although this homeowner's benefit from doing this may be great, the noise, smell, and the commercial traffic caused by these activities create a negative externality to the neighbors. The neighbors may have these activities banned legally; or they may get together and buy off their peculiar neighbor. That is, they may give the homeowner enough money to compensate for the loss of private benefit—up to the point at which the neighborhood's social benefit is equal to the animal keeper's private loss.

Can Externalities Be Internalized?

In most cases, government intervention is needed to make individuals recognize and act on spillovers. A person driving home at five o'clock in bumper-to-bumper traffic on the freeway says, "Why don't they put a toll on this road from four to six so people who *could* drive at off-peak hours would do so?" What the driver is saying is that at rush hour the marginal private cost of driving is less than the marginal social cost (the higher cost being due to noise, air pollution, drivers' frustration, time lost in traffic, and so forth). "They" refers, of course, to government.

Someone drives by a factory that is belching black smoke or an oil refinery that is dumping effluents into a river, and says, "Why don't they make them filter those exhaust gases or clean up that stuff before they dump it into the river?" Again, what the person is saying is that there is a negative externality that the government should impose on private business as a cost of operating. Other examples of these spillovers abound: building of low-cost housing for the poor, conservation of forest areas, reshaping of the land from which coal has been strip-mined. The feature common to most of these externalities is that they affect more than just a small group, and getting them done requires government action.

The balance between private and public property rights (Gabor Demjen/Stock, Boston)

Government and Property Rights

You can see that the market system produces some wrong signals, which both consumers and producers act on. When you take into account the social costs and benefits of using resources, you can see that our market system encourages people to consume too much of some things and not enough of others. Still, these wrong signals are among the mishaps, the accidental side effects, of a free democratic society. People are free to use their private property as they please. If they happen to allocate private resources inefficiently, others must bear it. After all, isn't private property sacrosanct? A look at our legal-economic system suggests that the answer is no.

A private property right—the right to use property according to the tastes of its owner—is not an unrestricted right. For example, if you own a piece of land, you have much freedom of choice as to how to use it. You can leave it vacant, or build something on it, or grow vegetables on it; you can sell it or lease it. The police will remove trespassers from it for you. Still, there are restrictions on your use of your property, though

396   Private Versus Public Costs and Benefits: Are They Always the Same?

they differ greatly from one community to another. You may not arbitrarily shoot someone who ventures onto your property. Some cities prohibit the burning of trash because of air-pollution and fire-control laws. If the area is zoned for residential uses only, you cannot build a store on your lot.

The important point is that each society must establish, by political means, a balance between private rights and social rights in the use of property. This is true even of a society like that in the United States, in which individuals control the use of most resources, and the benefits from using them also flow to individuals. Assignment of property rights in any society affects economic activity and the allocation of resources.

In our society, it is pointless to think only of private *or* social rights in property. There are both, of course, and where spillovers exist, when there are large cost or benefit externalities, people should ask the government to intervene to correct them. This does not mean, of course, that government ought to step in in each case. A well-kept lawn and garden are an external benefit to nonowners who walk by on the sidewalk. However, no one argues that government should subsidize lawns and gardens because they are a greater social than private benefit.

How Much Government Intervention Is Enough?

If governments should not intervene in every spillover, when *should* they intervene? Economic theory does not suggest a rule of thumb, except that marginal social benefit should equal marginal social cost. Certainly a spillover should be large enough to warrant using government resources to accomplish that social objective rather than another, both in terms of cost or benefit and/or in numbers of people affected. Admittedly, this is a very general principle, and leaves much to be desired as a precise means for choosing courses of public action.

The point is that once government intervenes in a spillover situation, it should allocate its own resources efficiently. It should try to make the marginal social benefit of reducing the externality equal to the marginal social cost of doing so. For example, if local governments set out to clean up the air, should they try to get rid of pollution? They should not, at least not as a matter of principle. In New York, the air-conscious city government, pressured by environmental groups, passed a regulation saying that landlords of buildings with oil heat had to use a more expensive higher-grade fuel oil because burning the cheap grades of oil created such a great amount of pollutants. When the landlords complied, they had to raise the tenants' rents to cover the increased costs of fuel. Then along came the fuel shortage in 1973, and the government relaxed the restriction because of the energy crisis. So landlords went back to using the old sludge-filled oil, polluting the air once again (and keeping the higher rents; although, to do them justice, their other expenses were steadily rising also).

As a government makes an effort to clean up the air, the area runs into diminishing returns (rising cost) as well as diminishing marginal benefit. Since there are many competing uses of public, as well as private, resources, beyond some point it becomes inefficient (uneconomic) to continue trying to clean up the air. The same argument applies to building low-cost housing, reconstructing the terrain surrounding strip mines, protecting endangered species of wild life, and so forth.

Spillovers and Government Production

When there are significant spillovers, should the government take over and start producing the goods so affected? As a rule, it should not. There is, however, a class of goods that economists call **public goods**. The use of these goods by one person does not reduce the amount other persons may use, *once the good has been produced*. Another characteristic of public goods, in contrast to private goods, is that no one can prevent individuals from using them. For example, military goods provide a service called defense. Once a nation produces an aircraft carrier, the benefits of defense are not transferable from one person to another. Each person "consumes" defense but does not reduce the amount of defense available to other citizens.

Even public goods, however, can become private, with the exception of goods like defense goods with costs and benefits that are *indivisible* (you cannot divide an aircraft carrier into 210 million pieces and give each citizen a piece of it).

A good example of how public goods become private goods is a television signal. Once the signal is broadcast, anybody with a television set in the viewing area can see the picture. The marginal cost is zero. One can assign the benefits to individuals, however, by (1) selling advertising time, the rates for which are based on the number of viewers; or (2) instituting pay television, in which subscribers pay for the programs they watch; or (3) saying that everyone must have an annual license for a TV set, and charging a sum of money for the license. (The British and other Europeans do this. With this system, there are no commercials.)

The lesson here is clear. Spillovers tend to generate arguments and cause people to agitate for government intervention. When the government does intervene, however, it does not necessarily supply the goods itself. Government has no more ability to produce steel with nonpolluting furnaces than private industry does. The role of government, therefore, should not necessarily be to produce steel, but rather to force private steel producers to internalize the full social costs of producing the steel. (We shall say more about this in the applications that follow.)

SUMMING UP

1. This chapter deals with two related subjects: (a) How prices are established in competitive markets, and (b) the difference between private (market) costs and benefits and social (nonmarket) costs and benefits.

2. There is only one *equilibrium price* in a competitive market. It is the price that clears the market or makes supply and demand equal. In a competitive market, supply and demand forces are independent of each other.

3. Any price above equilibrium results in *excess supply*. Any price below equilibrium results in *excess demand*. Competitive (independent) bidding by consumers and producers eliminates either excess supply or demand and moves price toward the equilibrium point.

4. A *private* (market) *equilibrium* establishes a relation between private benefits to buyers and private costs (including normal or entrepreneurial profit) to sellers.

5. Even where noncompetitive markets exist, the market achieves private equilibrium and rations output on the basis of price, incomes and tastes of buyers, and so on. There is no assurance, however, that private competitive or noncompetitive results are socially desirable.

6. In many cases the privately established prices of goods (and rates of production and consumption) do not reflect the "true" social costs and benefits of using resources. (For example, gasoline prices are not high enough to keep people from wasting gasoline or using it for frivolous purposes.) There is a *marginal private cost or benefit* and a *marginal social cost or benefit* for each good supplied. Where these two costs or benefits differ, there is an *externality* or *spillover* effect that measures the difference.

7. If the marginal private cost of supplying a good is lower than the marginal social cost of supplying it, the difference is a cost spillover or externality, and consumers act on prices that do not reflect the true social costs of supply. Consumers, therefore, use "too much" of the good. If there is an externalized social benefit associated with the production and consumption of a good, private citizens produce and consume "too little" of it.

8. Externalities *can* be internalized, but frequently the government must intervene to bring this about, since private individuals can rarely get together and internalize large differences between private and social costs and benefits. One way the government can intervene is by taxing private activities by an amount that makes their private cost equal to their public cost.

9. Government's role in the internalization of spillover is to ensure that producers of a good or service incorporate the full social costs and benefits in the price of the product. This does not mean that government should necessarily step in and produce the goods whenever spillovers exist, or that in order to ensure internalization, it should do away with private property rights.

10. Each society must establish, by political processes, a balance between private and social rights with regard to the use of property.

However, government does not have to become involved in all divergences between the two sets of rights, only in those in which the differences are great and that affect large numbers of people.

11. When government *does* intervene in spillover cases, it should do so to the point at which the marginal social benefit is equal to the marginal social cost.

QUESTIONS

1. What would happen to the full public equilibrium in Figure 17-2 if there were a negative benefit externality (if marginal social benefit were less than marginal private benefit)?

2. Think of some markets in which competitive conditions exist; then think of some in which *non*competitive conditions exist. Are equilibrium prices established in both?

3. Should economists advise the government to intervene in each situation in which spillovers exist? Why or why not?

4. Is there an air pollution problem in your area? How does it reflect spillovers? What kind of action (and how much) do you think the government should take toward reducing this pollution?

5. Are you, your family, your neighbors, or your friends involved in projects that involve external benefits? What are they, and how do they reflect spillovers?

SUGGESTED READINGS

See the Suggested Readings at the end of Application 17 (page 404).

Application 17

How Much Clean Air Do We Want to Buy?

Those who have read some of the horror stories and doomsday forecasts stacked on the shelves of bookstores are likely to feel that there should be no restrictions on cleaning up air (and water). Paul Ehrlich, author of several of these books, concludes that "Western society is in the process of completing the rape and murder of the planet for economic gain.... The days of plunder are drawing inexorably to a close."

Writing about population, in 1970, Ehrlich said that "our fragile planet has been filled with people at an incredible rate. By 1975 some experts feel that food shortages will have escalated the present level of world hunger and starvation into famines of unbelievable proportions." The famines are here, in Bangladesh and the Sahel area.

Dire Predictions and How to Live with Them

In the face of predictions like these, how can people ask "How much clean air do we want to buy?" They can for these reasons: (1) Dire predictions (the Club of Rome study, the books by Ehrlich and others with the same news) are based on extrapolation—usually linear—of recent statistics on use of resources and growth of population. Economists are wary of such extrapolations because they are based on the view that resources are static and that the rate of population growth in underdeveloped countries will remain the same. (2) Such views imply that private industries, in league with governments, are responsible for what Ehrlich calls "eco-catastrophe." Ehrlich refers to the proinsecticide campaign of the American petrochemical industry, implying that the oil industry operated in collusion with its "subsidiary," the Department of Agriculture.

Business: Culprit or Savior?

Let's consider cars. Think how often automobile manufacturers change styles. Many people turn in their cars every two or three years in favor of new models, because they feel that the old ones are out of style (although this approach may be changing). James M. Roche, former board chairman of General Motors, said in April 1970: "Planned obsolescence, in my opinion, is another word for progress." It may be good for business, but think of the waste. Such attitudes lead to the hopeless feeling that there are neither private (market) nor public-private solutions to the problems of pollution. We do not subscribe to this attitude.

Don't misunderstand. Economists are not optimistic enough to believe that quick or easy solutions to environmental problems can be found. They do, however, hold the following views:

1. The problems are basically economic in origin. Each year the United States uses a certain amount of input (raw materials, fuel, and so on) in producing our GNP. In consuming these goods and services, people dispose of waste products (throwaway bottles, factory wastes, worn-out cars, soaps, human excreta, plastic articles, paper, and so forth). This approach to explaining environmental problems is called the **materials-balance approach**.

2. So long as the earth's ecological systems were able to absorb these wastes and recycle them, clean air and water were free goods. They did not become scarce commodities, goods with a price, at the same time everywhere. The great industrial cities, such as Pittsburgh and Birmingham, England, were the first places to experience a scarcity of these goods. Then scarcity spread throughout the world, depending on factors such as wind patterns, water tables, rate of growth and density of population, and amount of industry.

3. Today, because of (a) population growth, (b) technological change (new powerful pesticides and fertilizers, leaded gasoline, detergents), (c) economic growth (more industrial output), and (d) lack of incentives to avoid pollution, these blessings of nature, clean air and water, have become scarce commodities, which must be priced. They must be rationed and allocated like other commodities. But this rationing will most likely not happen without government intervention.

The Price of Breathing

Clean air can be priced. St. Louis is an example. Economist Robert E. Kohn estimated the price (cost) of attaining statutory goals of air quality in the St. Louis airshed. One can draw a diagram of the situation, letting S represent the supply of clean air. This supply curve slopes upward because of rising marginal cost. That is because it becomes more and more difficult, with existing technology, to further reduce the amount of polluting particles in the air.

"No crowds, no traffic, no noise, no smog—this place gives me the creeps, Henry."

Limits on air pollution speak for themselves. (Philip Jon Bailey/Stock, Boston)

What about demand for clean air? Since clean air is a public good (its benefits apply to all), the demand for it must be "public." It must be a community demand. In Philadelphia, for example, economist Robert Ridker estimated Philadelphians' willingness to pay for clean air. He offered a sample group a choice of pure air (no pollutant), clean air in and around their own houses, and a community solution that would give the entire neighborhood clean air. Ridker found a downward-sloping demand curve. People would be willing to "buy" more clean air as the price of it fell.

How much clean air should a community buy? Look at Figure A17-1. People's preferences are reflected in D_C, community demand (which might be established by sampling or by voting). The supply of clean air is given by MC. (Supply differs from community to community because of varying economic and physical conditions.) The equilibrium amount (or degree) of clean air is E (midway between the "Pure air" and "Crisis pollution" points).

The cost of meeting this market-determined standard is C_0. Since clean air is a common or public good, it is indivisible so far as individuals are concerned. Therefore, the public would have to pay the costs, by (1) special taxes on polluters (that is, on businesses, automobile owners, trucking firms, and so on), or (2) selling "rights" to pollute at a fixed amount that would preserve Q_0, clean air. Presumably, a profit-maximizing business would not buy more rights to pollute than would be profitable. Ultimately, as the price of a fixed supply of pollution rights rose, it would become more profitable for the business to install antipollution equipment than to buy rights to pollute.

Enforcing Limits on Air Pollution: Hard Choices

This market approach does not satisfy everyone. For example, there are those who argue for laws that set limits on air pollution (such as the man-

FIGURE A17-1 Community Pricing of Clean Air

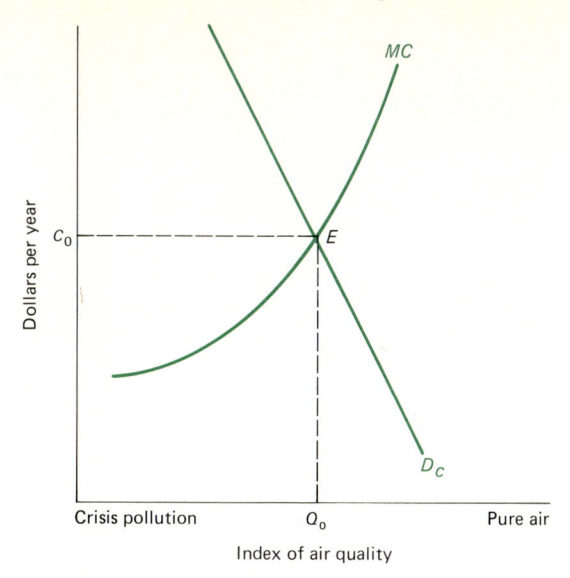

datory automobile emission standards set by the Environmental Protection Agency) or prohibit it entirely. These people feel that persuasive articles setting forth standards of pollution are too technical for consumers to appreciate. Informing consumers fully would cost too much and take too long. The government should therefore impose a set of public standards. People who espouse such legislation agree that the added costs of cleaning the air should be largely (or entirely) passed on to consumers, perhaps in the form of a special tax.

Some people maintain that neither of these approaches (consumer determined or legislation determined) are adequate. These people are not necessarily members of the doomsday groups. They simply believe that clean air has an esthetic value that the other groups overlook or undervalue. However, who is to determine esthetic standards if not the consuming public or its elected representatives?

SUMMING UP

1. Some people (the Club of Rome, writers such as Paul Ehrlich) believe that unrestricted economic growth and population increase are causing the destruction of the world's natural ecosystems and that our present-day industrial economies have a disastrous effect on the world environment.

2. Doomsday forecasts appear to be based on (a) linear extrapolations of statistics on use of resources and growth of population, and (b) the idea that private (market) and government action are responsible for "eco-catastrophes."

3. Economists, in general, hold the following views: (a) Environmental problems are economic in origin. They depend on nature's ability to absorb and recycle wastes created in production and consumption. (b) So long as the earth's ecological systems were able to absorb these wastes and recycle them, clean air and water were free goods. (c) Because of population growth, technological change, and lack of incentives to refrain from polluting, so many wastes have been created that the earth can no longer absorb and recycle them without the public's having to pay certain costs.

4. Economists maintain that one can put a price on environmental repair, including the cost of obtaining clean air. Experiments in St. Louis indicate that one can establish the prices of supplying certain levels of clean air and that the supply curves slope upward. In Philadelphia, economists found that they could determine community preferences or "demand" for clean air and that the equilibrium point for clean air is midway between pure air and crisis pollution.

5. Government could meet the costs of achieving the equilibrium amount of clean air by (a) putting special taxes on vehicles and industries that emit pollutants, or (b) selling a fixed (equilibrium) amount of "rights" to pollute (the rising price of these rights would ultimately induce firms to pay for air-cleaning equipment).

6. Another solution is for government to legislate standards for clean air and use taxes or special levies to pay the costs. This solution by-passes consumer tastes for clean air, but causes us to rely on the technical knowledge of experts and the collective decisions of elected officials.

7. Neither market nor government mechanisms for obtaining clean air satisfy the purists, who argue for pure air on esthetic grounds.

QUESTIONS

1. Economists and biologists come to very different conclusions regarding doomsday forecasts

about the future environment of the earth. Can you give reasons for these differences?

2. How much clean air would you be willing to pay for (either through taxes or in other ways) in your community?

3. Would you be willing to pay for more clean air as the price of it fell? Why?

4. When a community chooses to buy more clean air, what does it have to give up in return?

5. Which method (market or government) do you prefer for obtaining cleaner air and for determining how much of it to "buy"? Why?

6. Youngstown, Ohio, is the site of many steel mills, which spout tons of pollutants into the air of the city and pollute the Mahoning River, which borders Youngstown, to such an extent that there have been no fish in the river for fifty years. In March of 1976 the Environmental Protection Agency suggested a plan to clean up the air and water in Youngstown by forcing the steel mills to institute new antipollution devices. The plan, if carried out, would cost a quarter of a billion dollars. The television networks sent crews of reporters to Youngstown to poll the local citizenry (most of whom work for the steel mills) to find out how they felt about the Environmental Protection Agency's plan. The reaction of most Youngstown citizens was strongly negative: "No! If the EPA makes the steel companies clean up the air and the water, we'll lose our jobs. We don't need fish in that river! We don't need air that's any cleaner than we've got. We just want our jobs. Let the EPA keep hands off."

If you were a citizen of Youngstown, what would your attitude be?

SUGGESTED READINGS

Ayres, R.; A. V. Kneese; and R. D'Arge, *Economics and the Environment: A Materials-Balance Approach.* Johns Hopkins, Baltimore, 1970.

Barkley, Paul W., and David W. Seckler. "Market Failure: Externalities." In *Economic Growth and Environmental Decay.* Harcourt Brace Jovanovich, New York, 1972.

Deacon, Robert. "Environmental Quality: A View from the Marketplace." In *Economic Analysis of Pressing Social Problems*, by Llad Phillips and Harold L. Votey. Rand McNally, Chicago, 1974.

Ehrlich, Paul. "Eco-Catastrophe." Reprinted in *Readings in Introductory Economics*, by John R. McKean and Ronald A. Wykstra. Harper & Row, New York, 1971.

Friedman, David. *The Machinery of Freedom, Guide to a Radical Capitalism.* Harper & Row, New York, 1973.

Gintis, Herbert. "Consumer Behavior and the Concept of Sovereignty: Explanations of Social Decay." In *The Second Crisis of Economic Theory,* edited by Rendigs Fels. General Learning Press, Morristown, N.J., 1972.

Hoskins, W. Lee. "An Economic Solution to Pollution." *Business Review*, September 1970.

Kohn, Robert E. "Air Quality: The Cost of Capital and the Multi-Product Production Function." *Southern Economic Journal*, October 1971.

Lerner, Abba P. "The Economics and Politics of Consumer Sovereignty." In *The Second Crisis of Economic Theory*, edited by Rendigs Fels. General Learning Press, Morristown, N.J., 1972.

Mander, Jerry. "Six Months and Nearly a Billion Dollars Later, Advertising Owns Ecology." *Scanlan's*, June 1970.

North, Douglass C., and Roger Leroy Miller. "The Economics of the Automobile." In *The Economics of Public Issues*. Harper & Row, New York, 1973.

Ridker, Ronald G. *Economic Costs of Air Pollution.* Praeger, New York, 1967.

18

Pure Competition: One Extreme

Farmer Jones and General Motors—do they act the same way with respect to pricing their products and to deciding how much to produce, that is, their supply? Are the market conditions facing them both the same? Must Farmer Jones and General Motors compete with the same number and kinds of firms? Is Farmer Jones's ability to make profits the same as that of General Motors? After all, Farmer Jones, with six hundred acres of farmland, and the board of directors of General Motors, with their billions of dollars of investment and receipts and hundreds of thousands of employees, both operate enterprises for the purpose of earning profits.

Anyone would admit that the market conditions facing Farmer Jones differ considerably from those confronting General Motors. In this and the next three chapters, we will examine the different market conditions that confront Farmer Jones, or Pacific Telephone Company, or the corner drugstore, or even General Motors. When one understands these differing market conditions, one can analyze how these various firms behave with respect to pricing, production, profit, and loss. We can then begin to understand how firms with differing market conditions affect general economic activity.

In this chapter we will discuss the market classification known as pure competition. As you read through the chapter, you may get the impression that economists feel that pure competition is a good thing. But what about the agricultural industry? Farmer Jones produces in a competitive industry, in which the government continually interferes, trying to alter the competition. Does the government really want competition? Does Farmer Jones really want it? The problem is that due to all that interference, consumers must pay higher prices for food. In Application 18, we will explore what is often called the "farming mess."

Market Classifications

Obviously, firms in different industries encounter different market situations. The market milieu in which General Motors operates is quite different from the milieu of Farmer Jones, since the market situation for automobile firms is different from that for agricultural firms. Economists have grouped these differing market characteristics into four main types:

1. *Pure competition* concerns the highest degree of competition. (Theoretically, *perfect* competition is even more competitive than *pure* competition, because it embodies the condition of perfect knowledge. That is, "perfect competition," to economists, is a situation in which every firm and every consumer is perfectly informed about the economic situation in the market. However, here we shall restrict our discussion to the more realistic situation of pure competition.)

2. *Monopolistic competition* encompasses both competitive and monopolistic elements, but proportionally more competitive elements.

3. *Oligopoly* exhibits the elements of monopoly more strongly than monopolistic competition does.

4. *Pure monopoly* has minimal competitive elements.

The diagram below shows the four types as a continuum, ranging from the most competitive to the least competitive.

Most competitive ← Pure competition | Monopolistic competition | Oligopoly | Pure monopoly → Least competitive

One factor is *number of firms*. As the degree of competition declines, the number of firms usually declines.

In this chapter we will analyze the purely competitive industry. In the next three chapters we will deal with the other three.

Characteristics of Pure Competition

1. **Pure competition** assumes that no one firm or group of firms can affect market price by making this or that decision about production. No one firm can perceptibly affect price. In other words, no single firm—regardless of how much it may produce—has a share of supply big enough to affect price in the market by varying its output. Furthermore, there are no groupings of firms that can make collective decisions about out-

put. This means that there is no collusion among firms. In effect, then, each firm is independent of every other firm and is influenced only by factors that affect the entire market.

2. In a purely competitive industry all firms produce a **homogeneous product**, one that is so standardized that the consumer cannot differentiate between the output of the various producers. It is immaterial to the consumer *whose* product he or she buys. For example, to a wheat buyer, the grade-A red winter wheat of Farmer Nielson is the same as the grade-A red winter wheat of Farmer Gomez in the next county.

3. When industries are purely competitive, there is complete freedom of entry for new firms into the industry and complete freedom of exit for old firms from the industry. This ease of entry and exit ensures the highest degree of mobility of resources. This means that there are no restrictions (such as zoning restrictions, for example) that prevent firms from producing those commodities that yield the largest anticipated rate of profit.

4. A basic assumption of the purely competitive situation is that both buyers and sellers know enough about price and quantity to be able to make intelligent decisions. Buyers' or sellers' lack of knowledge cannot give any individual or group an advantage.

5. The purely competitive firm does not advertise, since its product is homogeneous and the consumer cannot distinguish between the output of the various firms. It would be foolish for Farmer Nielson to increase his cost by advertising, claiming that *his* grade-A red winter wheat is better than anyone else's, because buyers know this is not so. If advertising does succeed in convincing buyers that one firm's product is better than another firm's, the product is no longer homogeneous, and the firm is no longer a purely competitive one. Firms in a competitive industry may form an association, which may advertise the industry's product but not the product of any one firm. Ads telling us to drink milk, wear woolen clothes, or drink Florida orange juice are examples of this form of institutional advertising.

Pricing Decisions

Because of the above characteristics, the purely competitive firm cannot influence price by varying its output. It can sell all it can produce at the going market price, since its output is a negligible part of total supply. The firm, therefore, will not reduce its price below market price because that causes it to forgo revenue unnecessarily. And of course the firm will not raise its price above the market price, for that would mean that it would not sell any of its product. Conversely, since the product is a homogeneous one, the consumer's only consideration before buying it is price. In effect, the individual firm that is purely competitive has no pricing policy. The firm's price for its product is a given figure determined by the market as a whole. The firm has no control over price. No matter how much the firm produces, it receives the same price. Recall

In pure competition, the product is homogeneous. (Ellis Herwig/Stock, Boston)

that the purely competitive firm is, in effect, independent. It is not affected by other individual firms, but by the entire industry.

Output Decisions

The basic decision that all competitive firms must make is how much to produce. This decision is affected by the period of time under consideration. Let's analyze the firm's behavior, first in the short run and then in the long run.

We assume that, in a capitalistic system, any firm wants to produce at that rate at which its profits are the highest or its losses the lowest. In other words, in a purely competitive industry (as in any industry), the firm arranges its productive facilities—relating its costs to its revenues—so as to produce the amount that will maximize its profits or minimize its losses.

PURE COMPETITION IN THE SHORT RUN

In Chapter 17, we defined the *short run* as a period of time long enough to allow variations of some factor inputs, and therefore variations of production, but not long enough to allow variations in the size of the plant or in technology. (In some industries, the limiting factor is human capital. For example, in the field of medical care, the number of doctors is fixed.) In the short run, the firm has both variable and fixed costs. Also, in the short run, new firms cannot enter the industry because the time is not long enough to enable newcomers to build plants. In addition, there's not enough time for existing firms to expand or liquidate their existing plants. So plant size is fixed, but the rate of utilization of the plant is not.

One can approach the analysis of the firm in pure competition in two ways: (1) by comparing total cost and total revenue, and (2) by comparing average and marginal revenue and average and marginal cost. (These two approaches, of course, can be used for all the market classifications.) The more useful approach is the one emphasizing the relationships between average and marginal revenues and costs. In this chapter, which deals with pure competition, we will also include an analysis of total cost and revenues to give an indication of how one can use such an analysis. In Chapters 19, 20, and 21, which deal with the other market classifications, we will use only the marginal-cost, average-cost, and marginal-revenue approaches.

Total Revenue and Total Cost

Economic Profit. Recall our definition of an **economic profit** as being one that is above a normal profit. Then look at Table 18-1. It contains data on total revenues and costs for a purely competitive firm with a price of $10 for its product. (Note that profits are shown in column 12.) Figure 18-1(a) shows a total-revenue curve and a total-cost curve derived from Table 18-1. Beginning at output 4 on the curve, total cost lies below the curve for total revenue, and the firm makes an economic profit. Output will be at the level at which profits are at a maximum, at output 11. At that output, the distance between the total-cost curve and the total-revenue curve is the greatest. The firm earns an economic profit of $20.

TABLE 18-1 Price Competition: Revenues and Costs

1	2	3	4	5	6	7	8	9	10	11	12
Output	Price	Total revenue	Marginal revenue	Fixed cost	Total variable cost	Total cost	Average fixed cost	Average variable cost	Average total cost	Marginal cost	Profit
1	$10	$10		$5	$10	$15	$5.00	$10.00	$15.00		$−5
2	10	20	$10	5	19	24	2.50	9.50	12.00	$9	−4
3	10	30	10	5	27	32	1.60	9.00	10.60	8	−2
4	10	40	10	5	34	39	1.20	8.70	9.90	7	1
5	10	50	10	5	40	45	1.00	8.00	9.00	6	5
6	10	60	10	5	45	50	.83	7.50	8.33	5	10
7	10	70	10	5	51	56	.71	7.30	8.00	6	14
8	10	80	10	5	58	63	.62	7.20	7.82	7	17
9	10	90	10	5	66	71	.55	7.30	7.85	8	19
10	10	100	10	5	75	80	.50	7.50	8.00	9	20
11	10	110	10	5	85	90	.45	7.70	8.15	10	20
12	10	120	10	5	96	101	.41	8.00	8.41	11	19

Note: Short-run costs and revenues for a purely competitive firm that makes an economic profit.

Normal Profit. Recall our definition of **normal profit** as being a return to the entrepreneur that is just large enough to keep her or him producing. It must at least equal the entrepreneur's opportunity cost. That is, normal profit must at least equal what the entrepreneur could obtain from producing some other commodity or working for some other firm. Another possible situation would be one in which the firm obtains only a normal profit. This occurs at price $7.82. In Figure 18-1(*b*), price is $7.82 and total revenue is equal to total cost at output level 8. Remember that *a normal profit is included in cost* so that when total costs and revenues are equal, the firm receives a normal profit.

FIGURE 18-1 (*a*) Maximum economic profit is at output 11. The vertical distance from total cost to total revenue is greatest at output 11. (*b*) Firms obtain only a normal profit at output 8 (when price is $7.82). At output 8, the total-revenue curve is tangent to the total-cost curve. (*c*) At price $7.50, total revenue does not cover total cost. The least loss (the vertical distance from total revenue to total cost) occurs when output is between 8 and 9. Total revenue covers total variable cost, and the firm continues to produce in the short run. However, in the long run, it will leave the industry. (*d*) At price $6, total revenue is less than both total cost and total variable cost. The firm has a greater economic loss when it produces than when it shuts down, and in the long run it leaves the industry.

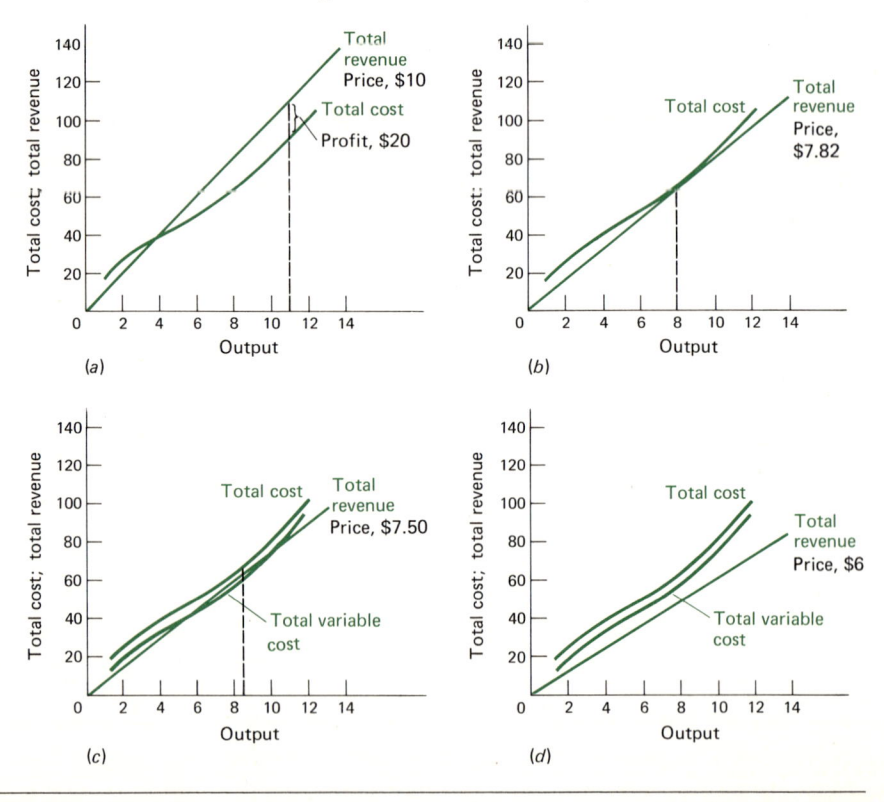

Economic Loss with Production. In Figure 18-1(*c*), at a price of $7.50, the total-revenue curve lies below the total-cost curve and so the firm sustains an **economic loss with production**. Total revenue, however, is greater than total variable cost, and the firm will continue to produce until it can **liquidate**. (By *liquidate*, we mean sell out entirely or convert all plant capacity to making some other product.)

Economic Loss Without Production. In Figure 18-1(*d*), at a price of $6, the total-revenue curve lies below the total-cost and the total-variable-cost curves. The **economic loss without production** is so great it exceeds total fixed cost. The firm thus decides to shut down.

Profit Maximization: Marginal Cost Equals Marginal Revenue

Economists conclude that **profit maximization** or **loss minimization** occurs at the level of production where marginal costs and marginal revenue are equal. This is only logical. Total profit is the difference between total revenue and total cost. When the marginal cost (the addition to total cost of producing one more unit) is less than the marginal revenue (the addition to total revenue that the firm derives from selling that one additional unit), it stands to reason that total profits increase. The firm is adding more to its revenue than to its cost. Thus, it will increase production as long as its marginal cost is less than its marginal revenue.

Now suppose the scale tips and marginal cost becomes greater than marginal revenue when the firm produces that one additional unit. Then total profits go down; more is added to cost than to revenue. So that puts the lid on that. A firm will not produce at any level at which marginal cost is greater than marginal revenue.

In summary: The firm continues to increase its output as long as the addition to output adds less to cost than to revenue (that is, as long as profit increases). But the firm does not produce when marginal cost becomes greater than marginal revenue (that is, when profit decreases). The point of maximum profits is the point at which the two, marginal cost and marginal revenue, are equal or MC equals MR. This applies whether the firm is incurring losses or making a profit.

Now let's illustrate this with numbers. We will use the data from Table 18-1 for a purely competitive firm with a price of $10 for its product (the firm takes this price as given). At output 8 (column 1) marginal revenue is $10 (column 4) and marginal cost (column 11) is $7. If the firm produces that one extra unit, profits (column 12) will increase by $3, to $17. For outputs 9 and 10, marginal revenue is still higher than marginal cost, and profit is increasing.

But now look at output 11. Marginal cost is equal to marginal revenue ($10 each). Here profit is at its highest: $20. (At output 10, profit is also equal to $20. Remember that normal profit is included in costs. The firm would produce output 11 because even though that output does not add to economic profit, it does add to normal profit.) Above output 11, marginal cost is greater than marginal revenue, and profit declines. Only at output 11—where marginal cost is equal to marginal revenue—is profit at its maximum.

Therefore, to maximize profits or minimize losses, the rate of output should be the rate at which marginal cost equals marginal revenue.

Remember that a *normal profit* is the return to the entrepreneur that is just large enough to induce him or her to continue producing that commodity, instead of engaging in some other economic activity.

There are four possible situations for the purely competitive firm in the short run: (1) The price per unit is high enough for the firm to make an economic profit. (2) The price per unit is just high enough to enable the firm to cover all costs, including a normal profit. (3) The firm does not receive a price high enough to cover all costs, but it is to its advantage to continue to produce in the short run. (4) The price per unit is too low to cause the firm to produce in the short run.

Stated briefly, the four situations are *economic profit, normal profit, economic loss with production,* and *economic loss without production.*

Situation 1: Economic Profit

Let's look at Figure 18-2. The line for average fixed cost per unit is not drawn, since it is the vertical distance from the average-variable-cost curve to the average-total-cost curve. The demand, average-revenue, and marginal-revenue curves are the same, and are perfectly elastic for this reason: The purely competitive firm lacks control over price. As we have said, price per unit is taken as given and is the same regardless of the output of the firm. Since each unit produced sells for the same price, average and marginal revenue are synonymous.

We assume that any firm's production goal is to maximize profits or minimize losses. The firm reaches this point when its output is such that marginal cost is equal to marginal revenue. Figure 18-2 shows that, at price $10, this profit maximum is at output 11. Total revenue is price $10 times output 11, or $110. Total cost is output 11 times cost per unit $8.15, or $90. Total profit *(TR − TC)* is $20. Now from Chapter 17 we know that a normal profit—that is, a profit large enough to keep the firm producing—is included in cost. Therefore that profit of $20 is a profit above normal, or an economic profit.

We can also analyze economic profit visually and in more general terms without using numbers. Figure 18-2 shows that price per unit is *P* (from the origin, along the vertical axis to point *P*). At that price one sees the curves for perfectly elastic demand, average revenue, and marginal revenue. To repeat, the quantity the firm produces is the amount that maximizes profits or minimizes losses. This quantity is the amount at which marginal cost equals marginal revenue. Figure 18-2 shows this rate at point *B*. Since quantity is measured on the horizontal axis, point *B* corresponds to quantity *A*.

Total revenue (or receipts from production) is price per unit times quantity, or the area of the rectangle $0PBA$. At quantity A, total cost per unit is measured by a perpendicular from A to the average total cost curve at point D. Since cost is measured on the vertical axis, cost per unit is C. Total cost is cost per unit C times quantity produced A, which is represented by the area of the rectangle $0CDA$. Total revenue, the area of $0PBA$, is larger than total cost, the area $0CDA$. Since normal profits are included in costs, the excess of revenues over cost, or area $CPBD$, is economic profit.

In a purely competitive market, firms have no barriers to entry in the long run. In the short run, there is not enough time for a company to expand the size of its plant, that is, to build new plants or expand existing ones. Herein lies the explanation for economic profit. In the short run, in a purely competitive industry, a firm can make an economic profit because other, newer firms cannot enter the industry and, by competing, reduce that profit.

Situation 2: Normal Profit

What about the purely competitive firm that has only normal profits in the short run? Figure 18-3 illustrates this situation.

The demand-average-revenue-marginal-revenue curve is perfectly elastic and tangent to the average-total-cost curve at its lowest point. The marginal-cost curve cuts the average-total-cost curve at its lowest point. Therefore, total revenue (price per unit P times quantity produced A, or the area of rectangle $0PBA$), is equal to total cost (average

FIGURE 18-2 Situation 1: Economic Profit for a Purely Competitive Firm (plotted from data in Table 18-1). Economic profits exist because price ($P=10$) is greater than cost per unit ($C=8$).

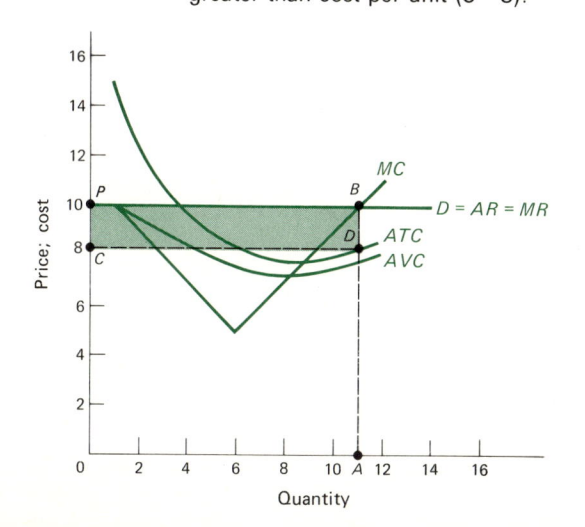

FIGURE 18-3 Situation 2: Normal Profit for a Purely Competitive Firm. The profit is only a normal one because price per unit is only just high enough to cover cost per unit (also P). Demand is tangent to the lowest point on the average total cost curve.

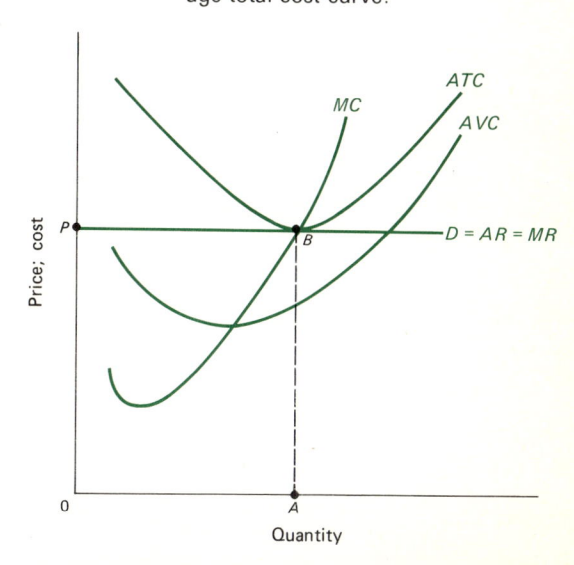

Profit Maximization: Marginal Cost Equals Marginal Revenue

total cost P times output A, or the area of rectangle $0PBA$). Since, as we said before, normal profit is included in cost, it can be seen that the firm receives only a normal profit.

The firm we are discussing is typical of the industry, and is at a stable position. The firm has reached its optimal level of output by producing at a level that maximizes profit. Remember that this is the short run, so firms cannot enter or leave the industry, because they do not have time. This same set of circumstances applies to all the other firms in the industry.

Situation 3: Economic Loss with Production

Situations 3 and 4 involve the possibility of economic losses in the short run. When a firm's in that kind of spot, the question is not just how much it should produce, but whether it should produce at all.

Remember that in the short run firms do not have enough time to liquidate their plants, so they incur certain fixed costs whether they produce or not. Since they have to pay these fixed costs regardless of output, revenues must be at least high enough to cover any additional or variable costs caused by production. Therefore, in the short run, the firm will produce as long as its variable costs are covered.

Figure 18-4 shows the relationship between revenue and cost for situation 3, in which the firm experiences economic losses. The price per unit covers variable costs per unit, but not total cost per unit. The firm thus produces in the short run, despite its economic loss.

To minimize losses, the firm produces the number of units at which marginal cost equals marginal revenue (output A). Price per unit is P and total revenue is the area of the rectangle $0PBA$. Average total cost per unit at output A is E, and total cost is the area of rectangle $0EDA$. Total cost (area $0EDA$) is larger than total revenue (area $0PBA$). Total economic loss is equal to the difference, or area $PEDB$. Loss per unit at output A is equal to PE.

Recall that this firm in the short run cannot liquidate and do away with all losses. All it can do is keep on producing, and incur its losses of $PEDB$. Or it can shut down. If it shuts down, it must still pay its fixed costs. Average fixed cost per unit at output A is the distance between average total and average variable cost, or FD. Total fixed cost is represented by the area of the rectangle $GEDF$. In this situation, the firm takes less of a beating if it goes ahead and produces. In other words, the firm earns more revenue by producing its product than it spends on the variable costs of producing it. Revenue covers all variable cost, plus some fixed cost. In the long run, however, this firm will have to either liquidate or vary the size of its plant.

Situation 4: Economic Loss Without Production

In situation 4, the firm's losses are greater than its fixed costs, so it minimizes its losses by shutting down and paying only its fixed costs. Figure 18-5 illustrates this situation.

The firm receives price per unit P. At this price, there is unfortunately *no* level of output at which average variable cost per unit is less than or equal to price. No matter what the level at which the firm might produce, its variable costs—that is, the additions to cost due to production—would always be higher than the revenues the firm would get by selling its output. If the firm were to produce anything, it would produce at the level of output at which marginal cost would equal marginal revenue at output A. Price per unit is P and revenue is area $OPBA$. At output A, the average variable cost per unit is F and the variable cost is area $OFCA$. Variable cost is greater than revenue.

At output A, average total cost per unit is E and total cost is area $OEDA$. Since revenue is area $OPBA$ and total cost is area $OEDA$, if the firm produces its usual product, it incurs economic losses equal to area $PEDB$. If the firm shuts down, it will have to pay all fixed costs. Figure 18-5 shows that average fixed cost at output A is the vertical distance from the average variable cost to the average total cost, or FE. Fixed cost is area $FEDC$. If the firm produces, its economic losses are area $PEDB$. But if it shuts down, its losses are only area $FEDC$. So the firm will shut down in the short run rather than produce its product.

FIGURE 18-4 Situation 3: Economic Loss with Production for a Purely Competitive Firm. In spite of its economic losses, the firm continues to produce, because price per unit (P) is less than cost per unit (E), but higher than variable cost per unit (G). If the firm produces, it loses area $PEDB$. If it shuts down, it must pay all fixed costs (area $GEDF$). So it loses less by keeping on producing.

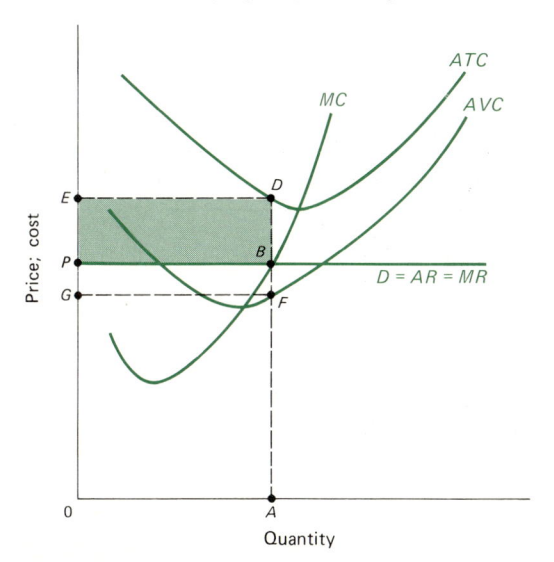

FIGURE 18-5 Situation 4: Economic Loss Without Production for a Purely Competitive Firm. The firm loses money and shuts down, because price per unit (P) is less than both average total cost per unit (E) and the average variable cost per unit (F). If the firm produced, it would lose area $PEDB$. This is greater than the fixed cost (area $FEDC$) that the firm has to pay if it shuts down.

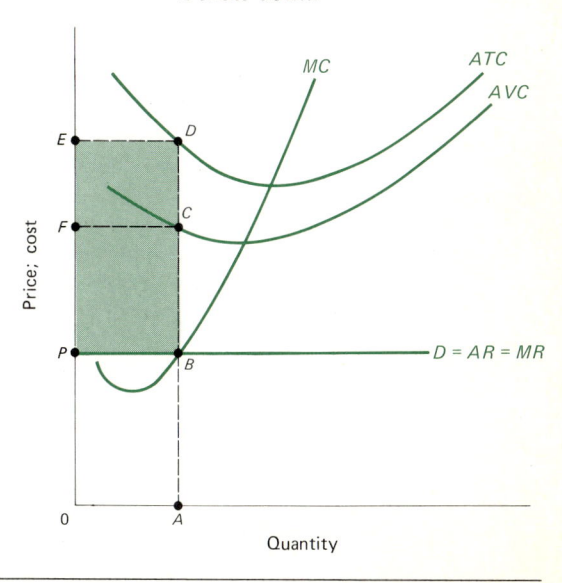

Profit Maximization: Marginal Cost Equals Marginal Revenue

Pure Competition, Short Run: A Summary

In the short run the purely competitive firm may encounter any one of four possible profit or loss situations.

Situation 1. Price is higher than average total cost, and the firm earns an economic profit. Figure 18-6 shows that price is *A* and that output *(MC = MR₁)* is *E*. Revenue 0*AIE* is greater than cost, and the firm has an economic profit.

Situation 2. Price, which is just equal to average cost per unit, is *B*, and quantity *(MC = MR₂)* is *F*. Revenue is equal to cost, and since a normal profit is included in cost, the firm gets only a normal profit.

Situation 3. Price is less than average total cost per unit but greater than average variable cost per unit. Figure 18-6 shows that price is *C* and output is *G (MC = MR₃)*. Revenue is less than cost, so the firm has to take a loss. However, revenues cover all variable costs plus some fixed costs. The firm loses less if it keeps on producing than it does if it shuts down.

Situation 4. Price does not even cover average variable cost. Figure 18-6 shows that price is *D*. If the firm were to produce at that price, its output would be *H (MC = MR₄)*. However, revenue does not cover all of variable cost, and thus, obviously, it does not cover the firm's fixed costs. The firm will be able to minimize its losses only if it shuts its doors and pays just its fixed costs.

In situations 3 and 4, the firm will in the long run either liquidate or adjust the size of its plant.

FIGURE 18-6 Summary of the Short Run for a Purely Competitive Firm. The four possible situations the firm encounters in the short run. At price *A*, the firm obtains an economic profit. At price *B*, it obtains only a normal profit. At price *C*, it incurs an economic loss, but continues to produce. At price *D*, the economic loss exceeds the fixed cost, and the firm shuts down.

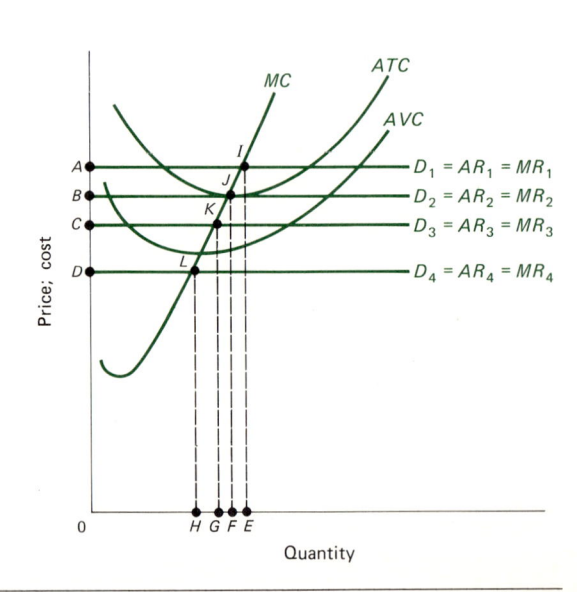

416   Pure Competition: One Extreme

Marginal Cost: The Competitive Firm's Short-Run Supply Curve

A supply curve such as that discussed in Chapter 3 shows the quantities a firm is willing and able to sell at various prices. In Figure 18-6, one sees that the marginal-cost curve above the minimum of the average-variable-cost curve is in fact the short-run supply curve for the purely competitive firm. At price A one can find the quantity the firm is willing and able to supply by following the perfectly elastic demand curve at price A to the marginal cost curve at I, or quantity E. The same applies to prices B and C and all other possible prices above the average-variable-cost curve. At prices below that curve, production will be zero, as the firm shuts down to limit its losses to only its fixed costs. Therefore, for the purely competitive firm in the short run, the marginal-cost curve above the average-variable-cost curve is equivalent to the supply curve. One can draw the supply curve for the whole industry in the short run by combining the relevant sections of all the competitive firms' short-run marginal-cost curves. (This is only substantially correct. In fact, as you saw in Chapter 16, as all firms increase the quantity they supply, some costs to all the firms in the industry may rise. This would increase cost to the single firm. For the moment, however, it is correct to add up the MC curves to obtain the industry's supply curve.)

PURE COMPETITION IN THE LONG RUN

You may recall that we defined the *long run* as a period of time long enough to enable firms to vary all factor inputs, including plant capacity, but not long enough for technology to change. In the long run, new firms can enter the industry and build new plants, and existing firms can expand plants and build new ones. In the same period of time, existing firms can do the opposite, that is, liquidate plants and leave the industry.

Figure 18-7(*a*) embodies the assumption that in the short run the firm reaps economic profits at price A and quantity C. In the long run, new firms, anxious to take advantage of the economic profits, enter the industry. And existing firms (if they are not at their long-run optimal scale) expand their plants. Naturally, this increases industry supply from S_1 at price A. See Figure 18-7(*b*). This expansion continues until supply increases to S_2 at price B. At price B with $D_2 = AR_2 = MR_2$, the firm makes only normal profits. At that point there are no incentives for additional firms to enter the industry.

Figure 18-8(*a*) shows that the firm incurs economic losses in the short run at price A. In the long run, such a firm may liquidate its plant and leave the industry. In Figure 18-8(*b*), supply S_3 for the industry decreases (shifts up to the left) and price increases. In Figure 18-8(*a*), as

FIGURE 18-7 Pure Competition: (a) The Firm. The long-run adjustment to an economic profit occurs when $D_1 = AR_1 = MR_1$ is shifted down as firms enter the industry and increase supply (part b) from S_1 to S_2. (b) The Industry. Price decreases to B. In part a, $D_2 = AR_2 = MR_2$ at price B results in only a normal profit.

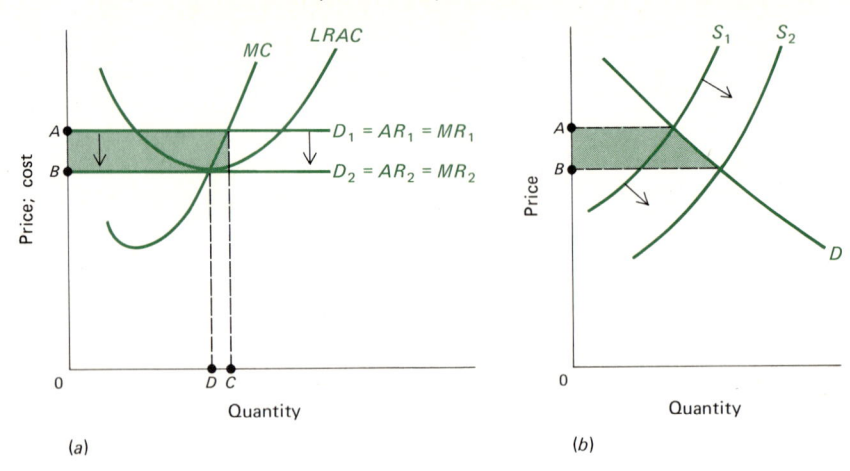

price increases $D_3 = AR_3 = MR_3$ rises to $D_4 = AR_4 = MR_4$. This cuts out economic losses and the firm makes only normal profits.

In long-run competitive equilibrium, firms receive only normal profits. As they enter or leave the industry, these firms change supply and thereby price, which eliminates economic profits or losses. Remember, though, that the long run is a *planning period*, not a period of actual production. Therefore, although each firm expects to reap economic profits, all firms tend to implement plans that result in a level of supply and a price that eventually make possible only normal profits.

Increasing-Cost, Constant-Cost, and Decreasing-Cost Industries

The above analyses of long-run equilibrium at normal profits were based on the assumption that the cost curves of the firms we are discussing do not change as the output of the industry changes. As you already know, and as the various cost curves show, costs within the firm do change as the firm varies output. Costs may also change when the output of the industry changes. As you saw in Chapter 17, these cost changes, which affect all the firms in the industry and which shift the cost curves up or down, are examples of what economists call externalities. They are a result of changes in factors external to the firms themselves. An **external economy** is a change originating outside the firm, caused by changes in output by the industry that reduce costs to the individual firm. A decrease in prices of materials or wages is an external economy. An **external diseconomy** is a change originating outside the firm, caused by changes in output by the industry, which *increase* costs of the individual

FIGURE 18-8 Pure Competition: (a) The Firm. The long-run adjustment to economic losses occurs when $D_3 = AR_3 = MR_3$ is shifted up as firms leave the industry and decrease supply (part b) from S_3 to S_4. (b) The Industry. Price increases to B, and $D_4 = AR_4 = MR_4$ at price B results in only a normal profit.

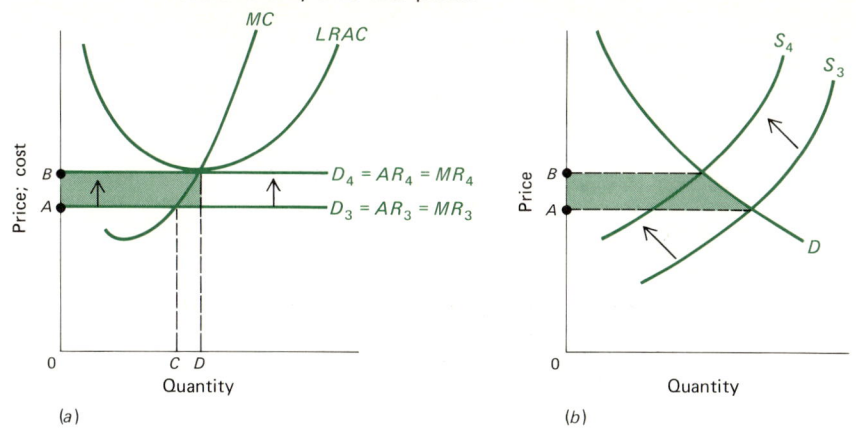

firm. An example is the need to use less well-trained labor because the better-qualified laborers have already been hired. This situation, as the firm's output increases, reduces the firm's efficiency and increases its costs.

One can define an industry in terms of how variations in output affect the costs of the individual firms within the industry. In an industry with increasing costs, the cost curves of individual firms shift upward as output increases in the industry as a whole. In an industry with decreasing costs, the cost curves of individual firms shift downward as output increases in the industry as a whole. In a constant-cost industry, the cost curves of individual firms remain stable as the output of the industry as a whole changes.

Increasing-Cost Industries

In an **increasing-cost industry**, as the output of the industry increases, external diseconomies (factors outside the firm) create increasing costs (shifting the cost curves of the individual firm upward). One common form of external diseconomy occurs when the industry has a significant share of the demand for its resource input. When the industry as a whole increases its output, demand for resources or raw materials increases, which has the effect of increasing the prices of the resources. This increase in prices of inputs increases costs to the firm at each level of output; that is, it shifts the cost curves of the firm upward. For example, Farmer Brown in Kansas demands such a small part of the total supply of fertilizer that any increase in demand for fertilizer to increase his output does not affect price. However, if all the farmers in the Midwest increased output, thus increasing demand for fertilizer, then the demand curve for fertilizer shifts to the right, thereby increasing the equilibrium price of fertilizer. Then the higher cost of

FIGURE 18-9 Long-Run Equilibrium, Increasing-Cost Industry. Two forces produce long-run equilibrium for a firm in an increasing-cost industry when the firm incurs an economic profit in the short run. The entry of new firms increases supply and reduces product price. $D_1 = AR_1 = MR_1$ falls to $D_2 = AR_2 = MR_2$. Also, increased industry supply increases the price of factor inputs, increasing the cost to the individual firm. $LRAC_1$ shifts up to $LRAC_2$.

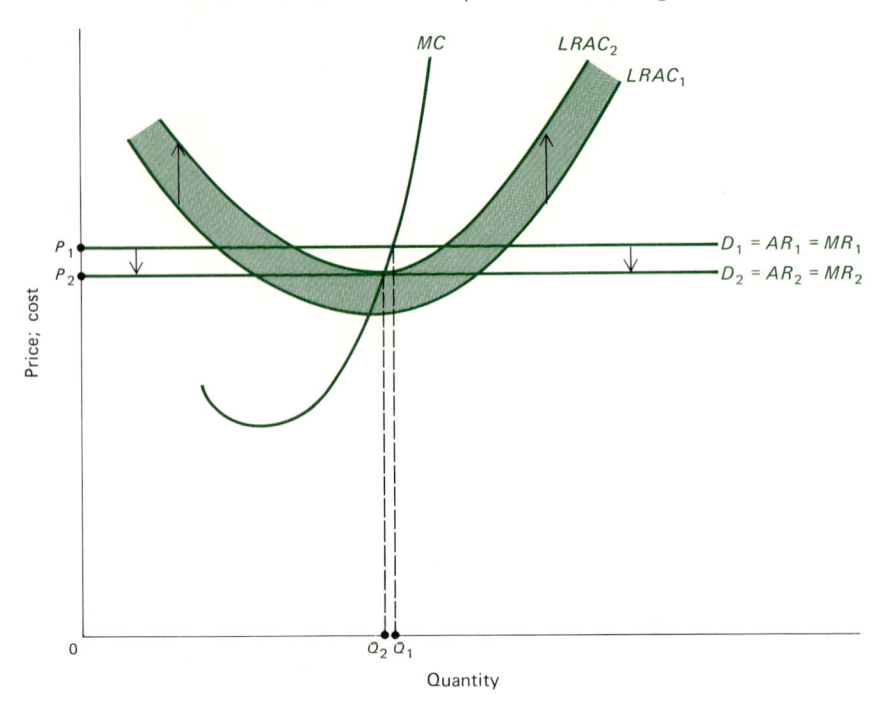

fertilizer causes a shift upward of the cost curves of poor old Farmer Brown, who is just doing his best to increase his output.

In the short run, for an increasing-cost industry, when there are economic profits, supply increases as new firms enter to take advantage of the economic profits. The addition of new firms has two effects, both of which lead toward the elimination of economic profits. The first you are already familiar with. Increased industry supply reduces the price of the product, shifting the $D = AR = MR$ curve down, to eliminate economic profits. Figure 18-9 shows that the curve $D_1 = AR_1 = MR_1$ shifts to $D_2 = AR_2 = MR_2$. At the same time, increased industry supply increases the demand for inputs of various factors, and the prices of these factors increase. Increased prices of factors in turn shift the cost curves of the individual firm upward, eliminating economic profits. In Figure 18-9, $LRAC_1$ shifts up to $LRAC_2$. In the long run, the reverse occurs if the firm has incurred an economic loss in the short run.

Constant-Cost Industries

In a **constant-cost industry**, the individual firm's cost curves remain stable as the output of the industry varies. External economies and diseconomies offset each other, or they are absent. A main explanation for a constant-cost situation is that the industry demands such a small part of the total supply of its factor inputs that variations in industry output do not affect their price. This leaves costs to the individual firm unaffected. For example, in any city, the neighborhood dry-cleaning outlets use labor that is primarily unskilled, and use only a small part of the total supply of the unskilled labor in the city. Any increases or decreases in the size of the dry-cleaning industry as a whole will not affect demand for unskilled labor, and thus the wage rate for unskilled labor is unaffected. If there is no increase in wages to labor, there is no increase in costs to the firm.

In the analysis of the long-run elimination of an economic profit depicted in Figures 18-7(a) and (b), we were assuming a constant-cost industry. The economic profit was eliminated in the long run by new firms entering the industry, thereby increasing the supply and reducing the price of the product. Falling $D_1 = AR_1 = MR_1$ in Figure 18-7(a) squeezes out the economic profit. The reverse occurs with an economic loss. In an increasing-cost industry, both falling product price and rising firm cost curves work toward the elimination of the economic profit in the long run. In a constant-cost industry, falling product price is the only factor that moves the firm to long-run equilibrium at only normal profit.

Decreasing-Cost Industries

In a **decreasing-cost industry**, as the output of the industry increases, external economies reduce costs to all the individual firms. These external economies include an increased supply of required skilled labor that may reduce wage rates, and reduced need for premiums to induce labor to come to underdeveloped areas as these areas begin to develop. Also with increased pressure from the growing industry, government may take action to improve transportation. For example, radar was developed during World War II, and after the war, was adapted to nonmilitary uses. At first, technicians skilled in radar were very scarce and wages paid to them were relatively high. As the industry expanded, this labor supply increased considerably and relative wages paid to technicians decreased.

Also, in a decreasing-cost industry, there are two factors at work: *changing product prices* and *changing costs*. In an increasing-cost industry, these two factors work together to eliminate profit. But in a decreasing-cost industry, these two factors work against each other to prolong the making of an economic profit. You can see this in Figure 18-10, on the next page. As new firms enter an industry and make an economic profit, the supply of an article increases and price P_1 falls. Thus also $D_1 = AR_1 = MR_1$ falls. This fall itself tends to eliminate profits. However, as the industry expands, external economies appear and the long-run average cost for each firm, $LRAC_1$, tends to fall. This fall by itself tends to increase economic profits. If costs fall more rapidly than product price, then economic profits increase. However, the long-run equilibrium in Figure 18-10 occurs because a decreasing-cost

FIGURE 18-10 Long-Run Equilibrium, Decreasing-Cost Industry. In a decreasing-cost industry with an economic profit in the short run, firms enter the industry and increase supply of the product while decreasing price. $D_1 = AR_1 = MR_1$ and P_1 shift down. At the same time external economies occur, decreasing the cost curves $LRAC_1$. Eventually the equilibrium situation of $D_2 = AR_2 = MR_2$ and $LRAC_2$ produces price P_2 and quantity Q_2.

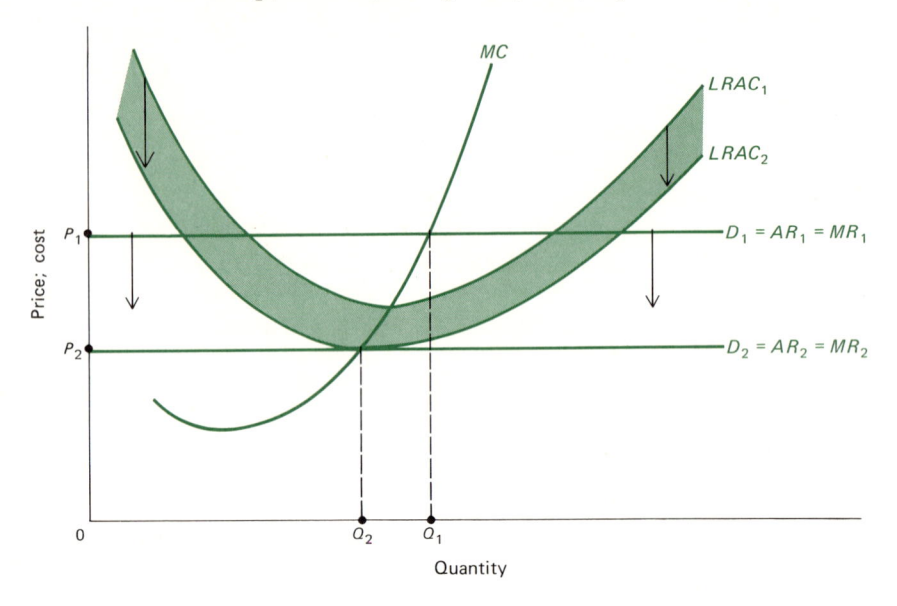

situation is only a temporary one. Eventually all decreasing-cost industries become either constant-cost or increasing-cost industries. For example, when the premium to bring workers to the wilderness areas need no longer be paid, the one-shot affair ends. When the government builds a road or railroad in the area of industrial activity, thus reducing costs to the firm, it is again a one-time occurrence. But the shift of an industry to a constant-cost or increasing-cost status must come about from the following: The industry grows to a level at which its share of total demand for its resources is so large that further growth increases demand and price of its input. This, in turn, increases costs.

In summary, then, firms operating in a constant-cost industry can achieve long-run equilibrium with only normal profits by shifting price, and thereby shifting demand, average revenue, and marginal revenue. For those operating in an increasing-cost industry, two factors eliminate economic profits or losses in the long run: changing product prices and changing costs. However, it may take a very long time for firms operating in a decreasing-cost industry to achieve long-run equilibrium, because decreasing prices tend to be offset by decreasing costs. Eventually, these industries become either constant-cost or increasing-cost industries, which assures them long-run equilibrium at normal profits.

Pure Competition: One Extreme

THE ADVANTAGES OF PURE COMPETITION

In conditions of long-run equilibrium, the purely competitive firm gets only a normal profit. When it reaches this point of normal profit, price (marginal revenue) is equal to marginal cost at the lowest point on the average cost curve (see Figure 18-11).

This equality $(P = MR = MC = AC)$ is important, because it is the basis for the analysis of the advantages of pure competition. Such an analysis sets forth the welfare conditions that many economists consider optimal. We are not using *welfare* in the usual sense here. In economic discussions, one can in large measure substitute *welfare conditions* for the term *advantages of competition*. These advantages are grouped under two main headings: (1) The purely competitive firm (and industry) produces at the most efficient level. (2) Competition forces industries to produce an array of products at prices just covering alternative cost of production.

Most Efficient Level of Cost

Competition forces the purely competitive firm to produce at the most efficient (lowest) level of unit cost. There are three main reasons for this:

1. The purely competitive firm has no control over price, so its marginal revenue curve is perfectly (or infinitely) elastic. Competition forces price to the point at which the firm can make only normal profits. Figure 18-11 shows that at that price the low point of the average-cost curve is tangent to the $D = AR = MR$ curve. This low point on the average-cost curve is also considered the level of **full capacity**, which is the level of production that can be achieved at the lowest per-unit cost.

If the firm in the long run chooses to produce less than this, excess capacity will accrue. If it produces more than this, it operates above

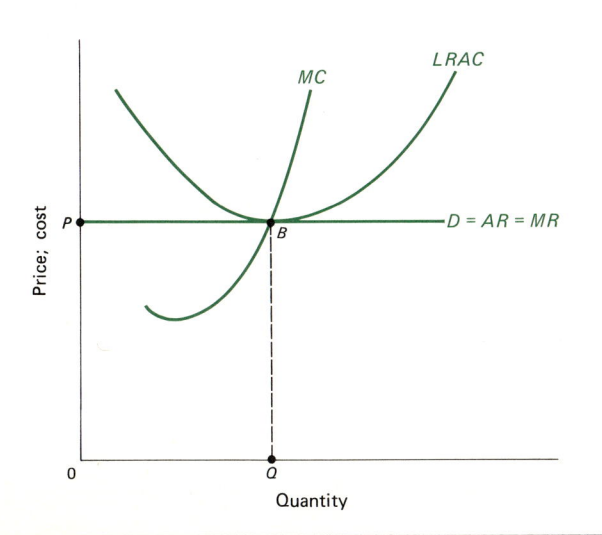

FIGURE 18-11 Long-Run Equilibrium, Purely Competitive Industry. In the long run, only a normal profit is possible. Price, demand, and marginal revenue are equal to marginal cost and average cost at *B*, which is the low point on the long-run average-cost curve. It is also the point of full capacity.

capacity. Excess capacity will also accrue if the firm fails to produce at the lowest average cost with the optimal size of plant. Competition forces a firm to strive for both optimal scale and optimal level of production on that scale. In other words, competition forces the firm to produce at the lowest level of cost, at the lowest point on the long-run average-cost curve. This is considered to be full capacity.

2. The purely competitive firm has to use the most up-to-date methods of production. If it does not, then its costs will be higher than those of other firms in the industry, and the normal-profit prices received by the other firms will cause the old-fashioned, technologically backward firm to have higher costs and fewer profits. Eventually it will incur losses. If Farmer Nielson is relatively slow to adopt a new improved strain of corn, his yield per acre falls below that of the rest of the industry (that is, the other farmers who are not slow). His cost per unit of corn produced is higher than the cost per unit to Smith, Brown, and Robinson. Competition will force the price of his corn down to the point of normal profits for all the others, who *are* using the improved strain of corn. The high cost to Farmer Nielson then results in an economic loss. So pure competition leads to up-to-dateness.

3. In pure competition the product is homogeneous: One product is like another. So firms are not justified in spending any money on advertising. Therefore, selling or advertising costs do not have to be added in to the costs of production. Of course, with respect to products that are produced in a purely competitive market, the consumer (that is, the public) knows a good bit about the product—enough to prevent price advantages resulting from buyer ignorance.

Most Efficient Combination of Products

The fact that an industry produces its output with the greatest efficiency does not necessarily mean that the output is composed of the kinds of products consumers most prefer. In a purely competitive market, however, competition forces an industry to produce an output consumers most prefer. Here again, the equality between price (P), cost (MC), and marginal revenue (MR) at the point of production is most important.

Price is what measures the worth of the product to the consumer at the margin. *Marginal cost* is what measures the opportunity cost to society of producing the last unit of the product. In other words, price measures the worth to the consumer of the last unit to be produced, while marginal cost measures the sacrifices of other products that consumers have to make for that last unit to be produced (consumers being society at large).

Now let's see what happens when price, marginal cost, and marginal revenue are not equal. When MC is greater than P, this means that consumers are sacrificing more of other goods *(MC)* than the value to them of the good received (P). Industry is producing more of the product than consumers really prefer. Where price is greater than MC, the opposite occurs. Industry is producing less of the product than consumers prefer, in terms of the sacrifice of alternative goods.

Because of (1) competition, especially by firms entering and leaving the industry, and (2) the desire to maximize profit, the purely competitive firm produces its product at the point at which $MC = MR = P$. This leads to equality between the degree to which the consumer values the product and the degree to which the consumer values alternative products. In other words, the composition of output is that which consumers prefer (given their incomes, tastes, and so on).

THE DISADVANTAGES OF PURE COMPETITION

We have discussed the advantages; now what about the *dis*advantages of pure competition?

Compared with markets of other kinds, the purely competitive market has a number of disadvantages. Let's look at three of the most important ones.

1. In pure competition, the product is homogeneous. In a society that has a desire for differences of style, homogeneity becomes a serious limitation. You cannot get 215 million Americans to wear identical padded Mao jackets. Differences based on varying styles provide the basis for product differentiation, and this will lead to a departure from pure competition.

2. The purely competitive system cannot adopt the technology existing in many industries and still remain purely competitive. Modern technology—based on assembly-line production, automation, and various feedback systems—requires such a large output in order to reach economies of scale that only a few firms can exist in each industry. If some agency (for example, the government) forces a purely competitive situation, the industries may have to sacrifice economies of scale or the opportunities to use modern technology. It is hard to imagine that enough firms can keep afloat in industries such as automobiles, steel, aluminum, oil refining, and so on, to make possible purely competitive pricing behavior. On the other hand, we do not know how many firms *are* required to create this situation.

3. Purely competitive firms are usually quick to adopt known improvements in technology. However, given today's financial climate for science and technology, it is unlikely that firms in a purely competitive industry will have the resources to engage in extensive research and development. To achieve positive results, research and development in science and technology require very large amounts of money. Only

fairly large firms can afford to spend that much. However, public agencies and nonprofit institutions do carry on much research and development. Imposing purely competitive conditions would surely shift more research and development money to such agencies. Indeed, big technological strides in highly competitive industries generally do originate outside the industry, as in agriculture and the garment industry, for example. Impressive improvements in agricultural productivity have originated from research by government agencies, as well as by manufacturers of agricultural equipment, fertilizer, chemicals, and seed. In the garment industry, improvement in sewing machinery has come from the equipment makers, not from the garment firms themselves.

An industry, therefore, that appeals to consumers on the basis of style or quality, or that gains significant efficiency from economies of large scale, or that needs large research facilities to develop technology, may move from a purely competitive market to a market with elements of monopoly power. As long as the industry gains such advantages, the loss of the advantages of pure competition may possibly be offset. However, the intensity of monopoly power may become so great that it outweighs the advantages.

One final note about the disadvantages of pure competition: The conclusion that a purely competitive system produces that combination of goods that consumers prefer takes into account only activities carried on in a market environment. However, as you saw in Chapter 17 and Application 17, in both competitive and noncompetitive markets, the process of production itself generates costs and benefits that we have not considered in our talk about markets. There are many social costs of production. Perhaps the most important and most pressing have to do with pollution.

THE RELEVANCE OF PURE COMPETITION

One may well ask: Why study the purely competitive model? Isn't our economy dominated by big business? *Is* there such a thing as a purely competitive industry?

One can defend the relevance of the purely competitive model on various grounds:

1. Certain industries do closely resemble the model. The contracting aspect of the garment industry is a good example. The contractor only produces the garments and does not design or sell them. The number of these contracting firms is large, their size small, and their capital requirements low, especially when compared with those of other manufacturing industries. We can most easily understand this industry's behavior in terms of the purely competitive model.

2. The purely competitive model provides an insight into how an industry can be affected by outside forces that distort its purely competitive structure. For instance, agriculture should, beyond a doubt, be considered a purely competitive industry. To understand the agricultural situation fully, one must have some understanding of the purely competitive model.

3. In order to understand the *im*perfectly competitive market structure, one must have some understanding of the purely competitive ones, because they provide the ideal to use as a yardstick for other market classifications. From the nineteenth century to the present, economists have used conclusions drawn from the purely competitive model to analyze capitalism. And one can understand certain elements of monopolistic markets best in terms of their departures from pure competition.

4. Essentially, the purely competitive model assumes an economic situation devoid of interference. It is a situation in a vacuum. But the physicist also makes similar assumptions and considers models in a vacuum. For example, the first step in understanding ballistics is the assumption that the projectile is traveling in a vacuum. Afterward, the physicist can make adjustments for real-world factors such as friction from the air, and direction and velocity of wind.

5. When you understand the purely competitive model, you can recognize the beneficial impact of increased competition. You can see how competition leads to lowered prices, costs, and profit margins, and how it increases the efficiency of allocation of resources. You need to understand the purely competitive model in order to grasp the arguments for stronger antitrust actions, for reduction of tariffs and import quotas, and for freer trade in general.

SUMMING UP

1. In the theory of the firm, the four major market classifications are pure competition, monopolistic competition, oligopoly, and pure monopoly.

2. *Pure competition* has the following characteristics: (a) There are so many firms that no one firm or group of firms has any control over price. (b) There is a *homogeneous product*. (c) There is complete freedom of entry into and exit from the industry. (d) There is full information for buyers and sellers. (e) There is no need for advertising by individual firms, because the product is homogeneous.

3. In the short run, two approaches can be used to analyze the behavior of the purely competitive firm as to output, price, and profit or loss: the comparison of total cost and total revenue, and the comparison of average and marginal revenue and average and marginal cost.

4. The level of output that the firm prefers is the one at which profits are at a maximum or losses at a minimum; that is, the output at which the vertical distance between the total cost and total revenue curves is at a maximum (for a profit) or at a minimum (for a loss).

5. An *economic profit* exists when the total-revenue curve lies above the total-cost curve. A *normal profit* exists when the total-revenue curve is tangent to (just touches) the total-cost curve. An *economic loss with production* exists when the total-revenue curve lies between the total-cost and total-variable-cost curves. An *economic loss without production* (a shutdown case) exists when the total-cost and total-variable-cost curves lie above the total-revenue curve.

6. Economists assume that all firms will produce at that level of output that maximizes profits or minimizes losses, which is the level at which marginal cost equals marginal revenue.

7. In pure competition, since the individual firm cannot influence price, no matter how much it produces, price does not vary with output. This means that the demand, average-revenue, and marginal-revenue curves are the same and are perfectly elastic for the firm.

8. In the short run, purely competitive firms face four possible profit-loss situations. (a) When price is greater than average total cost, the firm makes an economic profit. (b) When price is equal to average total cost, the firm makes only normal profits. (c) When price is less than average total cost, but greater than average variable cost, the firm incurs losses, but keeps on making the product. (d) When price is less than average variable cost, the firm shuts down and just pays its fixed costs. The reason these situations exist is that, in the short run, firms can neither enter nor leave the industry.

9. In a *purely competitive industry*, in the long run, only normal profit can exist.

10. In an *increasing-cost industry*, as firms enter in order to make profits, the cost of the product increases as the price decreases.

11. In the long run, in a *constant-cost industry*, firms stop making economic profits because new firms enter the industry, thus increasing supply of the product and reducing the price of it. When firms leave the industry, the remaining firms start making normal profits because the supply of the product decreases and the price of it increases.

12. In a *decreasing-cost industry*, as firms enter in order to make profits, the supply of the product increases as the costs decrease.

13. If an economy were composed wholly of purely competitive industries, resources would be allocated most efficiently to produce that combination of products consumers preferred most, given consumers' incomes, tastes, and so on.

QUESTIONS

1. Why would you classify general agriculture as a purely competitive industry? Discuss characteristics of the modern agricultural industry that do not seem to conform to the concept of pure competition.

2. Explain how the equality of marginal cost and marginal revenue maximizes profits or minimizes losses.

3. Explain why, in the short run, in a competitive industry, a firm continues to produce, even though it is taking a loss. Under what conditions will it shut down in the short run? What kind of firm will continue to produce for a long time in the face of economic losses?

4. Using diagrams wherever possible, explain the long-run equilibrium of a purely competitive firm in a constant-cost industry. Show what would happen to price, output, and costs if market demand were to (a) decrease, (b) increase.

5. Work out the long-run equilibrium (question 4) for a firm in (a) an increasing-cost industry, (b) a decreasing-cost industry.

6. In long-run equilibrium, what does $P = MR = MC = AC$ mean?

7. Explain why each of the following industries is or is not purely competitive: coal mining, production of high-fashion garments, wheat farming, automobile manufacturing. For those industries that you did not classify as purely competitive, what factors caused you to exclude them from the classification?

SUGGESTED READINGS

Friedman, David. *The Machinery of Freedom.* Harper Colophon Books, Harper & Row, New York, 1973.

Laidler, David. *Introduction to Microeconomics.* Basic Books, New York, 1974. Chapters 13 and 14.

Leftwich, Richard H. *The Price System and Resource Allocation.* Dryden, Hinsdale, Ill., 1973. Chapter 6 and 9, pp. 103-114 and 177-204.

Morrison, Donald M. "The Future of Free Enterprise." *Time,* February 14, 1972.

Stigler, George J. "Perfect Competition, Historically Contemplated." *Journal of Political Economy,* 65 (1957), pp. 1-17.

Stigler, George J. *The Theory of Price.* Macmillan, New York, 1952. Chapter 10, pages 160-186.

Stonier, Alfred W., and Douglas C. Hague. *A Textbook of Economic Theory.* Wiley, New York, 1972. Chapters 5, 6, 7.

Application 18

Do We Really Want Competition? The Farming Mess

We have just concluded that a big advantage of the competitive system is that it allocates an economy's resources in the most efficient manner (1) to produce goods at the lowest possible cost and (2) to produce that combination of products the consumer most prefers. However, throughout history, both in the United States and in other countries, governments have used many devices to interfere with market forces in that highly competitive industry, agriculture.

Agriculture in the United States seems to fit the characteristics of the purely competitive model. There are more than three million farmers, and none—even the largest—is big enough to affect supply noticeably. On the whole, farmers produce homogeneous products. These products are graded; but any farmer's wheat is much like other wheat of the same grade, and this is also true of eggs, milk, and meat. It makes little difference which farmer produced the product ultimately bought in a store.

Yet the government, since 1929, has actively attempted to influence the prices of farmers' products. It does so by manipulating supply, and to some extent demand.

Not only does the government interfere in the competitive agricultural market, but its agricultural policy seems to satisfy no one. Everyone criticizes it—consumers, economists, politicians, and many farmers. It is like the welfare program; it pleases practically nobody, but we cannot seem to get along without it.

Origins of the Agricultural Support Program

For more than twenty years prior to the depression of 1921, United States agriculture bloomed as never before. Before World War I, there was great foreign demand for U.S. agricultural products. The high immigration rate produced high domestic demand as well. During the war, foreign agricultural production decreased as Europe shifted its resources to producing war materials. This had the effect of further increasing foreign demand for U.S. farm produce. Agricultural prices increased faster than general prices, and farmers' real incomes rose. The mechanization of agriculture accelerated. Farmers who tried to increase their individual outputs by buying more land caused land values to rise rapidly. The dollar value of mortgages increased accordingly.

After the war, the picture began to change. Foreign agriculture slowly recovered, and so the overseas demand for U.S. agricultural products fell. Also, immigration halted because of new restrictions. The depression of 1921 was very severe, although it was short; and agriculture suffered greatly. Prices of agricultural products fell drastically—much further than prices in general. Farm incomes naturally fell too and remained below nonfarm incomes. This fact, coupled with high mortgage levels, put the U.S. farmer in a tight squeeze. Thus, one can see that U.S. agriculture was already depressed by the 1920s. The general depression of the 1930s only made things worse.

Farmers pressured the government for help, so in 1929 the government set up the Federal Farm Board, whose aim was to stabilize supply by storing oversupplies of farm products until they were needed. But this program could not counter falling prices and incomes, so Congress replaced it with the Agricultural Adjustment Act of 1933, which aimed at increasing prices by bringing about a forced—and artificial—reduction in supply. Ever since 1933, there has been a series of programs designed to do the same thing, in other words (1) to decrease the supply of farm produce by limiting acreage and withdrawing some land from production and (2) to increase the incomes of farmers relative to the incomes of nonfarmers. Therefore, the U.S. government, for the last forty years, has persisted in interfering directly in the competitive market of agriculture. What are the reasons for this policy?

No Bed of Roses: Agricultural Economic Problems

Demand

Agriculture, by its very nature, engenders fluctuating prices and unstable incomes. And both prices and incomes have to do with demand and supply. First, let's look at demand.

The demand for food in general is highly price inelastic. This means that when the price of a food product goes down, the quantity of it demanded increases by a smaller percentage than the percentage of decrease in price. Therefore, when the price of apples falls, the farmer's revenue from the apple crop also falls. Thus, farm prices and farm income are very sensitive to changes in quantities supplied. Food *in general* (1) has no substitutes, (2) is a necessity, and (3) is perishable—all factors causing inelasticity.

The demand for food also has a low income elasticity. (Remember that income elasticity measures the degree to which people's demand for an item increases or decreases with changes in their incomes.) For example, if income elasticity were equal to 1, a 1 percent increase in income would produce a 1 percent increase in demand for food. In the United States today, the income elasticity for food is around .2, which is very low. A person's income must increase by $5 before her or his demand for food increases by $1. As a person's income goes up, the percentage of it spent for food goes down. (This is only natural, since the *percentage* of income a low-paid worker spends on food is much greater than the percentage of income that a bank president spends on food.) In effect, the higher a person's income, the lower his or her income elasticity of demand for agricultural products. One can then say that the more highly developed an economy, the lower the income elasticity of foods. Therefore, there is little stimulus to growth in the demand for food in the U.S. economy even when there is economic growth and a general increase in income.

Thus, the demand for food is both price and income inelastic. Variations in supply have large effects on price. Figure A18-1 depicts a demand curve for food that is generally price inelastic, although it has different elasticities at each price. An increase of supply from S_1 to S_2 has a much greater impact on prices than on quantity.

Demand, as we have said, also tends to grow slowly. In the long run, the only factor that may increase demand for food (in other words, that may shift the demand curve up to the right) is an increase in the number of buyers because of population growth. Economic growth and increasing individual income have a minimal effect on demand for food because of low income elasticity. There is little likelihood that people will start demanding greater amounts of food. With all the articles stating that obesity is unhealthy, it is even possible that people's demand for food may lessen (though not our exports to other countries, including those with low per capita incomes). Variations in price expectations can have only a short-term effect. In brief, analyses of those factors affecting demand for food (or affecting the position of the demand curve) seem to indicate that the demand for food is relatively stable.

Supply: Short Run

Supply is the dominant force in determining variations in the agricultural marketplace. The

FIGURE A18-1 With a given shift in supply, the highly inelastic demand for food results in significant changes in price, with very little change in quantity.

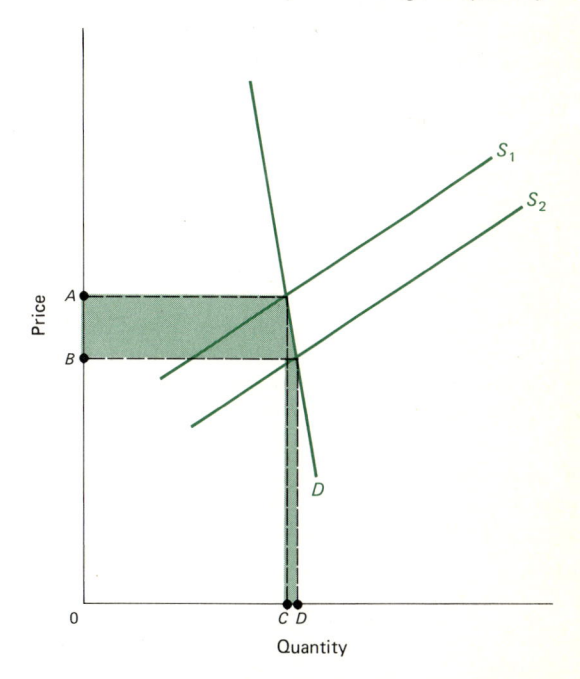

Farmers slaughtering calves to avoid selling them at a loss (Mark Perlstein)

factors affecting supply can be divided into long-run and short-run factors. In the short run, there are three main points to consider:

1. Agriculture is a highly competitive industry that encompasses a very large number of firms. No one firm (or group of firms) has any perceptible control over supply. Therefore, firms cannot artificially restrict supply in order to influence price, though some farm organizations try from time to time. The individual firm must sell at the prevailing market price. Unlike the situation in monopolistic and oligopolistic industries, in a competitive industry supply is outside the control of the individual firm or group of firms. When increases in supply reduce prices—and in agriculture, farmers' income—firms cannot band together and artificially restrict supply by concerted action to stop the falling trend of their incomes. It just won't work out.

The actions of the National Farmers' Organization during the 1960s is a case in point. In an effort to restrict supply and increase price, the NFO persuaded its member farmers to hold back from the market supplies of beef, milk, and various other products. Needless to say, the effort failed. So one must conclude that if supply is to be reduced artificially in order to stimulate income, the government must do the manipulating, and its strategies must apply to all of agriculture. Another possibility is a more rapid exit of farmers from agriculture.

2. Farmers' fixed costs run uncomfortably close to their total costs. There are high fixed costs of interest on land investment—either explicit in terms of interest charges on mortgages, or implicit in terms of imputed interest on owner-invested capital. The cost of maintenance and depreciation on equipment and buildings (these are

fixed costs) are also high. Because there are not many jobs available for farm families as an alternative to farm work, the farmer's family's labor must also be considered a fixed cost. Remember that firms that are losing money continue to produce in the short run if their losses are less than their fixed costs. Farmers with such a high proportion of their total costs fixed have less tendency to give up in the short run because they are losing money. Supply of food in the short run, then, tends to remain high despite farmers' economic losses. So supply of food, like demand for it, tends to be price inelastic.

3. Farmers can influence the total amount of certain foods available by controlling the amount of land and other resources they devote to production. Weather, however, can produce great variations in the expected levels of production, since a flash flood or a freak hailstorm can wipe out many square miles of ripe grain. And because weather varies so enormously from year to year, the supplies of foodstuffs also vary from year to year. Good weather can greatly increase supply, which can reduce both price and farm incomes. Bad weather may reduce supply and increase price and overall farm incomes. But this does not necessarily benefit the agricultural population as a whole. In fact, the only farmers who benefit from reduced supply because of bad weather are those who have escaped the bad weather; those who have endured the bad weather usually do not have enough product left to take advantage of these higher prices. For example, in 1974 farmers planted more acres of wheat than were planted in 1973. A drought caused the 1974 crop to be 15 percent *less* than the 1973 crop. A farmer can take out crop insurance. But in the long run, crop insurance is not an adequate solution to the age-old problem of the weather.

Supply: Long Run
According to the purely competitive model, in the long run firms enter an industry to compete for economic profits. When losses prevail, firms leave the industry. This means that in the long run, in a given industry, only a normal profit will exist. This assumption of normal profits is based on the mobility of resources; that is, resources usually move into and out of an industry quite readily.

In agriculture, however, resources are notoriously immobile, especially when it comes to leaving the industry. In other words, farmers tend to stick it out on the farm, come what may. There are two main reasons for this immobility, one economic, and the other social:

1. *The economic cause.* The uses of agricultural resources are highly specialized. There are few alternative uses, especially for such machines as grain combines, balers, and corn planters, or for such farm buildings as silos and barns. There are also few alternative uses for agricultural products. (What use are chickens for anything but food?) Even farm labor is fairly specialized. Although the level of skills demanded of a farm worker is relatively high, many of these skills are not needed once the worker steps outside the farm world. Many farm laborers in order to make a living elsewhere, as other than common labor, would need considerable retraining. In other words, alternative opportunities of resources now employed in agriculture are relatively scarce. In fact, many of these resources may be trapped in agriculture and have no alternative uses.

2. *The social cause.* Farmers may be reluctant to leave their rural environment. People find it hard to leave their friends and homes. And the different cultural and social conditions in urban areas may discourage farmers from leaving rural areas.

Continuity of Production
The agricultural industry has limited control over its own situation. In an assembly-line industry, management can plan output precisely, for each week, day, or even hour, because this kind of operation means continuous production. In agriculture, production is not continuous. The time needed to increase your output may vary from six months for raising pigs to three years or more for raising a fruit crop. In September, farmers must make decisions about the production of wheat that cannot be harvested until the following August. Decisions about how much land to plant with wheat are based on prices and projection of prices a year before the harvest. Not only can weather conditions change output drastically, but by the time the harvesting of the crop takes place, the projected output may be too little or too much to fit the situation.

Technological Change
Agriculture in the United States has seen rapid technological development over the last century, especially since World War II. Productivity has increased even more rapidly in agriculture than in manufacturing. However, this new technology

developed in large measure independently of individual farmers. The federal government, through the Department of Agriculture (established in 1861) and its encouragement of land-grant colleges (1864) and experiment stations (1888), was the most important contributor to these innovations. Suppliers of farm machinery, fertilizer and chemicals, and bug and weed killers also contributed significantly, and many of these businesses took advantage of technology first developed at the agricultural experimental stations.

This technological revolution tremendously increased farm laborers' productivity. In 1820, one farm worker produced enough to feed four people. By 1930, this had increased to ten. This increase was largely due to the shift from horses to tractors, which released millions of acres of farmland formerly used to raise food for the horses. By 1950, one farm worker's output could feed fifteen people. However, from 1950 to 1970, only twenty years, the number of people that one farmer could feed jumped from fifteen to forty-six, an amazing increase in labor productivity. Furthermore, many of the productivity-increasing innovations—especially plant breeding and the use of chemicals—enormously increased the yields of the land itself.

This dramatic development naturally increased the supply of farm products many times over. However, the benefits of this increased productivity have not been evenly distributed. Many farmers have neither the training nor the knowledge to utilize the new technology adequately, and their farms are too small to benefit from new machines and techniques. Also, many of the older farmers tend to be conservative. Thus, the difference in productivity between a farm of adequate size, with a proper complement of machinery, run by a farmer with modern skills and knowledge, and the small-scale farm with inadequate machinery, run by a farmer without up-to-date knowledge, is striking.

The Agricultural Support Program

Prior to the 1973 Agricultural Act, the government's farm-support program functioned primarily in three directions: (1) efforts to increase prices of farm products by reducing the supply, (2) efforts to remove land from production, and (3) efforts to stimulate demand for farm products.

The effort to stimulate prices follows the concept of **parity**. Parity, in agriculture, means manipulating agricultural prices so that the purchasing power of the money that farmers receive for their products in one year is equal to the purchasing power of the money they received for their products in some acceptable base year. The period from 1910 to 1914 is usually considered the golden age for U.S. farmers, so let's take this period as the base years.

Now, suppose that in 1910-1914 shirts were $2 apiece and wheat $1 a bushel. A farmer would have had to sell two bushels of wheat to buy one shirt. Now, say that in 1977 the same shirt cost $6. If 100 percent parity exists, wheat should be selling at $3 a bushel, so that the farmer would, as in 1910-1914, be able to sell two bushels of wheat and have enough money to buy one shirt. In other words, one compares an index of prices of farm products with an index of prices of products farmers bought in the base year, then seeks the same relationship for prices for, say, 1977 (or whatever year we're concerned about). Until the early 1970s, the trend was for the prices of what the farmers sold to rise more slowly than the prices of what they needed to buy. The government tries to support farm prices on the basis of parity; but it does not have to support them at 100 percent of parity.

"It's time he had a chemistry set if he's going to be a farmer."

Mechanizing agriculture (USDA Photo)

To support farm prices, the government has to keep them above an equilibrium level. In Figure A18-2, the equilibrium farm price is A, but this is too low for the government's goal of parity prices for farmers; the government wants price B. However, if the government just supports prices at B and lets it go at that, there is disequilibrium in the market. An excess supply, EG, is created, which the government must eliminate, or else it cannot maintain the price of B. To do this, it must either reduce supply to intersect demand at point C, or increase demand to intersect supply at point D, or a combination of both.

When you look at Figure A18-2, you can see that it is not enough for a government just to support prices. At the same time it has to restrict supply—which it has done by limiting the number of acres of certain products that farmers can plant. The government itself increased demand by buying up and storing millions of tons of agricultural products. Simultaneously, it set up programs (we'll talk about those later) to stimulate *non*government demand for these products.

Other government programs—the soil conservation program and the soil bank program—aimed at lessening the number of acres involved in the production of field crops. The government's soil conservation program, initiated in 1936, encouraged farmers to stop planting certain field crops on land threatened by soil erosion. At government expense, farmers planted the acres in grass, put in terraces, and began to follow the scientific methods of contour plowing. Quite literally, this program has conserved soil. The soil bank program, begun in the 1950s and phased out in the late 1960s, paid farmers to remove land from production.

A well-known government program aimed at directly stimulating demand for agricultural products is the food-stamp program. Low-income families can get stamps from the welfare department, take these to their local supermarket, and buy food with them. A second program calls for direct distribution of food to needy families. And, third, there is the free school lunch program, which also stimulates domestic demand. It has the additional virtue of providing many children in deprived areas with the only hot, balanced meal they get during the day. These programs have another function: They supplement the incomes of people who are in need. One could talk at length about which of the two functions—supporting demand for farm products or maintaining incomes of the poor—is the more important. But we shall not delve into that here.

Still another program stimulates foreign demand for American agricultural products. Under the foreign-aid program, famine-struck countries apply to the U.S. government for food. The United States has sent billions of dollars' worth of wheat and other grains to countries such as India.

Agricultural products with domestically supported prices are too expensive for many foreign countries to buy, however. So in order to keep its overseas customers, the U.S. government pays the difference between domestic and foreign prices. For example, when the United States shipped mammoth amounts of wheat to the Soviet Union in 1972, the government subsidized the sale, so that the Russians bought the wheat at cheaper prices than American consumers could buy it. In 1973, the nine countries in the European Economic Community, especially Great Britain, had a massive surplus of butter; in order to support butter prices and keep dairy farmers from going broke, the EEC bought up 400,000 tons of butter and stored it, meanwhile looking desperately for customers. Along came the Russians, happy to take it off their hands, if the price was right. So the EEC sold 200,000 tons of butter to the Russians at rock-bottom subsidized prices, which created the politically awkward situation of the Russian consumer's being able to buy British butter at a cheaper price than the British could.

Critique of the Agricultural Support Program

As you have probably gathered, the federal agricultural support program has a lot of flaws. It cannot seem to solve the problems of small operators, who comprise a majority of U.S. farmers. It places a heavy burden on consumers, in the form of high prices, at the same time that it penalizes consumers with the cost of taxes for running the program. And of course, in these times of worldwide food shortages, the federal food program fails to protect consumers from sharp increases in price brought about by enormous foreign demand.

A policy leading to direct support of prices instead of direct support of farmers' incomes puts a double burden on the general public, which has to pay higher-than-equilibrium prices for food and at the same time pay taxes to support the farm program. Figure A18-2 shows that, in order to achieve the price levels the Department of Agriculture considers desirable for agricultural products, the government must force the level of prices higher than it would be under conditions of free competition. In addition, these high, artificially supported prices generate surpluses that the government must deal with, at a cost that is, of course, passed on to the taxpayer.

Until the huge wheat deal with Russia in 1972, the U.S. government had to bear the main burden of dealing with American agriculture's huge grain surpluses. The government bought up the excess grain, built mammoth storage bins, and stored it.

The government's attempt to restrict supply by ordering farmers to limit acreage planted to certain crops and to reduce land under cultivation

FIGURE A18-2 Price Supports. Government efforts to support prices of farm products so that they are at *B*, above the equilibrium price *A*, generate an excess supply, *EG*. If the price *B* is to be maintained, either demand must increase or supply decrease.

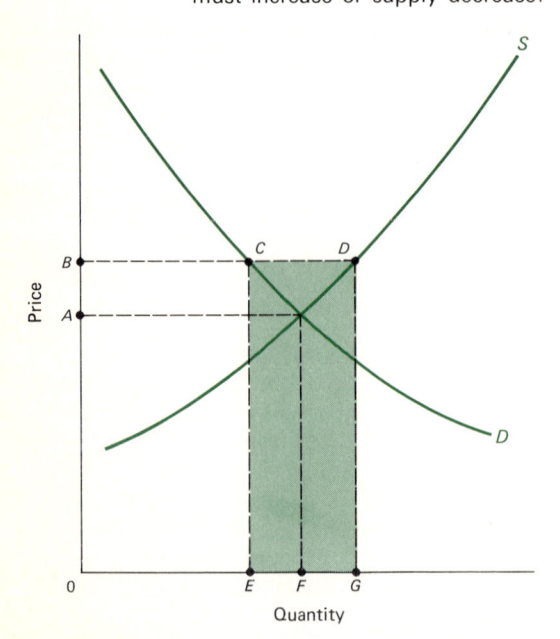

was ineffective until the late 1960s, for several reasons: (1) Farmers, reasonably enough, took their *least*-productive land out of production. This reduced the impact of acreage restrictions, since the land farmers stopped planting had a low yield anyway. (2) Farmers applied more fertilizer and used more pest-control measures on the higher-yield land, which was still under cultivation. Substantial increases in yields per acre resulted, which of course again thwarted the effort to reduce supply. In effect, under this acreage-reduction program, supply tended to increase, not decrease!

Other government programs aimed at reducing land in production were also ineffective in reducing agricultural supply. Because the soil conservation program reduced soil erosion, it increased long-run agricultural productivity. Farmers put into the "soil-bank" only their least-productive land and used the government money they received to buy more fertilizer and chemicals to increase the productivity of the land remaining in production. So the main effect of the soil bank program was to increase the price of a given piece of land by an amount comparable to the amount of money the farmer received for removing the land from production.

The programs designed to stimulate demand for farm products also did not do well. The school lunch program, the food stamp program, and the program for direct distribution of food to the poor have not been well funded and have suffered from too much local political interference. And they have not significantly affected demand for farm products, either.

The trouble is that not only the federal government, but also the local governments, must contribute money for the free-food programs, either by matching funds or by supplying facilities for distribution. So there has been local political manipulation in some areas. There were battles between city hall and welfare organizations in Boston, Syracuse, and Chicago—to name only a few cities—about who would control distribution of free food. And then there was the case in North Carolina in the early 1960s in which county supervisors stopped the distribution of free food because it was helping striking tobacco-field workers stay away from their jobs longer.

In the 1950s and 1960s the government shipped millions of tons of food to famine-stricken countries, yet even this was not enough to reduce the government's enormous stored surpluses significantly (although for both humanitarian and political reasons, the giveaway program was more than justified). However, after 1968, these shipments, plus the huge sales of grain to the Russians, finally did deplete the U.S. surplus grains and even drained away our normal reserves. In the early 1970s, grain prices increased sharply, which pushed up prices of agricultural products in general. And as of the mid-1970s, there are shortages of grain in many countries, and therefore shortages of food in general.

Did the Agricultural Support Program Help All Agriculture?

Not only did the federal farm support program put severe burdens on the consumer and taxpayer, but it did not solve the problem of low and unstable incomes for the majority of the farmers in the United States.

Many farmers just do not have enough resources—land, machinery, and skills—to be able to earn a "decent" living. Because the volume of their output and the size of their land holdings are inadequate, small farmers are helped only minimally by the farm-support program. Getting higher prices for their produce is not enough to bring their incomes to acceptable levels.

Low-income farmers are, in essence, welfare cases. In most areas, though, the fact that they own a farm keeps them from qualifying for welfare programs. Now suppose these farmers leave agriculture entirely and that their land is retired from production. Then the amount of farm products would drop off sharply and the farmers that remained would undoubtedly get higher incomes, perhaps high enough to make farming a profitable business for them.

Owners of relatively large farms can take full advantage of support programs. This shift from small, inefficient-size units to larger-size farms decidedly increases the efficiency of allocation of total resources. Technological change has made the small farm comparatively inefficient, and one should not bemoan its passing, at least on economic grounds. But on both ethical and economic grounds, it is hard to justify government subsidies to farmers who already have incomes considerably higher than the average American.

So farmers with too little income cannot get more; and farmers with big incomes get even bigger ones. As Alice would say, the situation is "curiouser and curiouser."

Since 1972: Where Have All the Surpluses Gone?

In 1963 the government's farm programs shifted strategy. Instead of supporting prices mainly by buying and storing farm surpluses, the government began to emphasize direct management of supply. It paid farmers to get them to withhold land from production. Table A18-1 shows the results. After 1963, stocks of wheat and corn held by the government's Commodity Credit Corporation (CCC) began to dwindle, and there were overall declines in grain stocks. In the 1960s as a result of direct government payments, farmers withdrew more than 50 million acres from the production of grains. These payments rose from approximately $1 billion in 1960 to almost $4 billion by 1972. In 1960 government payments as a percentage of net farm income were 6 percent, and by 1972 they had risen to 20 percent. Reduced acreage and low stocks of grain set the stage for the food shortages that began to appear in 1973.

Beginning in 1973 the prices of U.S. agricultural products increased more than 35 percent. Net farm incomes rose from a record $19.7 billion in 1972 to $25.2 billion in 1973. It now seems possible that food shortages will ultimately rival the energy crisis in importance. There appear to be four main reasons for the rise in food prices:

1. The large sale of wheat to the Soviet Union by the United States in late 1972

2. The marked decrease in the anchovy crop off Peru

3. The spread of price increases from wheat and anchovies to substitutes such as soybeans, oats, and rye

4. The increase in foreign demand for U.S. farm products because of devaluations of the dollar in 1971 and in 1973 (after devaluation, American food became cheaper than foreign food—but more about that in Application 26).

Wheat and the Soviet Union

In late 1972 the United States negotiated a whopping deal with the Soviet Union, by which the Russians bought, for more than $1 billion, one-quarter of the U.S. wheat crop, mainly from the 1972 harvest. The supply of wheat for 1972 was fixed by that time. This inelasticity of supply compounded the already strong inflationary pres-

TABLE A18-1 Wheat and Corn Held in Storage in the United States (millions of bushels)

Year	Wheat total	CCC	Corn total	CCC
1950–1954	544	382	752	324
1955–1959	1,031	947	1,322	937
1960	1,313	1,195	1,787	1,286
1961	1,411	1,243	2,016	1,327
1962	1,322	1,097	1,653	888
1963	1,195	1,082	1,365	810
1964	901	829	1,537	828
1965	817	646	1,147	540
1966	535	340	840	148
1967	425	124	823	139
1968	539	102	1,162	182
1969	819	163	1,113	295
1970	885	301	999	197
1971	730	366	663	97
1972	863	209	1,126	156
1973	428	7	707	4

Source: Agricultural Statistics, U.S. Department of Agriculture, 1974.

sures on wheat prices that resulted from the sale itself.

Figure A18-3 shows the supply-demand relationship involved in the Soviet wheat purchase. Price P_1 would have prevailed if there had been no sale to the Soviets. Because the wheat had to come out of the already partly harvested crop of 1972, the price rose to P_3. Price P_2 would have resulted if the sale had come from the 1973 crop, provided farmers had had enough warning to increase plantings. The reason that the price rose to P_3 was that the increase in wheat supplied had to come from the inelastic supply of 1972. As it was, wheat increased from $1.70 a bushel in July of 1972 to $5.00 a bushel in August of 1973.

Anchovies

Just at this juncture in history, nature caused a crisis that compounded the effect of wheat prices of the wheat deal with Russia. In 1972 there was a sharp decline in the anchovy harvest off the coast of Peru. Now anchovies, even though you associate them with pizzas and party canapés, are a major source of protein in animal feed. The decline in the supply of anchovies—estimated to be the equivalent of 150 million bushels of soybeans—obviously increased the price pressure on the livestock industry.

Substitutes

There are a number of close substitutes for wheat and anchovies in the diet of animals: soybeans, oats, rye, and corn. Therefore, it was inevitable that the price of soybeans, oats, rye, and corn would also climb sharply. (Remember that when the price of a commodity increases, there is an increase in the demand for close substitutes.) In only a year's time, soybeans went from $3.50 per bushel to $12.00, rye from $1.01 to $3.86, and oats from 80 cents to $2.06.

Exports

Lately, the United States has been exporting more and more farm products, largely because of the devaluation of the dollar, which has countered rising prices. For example, even though the United States sent all that wheat to Russia in 1972, our exports in 1973 rose even higher. In 1973 total exports of farm products increased 60 percent, with higher prices accounting for only 40 percent of the increase. All these exports have meant that the U.S. reserve stocks of grains have been depleted, and the United States is now trying to build up more reserves.

Legislation to Help the Farmer in the Mid-1970s

In 1973, under the pressure of rising prices, Congress passed some laws to try to help both U.S. farmers and the starving millions overseas. The main thrusts of this legislation were as follows: (1) Land withheld from production over the past decade was freed, at least temporarily. (2) Price supports were abandoned. (3) Direct payments were substituted for indirect supports. Each year the Department of Agriculture is to set target prices. Whenever prices fall below these targets, the government will pay the farmer the difference. The Department of Agriculture can decree the number of acres to be planted.

The fact that the farm program has boiled down to direct payments coupled with acreage restrictions does not mean that agriculture in the future will be nearly free from government interference. As long as prices remain high, farmers are not going to rock the boat. But though it seems unlikely, if the United States should again have huge surpluses and low farm incomes, government management of agricultural production—and thus government interference in the competitive agricultural market—may reappear.

Whether agricultural prices will someday be stabilized, if not reduced, depends on whether the world can effectually mobilize its resources for food production to meet growing world demands.

FIGURE A18-3 The Soviet Wheat Deal of 1972 (*Source:* Robert Heilbroner, *The Economic Problem Newsletter,* Winter 1973.)

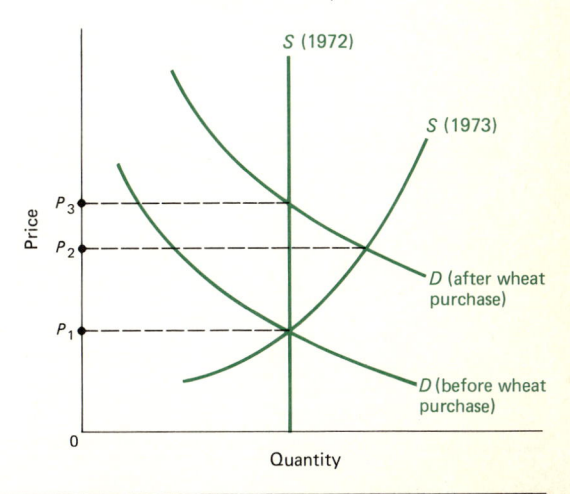

In the mid 1970s, the agricultural policy makers of Western Europe and the United States are faced with a real dilemma. For decades they have tried to restrict supply in order to keep farm prices and incomes high. But now food supplies need to be increased to reduce starvation in many areas of the world. Poor harvests in Russia and China in 1974, drought below the Sahara, famine in Bangladesh, low yields in India and other areas—all contribute to the world hunger crisis. But if full capacity is devoted to increasing output, agricultural prices may not rise fast enough to compensate for rising costs.

The big question is: Can government policy makers, who for so many years restricted supply to increase prices and farm incomes, reverse themselves and effectively increase supply? Can a free competitive agricultural market produce enough food to feed the hungry millions of the world, at prices that will enable farmers to receive a competitive rate of return on their investments? Can a free competitive market be restored without harmful economic dislocations?

SUMMING UP

1. Although pure competition is advantageous, governments—including that of the United States—have interfered in the workings of market forces in agriculture, the industry that comes closest to fitting the description of pure competition.

2. Since the depression of 1921, U.S. farmers have had unstable and relatively low incomes, compared with nonagricultural workers.

3. From the standpoint of demand, the reasons for agriculture's relatively shaky position are (a) price inelasticity of demand and (b) low income elasticity of demand. Therefore, as the supply of agricultural products increases, prices fall relatively more than quantity demanded rises, and farm incomes fall. Factors that tend to increase demand (changes in tastes, money income, population, expectations of future prices) are not strong enough to compensate for price inelasticity.

4. Among the factors determining agricultural income, supply tends to be dominant. Supply, however, tends to be highly variable, to resist decreases, and to have a strong tendency to increase.

5. Agricultural supply tends to be highly variable because (a) no one farmer or group of farmers can control supply, since conditions are purely competitive, (b) weather has an enormous and unpredictable effect, and (c) production of farm products is discontinuous.

6. The supply of agricultural products resists decreases for the following reasons: (a) In the short run, farmers have large fixed costs, so they have to incur large losses before they admit defeat and shut down. (b) In the long run, the farmer's resources are immobile, so the farmer stays on the farm, aware that job chances for a farmer in the nonfarm world are scant (opportunity costs are low) and that the personal and social costs of adjusting to a new environment would be great.

7. The great improvements in agricultural technology, stimulated by the Department of Agriculture and by industries that provide materials such as machinery, fertilizer, chemicals, and animal feed, have led in the long run to increases in the supply of farm products.

8. Before mid-1973, U.S. farm policy was based on a program of price supports, coupled with acreage restrictions and government purchases and storage of surpluses. The Department of Agriculture determined the price to be supported by using the concept of *parity* as a rule of thumb.

9. To increase demand and decrease supply of agricultural products, the government has (a) reduced supply by means of soil conservation, soil bank programs, and acreage restrictions, and (b) stimulated demand by means of food stamp and school lunch programs and by direct distribution of surplus foods to needy families.

10. A price-support program forces on consumers prices that are higher than equilibrium. When the government buys and stores surpluses, it has to tax consumers to pay for the program. The government's programs to remove land from production are ineffective, because the land that farmers remove from production is mostly less productive land. Restrictions on the number of acres a farmer can cultivate do not cut back supply because farmers concentrate on their more productive land and use more fertilizer and chemicals to increase its yield.

11. The government's demand-stimulating food programs are ineffective because there is not enough money available to make them work.

12. The millions of farmers who operate on a small scale have very low incomes, mainly because they do not have enough resources—land, machinery, and skills—to invest in their farms.

13. The rapid increases in farm prices that started in 1973 were due to (a) the sale of one-quarter of the 1972 wheat crop to the Soviet Union out of the fixed supply of 1972; (b) the loss of the equivalent of 150 million bushels of soybeans because of the decreased anchovy catch off Peru; (c) the spread of higher prices from wheat and anchovies to close substitutes such as soybeans, oats, and rye; and (d) the increase in foreign demand for U.S. farm products resulting from the devaluation of the dollar.

14. Legislation enacted in 1973 established target prices for farm products and guaranteed farmers direct payments of the difference between actual and target prices, provided that actual prices fell below the target; it also provided for continued government authority to dictate total acreage planted.

QUESTIONS

1. Using the theory of demand, explain the shape and degree of stability of the demand curve for food.

2. Using the theory of a firm in a purely competitive market, explain why low farm incomes have little effect on the output of an agricultural firm in (a) the short run, (b) the long run.

3. We maintain that the supply of agricultural products is highly variable in the short run and shows a long-run tendency toward increases. Why?

4. Explain why food prices began to increase so sharply in 1973. Do you think high prices are only temporary? Why?

5. Explain the two basic features of the agricultural legislation of 1973. Do you think it will solve the problems of agriculture?

SUGGESTED READINGS

Federal Reserve Bank of Chicago. "The Food Stamp Program." *Business Conditions*, July 1975.

Federal Reserve Bank of St. Louis. "The Russian Wheat Deal." *Monthly Review*, October 1973.

Harshbarger, C. Edward. "1974 Agricultural Outlook: How High the Summit?" *Monthly Review*, Federal Reserve Bank of Kansas City, December 1973, pp. 12-20.

Harshbarger, C. Edward, and Richard D. Rees. "The New Farm Program—What Does It Mean?" *Monthly Review*, Federal Reserve Bank of Kansas City, January 1974, pp. 12-14.

Hathaway, Dale E. *Problems of Progress in the Agricultural Economy*. Scott, Foresman, Chicago 1964.

Heilbroner, Robert. *The Economic Problem Newsletter*, Winter 1973.

Mayer, Lawrence A. "We Can't Take Food for Granted Anymore." *Fortune*, February 1974.

U.S. Department of Agriculture. *Farmer Income Situation*.

Zwerdling, Daniel. "The Food Monopolies." *The Progressive*, January 1975.

Pure Monopoly: The Other Extreme

Monopoly is a dirty word in the English language. Both U.S. history and English history are filled with condemnations of monopoly. English Common Law, the basis of U.S. law, treats monopolistic acts as restraints of trade and, therefore, as illegal. In 1886 the federal government created the Interstate Commerce Commission to regulate abusive actions of railroads. The Sherman Antitrust Act of 1890 was the first of a series of laws, including the Clayton Act of 1914 and the Robinson-Patman Act of 1936, that aimed at controlling monopoly and unfair competition. The Federal Trade Commission and the antitrust division of the Justice Department in Washington, D.C., are the federal "watchdogs" against monopoly. Whether such efforts successfully fight monopoly is not now the question, but they do testify to the low social esteem in which monopoly is held.

Books condemning monopoly abound: Loyd's *Standard Oil Trust* and Ignatseo Donnelly's *Caesar's Column* are examples from the beginning of this century. Baran and Sweezy's *Monopoly Capitalism* and Friedman's *Capitalism and Freedom* are present-day examples worthy of mention.

But what is monopoly? How does one define it? What are its characteristics? What is monopoly power? And, most of all, what does monopoly do that generates such disapproval?

In Chapter 18 we stated that pure competition is at one end of a scale measuring degrees of competitiveness. At the other end is pure and regulated monopoly. In this chapter we wish to define and then analyze the behavior and performance of monopoly.

Pure Monopoly: A Definition

First, in a **pure monopoly** there is only one firm in the industry, and it is not controlled by the government. Second, since there is only one firm in the industry, whether its product is homogenous or differentiated is irrelevant. Third, the monopoly must be able to maintain its position by producing a product for which there is no good substitute. (Some economists say that the term *pure monopoly* applies only where there are no substitutes. By this definition, pure monopoly is very rare. We shall use a less rigid definition for our purposes here.) Fourth, since there is only one firm in the industry, there must be complete barriers to entry. That is, it must be impossible for other firms to break into the field.

It is important that you be able to distinguish between *monopoly* and **monopoly power**. *Monopoly* means there is only one firm in the industry. **Monopoly power** means that one firm can influence the prices of its product. A monopolist has monopoly power. But monopoly power may be possessed by more than one firm in an industry. In this chapter, and also in later chapters, we shall explore the subject of monopoly power more fully.

Even though the pure monopolist is the only firm in the industry, there are still certain restraints on its ability to manipulate price and profits.

1. The monopolist, although not getting direct competition from other firms producing the same product, does run into competition from firms in industries that produce products with some degree of substitutability. For example, Polaroid used to have a monopoly on instant-copy cameras, but still had competition from firms making other *kinds* of cameras. (In a case like this, you must be careful how you define an industry. In the camera industry in general, Polaroid is one of a number of firms. In the field of instant-copy cameras, Polaroid was the monopoly firm as long as its patent was valid.) And Alcoa, before World War II, had a virtual monopoly on aluminum; yet the firm still had to worry about materials that afforded close competition, such as steel and tin. Alcoa thus used self-discipline; it set its prices low enough to prevent firms in other industries from being tempted to devise better substitutes for aluminum. In other words, the degree of monopoly is usually proportional to the substitutability of the monopoly's product.

The monopolist fully appreciates this form of competition. The recent merger between Hazel-Atlas Glass Company and Continental Can Company is a good example of efforts to reduce competition induced by product substitution.

2. Monopolists must avoid making enemies because they run the risk of political repercussions. They are not usually protected by anonymity. Both government and consuming public usually know what firms are monopolies. So the monopolistic firm must be careful in pricing, since both public and government know more about the monopolist's pricing policies than they do about the pricing of firms in less concentrated industries.

3. A monopoly is constrained by the demand for its product. Since it is the only firm in a given industry, it has complete control over supply; it can restrict or expand supply to obtain a target price. However, it does

not control *demand,* because all the buyers in the market determine demand. (It may, however, try to influence demand through advertising.) So although the monopoly influences price by controlling supply, it cannot determine the quantity that consumers will demand.

4. When it comes to profits, the monopolistic firm is restrained by cost conditions. Although by controlling supply, it can set any price, its lack of control over costs and over the quantity of product demanded limits its ability to earn profits.

Barriers to Entry

Let us repeat that the monopoly has complete control over supply, since it is the only firm in the industry. If it is to hang onto its monopoly position, however, there must be some mechanism that prevents other firms from breaking into the field. In other words, there must be absolute *barriers to entry.* The most important barriers to entry are:

1. *The entrenched firm's control of patents and secret processes.* The U.S. patent laws give a firm exclusive rights to produce a product or use a process for seventeen years. Thus, a patent is a monopoly right to control production of a product. Polaroid, until its patent rights expired, was the only firm that could produce the instant-picture camera. The United Shoe Machinery Company is another example. For many years it was the only firm producing shoemaking machinery, because it owned hundreds of patents on various machines that made shoes. And then there is Alcoa, whose original monopoly position in the aluminum industry was built on a patent right. (For an informative discussion of Alcoa's behavior, see Chapter 5 of Leonard Weiss's *Economics and American Industry.*)

2. *Economic warfare.* There are various kinds of economic warfare that can prevent firms from establishing themselves in an industry, or even eliminate firms that are already there. For example, the Standard Oil group, before 1900, used to eliminate competition by setting different prices in different regions. If they had a local competitor they wanted to get rid of, they cut prices in the competitor's region, while keeping their prices higher in the rest of the country. Eventually, these localized low prices, unjustified by cost differentials, drove local competitors into bankruptcy, after which the Standard Oil group raised its prices again.

3. *The entrenched firm's control of sources of supply.* A firm that has established itself strongly in a given field can create an effective barrier to entry into the field by other firms by gaining control of the supplies of raw materials. For example, U.S. Steel, when it was founded in 1903, controlled large amounts of soft coal and most of the coking facilities around Pittsburgh; furthermore, it controlled the Mesabi iron ore deposits. And prior to World War II, Alcoa was able in large measure to control the aluminum industry because it controlled the bauxite deposits in the United States.

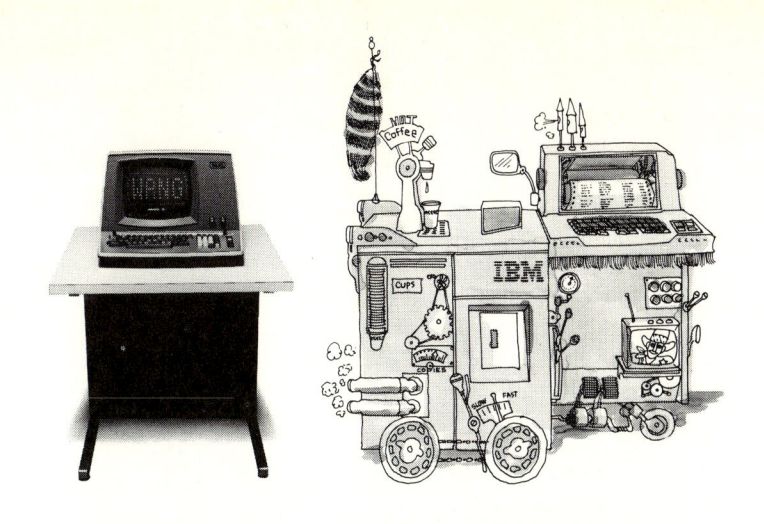

A lot of companies confuse the computer they need with the one they've heard about.

The Wang 2200 Line of Small Computer Systems and the IBM System 32.

The Wang 2200 Line fits any need. Small or large. Business or scientific. Because it's a complete product line, not just one computer.

The Wang 2200 Line comes with many different processors and 35 system peripherals. Which means there's a Wang computer system that fits your needs precisely.

With the IBM System 32, you must fit one size — large. And pay for capabilities you won't use.

The Wang 2200 Line starts at under $10,000. And it expands as you expand.

No matter how much computer you need, Wang can provide just that much. And whenever you need greater capability, it too will be exactly what you need.

All things considered, are you interested in the one computer system designed for you, or the one you've heard about?

For more information on the Wang 2200 Line of Small Computer Systems, please call (617) 851-4111 or write:
Wang Laboratories, Inc.,
Dept. **WSJ-2**, 836 North St.,
Tewksbury, Mass. 01876.

WANG
We happen to make a better small computer than IBM.

Wang Europe S.A., Buurtweg 13, 9412 Ottergem, Belgium

Another firm attempting to break into an industry (Courtesy Wang Laboratories, Inc.)

4. *Obstacles due to economies of scale*. In a number of industries, the technology required to produce the goods is such that a firm has to produce on a large scale in order to reach optimum scale and low cost per unit. For example, in the auto industry, optimum scale and lowest per-unit cost occurs around 250,000 units. This means that a new firm trying to break into the field would have to start production on a huge scale, and have enough demand for those cars they would sell; otherwise, cost

Barriers to Entry   445

per unit would be too high to be competitive. Furthermore, in any such large-scale industry, a new firm would need, from the beginning, a nationwide system of sales outlets, repair centers, and warehouses containing spare parts. These things are hard for a firm to achieve when it is just entering an industry.

5. *The problem of product differentiation.* To enter an industry, a firm may have to be able to differentiate its product from those of its competitors and obtain strong customer loyalties. This is a major barrier to entry. Established firms have the advantage here, since it costs less per unit of sales to maintain customer loyalty than to create it. Advertising is a crucial—and expensive—element in product differentiation. The substantially higher advertising costs that a new firm must pay are often a serious and formidable barrier to entry. The cosmetic industry is an example. Some cosmetic firms spend more than 30 percent of the value of their annual sales on advertising. (Until the federal government restricted cigarette advertising, the cigarette industry was an often-cited example of this sort of barrier-protected field.)

The automobile industry is another big advertiser. Its advertising campaigns must be national in scope to match the national market for cars. Consumer acceptance is created only gradually, over a number of years. The resulting high levels of expenditures for advertising are thus a deterrent to entry.

6. *Government-created barriers.* Government policy with respect to many actions—such as licenses, zoning, franchises, and import quotas (plus the patent right, already mentioned)—creates barriers to entry. Government-created restrictions on entry into taxicab services, bus transportation, telephone services, electricity, gas, and water production, to name but a few, have led some economists to conclude that the government has done more to create monopoly than to destroy it.

Governments, having created monopolies, have taken the responsibility of regulating most of them as to prices and other policies. Governments do this in order to protect the consumer from those who exercise monopoly power. Such government-created and government-regulated monopolies are called **regulated monopolies**. They include such industries as telephone, gas (for homes), electricity, and urban mass transit.

Note two things: (1) A monopoly is not the same thing as a large-scale firm. For one thing, there may be more than one large-scale firm in a given industry. Thus, they are not pure monopolies. For example, U.S. Steel and Bethlehem Steel are both large-scale firms, but both are in the same industry. They are not monopolies. (2) A pure monopoly may be a relatively small firm. Suppose that there's only one druggist, or one dentist, or one lumberyard in a small town. That drugstore and dentist and lumber yard are monopolies, because they are the only firms in their respective categories in town. So it is not size that makes a monopoly. It is the *size of the relevant market* that determines the size of the pure monopoly.

NEWS ITEM: JUSTICE DEPT. CASE AGAINST A.T.&T. COULD TAKE YEARS

"FIRST I COULDN'T GET A DIAL TONE, THEN I GOT CUT OFF. THAT WAS FOLLOWED BY A RECORDED MESSAGE. NOW THEY'VE PUT ME ON 'HOLD'."

Pure Monopoly *MR, AR,* and *D*

Since the monopoly is the only firm in the industry, it can control supply and can influence equilibrium price. Remember, however, that the monopoly cannot control the quantity the public demands. Indeed, since there are some substitutes for the monopoly's product, if the firm wishes to increase the quantity demanded, it has to reduce the price, to induce consumers to buy more. Therefore, in a monopolistic market, price to the firm must decline as output increases. This is unlike the case of a purely competitive market (in which price for the individual firm does not vary with output).

Let's look at a set of hypothetical demand data for a monopoly (Table 19-1). Note that as output increases, price decreases. (Remember that the price column is the same as the demand schedule.) *Total revenue* at first increases sharply as price falls. The increase becomes less rapid as output increases further. Total revenue reaches a maximum at output 6, and then begins to fall at output 7. *Average revenue* is simply total revenue (column 3) divided by output (column 1) and is the same result as the price or demand column. *Marginal revenue* is the change in total revenue due to a small, or one-unit, change in output. (We are assuming here that the monopolistic firm sets only one price for its product at each level of output.) Because the lowered price applies not only to the last unit sold, but to all units sold at that price and quantity, marginal revenue falls more rapidly than price (average revenue). As long as total revenue is increasing, marginal revenue is positive. This is true at rates of output from 1 to 5, inclusive.

When total revenue reaches a maximum (is greatest), marginal revenue is zero (at output 6). When total revenue is decreasing, marginal revenue is negative (at output 7).

By plotting the data in Table 19-1, one gets curves for demand (price, column 2), average revenue (column 4), and marginal revenue (column 5) as in Figure 19-1. The demand and average-revenue curves are equal and slope downward to the right, reflecting the fact that the monopolistic firm—in order to increase the quantity demanded by the consumer—must lower the price of the product. The marginal-revenue curve of the monopolistic firm—unlike that of the firm in pure competition, is not the same as the demand and average-revenue curves, but slopes downward more steeply, and is below them.

Elasticity of Demand

Table 19-1 and Figure 19-1 can be used to show the various ranges of elasticity on the monopoly's demand curve. Recall from Chapter 15, on elasticity, that if price declines and total revenue increases, demand must be elastic. When marginal revenue is positive (up to output 6), total revenue increases as price declines. Therefore, the portion of the demand curve vertically above the rates of output at which marginal

TABLE 19-1 Output, Price, and Revenue for a Monopoly

1 Output	2 Price or demand	3 Total revenue	4 Average revenue	5 Marginal revenue
1	10	10	10	10
2	9	18	9	8
3	8	24	8	6
4	7	28	7	4
5	6	30	6	2
6	5	30	5	0
7	4	28	4	−2

Note: Since the monopolistic firm's demand is the same as the industry's, in order to sell more, the monopolistic firm must lower price. In column 2, per-unit price declines as output increases. Average revenue (column 4) also declines, but marginal revenue (column 5) declines more rapidly. Marginal revenue is the change in total revenue for each unit increase in output. The reason it falls more rapidly is that the price decline applies to all units sold at that level, not just the extra unit.

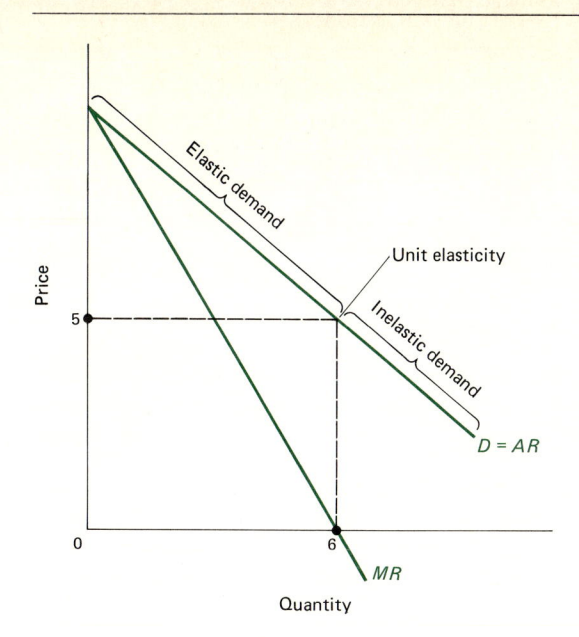

FIGURE 19-1 When marginal revenue is zero, demand is unit elastic. When marginal revenue is positive, demand is elastic. When marginal revenue is negative, demand is inelastic.

revenue is positive is elastic, as Figure 19-1 indicates. Keep in mind the fact that when price falls and total revenue is unchanged (at a maximum), elasticity is unitary. Table 19-1 shows that when price falls and total revenue is unchanged, marginal revenue is zero (output 6). Figure 19-1 shows that demand is of unitary elasticity at that output rate at which marginal revenue is zero. Again, remember that when total revenue decreases as price falls, demand is inelastic. Table 19-1 shows that at output 7, total revenue falls; as price declines, marginal revenue is therefore negative. You can see in Figure 19-1 that the part of the demand curve above the output rate at which marginal revenues is negative is inelastic.

Now let's summarize price elasticity on the demand curve (E_d).

1. Above output levels at which marginal revenue is zero, E_d is equal to 1 or is unitary.

2. Above output levels at which marginal revenue is positive, E_d is elastic (above the point of unitary elasticity on $D = AR$).

3. Above output levels at which marginal revenue is negative, E_d is inelastic (below the point of unitary elasticity on $D = AR$).

Pure Monopoly: Short Run

Now that we have examined the pure monopoly's demand and revenue curves, we can include its cost curves and analyze its behavior with respect to output, price, and profits. Let's first analyze the behavior of the pure monopolist just *in the short run*. (We will deal with the long run later on.)

Remember that, in the short run, firms can neither enter nor leave the industry. Therefore the monopoly encounters the same four possibilities that face the purely competitive firm:

1. When price exceeds average total cost, the monopoly will make an economic profit.

2. When price is just equal to average total cost, the monopoly will make only a normal profit.

3. When price exceeds average variable cost, but falls short of average total cost the monopoly will sustain a loss, but in the short run continue to produce.

4. When price is not high enough to cover average variable costs, the monopoly will sustain such a loss that it will choose to shut down.

Figure 19-2 shows the way the curves look for the pure monopoly that makes an economic profit. As in the case of pure competition, the monopolistic firm has maximum profits (or minimum losses) at the output at which marginal cost is equal to marginal revenue, at output A. The monopolistic firm determines the price, however, at the demand curve, not the marginal revenue curve. To find out what price the monopolist would set in order to sell output A, one draws a perpendicular

FIGURE 19-2 Situation 1: Economic Profit for a Monopolistic Firm. Price P is higher than average total cost, AE. Total revenue $OPBA$ is larger than total cost $OCEA$. The monopolistic firm makes an economic profit, in the short run, of $CPBE$.

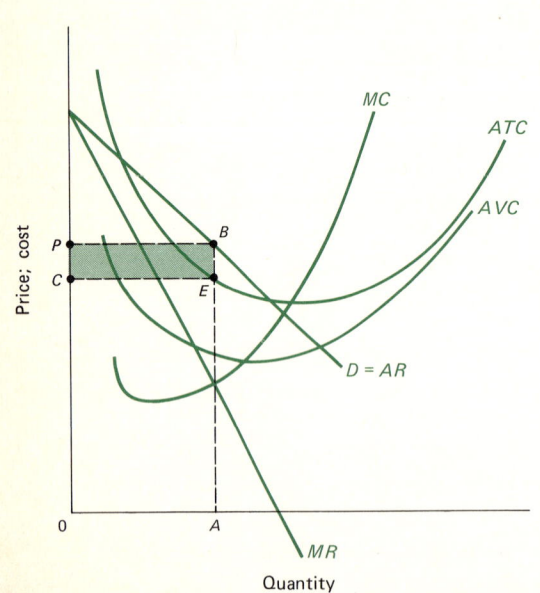

FIGURE 19-3 Situation 2: Normal Profits for a Monopolistic Firm. Price P is equal to average total cost, AB. Total revenue $OPBA$ is equal to total cost $OPBA$. The monopolistic firm, in the short run, makes only a normal profit.

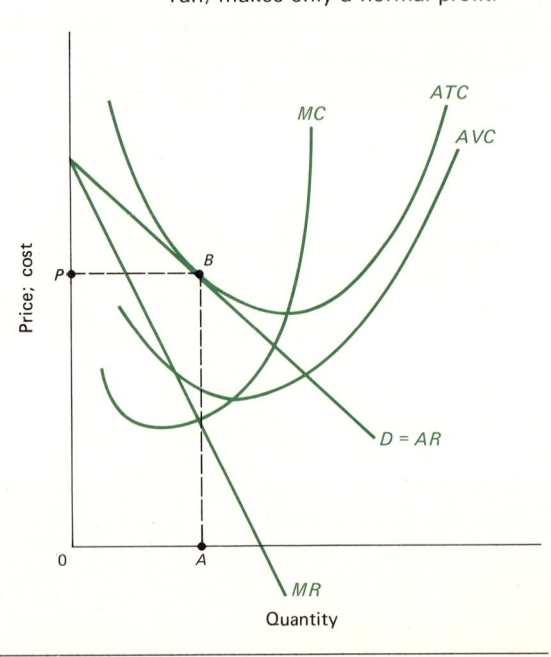

450 Pure Monopoly: The Other Extreme

from A to point B on the demand curve. To measure price, one draws a horizontal line toward the left, from B to the vertical axis, which hits the axis at P. So the monopoly's price is P. Total revenue is measured by the area $0PBA$. At output A, the monopolistic firm's average cost (cost per unit) is represented by a perpendicular from A to the average-total-cost curve at point E, or the distance $0C$. Total cost is represented by the area $0CEA$. So, since total revenues are larger than total costs, the monopoly makes a profit, which is represented by area $CPBE$.

Now we can see that in the short run economic profits can exist under both pure competition and pure monopoly. The reason is that firms cannot enter the industry in the short run.

Figure 19-3 shows the way the curves look for the pure monopoly that is making only a normal profit. Once again, equilibrium output is the output at which marginal cost is equal to marginal revenue (output A). The monopolistic firm determines the best price by drawing a perpendicular from A to the demand curve at point B; in other words, price P. Total revenue is area $0PBA$. Cost per unit is also the perpendicular

FIGURE 19-4 Situation 3: Economic Loss with Production for a Monopolistic Firm. Price P is less than average total cost $0C$. Total revenue is area $0PBA$; total cost is area $0CEA$. The loss, or area $PCEB$, is less than fixed costs, $GCEF$. *Moral:* In the short run, if price is between ATC and AVC, the monopolistic firm loses less if it keeps on producing than if it shuts down.

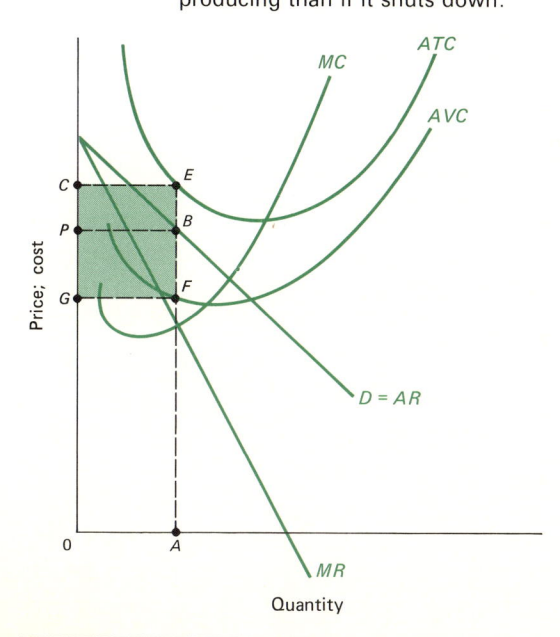

FIGURE 19-5 Situation 4: Economic Loss Without Production for a Monopolistic Firm. Price P is less than both average total cost AF and average variable cost AE. If the firm kept on producing, it would lose money (area $PGFB$). If it shut down, it would also lose (area $CGFE$). So in the short run, the monopolistic firm loses less by shutting down than by keeping on producing.

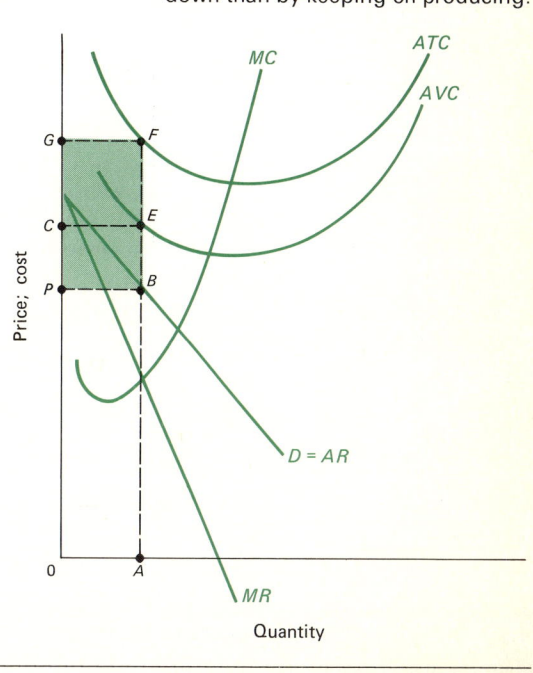

Pure Monopoly: Short Run   451

from A to the average total cost curve, or again AB. And so total cost is also area $0PBA$. Since revenue is equal to cost and a normal profit is included in cost, the monopolistic firm, in this situation, makes only a normal profit.

Figure 19-4 shows the third situation that the pure monopoly may encounter in the short run: the monopoly loses money, but keeps on producing anyway. Profit-maximizing output is still at the level at which marginal cost is equal to marginal revenue. One determines the monopolistic firm's price again by drawing a perpendicular from the equilibrium rate of output A to the demand curve at point B; price is P (that is, the equivalent horizontal distance along the vertical axis, or $AB = 0P$). Revenue (price × quantity) is then area $0PBA$. Cost per unit at output A is the perpendicular from A to average total cost, measured on the vertical axis; in other words, average total cost is $0C$ (or AE). Cost is then area $0CEA$. It is plain that cost exceeds revenue. The monopolistic firm's loss is the difference, or area $PCEB$.

In the short run, the monopolistic firm, just like the firm in pure competition, must decide whether to keep on producing or shut down. If the monopolistic firm gives up, shuts down, and stops production, it will still have to pay all fixed costs in the short run. If it keeps on producing and its losses are less than its fixed costs, it loses less by producing.

Figure 19-4 shows that fixed cost per unit is the vertical distance from the average-variable-cost curve to the average-total-cost curve at output A. Note that this can be measured on the vertical axis by GC. Fixed cost is then area $GCEF$. The amount of money the monopoly loses is less than total fixed cost, being only area $PCEB$. In this situation, in the short run, the monopolistic firm would continue production, but in the long run it would have to either liquidate or adjust its scale of production.

For example, if total fixed costs are 25, then 25 must be paid whether the firm produces or not. If the firm loses 15 by producing, it will be better off producing and losing 15 than shutting down and paying 25 in fixed costs. If the firm produces, it loses 15; if it shuts down, it loses 25.

Figure 19-5 shows situation 4, in which the monopolistic firm loses more money than the amount of its fixed costs by continuing to produce and so must shut down. At output A, the firm can get only price P for its product, which is less than average variable cost. If the firm keeps on producing, its losses will be area $PGFB$. If the firm shuts down, it will have to pay only the amount of its fixed costs (area $CGFE$). The monopolistic firm therefore loses less money (area $PCEB$) if it just gives up and closes its doors.

Pure Monopoly: Long Run

Remember, in the long run, in a purely competitive market, a firm can make only normal profit (profit just large enough to keep it producing). So many firms enter the market that no one can make any economic profit (profit above normal), while the exit of firms from the market tends to eliminate economic losses. In pure monopoly, in the long run, firms do not enter the industry, because of complete barriers to entry. Although a monopolistic firm may liquidate and avoid economic losses, economic profits cannot be eliminated by the entry of firms. If firms could enter, they would increase supply, reduce price, and reduce the economic profit.

In the case of a pure monopoly, in the long run, two possible situations can exist: (1) Because there is no mechanism to prevent firms from making an economic profit, they probably will make one. (2) Price may be so low that the monopoly can not make an economic profit. Therefore, the monopolistic firm can make only a normal profit. Economic losses cannot exist, because in the long run, a firm that incurs economic losses liquidates, and ceases to exist.

In the long run, the pure monopolistic firm will probably make an economic profit. Figure 19-6 shows that the output that would maximize the monopoly's profits would be the output at which marginal cost equaled marginal revenue at A. When that output corresponds to the demand curve, the monopoly's best price is at P. Revenue is area $0PBA$.

FIGURE 19-6 Economic Profit in the Long Run for a Monopolistic Firm. In the long run, the firm can make an economic profit, provided that price P is greater than long-run average cost $0C$. Total revenue (area $0PBA$) exceeds cost (area $0CEA$). There is thus an economic profit (area $CPBE$).

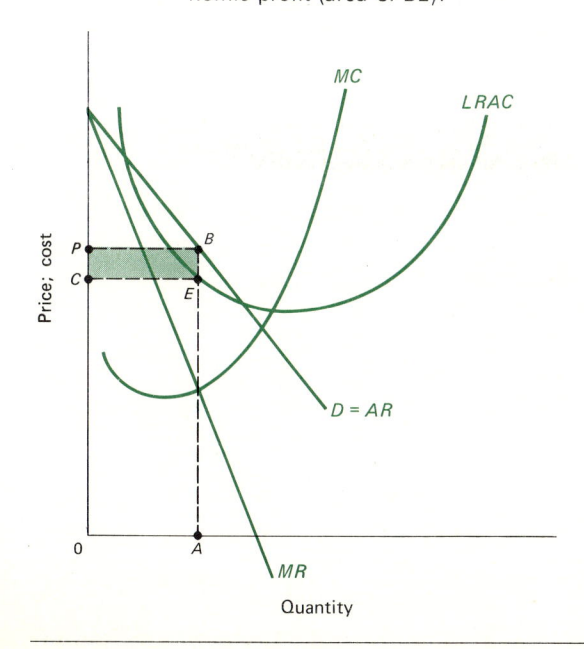

FIGURE 19-7 Normal Profit in the Long Run for a Monopolistic Firm. In the long run, the firm may make only a normal profit, provided that price P equaled average cost AB. Revenue and cost are both equal to area $0PBA$. Thus, the firm could make only a normal profit.

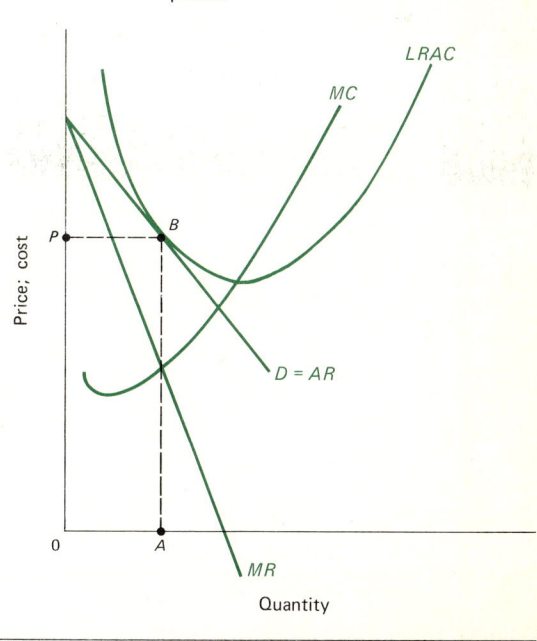

Pure Monopoly: Long Run   453

Average cost at output A is C; cost is then area $0CEA$. Since cost is less than revenue, the economic profit is area $CPBE$.

However, in the long run, the monopolistic firm may possibly earn only a normal profit. Figure 19-7 shows that the long-run average-cost curve ($LRAC$) is tangent to the demand curve at point B. The demand curve shows that the monopolistic firm could sell output A for price P. Revenue and cost are equal at $0PBA$, so the monopolist earns only a normal profit. If the monopolistic firm—perhaps by advertising—can shift its demand curve to the right, or if it can subdivide its markets and discriminate in price between one market and another, it can increase its profits.

Pure Competition Versus Pure Monopoly

Let's assume for the moment that cost curves are the same for both purely competitive and purely monopolistic firms. Figure 19-8 compares their relative performances. In this figure, marginal-cost and average-cost curves apply to both market classifications. For pure competition, the $D = AR = MR$ curve is horizontal to the quantity axis at P_c. For pure monopoly, these curves slope downward.

Under the above conditions, pure competition has the following advantages over monopoly:

FIGURE 19-8 Demand and Revenue Curves for Both the Purely Monopolistic and the Purely Competitive Firm. Pure competition is indicated by subscript c; pure monopoly, by subscript m.

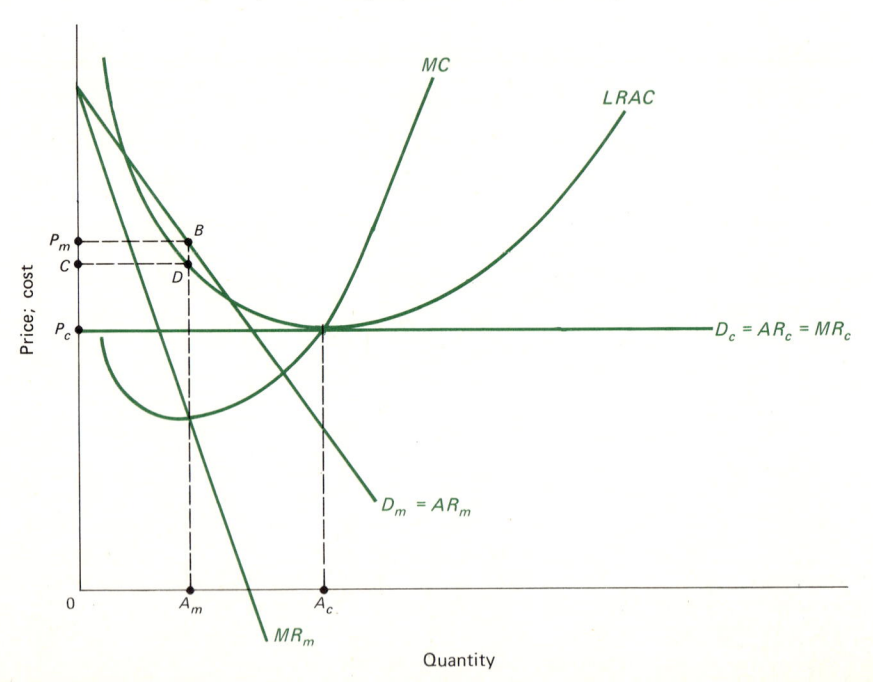

454   Pure Monopoly: The Other Extreme

1. Purely competitive firms produce a larger output (A_c) than firms that are pure monopolies (A_m) and sell it at a lower price, P_c, as compared to the monopolies' price of P_m.

2. Two facts apply to income distribution in circumstances of pure competition: (a) Because a purely monopolistic firm is likely to earn an economic profit and a purely competitive firm is likely to earn only a normal profit, profit is usually a smaller part of income under pure competition. (b) In pure competition each factor of production receives its competitive opportunity cost. But the pure monopoly's profit is only partly a payment of opportunity cost. Part of the monopoly's profit (its economic profit) is due to the control over prices of the product through the control over supply, which it exercises because of barriers to entry. Under pure competition, then, market earned incomes are based entirely on productivity. Under pure monopoly there are economic profits that are not based on productivity, but rather on the ability of monopolists to block entry and prevent reallocation of resources.

3. A purely competitive firm produces at the most efficient level of production, that is, at full capacity; in other words, at the low point on the long-run average-cost curve ($LRAC$). The purely monopolistic firm is not likely to keep on producing until it reaches the low point on the $LRAC$ curve because its demand curve is not horizontal, but slopes downward. So the purely monopolistic firm usually produces at some level less than full capacity. (Figure 19-8 shows this level at output A_m.) Therefore the purely monopolistic firm's costs per unit are higher than the purely competitive firm's costs per unit. Even if the monopolistic firm produces at minimum average cost (if its MR cuts the minimum point of long-run average cost), it will set a price above average and marginal cost and receive an economic profit.

Remember that the long-run average-cost curve encloses a series of short-run cost curves, each at a successively larger scale or size of operation. In the long run, the purely competitive firm uses the most efficient scale and also produces at the most efficient point (minimum average cost) on that short-run average-cost curve. Assuming that the monopolistic firm's cost curves are identical with those of the competitive firm, one finds that the monopolistic firm tends to use a scale smaller than the most efficient one and produces on that scale above minimum average cost. Thus, for the purely monopolistic firm, cost per unit is usually higher in the long run than for the purely competitive firm.

4. When there is pure competition, in long-run equilibrium, price equals marginal cost. Under these conditions, competitive firms allocate their resources most efficiently to produce that combination of goods that consumers most prefer. But when there is pure monopoly, price is higher than marginal cost. From the point of view of the whole economy, this means that the monopolistic firm has fewer resources allocated to its product than its consumers prefer. So the monopolistic firm

does not produce as much as consumers are willing to buy at the marginal cost of production. When price exceeds marginal cost, consumers place higher value on additional units of the product than on other products that can be produced from the same resources.

Technology and Monopoly

Technology affects purely monopolistic and purely competitive market situations in two ways: (1) It creates differences in economies of scale, and (2) it raises the question of which type of market most encourages technological development. In many cases, our assumption that cost curves are similar for both competitive firms and monopolistic firms may not be valid. In industries characterized by pure monopoly, modern technology often dictates a high level of output before a producer can realize all available economies of scale. If such an industry were to be subdivided into enough firms to establish pure competition, the volume of output per firm would not be great enough for all those small firms to realize the productive advantages, and hence the economies of scale, possible to users of that technology. In such a situation, pure competition may result in high costs, high prices, and low output.

Figure 19-9 shows a long-run average-cost ($LRAC$) curve for a firm that requires high levels of output in order to realize fully economies of scale. Recall that the long-run average-cost curve is a planning curve that encompasses a series of short-run average-cost curves, each representing a larger scale of operation. If there were only one firm in a given industry, it would operate on the short-run scale marked AC_m. But if that industry's output were split up among enough firms to achieve purely competitive conditions, it would operate on the short-run scale marked AC_p. So even if the purely competitive firm produced at a point at which MC equaled price, it may have a much higher price and will have a higher level of cost than the monopolistic firm.

FIGURE 19-9 Provided that the technology required a high output before the firm could realize economies of scale, AC_m would be the scale of costs for a monopolistic firm (only one firm in the industry). If the industry were divided into enough firms to qualify as a purely competitive industry, the individual firm would have scale AC_p. Obviously AC_p is much less efficient than AC_m.

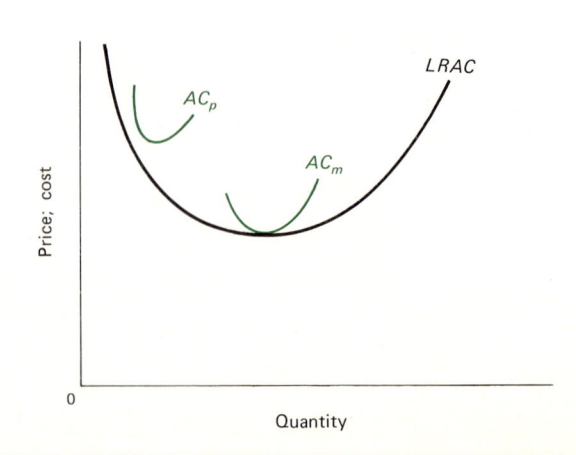

Some economists (including John Kenneth Galbraith, in his book *Economics and the Public Purpose*) imply that large-scale firms are necessary to ensure technological development. The big research and development facilities necessary to develop new techniques cost a lot of money. And money in such large amounts just is not in the budgets of smaller purely competitive firms. One could conclude that the larger the firm, the more it could spend on research and development and the greater the technological innovation would be.

But it isn't necessarily true that only the larger firms spend a great deal of money on research, or that they use their money to ensure technological development. Purely competitive firms often adopt technological innovations at a faster rate than monopolistic firms in order to keep ahead of their competitors. Such firms must be up to date in order to survive. The monopolistic firm does not have pressure from competitors to force it to adopt improved techniques. In fact, if the firm has plant and equipment that innovations would render obsolete, this factor alone slows the process of adopting innovations. For example, after World War II, the West Germans (who had lost most of their steel capacity during the war) had to develop new machinery, which included many innovative techniques in steel manufacturing. In the United States in the mid-1950s, steel companies began to borrow these techniques. But it was the *smaller* steel companies—not U.S. Steel—that did so first.

Some economists disagree with the theory that the larger the firm the more likely it is to make rapid technological advances. One study concludes that small and medium-size firms produce more innovations per dollar of research funds than larger ones do. In addition, large firms have little access to ideas from people actually working on the production line. The study claims that many creative discoveries came from individuals working alone or in small research facilities. Creative researchers are often nonconformists, and even first-rate discoveries may seem at first glance to lack any immediate practical application. In addition, bureaucratic inefficiency seems to blunt the impact of the inventions of large research organizations. The study concludes that for firms beyond a certain size technological productivity tends to decline. However, the "small" firms in this study were much larger than the typical purely competitive firm.

The relation between technological productivity and size of firms is even more complex. The smaller firms usually seem to pioneer in the early, low-cost, high-risk stages of an innovation. In the final development stage, when costs get higher but risks get lower, the larger firms come along and take over. We should also remember that much research and development work is undertaken or sponsored by government. To the extent that the results of this research (new processes, techniques) are made available to the public, they are as readily used by small firms as by large firms.

It is apparent that not only big firms sponsor research and development or adopt new ideas and put them into effect quickly. Competition makes the little firm run to keep up; the absence of competition enables

A regulated monopoly (Courtesy AT&T Photo Center)

the big firm to go slowly, and this factor slows the adoption of new ideas. Perhaps a purely competitive situation is not the ideal climate for rapid technological development. But neither is a purely monopolistic one.

Regulated Monopoly

As you recall, one barrier to entry into an industry is the existence of government induced monopoly. In some industries the consumer would not gain anything in terms of either lower costs or convenience if more than one firm produced the product or service in the same area. Examples are the public utilities, such as gas, electricity, water, telephone, and bus service. Governments (local, state, and federal) have recognized this and granted individual firms exclusive rights to produce in certain geographic areas. When it grants a monopoly, the government usually also promises to prevent the firm from exploiting the public with its monopoly power. (That is why these franchised companies are called regulated monopolies.) So the government establishes a commission to regulate

458   Pure Monopoly: The Other Extreme

these firms. The commission must assure the firms a normal profit, or "fair rate of return," or else they would not produce. At the same time, theoretically, the commission is supposed to set prices to prevent the monopoly from making economic profits.

Figure 19-10 shows that the unregulated monopoly maximizes profits at quantity A, that it charges price P, and that it makes an economic profit equal to area $CPBD$. Now suppose that the government declares this monopoly to be a public utility, and sets up a commission to ride herd on it. The utility commission, mindful of its duty to the public, sets a price that will ensure only a normal profit. (Recall that a normal profit exists when average revenue is equal to average cost.) A normal profit occurs at two points on Figure 19-10—point H and point G. Because it produces a normal profit at a much lower price and larger output than H, the commission chooses point G, and sets the price at P_1. Output is then going to be E. Cost will equal revenue, so this regulated monopoly will make only a normal profit. Note that the regulated monopoly produces more (E instead of A) and sells it at a lower price (P_1 instead of P) than the unregulated one.

Although prices are theoretically lower and output higher for the regulated than the unregulated monopoly, price is still greater than marginal cost. The purely competitive result that price equals marginal cost (the value consumers place on the last unit is equal to the sacrifices of other goods that are made to produce it) is still not duplicated by the regulated monopolist. The problem is to curtail monopoly profits by regulation.

Seems simple, doesn't it? The commission sets a price for the utility at which average revenue equals average cost, and the monopoly makes

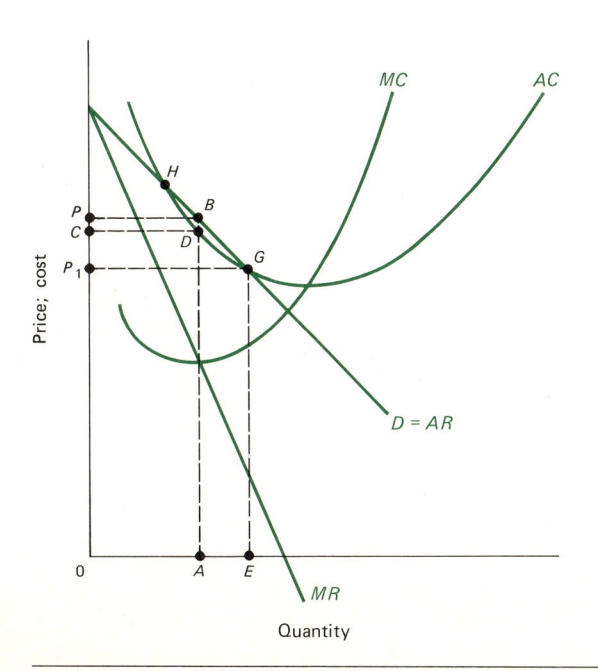

FIGURE 19-10 The pure monopoly produces at the point at which marginal cost equals marginal revenue, at A; price is at P. The regulating commission sets the output and price of the regulated monopolist at the point at which average revenue equals average cost, at output E and price P_1. Its revenue and also its cost equal OP_1GE; it gets only a normal profit.

Regulated Monopoly

only a normal profit. The commission periodically revises prices to adjust for changes in costs and demand.

However, when one tries to put this theoretical model into practice, there are problems. How does one compute "normal" profit? Is it the traditional profit for that industry? Or is it the profit a given firm makes in industries that contain other firms of comparable size? But an economic profit may already be built in. Should the commission compute depreciation at original cost or replacement cost? What about the value of good will?

Politics is perhaps the most important problem. Naturally, everyone assumes that commissions will regulate with impartiality. But the people on these commissions are political appointees. So there are always complaints that various regulatory commissions, federal and state, decide cases on the basis of favoritism, not facts, and that they do not pay attention to consumers or their interests.

Price Discrimination

Thus far, we have assumed that firms charge all customers the same price for their goods or services. But we have not discussed price discrimination. **Price discrimination** occurs when a firm charges different prices for a given commodity, despite the fact that the units of this commodity are physically homogeneous.

In its technical economic sense, price discrimination also occurs when prices are the same but the marginal cost of supplying each product is different. One product may have a larger profit margin than another. This form of discrimination, however, is often legal; a firm may take widely different profits on two different products and be within the law. To be technically correct, price discrimination exists when the price to consumer A divided by the marginal cost of that unit of product is not equal to the price to consumer B divided by the marginal cost of that unit. However, for our purposes, we shall consider price discrimination to exist when different prices are charged for different units of the same product. Price discrimination cannot take place under pure competition; it requires some form of monopoly power. But a firm that has monopoly power will not necessarily discriminate in pricing.

There are two main categories of price discrimination:

1. A firm charges the same consumer a different price for each unit sold to that consumer, and it is always the maximum price that the consumer will pay. This is called **perfect price discrimination**, and it is rare.

2. A firm charges different prices to different groups of buyers. This is the more usual case.

Conditions Necessary for Price Discrimination
1. A buyer who buys something for a low price cannot resell it to somebody else who had to pay more. For example, two buyers, A and B, each

buy a good; A pays 10 cents and B pays 20 cents. The firm must prevent A from reselling the good to B for *less* than 20 cents. Otherwise, reselling would create only one price for the good.

2. The price elasticity of demand for each consumer or for each submarket must be different. Only if these elasticities of demand are different can the price-discriminating firm increase its profits by charging different prices.

There are four conditions under which resale will not take place, and price discrimination is possible:

1. B doesn't know that A paid less.

2. B *knows* that A paid less, but doesn't care, because B feels that her or his good is better than the one that A bought.

3. The good is a service (such as medical care). If the same doctor operates on two patients, A cannot resell his or her $100 appendectomy to B, who must pay $500.

4. The two buyers are separated by distance or by legal restrictions. (In the case of distance, the difference in price may be only as large as the cost of transportation. In the case of legal restrictions, when the two buyers live in two countries, the difference in price may be only as large as the tariff.)

Graphic Analysis of Price Discrimination

You know by now that a firm will maximize profits by producing at the level at which marginal revenue equals marginal cost. When a monopolistic firm has the power to discriminate between buyers when it comes to pricing, it is operating in more than one market. So it will maximize profits by producing in each market that output at which marginal cost is equal to marginal revenue. If demand is equally elastic in the different markets, marginal cost and marginal revenue will also be equal at the same price. Therefore, in order for price discrimination to add to the profits of the firm, the elasticities of demand of the different markets or buyers must differ. When elasticities of demand differ, prices also differ.

If the firm can separate its market into two markets—one with an elasticity of demand D_2, greater than the other market's elasticity of demand D_1—the monopolist will discriminate in price between the two. Figure 19-11 assumes that marginal cost MC is horizontal for both markets. The monopolistic firm maximizes profits by equating marginal cost and marginal revenue in each market. The result is price discrimination, with a higher price P_1 in the market with the less elastic demand curve. The consumer with few alternatives has a less elastic demand curve and pays a higher price than the consumer with many alternatives.

Price discrimination is not profitable when elasticities are the same in both markets. For example, if price discrimination were applied to left-handed people at a bookstore, profits would not be increased. The price elasticity of demand for books is presumably the same for both

FIGURE 19-11 When two markets have different elasticities of demand, price discrimination increases profits.

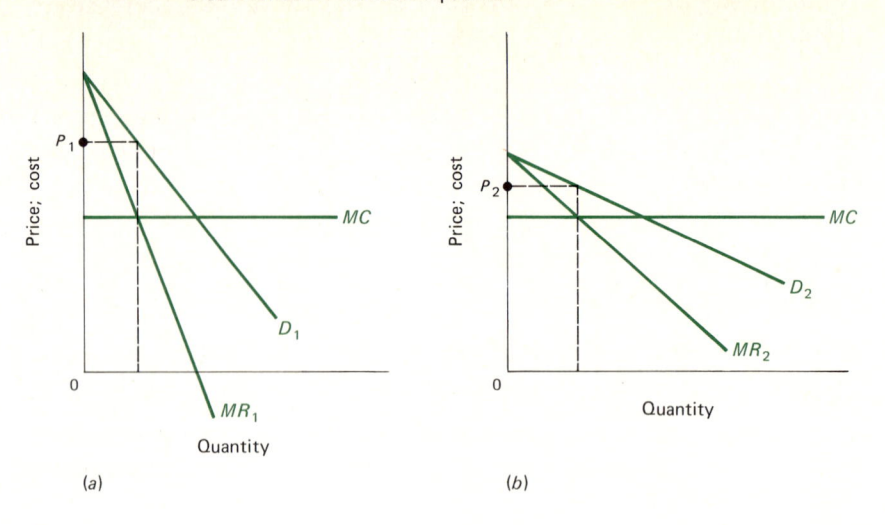

lefties and righties. With different prices, marginal cost and marginal revenue would not be equal and, therefore, profits would not be maximized.

An example of the use of price discrimination is the field of electric utilities, where price discrimination is common. The sector of the electricity market with the most inelastic demand is household use, since there are no effective substitutes for electricity for home lighting. For homes with low rates of consumption, price per unit of electricity is high. Demand for appliances such as electric ranges and driers is made more elastic because of this rate schedule. As a household uses more electricity, the unit price it must pay for electricity decreases, which encourages consumers to use more electric appliances. Because of regulation, much of the gain from price discrimination in the electric-utility industry is passed on to the consumer in the form of a generally lower level of prices. A reversal of this form of price discrimination may have begun in the late 1970s. For instance, California in 1976 approved a rate schedule for electricity and gas under which those households that use less of these energy sources will pay lower rates than those that use more. This move to reduce energy consumption in the interest of conservation may change the whole pattern of price discrimination in the energy industry.

Another example of price discrimination is in theaters. Differing areas of the theater have different elasticities because of more or less favorable positions. People's demand for good seats is inelastic. Thus seats in those locations cost more. Through price discrimination, theaters maximize their total profits.

SUMMING UP

1. The following are the characteristics of a *pure monopoly:* (a) There is only one firm in the industry, and it is not controlled by the government. (b) Since there is only one firm, whether its product is homogeneous or differentiated is irrelevant. (c) It produces a product for which there are no good substitutes. (d) There are complete barriers to entry of other firms. The pure monopolist that wants to manipulate prices and profits, is hampered by (a) competition from firms that produce substitutes, (b) fear of antagonizing the public and the government, (c) inability to control the quantity consumers demand (although the pure monopoly can control price), (d) lack of control over costs.

2. Six barriers that keep new firms from entering a monopolistic industry are (a) entrenched firm's control of patents and secret processes, (b) economic warfare, (c) the entrenched firm's control of sources of supply, (d) obstacles due to the necessity for large-scale production in order to achieve economies of scale, (e) higher cost of initiating consumer acceptance than of maintaining it, (f) government-created barriers to entry.

3. In pure monopoly, the monopolistic firm's demand is the same as demand for the industry as a whole. To increase the quantity consumers demand, the monopolistic firm must therefore lower price. As a result, the marginal-revenue curve lies below the demand-average-revenue curve, and falls more steeply.

4. In the short run, because plant capacity is fixed, the pure monopoly has the same four profit-loss possibilities as the purely competitive firm: (a) Price is higher than average total cost, and the monopoly gets an economic profit. (b) Price is equal to average total cost, and the monopolist gets only a normal profit. (c) Price is less than average total cost, but higher than average variable cost, and the monopoly takes an economic loss, although it continues to produce in the short run. (d) Price is less than average variable cost, and the firm shuts down.

5. A business firm—whether monopolistic or competitive—produces at the level of output at which marginal cost is equal to marginal revenue. Since marginal revenue lies below the demand curve, the monopolistic firm's price (which is established on the demand curve) is higher than marginal cost.

6. In the long run, there are two possible situations: (a) Firms cannot enter the industry because of barriers to entry; thus in a pure monopoly, the monopolistic firm will probably make an economic profit in the long run. (b) Sometimes prices are only high enough to just cover average cost; in that case the monopolistic firm will make only a normal profit. The firm cannot takes losses in the long run, because if losses continue the firm will liquidate.

7. When one compares the long-run equilibrium positions of the purely competitive firm and the purely monopolistic firm, assuming that their cost curves are the same, one finds the following: (a) The purely competitive firm produces a larger output than the purely monopolistic firm, at a lower price. (b) If the monopolistic firm and the purely competitive firm should produce the same output, the monopolist charges a higher price. (c) Under pure competition, only normal profits are earned, while under pure monopoly there probably will be economic profits. (d) Pure monopolists tend to produce at less than full capacity. (e) Since, under pure monopoly, price is higher than marginal cost, the amount of output produced by a monopoly is not the amount consumers most prefer.

8. In some industries, the consumer would be at a disadvantage—either in terms of cost or convenience—if more than one firm were to produce in a given area. So the government awards a franchise to one monopolistic firm. Such firms are regulated by the government, and are called *regulated monopolies.*

9. The regulatory commission tries to set a price at which the monopolistic firm earns only a normal profit. This price level is that amount of output at which average revenue (or demand) equals average cost, and leads to a lower price and higher output than that obtained under unregulated pure monopoly.

10. When a monopolist charges different prices for different units of a commodity, that is *price discrimination.* (a) The main condition necessary for price discrimination is that a buyer of a commodity be unable to sell it to someone else who has been charged a higher price for the same commodity. (b) Price discrimination can be profitable only if the elasticities of demand for each consumer or market are different.

11. A monopolistic firm—like any other business firm—when it wants to practice price discrimination, maximizes profit by producing things at a rate at which marginal cost equals marginal revenue in each market. If elasticities of demand differ in each market, the monopoly will charge different prices in each, equating marginal revenue to marginal cost in each market. The lower the elasticity of demand, the higher the resulting price.

QUESTIONS

1. In a pure monopoly, the monopolistic firm is the only one selling the product; therefore there are no constraints on what the firm can charge or on the profit it can make. Do you agree? Why?

2. Discuss various barriers to entry into an industry, explaining how they can engender a monopoly situation. Are any of these barriers socially desirable? Why?

3. Assuming that the same cost curves apply to both purely competitive and monopolistic firms, compare their relative performance in terms of price, output, and profit. Use diagrams. Since firms of both kinds produce at a level at which marginal cost equals marginal revenue, to what do you attribute the differences between their performances?

4. Discuss the relative degree and timing of utilization and development of technology in (a) a purely monopolistic and (b) a purely competitive system.

5. An alternative to pure monopoly is regulated monopoly. Analyze the ways price and output are determined under regulated monopoly and compare them to what happens under pure monopoly. Do you think regulated monopoly is a practical alternative to pure monopoly or near monopoly? Why?

6. Under what conditions is it possible for a monopolistic firm to practice price discrimination?

7. Draw diagrams and show at what levels a monopolistic firm would produce and what prices it would charge to consumers, if it were given the chance to practice price discrimination.

SUGGESTED READINGS

Bain, Joe S. *Essays on Price Theory and Industrial Organization*. Little, Brown, Boston, 1972.

Leftwich, Richard H. *The Price System and Resource Allocation*. Dryden, Hinsdale, Ill., 1973. Chapter 10.

MacAvoy, Paul W., ed. *The Crisis of the Regulatory Commissions*. Norton, New York, 1970.

Mansfield, Edwin, ed. *Monopoly Power and Economic Performance*. Norton, New York, 1968.

Stigler, George J. *The Theory of Price*. Macmillan, New York, 1966. Chapter 12.

Stonier, Alfred W., and Douglas C. Hague. *A Textbook of Economic Theory*. Wiley, New York, 1972. Chapter 8.

Weiss, Leonard. *Economics and American Industry*. Wiley, New York, 1967. Chapter 5.

Application 19

A National System of Nader's Raiders: Whose Interests Are Represented by Public Regulation?

Rachel, Rachel, I've been thinking
What a fine world this would be
If our problems could be solved by
                    Economic theory.

Regulatory Commissions: Imperfect Guardians of the Public Interest

If public utilities—and other industries that Congress and the President have defined as needing regulation—were administered according to theory, everyone would sleep better. If our politicians were all philosopher-kings (duly elected, of course), all consumers could feel so secure.

But theory does not rule, nor are our politicians philosopher-kings. Our regulatory agencies are part of our political system. Politicians appoint the people who serve on these commissions. Often groups of indignant citizens ask whose interests are represented by these regulatory commissions: the interests of industries the commissions are supposed to regulate or the interests of the consuming public?

One might say that the regulatory agencies should make the self-interest of both consistent. But many people believe that they don't do it very often.

The public has recently become aware of organizational problems in the commissions themselves, in the form of self-interest and self-perpetuation. Getting better-qualified people, or people not connected with the industry being regulated, would not solve the problem. It is unrealistic to expect that such regulators would behave differently, because in effect regulators may be representing their own interest.

One voice, Matthew Josephson, in *The Money Lords*, points out that nine out of eleven recently retired commissioners of the Interstate Commerce Commission (ICC) were hired as lawyers or executives by the very companies they had so recently been regulating. (The ICC is the oldest federal regulatory agency and has been regulating railroads since 1886.)

Another voice, David Hemenway (in an article on the ICC in the book *The Monopoly Makers*) goes much further. He says, "Although the nineteenth-century rationale for regulation has become largely obsolete, the lawyer-dominated commission has remained true to its original purpose, i.e., the stability of the system rather than the welfare of society."

Not only do ICC staffers, when they retire from the commission, go to work for the industry they have just been regulating, but also railroad and trucking officials approve the appointments of people to the Interstate Commerce Commission.

A factor that reinforces this tendency of the commission to identify with the industry it regulates is that neither consumers nor shippers can fight the industry without incurring very large legal costs. Representing the legal interests of the public has proved costly.

The Interstate Commerce Commission also prevents existing firms from effectively competing with each other within industries (railroad, trucking) or across industry lines, and severely restricts the entry of new firms by requiring them to show need for the additional facilities before it permits them to enter the field. The ICC is the biggest obstacle to increased competition in the industries it regulates, to the long-run health of these industries, and to the welfare of the consumer. Its purpose seems to be to preserve the status quo. One could say much the same thing about the Civil Aeronautics Board and *its* control over interstate airline flights.

Furthermore, the ICC cuts down efficiency. Its regulation adds unnecessary dollars to the transportation costs that the public must pay. In a paper presented at an antitrust conference in Washington in 1971, T. G. Moore, another critical voice, estimated that economic losses due to ICC regulations run as high as $4 to $8 billion per year. Here are some examples: (1) The ICC places restrictions on carriers with respect to commodities, routes traveled, and delivery points to such an extent that on return trips drivers often must haul back empty or near-empty trucks. (2) To prevent carriers from competing with each other, the ICC may require them to travel roundabout routes, a custom called *gateway restrictions*, which adds to their mileage and runs up transportation costs. (3) The ICC's control over the entry of new firms and its fostering of mergers has reduced competition and increased monopoly pricing. (4) Price discrimination, called *value-of-service pricing*, distorts the allocation of transportation facilities. (5) The absence of competition, plus the ICC's desire to maintain the status quo, has led to managerial laziness and to ICC opposition to cost-saving innovations.

In recent years, a great many people have been criticizing *all* the federal regulatory commissions. The critic who has received the most attention for the past ten years is a fearless gadfly named Ralph Nader. But there have been others. The late Senator Estes Kefauver, in his book *In the Hands of a Few*, written in the 1960s, severely criticized the Food and Drug Administration (FDA) for its offhand methods of testing and approving the marketing of drugs. He also objected to the FDA's slowness in removing potentially harmful drugs from the market.

A case in point is the drug thalidomide, a sleeping pill that European doctors often prescribed, because an overdose was not fatal. Only the caution and stubbornness of one woman, Dr. Frances Kelsey, employed in the FDA's drug-evaluation department, prevented the United States from the thalidomide disaster that struck West Germany and England. On the basis of the scantiest evidence and her own hunch that something was wrong, Dr. Kelsey refused to give a safety clearance to the drug. U.S. drug manufacturers, who wanted to market thalidomide in the United States, were impatient with the FDA for not giving the approval necessary and brought pressure to bear, calling Dr. Kelsey a stubborn, unreasonable, and stupid bureaucrat. She still held out. Months later, European doctors discovered that women who took thalidomide during pregnancy later bore horribly deformed babies. The United States missed this agony by a frighteningly slim margin.

One problem is that although FDA administrators get into trouble if they approve a bad drug, they may run into hostility if they withhold approval of a good one. In the thalidomide case, this caution proved justified. But how often has bureaucratic caution kept good drugs off the market?

Then there was the case of the *Wall Street Journal*, surely not a radical newspaper. In 1975 it ran a series of articles condemning federal regulatory commissions for their lack of concern for the welfare of the consumers they were supposed to protect. The articles accused the commissions of being primarily concerned with maintaining the status quo in the industries in their charge, and with restricting the competition that would lead to benefits to consumers in the form of lower prices and improved service. They singled out the Federal Power Commission specifically as being a strong offender.

Who Watches the Watchdog?

The group responsible for watchdogging the various commissions and agencies of the executive branch is Congress. If there is any validity to all these criticisms, the alertness of the watchdog (Congress) must leave much to be desired. Who watches the watchdog?

Ralph Nader, among others. In 1965 he published a book, *Unsafe at Any Speed*, which blasted American automobile manufacturers for selling cars that were often shoddy, and downright dangerous. The ensuing furor was such that Congress began a probe into Nader's accusations. In the course of the Congressional study, it was revealed that General Motors, outraged at being thus accused, had secretly hired private detectives to investigate Nader's private life, including his sex habits. Nader thus emerged a hero, and General Motors a villain. This may have had some influence on the passage of the National Traffic and Motor Vehicle Safety Act in 1966. Nader attracted a large following of idealistic people, and he and his team of associates have been leaders in the fight to keep the government honest.

Nader, wanting to protect the citizen-consumer from a profit-motivated corporate economy, set up two structures in his fight to obtain the necessary laws and to see that they were enforced. The first is Nader's Raiders, groups of people, mostly young, who investigate abuses in

"I only have a dime; who should I call first, your doctor, your mechanic, your insurance agent or Ralph Nader?"

corporations and in federal government, and lobby for their correction.

Nader also tried to encourage the formation of Public Interest Research Groups (PIRG) at the state level, so that the Raiders' activities directed at the federal government could be duplicated with respect to the state governments. Although PIRGs have been organized in a number of states, their effectiveness has been limited.

Nader himself is pessimistic about the effectiveness of his own work. Charles McCarry, in his biography of Nader, called *Citizen Nader*, comments that:

The bills with which Nader has been associated have all suffered an unhappy fate. The Natural Gas Pipeline Safety Act of 1968 resulted in the employment of one engineer to deal with five hundred thousand miles of pipeline; the Wholesome Poultry Act of 1968 has shortcomings analogous to those of the Wholesome Meat Act; the provisions of the Coal Mine Health and Safety Act of 1969 were so far from being enforced that some of its congressional sponsors brought a court action against the administration to compel its implementation (and lost); the Radiation Control for Health and Safety Act of 1968 has resulted in reforms more limited than Nader envisioned.

However, Nader and his groups have had some positive results. To name a few: Nader's book led to the passage of the 1967 Auto Safety Act. After two Raiders published a damning report on the Federal Trade Commission (FTC), President Nixon appointed a new Chairman, Caspar W. Weinberger, and the commission was overhauled. Nader's comments caused the FTC to make a strong attack on deceptive advertising. Two other Raiders, up in arms about the extreme levels of pollution from Union Carbide plants in West Virginia and Ohio, got that corporation to reduce its pollution to more acceptable levels.

McCarry sums up Nader's latest attitude with the following:

> He dreams of finding dedicated citizens to act as watchdogs over the Department of Agriculture and the rest of the federal bureaucracy. This seems to him the only possible way of assuring the honest operation of the government; he regards the Nixon Administration and the civil service as being joined in an alliance with the vested interests that is by its nature fatal to reform of almost any kind.

A Conclusion

It seems that many of our regulatory commissions and agencies, though paid to protect the public, are not primarily concerned with the welfare of the consumer. It also seems that Congress is not a very efficient watchdog of the consumers' interests with respect to these commissions. So we are left with a group of vigilant unpaid amateurs: Nader and his Raiders. They may not be the best organization to watch the watchdog, but, at least for the present, they seem to be running the only game in town.

QUESTION

How would you solve the problem of watching the watchdog?

SUGGESTED READINGS

Green, Mark J., et al., eds. *The Closed Enterprise System.* Grossman (a division of Viking/Penguin), New York, 1972. Especially materials on the Federal Trade Commission in Part III.

Green, Mark J., ed. *The Monopoly Makers.* Grossman (a division of Viking/Penguin), New York, 1973. Chapters 2, 4, 5, 6, and 7.

Hemenway, David. "Railroading Antitrust at the ICC." In *The Monopoly Workers*, edited by Mark J. Green. Grossman Publishers, New York, 1973.

Josephson, Matthew. *The Money Lords.* Mentor Books, New York, 1972.

Kefauver, Estes. *In the Hands of a Few.* Penguin Books, Baltimore, 1965.

McCarry, Charles. *Citizen Nader.* Signet Books, New York, 1972.

Moore, T. G. "The Feasibility of Deregulating Surface Freight Transportation." Paper presented at the Conference on Antitrust and Regulated Industries, Oct. 28-29, 1971. Brookings Institution, Washington, D.C.,

Monopolistic Competition: Most Small Firms

A man reminisces:

> When I was a lad in the 1930s I used to go food shopping with my mother. In those days there weren't supermarkets all over. We, my mother and I, would walk around the corner and down the block to a small collection of stores at the farthest corner. First we would go to the grocery and buy canned goods, paper products, and dairy products. Then we would walk next door to the fruit and vegetable store, and afterward to the meat store. We never went to the fish market on the block. (Mother was sure their fish wasn't fresh.) Once a week she took the bus to a fish market about ten blocks away.
>
> Each store was so small that customers had to stand outside if more than ten came at the same time. There were thousands of these small retail mom-and-pop stores in the city. Each had a special advantage in its own neighborhood, because my mother would go to strange stores only with reluctance, both on account of the inconvenience of going greater distances and also because she knew, trusted, and liked the local owners.

The above market situation, known as monopolistic competition, is what we are going to explore in this chapter. Monopolistic competition is a departure from *pure* competition. In Application 20, we will examine the question: Is monopolistic competition as close as we can get to competition?

What Is Monopolistic Competition?

Monopolistic competition includes strong elements of competition, but at the same time it has elements of monopoly power. The three main characteristics of monopolistic competition are (1) a large number of firms, (2) a differentiated product, and (3) relative ease of entry into the market (and exit from it).

Monopolistic competition: The corner store (Herb Moyer)

At one extreme of monopolistic competition, each firm in the industry acts independently of the others, so that the action of any one firm does not affect the actions of the others. Of course, a view more relevant to most examples of monopolistic competition is that any one firm may be in close competition with another one or with a few firms that are nearby, and it has to react when the others change prices. There is unrecognized interdependency between competitors that are in close interaction. They must react to each other's changes, especially changes in price. But a given firm is influenced only incidentally by firms that are farther away. For example, a Laundromat is influenced by other Laundromats that draw customers from its neighborhood, but not by Laundromats far enough away to be inconvenient to its customers.

The fact that there are many firms in a monopolistically competitive situation is a competitive element that restricts the ability of firms to control price through product differentiation. Significant differences in price between firms quickly lead customers to abandon the loyalties engendered by product differentiation and to buy from the firm that offers lower prices. ("Never mind that brand X comes in a prettier box than brand Y. Can I get brand Y a dollar cheaper?")

A second competitive element is the *relative ease of entry* into monopolistically competitive industries, which reinforces and maintains the competitive element of many firms in the industry, and also restricts a firm's ability to exploit product differentiation.

In purely competitive situations, there is complete freedom of entry. But in monopolistic competition, product differentiation can act as a barrier to entry, in that it can keep a monopolistically competitive firm from duplicating the product of another firm. Therefore, one cannot say that it is "complete" freedom of entry as in pure competition, but one must qualify this by saying "reasonable" freedom of entry.

The products produced in monopolistically competitive industries are differentiated. *Product differentiation* means that consumers do see differences between the output of different firms. This is an element of monopoly power, for it enables the individual firm to charge different prices from those of its competitors, because customers are loyal to the firm's product. Usually, the greater the differentiation, the greater the firm's ability to charge a higher price than its competitors. In other words, the greater the differentiation, the greater the monopoly power of a given firm. The basis for product differentiation varies: It may be a brand name, a store name, a difference in quality or services or timing of services, or most important, a difference in location.

The example at the beginning of this chapter of the mom-and-pop retail store embodies several forms of differentiation. The owners' personalities cause customers to either like or dislike them. The services they offer (such as delivery or credit) help draw customers also. But the most important form of differentiation is location. The grocery store around the corner is more convenient than the one ten blocks away. Locational differentiation, though it is not the only form of differentiation, is the most important form in a number of industries. This is true of Laundromats, gasoline service stations, dry-cleaning shops, and restaurants.

The individual firm in a monopolistically competitive situation knows that it can best reduce the intensity of the competition by accentuating differences in its product. When a firm puts a lot of effort and money into differentiating its product from everyone else's, strong product rivalry can develop.

Product variation should not be confused with selling efforts. Differences in location and in efforts to change the quality of the product are clear examples of variations in the product. When a pizza parlor not only has a good location but also takes special care and uses extra ingredients to make a good pizza, it is differentiating its product. If the pizza parlor advertises its pizza, it incurs selling costs. So in monopolistic competition one has to count in two more forms of costs that are added to production costs: (1) cost of creating product differentiation, and (2) costs of selling that differentiated product to customers.

Another force that affects a monopolistically competitive industry is advertising. In pure competition, an individual firm's advertising is ineffective because of product homogeneity. In pure monopoly, advertising merely creates public good will or stimulates general demand for the product at the expense of another industry's product; there is no interfirm advertising. In monopolistic competition, however, advertising that emphasizes the firm and its product may create or intensify existing differentiation. The greater the consumer acceptance created through advertising, the greater the firm's ability to differentiate its product, and the stronger the firm's monopoly power. The greater its monopoly power, the more it can vary its prices.

Advertising may affect the firm's demand curve in two ways: (1) It may increase demand for the firm's output, shifting the demand curve up to the right, as customers want more of the product. (2) It may cause

Advertising is crucial in monopolistic competition, especially when location increases interfirm rivalry. (Herb Moyer)

consumers to have a stronger attachment to the product, which reduces the degree of price elasticity of demand.

When a firm increases its monopoly power by stepping up differentiation of its product, it unfortunately increases its costs at the same time, even though it gains greater control over price. The firm must add to its ordinary production costs the costs of maintaining and intensifying product differentiation. These additional costs fall into two classes: (1) selling costs, often the biggest, which consist mostly of advertising costs, and (2) costs of changing the shape, color, package, and so on, of the product itself; for example, the cost of designing a new soft drink bottle.

Figure 20-1, on the next page, shows selling costs and costs due to product differentiation added to production cost for a monopolistically competitive firm. Both kinds of costs (undertaken in order to intensify differentiation) eventually suffer from diminishing marginal return. The reason is that a firm must make larger and larger expenditures to bring about an equal increase in differentiation. However, in monopolistic competition, firms are small, and each one services a limited local market. Advertising in monopolistically competitive industries is therefore primarily local in coverage.

Two points about advertising should be emphasized: First, many industries characterized as monopolistically competitive may do little if any advertising; for example, Laundromats, drugstores, dental services, and medical services. Second, some monopolistically competitive industries buy national advertising. Big brand-name oil companies advertise nationally, and local service stations benefit from this advertising. Many franchised businesses—such as Kentucky Fried Chicken and McDonald's—have national advertising campaigns that help the individual local firms.

What Is Monopolistic Competition? 473

FIGURE 20-1 Costs of Selling and Product Differentiation Added to Costs of Production for a Monopolistically Competitive Firm. Average cost (AC_1) = production costs; AC_2 adds selling costs to AC_1; and AC_3 adds cost of product differentiation to the other two costs.

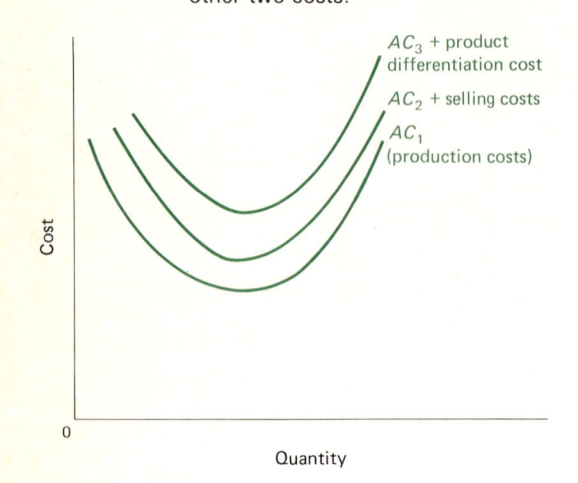

FIGURE 20-2 Demand Under Monopolistic Competition

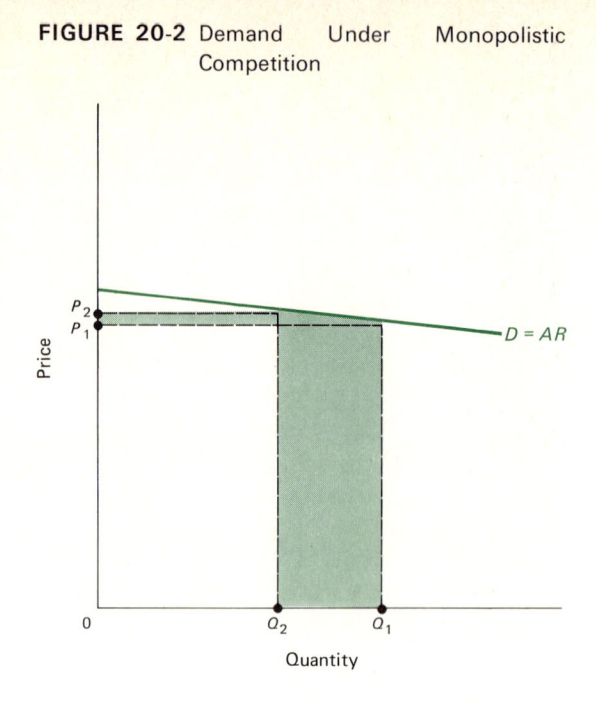

Monopolistic Competition: The Short Run

Recall that in pure competition the individual firm has no control over price. Therefore, the curves depicting its demand, average revenue, and marginal revenue are perfectly elastic at the market price. In pure monopoly there is no competition. Demand and average-revenue curves slope downward. Marginal-revenue curves fall still more sharply, and lie below the demand and average-revenue curves. The pure monopoly must lower price to increase quantity demanded. In monopolistic competition, on the other hand, the individual firm has some control over price, in the sense that it can raise its price and not lose all its customers. This control is due to product differentiation. Thus, the firm's demand (average-revenue) curve is not perfectly elastic, but slopes downward. However, since there are many firms in the industry and entry is easy, competition is strong and the individual firm's ability to vary price is restricted.

Figure 20-2 shows that this demand curve is not perfectly elastic. Price can increase from P_1 to P_2 and quantity sold may decrease only from Q_1 to Q_2. The firm does not lose all its customers. However, because of the competitive elements in a monopolistically competitive industry—large number of firms and ease of entry—this small rise in price results in a large fall in quantity demanded.

Now let's sum up the three market classifications discussed so far, assuming the same scale in a hypothetical diagram. In pure competition, the demand curve is perfectly elastic, and is represented by a horizontal line. In a monopolistic competition, product differentiation gives the firm some control over price, so the demand and average-revenue curve slopes downward. And, since price varies with quantity demanded, marginal revenue decreases more rapidly and lies below the demand, average-revenue curve. In monopolistic competition, the demand curve is not as elastic as in pure competition, but it is more elastic than in pure monopoly.

The monopolistically competitive firm, like the purely competitive and purely monopolistic firms, maximizes profits (or minimizes losses) by producing at the level at which marginal cost equals marginal revenue. In the short run, monopolistically competitive firms, like those in the other market classifications, cannot enter the industry by building new plants, and cannot expand existing facilities, and cannot liquidate their plants. (Remember, the short run is a time period too short to allow plant facilities to be expanded or contracted or liquidated, that is, converted to other kinds of production.) In the short run, then, the entry of firms and the expansion of facilities cannot cause a firm's economic profits to disappear. Also, in the short run, firms cannot liquidate existing plants. Thus, firms faced with economic losses must either produce or shut down and pay fixed costs. In the short run, the monopolistically competitive firm with a given set of supply (cost) conditions faces the same four possible profit or loss situations as firms in the other market classifications:

1. *Demand is great enough to generate an economic profit.* Price on the demand-average revenue curve is higher than average cost.

2. *Demand is high enough to generate only a normal profit.* Price is at the point at which the demand-average revenue curve is tangent to average total cost. Total revenue and total cost are equal. (Remember that a normal profit is already included in economic costs.)

3. *Demand may be high enough to cover at least variable cost and the firm incurs an economic loss.* But the firm will continue to produce in the short run, because price is greater than average variable cost. The economic loss the firm incurs by producing is less than the firm will incur if it shuts down and experiences a loss equal to total fixed cost.

4. *Demand may not be high enough to cover variable costs.* With such large economic losses, the firm shuts down in the short run. Price is less than average variable cost. By shutting down, the firm loses only an amount equal to its fixed cost, while if it continues to produce, it will lose more than its fixed costs.

The only difference in the diagrammatic presentation of these four situations is that in monopolistic competition the demand (average-revenue) curve is more elastic than it is in pure monopoly, but is not perfectly elastic, as it is in pure competition. By now you should be able to diagram the four possible short-run situations in monopolistic competition yourself.

Monopolistic Competition: The Long Run

In the long run, in monopolistic competition, firms can enter the field with reasonable freedom. If there are economic profits to be made in the industry in the short run, firms enter in the long run to take advantage of them. But the fact that more firms are dividing up the market reduces the public's demand for the product of each individual firm. This has the effect of squeezing out the economic profit. The economic profit is also squeezed out when firms engage in price cutting to gain customers. Economic profits are further drained away when firms intensify their efforts to differentiate their product, and in doing so increase their selling costs and costs of differentiation. In the long run, therefore, the result is usually only a normal profit.

So it is no surprise that Figure 20-3 shows the monopolistically competitive firm, in the long run, earning only a normal profit. Let's see why. The firm has very limited control over price, in spite of product differentiation, because there are many firms in the industry and there is ease of entry. In Figure 20-3, D_1 shows the firm's economic profits in the short run. In the long run D_1 falls to D_2, as firms enter the industry and subdivide demand. With D_2, profit-maximizing output will be at the level at which marginal cost equals marginal revenue. Output will then be A. To find the price that will be charged at output A, one draws a perpendicular to the demand curve and a horizontal to the vertical axis. Price is then P. Since the demand curve is *tangent* to the average cost curve, the average cost equals the price. Total cost equals total revenue, and the firm gets only a *normal profit*.

However, in long-run equilibrium, there is an exception to this presumption of only normal profit. In a monopolistically competitive situation, there is product differentiation. And a firm may differentiate its product from that of its competitors so greatly that other firms do not provide enough competition to take away its economic profit. Thus, in the long run, it is possible for a monopolistically competitive firm to earn an economic profit. For example, a long-run economic profit may be earned by a service station in an exceptionally good location, a restaurant with an outstanding chef, or a brand-name product that consumers prefer to other products, as the result of a successful advertising campaign.

Figure 20-4 shows what this looks like. Output is A (where $MC = MR$), and price is given by a perpendicular to the demand curve (AB), with price P. Cost per unit is a perpendicular to the long-run average-cost curve, or E. Total revenue, area $OPBA$, is greater than total cost, area $OECA$. The difference, area $EPBC$, is economic profit.

Note, however, that the most probable situation is one of tangency between $D = AR$, and $LRAC$. In this case there is only a normal profit. Some economists say that the economic-profit situation is really a case of oligopoly. (We shall discuss oligopoly in Chapter 21.) It is oligopoly in the sense that insufficient competition exists because there are few competing sellers located near the firm. The problem is too complex for us to draw any conclusions here.

FIGURE 20-3 Long-Run Normal Profit Under Monopolistic Competition

FIGURE 20-4 Long-Run Economic Profit Under Monopolistic Competition

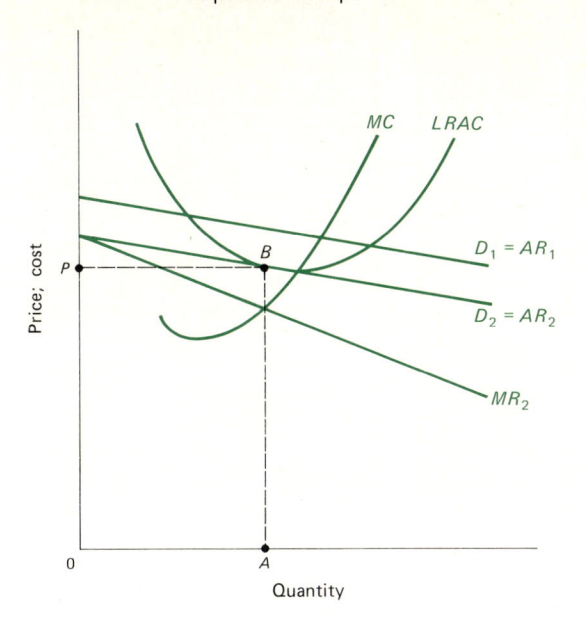

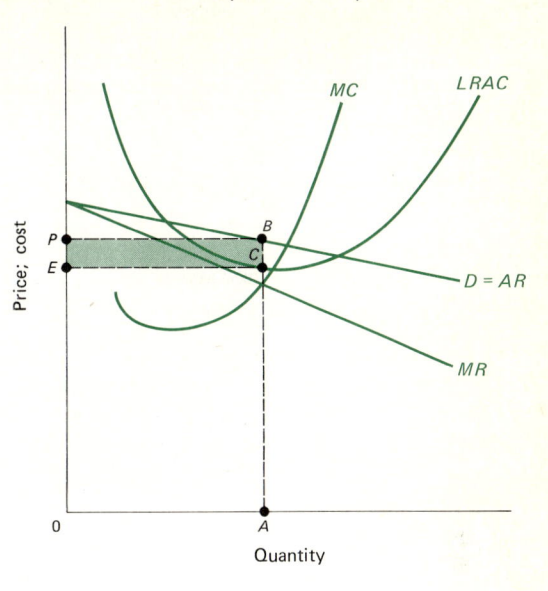

In the long run, there are no economic losses, because firms that take a loss leave the industry. Each of the firms that remain has a larger share of the market, because there are fewer of them. This shifts their demand curves upward and squeezes out the economic loss.

Monopolistic Competition: Economic Consequences

When you compare monopolistic competition with pure competition (Figure 20-5), bear in mind that many of the conclusions drawn from a comparison of pure monopoly and pure competition in Chapter 19 also apply here. Figure 20-5 is based on the assumption that the cost curves in the two classifications are the same.

When there is just normal profit (the most probable long-run situation in both monopolistic and pure competition), the price is lower (P_c) and the output higher (A_c) under pure competition than under monopolistic competition. Also, the monopolistically competitive firm produces at less than capacity (it has output less than that which corresponds to the low point on the long-run average-cost curve), and with higher levels of unit cost, than the purely competitive firm.

Since the typical firm in both market classifications is small, it is reasonable to assume similar cost curves. When we discussed pure monopoly, we had to consider the economic effects of differences in economies of scale and encouragement to technological innovation. These considerations generally are not relevant to monopolistic competition.

In monopolistic competition, facilities are rarely used at full capacity for any length of time. (Herb Moyer)

In monopolistic competition, there are higher costs than in pure competition, and production is at less than capacity. Many economists have characterized this failure to produce at capacity as the *waste of monopolistic competition.* For example, the facilities of most gas stations are hardly ever used to capacity for any length of time, even when there is plenty of gasoline. This is also true of Laundromats, restaurants, and grocery stores.

Note in Figure 20-5 that in monopolistic competition, the marginal-revenue curve lies below the demand curve. Since in order to maximize profits or minimize losses a firm must see that its marginal revenue equals its marginal cost, price is always higher than marginal cost. Therefore, in monopolistic competition, as in pure monopoly, companies do not obtain a socially efficient allocation of resources.

FIGURE 20-5 Comparison of Monopolistic Competition and Pure Competition. Subscript *m* indicates a monopolistically competitive situation; subscript *c*, a purely competitive one.

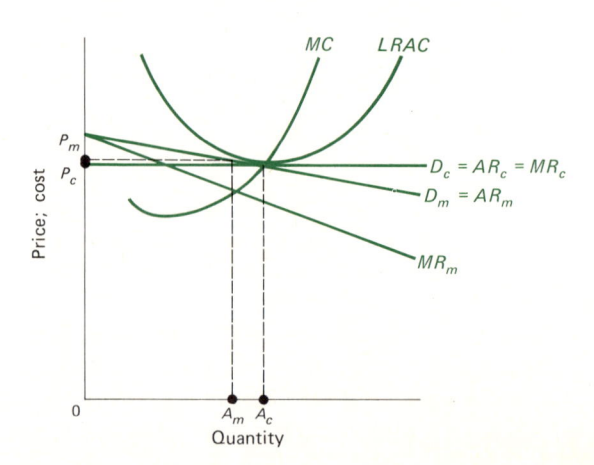

478 **Monopolistic Competition: Most Small Firms**

Remember that the condition that makes pure competition most attractive is that it ensures that resources are most efficiently allocated to produce that combination of goods consumers want. This is so because under pure competition (1) price equals marginal cost, (2) average revenue equals average cost, and (3) quantity produced is at the minimum point on the average cost curve. These conditions do not exist for the monopolistically competitive firm, because under monopolistic competition (1) price is higher than marginal cost and (2) quantity produced is at a point less than the minimum average cost. Therefore, one concludes that under monopolistic competition resources are not efficiently allocated.

However, one must keep in mind that the demand curve for a monopolistically competitive firm is highly elastic. The results—in terms of the relations between price, cost, and output—approach those of pure competition. In many monopolistically competitive industries, these differences may not be large enough to be significant. Furthermore, whatever inefficiencies do result from the monopolistically competitive situation may be interpreted as the cost society must pay to obtain the variety of choices that product differentiation gives the consumer.

SUMMING UP

1. The three main characteristics of *monopolistic competition* are that (a) the number of firms in the industry is large enough that the actions of one firm do not affect the actions of other firms, (b) the product is differentiated, so that the firm gains some control over price, and (c) there is reasonable ease of entry into the industry. In addition, a monopolistically competitive firm may gain advantages from advertising.

2. Because a given firm can vary its price without losing all its customers, the demand (average-revenue) curve is highly, but not perfectly, elastic, and the marginal-revenue curve lies below it.

3. In the short run, the monopolistically competitive firm faces the same four possible profit or loss situations as a firm in a purely competitive or a purely monopolistic situation: economic profit, normal profit, economic loss with production, and economic loss with shutdown.

4. In the long run, because of the large number of firms in a monopolistically competitive industry, the probability is that a firm will earn only a normal profit. However, because of product differentiation, a firm may make an economic profit. Economic losses do not occur, because any firms that might incur losses in the long run would instead leave the industry.

5. In comparison to a firm in pure competition, a firm in monopolistic competition has higher prices, lower output, and higher costs. Resources are not allocated efficiently because price is greater than marginal cost, and output is at a point that is less than the minimum point on the

average cost curve. However, because of the relatively high degree of competition, these differences may not be significant. Whatever costs or inefficiencies there are may be interpreted as the cost society must pay for the choices that product differentiation gives the consumer.

QUESTIONS

1. Define monopolistic competition, and discuss the importance of product differentiation. Give a number of examples of monopolistically competitive industries. In each case, what is the basis of its product differentiation?

2. Compare the curves for average and marginal revenue for firms in monopolistic competition to the average and marginal revenue curves for firms in pure competition and pure monopoly. Why are they different?

3. What are the possible long-run situations with respect to profits or losses for firms in monopolistic competition? Draw diagrams.

4. Assuming identical cost curves, compare the economic performance of a firm in monopolistic competition and a firm in pure competition in terms of output, profit or loss, and efficiency. Is the assumption of identical cost curves realistic? Why?

SUGGESTED READINGS

Bain, Joe S. *Essays on Price Theory and Industrial Organization.* Little, Brown, Boston, 1972.

Chamberlin, Edward H. *The Theory of Monopolistic Competition.* Harvard University Press, Cambridge, Mass., 1935.

Clower, Robert W., and John F. Due. *Intermediate Economic Analysis.* Irwin, Homewood, Ill., 1966.

Leftwich, Richard H. *The Price System and Resource Allocation.* Dryden, Hinsdale, Ill., 1973. Chapters 11 and 12.

Robinson, Joan. *The Economics of Imperfect Competition.* Macmillan, London, 1969.

Stonier, Alfred W., and Douglas C. Hague. *A Textbook of Economic Theory.* Wiley, New York, 1972. Chapter 9.

Watson, D. S. *Price Theory and Its Uses.* Houghton Mifflin, Boston, 1973.

Weiss, Leonard W. *Economics and American Industry.* Wiley, New York, 1967.

Application 20

Is This as Close as We Can Get to Competition?

Chapter 18 discussed the kind of market known as pure competition. Recall that the biggest advantage of pure competition is the efficient allocation of resources that occurs when marginal cost (what it costs the firm to produce one more unit of product) becomes equal to price (what the consumer is willing to pay for that last unit produced). But outside of agriculture, pure competition is rare. And even inside agriculture, government interference blurs the distinctions.

Monopolistic Competition: A Definition

Chapter 20 dealt with the kind of market known as monopolistic competition, and showed that this variety of competition is quite common in the world around us. Virtually all industries composed of small-scale firms fall in this category. Monopolistic competition applies especially to small retail stores and to industries dealing in consumer services. Examples are Laundromats, dry cleaners, small grocery stores or drugstores, restaurants, barber shops.

In the American economy, much of the competition we see around us can be classified as monopolistically competitive. So it behooves us to ask: Just how close to competition can we get here?

The main difference between pure competition and monopolistic competition is that products produced in purely competitive markets are *homogeneous*, while products produced by monopolistically competitive markets are *differentiated*. It is product differentiation that gives a firm monopoly power. When a firm has monopoly power, it can even raise its prices and still not lose all its customers.

Firms in a monopolistically competitive market are usually *small in scale*, and *large in number*. Therefore the individual firm cannot affect prices in the industry at large by varying the amount it produces, since it turns out only a small portion of the total supply. A single firm's ability to affect price depends only on how well it can differentiate its product. The greater the differentiation, the greater the firm's ability to vary its price.

Forms of Differentiation

Location

There's an old saying that if you want opportunity to knock, you must put your door where opportunity is likely to be. This is particularly true for the millions of small-scale businesses in a monopolistically competitive field. For them, *location* is a prime element in product differentiation. For example, for a Laundromat, location is the main form of differentiation. It also helps if the place is clean, if the machines work, and if the attendant is courteous. But these are small factors compared to location. If people must choose between two Laundromats in two different locations, charging the same price, they generally go to the one that is closer. Customers who live an equal distance from the two are indifferent. But if Laundromat A charges more than B, they go to Laundromat B. Laundromat B also gains the favor of all those who find the inconvenience of going to B less onerous than the extra price charged by A.

When location is what makes one firm's product differ from another's, competition reduces price differentials between the two firms, so that the only difference that remains is the inconvenience of travel. But to utilize their plant and equipment efficiently, both firms need a certain volume of business. Thus, they must draw customers from outside the immediate neighborhood. However, they cannot price discriminate by charging customers who live nearby a higher fee than customers who live far away. If they could, they could attract clients from a considerable distance. ("I can wash everything in the house for a buck and a half if I'm willing to drive all the way over to the Washeteria. Come on and help me lug all this laundry out to the car.") But Laundromats must offer one price to all comers. This is what we mean when we say that *a firm's ability to exploit the advantages of location is limited.*

Quality of Service

Quality of service is a second major form of product differentiation. A good cook can put a restaurant on the map, even if it's a little hole in the wall. On the other hand, even the dining room at the Ritz will eventually lose customers if the waiters have dirty fingernails and the waitresses are uppity. For a corner grocery store, differentiation may depend on how helpful the clerks are or on whether the roaches stay out of sight. In a barber shop or a hairdresser's, trade may pick up if there is an operator who, customers think, performs miracles with hopeless hair.

One cannot estimate the value people place on these forms of differentiation. Their impact varies, depending on people's utility schedules—in other words, on what it takes to satisfy them. People's feelings about these forms of product differentiation may be strong, weak, or indifferent.

Suppose Hungry Joe's Steak House raises its prices. People who are indifferent (or who make no particular identification with Hungry Joe's) take their business to the Steak Pit, across the way, where prices are a bit lower. No matter that the Steak Pit has a waitress who snarls when you ask for a spoon. All these customers want is a cheap dinner.

So when it comes to quality of service, here too *a firm's ability to exploit product differentiation is limited.* The reason is that those people with weak feelings about quality of service switch to cheaper products when price differentials widen. But to achieve efficient production, all firms must have a certain minimum volume of business. So competition, coupled with the fickleness of the public, limits a firm's ability to exploit these nonconcrete forms of differentiation.

There are many other means of product differentiation, advertising, for instance. Once a firm differentiates its product from that of its competitors, it can use advertising to intensify the difference by implanting it more strongly in the public's mind. This applies both to rational advertising, which gives needed information ("Our shop is right next to Grand Central Station"; "Our cleanser contains no abrasives") and irrational advertising ("Love that green box!"; "Don't squeeze the Charmin"). Advertising—if it is rational—does not create differentiation. It only magnifies it.

Because monopolistically competitive firms are small and operate in small areas, their advertising must be local in scope. Therefore, their ads are relatively low cost and do not offer much of a barrier to entry of new firms. And because of the large number of monopolistically competitive firms and the similarity of their products, advertising is not likely to be a great factor in reducing price competition among them.

Conclusions About Competition

Purely competitive markets and monopolistically competitive markets are very similar. Generally speaking, both consist of many small-scale firms. Both markets are easy for newcomers to break into. Purely competitive industries turn out a homogeneous product; monopolistically competitive industries turn out a differentiated one. The *nature* of the product is what makes the difference. So a monopolistically competitive firm cannot become a purely competitive one. A monopolistic competitor cannot overcome problems caused by differences in location (a gas station on a busy turnpike versus one on a lonely country road). Nor can people who offer personal services—such as barbers or clothes designers—make their services homogeneous. Nobody would even want them to.

It is possible for a firm to so differentiate its product that it can make an economic profit. It may take a great deal of advertising to achieve this differentiation. Or perhaps the product has considerable differentiation built into it (for example, a gas station at the intersection of two turnpikes or a restaurant with a top-notch chef). At any rate, the degree to which products can be differentiated is limited. The competition brought about by the large *number* of firms forces price to the point at which most firms can make only normal profits.

In brief, in many industries, for those products that can be differentiated, monopolistic competition is as close as we can get to competition.

QUESTIONS

1. What are the differences between pure competition and monopolistic competition?

2. Describe the different ways firms achieve product differentiation in various industries that may be called monopolistically competitive.

3. Name three monopolistically competitive industries, and state their chief form of product differentiation. Can these industries become purely competitive? If so, how? If not, why not?

4. Is monopolistic competition as close as we can usually get to competition in the United States? Why or why not?

SUGGESTED READINGS

Adams, Walter, ed. *The Structure of American Industry*. Macmillan, New York, 1971. Chapters 2 and 12.

Blackwell, Roger D. "Price Levels in the Funeral Industry." Reprinted in *Price Theory in Action*, 3d ed., edited by Donald S. Watson. Houghton Mifflin, Boston, 1973.

Stigler, George W. *The Organization of Industry*. Irwin, Homewood, Ill., 1968.

Weiss, Leonard W. *Case Studies in American Industry*. Wiley, New York, 1962. Chapter 5.

21

Oligopoly: Much of the Real World

Definition of Oligopoly

Back in 1953, President Eisenhower appointed Charles E. Wilson, then president of General Motors, as Secretary of Defense. When the appointment came before the Senate for confirmation, Wilson promised that he would sever all ties with GM before he took office. Senator Richard Russell, then chairman of the Senate Armed Services Committee, asked, "Would you make a decision adverse to General Motors?"

Wilson answered, in what has been the most quoted remark made by a businessman in the past half-century: "What's good for the country is good for General Motors. And vice versa."

Wilson's statement contained a great deal of truth, because one-sixth of the nation's jobs depend to some extent on motor vehicle production and use, and General Motors is the "big daddy" of the automotive industry.

The American automotive industry employs more than 811,000 workers, sells more than $35 billion worth of goods, and has more than $20 billion worth of assets. Its yearly output equals the GNP of Argentina or Belgium, and exceeds that of many countries. The four top firms in the automotive industry make 99 percent of all cars and trucks produced in the United States.

This same top-heaviness also occurs in other industries, aluminum, for instance. Alcoa has more than 46,000 employees, $2 billion in yearly sales, and assets worth $3 billion. The four largest firms in the aluminum industry produce 96 percent of the aluminum made in the United States. Steel is another example. The U.S. Steel Company employs more than 184,000, has sales of more than $7 billion, and holds assets worth more than $7 billion. The four largest steel companies in the United

States manufacture more than 50 percent of the steel produced in the United States.

Other examples are airlines, consumer durable goods (such as refrigerators and washing machines), and computers. In the banking business, with its more than fourteen thousand separately incorporated banks, the top five banks have more than $135 billion in assets. The top hundred commercial banks own 40 percent of the assets of all commercial banks. In retailing, that great bastion of competition, the top five corporations have sales of more than $30 billion.

So you can see that many industries in the U.S. economy are characterized not by pure competition, not by monopolistic competition, not even by monopoly, but by the dominance of a small number of firms. This market situation is called **oligopoly**. Its other characteristics are that it may have homogeneous or differentiated products and that it has substantial barriers to entry of other firms into the industry.

Oligopoly is a very important market model in this study because it fits much of the U.S. economy. Oligopoly encompasses the bulk of manufacturing and food processing. The automobile and steel industries, oil refineries, aluminum-producing industries, and many other industries are oligopolistic. To understand the American economy, one must understand oligopolistic markets.

Following this chapter, we will present some applications on oligopoly: case studies of the behavior of oligopolistic industries and the concept of the military-industrial complex.

Number of Firms: Small

In an oligopolistic industry, there are only a few firms that dominate the field. By few, we mean that the number of dominating firms is so small *that the actions of one affect the actions of all other firms in the industry.* This interaction is called **interdependency** and is recognized by the interdependent firms. That is, firms in oligopolistic industries know that they are interdependent as to policies of price and output.

Let's consider automobiles again. Four firms turn out 99 percent of the cars and trucks produced in the United States. The Ford Motor Company, to protect its own markets, must try to foresee what GM, Chrysler, and American Motors are likely to do with regard to pricing, styling, and other sensitive aspects of production. And how will these firms react to changes in pricing, styling, and other aspects by Ford? In other words, automobile companies are interdependent. Each reacts to the economic decisions of the others in the industry.

Of the twenty-two firms in the steel industry, as we said, the top four produce 50 percent of the output and tend to dominate the smaller firms. In the computer field, the number of firms is larger, but IBM is the dominant firm by far. And interdependence exists, though the federal government is trying to break IBM's dominance.

Product: Both Homogeneous and Differentiated

Some oligopolistic industries produce a homogeneous product and others differentiated products. An example of a homogeneous product is steel. Most steel items are produced according to specifications. The buyer specifies the desired strength, composition, weight, and shape of the steel product, and most steel companies can meet these specifications. Although different companies may offer their customers variations in the way of credit terms, delivery, or servicing, products made of steel are essentially homogeneous.

On the other hand, in the automotive industry, companies go to great lengths to turn out differentiated products. They want consumers to be able to distinguish one car from another on the basis of name, car name, styling, and quality. Intensive advertising magnifies these real and not so real differences.

However, firms in oligopolistic industries that produce homogeneous products do not have much chance to compete with each other, except by pricing. Oligopolistic industries that produce differentiated products (such as cars, washing machines, cigarettes, and computers) can always introduce tiny variations in their products and call attention to the difference by advertising. This lessens the necessity to compete with other firms' prices. Nonprice competition replaces price competition.

Barriers to Entry: Substantial

Since there are only a few firms in an oligopolistic industry, there must be substantial barriers to entry of new firms. In Chapter 19, on monopoly, we talked at some length about the various barriers to entry. In an oligopolistic industry, of the many barriers to entry, the following are most likely to keep out newcomers: (1) patents and copyrights; (2) technology that requires such high levels of output for the firm to reach economies of scale that new firms must start producing in enormous quantities; (3) various forms of economic warfare that can prevent new firms from entering the industry or force small, weak ones out; (4) costs of product differentiation (new firms may have to spend much more to get consumers to accept their product than existing firms spend to maintain consumer acceptance); (5) control of sources of raw materials by existing firms; and (6) various activities of government that restrict entry, either deliberately or incidentally.

Behavior of the Oligopolistic Firm

Oligopoly is the only kind of market that encompasses recognized interdependence between firms. How do rival firms react to decisions of other firms in an oligopoly?

There is no single set of reactions. Theorists have observed a variety of ways interdependent firms react and have set forth a variety of reactions not yet empirically verified. When we have discussed other kinds of markets, we have been concerned, in essence, with only one model of behavior in each classification. In an oligopolistic industry, there are as many ways that an individual firm can behave as there are assumptions.

Kinked-Demand Oligopoly

Assume that a given firm's competitors exactly match any price change it may make. Figure 21-1 indicates this by demand curve D_1 and marginal-revenue curve MR_1, which reflect this assumption. Price is initially at the point where D_1 and D_2 intersect. If the oligopolistic firm raises its price, and then all the other firms in the industry raise theirs too, the dashed portions of D_1 and MR_1 apply. Since all firms have raised their prices, the first firm won't lose customers to the others. However, consumers will certainly react to the higher prices by buying less of the commodity. So *all* firms in the industry will lose to some extent. Thus, to the first firm, demand for its product tends to be inelastic.

Now suppose that the first firm *lowers* the price it charges and that all other firms follow suit and cut their prices. Then the solid portions of D_1 and MR_1 apply. The first firm will not take customers away from the others because all the firms have matched the price decrease. However, all firms will gain somewhat, as the buying public reacts to the lower price and buys more of the product. This increase in quantity demanded

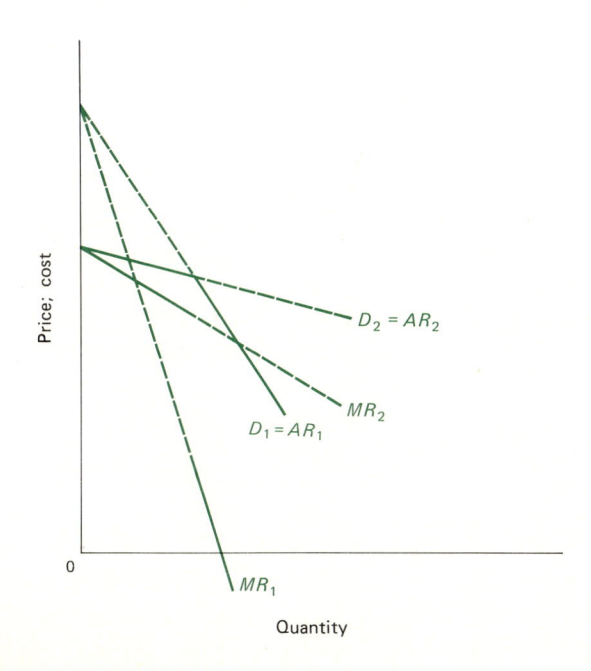

FIGURE 21-1 Kinked-Demand Oligopoly. The solid portions of both D_1 and D_2, and MR_1 and MR_2, depict the theory of *kinked demand*: in an oligopoly, other firms ignore a competitor's price increase, but match a competitor's decrease.

tends not to be great. So when other firms match both increases and decreases in price, the demand curve for the initiating firm tends to be inelastic. (Remember, however, that on almost all straight-line demand curves, the price elasticity of demand is different at each point.)

There is another way of looking at this situation. Suppose that the first firm's competitors do not respond at all when the firm changes its prices. Figure 21-1 indicates this by demand curve D_2 and marginal revenue curve MR_2. Price is initially at the same point described above. The oligopolistic firm raises its price, but this time the other firms in the industry do not follow suit; they hold their prices constant. And the solid portions of D_2 and MR_2 apply. Since the first firm is the only one to raise prices, its price is higher than that of the rest, and it will lose customers to its lower-priced rivals. So the solid portion of D_2 is relatively elastic, compared to D_1.

Now suppose that the first firm cuts its price, below the initial price. The other firms in the industry do not follow suit, but hold their prices constant. Then the dashed portions of D_2 and MR_2 apply. Since the first firm is the only one to cut prices, its price is lower than that of the others in the industry, and it will lure customers away from its now higher-priced rivals. So the dashed portion of D_2 is relatively elastic, compared to D_1.

Let's review: If a given firm cuts its price, then one would expect the other firms in the industry to match that decrease, to prevent the first firm from siphoning off their customers. On the other hand, if a firm *raises* its price, one would expect the other firms in the industry *not* to raise theirs to match, because they would all want to lure customers away from the first firm. So the price-raising firm would lose many of its customers to its lower-priced rivals. Therefore, a reasonable assumption about behavior of firms in an oligopolistic situation—and the one that explains the **kinked-demand curve**—is that rival firms in a given industry will match competitors' price decreases, but ignore their price increases.

How do demand and marginal-revenue curves based on this assumption look? In Figure 21-1, the intersection of D_1 and D_2 is the prevailing price. The first part of the assumption is that if one firm lowers its price, its competitors will do likewise (moving along the solid portion of D_1). In kinked-demand analysis, it is the solid portions of D_1 and MR_1 that are the relevant curves.

The second part of the assumption is that if one firm raises its price, its competitors will just look the other way and hold their prices steady (moving along the solid portion of D_2). In kinked-demand analysis, it is the solid portions of D_2 and MR_2 that are the relevant curves.

Note that there is a *kink* (or bend) at the prevailing price. Note also that there is a *gap* or *discontinuity* in *marginal* revenue. This kink and this discontinuity are due to the difference in expectations about the way firms will behave if one firm raises (or lowers) prices. In kinked-demand oligopoly, the demand curve above the prevailing price is relatively elastic, but below it is relatively inelastic. So the kink occurs because, at the prevailing price, any change in price causes a shift from a relatively elastic demand to a relatively inelastic one. As a result, there are two *MR* curves: one for the elastic and one for the inelastic portion of the demand curve, with a discontinuity between the two.

Price Inflexibility in a Kinked-Demand Oligopoly

Figure 21-2, still operating on the assumption of kinked demand, shows cost curves added to the demand and marginal-revenue curves. The marginal-cost (*MC*) curve must intersect the marginal-revenue (*MR*) curve within the discontinuous section, or else there is no equilibrium at price *P*. Thus, to maximize profits, the firm's output should be *Q* and its price *P*. Total revenue is area 0*PAQ* and total cost is area 0*BCQ*. Because of formidable barriers to entry and the unprofitability to any one firm of lowering prices when rivals are sure to follow, the firm makes an economic profit, in this case equal to area *BPAC*.

In a kinked-demand oligopoly, prices tend to be inflexible, for the following reasons:

1. If a given firm raises its prices, its competitors do not; and since demand is relatively elastic, the initiating firm's total revenue declines.

2. If a given firm cuts its prices, its competitors follow suit; and since demand is relatively inelastic, again the firm's total revenue declines. In addition, when firms try to match each other's price cuts, a price war may break out, as the initiating firm keeps trying to make its prices the lowest. If there is a price war, prices usually spiral downward for a time, which puts pressure on all the warring firms, because although they can't stand the heat, they can't get out of the kitchen.

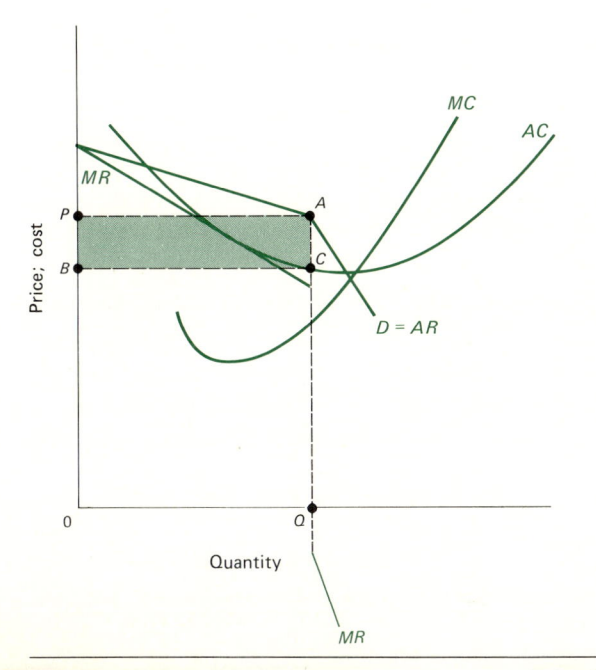

FIGURE 21-2 The Kinked-Demand Curve and Discontinuous Marginal-Revenue Curve Redrawn from Figure 21-1, with Cost Curves Added

Results of a price war in the used-car business (Daniel S. Brody/Stock, Boston)

3. The marginal-cost curve can shift within the gap or discontinuity in marginal revenue without changing the level of output or price at which marginal cost and marginal revenue are equal and profits are maximized. This means that costs can vary somewhat without prices changing. The only thing that triggers a price increase is a considerable increase in costs, which pushes the marginal-cost curve in Figure 21-2 above the discontinuity of the marginal-revenue curve. This increase in costs must be industry-wide, and the industry must recognize that the price increase is a result of that increase.

For example, suppose that the labor union that operates in an industry that is a kinked-demand oligopoly obtains wage increases that are enough to push up the marginal cost curve but not enough to get firms out of the gap in marginal revenue. Each individual firm would be reluctant to initiate the price increase for fear the others would not follow suit. If the wage increase were large enough to push marginal cost above the gap, each firm would see that its profits would be increased if it raised its price, regardless of whether or not its competitors raised theirs.

This kinked situation with its price inflexibility occurs most often during periods of general price stability or mild inflation, because supplies then are relatively plentiful and consumers can choose among competing firms. Companies that are trying to keep their customers hasten to match any price cuts by their competitors, but are reluctant to increase their prices.

However, during periods of significant inflation, when prices keep rising everywhere, these constraints evaporate. Supplies are scant and consumers have less choice, as well as less chance, to shift firms. The minute an initiating firm announces a price increase, its competitors imitate and raise theirs too. And after the prices are raised, all the companies are reluctant to lower prices and forgo the additional profits they can get from the raised prices. This pattern of response intensifies the inflationary spiral. (Think about oil, sugar, and paper prices in the mid-1970s.)

Until the energy crisis of 1973, many would have said that the oil industry was exhibiting kinked-demand behavior. The oil industry consisted of a group of large firms, seemingly without a price leader, and there was an even bigger group of small independents that at times tested the competitive situation. Even though all the oil firms tried hard, by advertising, to differentiate their products, gasoline is gasoline. When one oil company raised its prices, other oil companies used to resist the idea and hold the line on their own prices. Price wars, regional and national, used to take place, the most memorable being the national price war that broke out when Gulf introduced Gulftane—a gasoline with lower octane and lower prices than regular gasoline—in the mid-1960s. In North Carolina the price war lasted almost a month, and at one point brought about a general price fall of 10 cents a gallon. Gulf, in creating Gulftane, was using product variation as an offensive weapon against its competitors. The weapon brought on a price war.

To get around the restrictions and uncertainties of the kinked-demand situation, companies sometimes enter into various forms of cooperation, such as collusive oligopoly and price leadership.

Collusive Oligopoly: If You Can't Lick 'em, Join 'em

Covert Collusion

One way oligopolistic companies react to the uncertainties and inflexibilities of a noncollusive situation is to get together on the sly and agree to consult one another and set up mutually agreed-on prices, shares of markets, and so on. (Of course, it's against the law; but we're not talking about lawful behavior here.) Such agreements, either verbal or written, create a monopoly situation, one in which the whole industry functions in the same way as would a pure monopoly with several plants.

The more complex the market situation, the more complex these agreements must be. As long ago as the 1870s, the railroads' efforts to set up collusive arrangements involved intricate agreements, including multiple rate schedules and complex systems of market sharing. In the 1960s, there was a notorious collusive agreement between U.S. electrical-equipment producers, which eventually led to jail sentences for executives of some of the companies. During the years of active collusion, there must have been many secret meetings and reams of memos to enable the executives of the various firms to keep track of prices and market shares.

There are two major obstacles to making collusive agreements work: (1) During a recession—or, as it is politely known, a business contraction—many firms break these agreements as they scramble for the business that is growing less each day. (2) Many kinds of collusive agreements have been outlawed by the U.S. antitrust acts, beginning with the Sherman Antitrust Act in 1890, and therefore are not only unenforceable by a court, but would, if they became public knowledge, be subject to criminal prosecution. Covert collusive agreements—such as fixing prices and allocating market shares—are illegal per se.

Whenever several companies conspire to fix prices and other conditions of the market, it is as though they had combined and formed a monopoly without any one of them losing its independence. The revenue and cost curves of these firms form a composite that could very well be used to portray the monopoly model. These colluding firms make decisions as to prices and output that serve to maximize profits for the entire industry.

Despite the fact that covert collusion is illegal, the government and the courts have fostered monopoly-type situations that limit—or even eliminate—price competition in a number of fields. For example, the Civil Aeronautics Board, a Federal regulatory commission, sets the fares the airlines may charge on domestic flights. The New York City government not only restricts the number of legally licensed (medallioned) taxis in the city, but also fixes the price of becoming a cab driver by requiring high-priced license fees (New York has charged more than $32,000 for a hackney license). In addition, it regulates the fares that taxi drivers may charge. In professional baseball, the courts have approved a collusive agreement whereby a baseball club owns a player's contract, and whenever it wants to, it can sell the contract to another club. The courts condoned this practice, which makes impossible a free market for labor in pro baseball, on the grounds that this arrangement would in the long run benefit the sport. Some people feared that a free market for the players would mean the team with the most money would get the best players. This result would eventually lead to loss of competition among professional baseball teams entirely, since the top team would rise to the top and stay there, because it would earn the most money.

After the antitrust laws were passed, covert collusion became even more clearly illegal. Despite its illegality, however, covert collusion is always with us.

Price Leadership

American business people are noted for their ingenuity. To sidestep the illegality of covert collusion and still avoid the uncertainties and inflexibilities of noncollusive oligopoly, some industries have adopted the convention of price leadership, an arrangement by which the firms in an industry agree to let one firm be the leader. The agreement is usually a tacit one, naturally, but there are a number of oligopolistic industries that behave in such a way that everyone knows which firm is the price leader.

For example, in the steel industry, U.S. Steel used to function as the price leader. All that U.S. Steel had to do was issue a press release about forthcoming price changes, and the other steel firms would announce similar price changes. (However, in the last ten years the dominance of

"Hold your signature on that merger, Mr. Selmeyer. The Justice Department's changed its mind again."

U.S. Steel has waned. Leadership has been assumed at different times by several of the other large firms in the industry.)

In the early 1960s, when the late Senator Estes Kefauver questioned George M. Humphrey, head of National Steel, about this practice in Senate hearings on price leadership, he replied, "We match the price increases of U.S. Steel to meet the competition in the industry." When Kefauver pointed out that matching a price increase cannot be considered meeting the competition, this seemed to be beyond Humphrey's comprehension. (See Estes Kefauver's book *In the Hands of a Few*.)

The price leader must be careful when it sets prices that no other firm within the industry is so penalized that it revolts against the price-leadership agreement. A case in point was the announcement in April of 1962 by U.S. Steel that it was going to increase steel prices. President Kennedy attacked the price increase, saying it was against the public interest and it violated the implied terms of a labor management agreement that he had helped negotiate. Kennedy threatened to withhold government contracts from those steel firms that adopted the price increase. Two companies, Kaiser Steel and Inland Steel, bowed to Kennedy's wishes and announced that they would hold their prices steady. There was an implied promise that these companies would get preferential treatment by the government. But of greater importance was the fact that these firms were the last in the industry still negotiating with the unions. If they had raised their prices, they probably would have had to give their workers a fatter wage package. U.S. Steel had overlooked that fact in the timing of its own price increase, so, in that particular effort at price leadership, U.S. Steel muffed the job. No single steel firm dominates the industry now as U.S. Steel had since its formation in

1903. In addition, some of the smaller firms, such as Inland, have become more efficient than U.S. Steel. So challenges to U.S. Steel's leadership are more likely than ever, providing that some price leadership remains in the industry.

When there is price leadership, the only curves that affect price and production decision making are the curves of the price leader. Its curves are similar to those of a monopoly. However, the price leader must set prices at a level that is comfortable for all the firms in the industry.

Nonprice Competition

In a situation of kinked-demand oligopoly, prices are inflexible and price competition is infrequent. In a situation of collusive oligopoly, whether it involves covert collusion or just price leadership, there is no price competition at all. In other words, one seldom finds price competition in an oligopolistic industry. Firms in oligopolistic industries do compete aggressively for larger shares of the market. And since they use price competition infrequently in their struggle, they substitute various forms of nonprice competition, such as styling, services, quality, and advertising.

Styling
One common form of nonprice competition is variation in the styling of the commodity. One company differentiates its product from that of the others by changes in color and shape—that is, in style. For example, washing-machine manufacturers offer a selection of colors rather than only white, and build in an array of buttons, dials, and levers to attract buyers. Automobile manufacturers, of course, use styling as a tool of competition to such a degree that they spend billions to retool every year or so, just so their cars will look different.

Services
Variations in services rendered are another well-known form of nonprice competition in oligopolistic industries. For example, in the computer industry, software services vary, both in extent and quality. These services, which include items such as the training of staff and the offering of a number of standard programs, go along with the hardware and are important factors in determining sales. (IBM has a strong competitive advantage in these services.) Retail stores use delivery service and various kinds of credit terms to attract customers. All these are forms of nonprice competition.

Quality
Quality is one form of nonprice competition that definitely benefits the consumer: firms compete with each other by improving the quality of their products. For example, in the automobile industry, innovations such as power brakes, power steering, better gasoline mileage, and many other improvements have given their initiators competitive advantages. (Some representatives of the Chicago school of economics, a

group of economists whose thinking has been influenced by the work of Milton Friedman at the University of Chicago, say that if true differences in quality exist, there are really two different products. For our purposes here, it makes little difference whether the products are considered differentiated or close substitutes.)

Nonprice competition in the form of variations in styling, services, and quality may definitely benefit the consumer. Or they may be useless to the consumer and a waste of resources. The garment industry is notorious for manipulation by introducing new styles to make people feel that their present clothes are out of date, and for the waste of resources brought about by these changes in style. The automobile industry is no better. The social (or even economic) rationale behind the auto makers' compulsion to change body styles each year escapes many observers. The billions of dollars spent each year in order to change body styles seems a high price to pay for such variety.

Advertising
The most important form of nonprice competition in the consumer-goods markets is advertising. Rather than compete by lowering their prices, oligopolistic firms tend overwhelmingly to try to influence consumer demand by advertising. Let us now take a hard look at advertising. What are the pros and what are the cons?

The Case for Advertising. Five main arguments have been used to justify advertising on the grounds that it is beneficial to the consumer:

1. Advertising increases the demand for the firm's output, and as a result the price to the consumer decreases. Because of increased demand, the firm makes more of the product, which means that this increased demand has the effect of raising the level of output, and thus lowering the average cost per unit (on the assumption that initially average cost falls as output rises; in other words, that there are economies of scale). This decrease in production cost per unit may outweigh the increase in selling cost caused by advertising. Then the price to the consumer may decrease.

Figure 21-3 shows the situation graphically. Suppose a company does not advertise. Demand for its product is *B*, with cost *BA*. Then the company starts advertising, and the demand for its product increases (curve shifts to the right), so it increases output to *C*. "Cost" now includes both production and selling costs. However, the improved efficiency, due to economies of scale as output increases, more than compensates for the higher cost of selling the product. The average cost of making the product is therefore less (*CD*) *with* advertising than without (*BA*). Thus, there is a possibility that the company may cut its prices.

2. Advertising gives information that consumers need in order to make intelligent choices among competing products. There is such a large number of commodities and they have so many variations, that the consumer needs all the help possible. Who (and where) are the sellers?

FIGURE 21-3 An increase in demand for a product, brought about by advertising, can decrease the cost of it enough to offset the increased cost of selling it, and may make it possible for the company to sell the product for less.

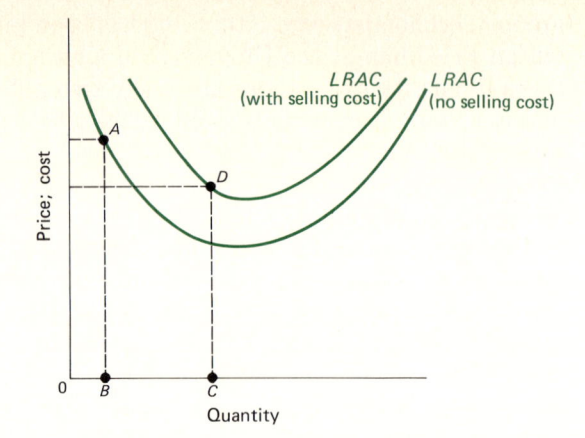

What does the product do? What are the differences between it and similar products? Advertising can provide this information; in some cases, advertising is the only source of it.

3. Advertising produces the money to support, partly or completely, the media for mass communication. Television is almost wholly supported by advertising, and thus is "free" to viewers. (Of course, American viewers must put up with the commercials. But in England and in other countries in Europe, although there are no commercials, TV owners must pay a high annual license fee for each set they own.) Newspapers and magazines would cost a lot more if they did not carry advertising. In other words, advertising provides "free" TV and makes possible newspapers and magazines that the public can afford to buy.

4. Advertising, as a side benefit, often conveys to the public helpful messages incidental to advertising the product. For example, toothpaste ads have stimulated better dental-care habits.

5. Advertising enables firms to differentiate their products. Consumers seem to like product differentiation. In other words, they like variety, and advertising enables firms to give them variety.

The Case Against Advertising. Now let's look at the opposite side of the coin, the arguments against advertising.

1. Advertising may increase an individual firm's demand and cause its output to increase, achieving economies of scale, so that production costs fall more than selling costs. In this way, advertising may enable the individual firm to cut its costs. However, advertising has a beneficial effect on the entire economy only if the increased demand (and thus the economies of scale) for the product of the individual firm that advertises is not diverted from rival firms, thus reducing the demand for *their* products, and increasing *their* costs. When an economy is at full employment, this diversion of demand may happen. Even when advertising does not stimulate the demand for a single firm's product, it causes changes in the composition of total demand. Since the public has only

just so much income, and the economy at full employment just so many resources, increased demand for a given product must mean a decline in the demand for some other commodity (or commodities) and a reduction in other firms' economies of scale. In other words, the benefits one firm gains from advertising may at the same time worsen the cost situation for some other firms. Society thus may not gain a *net* increase in efficiency (reduction in cost).

Even if production costs for an individual firm did fall more than selling costs increased, this decrease would benefit the consumer only if prices were to fall as a result. And companies lower their prices only if it is profitable to do so. So a new company that enters a monopolistically competitive industry can use advertising to stimulate demand and to gain economies of scale. When the monopolistic competitor runs into this competition, it cuts prices. But in an oligopolistic industry, since price competition is unlikely, the benefits of cost reductions may not be passed along in the form of lower prices. Furthermore, advertising increases the strength of product differentiation, which reduces, rather than increases, competition.

Most of the money spent on advertising does not lead to overall improved economies of scale. A lot of advertising is nonproductive; it is just a company's way of competing with others and retaliating against others that are making the same product.

Firms use competitive-retaliatory advertising as a substitute for price competition. It may surprise you to know that the various firms in a given industry work out a balance as to the relative intensity with which they will advertise. Periodically, however, an advertising war breaks out. For example, in the soap industry in the mid-1960s, an advertising war broke out between Procter and Gamble and Lever Brothers. Procter and Gamble wanted to take some share of the market away from the industry leader, Lever Brothers, and therefore launched a vigorous advertising campaign for their product, Dash. There were detergent ads everywhere, with washing machines ten feet tall. Lever Brothers fought back for their detergent All by showing a man messing up clean clothes and saying, "All outcleans them all." The net results were *no* improvement in economies of scale, a somewhat larger share of the market for Procter and Gamble, and tens of millions of dollars of advertising costs added to the cost of soap to the consumer.

Practically nobody would argue in favor of total elimination of advertising. However, if the present high levels of advertising could be scaled down to a level that would just maintain industry demand by providing useful information about products, and if the savings could be passed on to the consumer, then a great deal of advertising waste could be eliminated.

2. To the extent that an advertisement gives information the consumer needs in order to make rational choices, that advertisement is economically justified. However, a great deal of advertising does not impart information; in fact, some of it even puts out misleading information. For example, the Brylcreem ads do not give information by showing a

"The commercials will be on in a minute—we can say grace then."

beautiful woman squeezing out of a tube or a football player yelling, "I've come back." The late Senator Estes Kefauver, in his book *In the Hands of a Few,* cites several drug-company ads aimed at doctors that border on the fraudulent because they do not clearly label pictures of X-rays.

3. The argument that advertising provides "free" TV and cheap newspapers and magazines is not valid. The huge sums of money that companies pay out in advertising fees to the various media must come from somewhere; they are included in the prices of the products. (Some thoughtful observers have pointed out that when advertising "pays" for TV, it merely redistributes the cost of TV to many people who do not watch TV but use the products advertised.) The consumer pays for TV, newspapers, and magazines, not directly, but indirectly, when she or he buys the product advertised. The indirectness of this payment blurs the consumer's understanding of the link between costs and services. Furthermore, the consumer who pays, albeit indirectly, for the media does not have any control over the media. The advertisers not only do not really pay for the media, but they can, and often do, unduly influence what appears in the media.

(The question of who really pays advertising costs, like the question of who really pays excise or sales taxes, is more complex than this brief rundown would lead you to expect. Who does the actual paying depends to a great extent on the elasticities of demand and supply. However, if we assume that manufacturers have long-run costs that are constant, the conclusion that the costs of advertising by oligopolistic industries are passed on to the consumer is substantially correct.)

4. The argument that toothpaste ads have encouraged the public to form better dental habits may hold water, but advertising in other areas is not so beneficial. For example, television ads can encourage the public to form harmful habits: For years, until the recent ban on cigarette advertising on TV, the cigarette companies sold cancer along with their cigarettes. TV advertising also exercises subtle influences on the public's attitude toward women. The Comet cleanser and Folger coffee ads demeaned women by depicting them as being incapable of making a good cup of coffee or of cleaning a sink. Car advertisements feature beautiful women in scanty clothes along with the cars; this is one of the most blatant examples of the use of sex to sell a product. (We shall discuss economic implications of sex discrimination in Application 24.)

As we said, hardly anyone wants to ban advertising altogether, if only because advertising's information-giving function is a vital one in this complex economic world. However, there are a number of problems: (1) advertisers circulating misinformation, (2) nonsense ads and economic warfare through advertisements, and (3) high levels of retaliatory advertising.

Profit Maximization: Fact or Fancy?

In our analysis of the four market classifications, we assumed that any firm produces at the level of output, and charges the price, that will maximize its profits. In both purely competitive and monopolistically competitive situations, this assumption of profit maximization is probably valid. The pressures of competition and the fact that the individual firm has very little control over prices mean that most firms must seek profit maximization. (In monopolistic competition, the individual firm does have some ability to affect price, but very little.) However, some economic theorists doubt that in monopoly and oligopoly each firm aims at output and price that result in profit maximization. These theorists have summed up their doubts in the following six ways:

1. The individual firm, whether it wishes to maximize profits or has some other priority, does not have enough data accurately to compute demand, average revenue, marginal revenue, and marginal cost. Without this information, the firm will not know the level of output and price that will cause marginal revenue to equal marginal cost.

2. A firm may be afraid that the government will bring an antitrust action against it if it tries to maximize its profits. A firm that succeeds usually wants to expand, and presently it may be the firm that dominates a given industry, which may trigger an investigation or an antitrust suit. For example, during the mid-1960s, to avoid a possible antitrust suit, General Motors deliberately restricted sales in order to keep from increasing its percentage of the market.

3. A firm may want to avoid adverse public reaction, which is why monopolistic and oligopolistic firms may elect not to push their prices up

to the point of maximization. Since these firms are larger and fewer in number than others, they are more visible to the public. (Points 2 and 3 do not refute the assumption of profit maximization; they only point out that at times profit maximization is limited by noneconomic factors.)

4. Firms may decide not to try to maximize profits in the short run in order to keep profits low, and thus discourage potential rival firms from entering the industry, because despite the difficulties of entering monopoly and oligopoly industries, if the profits are high enough, some firms will try. (Not attempting to maximize profits is sometimes called *limit pricing*.) Here again, the assumption of profit maximization is not violated. The fact that some companies do not try to make maximum profits out of fear of potential competition only points up the complexity of estimating profit maximization.

For example, before World War II, Alcoa's long-run pricing policy was predicated partly on the idea of low prices, with the aim of discouraging potential competition. Also, in the funeral industry there is evidence that morticians used less than maximum prices to discourage new people from entering the funeral business. (See Leonard Weiss's book *Economics and American Industry*.)

5. Other considerations may be as important as profit maximization, or, more so. These considerations may include increasing the firm's share of the market and volume of sales. Some people have even argued that corporate executives might feel a sense of social responsibility that would reduce the drive toward profit maximization.

6. A serious challenge to the assumption of profit maximization comes from John Kenneth Galbraith's book *The New Industrial State*. At the risk of oversimplification, let's summarize Galbraith's argument: Big corporations are no longer run by individuals or by the stockholders or the board of directors. The major corporations are so large and present-day technology is so complex that it takes many interlocking groups and committees within the corporate structures to make decisions. This group decision making is dominated by what Galbraith calls the "technostructure," or people he calls **technocrats** who have the technical expertise to deal with the complex technology of the modern corporate economy. The technostructure controls the corporation, and profit policy is directed toward the self-interest of this technostructure. In effect, there is separation of ownership (the stockholders) and management; control is held by management.

Galbraith maintains that because of self-interest the technocrats have two aims: (1) The technocrats want to keep the stockholders from exercising control. The technostructure accomplishes this by seeing to it that the company earns a large enough profit both to maintain dividend payout (which keeps the stockholders quiet) and to hold enough retained earnings to keep the firm from having to borrow money for expansion. (2) The technocrats want to expand the technostructure's area of activity. Accomplishing this tends to lead to expansion of both sales and size of the corporation.

Whether Galbraith's assessment of the workings of major corporations is correct is too big a subject for us to try to resolve here. But even if we accept his description, it does not seriously refute the idea of profit maximization.

The technostructure must make enough profits to satisfy stockholders and to finance expansion. How much profit is enough? Galbraith does not say. However, there is no reason to conclude from his arguments that the technostructure would not use profit maximization as its guide in determining profit goals. Profit maximization, after all, generates the net revenue necessary for growth and the retention of control of the corporation.

Administered Prices

Often a given firm cannot estimate what its demand, average revenue, marginal revenue, and marginal cost will be. When such is the case, the firm may not follow the policy of marginal-revenue–marginal-cost pricing we have been discussing. The firm must then, through its administrative processes, decide on a pricing policy that is called **administered pricing**.

Administered pricing is the practice of setting price by a firm's administrative officers, and not through marginal-cost, marginal-revenue pricing.

One form of administered pricing is called **cost-plus pricing**. The firm first computes its variable cost, then its fixed cost, and finally decides the profit it expects to make per unit. It adds this per-unit profit to the variable and fixed costs. However, the question arises: When demand for a product varies, what should the profit margin be? This question constitutes a major problem in cost-plus pricing.

There are two alternatives: (1) The company can keep prices relatively inflexible and let the profit margin vary with changes in demand. (2) The company can vary prices and keep the profit margin fixed. When the prices of labor and materials increase, naturally the company must raise prices commensurately.

A big problem arises when demand falls and thus the firm's average cost per unit rises. (Remember that the average cost curve is U-shaped. If the firm is operating at average minimum cost or at a rate of output smaller than that, output decreases, and the average cost per unit rises.) Figure 21-4 shows that before the decrease in demand, output was A. After the decrease it was B. Note the increase in average cost, from C to D. If the firm's policy is for profits to be a fixed percentage of price, then the firm must increase its price as demand falls. Thus, one finds prices increasing during a period of adoption of such a policy, a fact that could in part explain the inflation during the recessions of 1958, 1969-1970, and 1974-1975.

FIGURE 21-4 Rise in Average Cost with Fall in Demand

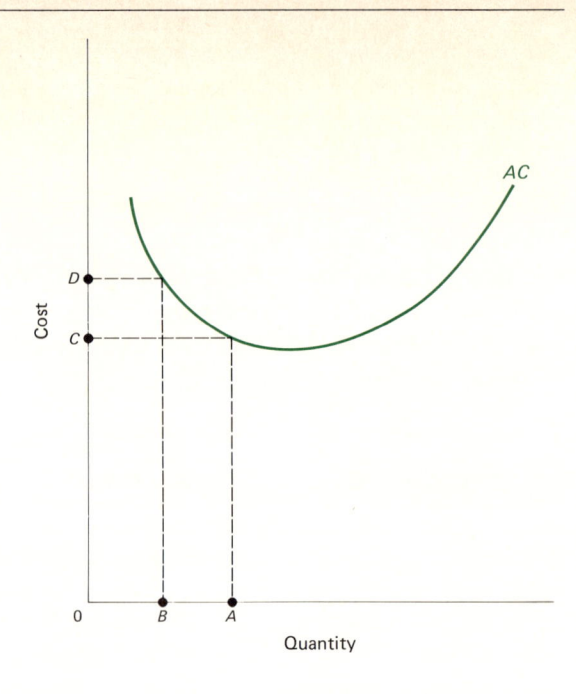

Another form of administered pricing is deciding what the price should be, given potential demand and desired output, and then deciding what the profit margin should be. What is left is the maximum allowable cost of producing the product. If a firm uses this method to decide on price, then increases in cost—due either to increases in the price of resources or decreases in demand—may show up first in a lessening of the quality of the product. For example, in the candy industry, the prices of candy bars have risen slowly, but candy bars have become smaller, to compensate for higher costs of production.

The problem of setting profit margins for different products, especially in a multiproduct firm (that is, a firm that produces a variety of products) is a complex one. Administered pricing, which is usually an effort to approximate profit maximization and to take into account the elasticity of demand, depends largely on the number of close substitutes available for a given product. For example, Alcoa, which produces a variety of products, varies its profit margin according to the degree of competition from other companies and other metals, that is, the elasticity of demand. The more inelastic the demand, the higher the profit margin. Also retail stores, in their effort to approximate profit-maximizing pricing, use cost-plus pricing as a rule of thumb.

Oligopoly Evaluated

On the whole, people criticize oligopolies for the same reasons they criticize pure monopolies. In an oligopoly, marginal revenue is less than average revenue (see Figure 21-2). Therefore, oligopolistic firms set their prices higher than, rather than equal to, marginal cost. As we have said, it is only when marginal cost and price are equal (as they are in purely competitive situations) that the economy is producing at optimum efficiency, that is, that resources are efficiently allocated to produce the combinations of output consumers will buy, given their tastes and incomes.

But in an oligopoly, there probably will be economic profits which some regard as unearned. These economic profits measure the degree to which a given firm can exploit its monopoly power. In a way, these "unearned" economic profits can be defined as the degree to which the consumer is being exploited.

Are costs higher in oligopolistic industries than in purely competitive ones? No one knows for sure. In many industries, technology is such that it takes a large operation to achieve economies of scale. In such industries, if enough firms entered the field to duplicate purely competitive conditions, each would be so small that it would not stand a chance of achieving most economies of scale. But are we really, in a practical sense, comparing oligopoly with pure competition? No, we are comparing fields in which there is little, if any, competition and fields in which there is a great deal of competition.

Chapter 20 discussed the size of the firm and its relationship to the rate of technological innovation. Some people, as you recall, argue that the present state of technology is such that it requires large research facilities and huge amounts of money to bring about innovations. Galbraith is one who takes this position, as an argument in favor of large-scale oligopolistic firms. Galbraith feels that oligopolies, in spite of their faults, foster improved technology because the larger the firm, the larger the amount spent for research, and thus the faster the development of technology.

Two other economists, J. D. Jewkes (see Suggested Readings at the end of this chapter) and Edwin Mansfield, take an opposing viewpoint. They argue as follows: (1) Medium-size and smaller firms (the smallest discussed is a thousand employees) have the highest proficiency in technological development. (2) During its early high-risk, low-cost phase, an invention is usually developed by smaller firms; then during the finishing, or low-risk, high-cost stage, it is taken over by larger firms. (For a fuller discussion of technology and size, reread Chapter 19.) So the more competition there is between firms in an oligopolistic industry, the lower the economic profit and the more urgent the drive toward technological innovation. The more firms, the greater the tendency toward price competition and away from nonproductive, nonprice competition.

Countervailing Power

In one of John Kenneth Galbraith's early books, *American Capitalism*, he introduced the concept of **countervailing power**, which he feels tends to minimize the abuses of oligopoly and monopoly situations. Galbraith says that there is monopoly power (some control over price) on both the sellers' and the buyers' sides of the market. Often, therefore, a monopolist or oligopolist deals with a monopsonistic or oligopsonistic buyer in the market. (**Monopsony** means only one buyer in the market. **Oligopsony** means a small number of buyers in the market.) These opposite forces negotiate the firm's output of a product, as well as its final price. Galbraith envisioned one firm with monopoly power forcing concessions from others, and in this way spreading out the gains from the exploitation of monopoly power. For example, a labor union, United Auto Workers, has enough power to force General Motors to share with the union, in the form of higher wages, some of its gains from the exercise of its monopoly power. Supermarket chains can force concessions from the large producers of processed foods. The government, which buys so much that it has enormous countervailing power, can obtain prices close to cost from the firms from which it buys (though the cost overruns in defense and other goods sold to the federal government lead one to be suspicious of the cost base against which the prices are set).

There are flaws in this argument, which you can probably see. The biggest flaw is that the general public—the consumer—has not been able to gain access to this grab bag of monopoly power. So the consumer ends up paying the price of monopoly power. Even the counterargument that business firms share their monopoly power with the public because of the countervailing power of labor unions fails because out of a labor force of more than 90 million and a population of about 215 million, only about 17 million people belong to labor unions.

The fact that oligopolistic and monopolistic firms get "unearned" economic profits from consumers by charging higher prices and by perpetrating the abuses of nonprice competition is a seriously inefficient element in the U.S. market system. (Several books stemming from Ralph Nader's consumer protection research lend powerful support to such a conclusion. One such book, *Corporate Power in America*, is edited by Nader and Green. In addition, Baran and Sweezy's book, *Monopoly Capitalism*, is a strong Marxist indictment of the structure of monopoly power in the U.S.)

SUMMING UP

1. The following are the characteristics of *oligopoly:* (a) There are so few firms in the industry that the actions of one firm affect the actions of all the others. (b) The product may be either homogeneous or differentiated. (c) There are substantial barriers to entry of new firms into the field.

2. *Interdependency* means that the actions of one firm affect the actions of other firms in the industry. Because of this interdependence, there are as many models of oligopoly behavior as there are theories about how firms react to the actions of others.

3. The *kinked-demand* model of oligopoly behavior is based on the assumption that firms follow each other in making a price decrease, but ignore a price increase. This difference causes a sharp kink or bend in the demand curve at the point that represents the prevailing price. Also, there is a vertical discontinuity in marginal revenue below the point that represents the prevailing price.

4. In the long run, because of barriers to entry, an oligopolistic firm is likely to make an economic profit, although it is possible that it will make only a normal profit. The exit of firms from the industry prevents the firm from suffering an economic loss.

5. In a kinked-demand model of oligopoly behavior, prices tend to be inflexible. (a) When one firm raises its price, other firms in the industry do not follow suit; demand is elastic and the initiating firm's revenue declines. (b) When one firm lowers its prices, other firms in the industry follow suit; demand is inelastic, and the firm's revenue declines. Furthermore, price wars may develop. (c) As witnessed by the discontinuity in the marginal-revenue curves, costs may vary and prices still remain the same.

6. A second model of oligopoly behavior is covert collusion, in which firms meet and set prices and market shares. This is illegal under the U.S. antitrust acts.

7. Another form of collusion is *price leadership,* in which one firm leads in setting prices and the other firms in the industry follow suit. The leader must be careful not to impose enough hardship on any firm to precipitate revolt.

8. Oligopolies that involve covert collusion and those that involve price leadership may approach a monopoly situation.

9. Since in an oligopoly price competition is infrequent, *nonprice competition*—including variations in styling, services, quality, and amounts of advertising of a given product—are widely practiced.

10. The following are arguments in favor of advertising: (a) Advertising can lead to increased demand for a product so that companies produce more of it, achieving economies of scale, so that the firm's production costs decrease more than its selling costs increase. This enables the firm to cut its prices. (b) Advertising conveys information consumers need in order to make intelligent choices. (c) Advertising pays for the media, either in whole or in part. (d) Advertising may convey messages beneficial to the public. (e) Advertising furthers product differentiation, thus giving the public greater variety.

11. The arguments against advertising are: (a) Much of advertising is nonproductive competitive-retaliatory advertising that does *not* create economies of scale. (b) A great deal of advertising does not impart information; in fact, sometimes it even disseminates misleading information. (c) The media's revenues from advertising are passed on to the consumer in the form of higher prices which the consumer must pay for

the product advertised; advertising also gives advertisers undue influence over the content of the media. (d) Advertisements may encourage unhealthful activities, such as consumption of tobacco and alcohol, and often present a demeaning or exploitative view of women.

12. Some theorists argue that not all firms strive to maximize their profits; these theorists give the following reasons for their contention: (a) Firms generally do not have enough data to compute their marginal revenue and marginal cost. (b) Firms may curb their drives for profit because they fear possible antitrust action. (c) Firms may elect not to maximize profits because they want to avoid adverse public opinion. (d) Firms may keep their profits lower than necessary to discourage new firms that might try to enter the industry. (e) Firms may give higher priorities to considerations such as increasing their shares of the market and volume of sales than to profit maximization. (f) The *technocrats* who control corporations have goals other than profit maximization. However, all these criticisms, rather than refuting the profit-maximization assumption, point up the difficulties of estimating and achieving it.

13. Some people feel that *administered pricing*, or the deciding on price by the administrative sections of a corporation, is necessary because most companies do not have enough data to compute their marginal revenue and marginal cost.

14. The market situation known as oligopoly is subject to the same criticisms as pure monopoly. People complain that, since for an oligopoly, marginal revenue is less than price, oligopolistic firms produce at less than optimum efficiency. The critics of oligopoly also say that consumers of products made by an oligopoly do not get the combination of output preferred, that oligopolists receive economic profits, that prices in an oligopoly are higher and output lower than in other market forms, and that excess capacity probably exists. Still under debate is the question of whether oligopolistic markets encourage innovation more than other kinds of markets do.

15. According to John Kenneth Galbraith's concept of *countervailing power*, a monopolistic firm on the selling side of the market often has to deal with a monopsonistic institution on the buying side of the market. In this way, gains resulting from the use of monopoly power are widely distributed. However, the largest group in the economy, the consumer, has no countervailing power.

QUESTIONS

1. Compare the role of advertising in monopolistic competition with the role of advertising in pure competition and pure monopoly.

2. What are the assumptions on which the kinked-demand oligopoly model is based? Draw a diagram of the model, showing a firm in profit-

maximizing equilibrium. Why is there a kink or bend in the demand curve and a discontinuity in the marginal-revenue curve?

3. Why are prices so inflexible in a kinked-demand oligopoly situation?

4. Why may the firms in an oligopolistic industry choose to collude on prices? Why will they follow a price leader? Are prices as inflexible in one situation as in another? Why or why not?

5. Compare economic performance in an oligopolistic market with that in a purely competitive one. Is oligopoly the best market structure for rapid technological development? Why or why not?

6. Do you think that advertising is beneficial to U.S. society as a whole? Give reasons for your opinions.

7. Do you think that the existence of countervailing power in oligopoly and pure monopoly neutralizes the exploitative aspect of monopoly power? Justify your conclusions.

8. You have just been appointed an economic adviser to the Antitrust Division of the Attorney General's office. Your first task is to present a position paper on the government's role in preventing the use of monopoly power. Write your own position on that question, remembering that (a) you are concerned with *government's* role in monopoly power, and (b) there are advantages and disadvantages that must be weighed. These have both economic and ethical implications. Be sure you explore both.

SUGGESTED READINGS

Bain, Joe S. *Essays on Price Theory and Industrial Organization.* Little, Brown, Boston, 1972.

Galbraith, John K. *American Capitalism.* Harvard University Press, Cambridge, 1956.

Galbraith, John K. *Economics and the Public Purpose.* Houghton Mifflin, Boston, 1973.

Jewkes, J., D. Sawyers, and R. Stillerman. *The Sources of Invention.* Macmillan, London, 1958.

Kefauver, Estes. *In the Hands of a Few.* Penguin, Baltimore, 1965.

Leftwich, Richard H. *The Price System and Resource Allocation.* Dryden, Hinsdale, Ill., 1970. Chapter 12.

Mansfield, Edwin. "Size of Firm, Market Structure and Innovation." *Journal of Political Economy,* 1963.

Means, Gardner C. "The Administered-Price Thesis Reconfirmed." *The American Economic Review,* June 1972.

Stigler, George J. "The Kinked Oligopoly Demand Curve and Rigid Prices." Reprinted in *Readings in Price Theory*. American Economic Association, Irwin, Homewood, Ill., 1952.

Stigler, George J. *The Theory of Price*, Macmillan, New York, 1952. Chapter 13.

Stonier, Alfred W., and Douglas C. Hague. *A Textbook of Economic Theory*. Wiley, New York, 1964. Chapter 9.

Weiss, Leonard W. *Economics and American Industry*. Wiley, New York, 1952.

Application 21

Oligopoly Behavior: Some Cases

What is the salient feature of the oligopoly-monopoly situation? The fact that the individual firm can pretty much determine what prices will be in the marketplace—at least as far as supply is concerned. This monopoly power—the ability to influence prices—takes a variety of forms. This application will illustrate some of them by citing actual cases of the exercise of monopoly power.

Case one takes a look at the drug industry and its use of patents and brand names, coupled with advertising. Case two deals with the bakery industry and its discrimination to eliminate local competition. Case three sheds light on the electrical-machinery industry and gives a specific example of covert collusion: the electrical-equipment price-fixing case in the mid-1960s.

Patents, Brand Names, and the Drug Industry

Here we shall be concerned only with the ethical-drug aspect of the industry; by *ethical drugs*, we mean drugs that can be sold only through a doctor's prescription. This creates a very unusual market situation: The person who orders a given drug (the doctor) does not pay for it, and the person who pays for it (the patient) does not order it. This relationship between doctor and prescription dominates the approach of the drug companies to their exercise of monopoly power. They aim their marketing activities at the doctor, not the patient.

The ethical-drug industry is divided into three submarkets. The first, and perhaps the best known, is patented drugs. Only a few large firms can afford the big expenditures for research, production, and advertising required in this field. These firms discover and patent new drugs. They also get, from foreign companies, exclusive licensing rights to produce drugs patented in other countries. So the market for a patented drug is purely monopolistic.

It was revealed in the early 1960s that the pricing of patented drugs bears little relationship to costs, either of production or of selling. Everybody had suspected this for a long time. What let the cat out of the bag was the testimony before a Senate committee investigating monopoly, which was headed by the late Senator Estes Kefauver. Drug companies admitted that a prime consideration in their pricing of a given drug is the value of the drug to the patient. In economics language, how inelastic is the demand for the drug? The drug firm considers this question when it sets its price. The more a person needs the drug to sustain life, the more inelastic the demand and the higher the price. In plain English, the drug firms charge what the traffic will bear.

Figure A21-1 shows two demand curves with their marginal revenue curves. Demand one (D_1) is more inelastic than demand two (D_2), indicating that the drug represented by D_1 is more a necessity (there are fewer substitutes) than the drug represented by D_2. With the same marginal cost, prices are higher for the drug with less-elastic demand (the drug that is more a necessity). This is a form of price discrimination.

Drug companies also use large amounts of advertising, for three reasons: (1) Doctors need information about the patented drug. (2) Drug companies want to condition doctors, through advertising, not to use lower-priced nonpatented drugs as substitutes, since a patient could not avoid buying the expensive patented drugs unless a doctor prescribed substitutes. (3) Drug companies want to condition the physicians to the brand name, not the generic or scientific name, of a given drug. Even long after a drug firm's patent has expired, physicians conditioned by years of advertising still prescribe the brand name, out of force of habit. Note that *all* this advertising is directed at the doctor, not the patient.

An example of the high prices of patented drugs is tetracycline, one of the antibiotics. In 1959, before the military medical supply agency responsible for bulk buying of drugs for the government asked for bids from Europe, tetracycline cost the average American 17 cents per tablet. By 1963, under pressure of foreign competition, drug firms had dropped their price to the government agency to 1.5 cents per tablet. In other words, drug firms were able to charge the government 1.5 cents per tablet, yet at the same time charge the public 17 cents a tablet.

Patent laws prevent the public from buying patented drugs in Europe. Yet in the early 1960s one-half to two-thirds of all prescriptions written were for drugs protected by patents. Thus, the consumer is trapped. A trend may be developing, however, to reduce this reliance of consumers on monopolistically priced brand-name drugs. For instance, in 1975, California enacted legislation permitting pharmacists to advertise drug prices and to substitute equivalent generic drugs for brand-name drugs prescribed (unless specifically forbidden by the physician writing the prescription). In 1976, the state went further and allowed the advertising of prescription-drug prices. In the absence of collusion between physicians and drug manufacturers, this may substantially reduce monopoly power in this industry.

A second submarket in the ethical-drug industry is nonpatented but brand-name prescription drugs. Here again, it is only the few large drug companies that can play the game. They need the size so that they can buy the advertising needed to establish the brand name in the doctor's mind. This is an oligopoly situation, with a differentiated product created and maintained by advertising.

There may be slight differences in quality between one brand of drug and another, but there is no price competition between competing brands. Almost all the competition is in the form of advertising. And because of this unique relationship between the doctor who orders the drug and patient who pays for it and uses it, all this advertising is directed at the doctor. In many ways, doctors are unusually susceptible to this advertising. Doctors are overworked and have trouble keeping up with the torrent of medical literature. Thus, they may take the easy way out by using the short, simple advertised brand name rather than the complex, rarely seen generic name. The pain killer, Darvon, is an example. Darvon is the brand name; its generic name is dextropropoxyphene.

FIGURE A21-1 Elasticity of Demand for Drugs

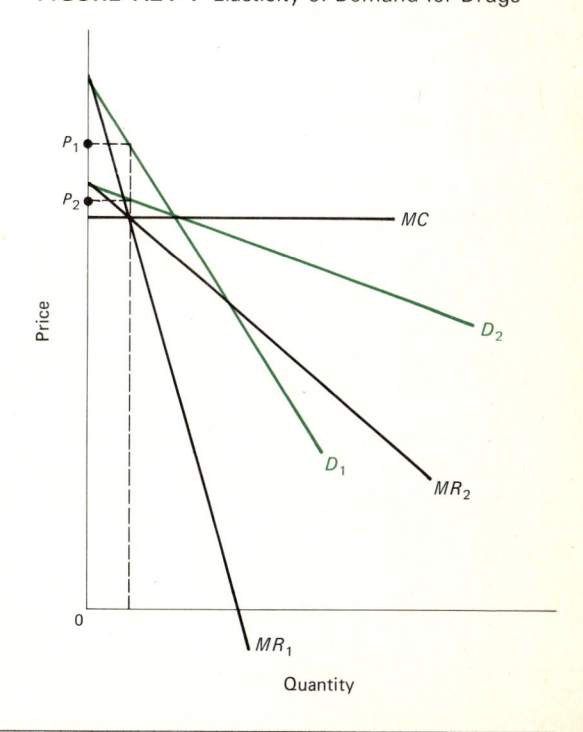

"Another thing, Hornby—stop referring to our product as a drug on the market."

Which name would *you* write on a prescription (especially if you had ten people waiting in your outer office)?

The third submarket in the ethical-drug industry consists of a flock of smaller-sized firms that bottle and sell drugs under their generic or scientific names. These small companies do not have the money needed to advertise enough to establish well-known brands of their own, so the competition among them is fierce. They sell their products mostly to institutions such as hospitals, clinics, and government agencies. These institutions—after decades of such buying for the contents rather than the brand name—find little difference between generic drugs and brand-name drugs. But though differences in quality are insignificant, differences in price are enormous. For example, in 1960 one could buy penicillin for half a cent per tablet if the doctor prescribed it by generic name, but it cost 20 cents per tablet if prescribed by brand name. During the same era, a patient paid $40 a thousand for tablets of the stimulant Dexadrene (a brand name), but if the doctor prescribed it under its generic name, it cost only $2 per thousand.

This difference in price is mainly due to the astronomical levels of profit of the drug companies. Senator Kefauver's committee investigated the finances of twenty-two drug companies in the early 1960s. The drug companies admitted that for each dollar of sales, 32 percent was cost of production, 25 percent was advertising cost, and only 6 percent was the cost of research and development. Profits amounted to a whopping 37 percent of sales. If the drug companies can advertise enough to convince the physician to prescribe their brand-name drugs, they earn enormous profits.

The fact is that the big drug companies in the United States use patents to create a monopoly. In turn, they use price discrimination through brand names in order to extract an economic profit from people who need the drugs to be healthy. These companies achieve their ends by aiming their brand-name advertising at the doctors, who order prescription drugs for their patients.

The Predatory Use of Monopoly Power: The Bakery Industry

In any market system, the existence of many firms in an industry stimulates competition and thus offers the greatest protection to the consuming public. Many companies are vying for the consumer's business, and this means competitive prices and constant improvements in the product. However, in many such industries, the small independent producer is being squeezed out by a few large firms, often because the big firms are able to exercise greater economic power, not because the little operator is inefficient. The bakery industry is an example. (The brewery industry has very similar conditions.) Once again, the late Senator Estes Kefauver's excellent book *In the Hands of a Few* gives us an insight into the exercise of monopoly power.

For many years, the wholesale bakery industry was a haven for the small firm. In 1958, there were 5,300 firms producing bread for the wholesale market, but the industry was becoming increasingly dominated by the large firms. The four largest bakery firms had a 22 percent slice of the market, and the eight largest a 37 percent slice. In the years since, the trend has been for the large firms to take more and more of the market, squeezing out the small producer.

This increase in share of the market by a few large firms is not due to superior production methods or greater efficiency on their part. Bigness does not mean technological advantage. In fact, most branch plants of large chain bakery firms are no larger than the plants of the independents, and many are smaller. Bread must be eaten soon after it is baked. Besides, shipping it any distance sharply increases the cost. Therefore, one must examine reasons other than production efficiency to find out why these large firms dominate the market.

The problem can be approached from another direction: barriers to entry. In the bakery industry, these barriers, from the point of view of scale requirements, are weak. A plant of efficient size does not require a large capital investment. The barriers lie in other areas: advertising and predatory pricing policies. Because of low-scale barriers, the larger firms engaged in active exercise of monopoly power are continually faced with actual or potential competition.

The large firms have expanded at the expense of the single-plant independents because they can exploit their economic power: They have the advantage of multiplant, multimarket operations. The single-plant, single-market bakers must meet all competition in the one market that provides all its profits, but the megabakery firm can create safe and profitable markets in which there is nonprice competition. The big firm can act vigorously to undercut the little independent firm struggling in its small, single market. When a big firm strikes a market in which there are no independents, it can peg its prices high, and make large profits. Then, in markets that do have small independents, the big firms can afford to cut their prices. It is no wonder that the little independents, up against this competition, find it difficult to survive.

Therefore, in the wholesale bakery industry, there are two types of markets:

1. *Markets in which there is nonprice competition.* These markets are mostly in large cities, in which big firms fight to grab the business, but hardly ever engage in price competition. There may be a kinked-demand situation, which means inflexible prices. Only under rare conditions is there a price war, but there's generally some form of price leadership.

2. *Markets in which a large firm sets up shop in a new market area containing small, single-plant firms.* The competition is vigorous, and often unfair and destructive. It is hard for the little independent to compete, not because it is inefficient, but because the large firm unfairly exercises price discrimination, which it is able to do because of

The bakery industry at the consumer's level (Ann Leyhe)

the distance between the low-price and the high-price markets. For example, a consumer will not travel from the high-price market in Philadelphia to the low-price market in Allentown just to save 10 cents on a loaf of bread.

Kefauver cites a variety of other ways in which the large multimarket bakery can discriminate. Here are some of them:

1. When a branch of a big firm is servicing a market in which competition is strong—that is, in which independent single-plant firms are operating—the branch plant charges lower prices than its competitors.

2. A single plant of a large baker sends its bread trucks out on a number of routes. They may charge different prices for bread on different routes. Surprisingly, they charge consumers who live close to the plant in urban areas generally higher prices than they charge consumers who live in the suburbs. Kefauver found that the lower-price routes were correlated with the presence of independent, one-plant firms. Differences in cost could not account for the differences in price. If anything, transporting the bread further increased the cost per loaf.

3. Another form of competition that is a low blow to the independents is "stales clobbering." Retail stores return their unsold bread to the bakery that made it. Naturally, bakeries try to keep these returns to a minimum. However, customers in a retail store tend to buy bread from the highest pile on a shelf. The giant bakery firm puts huge piles of bread on the grocers' shelves—much larger amounts than they expect to sell. The consumer, plucks a loaf from the big pile, leaving the smaller pile of the independent baker to grow stale, and reducing the small baker's sales. If the independent tries to fight back by increasing the piles of *its* bread, it only increases the amount of unsold bread that will be returned to it.

4. The branch of the large firm has enough resources behind it to give larger discounts to retail stores than the small independents do.

5. Promotional allowances to grocery stores by the large chain bakeries can offer damaging competition to independents. Some of these allowances are for legitimate promotional activities, but others are really only another form of discount or kickback offered to the retail store.

Large chain bakeries try to justify these practices by saying that they are just meeting the competition in a given market. In economics, this means that increased competition increases the elasticity of demand to the large firm. The large firm price-discriminates in order to maximize its profits by making its marginal revenue equal its marginal cost. This means higher prices in the less elastic markets (urban nonprice-competitive markets); in Figure A21-1, D_1 and P_1. And it means lower prices in the more elastic markets (nonurban competitive markets that nourish single-plant independents); in Figure A21-1, D_2 and P_2. The single-plant independents say that they can meet any competition based on relative productivity. But the fact that multimarket chain bakeries can make their profits in markets in which there is no price competition, while at the same time undercutting the independents in their single-market area, puts a heavy burden on the independents.

Covert Collusion: The Case of the Electrical-Equipment Manufacturers

In 1961 a major scandal rocked the business world, especially the electrical-equipment industry. Executives from all the firms in the industry were convicted of violating the Sherman Antitrust Act by conspiring to fix prices, shares of the market, and other aspects of the industry. These executives, the *Wall Street Journal* pointed out, were not criminals; they were respected members of their communities. But white-collar criminals are often members of the power structure. Why did they commit such a violation of the law? And how did they do it?

The stimulus of World War II and the Korean War caused the electrical equipment industry to build up a lot of excess capacity. At the same time, price competition was fierce, degenerating at times into price wars. This was especially true in 1955, the year of the so-called "white sale," when prices were cut by up to 50 percent. This happened again to a lesser extent in 1957. Profits dropped; some firms even suffered losses.

Since orders for electrical equipment, when they came along, were mostly large, the industry suffered from a feast-or-famine market. Individual orders were crucial to small firms struggling for survival, and there was great instability in the industry as a whole. The threat of bankruptcy hung constantly over the smaller firms.

The result of the white sale of 1955 was that General Electric and Westinghouse—the two biggest firms—gained an even larger share of the market. Some of the smaller firms complained to the antitrust division of the Justice Department, and there was talk of a possible antitrust suit by the government against GE and Westinghouse. Ironically, this very threat of antitrust action caused GE and Westinghouse to try to stabilize the markets to protect the smaller firms.

Executives are always under pressure to produce more and more; that is, to make profits for their corporations. In the highly competitive world of electrical equipment, the executives realized they could do this by reducing the intensity of the competition. With the firms' excess capacities and large fixed costs, and with the complexity of the industry and the prevalence of the custom of making firms submit sealed bids, price leadership was simply not practical. The only alternative seemed to be collusion: the under-the-table agreement.

The motives behind this secret agreement to fix prices included the following:

1. To stabilize the market by reducing the competition that was causing losses.

2. To fix prices so as to raise the overall level of profits to all companies.

3. To avoid antitrust action by guaranteeing shares of the market to all firms at prices profitable to the smaller firms.

The *Wall Street Journal*, in January of 1962, said that the social environment of the executives involved in the conspiracy helped explain why the conspiracy came into being. The executives of all these companies came out of the same kinds of colleges and had the same work experience. They were all engineers who, at some point on their way up the corporate ladder, left practical engineering for sales. All had worked in more than one firm in the industry, and the larger corporations (especially General Electric and Westinghouse) provided executives for the smaller ones. They all thought alike, knew each other, and were typical organization men. During their professional meetings, they began to discuss their problems: How to stabilize the market by eliminating competition?

Thus was the conspiracy born. These men undoubtedly knew that what they were doing was illegal, but they also undoubtedly did not consider it immoral. Their problem was not simply to meet and fix prices; it was more complicated. They had to set up shares of the market, and make up a system of rotation on sealed bids, so that one company would be the low bidder at one time, another at another time, and so forth. The complexities of the market required that they construct a regular bureaucracy to carry out the conspiracy in the various kinds of equipment markets. All this meant frequent meetings, consultations, and memos. No wonder the Justice Department uncovered the conspiracy!

There is evidence that the bureaucracy had a hard time keeping the conspirators in line as to prices. Collusive agreements are inherently unstable because of the attractiveness of cheating. Some firms seemed to have joined the conspiracy more for the purpose of snooping and finding out what the others' prices were going to be than of cooperating with the other firms. Since collusion is illegal, violation of the collusive agreements could not be enforced. When there is gang rule, any miscreant company can defy the illegal organization.

Violations of the ground rules about shares of markets were less of a problem. However, the bosses had to work out complex systems of sharing the market, dividing the market as to different kinds of equipment and also as to different sections of the country. Sometimes firms balked at the system, and so the executives had to work out new methods of dividing the market. At one point, they had to rework their figures on shares entirely in order to account for the entry of a new firm into the conspiracy.

All in all, the problems of setting up and operating the collusive conspiracy were difficult, complex, and cumbersome. The need for secrecy and the clear illegality of the conspiracy obviously added difficulties, both administrative and psychological. However, the fact that the conspiracy was formed and did function for more than four years, even in the face of all these difficulties, shows just how great may be the aversion of corporate executives to a competitive situation.

SUMMING UP

1. This application considers three industries in which certain companies exercise monopoly power: drugs, bakeries, and electrical equipment.

2. In the ethical-drug industry, a unique situation affects the exercise of monopoly power. The doctor orders the drugs, while the patient uses the drugs and pays for them. Thus, all advertising for ethical drugs is aimed at the doctor, not the patient.

3. There are three submarkets in the ethical-drug industry:
   a. *Patented drugs.* These are sold in a pure-monopoly market, in which profit maximization underlies pricing policies. Drug companies advertise heavily, so that doctors will keep on prescribing drugs by brand names, not by generic names.
   b. *Brand-name drugs.* This is an oligopolistic market in which brand-name drugs are the differentiated products. Companies spend huge sums in order to condition the physician to prescribe the brand names, not generic names.
   c. *Drugs sold under generic or scientific names.* Small companies that bottle and sell drugs under their generic names offer the only competition to the oligopolistic market of brand-name drugs. These companies compete fiercely, and the product they produce is essentially a homogeneous one.

4. The wholesale bakery industry is gradually becoming concentrated in the hands of a few giant bakery chains. The basic device these large firms use is price discrimination between one market area and another. The big multiplant, multimarket firm little by little drives the small single-plant, single-market firm out of business by selling its bread for a lower price in the market serviced by the single-plant, single-market firm. The big company is able to maintain its overall level of profits by charging a higher price in its other markets.

5. This price discrimination according to markets places the single-plant, single-market firm at a serious competitive disadvantage—not because of any lack of productivity, but because of its small size.

6. The 1961 case of price fixing by the manufacturers of electrical equipment is an example of covert collusion on prices, shares of the market, and other economic aspects of an industry. The electrical-equipment manufacturers needed covertly collusive agreements because the sealed-bid system of pricing made price leadership impossible.

7. The chief motives for price fixing were (a) to stabilize the market by eliminating the competition that was causing losses, (b) to fix prices so as to raise the overall level of profits, and (c) to avoid possible antitrust action by guaranteeing shares of the market to all firms at prices profitable to the smaller firms.

8. The executives involved were all organization men from similar backgrounds. They knew that what they were doing was illegal, but they apparently did not consider it immoral.

QUESTIONS

1. Of the three cases of the use of monopoly power discussed here, which industries used price discrimination? How did it work?

2. How was advertising used in each case?

3. Was the consumer hurt by the exercise of monopoly power in each case? If so, how?

4. From your own knowledge, sketch at least one more example of the exercise of monopoly power, using the three cases as models.

SUGGESTED READINGS

"The Drug Industry's Clouded Future." *Business Week*, November 23, 1974.

Ehrenreich, Barbara, and John Ehrenreich. *The American Health Empire*. Vintage, New York, 1971.

Kefauver, Estes. *In the Hands of a Few*. Penguin Books, Baltimore, 1965.

Kessel, Reuben A. "Price Discrimination in Medicine." Reprinted in *The Daily Economist*, edited by Harry G. Johnson and Burton A. Weisbrod. Prentice-Hall, Englewood Cliffs, N.J., 1973.

Sampson, Anthony. *The Sovereign State of ITT*. Fawcett, Greenwich, Conn., 1973.

Wall Street Journal, January 10 and January 12, 1962.

Weiss, Leonard W. *Economics and American Industry*. Wiley, New York, 1961.

Application 22

The Military-Industrial Complex: Myth or Reality?

Ten Propositions About the Military-Industrial Complex

Perhaps the most vocal critic and innovative analyst of what President Eisenhower called the military-industrial complex is Seymour Melman, professor of industrial management at Columbia University. Melman assembled some of his own writings and those of others in a book called *The War Economy of the United States*, which supports a startling analysis of the relationship between the defense establishment and the firms producing materials for that establishment. One important reason for reviewing Melman's book in this application is that this viewpoint is rarely mentioned in texts on the principles of economics. It is a view that deserves a wider audience. This application will explore the book's startling and provocative premises. Melman sums up the analysis by stating ten propositions:

Proposition 1. The military-industrial firm is not autonomous.
Proposition 2. The military-industrial firm is controlled by a state management.
Proposition 3. The military-industrial firm does not minimize cost.
Proposition 4. The military-industrial firm is not a profit-maximizing entity.
Proposition 5. The state management is a new concentration of industrial control.
Proposition 6. Gross national product is composed of productive and parasitic growth.
Proposition 7. Economically parasitic output produces price inflation.
Proposition 8. Foreign military spending endangers the value of the dollar.
Proposition 9. The cost of the military system entails a large opportunity cost for American society.
Proposition 10. The military-industrial firms, as a group, lack flexibility for conversion to civilian work.

Melman's book is 242 pages long, and our discussion here must be brief. But we will try to include the most important points.

The Military-Industrial Firm: Is It a Free-Enterprise Firm?

Propositions 1 through 4 are most interesting, especially when we view them in relation to our theory of the firm (Chapters 18-21). What these propositions are saying is that the military-industrial firm does not conform to the usual picture of the firm. The military-industrial firms are special, and must be viewed from a different perspective. One writer, John F. Gorgol, feels that one should not even view them as free-enterprise firms, for the following reasons:

1. The military-industrial firm deals with a monopsonistic buyer (remember a monopsony is a market situation in which the products or services are bought by only one buyer). That buyer is the government. There is no other source of demand. Therefore, the military-industrial firm has lost its independence; it is dependent on the demand, in terms of both quantity and composition, of the Department of Defense.

2. The monopsonistic buyer, the Department of Defense, in effect controls the major decision-making processes of the military-industrial firm.

In 1961 Secretary McNamara established under the Secretary of Defense an administrative office that coordinates procurement by all branches of the service. This office, acting through the Armed Services Procurement Regulations, controls most areas that one would consider the decision-making prerogatives of a free-enterprise firm. The regulations (plus specific contracts) prescribe what is to be produced, state standards of product acceptability, answer questions about subcontracting, define how goods are to be produced and in what quantities, and give details of distribution, prices, working capital requirements, and investment in plant and research.

You can see that these regulations, plus the specific contract and the auditing procedures, usurp broad areas of decision making from the military-industrial firm's management. In Melman's view, the military-industrial firm becomes

"Straighten up there, soldier, and try to look like part of the military-industrial complex."

a branch plant, so to speak, of the Department of Defense.

3. The military-industrial firm is not concerned with minimizing cost. Since the Department of Defense controls so much of decision making, the firm's management may have neither the ability nor the incentive to minimize costs. The absence of competition, plus the cost-plus price system, does away with a firm's incentives to cut costs.

4. The military-industrial firm is not a profit-maximizing firm; it has no control over its price. The Department of Defense, either by negotiating the price with the firm or by agreeing to a cost-plus price, sets the price. The Department of Defense views the profit part of the price as simply part of its cost. At no point does the military-industrial firm have enough control to vary its decisions as to output, quality, cost, or price; so how is it going to maximize profits?

Proposition 5, in effect, summarizes all this. Since 1961 the Department of Defense, by authorizing and coordinating procurement, has gained control over a vast economic empire. Within this economic empire, corporations, though nominally privately owned, are coordinated much like branch plants or divisions of a giant corporation. Melman and his associates maintain that it is not the military-industrial firms that control the Pentagon, as some maintain, but rather the Pentagon that controls the military-industrial firms. Melman says:

> By 1968 the Department of Defense industrial system supplied $44 billion of goods and services. This exceeded the combined net sales (in billions) of General Motors ($22.8), General Electric ($8.4), U.S. Steel ($4.6), and DuPont ($3.4). Altogether, this constitutes a form of state capitalism operating under the Department of Defense—hence the designation "Pentagon capitalism."

Growth: Is It Parasitic or Productive?

In proposition 6, Melman defines "parasitic growth" as output that neither contributes to consumption nor increases capital. Significantly, he leaves out military production altogether; it does not fall in either category, he feels. *His critics argue that military production does provide a service: defense or military security.*

Proposition 7 says that parasitic output contributes to inflation because it provides neither a good for consumers to buy nor capital to bring about increased capacity. It uses up resources that are "wasted," and therefore reduces effective supply, which leads to inflation.

In evaluating this position, let us bear in mind that if the government gets the purchasing power to produce these goods by expanding federal debt or by increasing the supply of money, it *is* inflationary to produce them. However, if the government uses taxes to buy them, or if the new expansion of federal debt transfers purchasing power that would otherwise have been used for either consumption or the creation of new capital, producing these goods is not inflationary. Furthermore, military expenditures can be inflationary only under conditions of full or near-full employment.

Proposition 8 blames military spending outside the United States for much of our balance-of-payments problem and for the gradual depreciation of the dollar versus foreign currencies. (The dollar was devalued twice in the early 1970s. In December 1971 it was devalued by 8.5 percent and in February 1973 by 10 percent—a total of 18.5 percent devaluation in fourteen months.) One cannot deny that maintaining peace-keeping troops on foreign soil is expensive.

Since 1950, our foreign military expenditures—principally in Japan, Southeast Asia, and West Germany—have put an average of about $2 billion a year into foreign hands.

The opportunity cost of our military system (proposition 9) is indeed large, from two points of view. First, we could have used the enormous resources eaten up by the military machine to produce consumer goods or capital to expand capacity. For example, about 8 percent to 9 percent of the labor force is directly involved in the military-industrial complex. (How much better off everyone would be if they were working to build houses, schools, or hospitals.) Second, the military-industrial firms use a large proportion of our engineers and scientists—more than half of our technical research talent. At times we have had a shortage of these skilled people for civilian production, and this has slowed our rate of technological progress and productivity.

The opportunity cost of military expenditures is indeed high. The question is whether the services, in terms of increased security, are worth the cost. Can one reduce the expenditures without reducing the services rendered? The answer to this question lies outside the field of economics.

Melman's proposition 10 deals with the flexibility of the military-industrial firms. He says that they "lack the flexibility for conversion to civilian work." The people who manage the military-industrial firms lack the training and experience to switch over to producing goods and services for the public. They do not know how to compete in the market and lack the cost consciousness they would need to be succesful outside the Department of Defense's market.

Some Conclusions

Our presentation has of necessity been brief—too brief to explore the many complexities of the arguments of Melman and his associates, or to criticize their position. We have outlined only some of their more provocative arguments, enough to set you thinking about the effect of our military expenditures on the American economy.

Melman and his colleagues deny that the military-industrial firms use political influence to determine the actions of the Department of Defense. They say that the Department of Defense controls the military-industrial firms and that it has created a huge industrial empire to feed the Department of Defense managers' needs. However, some people see the reverse relationship and claim that the lobbying done by defense suppliers and the hiring and rehiring of Department of Defense managers and former executives by defense firms are too coincidental not to be suspicious. If Melman is right and the Department of Defense has created and is controlling a vast industrial complex of unheard-of proportions, then the political implications of such power are at least as serious as the economic. Policy alternatives would have to begin with breaking these relations. And, as a first step, a complete overhaul of the managerial structure of the Department of Defense itself would be required.

QUESTIONS

1. Who controls whom? Do the military-industrial firms control the Department of Defense, or vice versa?

2. Leaving aside the question of the need for national defense, is the existence of the military-industrial complex a benefit to the American economy? Why, or why not?

SUGGESTED READINGS

Mansfield, Edwin, ed. *Defense, Science, and Public Policy.* Norton, New York, 1968.

Melman, Seymour. *Our Depleted Society.* Dell, New York, 1965.

Melman, Seymour. *The Peace Race.* Ballantine and George Braziller, New York, 1962.

Melman, Seymour. *Pentagon Capitalism.* McGraw-Hill, New York, 1970.

Melman, Seymour, ed. *The War Economy of the United States.* St. Martin's, New York, 1971.

22

The Factor Markets: Not Only Products Are Sold

Chapters 18 through 21 discussed the way *product* markets operate—in categories from pure competition to pure monopoly. We said that prices of resources and productivity of resources are the two things that determine costs of production, and therefore the supply of products. In this chapter and in Chapter 23, we will show how *factor* markets work, how the prices of factors, that is, resources such as wages for labor and interest payments on capital, are established. You should then have a complete picture of the operation of the market system.

What Are Factor Markets?

Picture the many boards of directors of companies across the length and breadth of the United States. Imagine them sitting in boardrooms, making decisions about how much to invest and about how much steel, how many refrigerators, how many tons of bananas or vats of wine or thousands of shoes they will produce next year. These people—few in number, relatively speaking—determine the U.S. output of goods and services. They govern the supply side of product markets. Each adult, on the other hand, participates in the **factor markets**, those markets in which the prices of resources—labor, capital, land, and entrepreneurship—are set. Indeed, all market incomes are derived from these factor markets.

Most people get "income" from wages or salaries. Others—a growing number—get income from interest, rents, or profits. The entire market incomes of a society are made up of these four kinds of payments. Of course, market incomes are not the only income sources in a society. Government transfer payments (unemployment compensation, food stamps, and so on) supplement these market incomes.

The factor markets: Workers as factors of production (UPI)

Factors: Supply and Demand

The prices of factors, like the prices of products, are determined by supply and demand. If you have a firm grasp of these concepts from earlier chapters, this section will be easier for you. We are not going to simply repeat the analysis, however, because there are important differences between supply and demand in the product market and supply and demand in the factor market. In this chapter, we are going to concentrate on the *demand* for factors of production. In Chapter 23, we will examine the *supply* and pricing of factors.

What Determines the Demand for Factors?

Demand for a product depends on the utility or satisfaction people expect to get from it. Demand for a factor, however, is an indirect or **derived demand**. That is, it is derived from the expected demand for a given product that the factor produces. You buy a new car because of the satisfaction you will get from it. The Ford Motor Company builds a new assembly plant, not because its officers derive satisfaction from looking at it, but because they have certain expectations about the demand for new cars that this plant can help to satisfy.

Three things determine the demand for any factor of production and can shift the demand curve for it. Only a change in the *price* of a factor can cause a change in the *quantity demanded*. However, a change in any of three determinants will change the demand for the factor.

1. *The amount of product demanded.* Suppose that Americans' demand for cars increases. Then the demand for steel, aluminum, rubber, and labor time of automobile workers will increase. So will the demand for many other things that are used in automobile production. This also works in reverse. For example, some years ago, the Roman Catholic Church in the United States relaxed its ban on eating meat on Friday. The result was a decrease in the demand for fish (with a corresponding increased demand for meat). This meant a decreased derived demand for the labor of fishermen, for fishing boats and equipment, and for all factors used to harvest and process fish.

2. *The productivity of resources.* People who are running businesses hire the most productive resources (factors) they can and combine them in the most productive ways they can. The most productive resources are the "first hired and the last fired." And as a resource's productivity increases, so does the demand for it. Many things influence the productivity of a resource: (a) the productivity of other resources ("This machine makes it possible for me to turn out twenty times what I used to by hand"); (b) technology ("This *new* machine is a lot faster than the old one"); (c) managerial ability ("Our new boss sure knows how to get the work out"); and (d) the skills and innate abilities of labor.

3. *The prices of other factors of production.* Let's assume that firms seek to maximize profits. To do this, they try to produce their product at the least possible cost and at the most profitable rate. Therefore, in combining resources, they must consider not only relative productivity of factors but also relative prices of factors. Much of the amazing development of technology in the United States is due to the efforts of American businesses to find new machines and capital-intensive processes that will reduce the unit costs of production. This has bad as well as good features. A lot of what is called *technological unemployment* (the displacement of labor by capital) can be blamed on the relatively faster increase in the cost of wages (because of pressure by unions and minimum wage laws) than in the cost of capital.

An Example of Factor Demand

The Universal Study Guide Company is a profit-maximizing firm. For simplicity, let's say that it is a pure competitor in both its product market and its factor market. This means that it is unable to influence either the price of study guides (those all-purpose study aids for college students) or of labor (the variable factor used in producing the guides).

How many workers will Universal Study Guide hire? It will maximize its profits by producing up to the point at which marginal revenue equals marginal cost. We have assumed that labor is the firm's only variable cost. Thus it will hire workers up to the point at which laborers will no longer add to its profits. (In other words, at some point more workers will begin to add more to the firm's cost than to its revenue.) To establish this point, we must introduce a new concept: **marginal revenue product** *(MRP)*, which is the change in total revenue associated with a change in the use of the variable input. Table 22-1 gives numbers to show the importance of *MRP* to the Universal Study Guide.

TABLE 22-1 Demand for a Resource (Labor) by Universal Study Guide Company in a Purely Competitive Market

1	2	3	4	5	6
Units of variable resource (labor = L)	Total product (TP = output per day in thousands)	Marginal physical product ($MPP_L = \Delta TP/\Delta L$)	Product price (P)	Total revenue (TR = TP × P)	Marginal revenue product (MRP = VMP = $MPP_L \times P$)
0	0		$2	$ 0	
		30			$60
1	30		2	60	
		27			54
2	57		2	114	
		24			48
3	81		2	162	
		20			40
4	101		2	202	
		18			36
5	119		2	238	
		15			30
6	134		2	268	
		12			24
7	146		2	292	
		10			20
8	156		2	312	
		8			16
9	164		2	328	
		5			10
10	169		2	338	
		0			0
11	169		2	338	

Column 1 of Table 22-1 shows units of labor (L) hired to produce study guides. These workers represent successive equal units of labor. Thus, they enable us to observe the operation of the **law of variable proportions** (or diminishing marginal productivity). As a firm uses successive equal increments of a variable input in conjunction with a fixed input (or inputs), beyond some point the additions to output attributable to the variable input will diminish.

Column 2 shows total product (TP). It shows the way output increases through the tenth unit. Up to that point, each additional unit of labor produces some added product. The eleventh unit of labor, however, does not produce anything. Perhaps, the worker must wait to use a machine. Note, though, that the diminishing output is not the "fault" of the last worker, nor is it the result of a decrease in the quality of that input; it is caused by the *combination* of inputs, fixed and variable alike.)

Column 3 represents the **marginal physical product (MPP_L)**. This is the addition to the output of study guides on the part of the last unit of labor. You can see that MPP_L keeps decreasing until, finally, when Universal Study Guide hires the eleventh unit of labor, MPP_L reaches zero. Perhaps this result was not immediate. Initially, the MPP might have increased, or at least remained constant. But finally, it goes toward zero.

Column 4 shows that Universal Study Guide accepts a competitive study guide price of $2. This is the price at which the firm can sell all the guides it produces with the labor it hires. Total revenue (column 5) is the product of price (column 4) times output (column 2). Total revenue rises along with output. It also reaches a maximum when total product does. This happens when the tenth unit of labor is hired. Marginal revenue product (MRP) is the addition that each extra unit of a resource (labor, in this case) makes to total revenue. You can see that MRP keeps getting less and less for Universal Study Guide, as it hires more and more workers. It follows that if the firm faces a price of its product that is constant due to competition and has a constantly decreasing MPP it is bound to have a diminishing MRP. MRP is the same here as value of marginal product (MPP × price of study guides), since the marginal revenue of study guides is the same as their price.

How much labor will Universal Study Guide hire? Table 22-1 does not give this information. One can assume that the firm will hire whatever amount of labor is most profitable. The profitability of labor is determined by the relation between what labor adds to the firm's *cost* and what it adds to the firm's revenues. To figure profit on the use of labor, therefore, cost (price paid to labor times amount hired) is subtracted from revenue (price of product times output produced). Remember that we are assuming a simple marketplace in which Universal Study Guide both hires labor competitively and sells its product competitively. So not only is there a constant price ($2) for study guides, but there is also a constant wage for labor (not determined by Universal Study Guide).

Chapter 23 will look into the intricacies of wage determination. For now, suppose that Universal Study Guide can hire all the workers it wants to—all that it can profitably employ—at the going wage. (We will not yet take into account unions, minimum wage laws, company towns, and such considerations.) We will first examine a simple, purely competitive market process, and then add real-world complications.

Figure 22-1 shows the market process with the marginal revenue productivity of labor (MRP_L) plotted from the data in Table 22-1. Remember that every time Universal Study Guide hires an additional laborer, MRP_L declines because of diminishing marginal physical productivity. Since the firm sells study guides competitively, this is a special case of MRP.

In the special competitive case, marginal revenue productivity ($MPP \times MR$) is the same as **value of marginal product** ($VMP = MPP \times P$): what each additional unit of the resource (labor) contributes to the output of the firm, in dollars. This is true because under competitive market conditions $P = MR$. In other words, study guides sell for $2 apiece no matter how many of them the firm makes. Later on, we will make Universal Study Guide a noncompetitive firm to see what happens when price is less than marginal revenue. To review the changes that occur in a firm's product market when there is no pure competition, reread Chapter 19.

The Universal Study Guide Company has the $MRP_L = VMP_L$ of Figure 22-1. How much labor will it hire? Well, that depends on the price of labor (P_L). Let's suppose that the going wage for study guide workers is $30 per day. This constant wage is also the marginal cost of labor (MC_L), or the **marginal resource cost** of labor (MRC_L), which is what it costs to hire one more unit of the resource, labor, shown by the dashed line $MC_L = MRC_L = P_L = S_L$ (marginal cost of labor equals marginal resource cost of labor equals price of labor equals supply of labor).

The most profitable number of workers to hire is six, because the sixth worker hired adds the same to revenue as to cost, $30 to each. Universal Study Guide will hire the sixth unit of labor and no more. If it hired fewer workers than this, it would be giving up some profits; if it hired more than this, its profits would begin to decrease.

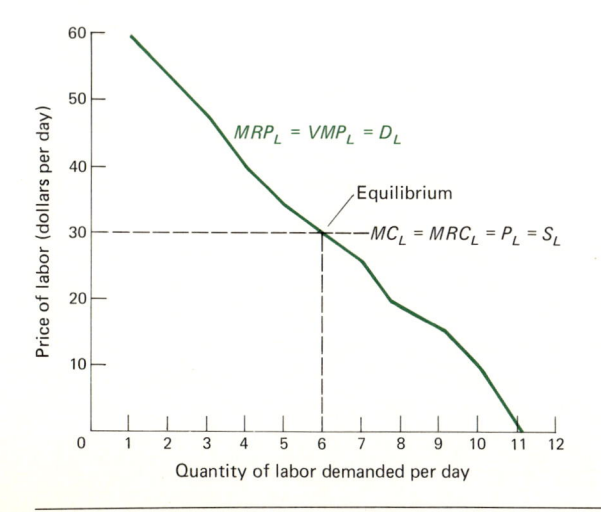

FIGURE 22-1 The Equilibrium Demand for Labor by the Universal Study Guide Company in a Purely Competitive Market

An Example of Factor Demand

Again, you have encountered the old law of supply and demand. MRP_L or VMP_L, once the marginal physical productivity of labor declines, is the competitive firm's demand curve for labor. And MC_L (MRC_L) is the competitive firm's perfectly elastic supply curve for labor. Supply and demand are equal at the equilibrium point—where there is neither excess demand nor excess supply.

To Maximize Profit, Minimize Cost

In Chapters 16 and 17, we examined business firms' average- and marginal-cost curves. Yet how do we know that those are the firms' costs? We assume that Universal Study Guide will make every effort to maximize profits. Therefore, it combines its resources in such a way that *cost is minimized,* for any rate of output. Since profit is total revenue minus total cost, the firm will wish to produce any output with the least cost.

Here's a general rule about minimizing cost: Resources are combined at least cost when a dollar spent on one input yields the same amount of output as a dollar spent on any other input.

Suppose that Universal Study Guide, for example, has two variable inputs—labor (L) and capital (K). The firm decides to juggle the ratios of these two inputs and see what happens. So it spends a dollar less on capital, which means that it has to give up ten guides ($MPP_K = 10$). It takes that extra dollar and spends it on labor. This leads to a gain of twelve guides ($MPP_L = 12$). So its net gain is two study guides. In this trial-and-error way, the firm keeps on juggling, until it establishes the following equilibrium (least-cost) relationship:

$$\frac{MPP_K}{P_K} = \frac{MPP_L}{P_L}.$$

This stack of letters says that the marginal physical *product* of capital divided by the *price* of capital is equal to the marginal physical *product* of labor divided by the *price* of labor. This is just a restatement of the general rule about minimizing cost, and it applies to points on the curves that show a firm's average and marginal cost. (Remember that the rate of output that is profit maximizing also requires that $MRC = MRP$.)

Demand for a Resource by the Market as a Whole

You have seen that the competitive firm's demand for an input is the same as the marginal revenue product of that input, or the value of marginal product. You can find out the demand for the whole industry by adding the demand of each firm at each likely price. But you can do this only so long as there are no **resource externalities**, changes in *costs* of resources that are not attributable to the actions of a single firm.

Suppose that the wage rate of labor used in producing study guides falls from $30 to $26 a day (a whole class graduates with study-guide-making skills and depresses the wage). Table 22-1 suggests that Universal Study Guide will take advantage of cheaper labor and hire one more laborer at the new wage rate (to make $MRP = MRC = \$26$). Now suppose, however, that *every* study guide manufacturer acts on the new wage rate, and starts to hire more labor. The *entire* guide industry may not hire labor competitively. If so, the industry's wage rate is bid up (an increasing-cost industry). The higher wage causes guide makers' marginal resource cost to rise. This reduces the equilibrium quantity of labor each firm demands. So to find out how much labor the industry demands, we add the equilibrium quantities of labor demanded by all these firms after the externalities are incorporated. The world is not a simple place even for a firm operating in a purely competitive market.

Elasticity of Demand for a Resource

The **elasticity of resource demand** is the rate at which the quantity of a resource demanded changes as the price of the resource changes. (You can remember this definition if you connect *elasticity* to the amount of *stretch*, or change.)

Imagine that you are president of Universal Study Guide, and you must watch the prices of all the factors closely, so you can juggle your production schedule to maximize profits. The elasticity of your demand for one of these factors—labor—as the wage rate changes is determined, basically, by four things:

1. *The rate at which the* MPP *of the factor (labor) declines.* The amount of this marginal physical product depends on the technology of the production process. The less rapidly labor's *MPP* decreases as Universal Study Guide adds labor, the less elastic the firm's demand for labor.

2. *The price elasticity of demand for the final product (guides).* Since the demand for this resource is a derived demand, if a small change in product price causes a large change in quantity demanded (if the price elasticity of demand for the final product is large), there will be a large change in the quantity of labor hired to produce study guides. In general, then, the greater the price elasticity of demand for the final product produced by the input, the greater its resource elasticity of demand (the two elasticities are positively related).

3. *The proportion of the total cost of production represented by the factor.* Suppose labor costs make up 70 percent of the cost of producing guides. And say the guide makers' union demands a 5 percent wage increase. If Universal Study Guide grants this increase, it will increase the firm's average and marginal cost. So the firm will reduce the quantity it produces, which will cut down on the supply of guides available. The market price will go up, and the public will buy fewer guides. If this happens, there will be a significant decrease in the quantity of labor Universal

Study Guide demands. In other words, the greater the proportion of total production cost accounted for by the factor, the greater its resource elasticity of demand. (The two factors—percentage of resource cost and factor elasticity of demand—are positively related.)

4. *The degree of substitutability for the factor.* Suppose that the Bleep Company (unlike Universal Study Guide) employs a large number of variable factors. The elasticity of demand of the Bleep Company for any *one* factor will be greater. Universal Study Guide, on the other hand, uses only one variable factor (at least in the short run) and only two, even in the long run. This causes the firm's MRP_L (see Figure 22-1) to be relatively steep. That is, there is no substitutability, because Universal Study Guide cannot substitute something else for labor. Thus, the less substitutability of one factor for another, the greater its price elasticity of demand. (Substitutability and elasticity of resource demand are inversely related.)

Income Distribution: Fair or Unfair?

According to the theory of marginal productivity, resources under competitive market conditions will be paid an amount of money equal to their marginal revenue product (or the value of their marginal product). In other words, people will be paid what they contribute in value to the output of the nation. This conclusion has led some advocates of competitive capitalism to argue that competitive markets lead to a "fair" or "just" distribution of income. Justice, in this case, means people are paid on the basis of their economic contributions.

Most economists would say that there are problems in this, for the following reasons:

1. *It is difficult (if not impossible) to separate the productivities of resources or to measure their contribution to output.* The theory of marginal productivity has a built-in assumption that one can identify and quantify the changes in output attributable to hiring more or less of an input. But when you get down to cases, the productivity of one unit of labor (or other kind of factor) depends not only on its own productivity, but the productivity of the capital (and other resources) with which it works. Even if paying resources their value of marginal productivity were regarded as equitable, it would be difficult to establish how *much* they should be paid.

2. *Economists shy away from talking about a "just" or "fair" distribution of income.* Who is to say that one income distribution is fairer than another? Words like *just* and *fair* are value-laden. What is fair in the mid-1970s in the United States may well be unfair at another time or to other people. So economists concentrate on price stability, growth, and other implications of income distribution.

The theory of marginal productivity is useful as a guide to the firm's profit-maximizing demand for resources. But don't try to read more into it than that.

Demand for Resources Among Monopolistic Firms

Industries in which products are sold noncompetitively demand resources too, of course. Suppose that Universal Study Guide, by a combination of financial acquisition and merger, becomes the only producer of guides. Away from the sweat and bustle of competition, Universal Study Guide becomes monopolistic. (We will also assume that the Justice Department does not intervene to invoke the antitrust laws against guide makers.)

Since demand for resources is derived from demand for products, changes in Universal Study Guide's demand for products determine what happens to its resource demand, now that it is no longer in a competitive market. For the time being, for convenience, we shall continue to assume that both the firm's supply of resources and its own demand for resources are competitive. (That is, its marginal resource cost is equal to the competitively determined resource price.)

Now that Universal Study Guide is noncompetitive, it has a solid percentage of the market demand for study guides. Think back to Chapter 15. Remember the discussion of diminishing marginal utility and of income and substitution effects? If so, you will also recall that the curve depicting market demand shows an inverse relationship between price and quantity demanded. When price goes up, quantity demanded goes down. If a firm wants to sell more of a product, it must lower the price. When Universal Study Guide was in a purely competitive market, the demand curve for its product was perfectly elastic. However, as a monopolist, it must deal with a demand curve *less* than perfectly elastic. In fact, the curve slopes downward.

Accordingly, for these new demand conditions, let's recalculate Universal Study Guide's demand for labor. Table 22-2 gives the overall picture. Note two things: (1) We are assuming that the marginal physical productivity of labor is the same to Universal Study Guide whether the firm is competitive or noncompetitive. (2) We are assuming, to simplify the market picture, that Universal Study Guide, now that it is a monopolist, is not really a bigger firm than it was as a competitive firm (its cost curves are the same). It is simply the only seller in the study guide market.

Now let's see what happens to Universal Study Guide's hiring practices when it moves from a competitive to a noncompetitive situation. Its choices about hiring labor (column 1) are the same in a noncompetitive situation as they were in a competitive one. Actually, this is unrealistic. Because if the whole study guide industry were to become monopolistic, and if market demand stayed at the same level as before, the firm that is still in the running would probably be larger. So it would hire more labor and produce more guides than it would if it were a smaller, competitive producer.

The simplified picture here, however, enables us to observe what happens to a firm's demand for labor solely as a result of having no competition in the market. Columns 2 and 3 remain the same (by assumption) when Universal Study Guide becomes a monopolistic firm.

However, column 4, product price, is different. As Universal Study Guide produces and sells more and more guides, their price falls. Because the price goes down (because the firm does not take price as given), the *marginal revenue product* ($MPP_L \times MR$) is no longer the same as the *value of marginal product* ($MPP_L \times P$). The reason is that MR is less than P. Note that monopolistic Universal Study Guide's MRP is now less for *each* amount of labor hired (up to the point at which $MPP = 0$) than it was under competition.

In other words, for a monopolist, hiring more labor does not produce as much additional revenue as it would for a competitive firm.

Figure 22-2 compares the two situations. The $MRP_L = VMP_L$ curve for competition is the same as it was for the competitive situation in Figure 22-1. The former equilibrium rate of employment was six workers per day. At this level, Universal Study Guide's marginal revenue product for labor was equal to its marginal resource cost, or the daily wage paid to those extra workers (shown by E_c, or the equilibrium point in a situation of competition, in Figure 22-2).

TABLE 22-2 Demand for Resources by Universal Study Guide Company in a Pure Monopoly

1	2	3	4	5	6
Units of variable resource	Total product (TP = output per day in thousands)	Marginal physical product ($MPP_L = \Delta TP/\Delta L$)	Product price (P)	Total revenue (TR = TP × P)	Marginal revenue product ($MRP = \Delta TR/\Delta L = MPP_L \times MR$)
0	0		$2.00	$ 0	
		30			$57.00
1	30		1.90	57.00	
		27			45.60
2	57		1.80	102.60	
		24			35.10
3	81		1.70	137.70	
		20			23.90
4	101		1.60	161.60	
		18			16.90
5	119		1.50	178.50	
		15			9.10
6	134		1.40	187.60	
		12			2.20
7	146		1.30	189.80	
		10			−2.60
8	156		1.20	187.20	
		8			−6.80
9	164		1.10	180.40	
		5			−10.40
10	169		1.00	169.00	
		0			0
11	169		1.00	169.00	

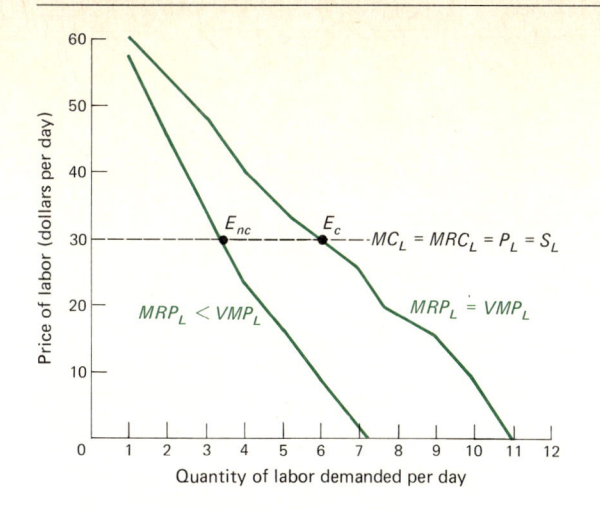

FIGURE 22-2 The Universal Study Guide Company's Equilibrium Demand for Labor Under Conditions of Competition (E_c). As compared to its equilibrium demand for labor under conditions of *non*competition (E_{nc}).

Now Figure 22-2 shows the new (noncompetitive) marginal revenue product of labor (column 6 in Table 22-2) plotted to the left of the competitive one. Labeled MRP_L, it reflects the fact that labor's marginal revenue product declines with a falling product price, as the firm sells more and more study guides. Remember that labor's competitive wage ($30 per day) is still the same. Now E_{nc} shows the new employment equilibrium in a noncompetitive product market situation: between three and four units of labor per day. Remember that we are assuming here that the output of study guides and units of resource are completely divisible. If they are not divisible, the firm will hire the third worker, but not the fourth, since the fourth will add less to revenue than to cost.

Remember that the demand for labor is derived from the demand for products. A noncompetitive seller finds it profitable to produce less of the product and hire less labor than a competitor would. The public buys fewer guides and Universal Study Guide hires fewer workers than it would if it were operating in a purely competitive market.

SUMMING UP

1. This chapter deals with the operation of *factor markets*, especially the way the *demand* for factors, or resources, of production (labor, land, capital, and entrepreneurship) is established. It is as important to understand factor markets as it is product markets, since factor markets are the source of our entire market incomes and provide the inputs to create all output.

2. Factor prices, like product prices, are determined by supply and demand. However, there are important differences between the pricing of factors and the pricing of products.

3. Demand for factors, unlike demand for products, is a *derived demand*. That is, a firm bases its demand for factors on the anticipated demand for its products.

4. Three things that determine the demand for a factor of production are (a) the amount of demand for the end product, (b) the productivity of the resource (which is influenced by the productivity of other resources, technology, managerial ability, and labor skills), and (c) the (relative) prices of other factors of production. (For example, much technological unemployment is due to the fact that labor's wages have risen faster than the cost of capital.)

5. A profit-maximizing firm hires a factor of production (such as labor) up to the point at which that factor adds as much to revenue as it adds to cost.

6. *Marginal revenue product (MRP)* is the addition to total revenue associated with a change in the use of a variable input. *The law of variable proportions* (or diminishing returns) says that when a firm uses successive increments of a variable input in conjunction with a fixed input, increases in output diminish beyond some point. Thus, the law of variable proportions affects *MRP*. Even when factor prices are competitive (constant to the individual firm), *MRP* ultimately diminishes.

7. For a competitive firm, the marginal revenue product of a factor of production equals the firm's demand for that factor. The competitive firms' supply schedule of that factor is the same as the *marginal resource cost (MRC)*, or price of the factor. The profit-maximizing competitive firm hires enough of the factor to make the *MRP* of the factor equal to its *MRC*.

8. A profit-maximizing firm tries to produce any rate of output (including its most profitable one) with the least total cost. To minimize cost, it employs resources until the point at which the marginal physical productivity per dollar spent on each resource is equal:

$$\frac{MPP_L}{P_L} = \frac{MPP_K}{P_K}.$$

9. One obtains the total demand for a resource by adding the individual firms' demands at each price. This method works so long as there are no *resource externalities*, or changes in costs of resources that are not attributable to the actions of the individual firm. If resource externalities exist, one must incorporate changes in costs of firms from industry demand changes in order to determine the change in each firm's demand for a factor.

10. The *elasticity of resource demand* is the rate at which the demand for a factor of production changes as its price changes. This elasticity of demand depends on four factors: (1) The rate at which the MPP of the factor declines as a firm uses more of it. (b) The price elasticity of demand for the final product the factor is used to produce. (c) The

proportion of the total cost of the product that is represented by the factor in question. (d) The degree of substitutability for the factor.

11. Some people say that competitive capitalism produces the "best" distribution of income because, according to the theory of marginal productivity, each factor of production is paid what it is "worth," its *value of marginal product* (or what it contributes to the revenue of the firm). Economists discount this argument for the following reasons: (a) It is difficult to separate the productivity of one input from the productivity of another. (b) Economists do not like value-laden normative terms like *best distribution*, since no one really knows what the best distribution is.

12. If a firm that has been selling its products in a competitive market becomes a *non*competitive seller, it gains control of a significant part of the market demand. It obtains monopoly power. Then, in order to sell more of its product, it must lower the price. Even if the noncompetitive firm uses resources with the same productivity as the resources used by the competitor, marginal revenue productivity (marginal physical productivity times change in marginal revenue) for the monopolist is less than value of marginal product (marginal physical product times product price). The reason is that when a firm has to lower the price at which it sells its product, the price of the product is more than the firm's marginal revenue.

13. Even if the supply of a given resource remains competitive, firms that sell their products on a noncompetitive basis hire less of the resource, since they find that it produces less revenue for them than it does for a competitive seller. This means that monopolistic firms do not employ enough of the resource to produce the product most efficiently, or to produce that amount of it that will yield the maximum satisfaction to consumers.

QUESTIONS

1. What do *factor markets* mean to you? If you have participated in these markets, which one(s)? If not, which do you expect will be most important to you during your economically active life?

2. How do supply and demand work to determine the amount of a factor of production a firm in a competitive market employs? What does *marginal revenue productivity* have to do with competitive demand for a resource?

3. What is the difference between *value of marginal product* and *marginal revenue product*? Under what conditions are they the same? Does it seem likely to you that they are often the same in reality?

4. Would the problem of technological unemployment be eased if we allowed the competitive market system to function more completely? Why, or why not?

5. What would happen to the demand for factors of production if we enforced the antitrust laws more vigorously against noncompetitive firms? Would this be true for noncompetitive firms that are, for technological reasons, more efficient than competitive ones?

6. In the argument that competitive capitalism leads to the "most desirable" distribution of income, what considerations are left out?

7. Suppose that you are a professional football player. Would you want to see abolished the reserve clause binding you indefinitely to the team with which you have a contract? Why?

SUGGESTED READINGS

Burck, Gilbert. "The Myths and Realities of Corporate Pricing." *Fortune*, April 1972.

Kennedy, William. "Work and Dissatisfaction: Is Money Enough?" In *Economic Analysis of Pressing Social Problems*, edited by Llad Phillips and Harold L. Votey, Jr. Rand-McNally, Chicago, 1974.

Lancaster, Kelvin. "Distribution and the Price System." In *Modern Economics: Principles and Policy*. Rand-McNally, Chicago, 1973.

Neale, Walter C. "The Peculiar Economics of Professional Sports." In *The Daily Economist*, edited by Harry G. Johnson and Burton A. Weisbrod, Prentice-Hall, Englewood Cliffs, N.J., 1973.

North, Douglass C., and Roger Leroy Miller. "The Economics of Baseball, Basketball and Football." In *The Economics of Public Issues*. Harper & Row, New York, 1973.

Rothenberg, Simon. "The Baseball Players' Labor Market." In *The Daily Economist*, edited by Harry G. Johnson and Burton A. Weisbrod. Prentice-Hall, Englewood Cliffs, N.J., 1973.

Application 23

How Much Education Should We Buy?

> An educated person is one who voluntarily does more thinking than is necessary for his own survival.
>
> — Anonymous

Ever since the days of the early settlers in the United States, people have believed in the power of widespread public education to guide everyone to a better way of life. Education has many advantages other than economic ones. It transmits the national culture to the next generation. It creates a more informed electorate. (Frederick the Great said, "An educated people is easily governed.") Nonetheless, education raises economic issues. Governments must set up and finance public education at all levels, from the elementary school through the university. In this application, we will examine some of these issues, especially those that deal with *how much* education the public should buy.

Table A23-1 shows that in the four decades between 1930 and 1970 we spent an increasing percentage of our money on education. Not only did the absolute amount of money spent on education increase by more than 2,000 percent in this period, but also the *percentage of GNP* spent on education more than doubled. Most of the percentage increase occurred after 1950 (from 3.4 percent of GNP in 1950 to 7.6 percent of GNP in 1970). Note also that in the same period (1) capital outlay (plant and equipment) declined from over 17 percent of total outlay to about 13 percent in 1970, (2) expenditures for both public and private education grew at about the same rates (although growth for private schools has been slightly slower), (3) expenditures for public higher education (beyond twelfth grade) grew much more rapidly than expenditures for private higher education.

Ever since the academic turmoil on campuses in the United States in the 1960s, people have begun to question the wisdom of committing so

TABLE A23-1 U.S. Expenditures* on Schools by Type of Control and Level of Institution, 1930–1970 (millions of dollars)

Control and level	1930	1940	1950	1960	1970
Total	3,234	3,200	8,796	24,722	70,600
Percent of GNP	3.1	3.5	3.4	5.1	7.6
Current expenditures	2,700	2,833	7,229	20,603	61,300
Capital outlay	534	367	1,567	4,120	9,300
Public	2,656	2,697	7,057	19,447	57,300
Percent of total	82.1	84.3	80.2	78.7	81.2
Elementary and secondary	2,367	2,364	5,883	15,613	41,000
Higher education	289	333	1,174	3,753	16,300
Private	578	503	1,739	5,275	13,300
Percent of total	17.9	15.7	19.8	21.3	18.8
Elementary and secondary	237	203	790	2,412	4,700
Higher education	341	273	949	2,863	8,600

* Expenditures include current expenditures, interest, and capital outlays.

Source: Adapted from Douglas Windham, "The Economics of Education: A Survey," in *Contemporary Economic Issues*, edited by Neil W. Chamberlain, Irwin, Homewood, Ill., 1973.

"Amazing when you think of it. $11,365.42 worth of knowledge in you and you don't look a bit different."

large an amount of national resources to education. This doubt has taken many forms. School budgets have been tightened. Many communities have voted down bond issues for new schools. These symptoms may stem in part from the recession of the mid-1970s and the slowing-down of population growth (which has led to too many school buildings and to the closing of many schools). From an employment viewpoint, many Americans are "overeducated." That is, they have been educated only to hold jobs that require lesser technical skills than their educational backgrounds have given them.

Are we overinvesting in educating people? Economists in recent years have come to identify a fifth factor of production to add to land, labor, capital, and entrepreneurship. The fifth factor, **human capital**, refers to the improvement in labor skills (increase in marginal physical productivity) that is attributable to education or other training. Economist Burton A. Weisbrod says that since 1900, total U.S. expenditures on education have increased four times as rapidly as expenditures on physical plant and equipment. It is possible, therefore, that the United States is investing too much in human capital, as opposed to other resources.

What is the "correct" amount of social investment in education (or human capital)? Douglass C. North and Roger Leroy Miller point out in their book *The Economics of Public Issues* that the "correct" amount is the one at which "the social return on investment in human capital is equal at the margin to other types of social investment" (that is, the opportunity costs of capital are equated at the margin). In other words, one must compare the social costs and benefits of investment in education with the social costs and benefits of other types of investment.

The social costs of education are (1) costs borne by students (such as room, board, books, and tuition); (2) costs borne by the public in the form of subsidies (collected through property taxes, appropriations by state legislatures, and so on); and (3) the opportunity costs to students, or what they could have earned if they had held full-time jobs during the time they were in school (research has shown this to be about half of total educational cost).

The social benefits of education are (1) that people with education have higher lifetime earnings than they would have without their education; (2) that education has value as a consumer good (it makes possible greater enjoyment of books, music, paintings, and so on); and (3) that society gains external benefits by having better educated citizens (there is less crime, voters are better informed, taxpayers are able to make out their own tax returns, and so on).

However, to determine the present value of these costs or benefits, you must discount back to the present both the *stream of costs* (the flow of costs over the educational lifetime of students) and the *stream of benefits* (the flow of benefits over the expected lifetimes of students). Think of it this way: A dollar in hand today is worth more than a dollar promised to you a year (or five or ten years) from now because of the interest you can earn over the future period on the dollar held now. The same is true for society as a whole. It, too, can enjoy the power of compound interest. It therefore must discount future dollars in favor of present dollars.

The difficulty with ensuring that the social costs and benefits are equal at the margin—that is, that the nation is buying the "correct" amount of education—lies in the fact that there are three potentially different assessments of costs and benefits. Students make one assessment, their parents make another, and government makes a third. Rates of return are likely to look different to each, because students often pay very little of even the direct costs of their education. Therefore, the benefits, in terms of added lifetime income (plus psychic benefits), almost always exceed the costs. (Students, of course, rarely make these decisions until they are of college age.) The parents usually bear most of the direct costs of education. These costs are often large for private elementary and high schools, as well as for colleges. Thus, parents derive mainly psychic returns, such as seeing their children graduate from college, or knowing that their children are more secure economically. Since these psychic returns are mental and emotional, the rates of return for parents are difficult to estimate.

Therefore, there is a possible divergence between rates of return on investment in education to students and to parents. However, the **private rates of return**—those that do not take into account indirect social costs and external benefits—are impressive. In a paper entitled, "Human Capital: Policy Issues and Research Opportunities," T. W. Schultz estimated percentages of return per dollar of investment in education as follows:

Type of education	Rate of return
All U.S. education	10–15%
Primary education	35%
Secondary education	25%
College education	15%
Graduate education	15%

These rates depend on the rate at which one discounts future income. Nonetheless, these rates are greater than the average rate of return on capital investment in the United States. The increase that education seems to bring to lifetime income alone ($350,000 for a high school graduate versus $586,000 for a college graduate) appears to warrant a high rate of private investment.

One must not, however, assume that *all* the increased earnings are due to education. It may well be that those with higher levels of education have greater abilities to begin with (higher marginal productivity). Even in the absence of the educational difference, there might still be some differences in income. The very high rate of estimated return on investment in primary education suggests that money invested in U.S. education should be reallocated so that a greater percentage of it goes to primary schools. Remember, though, that these rates are based on a given stock of capital. The figures do not suggest that such rates would hold true for all levels or all flows of capital into education.

What about the return to society at large on investment in education? The public, by paying taxes, puts up a considerable part of the costs of both private and public education (in 1967-1968, 35.2 percent of private higher education revenues and 78.2 percent of public higher education revenues). To what extent should the public subsidize the education of individuals? The economist's answer is that the public should subsidize to an extent sufficient to exhaust the *externalities* of education, so that the supply of education is increased and the price of it is reduced to the point at which the *socially* desirable amount of education is "produced and consumed."

According to economist Donald Winkler, the arguments in favor of public subsidization of education are based on the following considerations. All but the first two have some externalities attached to them.

1. *Imperfections in the capital market.* Some argue that education must be subsidized because low-income students cannot go into the capital market and borrow the money to "buy" an education (what collateral could they offer?).

2. *Income redistribution.* Those who believe that income should be distributed more "equitably" feel that educational subsidies are a useful means of doing this. Subsidies can both transfer income directly to low-income people and broaden the base of human capital (raise the productivity of low-income people). This causes future income to be distributed in a more nearly equal manner. (A study of higher education in California during the 1960s suggests, however, that educational subsidies redistributed income in favor of middle- and upper-income groups.)

These two arguments are not very convincing to most economists. After all, even if capital markets were perfect (that is, even if each individual had equal access to them), and even if income were redistributed to fit some particular notion of what is right, people might still underinvest in education because they could not take advantage of the *social* benefits of education. (They could not appreciate the value of education to the public.) The remaining arguments for subsidizing education rest, therefore, on externalities.

3. *Economic growth.* A well-known study by Edward Denison concluded that 23 percent of the economic growth of the United States between 1927 and 1959 was attributable to increased human capital. Other, more recent studies generally confirm this. Remember though, from Application 14, that growth produces negative externalities (in the form of pollution). Here we are mainly concerned with the net benefit of subsidizing education and the effect of this subsidy on economic growth.

4. *Reduced crime rates.* The opportunity cost of committing a crime is higher to educated people than to uneducated people. Thus, educated people are much less likely to commit crimes. (Winkler reports that, in 1960, 9.6 percent of the American population had completed four years of college, but less than 1 percent of the criminal population had that much education.)

5. *Improved learning environment.* The greater the degree of education of parents, the more readily their children, and their children's peers, learn. This is a benefit to society.

6. *Better citizenship.* There is evidence that educated people participate more actively in politics and, in this sense, are better citizens. One cannot place monetary value on good citizenship, but surely it benefits society significantly.

7. *Career orientation.* A degree certifies to society that a student has satisfactorily carried out certain programs of study. If it were not for this system, businesses and government agencies would have to pay the costs of this certification, of finding out what career the student was best suited for.

8. *Higher tax returns and lower transfer payments.* A 1972 study shows that college-educated people paid higher taxes on their (same) incomes than people who were not college educated. Educated people are also probably more able to prepare their own tax returns than noneducated people.

To summarize, parents, students, and governments have their own estimates of the costs and benefits (rates of return) that they derive from investment in education. Because the divergence between these estimates may be large, it is unlikely that U.S. investment in education is both socially and privately the "correct" amount.

SUMMING UP

1. The effects of education are both economic and noneconomic. But the "correct" amount of education that individuals and society should buy is a matter subject to economic analysis.

2. Since 1950, the United States has spent an increasing percentage of its gross national product on education, both public and private. In recent years, there have been discussions of whether the United States is investing too much in education.

3. Economists view expenditures on education as investment in *human capital,* which refers to the improvement in labor skills (increase in marginal physical productivity) attributable to education. A society should invest in education, as in anything else, up to the point at which the marginal social cost is equal to the marginal social benefit.

4. The social costs of education are (a) direct costs borne by students; (b) costs borne by the public in the form of subsidies; and (c) the opportunity costs to students, the income given up by students who do not work because they are in school. The social benefits are (a) the higher lifetime earnings attributable to education, (b) the value of education as a consumer good, and (c) the external benefits to society of having an educated populace.

5. The costs and benefits of education can be spoken of as *streams,* or flows over time. To establish the present value of each cost and benefit, one must discount it back to the present time. This is because of the opportunity cost (lost interest) of investing in the future.

6. Students, parents, and governments see costs and benefits differently. More education may be highly beneficial to a student who pays little of its cost. But it may or may not be beneficial to parents or to the government. The government alone can incorporate the external benefits of education.

7. Data suggest that the *private rates of return* on education—those that leave out the social costs

Is higher education worth it? (Ellis Herwig/Stock, Boston)

and benefits—are high for all levels of education (at least as high as for other forms of capital investment).

8. The arguments that education brings social benefits that warrant public subsidization are based on the following considerations: (a) Imperfections in the capital market make borrowing to buy an education impossible for low-income students. (b) Educational subsidies lead indirectly to income redistribution. (c) Increased human capital leads to economic growth. (d) Education reduces crime rates. (e) Education improves learning environment. (f) Education leads to better citizenship. (g) Education provides career orientation. (h) Education eventually produces higher tax returns and lower transfer payments. (The last six of these benefits represent external benefits to society.)

9. Because of the divergences between the estimated costs and benefits to students, parents, and government resulting from investment in education, it is unlikely that U.S. investment in human capital is the "socially correct" amount.

QUESTIONS

1. Do you, as a *consumer* of higher education, consider it a desirable good? Why or why not?

2. Since you are an *investor* in higher education (at least you are paying some of its direct costs), what do you think will be your rate of return when you get an A.B. degree? What about an M.A., or a Ph.D.?

3. Do you think that the rate of return on investment in your education is the same to your parents or to your state government as it is to you? Why or why not?

4. What do you think will happen to the rate of return on educational investment as the United States approaches zero population growth?

5. Do you think it is legitimate to view people as human capital? Why or why not?

6. Given the rates of return on investment in education that you have seen, would you (or society) be better off investing in education, in corporate

bonds, in a new highway system, or in an income-maintenance plan?

SUGGESTED READINGS

Blaug, Mark, ed. *Economics of Education*, Penguin, Baltimore, 1968.

Denison, Edward F. *The Sources of Economic Growth in the United States and the Alternatives Before Us*. Committee for Economic Development, New York, 1962.

Hansen, W. Lee, and Burton A. Weisbrod. *Benefits, Costs and Finance of Public Higher Education*. Markham Publishing, Chicago, 1969.

Hansen, W. Lee, and Burton A. Weisbrod. "The Distribution of Costs and Direct Benefits of Public Higher Education: The Case of California." *Journal of Human Resources*, Spring 1969.

Mundel, David S. "Federal Aid to Higher Education: An Analysis of Federal Subsidies to Undergraduate Education." *The Economics of Federal Subsidy Programs, Part 4, Higher Education and Manpower Subsidies*. Joint Economic Committee, G.P.O., Washington, D.C., 1972.

North, Douglass C., and Roger Leroy Miller. "The Economics of Indentured Servants." "The Economics of Lower Education." In *The Economics of Public Issues*, 2d ed. Harper & Row, New York, 1973.

Schultz, T. W. "Human Capital: Policy Issues and Research Opportunities." Human Capital Paper No. 70:10. University of Chicago, Department of Economics, 1971.

Shaffer, H. G. "A Critique of the Concept of Human Capital." *American Economic Review*, 52, No. 4 (1961). Reprinted in *Economics of Education*, edited by Mark Blaug. Penguin, Baltimore, 1968.

Thurow, Lester C. "Education and Economic Equality." *The Public Interest*, Summer 1972.

Weisbrod, Burton A. "Investing in Human Capital." In *The Daily Economist*, edited by Harry G. Johnson and Burton A. Weisbrod. Prentice-Hall, Englewood Cliffs, N.J., 1973.

Windham, Douglas M. "The Economics of Education: A Survey." In *Contemporary Economic Issues*, edited by Neil W. Chamberlain. Irwin, Homewood, Ill., 1973.

Winkler, Donald R. "Higher Education: Should Students Pay Their Way?" In *Economic Analysis of Pressing Social Problems*, edited by Llad Phillips and Harold Votey, Jr. Rand McNally, Chicago, 1974.

23

How Prices of Factors Are Set

Chapter 22 focused on the *demand* for resources, or factors of production. You saw that demand for resources is a derived demand and that it decreases as competition in the product markets becomes less. This happens because noncompetitive, profit-maximizing industries produce less and hire fewer resources than competitive industries. Throughout Chapter 22, however, we assumed, in order to simplify, that even for noncompetitive producers, a firm's **supply of resources** (the quantities offered to it at various prices) is competitively determined. Actually, as everyone knows, that is not usually the real situation. Imagine General Motors being unable to influence the wage rate of automobile workers.

So we will drop the assumption of pure competition in the factor markets. First, we will discuss noncompetitive supply and pricing of labor and see how it differs from competitively determined supply and pricing of labor. Then, we will discuss rents, interest, and profits in the same way.

Wages: Competitive Versus Noncompetitive

Labor is a commodity just like steel or oil or plant capacity. All manufacturers must buy it. Now, to analyze the supply of labor, we are going to make an assumption about the relation between wage rate and the quantity of labor time supplied. Our assumption is that *the quantity of labor time supplied increases as the wage rate rises*. The labor supply curve in Figure 23-1 reflects this assumption. It shows that at any higher wage, more labor time will be available than at any lower one. For example, if the wage paid to skilled operators of certain machines is $6 per hour, laborers are willing to work approximately thirty hours per week. But if the wage goes to $10 per hour, they will work fifty hours per week. The reason is that most people want more money income, at least in a developed economy in which desirable goods and services are everywhere available and widely advertised. With a higher wage, they can get more of these goods and services (at a given level of retail prices). We arrived at this hypothetical labor supply curve by adding the quantities of labor time offered at each wage rate for all individuals possessing this given skill. Now one may draw the conclusion that the labor supply curve for each individual is also an upward-sloping line. But that is not necessarily so.

Consider the labor supply curve in Figure 23-2, which economists call a **backward-bending labor supply curve**. Here the individual is willing to work more hours as the wage rate rises, but only up to a certain point (the point at which the wage rate reaches $8 per hour). Above $8, the amount of labor time offered declines (the curve bends backward). The reason is that there is a tradeoff between the *marginal utility of income* and the *marginal utility of leisure*.

Imagine your own labor supply curve. If your wage rate were to rise, you would be willing to work more hours per week (the *income effect* of the wage increase). To do so, you would have to sacrifice an equal amount of leisure, such as going to the beach, reading, visiting friends, or whatever (the *substitution effect* of the wage increase). You would continue to give up the leisure (whose marginal utility increases as you have less of it) and acquire more money income (whose marginal utility diminishes as you have more of it) up to the point at which the marginal utilities of the two are equal (at a wage of $8). At a wage above $8, if you

FIGURE 23-1 Supply Curve for One Kind of Labor

FIGURE 23-2 Backward-Bending Individual Labor Supply Curve

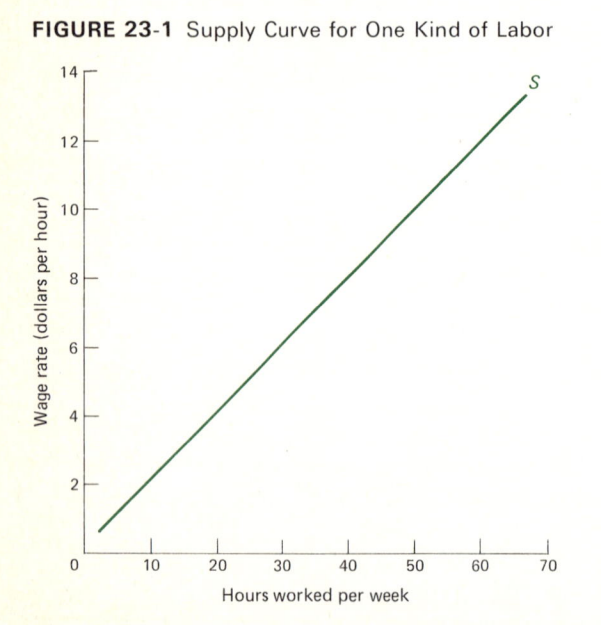

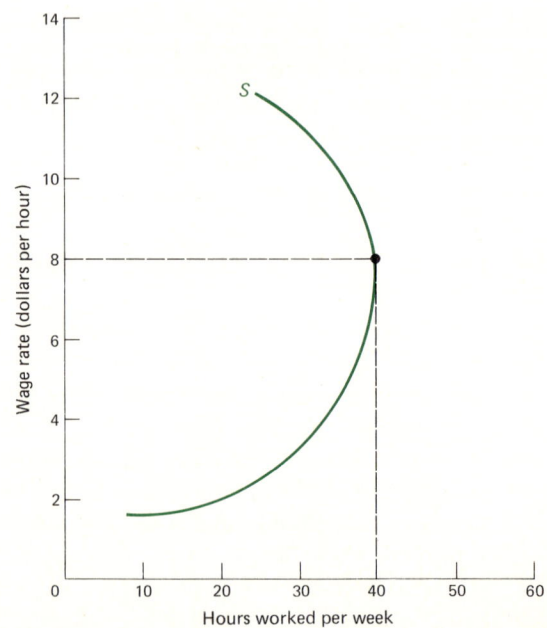

That necessary commodity: Labor (Courtesy Ford Motor Company)

were like the person in Figure 23-2, you would begin to substitute leisure for money.

Perhaps you are not used to thinking of leisure as being a good. Nonetheless, you *can* treat it as such. Indeed, if you are to understand the supply of labor, you *must* treat leisure as a good. If the price of leisure (the amount of money you give up to get it) rises, you will substitute money income for leisure (the substitution effect). But as your income grows, you demand more leisure, since most people have a strong taste for it (the income effect). The steady growth of productivity in the United States in the twentieth century has raised U.S. incomes. Today Americans often choose to trade off a significant part of potential income for additional leisure. The declining average workweek in the United States is evidence of the trend toward more leisure.

Even though there is a *backward-bending labor supply* curve for individual laborers, there is an *upward-sloping labor supply curve* for labor in general (Figure 23-1). The reason is that the labor market is made up of many people, each having different tradeoffs between income and leisure. That is why the individual curves do not all bend backward at the same wage. There are always some individuals who abide by the Protestant ethic. Because of these workers, who will respond to a higher wage by working more hours, the labor supply curve is most likely to be upward sloping, so we will use that shape in our analysis of labor markets. It is a convenient assumption at this point.

Why Not a Single Wage Rate?

We have been talking about the labor market as if there were just *one* going wage rate. We know this is not realistic. The principles of labor pricing we are going to discuss here are valid in any labor market. But we must account for the fact that, in reality, there are many different wage rates. Laborers with different skills are paid at different rates. (The mechanic does not earn the same rate of pay as the chairman of the board of General Motors.) Even laborers with the same skills are often paid differently. The difference may be due to location (wages are higher in New York than in Mississippi) or to discrimination (Jane Mechanic often does not earn as much as Jack Mechanic). Let's examine some reasons why.

Different Skills and Different Supplies of Skills

The innate abilities of each human being differ from those of every other human being. Add to these differences the variations in training, experience, and education. All these factors account for the variations in wages earned by people in different occupations and professions. These factors also account for differences in the wage scale paid to people within the same labor market. For example, it does not take as long or cost as much to acquire the skills of a mechanic as it does to acquire the skills of a physician (even though the skills of a mechanic are often substantial). It takes even longer—and costs even more—to become a neurosurgeon than to become a general practitioner.

Part of the difference in wage levels derives from the *elasticity* of supply of the labor involved. For example, in the United States, physi-

FIGURE 23-3 Hypothetical Supply and Demand for Physicians

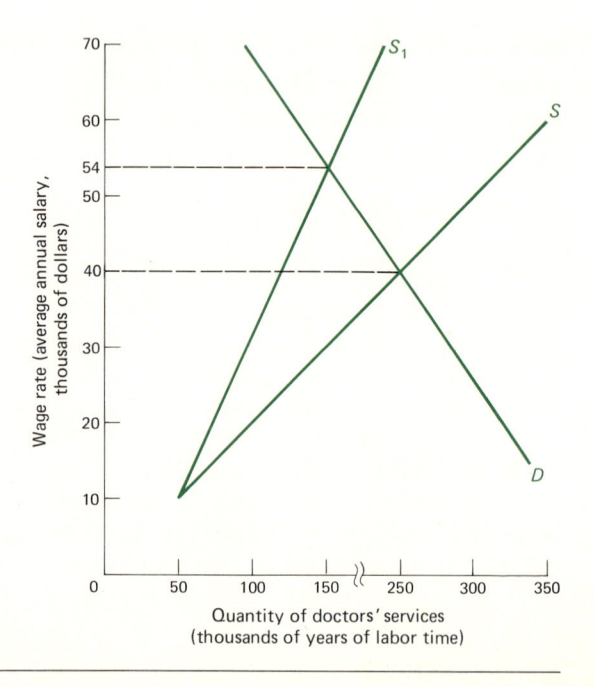

542   How Prices of Factors Are Set

cians are the highest paid of all professional groups for the following reasons: (1) Their education and training cost a great deal. Their high salaries are a "payout" to the private and public investment in human capital. (2) The supply of physicians is very inelastic.

Figure 23-3 illustrates this point. Here D stands for people's demand for the services of physicians. S and S_1 stand for two different supply conditions of medical services, S_1 being much less price-elastic than S. (The quantity of physicians' services rises less rapidly with their price along S_1.) The American Medical Association, by its power to certify hospitals and medical schools and by its control of state licensing of physicians, can reduce the elasticity of supply of physicians. It can thereby cause physicians' salaries to be $54,000 per year (where $S_1 = D$) rather than $40,000 per year (where $S = D$).

The medical profession is not unique, of course, in its ability to restrict the elasticity of supply of its members. Trade unions exert the same kind of control. The point is that:

Few resources are in perfectly elastic supply, but the less elastic the supply of a resource, the higher its wage (or other payment), for a given demand condition.

Different Wages and Same Skills

Sometimes people with very similar skills (for example, workers in the construction and home-repair industries) receive very different wages. The reasons are as follows:

1. *Short-term increases in the demand for one skill as opposed to another.* Sometimes there is not freedom of entry into a field of labor (as when a bricklayers' union will not admit new members). However, if there is freedom of entry, movement from one area of skill into the other should reduce these differentials.

2. *Wage and job discrimination.* In **wage discrimination**, employers *pay* employees on some basis other than their productivity, such as age or sex. Thus, the difference in wages derives not from a difference in productivity but from difference in non-market-induced demand. In **job discrimination**, employers *hire* employees on some basis other than their productivity. (For example, whites are hired, but blacks are not, or men are hired, but women are not. Sometimes only a token number of a minority group are hired.) (Application 24 will show how useful the supply-demand tools of the economist are in analyzing the effects of this market behavior.)

3. *Nonmonetary considerations in job decisions.* For example, if you get a Ph.D. in economics, you may decide to take a lower salary as a college professor than you could earn by getting a job in government or business. Presumably, the difference in wage is not as important to you as your enjoyment of teaching or the prestige attached to a professorship.

4. *Immobility of labor.* There are reasons (often self-imposed) why people will not move to better-paying jobs. ("Nobody's going to make me

move away from good ol' River City. I'd die of homesickness in six weeks.") This attitude can cause an oversupply of a skill in a given area, and depress the wage rate below what it is in other areas. This kind of immobility often hampers the efficient working of markets. But since it results from people exercising their democratic right to the pursuit of happiness, a free society must tolerate it.

How Wages Are Set: Competitively Priced Labor

Wages are the price one must pay for that necessary commodity, labor. Let's review the way a wage is set competitively and the way both competitive and noncompetitive firms respond to it.

Figure 23-4 sets forth the facts in readily understandable form. For convenience, we will continue to use study guides as an example.

Figure 23-4(a) shows what happens when the competitive factor market sets the wage scale. The independent influences of supply and demand determine the equilibrium wage rate. The supply curve of labor, S_M (or market supply) slopes upward, for reasons we have already discussed (income versus leisure). We are assuming for simplicity that there is no union and no minimum-wage law. There are only laborers, independently wanting to work. Each has her or his own tradeoff values between income and leisure. To figure out the overall demand for labor (D_M or market demand), we add the demands of all the single firms across the range of possible wage rates. Figure 23-4(b)'s curve showing these demands slopes downward because of the diminishing marginal physical productivity of labor. No single firm, by varying the amount of

FIGURE 23-4 Competitive Wages and Responses of Firms to Such Wages. (a) Wages set by the market; (b) Hiring by competitive and noncompetitive firms.

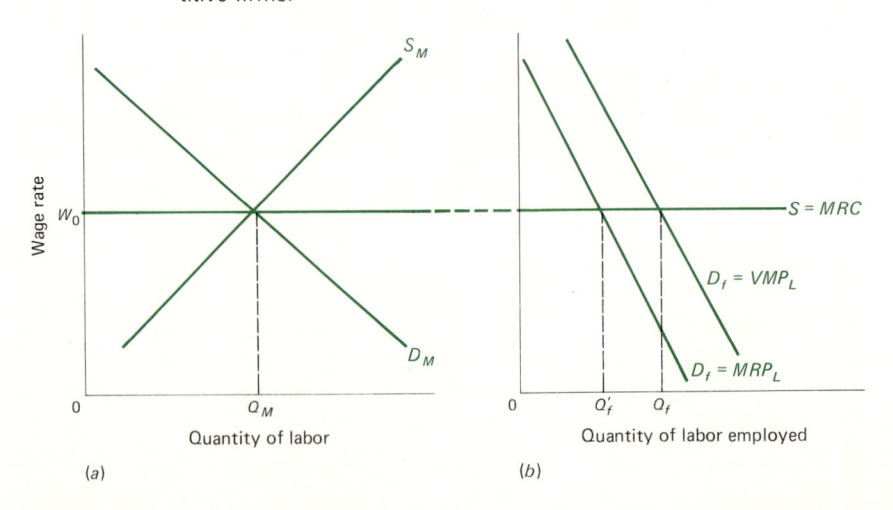

544   How Prices of Factors Are Set

labor it hires, can influence wages in general in the market as a whole. The equilibrium (market-clearing) wage is W_0. At W_0, there is neither excess supply nor excess demand, and industry employs Q_M of labor.

Figure 23-4(b) shows that each firm that hires this kind of labor takes W_0 as given. Since it can't influence the rate of the wage, the firm's supply of labor is perfectly elastic, and is represented by the straight line $S = MRC$ (supply equals marginal resource cost). Each time the firm hires one more laborer, it adds the same amount to its total costs.

Universal Study Guide, as you remember, is a profit-maximizing competitive firm. The value of its marginal revenue product (its marginal physical product times its product price) is equal to its demand for labor. Therefore, it will hire one worker, then another—up to the point at which *marginal resource cost* (*MRC*), the amount that one additional laborer adds to total cost, is equal to *value of marginal product* (*VMP*), the amount that the one additional laborer adds to total revenue.

When both product and factor markets are competitive, Universal Study Guide will hire Q_f of labor. (Q stands for "quantity" and f stands for "factor.") Labor is paid its *VMP* and consumers get the number of study guides they want. That is, they get all they are willing and able to buy at a price that just covers Universal Study Guide's opportunity cost of using labor (and all other resources, as well).

Suppose now that the study-guide industry goes through an upheaval. There are mergers and consolidations. As a result, each study-guide manufacturer ends up with a certain amount of monopoly power. Each firm now has the ability to influence the price of study guides through its own decisions about production. Look at Figure 23-4(b). See those downward-sloping demand curves, D_f (*D* for "demand" and f for "factor")? That is Universal Study Guide's factor demand curve. You can see its predicament. In order to sell more guides, it must lower the price of each one (the marginal revenue from study guides will be less than their price). And, as a result, *MRP* will be less than *VMP*.

In the real world, the downward-sloping demand curve is a fact of life for most producers of goods and services. In other words, as a firm hires another worker, and then another, and then another, the advantage becomes less each time. Each additional worker adds less to the firm's revenue than the one before. The reason is that the market value of the product goes down, and then goes down some more, each time the firm produces additional units of it.

Labor's contribution to revenue becomes marginal revenue product MRP_L (marginal physical product times marginal revenue). This is less than VMP_L (MRP_L curve lies to the left of the VMP_L curve). The Universal Study Guide hires labor competitively, so it makes W_0 (its *MRC*) equal to MRP_L and hires Q'_f laborers, fewer than it used to hire. Its decrease in laborers does not significantly affect the total employment picture, however, since Universal Study Guide, by assumption, hires an insignificant number of workers. Consumers, however, now get fewer guides than they would prefer, and it is likely that the price will rise.

How Wages Are Set: Noncompetitively Priced Labor

How can a situation with a *lack* of competition develop in the labor market? Noncompetitiveness enters into the labor market in three main ways:

1. A company may grow so big that it hires a significant part of the supply of a specialized type of labor. It will then no longer accept the wage rate as given. Instead, it will bid for labor and affect the wage rate because it is a monopsonistic firm. A **monopsony** is a market situation in which there is *only* one buyer of a given resource. Types of buying power can range from monopsony, to oligopsony (a *few* buyers), to monopsonistic competition (*many* buyers), to perfect competition. For simplicity, we will treat here only the case of a monopsony.

2. Laborers may organize a union (a labor monopoly) and bargain for their wage (with either competitive or noncompetitive producers, often in response to monopsony power).

3. Government may intervene in the labor market to create or reinforce noncompetitive conditions. For example, the government sets minimum wage levels.

In an effort to formulate a set of principles to explain modern labor conditions, we will examine these influences. We will also examine some of them in combination with others.

Monopsony

Suppose that Universal Study Guide Company becomes a monopsonistic firm. This puts the company in a class with the owners of a baseball club, which has a reserve (or option) clause in its contracts with its players, requiring them to bargain exclusively with that one club. This has a heavy impact on the supply of labor, the equilibrium quantity of labor it will demand, and the wage rate it will pay. Figure 23-5 will help you to visualize all this.

If you remember our discussion in Chapter 22 of the USG Company as a noncompetitive seller of guides, you will see that the *marginal revenue product of labor* (MRP_L) is equal to the Universal Study Guide's *demand for labor*. The amount of labor the company will employ varies *inversely* with the wage rate. (The lower the wage, the more hired.) Suppose that Universal Study Guide has a factory in a small company town. Universal Study Guide is the *only* firm in the area that hires workers with this kind of skill. Since the study guide factory is the only place for local workers to get a job, Universal Study Guide is the only bidder for labor. In order to hire more workers or get the staff to work a longer week, it must be willing to pay a higher wage. Therefore S_L is Universal Study Guide's supply of labor.

Now monopsony has entered the picture. Universal Study Guide's marginal resource cost of labor, MRC_L, shows what happens. Since Universal Study Guide can hire more labor only if it pays a higher wage than before, MRC_L is greater than the wage at any level of employment.

For example: Joe Doakes will work forty hours a week for $5 per hour. To get men to work a fifty-hour week, Universal Study Guide has to pay $6 per hour. So that extra ten hours is going to cost Universal Study Guide $100 per worker rather than $50. Thus MRC_L is drawn above S_L in Figure 23-5. (In other words, for each Q, level of employment, the *added* resource cost is greater than the wage associated with that amount of employment.)

How much labor will Universal Study Guide hire? What will be the equilibrium wage? If Universal Study Guide were still a competitive employer (though a monopolistic producer of guides), it would hire Q_0 of labor. At equilibrium point E, the supply of labor, S_L, would equal Universal Study Guide's demand for labor, MRP_L. The competitive wage would be W_0. But when Universal Study Guide becomes a profit-maximizing monopoly and monopsony, its marginal resource cost of labor (MRC_L) becomes equal to the marginal revenue of labor (MRP_L) at E'. The new equilibrium rate of employment is Q_1. Employment falls, and wages fall to W_1. (The supply curve S_L is the curve that indicates what must be paid to obtain a particular amount of labor.)

The general conclusion is this: Monopsony, or strong buying power in input markets, leads to fewer jobs and lower wages than exist in competitive input markets. When you get a combination of monopsony and product monopoly, both influences tend to reduce output, reduce employment, reduce wages, and *raise* prices.

From a technical viewpoint, monopsony tends to cause exploitation of factors. Look at Figure 23-5. Labor is paid Q_1G (or W_1). Labor's marginal revenue product is Q_1E'. So GE' represents the exploitation of labor. In other words, the employer is not paying the workers the value of what they contribute to the revenue of the firm. This is the exploitation due to monopsony.

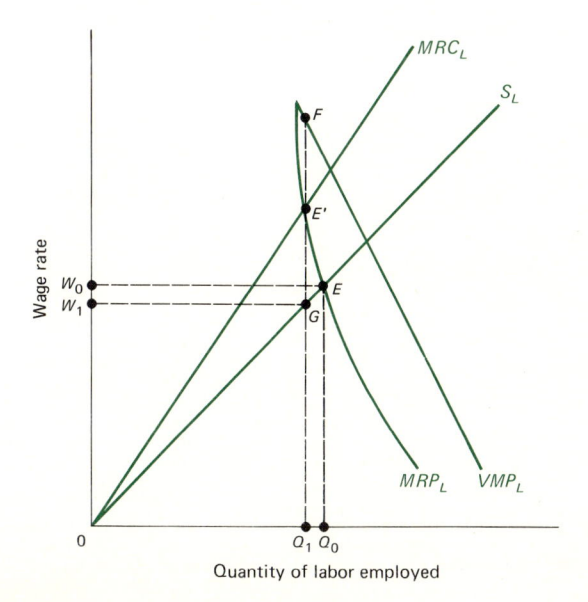

FIGURE 23-5 Determination of Wages in a Situation of Monopsony

One reaction to monopsony power (James Nachtwey)

Furthermore, labor is not paid its value of marginal product (Q_1F). This is the value that a *competitive* market would place on the productivity of that labor. Therefore $E'F$ represents the exploitation caused by monopoly power. However, if conditions as to labor and products were both fully competitive, there would be more jobs available and wages would move to a level at which $S_L = VMP_L$. In other words, the supply would equal the demand.

Collective Bargaining
In the past, there have been two main reactions to monopsony power. One has been the organization of laborers into *unions* that is, collective bargaining units. The other has been government intervention to counteract monopsony power. To be effective, a union must exert some degree of monopoly power. Where there is a **closed shop**, the union demands that people join the union before they can work at the study guide factory. In such cases, the union itself may be a pure monopoly. In other words, it is the only seller of labor services to a firm or industry.

Let's introduce a union with a monopoly supply of labor into our company town. Amalgamated Guide Workers has a monopoly on labor. The Universal Study Guide Company has a monopsonistic position with regard to hiring the union's members. So one monopoly is face to face with another—a *bilateral* monopoly.

Figure 23-6 shows the range of wages and employment. The supply and demand relations are the same as in Figure 23-5. Universal Study Guide wants to hire Q_1 guide workers and pay them a wage of W_1. What wage will the workers' union try to get? Presumably, W_2 (at which $MRC_L = MRP_L$). At that wage level, labor would be paid its marginal revenue product, or the value of what it contributes to the revenues of the firm.

The bilateral monopoly model shows that wages will fall in the range between W_1 and W_2. That is, the wage will be between the *MRP* of labor and the wage that will just bring forth the equilibrium (profit-maximizing) number of laborers. This model does not show precisely what the wage will be. The actual wage will depend on the relative bargaining strength of labor and management.

One *possible* result of this bargaining process is a wage of W_3. Look at Figure 23-6 now, and follow this. If W_3 is the wage settled on, the Universal Study Guide Company's marginal resource cost becomes $W_3 CDMRC_L$. The wage W_3 is what the company pays to all labor hired, out to point *C* on the supply curve. At this wage of W_3, the union will not supply any more than Q_2 of labor. If Universal Study Guide decides to hire more labor, it must pay overtime (look at S_L and MRC_L). A wage of W_3 will cause Universal Study Guide to behave like a competitive employer. It will hire more workers up to the point at which the wage (now MRC_L) equals marginal revenue product.

FIGURE 23-6 Bilateral Monopoly in the Study-Guide Industry

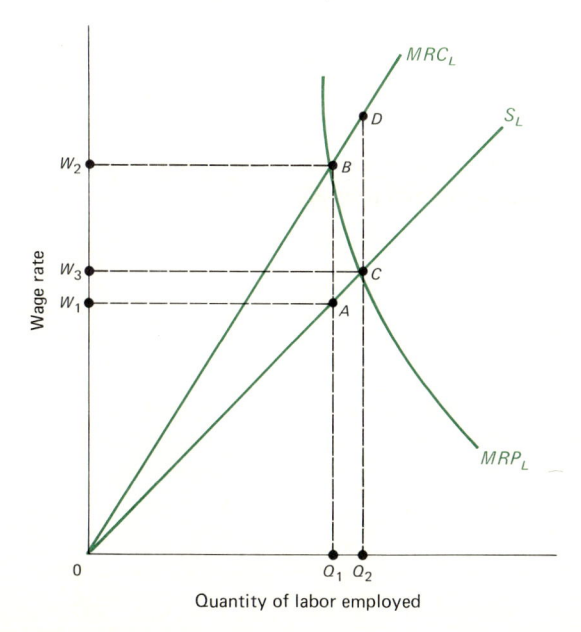

From this model, one learns an important fact. When monopsonistic firms bargain with monopolistic unions, the wages that result may eliminate some (theoretically, even all) of the monopsony power the firms have. However, even monopolistic unions cannot, by bargaining, get a wage that will eliminate the product-market monopoly position of firms. That is, the unions cannot *force* firms to produce enough to make wages equal the value of the marginal product of labor. (There is one exception: When a union bargains about wages with a firm that *is* a competitive product seller, it can make the wage equal to the value of marginal product of labor. Even in this case, though, the union has not changed the market for the firm's product, nor has it eliminated monopoly power. It has simply caused the firm to hire the most profitable amount of labor, and it has eliminated any monopsony power that the firm might have had. Examples of this are the construction industry unions that deal with independent competitive contractors.)

We can see this in Figure 23-6. If the union were able to bargain away the monopoly position of the firm, it would try for a hypothetical wage W_4, which would be a wage equal to the value of marginal product of labor (MPP_L × price of study guides). If this were to happen, a point E would be the new equilibrium point and Q_3 would be the new amount of labor employed. In other words, this situation (which cannot exist in a bilateral monopoly) points up the fact that even eliminating monopsony does not generate the level of employment and wage that competitive product markets do.

The Government Steps In

The third influence on wages is the government. Government may wield this influence by enacting minimum-wage legislation. There are many arguments in favor of minimum wages, but from the economist's point of view, two deserve attention:

1. Minimum-wage laws counteract the monopsony power of business firms by setting wages at a level that more nearly equals the marginal revenue product of labor.

2. Minimum-wage laws force employers to pay laborers socially acceptable and "equitable" wages, particularly in industries in which laborers are not organized. The problem with this argument is that it represents a value judgment about what is "equitable." As you have seen before, there is no unique distribution of income that is equitable. There is also no uniquely "equitable" wage.

Let's examine Figure 23-7, which deals with the first point. Suppose that the study-guide industry had not been unionized. Instead, suppose that Congress sets a minimum wage at W_m. The senator who wrote the bill says that the purpose of the law is to ensure a "decent" income for any worker whose output is shipped across state lines. (This includes the workers in the guide industry.) Before the minimum-wage law was enacted, the equilibrium wage paid to guide workers would have been W_e. At that wage level, demand (MRP_L) would have equaled supply (S_L). Now the senator pushes the bill through Congress, setting W_m (perhaps

$3 per hour) as the minimum wage. This means that the supply of laborers (S_L) who are willing to work below the minimum wage (W_m) no longer has any bearing on the level of employment, since no one can work legally for less than W_m. Thus, W_m becomes labor supply (S_L) and marginal resource cost (MRC), up to the point at which $W_m = S_L$.

What happens to employment? It falls from Q_e (where $S_L = MRP_L$) to Q_m (where $W_m = MRP_L$). Now you will notice an unpleasant fact of life. At the minimum wage there is substantial *involuntary unemployment*. At wage W_m, firms employ only Q_m of labor, even though workers are willing to supply Q'_m. So the passing of the minimum-wage law means that the actual rate of employment falls below the level that prevailed before the law was enacted. The government has raised the wage above the marginal revenue product of many workers. This is the most important drawback to minimum-wage legislation.

You can see that, in a market economy (as opposed to a command economy), the government can legislate wage rates by passing laws, but it cannot legislate the number of jobs available. This means that it cannot legislate the market incomes of the populace.

Other Factors of Production

We have established some general principles of supply and demand as they affect the pricing of labor. Now we will extend those same principles to the pricing of *land* (rents), *capitals* (interest), and *entrepreneurship* (profits).

FIGURE 23-7 Effect of Minimum-Wage Legislation

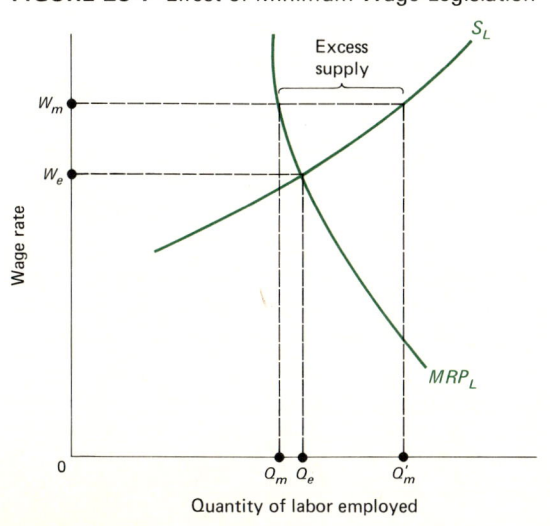

FIGURE 23-8 How Land Rents Are Determined

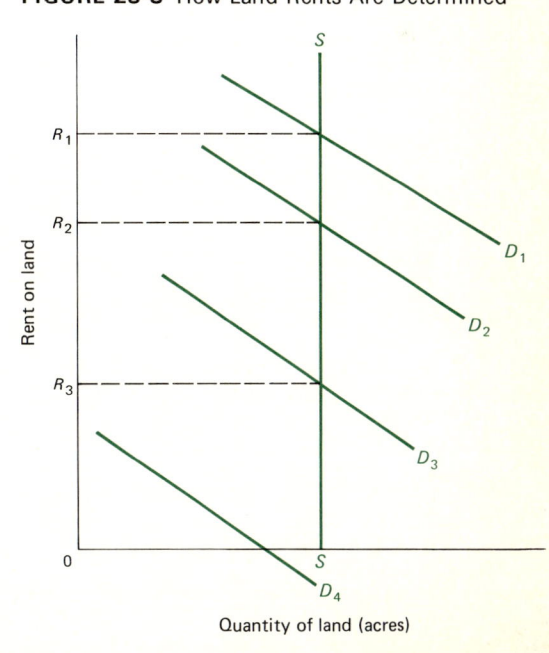

Land and Its Rent

Will Rogers used to say, "Buy land. They ain't makin' any more of it." That, in fact, is a peculiar feature of land. Unlike many other resources, land is nonreproducible. There is only so much of it. Of course, you can clear land that is covered with trees or boulders. Or you can wall off parts of the sea, and thus reclaim land from the water. By such methods, you may in the long run slightly increase the supply of land. But from most standpoints, one can assume that the supply of land is fixed, or perfectly inelastic.

Economists refer to the payment made for *any* resource whose supply is perfectly inelastic as **economic rent**. Calling it "economic rent" keeps people from getting it mixed up with the popular use of the word *rent* (as in "I paid the rent on my apartment"). Rent in this popular sense, though, includes the interest on borrowed capital, the profit that accrues to the entrepreneur, the wages paid to the gardener, and so on.

What determines the price of land, or the price of any resource with inelastic supply? *Demand* does. Figure 23-8, on the previous page, shows how this works. S is the supply of a certain type of land. There is just one acre of it in the middle of a big city, so the supply is perfectly inelastic. D_2 is the initial demand for this land, and R_2 is the equilibrium rent. (Let's say that this is a competitive market, and that all this land is equally productive, so there is *one* rent.) Now demand increases to D_1. There can be no increase in quantity, so the rent rises to R_1. Similarly, if demand decreases to D_3, rent declines to R_3.

But now suppose that there's a large supply of this land. The supply is then great relative to the demand. (Look at demand curve D_4 in Figure 23-8.) Since the demand for land is not as great as the supply at any price, the land will not command a price. It is, in fact a **free good**, one whose price is zero. This condition may actually exist today in some frontier areas. It existed in parts of the United States in the eighteenth and nineteenth centuries, when families who were willing to endure the hardships of homesteading could take up farming on unused land, including "free" land owned by the federal government. (Even this land was not entirely free, because settlers had to clear it and so forth.) Obviously, this is not common in market economies today.

Rents as Signals: Valid or Not?

Prices established in markets (rather than being arbitrarily set elsewhere) are useful signals to indicate where too many or too few resources are being used. In other words, prices serve to gauge the efficiency of an economy. If wages rise in one area or in one occupation, workers find out about it. To workers, it is a signal to move to that area or retrain for that job (assuming that there are not any market or government barriers). Interest rates and rates of profit act as signals, too, in much the same way.

Can rents on land serve this same function of fitting supply to demand? The answer has two parts:

1. In the aggregate, the answer is no. No matter how high or how low

rents are, landowners cannot rush into the market and supply more or less land. The supply of land is fixed. In this sense, rents on land are a *surplus* (some say *unearned*). They do not act as an incentive to make the market operate more efficiently.

In the aggregate, land is a gift of nature. Rent is certainly not necessary to ensure the supply of it. Therefore, should rents be paid on land? Some people say no. The most famous proponent of doing away with land rents was the American economist Henry George, who, in a book *Progress and Poverty* published in the 1880s, argued that taxing away rents completely would not change the availability of land or impair the working of the economy. George believed that as an economy developed (as it gained more people and as people got higher incomes), the demand for land would grow (as from D_2 to D_1 in Figure 23-8) and rents would rise. George pointed out that these payments would not be the result of productive activity on the part of landowners. Rather they would come about because of the fact that supplies of land were fixed. There could never be increases in supply. Henry George argued that a single tax on land could replace all other forms of taxation, without ill effect on the economy. The burden of the tax would fall entirely on the landowner. Suppose that rents on land rose from 0 to R_3 (Figure 23-8). A tax of $0R_3$ would eliminate the rent increases. And the tax would not affect the supply of land or the price of it. People who agreed with George (and there were many) became known as "single taxers."

The reasoning of the single taxers is subject to criticism, though. For one thing, it is hard to separate rents on land from payments for other factors. How much of the payment to a landowner is for ownership of the land? How much is for improvements on it? Would a single (land) tax really finance governments? Almost certainly it would not—not a modern government, anyway. Finally, how can one say that rent on land is unearned, while at the same time saying that capital gains (which usually result from no productive effort on the part of the gainer) are earned? Let's say that your grandmother bought a thousand shares of Coca-Cola stock in 1910 for $5,000, and that it is worth $5 million today. Did your grandmother *earn* this increase in capital value any more than a person who bought a parcel of land in downtown Boston in the same year earned the increase in value of that land?

2. For particular parcels of land rather than the total supply of land, the answer is less clear. Perhaps you use your land to put up an office building. Your neighbor uses a similar tract of land to plant an apple orchard. You receive a higher rent on your land than your neighbor receives. This is the concept of *relative rents*. Consumers and producers evaluate the worth of land according to the use to which it is put. Relative land rents thus serve as signals to indicate the most value-producing uses of land. Even so, once the rents exist, they can indeed be taxed away without affecting the supply of land.

This fact has been noted by many cities. City councils have historically structured their tax systems in favor of taxes on land instead of taxes on the incomes of individuals or businesses. It may interest you to know that in 1974 (according to the *New York Times*), Americans paid about $51 billion in property taxes. The Tax Foundation said that this was about double what Americans paid in 1965. (The average tax was $118 per person in 1965, but about $237 per person in 1974.)

Capital and Interest Rates

There are two forms of capital: **physical capital**, or the tools and instruments of production (plant, machinery, and the like); and **financial capital**, or money that has been saved and that may be supplied to firms that want to invest it in physical capital. Here we will discuss the *financial* capital market (the capital-goods markets function like other product markets).

The market that deals with financial capital is like other markets in that it is influenced by both supply and demand. The supply of capital is the savings of a society, the private savings of individuals and businesses. Businesses often finance their investments out of their retained (nondistributed) earnings. To the extent that they do this, they do not actually go to the capital markets to obtain financing. Even so, the opportunity cost to them is the interest rate, which is what they *could* have earned if they had supplied these funds to the capital market, rather than retaining them and using them internally.

We shall assume that the quantity of capital supplied does respond to changes in interest rates. Remember that interest rates are the prices that banks and other institutions pay to savers. Interest rates are also the prices that firms must pay to borrow funds. This means that as the interest rate increases, the amount of loanable funds available to business firms also increases. When interest rates are very high, savers increase their efforts to save.

A firm's *demand* for funds depends on the relations between the cost (price) of borrowed capital and the return expected by the firm (the marginal revenue product of capital). As long as a firm's return on its capital investment is greater than the interest rate, the firm will borrow—presumably up to the point at which the two are equal. That is, it will borrow until its MRP_K (marginal revenue product of capital) is equal to R_K (the rate of interest on the borrowed capital).

Figure 23-9 shows how interest rates are determined. In this illustration, the equilibrium interest rate is 8 percent. At this rate, according to the loanable-funds theory, supply equals demand (the sum of the demands of individual firms). But there is not one interest rate, but many. Why do interest rates vary? Variations may be traced to the following four factors:

1. *Risk*. The greater the chance that a borrower will default on a loan, the higher the interest rate needed to protect the lender against this risk. New York City must pay a higher rate to borrow (that is, to sell its bonds) than the state of New York does (which is still higher than that of some of the other states, such as California).

2. *Liquidity*. The harder it is to dispose of a debt instrument, that is, to

convert it into money, the greater the risk of loss and the higher the interest rate.

3. *Length of loan.* The longer the period of time of the loan or debt instrument, the higher the interest rate.

4. *Competitiveness.* The more competitive a particular capital market is, the lower the interest rate in that market.

Government and the Capital Market

Governments (especially the federal government) are involved in all the factor markets in the United States. However, they have a special concern for the capital market and the level of interest rates. Chapter 13 discussed the way the Federal Reserve System uses its powers to affect the supply of money and the interest rates (including the discount rate, or the rate that commercial banks pay to borrow money from the Federal Reserve). The government itself is a major demander of funds in the capital market. The funding and refunding of the federal debt is accomplished primarily in these markets, and the buying and selling of federal debt have a major effect on interest rates. When the government is borrowing heavily, individuals sometimes have difficulty obtaining a mortgage loan. Much of the supply of loanable funds is used up by government.

You can see that interest rates are not only prices that ration the supply of capital. They also have a strong effect on investment, home building, and the economy as a whole. The government, therefore, does not allow interest rates to seek any level that is warranted by supply and demand. The Federal Reserve, by using its power over the discount rate, can manipulate the rates of interest everyone must pay. The

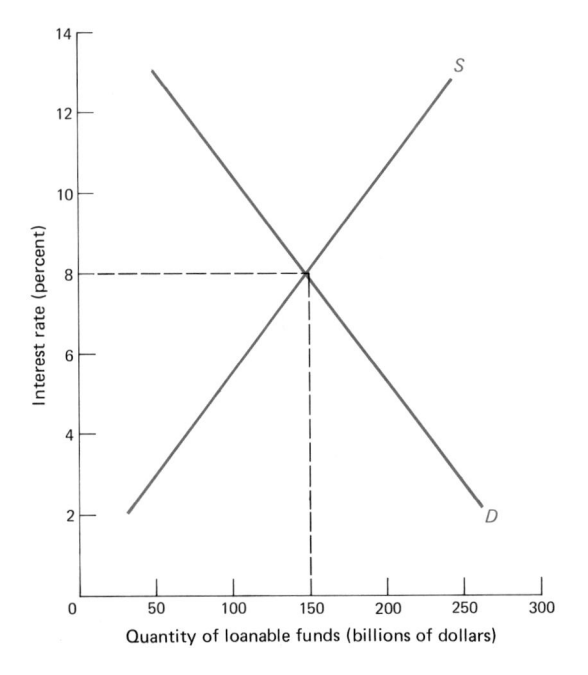

FIGURE 23-9 How Interest Rates Are Determined

interest rate is considered too important to be allowed to find its own level in a free market.

Entrepreneurship and Profit

Entrepreneurship is the function of organizing labor, land, and capital into a firm capable of producing and marketing a commodity or service. Economists regard it as a separate factor of production. The payment received by entrepreneurs is called **profit** (a return that is over and above normal profit, which is the return on invested capital). Remember that the "profit" referred to here is **economic profit**, which is the difference between a firm's total revenue and its total cost (the figure called "total cost" includes a normal profit).

The pursuit of profit is the principal motivation for entrepreneurs to perform their function. (However, vanity, the pursuit of power, and other less easily measured factors undoubtedly play a role as well.)

Let's consider one entrepreneur, Martin Bloggs, a part-time inventor. After years of work, he has come up with the all purpose study guide. He leaves his dull job with Ajax Publishers and sets out to found the Universal Study Guide Company. He borrows from banks; he hires labor, leases land and a building, buys machinery, and starts producing guides. Will he make an economic profit? If so, what will lie behind it? To answer, let's look at three interrelated theories of economic profit:

Monopoly Power. You have seen that economic profit cannot exist in the long run in a competitive market. If a firm has continued or long-term economic profits, it has some **monopoly power**. Let's say that Martin Bloggs gets a patent on Universal Study Guides. No one else can produce them (with his process) for seventeen years. He also trademarks the name of his product. This legal monopoly prevents, or retards, the entry of other firms into the study-guide industry. It also causes the output of guides to be lower and the prices of them higher than would be the case if there were competition. For example, instant-copy (Polaroid) cameras were very expensive when Dr. Land started producing them years ago. When the patents ran out and other camera companies leaped in with their models, prices went down.

What can be done about these profits that accrue to a monopolist? We have examined the options in other chapters, but they bear repeating:

1. Those high rates of profit can be relied on to act as incentives to attract others to produce similar products. This increases the competitiveness of the market. For example, for years before Polaroid's patent ran out, Kodak worked feverishly to produce its own instant-copy camera.

2. Antitrust laws, government contracting, and whatever other tools are available can be used to attack the source of monopoly power. For example, after World War II, to weaken the monopoly power of the Aluminum Company of American (Alcoa), the government sold alumi-

num plants to two new firms, Reynolds Metals and Kaiser Aluminum.

3. Monopoly power (in both product and factor markets) can be recognized as an inevitable consequence of barriers to entry into both product and factor markets and dealt with by directly involving government in the market system. This can be done through controls on wages, prices, and profit (this has been done before, as in World War II). Some economists, notably John Kenneth Galbraith, argue that the United States should be doing this today.

Innovation. Joseph Schumpeter, an economist at Harvard, said that **innovation**—introducing new products or new processes—is what causes an economy to *develop*, rather than just grow. So one could view economic profit as a temporary repayment to people who perform this unique function. Martin Bloggs (or Edwin Land, or Henry Ford) thus earns a high short-term profit *as a result of* throwing the market system off kilter by introducing innovations. As others enter the new industry, or use the new process and increase the supply of the product, these profits will disappear. (For some, there may even be losses in the long run.)

Risk and Uncertainty. When Bloggs starts producing guides, he may run into all sorts of problems. His *risks* include industrial accidents, deaths of executives, bad debts, and so forth. Bloggs can, if he wants, buy insurance against these risks. But there is no protection against *uncertainty*. For example, no one can sell Bloggs an insurance policy against having the foreman decide to go off and join a commune in the middle of filling an important order.

Once uncertainty enters the picture, both losses and profits become equally possible. "Playing the game" for profits is an important incentive for entrepreneurs.

Is Profit Earned?

It is necessary to pay people back for introducing innovations. It is necessary to pay them back for enduring the strain of facing uncertainty. On the basis of these concepts (and even on the basis of legal rights, such as patents), economists often say that short-term economic profits are earned. They are earned in that they are a necessary incentive. They bring to our society important, perhaps indispensable, economic functions, entrepreneurship, and innovation.

We should note that Marxists ("radical" economists in general) do not agree on this. Strict Marxists (including Marx himself) and some neo-Marxists hold to the *labor theory of value*: They believe that all value is based on the *amount of labor involved in production*. They say that monopolists cause laborers to work longer hours and do not pay them what their contribution to the product's value is worth. The monopolist retains the difference between the laborers' pay and the value of their contribution. This difference is called **surplus value**. It is not the same as economic profit. According to Marx, as long as there is a system of private ownership, surplus value will not be eliminated.

SUMMING UP

1. In this chapter, we discussed competitive and *non*competitive pricing, not only of labor but of land, capital, and entrepreneurship. These elements are called factors. Payments to factors are *wages, rents, interest*, and *profits*.

2. Wages are determined by the supply of and demand for labor. The quantity of labor supplied rises as the wage rate increases. Therefore, the supply curve of labor slopes upward. The supply of labor also depends on people having a positive marginal utility of income. In other words, it depends on people wanting more income with which to buy goods and services.

3. The labor supply curve of each individual does not always slope upward. The curve may bend backward if people satisfy themselves that they have enough goods and services. They may decide to trade off some income for more leisure Thus, above a certain wage rate, as wages go up, workers may offer to work less rather than more.

4. Leisure can be treated as a good. The demand for leisure as a tradeoff for income results from the *income effect* (our demand for leisure changes with changes in our incomes) and the *substitution effect* (the quantity of leisure demanded changes as its price changes).

5. In spite of *individual backward-bending labor supply curves,* the curve for the *total* supply of labor slopes upward, because all individual labor supply curves do not bend backward or bend backward at the same wage rate.

6. Also, various types of labor may command different wage rates, even for persons with similar skills. The difference in wages may be due to *location* (you can make more money repairing air conditioners in New York city than in Alaska) or to *discrimination* (male mechanics make more money than female mechanics).

7. Much of the difference in wage rates derives from differing elasticities of supply of different kinds of labor. In the United States, physicians have the highest incomes of any professional group. Part of this income differential is due to the inelastic supply of physicians.

8. People with very similar skills sometimes receive widely differing wages. The usual reasons are: (a) *Short-term increases in the demand for a given skill.* (b) *Wage and job discrimination.* For example, employers may refuse to hire any, or hire only a few, women workers or members of racial minorities, and after hiring, employers may pay women and minority workers less than the other workers. (c) *Nonmonetary considerations.* The satisfaction of performing some jobs may transcend monetary reward; for example, a college professor may accept a fairly small salary because the personal satisfaction of teaching outweighs a larger salary in the business world. (d) *Immobility of labor.* People may not move to better-paying jobs.

9. In a competitive situation, wages are set by the twin influences of supply and demand. A profit-maximizing firm that is a competitive seller of its products will hire enough labor to make the laborers *value of marginal product* (marginal physical product times product price) equal to their *marginal resource cost* (the addition to total cost attributable to the hiring of additional labor). Marginal resource cost is also equal to the wage rate, since, to a competitive employer, the wage is a constant, given factor.

10. If firms start to sell their products noncompetitively, the demand curve for their products begins to slope downward. To sell more of their product, they must reduce the price. Therefore, each time they hire an extra laborer in order to produce more of their product, the profit they gain from hiring that extra laborer becomes less and less. Now, noncompetitive monopolist firms will hire just enough labor to make the competitive wage (marginal cost) equal to the marginal revenue product (marginal physical product times marginal revenue). Since marginal revenue is less than the price of the product, the firm hires fewer and fewer laborers until finally consumers get less of the product than they would buy if markets were competitive.

11. Noncompetitiveness finds its way into the labor market in three main ways: (a) a firm may become *monopsonistic*, the only employer around to hire a particular type of laborer. (b) Laborers may organize a union, which is a monopolistic seller of labor's services. (c) Government may intervene in the labor market, by means of such devices as minimum-wage laws.

12. Monopsonistic firms must hire laborers in a market in which the curve showing the supply of labor is an upward-sloping one. In order to hire more and more workers, the monopsonist must pay a higher and higher wage. Therefore, the monopsonistic firm's marginal resource cost is not equal to the wage rate, but is greater than the wage rate. The profit-maximizing monopsonistic firm (which also has a monopoly on a given product) will hire just enough labor to make the marginal resource cost equal the marginal revenue product. Thus, monopsony, as compared with pure competition in the factor market, means that (a) the number of workers hired by a firm or industry falls off, and (b) the wage rate falls, since the wage rate becomes less than the value of the workers' marginal revenue product.

13. When a *monopoly* exploits labor, it pays workers less than the value of their marginal product. When a *monopsony* exploits labor, it pays workers less than the value of the workers' marginal revenue product.

14. When workers organize a union (and thus gain a monopoly on a certain kind of labor) and come face to face with a monopsonistic firm, the situation becomes a *bilateral monopoly*. When the two bargain and establish a wage, the figure they arrive at will be somewhere between the marginal revenue product of labor and the wage that will call forth just the equilibrium amount of labor demanded (indicated by the supply

curve of labor). The exact level of wages depends on the relative bargaining strength of labor and management.

15. One thing that *may* come about as a result of bilateral monopoly is that the wage rate will do away with monopsony power and bring about a wage that is equal to the marginal revenue product.

16. Minimum-wage laws are not the ideal solution. They may lead to a decline in employment and in workers' wages. If the minimum wage is enforced, the higher marginal resource cost may cause firms to hire fewer laborers, and even, in the long run, to substitute capital for labor. This leads to an oversupply of labor. If workers cannot find jobs elsewhere, unemployment or underemployment soon becomes a problem.

17. Land—unlike other resources—cannot be increased. It is therefore in inelastic supply. Economists refer to the payment made to any resource whose supply is perfectly inelastic as *economic rent*.

18. The price of land, like the price of any resource with inelastic supply, is determined by the demand for it. If demand increases sharply, rents increase sharply. If demand decreases sharply, rents decrease sharply. If the supply of land is very large relative to the demand for it, the rent will be zero. In this situation, land becomes a *free good* (as it is in some frontier societies).

19. In the aggregate sense, rents on land are not a valid indicator of the efficiency of an economy. No matter how high rents are, no one can add more land to the total supply. This has led some economists to argue in favor of taxing away all land rents. This idea has met with heavy criticism.

20. When it comes to particular parcels of land, *relative rents* (that is, rents that vary according to the use to which the land is put) do indicate which uses of land are the most profitable. Even so, these rents can be taxed away without affecting the supply of land.

21. There are two kinds of capital: *physical capital* and *financial capital*. The markets for financial capital are resource markets, whose *supply* comes from private (household and business) savings. The *demand* for financial capital comes from households, businesses, and government. Businesses will demand capital (that is, borrow money) as long as the marginal revenue product of the capital they borrow exceeds or is equal to its cost (the rate of interest, which is what it costs to borrow money).

22. The loanable-funds theory holds that the interest rate (the price of capital) is the rate that makes supply of funds equal to demand for funds.

23. There are many interest rates. Differences in rates depend on (a) risk, (b) liquidity, (c) length of loan, and (d) competitiveness in the capital markets.

24. One reason that governments intervene in capital markets is that interest rates do more than just ration the supply of capital. They also affect investment and the performance of the economy as a whole.

25. *Entrepreneurship* is the function of organizing labor, land, and capital into a firm capable of producing and marketing a commodity or service. The return to the entrepreneur who does this organizing and operating is called *economic profit*. There are three reasons why economic profit exists: (a) *Monopoly power*. A monopolist's patents, for example, are barriers to entry preventing movement of other firms into the field, which would drive prices down to competitive levels. (b) *Innovation*. The entrepreneur introduces new products or processes. *Profit* is a short-term reward for performing this function. (c) *Risk and uncertainty*. The entrepreneur must assume risks and bear the strain of uncertainty. It is just as possible to have losses as profits, and the entrepreneur who runs such a risk in pursuit of profits must be rewarded.

26. Many economists say that short-term economic profits are a necessary incentive to entrepreneurship and to the introduction of innovations, especially in view of the uncertainty and risks. Radical economists do not agree. Some Marxists hold to the *labor theory of value*. They feel that privately owned firms do not pay workers according to the amount they contribute to the value of the final product. The difference, *surplus value*, is a profit that the firm retains. This profit by the firm comes from private ownership.

QUESTIONS

1. What does your own labor supply curve look like? As the rate of your wages changes, what factors affect your willingness to work?

2. What is a backward-bending supply curve of labor? Do you think that it probably does exist in the real world? If so, why?

3. Which factors determine the wide range of wage rates you see in the world around you? Which factors do you think are most responsible for differences in wages for individuals with (a) the same skills and (b) different skills?

4. If you were offered a job doing the thing you most enjoy, would you take a lower salary for that job than for a job that was humdrum or unpleasant? If so, what would you call the difference between the amount of money you would earn at the enjoyable job and the amount you would earn at the dull one?

5. If you were running things, what would you do to reduce the monopsony power of certain employers? Have unions done a good job of reducing employers' monopsony power? Have minimum wage laws?

6. Do you think heavy taxation of land can (a) provide a significant part of government's revenues? (b) be an efficient—and equitable—source of revenue?

7. Think about Liberace and "Catfish" Hunter. Do you consider part of their salaries rent? Why? Is it earned?

8. What accounts for the wide range of interest rates? Should all these rates be the same?

9. Do you think that the profits entrepreneurs get are necessary to the successful functioning of the American economy? Why or why not?

SUGGESTED READINGS

Albrecht, William P., Jr. *Economics*. Prentice-Hall, Englewood Cliffs, N.J., 1974. Chapters 31 and 33.

Heyne, Paul T. "Productive Resources and Economic Rent." In *The Economic Way of Thinking*. Science Research Associates, Chicago, 1973.

Lekachman, Robert. "Academic Wisdom and Union Reality." In *The Second Crisis of Economic Theory*, edited by Rendigs Fels. General Learning Press, Morristown, N.J., 1972.

North, Douglass C., and Roger Leroy Miller. "Basketball and Football." "The Economics of Medical Care." "The Economics of Baseball." In *The Economics of Public Issues*. Harper & Row, New York, 1973.

Spencer, Milton H. "Determination of Factor Prices." In *Contemporary Economics*. Worth, New York, 1974.

Application 24

Wages, Incomes, and Economic Discrimination

In Chapters 22 and 23, we discussed the fact that under "ideal" (competitive) market conditions, the wages or salaries of workers would equal their *VMP*, value of marginal product. You arrive at this *VMP* by multiplying the marginal physical product by the price of the good the workers produce. But even in an economy in which workers' wages are equal to their *VMP*, all workers will not have equal market incomes, because one worker's productivity differs from another worker's, even if they both hold the same sort of job in the same field.

Another fact we discussed was that monopolistic conditons of production give rise to wages that are equal to *MRP*, marginal revenue product. *MRP* is marginal physical product multiplied by the marginal revenue the firm gets from selling the additional goods that additional workers produced.

Now recall that the wage differential between *VMP* and *MRP* is called **exploitation**, which represents the firm's failure to pay workers what they contribute to the value of their marginal product. We said that some exploitation might be offset by workers engaging in collective bargaining (which is a sort of bilateral monopoly). Whatever exploitation remained, however, would be uniformly felt in a market. It would apply to all workers who were employed. And employment would hinge strictly on the profit-maximizing behavior of firms.

When we look at job and wage structures in the world around us today, two things stand out: (1) The differences between the wages paid to one worker and the wages paid to another are greater than one can explain in terms of differences in their productivity. (2) All people in the labor force do not have equal opportunities for jobs. How can we explain this market behavior? Increasingly, economists have turned to *economic discrimination* as the clue.

What Is Economic Discrimination?

Economic discrimination is a state of affairs in which firms deal with people as consumers and producers of goods, or buyers and sellers of resources, on the basis of something *other* than market considerations. We have already mentioned (in Chapter 19) one form of economic discrimination—the kind people practice in the pricing of goods and services. Now we are going to examine two different forms of economic discrimination: job discrimination and wage discrimination. **Job discrimination** is the situation in which firms hire (or do not hire) workers on the basis of some consideration other than their productivity (their race, sex, age, religion, or whatever). **Wage discrimination** is the situation in which firms pay people wages that are lower than the wages would be if the firms were considering only people's productivity. (This form of discrimination is also based on such factors as race, sex, age, and religion.)

It is hard to identify these forms of economic discrimination, and even harder to measure them or determine how much discrimination is still being practiced. There are two aspects of discrimination to look for: **present discriminatory activity** (PDA), or current practice of basing jobs and wages on criteria other than productivity, and the **results of historical discrimination**, or the effects on today's jobs and wages of economic discrimination in the past. We will illustrate both.

Suppose that Thelma Smith, a black woman, is job hunting. (We are assuming that she is intelligent, capable, honest, healthy, and willing to work hard.) If firms will not hire her because of her race and/or sex, she is the victim of *job discrimination*.

But suppose that she does get a job. However, the firm pays her less than they pay her white, male coworkers. Then she is a victim of *wage discrimination*. In both cases, the results are due to *present discriminatory activity*.

Now suppose that she is not a victim of present discriminatory activity. Suppose she gets a job that uses all her skills, and that the firm pays her the same wage as her white, male coworkers. Is it possible for there still to be discrimination, even though there is no PDA? Yes. Because if Thelma Smith has in the past been denied access to good education on account of her race or sex, her skills may be less than they otherwise would have been. This *result of historical discrimination* represents an underinvestment in human capital. The discrimination she suffers from is not her employer's fault. It results from a body of social preferences and prejudices gradually built up over centuries past. Around these preferences and prejudices has grown a whole lore of snobbish and unfounded convictions. ("Woman's place is in the home. She shouldn't be out driving a truck or managing a company." "Women don't need to be paid the same as men. After all, they have husbands to support them. They only work to supplement the family income." "Black people have natural musical and athletic ability, but they don't have the drive to become entrepreneurs." And so forth.)

Understanding Discrimination

You can see the direct economic effects of job discrimination in the supply-and-demand conditions of labor markets. It will help you to understand discrimination, therefore, if we use some supply-and-demand tools of analysis. One of these is called **crowding theory**. This is the theory that economic discrimination leads to groups of people (women, blacks, Chicanos, and so on) being crowded *into* certain occupations, and *out of* others. For example, in the United States, the great majority of elementary-school teachers are female. The vast majority of physicians are male.

Figure A24-1 shows how crowding affects wages. In Figure A24-1(a), D_t represents demand for teachers, S_m represents the supply of male teachers, and S_{m+f}, the supply of male plus female teachers. Since most elementary-school teachers are female, the result is that women are crowded into this field. The wage is W_1. If there were no crowding—if women were able to get jobs in all fields on the basis of their abilities and preferences—the supply of female teachers would be reduced. The total supply might fall to some level such as S'_{m+f} and the wage might rise to W_2.

Figure A24-1(b) shows what happens to wages in those labor markets from which women (or blacks or Chicanos) are largely excluded. The supply of male physicians is S_m and total supply is S_{m+f} (which reflects the fact that most doctors are male). Demand for the services of doctors is D_d and the wage is W_1. If crowding did not exist, more women would become M.D.'s. The supply would increase to some level such as S'_{m+f} and the wage would move to some level such as W_2. A thought-provoking fact is that in the Soviet Union seven out of ten physicians are women; in the United States (as of 1973) one out of twelve physicians was a woman.

What Are the Consequences of Crowding?

1. Wages in those occupations into which people are crowded are lower than they would be if productivity and personal preferences were the factors that dictated people's choices of jobs.

2. The result of item 1 is that the relative income positions of certain groups are strongly affected. Groups crowded into low-paying occupations have much lower average incomes. (For example, in 1972, the median income of blacks in the United States was $7,106. The median income of whites was $11,549.)

3. Society loses as a result of these factors. Present discriminatory activity causes people to be shunted into jobs that do not fully utilize their skills. For example, a woman who is a trained chemist and is forced to take a job as a typist because of crowding has a lower marginal revenue product as a result. Society is thus misallocating its resources. (This is one source of underemployment.) The results of historical discrimination mean that society loses because it underinvests in human capital. It fails to educate groups of people that are crowded. Thus, society must forgo the higher productivity and full-employment GNP that it could enjoy if there were no results of historical discrimination. (For example, in 1972, 8.3 percent of blacks were college graduates whereas 19.9 percent of whites were college graduates.)

Unequal Wages for Equal Jobs

Crowding does explain why some people are excluded from some jobs, or have slight chance of entering some fields of endeavor. But it does not explain why people who work at the same jobs, and have the same skills, do not all receive the same pay. Figure A24-2 will help you understand this. There S_{m+f} represents the supply of male plus female labor with a given skill, D_m represents employers' demand for male workers with these skills, and D_f represents the demand for female workers with the same skills. (Note that we are assuming that the skills of the two sexes are the same. If they were not, we could not consider them as part of the same labor market.)

As we saw in Chapters 22 and 23, the demand for a factor of production depends directly on that factor's marginal physical productivity and on the price of the product it is hired to produce. Since there is no difference between these factors for men and for women in the same labor market, the difference between the two demand curves in Figure A24-2 must be attributed to a "taste for discrimination" on the part of employers. In this case, both males and females will be employed,

FIGURE A24-1 Effects of Crowding on Wages. (*a*) Elementary-school teachers; (*b*) Physicians.

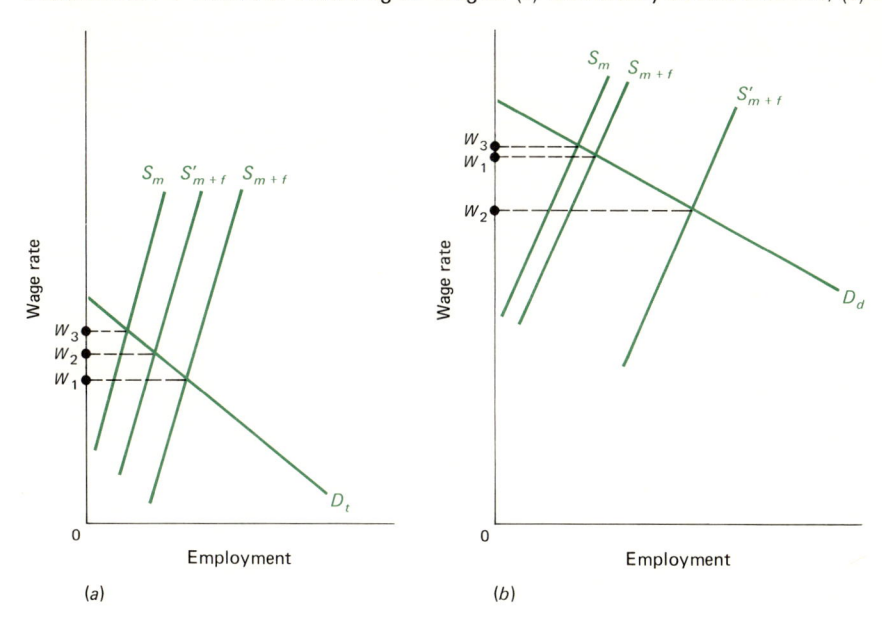

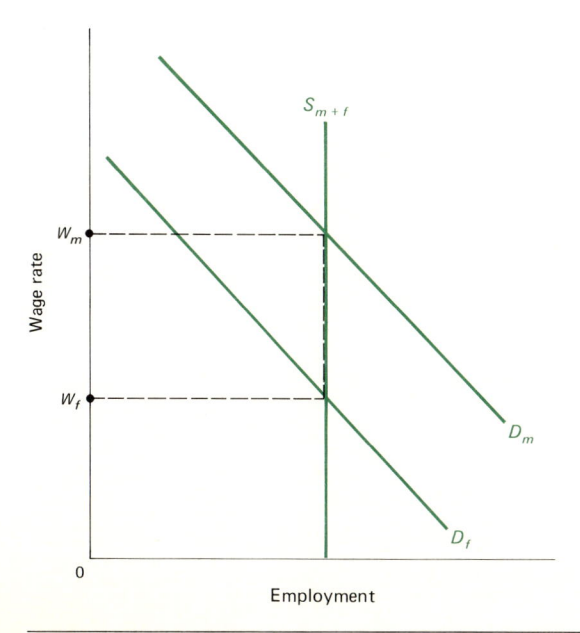

FIGURE A24-2 "Taste for Discrimination" and Wages

Unequal Wages for Equal Jobs 565

but males will be paid W_m and females W_f. (Here we are assuming, for the sake of simplicity, a supply of labor that is perfectly inelastic.)

What are the consequences of the wage discrimination shown in Figure A24-2?

1. The distribution of income is skewed in favor of men and against women, even when discriminating firms employ women on a supposedly equal-opportunity basis.

2. Figure A24-2 shows no underemployment (loss of productivity). However, there is a new form of economic exploitation, to add to that discussed in Chapter 23. It is the exploitation that exists when labor is paid less than its value of marginal product or marginal revenue product. This new form is due to wage discrimination. It is reflected in $W_m - W_f$, which is the difference between the wage paid to men and that paid to women. (For example, in 1971, the median income of male managers, officials, and proprietors was $13,087. The median income of females in the same jobs was $8,970.)

Table A24-1 gives further evidence of male-female wage discrimination. It also shows the relatively small percentage of women in occupations other than clerical or service work. This *implies* (but does not *prove*) a certain amount of job discrimination.

A Note of Caution

Our analysis of discrimination in jobs and wages between men and women is based on the assumption that both groups are equally productive. But if women appear to be more prone to absenteeism or to have a faster rate of job turnover (due to pregnancies, necessity of caring for children, and so forth), then they are presumed to be less desirable than men as employees. Table A24-1 shows that part of the lower hiring rate and lower wage of women is due to the response of profit-maximizing employers to a more expensive resource and not to exploitation or job discrimination. Also, women in many occupations presently tend to work fewer hours than men; this accounts for part of the difference in their incomes. Finally, our analysis has implied that it is only employers who practice job and wage discrimination. But research indicates that **customer discrimination**—job and wage discrimination resulting from the tastes of buyers, such as a preference for being waited on in restaurants by men or by whites—may be just as influential in explaining employers' discrimination. However, there is evidence that, even after all the above factors are taken into consideration, about one-fourth of the 40 percent wage differential between men and women is indeed attributable to discrimination.

TABLE A24-1 Median Income by Occupation and Sex, 1971

Occupation	Median income in occupation	Male median income	Female median income	Percent of male labor force	Percent of female labor force	Females as percent of occupation
Managers, Officials, and Proprietors	$12,192	$13,087	$8,970	15.8	6.4	14.6
Professional and Technical	11,395	12,842	8,515	15.7	18.6	33.4
Sales Workers	9,883	11,122	4,681	6.2	4.2	22.3
Craftsmen and Foremen	9,884	9,779	5,493	21.6	1.4	2.7
Operatives	7,274	8,069	4,884	17.7	13.9	25.0
Laborers (except farm)	6,932	7,083	4,486	4.8	.6	6.1
Clerical Workers	6,904	9,512	5,820	6.9	39.3	70.6
Service Workers	6,090	7,484	4,375	6.9	13.3	44.8
Farmers and farm managers	n.a.	4,915	n.a.	3.4	.2	2.2
Farm workers	n.a.	3,806	n.a.	1.0	.3	10.8
Private household workers	n.a.	n.a.	2,328	n.a.	1.7	n.a.
	n.a.	$9,631	$5,701	100.0	100.0	29.6

Source: Adapted from Mary Hamblin and Michael J. Prell, "The Incomes of Men and Women: Why Do They Differ?" *Monthly Review,* Federal Reserve Bank of Kansas City, April 1973.

"It seems to me the majority of people in this country belong to some minority group!"

What Can Be Done About Discrimination?

People in the United States have long believed that American society is a melting pot, that minority groups ultimately become absorbed into the mainstream of the economy. This idea may have been valid for males in the earlier minority groups (for example, Irish immigrants in the nineteenth and early-twentieth centuries). But it does not seem to be working as well for other groups: blacks, Chicanos, Puerto Ricans, women, older Americans. If time will not solve the problems of economic discrimination, what other remedies are there?

Public Action

Laws against economic discrimination go back to the early history of the United States. The Fourteenth Amendment to the Constitution prohibits some forms of discrimination. The controversial Equal Rights Amendment would do away with others. Civil rights legislation of the 1960s (especially the Civil Rights Act of 1964) outlawed discrimination in employment on the basis of race or sex. The Equal Employment Opportunity Commission in 1972 gained the power to sue employers for noncompliance. Today, all employers with more than fifty workers who hold federal contracts of $50,000 or more are required by law to have affirmative-action employment plans. However, there is no way of knowing as yet how successful these legal efforts have been—or may be in the future.

Moving more vigorously toward the goal of full employment is another way to help end wage and job discrimination. In all likelihood, it would create more opportunities for minority groups and women than it would for whites and males. The reason is that when times get hard, it is minorities and women that are the "last hired, first fired." This is true, at least, of private employers. Public employers (government at the federal, state, and local levels), however, when they create jobs to help ease an employment gap, tend to hire both minorities and women to a disproportionate extent.

Private Action

Some economists (notably, Milton Friedman) argue that *competitive pressures* on profit-maximizing employers do a lot to reduce job and wage discrimination. Competitive firms that exhibit a "taste for discrimination" find that their workers' productivity is lower and their costs higher. Ultimately, they must either abandon discrimination or be driven out of the marketplace. (These economists concede, however, that monopolistic employers do not necessarily succumb to these pressures.)

Unions

Unions may hold out hope for minority and female workers. Some blacks and women, however, have found it hard to join unions. Examples are trade unions, such as plumbers, electricians, and the construction trades. The industrial unions (automobile workers, steelworkers, and so on) have, on the other hand, racked up a good record of admitting, and helping, minorities and women.

Creating Entrepreneurs

The picture looks brighter when minorities and women become entrepreneurs. The idea of black capitalism is gaining strength everywhere, for example; and black employers will not discriminate against blacks (presumably). Nor will women employers discriminate against women (presumably). Hence, there are an increasing number of such organizations as the Women's Bank of New York, which opened its doors in 1975.

SUMMING UP

1. When employers pay employees less than the employees' value of marginal product, *exploitation* exists.

2. *Economic discrimination* consists in dealing with people as consumers and producers of goods, or as buyers and sellers of resources, on the basis of considerations *other* than market considerations.

3. A person who can not get a job because of race or sex (or some consideration other than nonproductivity) is a victim of *job discrimination*. A person who has a job but is paid less than others of equal productivity is a victim of *wage discrimination*.

4. Economic discrimination arises from two sources: (a) *present discriminatory activity* (jobs and wages not based on productivity), and (b) *results of historical discrimination* (effects on present economic situation of previous discrimination).

5. *Crowding theory* analyzes the effects of discrimination on the basis of supply and demand. *Crowding* refers to the shunting of women and members of minority groups into certain occupations, and keeping them out of others. The result is that wages in the "crowded" occupations are lower than they would otherwise be and higher than they would be in the "uncrowded" occupations, which are dominated by males and whites. Also, income is distributed in favor of whites and males.

6. Society loses as a result of crowding because it does not fully utilize the productivity of women and minorities. This loss of productivity reduces the full-employment GNP.

7. When employers pay unequal wages to persons of equal productivity, it is usually because the employer has a "taste for discrimination." Such a taste results in two different demand conditions, one for whites or males, or both, the other for women or minority workers, or both. The effect is to cause women and minorities to be paid a lower wage. The difference between the wages of the two groups is a form of wage exploitation based on race or sex.

8. Wage discrimination, unlike job discrimination, does not result in loss of productivity, or in underemployment. It does, however, skew income away from women and minority groups.

9. The idea of the melting pot does not appear to be working rapidly to end job and wage discrimination against women and members of minority groups. The remedies are public action or private action.

10. Public action against discrimination may take the form of legislation, or it may take the form of moving toward full employment. Private action may take the form of (a) letting competitive pressures eliminate discrimination, (b) encouraging union membership for women and minorities, or (c) encouraging women and minority-group members to become entrepreneurs, who will not discriminate (presumably) against their own kind.

QUESTIONS

1. If we as a nation moved vigorously to create a more competitive economy, would we eliminate much economic discrimination? Why or why not?

2. The melting pot worked to eliminate economic discrimination in the past. Why is it unlikely to do so or do so rapidly, in the situation that exists today?

3. Some radical economists claim that economic discrimination is the product of capitalism. Do you agree? Why or why not?

4. Will it be easier to reduce economic discrimination against women in the future than against blacks and members of other minority groups? Or will it be harder? Give reasons for your answer.

5. Do you think that black capitalism or female capitalism will succeed in reducing or eliminating economic discrimination? Why or why not?

SUGGESTED READINGS

Albrecht, William P., Jr. "Discrimination." In *Economics*. Prentice-Hall, Englewood Cliffs, N.J., 1974.

Ashenfelter, Orley. "Racial Discrimination and Trade Unionism." *Journal of Political Economy*, May/June, 1972.

Becker, Gary L. *The Economics of Discrimination*, 2d ed. University of Chicago Press, Chicago, 1971.

Bergman, Barbara R. "The Effect on White Incomes of Discrimination in Employment." *Journal of Political Economy*, March/April, 1971.

Chinitz, Benjamin. "Urban Economies: The Problem of the Ghetto." In *Perspectives in Economics: Economists Look at their Fields of Study*, edited by Alan A. Brown, Egon Neuberger, and Malcolm Palmatier. McGraw-Hill, New York, 1971.

Elliott, A. Wright. "Black Capitalism and the Business Community." In *Black Economic Development*, edited by William F. Haddad and G. Douglas Pugh. Prentice-Hall, Englewood Cliffs, N.J., 1969.

Hamblin Mary, and Michael J. Prell. "The Incomes of Men and Women: Why Do They Differ?" In *Annual Editions, Readings in Economics, 1974/1975*, Dushkin, Guilford, Conn., 1974.

Mansfield, Edwin, ed. *Economics, Readings, Issues, and Cases*. Part 7, "Income Inequality, Poverty, and Discrimination." Norton, New York, 1974.

Mermelstein, David, ed. *Economics: Mainstream Readings and Radical Critiques*, 2d ed., Part 3(b), "The Political Economy of Black America." Random House, New York, 1973.

North, Douglass C. and Roger Leroy Miller. "The Economics of Exploitation and Discrimination." In *The Economics of Public Issues*, Harper & Row, New York, 1973.

Tobin, James. "On Improving the Economic Status of the Negro." Reprinted in *Economics: Readings in Analysis and Policy*, edited by Dennis R. Starleaf. Scott, Foresman, Glenview, Ill., 1969.

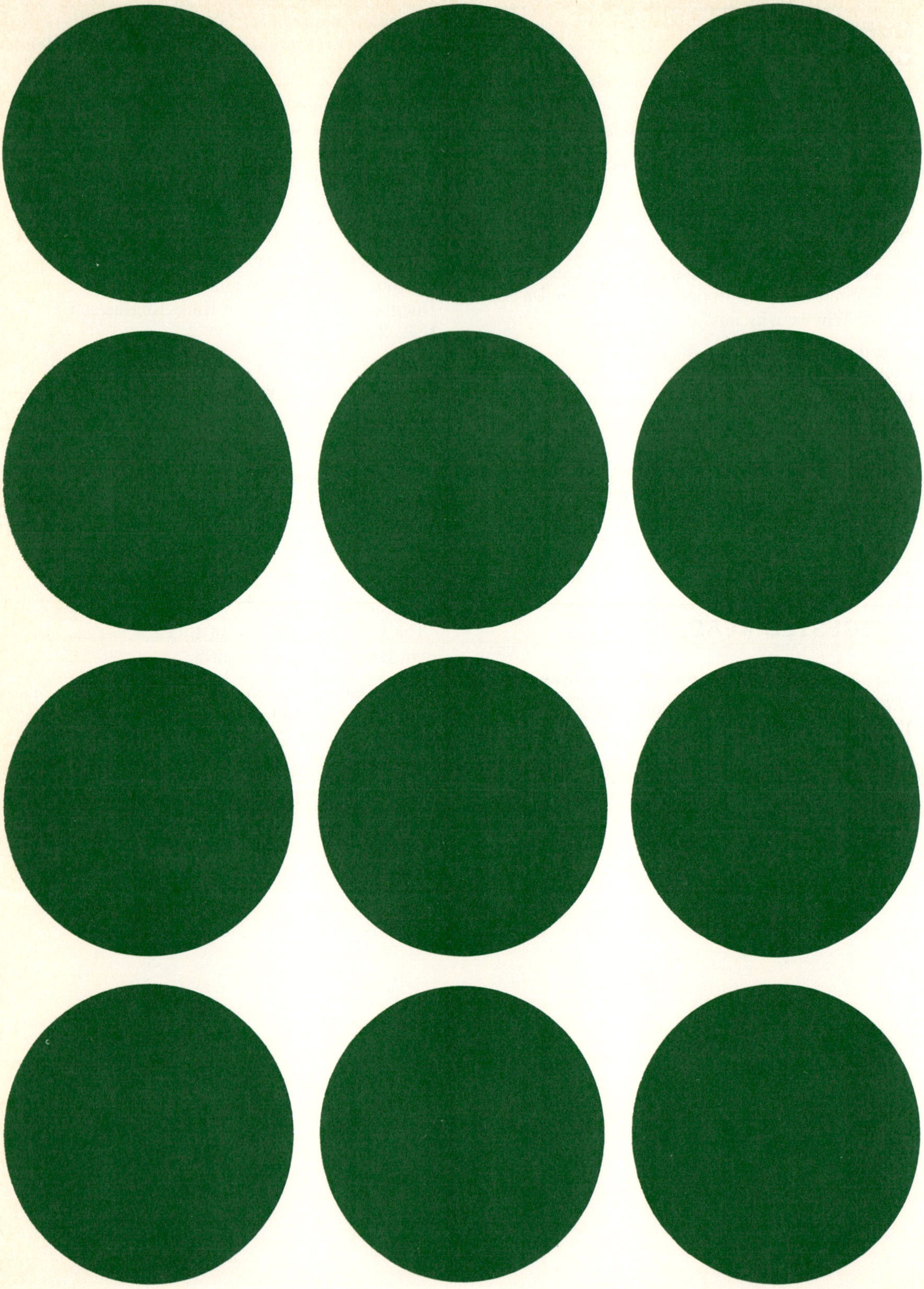

PART THREE

And Now the Rest of the World

We are now ready to tie in the economy of the United States with the economies of other nations. We will discuss trade with other countries and how the United States pays for it. We will examine the advantages of trade, the pressures that prevent nations from practicing unrestricted trade, and the exchange of national currencies. We will present arguments about whether trade results in economic development and whether countries should base their trade policies on short-term changes in their ability to sell to other countries as much as they buy from other countries (a problem faced by the United States in recent years). And it is fitting to end the book by comparing the American economy and its mixed-market, public system with other economic systems: with socialist economies in general (Chapter 26) and the Soviet Union in particular (Chapter 27).

24
Patterns of International Trade

In the preceding chapters, we analyzed the many aspects of a *single* economy. (The sole exception was Chapter 2, which dealt with scarcity and other economic factors common to *all* economies.) Most of our discussions began with abstract ideas; then we added the complexities of reality. We introduced each topic this way because it is easier to see a tree without the forest around it. Then we put in the forest, a little at a time. Finally, by the end of each discussion, we had built a model that was applicable to a wide range of problems.

Now we will remove the last, and most significant, of the simplifying assumptions: that the United States is an economic island unto itself. Everyone is aware that the United States does indeed trade with other nations. In 1973, U.S. imports and exports together totaled $145 billion.

What Is Trade?

Trade consists of **exports**—commodities and services sold to other nations—and **imports**—commodities and services bought from other nations. Suppose that a dealer in San Francisco imports a Datsun. The price the importer pays (plus any shipping charges paid to foreign shippers) is added to the total of U.S. imports. Similarly, when a Japanese grain dealer imports American wheat, the payments that U.S. wheat sellers receive (plus any payments to our own shippers) are added to the total of our exports.

Thus international trade is made up of both **visible items** and **invisible items**. The visible items are the commodities (cars, wheat, television sets, petroleum, machinery, and so on) that are exported and imported. Invisible items are the services, including financial services (services of

Export and import at work: Freighter taking on wheat for Japan after unloading Japanese automobiles (Courtesy Harry Gilmour/Port of Seattle)

exporters and importers, ship rentals, cost of financing, and so on) which are exported and imported.

How Important Is Trade?

At this point, you may say, "Look, the United States is a big nation; it produces a great variety of goods and services and has vast natural resources. Surely, trade with other nations isn't all that important to us. Why devote a whole chapter to it?"

To begin with, think back to Chapter 9 in which we said that the GNP (which very strongly affects the level of employment) is

$$GNP = C + I + GX.$$

This equation says that our gross national product is composed of consumer spending, investment spending, and government spending. Now, let's add a fourth element to GNP: **net foreign trade**. *Net foreign trade is the difference between exports (X) and imports (M)*. So net foreign trade equals X minus M (NFT = $X - M$). Therefore, GNP is now

$$GNP = C + I + GX + (X - M).$$

Whenever $X - M$ is positive (that is, when exports are greater than imports), a country has a favorable balance of trade. Then aggregate demand increases and GNP *increases by a multiple amount* (other things being equal). It does so because just as there is a multiplier when there are changes in C, I, or G, so is there a multiplier when there are changes in foreign trade. This is called the **foreign-trade multiplier**, the change in GNP resulting from a change in net foreign trade:

How Important Is Trade? 573

$$\frac{\Delta \text{GNP}}{\Delta (X - M)}.$$

(See Chapter 8 for a review of how the multiplier works.) Remember that the size of the multiplier depends on the marginal propensity to save and the marginal propensity to consume.

Whenever $X - M$ is negative (that is, when imports are greater than exports), there is a negative balance of trade. Then aggregate demand decreases, and GNP *decreases by a multiple amount* (other things being equal). In other words, net foreign trade (the **balance of trade**) exerts a powerful influence on a nation's overall economy. How great this impact is depends on the size of the net foreign trade ($X - M$), and on the size of the foreign-trade multiplier. Table 24-1 shows how the United States has fared in foreign trade in recent years.

You can see that, since 1960, net foreign trade has had a positive influence (exports greater than imports) on U.S. GNP and thus on employment. Only in three recent years (1971, 1972, and 1974) has $X - M$ been negative. Part of that negative balance can be chalked up to U.S. involvement in Vietnam. There was also a high income elasticity of demand for imports. This, coupled with the monopolistic oil-pricing policies of OPEC, created a negative foreign-trade effect on U.S. GNP. But in 1975, exports exceeded imports, thus helping the U.S. recovery from the recession of 1974. This positive foreign trade also added to GNP and caused employment to expand as the dollar volume of our exports (such as wheat, cars, and machinery) exceeded the value of our imports (such as oil, cars, and textiles).

TABLE 24-1 U.S. Foreign Trade and Net Foreign Trade 1960–1974 (billions of dollars)

	Exports (X)	Imports (M)	Net foreign trade (X − M)
1960	19.7	15.1	4.6
1961	20.2	14.8	5.4
1962	21.0	16.5	4.5
1963	22.5	17.2	5.3
1964	25.8	18.7	7.1
1965	26.7	21.4	5.3
1966	29.5	25.6	3.9
1967	31.0	26.9	4.1
1968	34.1	33.2	0.9
1969	37.3	36.0	1.3
1970	42.7	40.0	2.7
1971	44.1	45.6	−1.5
1972	49.7	55.6	−5.9
1973	71.3	69.5	1.8
1974	98.5	100.9	−2.4

Source: International Economic Report of the President, 1974; Department of Commerce.

Is Trade as Important to Us as to Others?

Perhaps you are saying, "All right, granted that foreign trade *can* have an effect on the U.S. economy, is the effect really important compared to the other factors that influence jobs and GNP?" Table 24-2 shows that for the United States, exports make up a smaller percentage of GNP than they do for the other nations listed. Exports are only 4.5 percent of U.S. GNP, but for the other nations, which account for a large part of the world's trade, the figure ranges up to 19.6 percent (Canada).

Do these figures mean that trade is relatively unimportant to the United States? The answer is, emphatically, *no*—for the following reasons:

1. The 4.5 percent represents an important part of demand for U.S. output and thus demand for labor (jobs) and other resources. If this foreign market for U.S. goods were to disappear, it would mean not just a 4.5 percent reduction in GNP, but a much larger reduction. (The size would depend on the foreign-trade multiplier.)

2. This additional 4.5 percent demand enables American firms to operate more efficiently and to achieve economies of scale that might not otherwise be possible. Because of this international trade, manufacturers are able to lower their costs. They pass on this saving to consumers, in the form of lower prices (both for exported goods and for goods produced in the United States from exported inputs).

3. In recent years, the percentage-of-GNP figure for foreign trade has grown (from about 4 percent prior to 1972). In 1975, exports made up 7 percent of GNP. Early in U.S. history, trade was very important to the economy of the United States. Then, as the United States came of age, the importance of foreign trade declined. Now, there seems to be a resurgence of international trade as a mainstay of the U.S. economy.

4. One big reason for the increased importance of trade is the growing dependence of the United States on imports of raw materials. The

TABLE 24-2 Exports in Relation to GNP for Some Industrialized Nations, 1970 (billions of dollars)

Nation	Exports	GNP	Exports as percentage of GNP
Canada	$16.7	$ 85.0	19.6
Italy	13.2	93.2	14.2
United Kingdom	19.4	121.0	16.0
France	18.1	147.5	12.3
West Germany	34.2	186.4	18.3
Japan	19.3	201.0	9.6
United States	43.2	970.0	4.5

Source: United Nations Statistical Yearbook.

United States now has to import about 40 percent of the petroleum it uses (although in the 1940s it was an exporter of oil). And although the United States has huge mineral resources, it must import 100 percent of the chromium and tin it uses, as well as between 90 percent and 100 percent of such minerals as cobalt, manganese, platinum, and nickel. In other words, the United States *needs* foreign trade for the sake of our own industrial economy.

Of course, the United States must pay the countries from which it imports in their own currencies. Japanese business firms want yen, not dollars, so that they can pay their workers. In turn, to earn these foreign currencies, the United States must export its own goods and services.

The Gains from Trade

You may (if you are in favor of isolation for the United States) still be doubtful about the necessity of foreign trade. You may argue as follows: "Apart from those needed minerals (and we can probably find substitutes even for them in the long run), I fail to see that we are necessarily better off because of trading. After all, we can use those Keynesian tools to achieve full employment, even without trade. Surely if we made the effort, we could produce just about everything we want. Where is the advantage to be had from trade?"

Some people actually do argue that way, and the answer is not obvious. The United States is among the few fortunate nations. It probably could—from a technical point of view—achieve **autarky**, economic self-sufficiency. Most food can be grown in the United States—even tropical fruits. And, if the President of the United States is right, the nation can achieve self-sufficiency in energy, too, within the next decade. But is complete self-sufficiency necessarily desirable—for the United States or for any nation? Most economists say no, for reasons we shall now examine.

Trade and Comparative Advantage

In discussing trade among nations, one immediately encounters two terms: the **absolute advantage** and the **comparative advantage** that each nation has in producing things. We can best define these terms by an example.

Let's say that you are a graduate engineer, and you set up a small business of your own. You have an assistant named Pat Bloggs, who does the filing and other routine jobs in your office. You pay Bloggs $30 a day to perform these tasks, while you, as a professional engineer, earn $100 a day. After a particularly hellish week, in which drawings have gone to the wrong firm and correspondence has been mislaid in the wrong folders, you review the operation of the office. You realize that you can do these routine chores much more efficiently than Bloggs. Thus you have an *absolute advantage* over Bloggs. Should you fire Bloggs and do the job yourself? No! The $100 a day you earn as an engineer reflects your marginal revenue productivity (*MRP*); the $30 reflects Bloggs's *MRP*. Therefore, you should stick to your specialty of engineering, because in this you have a *comparative advantage*. In other words, you are relatively more productive as an engineer than as an office assistant. There is a lesson to be learned here. Even a person with an absolute advantage in doing *every* task should specialize in that field in which her or his comparative advantage lies.

We demonstrated how this principle works when we were discussing the market system of a single country: for efficiency's sake, resources should move to their most productive alternative uses. A city could hire engineers to sweep the streets, and they would probably do a great job. But it would be foolish for a society to employ its engineers in this way, since their comparative efficiency is greater when they are building roads, bridges, and offshore drilling rigs.

Now let's apply this idea of comparative advantage to trade between nations. In the real world, international trade involves many nations and thousands of commodities and services. To keep things simple in this illustration, though, we shall deal with only two nations, the United States and Nicaragua. We will examine the trade in only two commodities that each country can produce—tractors and bananas. Discussing additional goods and countries would not change the basic principles; it would just make the relationships more complex.

Table 24-3 shows the production-possibilities schedules for the United States and Nicaragua. Each country is capable of producing both bananas and tractors. However, note that the rate at which tractors can be traded off for bananas (that is, the rate at which the output of tractors decreases as the output of bananas increases) is very different for the two countries. The reason is that growing bananas is easy for Nicaraguans, but it is not so easy for Americans. The United States does not have the proper climate.

Figure 24-1 illustrates the production possibilities for the two countries. Unlike the production-possibilities curves in Chapter 2, these "curves" are straight lines. That is, they reflect a constant rate of exchange of tractors for bananas (we are assuming that the cost of producing each item is constant). Later in this chapter, we will discuss

TABLE 24-3 Production-Possibilities Schedules, United States and Nicaragua

\multicolumn{2}{c	}{United States}	\multicolumn{2}{c}{Nicaragua}
Units of tractors	Units of bananas	Units of tractors	Units of bananas
50	0	0	100
40	5	5	80
30	10	10	60
20	15	15	40
10	20	20	20
0	25	25	0

FIGURE 24-1 Production Possibilities for (a) the United States and (b) Nicaragua

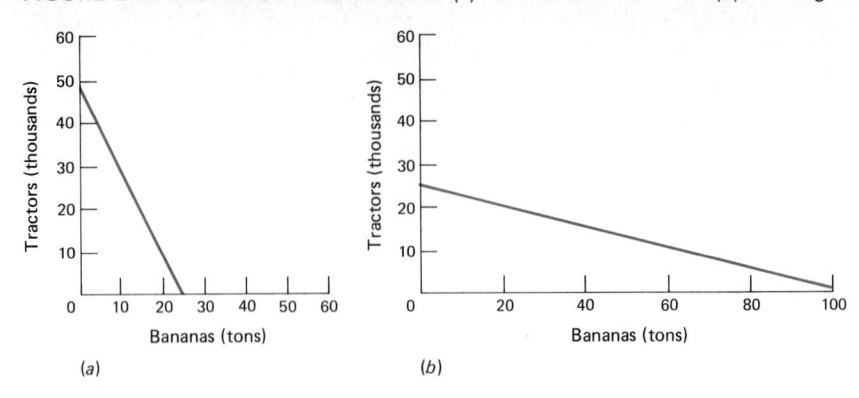

production-possibilities curves that are concave to the origin (as in Chapter 2) and reflect increasing real cost.

Let's say that Nicaragua decides to produce tractors itself, instead of importing them. It can produce 5 units of them (5,000 tractors), but to do so it must give up 20 units of bananas (100,000 − 80,000 tons). So Nicaragua's internal exchange rate is 1 unit of tractors equals 4 units of bananas ($1T = 4B$).

Now the United States, on the other hand, in order to produce 10 units of tractors (10,000 of them), has to give up only 5 units of bananas (5,000 tons). Its internal exchange rate is $1T = \frac{1}{2}B$. It is this difference between internal rates of exchange that provides the basis for mutually beneficial trade between nations.

In this instance, the United States can produce 1 additional unit of tractors and give up only $\frac{1}{2}$ unit of bananas. Nicaragua can produce 4 additional units of bananas while giving up only 1 unit of tractors. Both countries can have more of both bananas and tractors if they trade with each other than they can if they rely on their own individual production possibilities.

To put this in a slightly different way: Trade brings about a new exchange ratio. The United States will be able to get $\frac{1}{2}$ unit of bananas while giving up less than 1 unit of tractors. Nicaragua will be able to get 1 unit of tractors without giving up as much as 4 units of bananas.

The Terms of Trade

It has been established that the United States should specialize in producing tractors, and Nicaragua should specialize in bananas. Now the **terms of trade** (the relation between export prices and import prices) must be decided. That is, a ratio must be determined at which Nicaraguan bananas will be exchanged for U.S. tractors. There must be an advantage for each country. The Americans must get more than $\frac{1}{2}$ unit of bananas for each unit of their tractors, and the Nicaraguans more than 1 unit of tractors for 4 units of their bananas.

Each country must get more for its products in the world market than it would if it had sold them domestically. If both countries are to benefit, the actual exchange rate must lie between

$$1T = \tfrac{1}{2}B \text{ (preferred by Nicaragua)}$$

and

$$1T = 4B \text{ (preferred by the United States)}.$$

The exact terms of trade will depend on the market demand for both products. Market demand depends on the degree to which one can substitute other products for either commodity, and on the relationship of demand to supply. If there are no good substitutes for tractors, and if demand for them is greater than supply, the exchange rate (terms of trade) will be in favor of the United States. If conditions are reversed, the terms of trade will be favorable to Nicaragua.

Suppose that the exchange rate moves to $1T = 2B$. Figure 24-2, on page 580, shows what happens to production and consumption in both countries. Look at the replotted production-possibilities curves of both countries. The colored lines (called consumption-possibilities curves), indicating consumption after trade, show what each country can consume if it specializes in the good in which it has a comparative advantage and exports part of its output. For example, at point A', if the United States consumes 40,000 of its tractors and exports 10,000 to Nicaragua, it can import 20,000 tons of bananas in exchange. Thus, it can have 40 units of tractors plus 20 units of bananas, as opposed to 40 units of tractors and 5 units of bananas before trade (point A).

Likewise, at point B, Nicaragua, before exchange, can produce and consume 20 units of tractors and 20 units of bananas. With trade, it has 20 units of bananas and exports its remaining 80,000 units of bananas for 40 units of tractors, a combination that is much better (point B').

The important result that Figure 24-2 enables us to visualize is this:

As long as a nation has a comparative advantage in producing some things, it should specialize in producing those things. It should then export part of the goods for which it has a comparative advantage. By so doing, it will have more to consume.

This is true even if the nation has an absolute advantage in producing everything it consumes.

What Determines Comparative Advantage?

Since we have shown that comparative advantage is the basis for trade, we had better examine the factors that determine a nation's comparative advantage. Are nations locked into a particular comparative-advantage position, or do their positions change?

FIGURE 24-2 Production-Consumption Possibilities for (a) the United States and (b) Nicaragua (after trade)

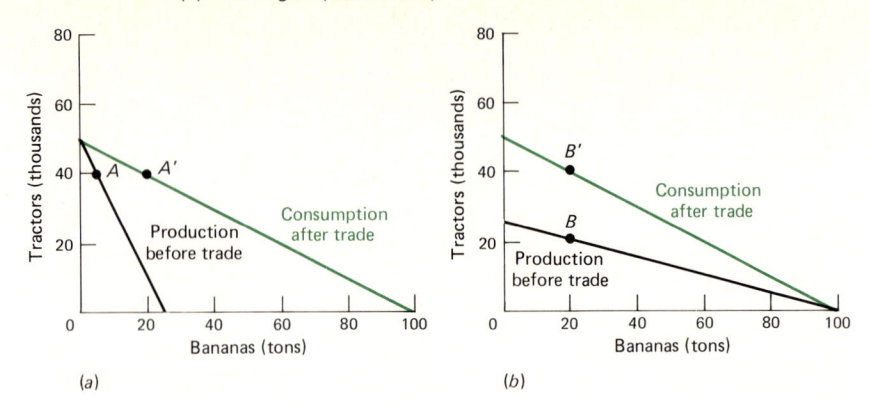

First, *nations have differing comparative advantages*, for the following reasons:

1. Different nations have different endowments of natural resources, both in quantity and quality. For example, the United States, Canada, the Soviet Union, and the People's Republic of China have large quantities (although different proportions) of relatively high-grade resources (petroleum, mineral deposits, topsoil, and so on).

2. Different nations have different physical features (mild or extreme climate, many or few natural harbors).

3. Different nations are at different stages of development of markets. For example, the United States, Japan, and the countries in Western Europe have well-developed capital markets, reflecting large supplies of savings that can be transformed through investment into capital.

4. Different nations have different supplies of labor. For example, China and many other underdeveloped nations have large supplies of labor.

A country tends to specialize in products (or services) that intensively use those resources in which it is relatively rich.

Second, *the comparative advantages of nations change*. Nations are not locked into a position with respect to comparative advantage. For example, the United States began as a nation rich in land and short of capital and labor. Today, it is relatively rich in capital and land, and relatively short of labor. (This has nothing to do with our unemployment rate. It means that, as the United States presently produces things—even at full employment—capital and land are abundant relative to labor.) Up until the Civil War, the United States specialized in land-intensive agricultural exports (cotton, tobacco, rice, and so on). Today it specializes in exports that are capital-intensive and land-intensive. For example, in 1973, 50 percent of U.S. exports were comprised of machinery, transportation, services, equipment, chemicals, goods manufactured of iron and steel, and nonferrous metals—all fairly capital-intensive. Another 12 percent were grains and cereals, which are land-intensive. Thus, 62 percent, nearly two-thirds of U.S. exports, were derived from processes that were capital- and land-intensive. On the other hand, the United States imports many things (coffee, cocoa, inexpensive textiles, handicrafts) that are relatively labor-intensive.

There are many arguments about changing the comparative advantages of countries, especially about whether comparative-advantage trade tends to help the poor trading nations to develop. In Application 25, which follows this chapter, we will examine some of these arguments.

Increasing Costs and Other Cautions

In the case involving the United States and Nicaragua, we concluded that each would produce only its most advantageous good, tractors or bananas. We showed that bilateral exchange between the two nations would make both better off in terms of the quantities of the two goods available for consumption. There are some qualifications to the argument, however.

1. As each country reallocates its resources from the disadvantageous good to the advantageous one, it may run into *increasing costs*. For example, as the United States produces more tractors, the cost (in bananas not produced) may rise, until it reaches a point at which it would be better off if it produced some bananas of its own rather than always exchanging tractors for Nicaraguan bananas. Nicaragua, whose costs of producing bananas also rise, may be better off producing some of its own tractors. The point is that increasing costs cause international specialization to be less than complete.

2. When two countries specialize in making things in which they have a comparative advantage and then trade with each other, achieving the greatest possible production, we assume that there is full employment in the trading nations. However, at times this trade means reallocating resources, and when this results in unemployment, the countries' output may fall below the production-possibilities curve. So it is not always desirable for a country to trade. But as we have mentioned earlier, there are various macroeconomic (fiscal and monetary) tools that a nation can use to restore full employment, and there are microeconomic tools that can be used to reallocate resources (job retraining, for example). Thus, many economists feel that the risk of creating unemployment is not a compelling reason to forgo trade.

3. The principle of comparative advantage depends heavily on *competition* in international trade. If the tractors are produced by a monopolistic firm but the bananas are exported by competitive firms, Nicaragua may not fully reap the benefits of trade. If monopolistic export boards (perhaps government ones) negotiate the terms of trade (American wheat for Russian oil, for example), one cannot tell what the outcome will be. This was also true of bilateral monopoly (Chapter 23). The end

result depends on the relative skills and bargaining strengths of the participants.

4. If there are *externalities* (Chapter 17), the terms of trade may not reflect the real costs of production. The countries may produce and exchange either too little or too much. (Suppose that the tractor factories pollute the water and air and that their costs do not reflect the added social costs of cleaning up the environment.)

5. The principle of comparative advantage depends on the fact that relative prices (the American price of tractors and the Nicaraguan price of bananas) reflect relative scarcities of resources in each nation. If the prices do not reflect these scarcities, an international (as well as domestic) misallocation of resources occurs. Suppose that the United States subsidizes the tractor industry. Then international prices of tractors (the terms of trade) would not reflect underlying relative scarcity and companies would produce more tractors than is efficient (and trade them). (Americans would, in effect, be producing tractors when they should be producing bananas.)

6. The biggest obstacle to trade being conducted according to comparative advantage is **protectionism**, the government's effort to protect domestic firms or industries from free international trade. Consequently, there has been little free trade in modern times (or indeed at any time).

The Means of Protection

There are two means by which countries usually intervene to protect their own industries from overseas competition: tariffs and quotas.

Tariffs

The most common means of protection are **tariffs**, which are taxes on imported goods. Figure 24-3 shows how a protective tariff works and also shows its effects on trade and prices. Before trade begins, the U.S. demand for bicycles is $D_{U.S.}$ and the supply is $S_{U.S.}$. Equilibrium price is P_1 ($D_{U.S.} = S_{U.S.}$). At this price, Q_1 of bicycles are sold. (Presumably, bicycles are goods in which this country has a comparative disadvantage.) Now trade opens up. The United States begins to import foreign bicycles (from Japan, Italy, and France). Supply of bicycles increases to $S_{U.S.\ \&\ foreign}$. Equilibrium price falls to P_2. The supply increases until the price of bicycles in the United States is equal to the price of bicycles abroad (not including transportation costs). As long as the American price is higher, foreign producers will continue to export bicycles in order to sell in the more profitable American market.

Now suppose that the bicycle manufacturers complain to Congress, as the Bicycle Manufacturers' Association did in 1972. They argued as follows:

> A deluge of imported bicycles into the United States has increased imports from 19.8 percent of our market in 1964 to 37.1 percent in

1972. We don't feel our business should go down the drain. Standards must be established that would automatically impose restrictions on imports competing with American products.... This is not protectionism.

Let's say that the bicycle lobby convinces Congress that this argument is valid, so that Congress levies a tax—a tariff—on imported bicycles. The tax, which is equal to AB in Figure 24-3, increases the cost of imported bicycles and reduces the supply to S_{at} (supply after tariff). The new equilibrium price is P_3, which is higher than the international price (by $P_3 - P_2$). The number of bicycles sold goes down (by $Q_2 - Q_3$). Note that part of the gain to consumers from all the foreign bicycles coming into the country is eliminated. If the tariff had been higher, imports might have ceased altogether, and supply might have fallen back to $S_{U.S.}$. Then price would have gone back up to P_1 (with only Q_1 sold).

So the tariff hurts consumers, because now they must buy bicycles at a price higher than the international price, and they are getting fewer bicycles. The tariff also hurts foreign bicycle manufacturers, because the net price they receive (after paying the tariff) is P_4. The total revenue to the U.S. government from the tariff is shown by the shaded area. This is the unit tariff per bicycle ($P_3 - P_4$) times the number of bicycles imported ($Q_3 - Q_4$). (At price P_3, American manufacturers supply Q_4.)

Is anyone better off as a result of the tariff? Yes, the American bicycle manufacturers are. They do not have to pay the tariff, so they keep the full price (P_3) of their product. This is higher than P_2, which is the price foreign makers have after they pay the tariff. The federal government is better off by the amount of revenue (the shaded area). The tariff, in other words, represents a loss in income by consumers, which is transferred to the government and firms.

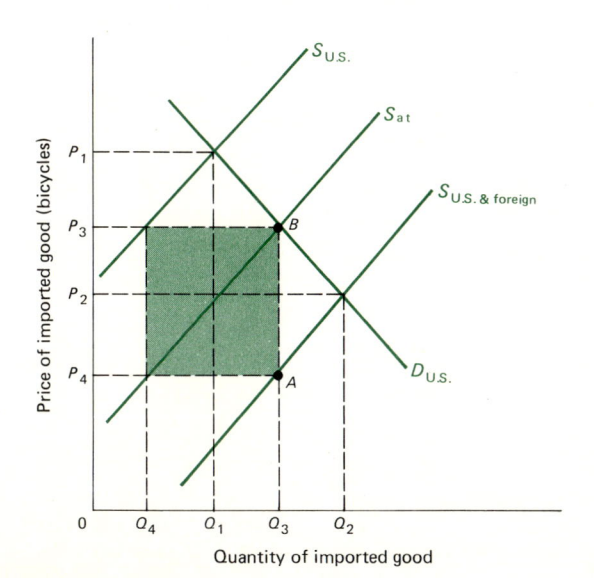

FIGURE 24-3 How a Protective Tariff Works

The Means of Protection 583

"He wasn't even warm—was he, Mom?"

Two points about tariffs should be emphasized: (1) When the government imposes a tariff, it makes a *net addition to domestic monopoly power*. The bicycle manufacturers had been getting a competitively set international price for their product. Now they are getting a monopolistically set price instead. (Though in this case the government, rather than private business, is the agent that sets the price.) Thus, tariffs defeat our objective of having a competitive market system. (2) When the government imposes a general tariff (or other trade restriction), it *reduces the number of good substitutes that consumers have for domestically produced goods*. This, in turn, may make the demand ($D_{U.S.}$) *more price inelastic* and (because it increases monopoly power) cause prices to rise by a greater amount than the amount of the tariff itself.

Quotas

The second major means the government uses to protect its industries against competitors from abroad is **quotas**, that is, restrictions on the quantity of goods that may be imported or exported. In one way, the effects of quotas are much like those of tariffs. Look again at Figure 24-3. Suppose that Congress, instead of enacting a tariff, had said that only $Q_3 - Q_4$ bicycles could come into the United States. Supply would still have dropped to S_{at} (or S_{aq} to stand for "supply after quota"). Total supply (Q_3) would have been domestic supply (Q_4) plus foreign supply ($Q_3 - Q_4$). Consumers would be affected just as adversely and U.S. bicycle makers would still get the higher price, P_3. The difference is that *a quota is not a revenue-producing device* (the shaded area would not exist), so the government would not get any extra money. Foreign bicycle makers would get the same price as domestic makers, P_3 (less transportation costs, of course). So nobody benefits much, except of course, American bicycle makers.

The most extreme form of a quota is an **embargo**, which is an absolute prohibition against importing a good. If Congress had imposed an embargo on foreign bicycles, supply would have reverted to $S_{U.S.}$. Price would have risen to P_1 (domestic producers would have been restored to whatever monopoly power they originally had).

Embargoes are relatively rare in American history. In 1808, during the Napoleonic wars, President Jefferson imposed one. After 1962 the U.S. government embargoed trade with Cuba (no Cuban cigars, sugar, or rum). Until a few years ago, there was a U.S. embargo on trade with the People's Republic of China; there is still one with Rhodesia. It is worth noting that when embargoes are lifted, they are usually lifted in the interests of political expediency (détente, for example) rather than in the interests of free trade. (It reminds one of the remark made recently by Neil McNeil, of *Time* magazine, about the difference between a politician and a statesman: "A politician looks to the next election. A statesman looks to the next generation.") Embargoes are usually short-term political penalties against antagonistic nations.

Arguments in Favor of Protection

As we have pointed out, the United States has rarely if ever practiced completely free trade. (Neither have other countries.) Americans always say they believe in competition. But they seem to argue against it when it is to their financial advantage. Economists in general—most U.S. economists, that is—sing the praises of free trade. But apparently, the economists who make public policy cannot convince the government. (Few members of Congress are economists. And no economist has ever been President of the United States.) Since so much protectionism exists, there must be some strong arguments in favor of it. Let's examine the major ones.

The Infant-Industry Argument

The infant-industry argument is as follows: Industries that are just starting cannot meet the pressures of competition by similar, already established industries located in other, more industrially mature countries. Such infant industries deserve the protection of a tariff or other protective device. They must be sheltered until they have become big enough to take advantage of the economies of scale.

This argument may seem reasonable. However, there are opposing arguments: (1) Tariffs, once enacted, are extremely hard to abolish. For example, the bicycle industry still enjoys tariff protection. So do the automobile and steel industries and many other U.S. industries that are hardly infants. (2) If an industry needs to be protected before it is mature, direct government subsidies are preferable, since they make the costs of such protection explicit. (3) The logic of the infant-industry argument is difficult to apply, since it is hard to know (in either a developed or underdeveloped nation) *which* infant industries will (and should) survive. Short of pursuing a goal of autarky, a nation must choose *which* infant industries to put into its protective incubator.

The National-Security Argument
The national-security argument is as follows: The United States can never really be certain of the supply of a good produced in a foreign country. The nation cannot even depend on its present friends to help in a tight spot. This means that, when it comes to military hardware, U.S. security must take precedence over U.S. economic efficiency.

This argument is difficult for economists to judge, since there are no objective criteria by which to evaluate the tradeoff between increased national security and decreased industrial efficiency. Economists can only identify the costs involved in (1) levying tariffs or (2) directly subsidizing firms that make military hardware. Almost all economists would probably say that direct subsidies are preferable, because they identify the costs involved.

The Cheap-Foreign-Labor Argument
The cheap-foreign-labor argument can best be summed up in an example. The American textile industry must be protected from imported Japanese and Korean textiles. Wages in Japan and Korea are so low that American firms cannot price their textiles low enough to compete. Although this argument is persuasive to many people, it is irrelevant to economists because (1) the higher wages of Americans presumably reflect higher marginal productivity; (2) it is socially inefficient to have an American firm that cannot compete with labor-intensive imports try to do so; and (3) it is less costly to retrain labor and reallocate resources to more efficient uses than it is to protect an inefficient industry. (However, remember the exception: the national-security argument.)

The Macroeconomic-Employment Argument
The macroeconomic-employment argument is that during hard times the United States can "export" some of its unemployment. (This is also sometimes called a *beggar-thy-neighbor* argument.) Large segments of the business community (except big importers) and of labor often support this idea. The principle is to create more jobs at home by excluding, or sharply restricting, imports. Such an increase in domestic demand for formerly imported goods causes the foreign-trade multiplier to move us toward full employment.

Has the United States followed the beggar-thy-neighbor principle? Figure 24-4 shows what has happened to tariffs during our "hard-times" periods. You can see that tariffs have been high during most recession and depression periods, such as the mid-1870s, 1890s, early 1900s (though they were falling then), and 1921. They were especially high in the early years of the Great Depression (the Hawley-Smoot tariffs, in 1930, were the highest in modern American history). The purpose of the so-called Tariff of Abominations (1828) was to protect U.S. infant industries such as textiles and iron. Tariffs have from time to time protected American makers of every sort of commodity. Cheese, watches, cameras, musical instruments, and machinery are some that come to mind.

Economists usually feel that a beggar-thy-neighbor action is not likely to succeed. Even if it does work, the cost is great because such actions invite retaliation by other countries. (If the United States raises its tariff on bananas, Nicaragua will raise *its* tariff on tractors.) A trade war is likely to result and every nation will be hurt. The reason is that as tariff walls go up, governments try to stimulate domestic demand, through tax cuts, increased government spending, and lowered interest rates. Assuming that previous international trade has reflected a comparative advantage, the United States will increase its domestic output, substituting homemade products for imported ones, at the expense of efficiency. Without trade, even if the United States reaches full employment, there will be relative inefficiency in the industries producing these products. Thus, the level of U.S. production of goods and services will be lower than if the tariff had not been introduced.

FIGURE 24-4 History of American Tariffs (*Source:* U.S. Department of Commerce, *Historical Statistics of the U.S.* and *Statistical Abstract of the U.S., 1972.*)

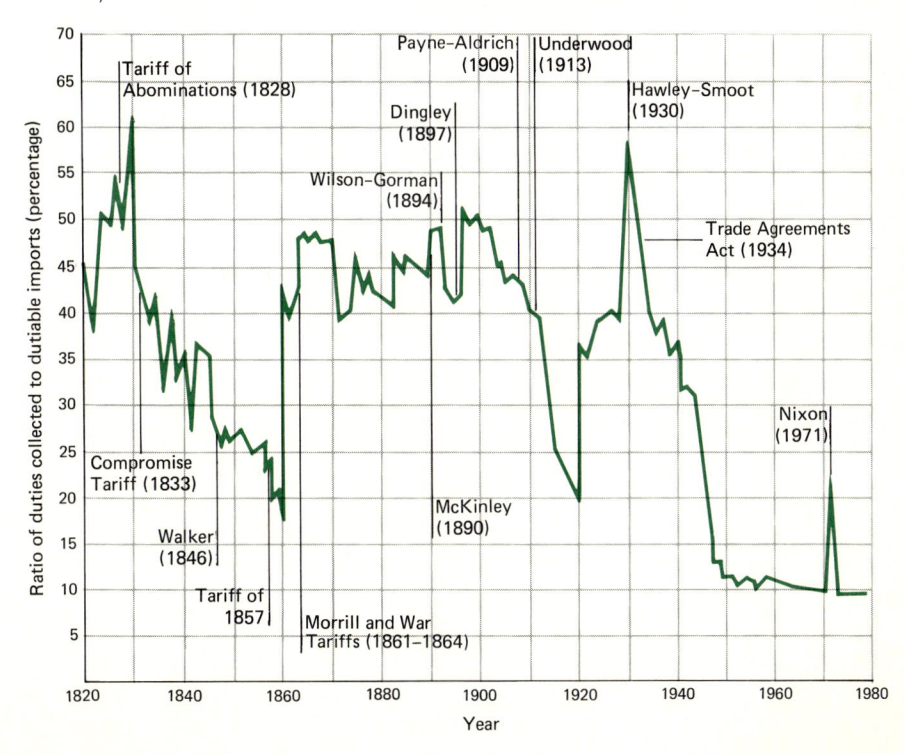

The macroeconomic-employment argument (Dick Brehl for Time, Inc.)

Free Trade: A Reprise

In general, then, a nation that is trying to get the greatest mileage out of the full-employment use of its resources is better off if it lets trade remain free. When a nation, for reasons of national defense, puts up a protective wall, the form of this protection should be clear and explicit (for example, direct subsidies) so that all the citizens will be aware of the costs of protection.

Chapter 25 will show how international trade is financed. We will also look at some of the problems a nation encounters when it introduces export-import prices and payments for trade.

SUMMING UP

1. International trade is the final link in the chain of principles related to the market system.

2. Trade consists of *exports*—commodities and services sold to other nations—and *imports*—commodities and services purchased from other nations. Exports and imports consist of both *visible items* (commodities) and *invisible items* (services).

3. *Net foreign trade* is the difference between exports (X) and imports (M); it is a part of aggregate demand. Thus

$$\text{GNP} = C + I + GX + (X - M).$$

Foreign trade is important, even to a diversified economy such as that of the United States, because of the *foreign-trade multiplier* effect, which is the change in GNP resulting from a change in net foreign trade.

4. Net foreign trade can exert a powerful macroeconomic influence on the level of income and employment. This is so even in the United States, in which exports (and net foreign trade) form a smaller percentage of GNP than they do in many other major trading nations. (However, in dollar volume, the United States is by far the largest international trader.)

5. In modern times, the United States has usually run a trade surplus ($X>M$). In 1971, 1972, and 1974, however, it had a trade deficit ($X<M$).

6. Trade is important to the United States for these reasons: (a) Trade constitutes an important part of demand for U.S. output, and hence demand for labor (that means more jobs) and other resources. (b) Demand that results from trade enables many U.S. industries to operate more efficiently and on a larger scale. (c) The percentage of U.S. GNP represented by trade has grown in recent years. This reflects a greater interdependence with other nations. (d) The United States needs imports of raw materials, such as certain key minerals, in order to operate many industries.

7. *Autarky* (economic self-sufficiency), although it is technologically possible for the United States, is economically unwise, because the United States, by specializing in items in which it has a comparative advantage, can realize gains from trade.

8. *Absolute advantage* refers to a nation's ability to produce all of a good it consumes more efficiently than any other nation. (Some nations have an absolute advantage in all goods.) *Comparative advantage* refers to a nation's being more efficient in producing some good or goods than in producing others (even though the nation may also be absolutely more efficient than its neighbors in producing everything).

9. At any given time, nations have certain production possibilities. These are reflected in their production-possibilities curves (assuming full employment and given technology). So long as any two nations have different internal rates of exchange (tradeoffs) between producing the same two goods, it is mutually beneficial for each to specialize in producing the good in which it has a comparative advantage.

10. By specializing in producing those things in which it has a comparative advantage, and by trading what it does not consume to other nations for goods in which *they* have a comparative advantage, a trading nation can have more goods to consume (the consumption-possibilities curve will be above the domestic production-possibilities curve).

11. Comparative advantage derives from (a) different endowments of natural resources, (b) different physical features (climate, harbors, and so on) (c) different stages of development of markets (for example, some nations have well-developed capital markets), and (d) different supplies of labor.

12. Comparative advantages change, sometimes dramatically. The United States began with a comparative advantage in land-intensive commodities, which it exported. Today it has a comparative advantage in capital-intensive as well as land-intensive goods.

13. If nations run into increasing costs as they specialize, the specialization will not be complete. They will produce a wider variety of goods. (For example, Nicaragua will produce some of its own tractors, the United States will produce some of its own bananas.)

14. Some people disapprove of foreign trade because of the unemployment that occurs when resources (especially labor) must be reallocated as a result of foreign trade. To economists, this is not a compelling argument against trade. They point to the macroeconomic tools that can be used to increase employment, and the microeconomic tools that can be used to reallocate resources (for example, job retraining).

15. Comparative advantage depends on competition. When competition does not exist, or when nations with equal advantage do not trade competitively with each other, some of the benefits of comparative-advantage trade are lost.

16. Trading nations that are burdened by *externalities* may produce and trade too much or too little for comparative advantage to work. Prices for goods exported must accurately reflect relative scarcity of resources.

17. The theory of comparative advantage depends on relative prices reflecting relative scarcities of resources in each nation. If prices do not reflect these scarcities, an international misallocation of resources occurs.

18. The biggest obstacle to free trade is *protectionism*, the effort to protect farmers and industries from the competition from lower-priced goods imported from foreign countries when there is free international trade.

19. The two major means of protectionism are (a) *tariffs*, which are taxes on imported goods, and (b) *quotas*, which are limitations on the quantity of imports.

20. Tariffs and other trade restrictions reduce the supply of goods and raise the prices charged consumers. They also add to the monopoly power of domestic producers, and they may reduce the number of good substitutes available to consumers, making domestic demand for a good more inelastic. One thing in their favor is that they produce revenue for governments.

21. *Quotas* do not produce revenue for governments. Otherwise the effects of quotas are similar to those of tariffs. They reduce supply, raise prices to consumers, and enhance the monopolistic position of domestic producers. The most extreme form of quota is an *embargo*, an absolute prohibition against importing a certain good or trading with a certain country.

22. Arguments in favor of protectionism are as follows: (a) the *infant-industry* argument (firms that are new and small need to be protected until they are large enough to compete with more established firms in foreign industries); (b) the *national-security argument* (uncertainty of foreign supply, plus need for a reliable source of military hardware, means that domestic producers must be protected, even if they are inefficient); (c) the *cheap-foreign-labor argument* (domestic firms that must pay high wages should be protected against imports from countries in which wages are low); and (d) the *macroeconomic-employment argument* (recessions and depressions can be "exported" if a nation puts up barriers to trade that reduce imports without reducing exports).

23. Economists generally reject these arguments that favor protectionism, with the exception of the national-security argument, for which there is no objective basis for evaluation. However, even in the case of protection given to industries producing goods needed for national security, economists feel that there should be direct subsidies instead of tariffs, so that cost of protection could be clearly identified.

24. Beggar-thy-neighbor tariffs are likely to be ineffective, even counterproductive. When one nation sets up high tariffs, other nations retaliate. As a result, without specialized trade, nations have fewer goods and services to consume, even when they have full employment.

25. Free trade is in the best interests of a nation that wishes to have maximum production *and consumption*, with the full employment of its resources and technological capability.

QUESTIONS

1. What imported goods do you often buy? How would you be affected if the United States restricted international trade or stopped trading with other nations entirely?

2. Why are most production-possibilities curves *not* straight lines? What happens to international specialization when such curves are truly curves?

3. Consider the following hypothetical production-possibilities schedules for the Soviet Union and the United States:

	Soviet Union		United States	
	Units of oil	Units of automobiles	Units of oil	Units of automobiles
	100	0	0	500
	80	40	30	400
	60	80	60	300
	40	120	90	200
	20	160	120	100
	0	200	150	0

    a. Plot the production-possibilities curves.
    b. Is there a basis for mutually beneficial trade between the two countries?
    c. What will determine the terms of trade that are established between the two countries?

4. Give reasons why, in your opinion, the beggar-thy-neighbor tariff (Smoot-Hawley tariff) of 1930 failed to stimulate American recovery between 1930 and 1934.

5. What happens to the trade from either developed or underdeveloped nations when monopoly export and import agencies are set up? Why?

6. Evaluate the following statements:
    a. "Free trade forces domestic producers to pay attention to consumer tastes and needs."
    b. "Free trade would be desirable, but we can't afford to rely on the Russians, or the French, or even the British, for our military hardware."
    c. "High tariffs to create more jobs will work for the United States because other, less-powerful nations wouldn't dare retaliate."
    d. "In several recent years, the United States has run a trade deficit. What we should do to counteract this is to buy less from abroad."

SUGGESTED READINGS

Adams, Walter. "The New Protectionism." *Challenge*, May-June, 1973.

Council of Economic Advisers, *International Economic Report of the President, 1974*. G.P.O., Washington, D.C., 1974.

McElheny, Victor K. "In 3 Years Détente Has Produced No Massive Exchange of Advanced Technology." *New York Times*, June 27, 1975.

Meier, Gerald M. *Problems of Trade Policy*. Oxford University Press, New York, 1973.

Miller, Roger Leroy, and Raburn M. Williams. "The Economics of Buying a Volkswagen Instead of a Ford." In *The Economics of National Issues*, Canfield, San Francisco, 1972.

Snider, Delbert A. *Introduction to International Economics*, 5th ed. Irwin, Homewood, Ill., 1973.

Application 25

Does Trade Create Development?

Application 2 discussed the fact that economic development has always been a great problem for most of the world. Economic development is the long-term process that improves the material well-being (or real per capita income) of people. If this is tied to the fact that every nation, rich or poor, engages in trade with other nations, the following question emerges: Can international trade provide the primary basis for the economic development of the emerging, or poor, nations?

The Relation Between Trade and Development

To answer this question, we must establish a relation between exporting-importing and the increase in productivity (see Chapters 2 and 14) that is the key to development. Opinions are divided about whether trade—especially trade based on comparative advantage—enhances economic development. In this application we will examine some of the controversies surrounding this subject.

The Classical View
Early economists, including Adam Smith and David Ricardo, believed that trade was essential to economic development, or to what Smith called "the wealth of nations." Writing about a country's efforts to produce things that it could import more cheaply, Smith said, "The value of its annual produce is certainly more or less diminished, when it is thus turned away from producing commodities evidently of more value than the commodity which it is directed to produce."

This idea of maximizing the wealth of a nation through trade, however, is based on a static situation (*static* meaning timeless). Much of the argument over its validity arises from the distinction between the static economic position of a country at a point in time, and the improvement (or deterioration) in the country's position that occurs over time. Let's illustrate the difference between these two perspectives.

The United States, early in its history, starts out with a certain endowment of land, labor, capital, and entrepreneurship. For simplicity, assume that all its resources are integrated into the market system. Now ask yourself the following questions: (1) In any given year—for instance, 1840—will the per capita national income be higher if the United States follows a policy of free trade? Or will it be higher if it imposes restrictions on trade? (2) Which policy—restricted trade or unrestricted trade—will cause income to grow faster from one date to another (for instance, from 1840 to 1890)?

Figure A25-1 will help you visualize the answer. It shows that in 1840 the United States could have two levels of per capita income: $120 or

$140. The $120 figure corresponds to the level if the government enforced protective practices (such as tariffs or quotas). It represents many possible levels of income resulting from different combinations of trade restrictions. Each of the combinations causes resources to be used in ways that are *less* productive than would be the case if there were free trade, or if there were comparative-advantage trade. The $140 represents the *free*-trade case.

Therefore, the answer to question 1 is that at the outset of its development, a nation will have a higher income if it engages in free trade and utilizes all its resources on the basis of comparative advantage.

Now what about *growth* as it relates to international trade? Which policy—comparative-advantage (free) trade or some sort of protective tariffs or quotas—would yield the United States the greater growth in income during the period from 1840 to 1890? Adherents of the classical economic view say that comparative-advantage trade would give the greatest growth, because a nation that trades according to the principle of comparative advantage allocates its resources to their most productive uses. Thus, as we saw in Chapter 2, the nation is maximizing its productivity. With free trade, as income grows (along $(Y/P)_{ft}$ in Figure A25-1), the size of the nation's market grows. There is specialization and division of labor. Capital and productivity increase.

Reservations About the Classical View

There are objections to the above scenario. Some economists feel that a policy of comparative-advantage trade is not, in the long run, the best policy for developing nations. They feel that one cannot prove an explicit relationship between growth and free international trade. Economist Hollis Chenery is one of the doubters. Chenery, for a long time an official who has worked on U.S. aid to developing nations, feels that there are five reservations that point to the wisdom of modifying comparative advantage as a policy, to enhance economic development for emerging countries:

1. *Factor costs.* The benefits of comparative advantage depend on factor markets producing equilibrium prices of resources. This means that the prices reflect "true" relative costs of production. Consider the imperfections in labor or capital markets that one sees in developing countries (for example, the United States in the nineteenth century or Brazil today). As development takes place, markets perform more efficiently. There are often dramatic changes in factor costs, and thus in comparative advantage.

2. *Export markets.* Comparative-advantage trade gives rise to specialization. Underdeveloped countries usually come to specialize in producing—and exporting—just one, or a very few, raw materials. Then they must import food and raw materials that they do not produce, along with manufac-

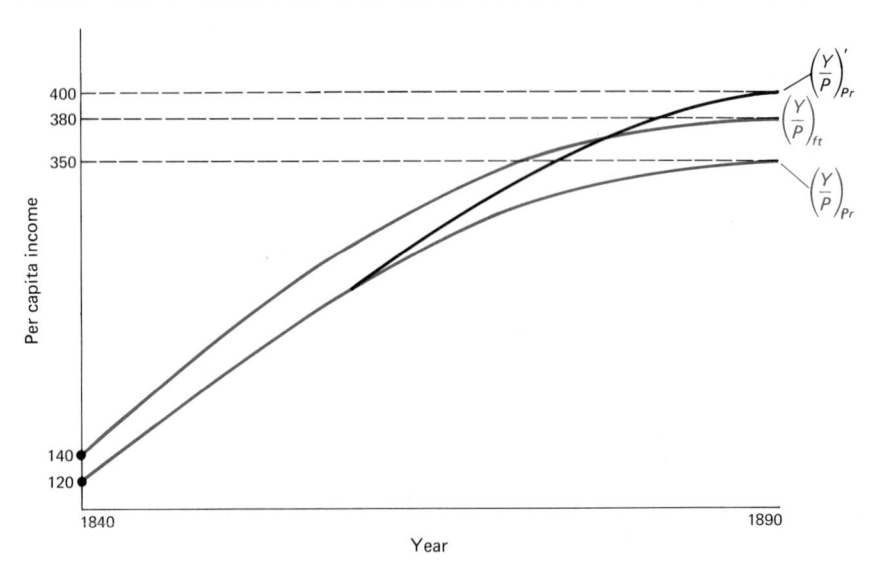

FIGURE A25-1 Growth Paths of the United States: Free Trade and Protectionism

tured (and semimanufactured) products. The result is an unstable economy, which is tied to the fluctuating prices of raw materials. (For example, the world price of copper plunged 65 percent in the early seventies. Chile, which produces one-eighth of the world's copper, suffered acutely.) You can see that following a policy of comparative-advantage trade makes it hard for an underdeveloped nation to keep its economy stable. In addition, price and income elasticities of demand for these countries' raw materials are low, though data are conflicting. (When the price of copper falls on the world market, and a country's chief export is copper, it cannot make up for the drop in price by selling a greater quantity to its industrialized neighbors.) So the terms of trade, the ratio of export prices to import prices, militate against the exporter of the raw material. The reason is that the poor nation—for example, Chile—must continue to import manufactured goods, whose prices (compared to the price of the exported copper) are now relatively much higher.

Many economists fail to see factors 1 and 2 as being necessarily valid arguments against a developing country's specializing in just a few raw-material exports. In their view, a developing nation's rate of return on investment in its raw material is greater than the rate of return it *would* get if it tried to build up other internal projects, such as factories, even after correcting for factor costs and fluctuating world prices.

3. *Productivity changes.* Manufacturing, by its very nature, increases the supply of factors more than the production of raw material does. Manufacturing enhances the skills of labor and management more than agriculture does. So some economic advisers urge a developing nation to stress manufacturing, even at the expense of comparative-advantage exports. Others disagree, asking whether such an advantage exists. Perhaps, they say, the developing nation could make as much headway by concentrating on agriculture as by concentrating on manufacturing. All agree, however, that the nation must make allowances for productivity changes in allocating its resources—even if it does not, in the long run, opt for manufacturing as the area of concentration.

4. *Dynamic external economies.* As an industry grows, its costs fall. Or demand for its output increases. As a result, the costs of other industries may also fall. There may, in fact, be a whole group of investments that are profitable *only if they are undertaken together.* Comparative advantage, manifested in market signals such as equilibrium prices, does not under these conditions indicate to a nation how it should allocate its resources. Suppose, for example, that the underdeveloped nation increases its investment in industry and realizes certain of these external economies. This will reduce the costs of more than one industry. But, some economists say, perhaps it would have realized even more external economies if it had allocated its capital to comparative-advantage agriculture. For example, it could have built fabricating plants, including expanding the production of the raw material.

5. *Uncertainty and flexibility.* Some economists feel that changes in the market can happen so quickly, and are so hard for policy makers to foresee, that a diversified economy—one that can quickly adjust to changes in supply and demand—is better (and certainly more flexible) than one that relies on a single product, or only a few products. Economist C. P. Kindleberger feels that the terms of trade now discriminate against the raw-material-exporting nations and favor the industrialized nations, because the raw-material-exporting nations lack flexibility. So it seems that a developing nation might be well advised to sacrifice some short-term efficiency in the interests of longer-term flexibility, and a capacity to adjust more rapidly to changes in world supply and demand.

The Implications for Trade Policies

For years the underdeveloped nations have been asking for international trade policies that would recognize the special problems that (they maintain) these five factors of international trade have imposed on their usually undiversified economies. Since the United Nations Conference on Trade and Development (UNCTAD) meeting in 1964, the developing nations have been making frequent pleas for special trading privileges. These privileges, if granted, would mean that the world would move away from free (market-determined) comparative-advantage trade. Or rather, it would make a *further* move away from it, since neither industrialized nor raw-material-exporting nations have ever followed a strict policy of free trade and comparative advantage.

In 1975 both the industrialized and the developing nations (including the members of OPEC, the Organization of Petroleum Exporting Countries) held an economic conference in Paris. There the low-income countries renewed their efforts to obtain special trading privileges. This time they seemed to be making progress. One of the chief reasons was OPEC's quadrupling of world oil prices in the early seventies. Not only did the United States, Western Europe, and Japan have to pay these quadrupled prices, but the poor nations had to pay them as well. Figure A25-2 shows that the less-developed areas, and those called here the "primary producing countries," were hurt the most. The reason is that these countries could not expand their earnings from their own exports enough to meet the swollen cost of oil and petroleum products. Secretary of State Kissinger recognized this in his address to the United Nations in 1975, when he spoke of the need for a "new economic order" of cooperation between the rich and the poor nations.

Trade consists of more than goods and services. The flow of short-term and long-term investment funds—the results of the operation of international capital markets—is *very* important to developing nations. Beginning in 1975, a definite trend began to appear in the international capital market. Large amounts of investment capital for manufacturing began flowing into the countries in Latin America, Southeast Asia, and the Mediterranean basin. The reason was that labor costs were rising much faster in the industrialized nations than in the low-income nations. So there was a shift in their comparative-advantage positions.

In January of 1976 a new factor appeared. The International Monetary Fund (IMF), in a meeting of its leaders in Kingston, Jamaica, proposed a new plan (which must be ratified by member governments). According to this plan, the IMF will sell off one-sixth of its gold holdings, in order to create a special fund available for loans to the underdeveloped nations. At the UNCTAD conference in Nairobi, Kenya, in May 1976, the United States supported a proposal to create a $7.5 billion program to aid poor countries through

FIGURE A25-2 Balance of Payments of Principal Areas. Solid color indicates the capital account; color outline, the current accounts (*Source:* International Monetary Fund, *IMF Survey,* Annual Reports Issue, August 25, 1975. Reproduced by permission of the publisher.)

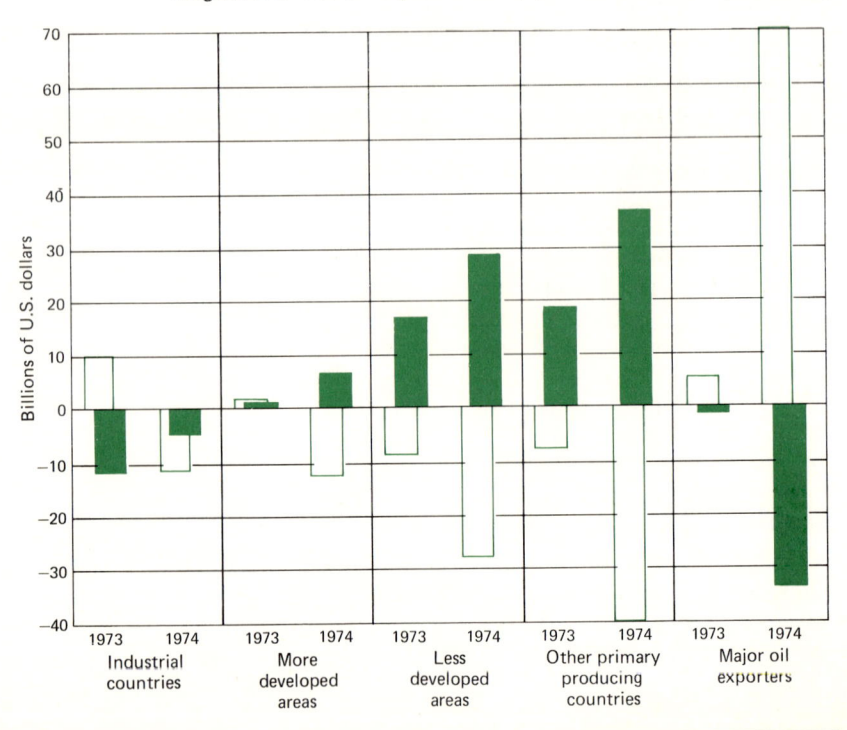

stabilizing the prices of their raw-materials exports and through other means.

So it appears that there will be many changes in the next few years in the trading relationships of nations, with respect to both commodities and finances. One cannot foretell the exact nature of these changes. But it seems likely that there will be a further departure from comparative-advantage trade. It will be interesting to see how—in terms of the five factors enumerated by Chenery—these changes will affect the development of the world's low-income nations.

SUMMING UP

1. Policy makers today must face a major question: Can international trade provide the primary basis for the economic development of poor nations?

2. Views differ as to the relation between trade and development. Classical economists (Adam Smith, David Ricardo) felt that comparative-advantage trade was essential to increasing output and maximizing the wealth of a nation.

3. Much of the debate over the relation between trade and development involves the distinction between the static principles of comparative advantage and the dynamic principles of growth.

4. One can show that, in a static sense (that is, at a point in time), a nation can maximize its output if it allocates all its resources to their most productive uses. However, there is no assurance that if a nation does this, the growth of its output over a period of time will be greater than it would have been if it had departed, selectively, from comparative-advantage trade.

5. Those who argue in favor of the policy of comparative advantage must face five main reservations: (a) *Factor costs*. Imperfections in the factor markets of underdeveloped nations cause their factor costs not to reflect their real relative cost. (b) *Export markets*. Comparative-advantage specialization on the part of the poor nations may result in unstable economies. Low income and price elasticities of demand for raw-material exports may turn the terms of trade against the nation that specializes. (c) *Productivity changes*. In an economy based on manufacturing, the skills of labor and management increase and diversify more rapidly than they do in an economy based on agriculture. (d) *Dynamic external economies*. Several investments—a whole package of them—may have to be made simultaneously in order to make them succeed, or pay off. This is more likely to happen in an industry-based economy than in an agriculture-based economy. (e) *Uncertainty and flexibility*. A diversified economy is more flexible, and can adjust more readily to changes in supply and demand, than an economy that specializes in a few raw-material exports. Thus, it can better resist the effects of worsening terms of trade.

6. Economists generally discount points a and b as reasons to abandon comparative-advantage trade. However, they must take into account factors c, d, and e when they are working out trade policy, and this may force them to call for significant deviations from free trade.

7. For years underdeveloped countries have been pushing for special trade and finance privileges. Their struggle attracted wide publicity in the 1960s, and even more publicity after OPEC's quadrupling of the world oil prices in the early 1970s. The IMF has proposed a reorganization of international finance, in which one-sixth of IMF's gold will be sold off, and the proceeds used to make loans to the underdeveloped countries. This and other changes, not yet possible to foresee, may mean a further departure from the policy of comparative-advantage—or free–trade.

QUESTIONS

1. What are the differences between the static view of comparative advantage and the dynamic view of growth?

2. If you were recommending economic policy to a developing low-income country, at what point would you recommend that it follow a policy of comparative-advantage trade, and at what point would you recommend that it sacrifice a certain amount of efficiency in the use of its resources in order to achieve more growth?

3. Consider an underdeveloped country (for example, Chile), and suppose that it primarily exports one raw material (for example, copper). How can low price and income elasticities of demand for copper affect Chile's export earnings, its

ability to import other, necessary goods, and its terms of trade?

SUGGESTED READINGS

Cameron, Rondo. "Some Lessons of History for Developing Nations." Reprinted in *Economics: Readings in Analysis and Policy*, edited by Dennis R. Starleaf. Scott, Foresman, Glenview, Ill., 1969.

Chenery, Hollis B. "Comparative Advantage and Development Policy." *American Economic Review*, 51:1 (March 1961). Reprinted in *Economic Development: Readings in Theory and Practice*, edited by Theodore Morgan and George W. Betz. Wadsworth, Belmont, Calif., 1970.

Council of Economic Advisers. *International Economic Report of the President, 1974*. G.P.O., Washington, D.C., 1974.

Frank, Isaiah. "New Perspectives on Trade and Development." *Foreign Affairs*, April 1967.

Hirschman, A. O. *The Strategy of Economic Development*. Yale, New Haven, Conn., 1958.

International Monetary Fund. "Developing Country Payments Crucial, Fund Warns." *IMF Survey*, Annual Reports Issue, August 25, 1975.

Johnson, Harry J. *Economic Policies Toward Less-Developed Countries*. Brookings Institution, Washington, D.C., 1967.

Knudsen, John W. "International Trade Benefits and Economic Policy." *Monthly Review*. Federal Reserve Bank of Kansas City, September/October, 1970.

Myrdal, Gunnar. *Asian Drama: An Inquiry into the Poverty of Nations*. Allen Lane, Penguin, London, 1968.

Pincus, John. "Trade Preferences for Underdeveloped Countries." Reprinted in *Economics in Action*, by Shelley M. Mark, 4th ed. Wadsworth, Belmont, Calif., 1969.

Prebisch, Paul. "Toward a New Trade Policy for Development." *Report by the Secretary General of the United Nations, Conference on Trade and Development*, United Nations, New York, 1964.

Singer, Hans W. "The Distribution of Gains Between Investing and Borrowing Countries." Reprinted in *Economic Development: Readings in Theory and Practice*, edited by Theodore Morgan and George W. Betz. Wadsworth, Belmont, Calif., 1970.

Smith, Adam. "Restraints on Foreign Imports." In *The Wealth of Nations*, Vol. I. Reprinted in *Readings in Introductory Economics*, edited by John R. McKean and Ronald A. Wykstra. Harper & Row, New York, 1971.

Sodersten, Bo. *International Economics*. Harper & Row, New York, 1970.

"Toward a Third World Bank," *Time*, May 17, 1976.

25 Paying for International Trade

Chapter 24 dealt with the theory of international trade in general terms. We examined the bases for trade between nations: (1) comparative advantage and (2) protectionism. Trade based on barter *is* possible; for example, the United States has exchanged destroyers with the British for military bases and is negotiating to exchange wheat with the Russians for oil. But barter is very rare among modern economies. Virtually all international trade today requires that money change hands.

An Example of Money Exchange

The American Aluminum Company agrees to sell $500,000 worth of rolled aluminum to the German Automobile Company. Suppose also that the **rate of exchange**, the price at which deutsche marks can be exchanged for American dollars, is 4 deutsche marks per dollar. (Later we will see how this rate is established.) The German importer, in other words, owes 2 million marks to the American Aluminum Company. Let's follow this transaction through the banking system in both countries:

1. German Automobile writes a check on its Hamburg bank for 2 million marks, and mails the check to American Aluminum.

2. American Aluminum cannot pay its workers and creditors in German marks; it needs dollars. Therefore, it sells the check to a New York bank that has a correspondent relation with a German bank.

3. Now American Aluminum has a $500,000 deposit in the New York bank. The New York bank deposits the check from German Automobile in its correspondent bank in Hamburg and becomes the owner of a claim to German marks.

In other words, an American company's exports of a commodity create a demand for dollars. When this demand is fulfilled, more

Virtually all international trade today requires that money change hands. (Clif Garboden)

foreign currency is available to people in the United States who need it.

When a U.S. company imports something, the process is reversed. The American company must obtain a supply of the currency of the country from which it is buying the goods. The supply comes from foreign currencies that American firms have earned through their exports. Thus, German marks are available to pay for U.S. imports of Volkswagens because Americans have exported wheat (and many other commodities) to Germany. In other words, *in order to be able to pay for its imports, a country must also have exports.*

A Good International Monetary System

This two-country illustration, although it is correct, makes the financing of international trade seem simple, and it is not. Financing trade is quite complex. It involves intricate relationships between the domestic economies of more than a hundred independent nations that exchange goods and services. In short, it involves the international monetary system.

Chapter 11 set forth the characteristics of a good money system in a *domestic* economy. Now let's examine the characteristics of a good money system in an *international* economy. One feature that is absolutely essential is that the system expedite the trading of goods and services. (After all, barter is no more feasible in international trade than it is in domestic trade.) By what criteria is a system of payments judged?

1. *The system must strike a reasonable balance between stability and growth in international trade and stability and growth in the individ-*

ual nations that engage in it. The economy of the United States (or Britain, or any other nation) should not have to absorb shocks to its own employment and investment situation in order to accommodate changes in its international trade position, or that of other nations. (Later in this chapter, we will discuss the gold standard, which forces exactly such adjustments.) The present set of monetary arrangements, although it is a great improvement over the gold standard, may still force some countries to make drastic adjustments in their internal economies in order to handle their international payments.

Essential to this requirement of reasonable balance is consistency of action. Once the rules for international financial transactions have been made, all the participating nations must play by the rules. The system may force a nation to make adjustments that conflict with its political and economic objectives, or even threaten the political survival of its government. (For example, it may have to raise interest rates, lower investment, and create unemployment.) If the system demands too many adjustments of this sort, nations will probably not adhere to it consistently. Then the system will become unstable.

2. *The system of payments must be equitable.* It is hard for nations to agree on how the costs and benefits of a system are to be distributed so that there is equity for all. Many nations, especially the underdeveloped ones, feel that present international financial arrangements are inequitable. They claim that they do not have enough control over decisions about the availability of capital and credit, and about who is to bear the costs of financing. An agreement on equity will be difficult to achieve in any revision of the International Monetary Fund (whose workings we will describe later).

3. *The system of payments must be efficient*, just as any other system of markets must. One measures the efficiency of an international system of payments in terms of the effect of that system on the cost of trade. An efficient system encourages trade by making the means of financing exports and imports readily available, and by reducing the risks of trade (unanticipated changes in exchange rates, for example).

Determining Equilibrium Exchange Rates

An **equilibrium exchange rate** is the rate of exchange between two currencies that clears the market or eliminates excess supply or demand. This rate will change only as the supply of or demand for the currencies changes. Like any other price, the exchange rate may be established in one of two ways: (1) It may be freely floating, that is, established by impersonal market forces (competition). (2) It may be fixed, that is, administered (determined by certain individuals or agencies). Here are some of the ways exchange rates are determined and export-import equilibrium established:

Freely Floating Exchange Rates
Let's take as an example the exchange rate between the dollar and the

deutsche mark. With a **freely floating exchange rate**, the exchange rate is established through the interplay of supply and demand. Figure 25-1 illustrates this interplay.

The curve D_0 is the American demand for marks. It slopes downward because as the dollar price of marks falls (as a dollar buys more marks), German goods (Volkswagens, Rhine wine, cameras, binoculars, and so on) become cheaper for Americans to buy. When that happens, Americans demand more marks, so they can buy more German goods. The curve S_1 is the supply of marks. It slopes upward because as the dollar price of marks rises (as marks buy more dollars), American exports become cheaper for Germans to buy. When that happens, Germans demand more dollars, so they can buy more American goods (cars, machinery, wheat, and so on). The Germans pay for their purchases with checks drawn on German banks.

The exchange rate is free to seek its market level, the level at which quantity supplied equals quantity demanded. Here it is at .40, which is 2.5 marks to the dollar ($\frac{1}{.40} = 2.5$). In other words, a mark will buy four-tenths of a dollar. The equilibrium quantity of marks in Figure 25-1 is 10 billion.

Now what if a disequilibrium—a fluctuation that throws things off balance—develops in this market? Suppose that Detroit auto makers, in a surprise move, announce a big increase in prices. (If the price increase had been anticipated, it would have been reflected in D_0—the original demand for marks.) Higher prices for Detroit-made cars mean that German cars are now cheaper by comparison. As a result, the demand for marks shifts upward (people want to buy more Volkswagens and Mercedes Benzes). But now there is a disequilibrium. At the present exchange rate (.40), only 10 billion marks are supplied, but foreign-exchange buyers now want nearly 20 billion.

When the exchange rate is freely floating, the excess demand of 10 million marks is taken care of by dealers who bid up the dollar price of the mark. (There are foreign exchange markets and dealers in nearly

FIGURE 25-1 Freely Floating Exchange Rate (dollars versus marks)

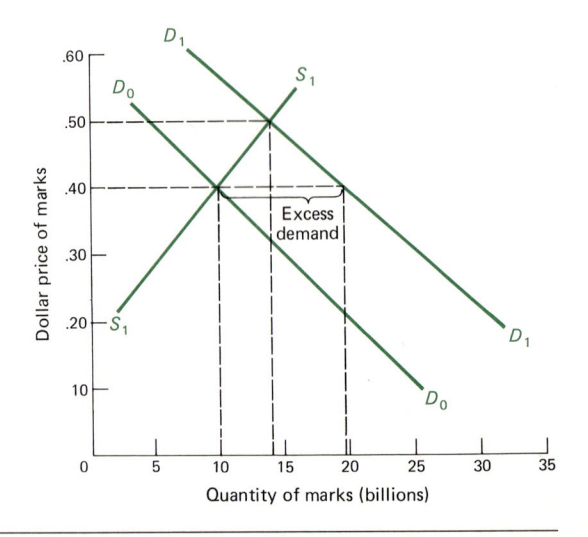

Paying for International Trade

Exchange rates in flux: German currency dealer with board listing exchange rates for various currencies against the mark (Wide World Photos)

every major city in the world.) The mark then costs more to buy. When the rate of exchange rises to .50 ($\frac{1}{.50}$ = 2 marks to the dollar), excess demand is eliminated. Remember that the additional quantity of marks supplied is forthcoming because, as the mark appreciates in value, Germans buy more of relatively cheaper American goods (ironically, they even buy the now relatively cheaper American cars).

Let's look at the advantages and disadvantages of allowing the value of currencies to float freely. The *advantages* are those of a competitive market: (1) The system responds quickly to changes in supply and demand. (2) Disequilibriums in payments are readily resolved; for example, the excess demand that appeared when Americans wanted to buy more German goods (Figure 25-1).

The *disadvantages* of the system are as follows: (1) The rate of exchange may be very unstable. This instability may inhibit trade, because a buyer who orders an imported article will soon stop buying if large changes in the exchange rate make the article cost more when it is delivered than when it is ordered. (2) Some countries depend heavily on international trade to provide jobs and investment capital (especially

Determining Equilibrium Exchange Rates 603

underdeveloped countries, in which the foreign-trade sectors dominate the economies). In these countries, wide swings in exchange rates can cause very destabilizing changes in exports and imports. (3) A nation's terms of trade can change quickly and sharply. Terms of trade are the amounts of exports a nation must have in order to maintain a given level of imports. Wide variations in the values of currencies can cause either variations in imports or disruptive efforts to adjust exports. In either case, destabilization may result.

Some economists (but not all) have serious reservations about allowing the exchange rate to fluctuate freely. In 1973, Arthur Burns, chairman of the Federal Reserve Board, testified before Congress and gave four reasons for his skepticism: (1) Freely floating rates are an academic dream that causes people to demand protection through government controls or government intervention in the money market. (2) Floating rates may lead to political friction. If other nations suspect that the rates are being manipulated, they will take retaliatory steps. (3) Floating rates increase people's uncertainty and thus inhibit trade. (4) Floating rates make it harder for the government to implement domestic fiscal and monetary policies that are suitable.

Other economists (such as Milton Friedman) believe that fears such as these about the dangers of floating rates may be exaggerated. They say the following: (1) Where the policy of floating rates has been tried (as it has with the U.S. dollar, beginning in 1971), there have not been any enormous swings in rates. The apparent reason for this is that speculators in foreign exchange, who anticipate changes in supply or demand and move to profit from them, stabilize the market. (2) Although freely floating rates do increase business uncertainty, this is a price worth paying in exchange for the above-mentioned benefits of the system.

In the United States, there seems to be strong political support for continuing to float the dollar. The Secretary of the Treasury, reporting to Congress in April of 1975 about the freely fluctuating dollar, said, "The dollar has been one of the most stable of the major currencies during this past four-year period." He said that he opposed any effort to fix exchange rates, or to stipulate the range within which the rates can move.

Fixed Exchange Rates

Some people favor complete stability of exchange rates. **Fixed exchange rates** mean a system of payments based on fixed and agreed-upon relationships between the world's currencies. To see how this works, refer again to Figure 25-1. Suppose that at the fixed rate of 2.5 marks to the dollar, there is an excess demand of 6 billion marks. The U.S. and German governments (perhaps dealing through an international agency) are committed to maintaining the 2.5 : 1 rate. The additional marks come from somewhere. Since the market will not supply them at the fixed rate, governments or international agencies must.

The additional marks can come only from **international reserves**, supplies of currency available to finance international trade. (In the past it was gold.) It is possible, of course, that the German central bank, the Deutsche Bundesbank, might lend the marks to the Federal Reserve System. The Federal Reserve, in turn, would make them available to American commercial banks. Alternatively, there might be an international agency such as the **International Monetary Fund (IMF)**, which has reserves of dollars, deutsche marks, Swiss francs, British pounds, claims to gold, and all other major currencies. The IMF makes loans to the Fed and through the Fed to our commercial banks.

Note: Fixed exchange rates require large currency reserves. In the face of growing world trade, they require *increasing reserves*, if banks are to be able to take care of fluctuations in demand for currencies.

The chief advantage of fixed exchange rates is that they lend stability to world trade. Fixed rates reduce uncertainty about international prices. If you want to buy a German car and you know that the banking system is committed to a 2.5 : 1 exchange rate, you can plan your purchase even if the car is not actually delivered to you until months later. This stability provides a favorable climate for the growth of trade.

Even fixed exchange rates are not necessarily fixed forever. For example, the German government may decide that subsidizing German exports to the United States is not in Germany's best interests. The U.S. government may decide that at the 2.5 : 1 rate its exports to Germany are too low. The international reserves needed to finance this trade imbalance may run dangerously low. The two countries, by mutual agreement, may change the rate to 2 marks to the dollar (which will equilibrate the exchange market shown in Figure 25-1).

Adjusting Economies to Fluctuations in the Exchange Rate

One can trace the origin of an exchange-rate disequilibrium (such as the excess demand in Figure 25-1) to changes in economic conditions in the exporting and importing nations. Figure 25-2 gives you the situation at a glance.

Suppose that the dollar-mark exchange market is initially in equilibrium. The demand for marks is D_0, supply is S_1, and the exchange rate is 2.5 : 1 (that is, the mark is equal to 0.4 dollars). Ten billion marks are exchanged. Now, suppose that inflation hits the United States. The rapidly rising prices of American goods make German imports relatively cheaper. As a result, American demand for marks to finance purchases of German goods rises to D_1. At the old exchange rate, there is an excess demand of 6.5 billion marks (16.5 − 10). If the dollar-mark rate is *not* freely floating, and if there is no system of international reserves to finance the payments deficit at existing exchange rates, two things may happen.

1. The excess demand may be treated as a rationing problem. People demand more marks than the amount of marks available at the going

exchange rate. So to "ration" marks, a nation might set up a system of **exchange controls** (perhaps an agency acting through its central bank). The agency could establish priorities to determine who should get the available marks. In effect, this would mean determining what kinds and quantities of German goods could be imported into the United States (perhaps Volkswagens, but no Mercedes Benzes, or perhaps machinery, but no cars at all). Presumably, these priorities would reflect certain national goals.

The main advantage of this approach to managing fluctuations in the exchange rate is that it enables countries to hold to a fixed exchange rate (with the aforementioned stability of trade), while at the same time ensuring that national import priorities are consistent with domestic economic priorities. The main disadvantages are that it does not allow the market to work, and that it imposes public tastes and preferences in place of private ones. (No matter how much you might like to import a Mercedes, you cannot, because it is important to the country to import farm machinery.)

The United States has never used exchange controls, although many underdeveloped countries have. Low-income countries, unlike the industrialized nations, must import much of their capital. They do not have the domestic markets to provide it, and they cannot afford to import expensive consumer goods at the same time.

2. The deficit in payments (or the excess demand) shown in Figure 25-2 may be taken care of by adjustments in income and employment in the economy of the country that is demanding "too much" foreign currency.

FIGURE 25-2 Exchange-Rate Equilibrium Maintained Through Macroeconomic Adjustment

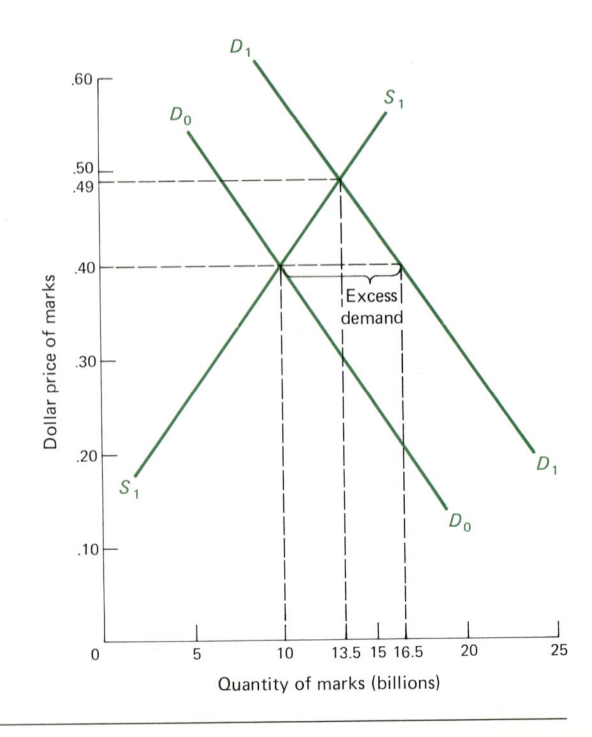

In this case, inflation in the United States is causing the excess demand for marks. To counter this demand, the United States must use the macroeconomic adjustment of **deflation**, which is a general lowering of prices. To accomplish this, the government may reduce aggregate demand by increasing taxes. It may also reduce government spending and raise interest rates. Or it may adopt any of the combinations of means that we discussed in Chapter 9. (Of course, a tax on imports could correct the relative imbalance in prices between the two countries, but this victory would be at the price of free trade.)

If the United States follows a deflationary policy and aggregate demand does decrease, money incomes will certainly decrease also. Now let's assume that the demand for imports has a strongly positive income elasticity. (Americans, like most people, have a strong taste for imported goods.) Demand for imports, and for German marks, will fall. If the decline is strong enough, D_1 in Figure 25-2 may shift back to D_0, and the dollar-mark ratio may again find its equilibrium at 2.5 : 1.

The main advantage of tying a nation's economy to its exchange-rate position is that it practically guarantees stable rates of exchange. (Remember that stable exchange rates are desirable because they enhance trade and make possible longer-term planning for trade.) The main disadvantage of such a policy is that the nation has to pay a price for this stability of exchange rates and equilibrium of payments. Most economists believe this price is out of proportion to its worth. It is truly letting the tail wag the dog. In the example here, the United States would have to deflate its economy deliberately—with all the effects it would have on income distribution, jobs, savings, and investment. Even if the United States had been at full employment before the government introduced the fiscal and monetary measures necessary to bring about deflation, there would soon be some significant changes in prices, incomes, and employment. But suppose that the United States had been suffering significant unemployment, coupled with inflation, as it has in recent years and the government came along and put through these measures. Then, deflating the economy would just add to the unemployment problem, thus curing an external problem by worsening an internal one. Few countries would be willing to pay such a price for stability of exchange rates.

The Gold Standard

In the past, the system of fixed exchange rates was tied to the **gold standard**. The gold standard provided for the rates of exchange of most of the world's currencies for about fifty years before World War I, and in varying degrees up until the Great Depression of the 1930s. Under the freely convertible gold standard, nations could be sure of two things:

1. Each trading nation permitted unrestricted exports and imports of gold.

2. Each nation defined its own currency in terms of a specific quantity of gold, and guaranteed to convert any claims to that currency into gold at the defined rate.

Under the gold standard, each currency was defined to be worth so many grains of gold. For example, the German mark might be defined as 10 grains of gold and the American dollar as 25 grains of gold. Therefore, the dollar would be worth 2.5 marks. No one would pay more than 2.5 marks to get a dollar, or sell a mark for less than 40 cents, because the dollars (or marks) could always be converted into gold at the official rate. People could take their dollars or marks down to the bank and get gold for them. (Here we are ignoring the cost of moving gold—actually physically moving it—from one nation to another: transporting, insuring, and handling it.)

Suppose that the United States was operating on the gold standard and there was a disequilibrium of payments (see Figure 25-3). The United States is committed to exchanging dollars for gold at 25 grains of gold per dollar. But it is *not* bound to keep the dollar-mark exchange rate constant. At first, therefore, the excess demand for marks at 40 cents apiece (distance AB, or 10.5 billion marks) causes the dollar price of marks to be bid upward (depreciating the dollar). At some price—let's say 40 cents per mark plus the cost of transferring gold (shown arbitrarily as 45 cents to the mark)—it becomes cheaper to buy gold in the United States, at the fixed price, and ship it to Germany to pay for imports than to buy marks with dollars to pay for the imports. This price is called the **gold-flow point**.

Let's suppose that the dollar price of the mark (Figure 25-3) rises beyond the gold-flow point. Gold begins to flow from the United States to Germany. Under the gold standard, the United States government backs its dollars by gold and must redeem them for gold. Since there is now less gold to back the currency, the money supply in the United States must be reduced.

The contraction in the money supply leads to a decline in the volume of transactions. Banks call in their loans, refuse to renew loans, and tighten credit. If this is not clear to you, remember the equation of exchange,

$$MV = PQ.$$

Recall that M = supply of money; V = velocity of circulation of money (the number of times it changes hands in a given period of time); P = price level; and Q = quantity of goods sold. When M declines (other things being equal), $P \times Q$ (the net national product, NNP) decreases. As NNP falls, employment and incomes decrease too. In effect, there is a deflation. Assuming a positive income elasticity of demand for German goods, the demand for imports (and German marks to pay for them) diminishes. The American demand for marks, D_1, will shift to the left, to D_2.

Now let's switch to Germany, where the gold is flowing in. The equation of exchange works in a direction that is the reverse of what is happening in the United States. More gold means a larger supply of money, M. Therefore, MV equals PQ at a higher level of transactions. Either prices (P) will rise, or quantities of goods sold (Q) will rise, or both. In either case, the German economy is inflated toward full employment, or even beyond it. This will increase German demand for American imports, and thereby increase the supply of marks available to the United States. The supply of marks, S_1, shifts to the right, to S_2 in Figure 25-3.

In the long run, equilibrium is restored. The changed supply of marks again becomes equal to the demand, at the previous exchange rate of 40 cents to the mark. The equilibrium quantity of marks exchanged must be between A and B: in this instance at C (15.5 billion marks).

The United States and other leading trading nations have not used the gold standard since the 1930s. Yet there are still those who advocate its return. Not long ago, the government of France came out in favor of it. The gold standard thus remains a source of controversy.

The advantages of the gold standard are the following: (1) It is automatic; any imbalance in relations between currencies sets in motion corrective gold flows. (2) It stabilizes exchange rates, and thereby makes possible long-term planning for trade. (3) Some economists maintain that gold flows make a nation practice economic self-discipline, live within its own (gold-determined) means, and refrain from forcing other nations to subsidize its consumption of goods.

The disadvantages of the gold standard are the following: (1) It causes domestic economic policy to be tied to international trade (the

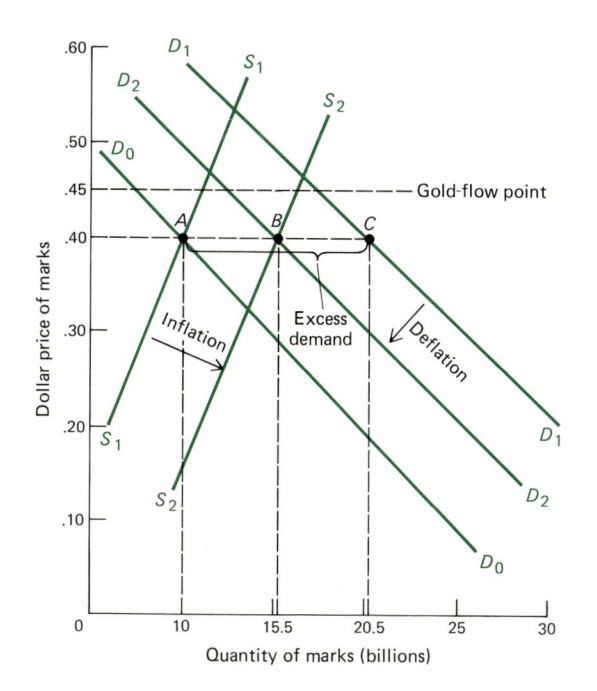

FIGURE 25-3 Exchange-Rate Equilibrium Under the Gold Standard

tail-wagging-the-dog argument). (2) It causes the volume of trade to be tied to the supply of an exhaustible resource, gold, which is in inelastic supply.

Postwar International Exchange Arrangements

Most present-day arrangements for financing trade stem from a meeting that the Allied nations (the United States, Britain, and France) held at Bretton Woods, New Hampshire, in 1944 (there were many other nations present as well). The Bretton Woods conference set up two basic trade features: (1) a system of adjustable pegs for exchange currencies, (2) the International Monetary Fund (IMF) to oversee the operation of the **adjustable-peg system**, a system of exchange in which currencies are pegged, or are not allowed to change in value by more than a specific percentage.

The nations that met at Bretton Woods sought to create relatively fixed exchange rates, which could be maintained. Each currency was to be valued in terms of both gold *and* U.S. dollars. Currencies could vary from these parities by no more than 1 percent. Exchange rates could be changed, however, when countries found that there was a "fundamental disequilibrium" in their payments position. But the Bretton Woods conference failed to define the term *fundamental disequilibrium*.

So, beginning in the 1950s, countries such as the United States began to run long-term deficits in payments, with no changes in exchange rates. They did this by drawing on gold reserves—reserves held by the IMF—and by borrowing from the central banks of other countries. Thus, they were without the automatic, self-correcting, adjustment mechanism that had existed under the gold standard (a good feature, for all its other flaws). This went on until 1971, when President Nixon devalued the dollar and set it free from the pegged rate.

During the 1960s, pressure for change in the international money system began to develop. The countries that had to absorb the excess dollars created by U.S. balance-of-payments deficits began to be dissatisfied with the terms of the Bretton Woods agreement—and with good reason: Speculators in the late 1960s were moving huge amounts of money out of dollars and into strong currencies such as German marks.

One modification of the system was the creation of **special drawing rights (SDRs)**. By using SDRs, countries with deficits could borrow so-called paper gold from the IMF to finance their imbalances of payments. This made it possible for the exchange system itself to finance trade. But it did nothing to establish equilibrium relations between the world's major currencies.

A second modification was to allow currencies to establish a supply-demand equilibrium through freely floating against each other. The dollar, as you know, led the way in doing this, in 1971.

The system of freely floating rates that is presently in force seems to work reasonably well. It does not satisfy Arthur Burns, Chairman of the Federal Reserve, and others like him, who want more stability in the exchange rate for dollars. Other people, such as Secretary of the Treasury Simon, who want supply-demand relationships to dictate exchange rates, praise the present system.

The Rambouillet Conference

In November of 1975, in the little village of Rambouillet near Paris, there was an economic conference of the so-called six giants—the United States, France, Britain, West Germany, Italy, and Japan—the most industrialized nations in the world. Among them they control half the world's international trade. The leaders of these countries declared their intention of cooperating in the future to prevent wide swings in the values of their currencies. The system of open trading was to continue, but whenever the values of currencies appeared to fluctuate strongly, the central banks of all the countries would cooperate to prevent it. They would step in and buy and sell currencies in such a way as to prevent drastic changes in values. This cooperation by the powerful national banks may work more efficiently than past systems.

The agreement on more active intervention by central banks was essentially a compromise between the United States, which felt that market forces should continue to guide currency movements, and France, which had sought a return to the fixed-rate system such as existed from 1945 to 1973.

The Rambouillet conference, like the 1933 economic conference in London, marked an effort by the industrial giants to cooperate in solving the world's economic ills. Their jointly issued statement stressed their desire to help the developing countries to attain a higher level of international trade and to embark on a new era of growth.

The Balance of Payments

Up to now, we have dealt with trade as a process of exporting and importing goods and services and paying for them directly with currency, but there is more to international trade. Not only goods and services move between nations. Capital flows. There are also other movements.

Each nation puts together an annual acounting of all its trade transactions (including trade in goods and services). This is called its **balance-of-payments statement**. This national statement is like a firm's profit-and-loss statement. It reveals not only what is bought and what is sold, but also how any difference between the two is financed. Table 25-1 shows a balance-of-payments statement for the United States.

By definition, the balance of payments must balance. A nation, like a firm or a person, must somehow find a means to pay for everything it buys. Let's look at these accounts to see how the United States paid for all the things it bought (imported) in 1974.

TABLE 25-1 The United States Balance of Payments, 1974
(billions of dollars)

Item	Credits (+) Debits (−)	Balance
A. Current account		
1. Merchandise	− 5.5	
2. Military transactions	− 2.1	
3. Travel and transportation	− 2.7	
4. Investment income	+10.1	
5. Other services	+ 3.8	
6. Remittances, pensions, other tranfers	− 1.7	
7. U.S. government grants (excluding military)	− 5.5	− 3.6
B. Long-term capital account		
8. United States government	+ 1.1	
9. Private	− 8.4	− 7.3
C. Basic balance		
(balance on current account plus long-term capital)		−10.9
D. Short-term capital account		
10. Nonliquid private	−12.9	
11. Allocations of SDRs	0.0	
12. Errors and omissions	+ 4.8	
13. Liquid private	+10.7	+ 2.6
E. Balance to be financed		− 8.3
F. Official reserve transactions balance		
Financed by changes in:		
14. Liquid liabilities to foreign official agencies		+ 8.5
15. Other marketable liabilities to foreign official agencies		+ 0.6
16. Nonliquid liabilities to foreign official agencies		+ 0.6
17. U.S. official reserve assets, net (gold, SDRs, convertible currencies, gold tranche position in IMF)		− 1.4
United States net total		0.0

Source: *Federal Reserve Bulletin*, August 1975.

The Balance-of-Payments Statement

A. *Current account.* The current account is like a family's calculation of current income and expenses. It includes both visible items (exports and imports of merchandise) and invisible items (services, including financial services). The biggest item, a visible item, is (1) merchandise exports and imports. In 1974, the United States exported $98.3 billion and imported $103.8 billion worth of merchandise. This means that imports of merchandise were greater than exports by $5.5 billion. Thus, the United States had a *balance-of-trade deficit*. (Remember, though, that this is only a part of the balance of payments.)

Much of the Arab oil riches invested in the United States become a plus in our balance of payments. (Settimio Garritano/Sygma)

Other items in the current account include (2) military transactions (military materials are treated separately from other "merchandise"); (3) expenditures for travel and transportation (Americans abroad spent $2.7 billion more than foreigners spent here); (4) Investment income (Americans earned and returned $10.1 billion more on their foreign investments than foreigners earned and returned on their investments in the United States); (5) other services (fees and royalties associated with investments abroad); (6) remittances, pensions, and so on (America sent $1.7 billion more to Americans—or relatives of Americans—living in other countries than other countries sent here); and (7) U.S. government grants of $5.5 billion (for example, a $2 billion economic assistance loan to India). That is all outgo. No one gave grants to the United States.

When the credits and debits for 1974 were added up, the United States had a current account deficit of $3.6 billion. How did the United States pay for it? One way was through long-term capital inflows.

B. *Long-term capital account.* This is a part of what is called the **capital account**, which is made up of both long-term and short-term capital flows. *Long-term capital movements* refers to long-term investments in the United States by foreigners. It also means investments abroad by Americans. In 1974, private capital flowing out of the United States accounted for a major deficit ($8.4 billion). At the same time, government capital (mainly foreign currencies held by the U.S. government) increased by $1.1 billion.

C. *Basic balance.* The combination of a nation's current account and its long-term capital account is often referred to as its *basic balance.* In 1974, the basic balance of the United States showed a deficit of $10.9 billion. This amount had to be financed.

D. *Short-term capital account.* Movements of capital occurring in response to changes in short-term economic conditions (those expected to be temporary) are called short-term capital movements. Suppose that short-term interest rates in Germany or Japan, for example, go up until they are higher there than here. Such a change may cause holders of liquid funds to move them to a country in which they will earn more. Table 25-1 shows that capital moved this way consists of (10) nonliquid private capital (the U.S. had a net outflow of $12.9 billion); (11) allocations of SDRs (the United States had zero); (12) errors and omissions (these are speculative movements of capital that are hard to account for specifically); and (13) liquid private capital ($10.7 billion came into the United States from private sources).

E. *Balance to be financed.* Overall, short-term movements of capital were a net plus to the United States in 1974. They reduced the deficit or balance to be financed to $8.3 billion.

F. *Official reserve transactions balance.* The account labeled **official reserve transactions balance** shows how the United States met its payments to the rest of the world. Mainly, it did so by borrowing from official agencies (usually central banks), by persuading them to hold more dollars ($8.5 billion more). Also, the United States sold some government debt ($0.6 billion) and some nonliquid liabilities to foreign agencies ($0.6 billion). Finally, the United States requested the IMF to allow a buildup of $1.4 billion in official reserve assets (mainly $1.27 billion in the U.S. **gold tranche position**, which represents the amount of gold the United States can borrow from the International Monetary Fund).

The Balance of Payments in Summary

As you can see, there is a lot of detail in the balance of payments. For an overview of it, let's put it in capsule form (Table 25-2). The six major accounts are shown again, without the previous detail. A, the current account, shows a deficit of $3.6 billion. To this is added B, the long-term capital account, which has a deficit of $7.3 billion. Together (A + B) they form the basic balance, which shows a deficit of $10.9 billion. The short-term capital account (D) has a surplus of $2.6 billion. The balance to be

TABLE 25-2 The United States Balance of Payments, 1974, Summary Form (billion of dollars)

Item	Credits (+) Debits (−)
A. Current account	− 3.6
B. Long-term capital account	− 7.3
C. Basic balance (A + B)	−10.9
D. Short-term capital account	+ 2.6
E. Balance to be financed (A + B + D)	− 8.3
F. Official reserve transactions balance	+ 8.3
Balance of payments (E + F)	0

financed is the sum of A + B + D, or $8.3 billion. The balance (again, there *must* be one) comes from the official reserve transactions balance (F). The balance of payments (E + F) equals zero. In other words, the United States in 1974, as in every other year, has financed all its international trade.

The U.S. Balance-of-Payments Deficits

Figure 25-4 shows that since the late 1940s the United States has had deficits (amounts to be financed) in the balance of payments for most years. The exceptions were 1959 and 1971, when there were surpluses. The United States has had these deficits in spite of the fact that (except for three recent years), there has been a surplus in the U.S. balance of trade. Therefore, the problem seems to be primarily in the *non*merchandise export-import position. Because the dollar's exchange rate is free to float, and because American goods have become relatively cheaper and easier to export, the trade (merchandise) deficits of 1972 and 1974 seem to be disappearing.

A longer-term problem that the United States has yet to solve is how to finance its overseas military commitments, foreign aid, tourist travel, and other kinds of expenditures without running a massive payments deficit, such as the huge one in 1971. Some people feel that the United States should retrench or withdraw from some of these foreign commitments (perhaps persuade allies to take on more of them). Others feel that this is not politically feasible. They believe that the United States must find a system of payments that accommodates our international role. This conflict between political and military roles and balance of payments promises to be a troublesome problem for years to come.

Huge movements of capital, both short-term and long-term, have put pressure on the dollar and weakened its exchange position in several recent years. One of the difficulties in dealing with short-term capital

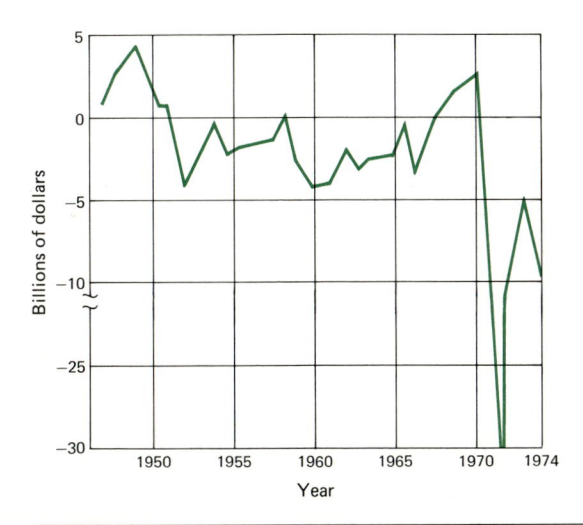

FIGURE 25-4 United States Balance of Payments, 1946–1974

movements (notice the $12.9 billion outflow in 1974) is created by the **multinational corporations (MNCs)**, which operate all over the world and know no national boundaries. They not only produce in many countries, but they finance themselves in whatever currency is convenient. (In 1971, they held an estimated $268 billion in short-term liquid assets.) They can move huge sums from one currency to another. Not even buying and selling by the central banks (including the Federal Reserve) can prevent these movements. (In 1971, by comparison, the central banks held only $68 billion in short-term liquid assets.) Some people believe the actions of the MNCs are logical and designed only to protect the value of their assets and maximize their profits. Others think that the MNCs destabilize the world's exchange markets, and may even contribute to the world's recurrent financial crises. One question the nation must decide in the future is whether the government should try to control the international financial activities of these corporations, and if so, how?

SUMMING UP

1. Very little international trade is carried out by means of barter. Nearly all of it requires a means of monetary payment, a money exchange system.

2. The conversion of currency of one nation to that of another is carried out by the international banking system and by specialized dealers. For example, a person importing a pair of shoes from Italy can mail a check to the Italian exporter. The exporter deposits it in a bank in Italy and gets a certain amount of lire for it. The Italian bank gets a claim to dollars from its correspondent bank in the United States.

3. The money exchange system enables exporters and importers to end up with the kind of national currency (dollars, marks, yen, and so on) that they need.

4. Exports by the United States create a demand overseas for dollars to pay for them. When a French firm imports American goods, for example, it creates a supply of claims to francs with which Americans may pay for their imports from France. In other words, *a country that wishes to export must import, in order to create the claims to currency necessary for it to trade.*

5. A good international monetary system has the following characteristics: (a) It establishes a balance between stability and growth in international trade and stability and growth in each of the trading nations. (b) It is equitable and ensures that each nation will have access to foreign exchange, and that each will help bear the costs of operating the exchange system. (c) It is efficient and thus enhances the growth of international trade.

6. There are two kinds of exchange rates: (a) freely floating and (b) fixed.

7. A *freely floating exchange rate* is determined by the supply of a currency and the demand for it. The *equilibrium exchange rate* is the rate at which quantity supplied and quantity demanded are equal. This means that there is no excess demand or excess supply.

8. The advantages of a freely floating rate are that (a) the rate responds quickly to changes in supply and demand, and (b) imbalances or disequilibriums in payments are readily resolved. The disadvantages are that (a) there can be great instability in rates; (b) there can be great instability in savings, investment, and prices in countries that depend heavily on foreign trade; and (c) there can be sudden changes in *terms of trade*, requiring a country to make a reallocation of resources so that it can export more, in order to continue to import.

9. Economists differ on the merits of freely floating exchange rates. For the time being, however, the United States seems committed to letting the dollar continue to float.

10. *Fixed exchange rates* mean that the currency of a country keeps the same value with respect to the currencies of other countries. The main advantage of fixed rates is stability; they permit longer-term planning for trade. The main disadvantage is that supply and demand are not allowed to work freely. Also, fixed exchange rates require a system of *international reserves* to fill excess demands.

11. Fluctuations of exchange rates derive from changes in economic conditions in the exporting and importing nations. Excess demand can be handled by (a) introducing *exchange controls* (rationing of currencies) or (b) by adjusting the economy of the country suffering the disequilibrium so that the domestic cause is eliminated.

12. Underdeveloped nations often use exchange controls. They determine who shall have access to the limited foreign exchange available. The advantage is a stable exchange rate. The disadvantage is that exchange controls impose a set of public tastes on what would be the private tastes for imports. The government decides what is best for the country to import.

13. Adjusting a country's domestic economy to eliminate excess demand for foreign exchange means adjusting domestic prices, incomes, and employment. Although a nation may use such means to establish exchange-rate equilibrium, it is a drastic solution. Most economists feel that it creates a major problem (unemployment) in order to solve a lesser problem for which other solutions exist.

14. Under the freely convertible *gold standard*, which has not been used since the 1930s, currencies are valued in terms of grains of gold. Each currency has a value in terms of gold as well as in terms of other currencies. In order for the gold standard to work, the exchange value cannot deviate much from the gold value. If it does, people buy gold and

ship it overseas to pay for traded goods, rather than using currencies to pay for them.

15. The *gold-flow point* is the exchange rate at which it is cheaper to ship gold in payment for traded goods than to buy currency.

16. The equation of exchange ($MV = PQ$) shows that flows of gold, once set in motion, cause an expansion in countries receiving gold and a contraction in those losing gold. These changes alter prices in the two countries, and also alter the demand for foreign exchange. This automatic mechanism ensures that exchange rates ultimately return to their original equilibrium.

17. The *advantages* claimed for the gold standard are that (a) it operates automatically, (b) it stabilizes exchange rates, and (c) gold flows impose an economic self-discipline on nations. The *disadvantages* claimed for the gold standard are that (a) it ties a nation's internal economic policy to the balance of its foreign payments (the tail wags the dog), and (b) it ties the world's volume of trade to the inelastic supply of an exhaustible resource.

18. The Bretton Woods Conference in 1944 established (a) an *adjustable-peg system* for international currencies, and (b) an *International Monetary Fund (IMF)* to administer the system.

19. The system of pegging currencies meant that they could change in value by no more than 1 percent. The world no longer uses this currency-pegging system. However, the International Monetary Fund still exists. It administers a system of *special drawing rights (SDRs)*, through which countries with balance-of-payments problems can borrow from the IMF.

20. The freely floating exchange rates now in use appear to work reasonably well. Actions of private speculators, who buy and sell currency, may have helped to prevent too exaggerated fluctuations. Also, the six giants (the world's most industrialized nations) pledged, at the Rambouillet conference in 1975, the cooperation of their central banks in acting quickly to prevent wide swings in the values of currencies.

21. Each nation annually prepares a *balance-of-payments statement*, an accounting of its international purchases and sales, plus an explanation of how it has financed any deficit payments.

22. A balance-of-payments statement lists (a) current account (visible and invisible items of trade), (b) long-term capital account (for long-term investments, both public and private), (c) basic balance (balance on current account plus long-term capital), (d) short-term capital account (for temporary changes in the market, such as short-term movements due to changes in interest rates in various countries), (e) balance to be financed, and (f) *official reserve transactions balance* (what the nation borrows from other nations, changes in its gold holdings, and so on). A nation's official reserves change when it has a payments deficit or surplus.

23. For most years since the late 1940s, the United States has had a deficit in its balance of payments. Recently, this deficit has been due partly to a *balance-of-trade deficit* (merchandise exports minus imports), and partly to military commitments abroad (Vietnam, NATO, and so on) and to private foreign investment and our foreign aid program. Our trade position appears to be improving. Prices of things we export have been falling relative to prices of other nations' export items. Even so, the deficit in our balance of payments continues.

24. One main problem the United States has had to contend with has been a short-term capital outflow, a movement away from the dollar. Some observers feel that the *multinational corporations (MNCs)* accentuate this outflow by their speculative actions and would like to see these actions curbed. Others view the actions of the MNCs as logical business activity, designed to maximize profits for the firms, and therefore as understandable.

QUESTIONS

1. Do you think the United States should continue to let the American dollar float against other currencies, or should it go back to some sort of pegged or fixed exchange rate system? Why?

2. Evaluate the following statement: "A nation cannot for long export (sell its goods to others) unless it imports (buys from others)."

3. What were the problems associated with the gold standard? What were its advantages?

4. Why is it correct to say that a nation's balance of payments *must* balance? What are the main balancing items?

5. What are the advantages and disadvantages of (a) fixed exchange rates? (b) freely floating exchange rates?

6. Suppose that the Secretary of the Treasury calls you in and says, "I have to go before the Joint Economic Committee of Congress and present a good argument for why the dollar should be allowed to float on world currency markets. What's the best argument I can make?" What would your response be?

SUGGESTED READINGS

"Exchange Rate Policy and International Monetary Reform." Joint Economic Committee, 94th Congress, First Session. G.P.O., Washington, D.C., August 1975.

"How Well Are Fluctuating Exchange Rates Working?" Hearings Before the Subcommittee on International Economics of the Joint Economics Committee, 93rd Congress, 1st Session. G.P.O., Washington, D.C., 1973.

Ingram, James C. *International Economic Problems*, 2d ed. Wiley, New York, 1970.

Miller, Roger Leroy, and Raburn M. Williams. "The Economics of Helping Ford Motor Company and United States Steel." "The Economics of Letting the Dollar Float." "The Economics of the Dollar Standard." In *The Economics of National Issues*. Canfield, San Francisco, 1972.

"Multinationals Find the Going Rougher." *Business Week*, July 14, 1975.

"Nontariff Distortions of Trade." Committee for Economic Development, New York, 1969.

Joint Economic Committee. "Simon Testified on Value of the Dollar and Outlines Exchange Rate Policies." *Notes from the Joint Economic Committee*, Vol. I, No. 7, Washington, D.C., April 4, 1975.

"The U. S. May Join the Commodities Club." *Business Week*, September 15, 1975.

Application 26

Politics and the Balance-of-Payments Problem

Reasons Behind Import Restraints

Whenever the United States buys more goods and services from other countries than it buys domestically, it has a deficit in its balance of trade, and there is a cry to "buy American!" Various people, union leaders and business executives alike, exhort the citizenry to either buy products made in the United States or to impose restrictions on imports. In fact, firms or industries may urge this at any juncture, whenever foreign producers begin to take away any sizable share of domestic sales from American industry. In the late 1960s, for instance, lobbyists for both the steel and automobile industries worked hard in Washington, trying to get Congress to impose import restrictions on European and Japanese steel and cars. (Detroit watches with gloom the import figures on Volkswagens and Datsuns, Volvos and Saabs, Opels and Peugeots, Fiats and Hondas and Toyotas.)

Up until the Great Depression of the 1930s, there was rarely much attention paid to the buy-American slogan. A country's nervousness about excessive imports usually comes out during hard times. But in the early 1970s (1971, 1972, and 1974), there were large deficits in U.S. goods and services and U.S. current account (including U.S. government grants). The United States had not had such a continuing deficit in its balance of trade since 1893.

Thus, in the early 1970s, people began to agitate for a new protectionism. Actually, pressure in this direction had been building up all during the 1960s. Inflation—largely due to the big federal deficits resulting from the Vietnam War—was pushing up prices in the United States faster than prices were rising in Western Europe and Japan. The purchasing power of the dollar fell, relative to the purchasing power of foreign currencies. This lowered value meant that American exports were more and more at a price disadvantage, while at the same time foreign products were selling briskly in the United States. After all, they had a price advantage.

In 1969, the United States negotiated a "voluntary" set of import restraints on steel, whereby Japanese and Western European steel makers were subjected to certain export restrictions enforced by their own governments. In 1971, similar export restrictions were imposed on textiles, chiefly textiles coming from Taiwan, Korea, Japan, and other nations of Southeast Asia.

A new aspect of the import tax situation opened up in January of 1976, when the U.S. Supreme Court overturned an 1871 decision that forbade states and cities to collect any taxes on imports. Until 1976, only the federal government could tax imports. Now the cash-hungry states and cities had a new avenue of tax revenue open to them: import taxes. Long-term reactions to this are as yet unclear. It is possible that some states will decline to tax imports at all, advertise themselves as a sort of duty-free state, and thus attract business.

Who Pays and Who Benefits?

Restrictions in the form of tariffs or quotas have usually been imposed for the purpose of saving the jobs of workers in the United States. In 1975, one labor leader put it this way:

> More than a million American job opportunities have been lost through the export of American technology, machinery, and money to low-wage areas. But the international operators, not the American consumer, get the benefit from low-wage imports.

Economists, on the other hand, have estimated that the cost of both tariff and nontariff restrictions (including voluntary export controls) is between $10 billion and $20 billion per year. This figure reflects the higher prices resulting from import duties (for example, there is a 12 percent import tax on cars). It also reflects the higher prices resulting from a lowered supply and a less competitive market in the United States for cars, steel, cattle, meat, dairy products—and all the other goods protected by high tariffs. For example, economist William Albrecht says:

> Between 1969, when the quota system was first introduced, and 1972, steel companies increased their prices five times as much as they had in the preceding eight-year period, despite the fact the industry was experiencing declining demand and had unused capacity of 25 to 50 percent.

To the extent that this heightened price structure may be generalized to apply to many industries, one could say that it is indeed the American consumer who suffers as a result of these import restrictions. Even a consumer who has lost a job because of competition from cheap imports is worse off. After all, the jobless consumer, who very much needs bargains, cannot buy cheap shirts made in Taiwan or cheap shoes made in Korea or low-price beef from Argentina.

The Big Push: The Burke-Hartke Bill

In 1973 and 1974, organized labor (joined by certain elements of American industry) pushed for the adoption by Congress of the Burke-Hartke bill. This bill would not only have regulated multinational corporations, but would also have imposed mandatory import quotas on many manufactured goods. The amount of support for this bill shows how much pressure builds up in favor of protectionism whenever trade deficits occur. The bill, however, did not pass.

At the same time that the pressure in favor of quotas and tariffs was building up in the Congress, the Joint Economic Committee was putting forth a new initiative to *liberalize* international trade. The majority of the committee recommended in 1973 that "industrial nations should agree to abolish gradually all permanently statutory tariff barriers over the next ten to twenty years." The committee did acknowledge, however, that temporary tariffs might be necessary to "safeguard domestic producers."

1975: How a Deficit Becomes a Surplus

It is very hard to forecast what net exports (exports minus imports, or $X - M$) are going to be. The reason is that the supply-demand influences that determine $X - M$ are much less amenable to influence by the United States (or by any other single nation) than the domestic supply-demand factor, which responds (to a greater or lesser degree) to the government's monetary and fiscal policy, or to a wage-price policy. There was an unexpectedly high deficit in $X - M$ for 1974: $5.5 billion (the Joint Economic Committee had forecast a zero deficit). But this turned into an equally unexpected $X - M$ *surplus* of about $10 billion in 1975. This was the largest merchandise trade surplus in American history.

Several events caused this dramatic change. For one, there was a change in the positions of the United States, Western Europe, and Japan with respect to export prices. Inflation, which had been the enemy of U.S. trade in the late 1960s, now became the friend, because the U.S. rate of inflation was much less severe than the rate in other countries. Japan, for instance, had a 25 percent inflation through much of 1974 and 1975. Western Europe had high rates also. But in 1975 the U.S. rate of inflation had fallen to between 7 and 8 percent. Thus, American goods became relatively cheaper than those of other industrialized nations. U.S. bumper grain crops also helped enormously to bolster the U.S. balance of payments, coinciding as they did with bad weather and crop failures in the Soviet Union and in other nations.

What Happened to Protectionism?

The dramatic turnabout in the trade position of the United States muted the cry for protectionism. Although unemployment in the United States remained high (more than 8 percent at the end of 1975), almost no one was blaming it on cheap foreign goods from low-wage nations flooding American markets and causing American workers to be displaced. Now the export sector seemed to be the healthiest part of the economy. Labor leaders turned their attention to domestic economic policy. They demanded more rapid growth of the money supply and more job retraining programs—rather than restrictions on foreign trade.

The Lesson to Be Learned

There are several things one can learn from the recent unusual balance-of-trade situation. First, the United States should not formulate foreign economic policy on the basis of short-term variations in its trade position. This can change so quickly, and the changes are so hard to forecast, much less control, that the situation may change by the time the policy is implemented. Second, protectionism (of the sort proposed in the Burke-Hartke bill) is nearly always self-defeating. If the United States had gone ahead and enacted that bill's drastic import-quota system, Western Europe and Japan would assuredly have retaliated. They would have put import quotas of their own on the things the United States wanted to sell to *them*. U.S. exports would then have declined. The balance-of-trade turnabout of 1975 would never have taken place. Tariffs and quotas have a way of boomeranging.

In general, then, economists rarely espouse the cause of protectionism. (At the time of the debate over the Burke-Hartke bill, almost no one was advancing the defense argument, the lone argument economists might accept in support of the bill.) When industries find that they can no longer maintain a competitive cost position with respect to foreign suppliers, economists' advice is usually "Retrain labor! Reallocate resources!"

SUMMING UP

1. When any nation experiences a deficit in its balance of trade (that is, when it exports less than it imports), citizens are urged to buy locally made products, and people call on the government to impose either voluntary or mandatory controls in order to limit imports of foreign goods.

2. In the late 1960s, two factors emerged that affected the U.S. trade position: (a) The inflation rate in the United States was greater than the inflation rate in other industrialized nations that were our customers. That made it more difficult to sell American goods abroad. (b) As a result of factor a, the United States had to negotiate "voluntary" import quotas on foreign steel, textiles, and other goods.

3. Labor leaders maintain that protectionism is necessary to guard American workers against

competition from low-wage areas of the world. They also claim that low-priced foreign imports do not benefit American consumers; they benefit international (multinational) manufacturers. Economists, however, estimate that direct and indirect controls cost American consumers between $10 and $20 billion per year. They maintain that such import controls not only add to the costs of goods, but also enhance the monopoly power of domestic producers.

4. In 1973 and 1974, leaders of both labor and industry pushed the cause of the Burke-Hartke bill, by which the government would have imposed controls over multinational corporations, as well as severe import quotas on a wide variety of goods. At the same time, the Joint Economic Committee was recommending the gradual elimination of permanent import controls.

5. In 1975, the United States (on the heels of a $5.5 billion trade deficit in 1974) experienced an unexpected surplus in its balance of trade of $10 billion, the largest surplus in American history. The reason was that inflation in the United States was now running at a slower rate than in other industrialized nations. American exports thus grew rapidly, helped along by a large increase in food exports resulting from bumper crops. As a result, the pressure for protectionism in the United States declined.

6. One can learn two things from the recent U.S. balance-of-trade experience: (a) The United States should not base its foreign economic policy on short-term changes in its trade position, because its trade position can change dramatically and is difficult to predict. (b) Protectionism (epitomized by the Burke-Hartke bill) is almost bound to be self-defeating, since it invites retaliation by foreign customers for U.S. exports.

7. Economists rarely support protectionism. Most feel that retraining of labor, plus reallocation of resources, is the way out for an industry that cannot compete with cheaper imports from low-wage areas of the world.

QUESTIONS

1. From the standpoint of value, the United States has a greater volume of international trade than any other nation. In the face of this, why would a protectionist policy with respect to imports almost certainly cause other nations to retaliate?

2. Evaluate this statement: "American workers earn high wages. The government must protect them against the imports of goods that are from low-wage countries."

3. What groups are likely to pay the bill for protectionism?

4. In what ways is a policy of retraining workers and reallocating resources preferable to a policy of protecting (by tariffs and quotas) a firm or an industry that is inefficient, relative to foreign firms or industries?

SUGGESTED READINGS

Adams, Walter. "The New Protectionism." *Challenge*, 1973.

Albrecht, William P., Jr. "The Cost of Trade Barriers to Consumers." In *Economics*. Prentice-Hall, Englewood Cliffs, N.J., 1974.

Bastiat, Frederic. "Sophisms of Protection." Putnam, New York, 1874.

"Big Money Shifts to Some Developing Areas." *Business Week*, August 18, 1975.

Chaikin, Sol C. "Boldness Will Pay Off: We Should Try Several Job-Creating Programs at Once." *Viewpoint, an IUD Quarterly*, 5, No. 2 (2d. qtr., 1975). Industrial Union Department, AFL-CIO, Washington, D.C.

Hazlitt, Henry. "The New Protectionism." *National Review*, May 20, 1969.

Miller, Roger Leroy, and Raburn M. Williams. "The Economics of Helping Ford Motor Company and United States Steel." In *the Economics of National Issues*. Canfield, San Francisco, Calif., 1972.

A New Initiative to Liberalize International Trade. Report of the Subcommittee on International Economics, Joint Economic Committee. GPO, Washington, D.C., 1973.

Ross, Irwin. "Labor's Big Push for Protectionism." *Fortune*, March 1973.

"Seeking an End to the Global Slump." *Time*, November 17, 1975.

Other Economic Systems in Theory

Throughout this book we have been analyzing an economic system that is characteristic of the United States: *capitalism*. To put this view of a capitalist economy in perspective, let's conclude our introduction to economics by examining other economic systems.

First, we will briefly summarize capitalism, tying in much of the material already presented. Then we will look at the basic elements of utopian socialism, Marxist socialism, and anarchism—we cannot discuss these theories in great depth, but we will present their essential points.

CAPITALISM

A system based on **capitalism** has two essential components:

1. Most of the means of production are privately owned.

2. Economic decisions are expressed through a system of interrelated markets.

By private ownership of the means of production, we mean that the legal owners of the capital (machines, buildings, and so on) producing the goods and services in an economy are *individuals* in that society. This definition allows for the existence of corporations, since they are owned by stockholders. In addition, it allows for government ownership. But the amount of capital owned by the government must be a small percentage of the total means of production. Therefore, the fact that in the United States governments own schools, hospitals, parks, and so on does not mean the U.S. economy cannot be labeled *capitalist*.

The statement that economic decisions in a capitalist society must be expressed through markets does not mean that these markets must be purely competitive, although they may be. However, from the chapters dealing with the theory of the business firm (Chapters 18 through 21), you know that many U.S. markets are not purely competitive. In the American economy, monopoly power exists in varying degrees. Large corporations often have a good bit of control over the prices at which they sell. Furthermore, certain buyers may also have monopoly power over price; for example, large corporations that buy raw materials and semifinished and finished products for resale. The U.S. government, especially the Department of Defense, exercises substantial monopsony power. Labor unions, as sellers of labor in the factor market, also exercise monopoly over the price of *that* resource. The point about capitalism is not who controls the markets, but the fact that *markets exist.* Capitalism is not the same thing as a competitive free-enterprise market system.

To make it possible for the two essential criteria of capitalism to exist, a society must establish a legal framework to support them. Two basic elements in this legal framework are (1) *the right of private ownership* and (2) *the legal enforceability of contracts.*

Economic Advantages Claimed for Capitalism

In Chapter 18, we said that economists have concluded that a purely competitive system of markets allocates resources most efficiently to produce (within the limits of the market) the combinations of goods and services chosen by consumers. The reason is that in the long run, under pure competition, price equals marginal cost for each firm. Therefore, the value that the consumer places on the last unit of a good (price) is equal to the opportunity cost of producing that good (marginal cost).

However, in the U.S. economy, purely competitive markets are rare. Most markets exhibit some degree of monopoly power. Demand and marginal revenue are not synonymous, and price must be higher than marginal cost. Therefore, in the absence of pure competition, there is not the efficient allocation of resources that would produce what consumers would most like to have.

When one tries to defend capitalism as a way of life and is deprived of the justification of efficient allocation, one must look for other arguments. These arguments begin to rest on shaky ground, and it is very difficult to obtain adequate enough data to reach definitive conclusions.

Defenders of a capitalism marred by monopoly power take a variety of positions. Some claim that monopoly power is not very significant. (See Chapter 21 for evidence on the quantitative importance of monopoly power.) They also say that today's technology requires large firms with their accompanying monopoly power, and that the efficiencies gained from large scale offset the misallocation. They say that if it were not for these large firms with their monopoly power, U.S. society would not have such advanced modern technology, because such technology requires large amounts of money for research and development.

They claim that the thorn of monopoly power is worth the rose of improved technology and productivity.

Some defenders of capitalism claim that **countervailing power** (monopoly power on both buyers' and sellers' sides of the market) and government power disperse the gains from monopoly power. (Chapters 19 and 21 contain more detailed discussions of technology and countervailing power.)

Then there is the argument that the profit motive provides a most powerful incentive for increasingly efficient production. Thus, under capitalism, the freedom to pursue one's own interests not only maximizes economic well-being, but also is the best protection of general freedom for a society.

When one looks to history to demonstrate the comparative economic advantages of capitalism versus other systems, one reaches an ambiguous conclusion. It is true that the capitalist countries of Western Europe, Japan, and the United States have shown an astonishing record of economic growth over the past two hundred years. However, over a much shorter period of time, the Soviet Union, and perhaps the People's Republic of China have also shown impressive growth. (See Chapter 27 and Application 27 for a further discussion about growth in the Soviet Union and China.) And if one also considers the pattern of income distribution under capitalism and collectivism, the latter appears to produce a more even distribution of income.

Economic Disadvantages of a Market System

Even if one assumes a capitalistic system composed of purely competitive markets that allocate resources with utmost efficiency, there are still two serious drawbacks (see Chapter 18):

1. Consumers decide what will be produced on the basis of how much money each one has to spend. Therefore, for those in poverty, who have needs but who do not have much purchasing power, the market does not supply goods.

2. Business firms, in setting prices, fail to include in their calculations the external costs (and benefits) that result from production but that are not part of the private costs of production or consumption. The most notable of these external costs are pollution and other forms of damage to the environment. *Note:* Communist countries are by no means untarnished in this respect. The same kinds of externalities appear to occur in socialist economies such as the Soviet Union.

In order to deal with the problems of poverty and ecological damage, governments must devise means of interfering with or supplementing market decisions. Most economists agree that the need for full employment and greater stability of prices demands government interference in economic decision making. Yet when government does interfere in free-enterprise markets, the doomsayers cry, "Socialism!"

SOCIALISM

Because of the many different kinds of socialist theory, it is difficult to give a precise definition of **socialism** that can encompass all varieties. Here we will describe the most important ones: utopian socialism, Marxist socialism, Leninism, and democratic socialism. One feature common to all is the belief that the means of production should be under some form of social ownership or control, the control to be in the hands of either the government or various cooperative groups.

Utopian Socialism

The earliest socialist view was **utopian socialism**, which proposed communities in which people lived and worked together without economic distinctions. "Utopian" is a good description of this form of socialism, because the word *utopia* means an imaginary place in which everything is perfect—laws, government, and social conditions. The three founders of this approach to socialism were the French Comte de Saint-Simon and Charles Fourier, and Englishman Robert Owen. All three began writing at the beginning of the nineteenth century; each proposed a different kind of community, in which people would live and work together without economic distinctions. They offered these utopian communities as their solutions to the economic and social problems of the time.

Saint-Simon
The French aristocrat, the Comte de Saint-Simon (1760-1825), who was the founder of French socialism, began in 1802 to formulate a social philosophy that pictured the French Revolution as a conflict between the producing classes (the **proletariat**, or laboring class, and the bourgeoisie, or middle class) and the "idle" classes (the aristocracy and the clergy). Above all, Saint-Simon was concerned about the welfare of the working-class poor. He saw the middle class and the laboring class as working together to establish a society based on reason and moral justice. Remembering the Reign of Terror in 1793-1794, when the masses in Paris (and in other French cities) beheaded seventeen thousand people during the French Revolution, Saint-Simon did not believe the proletarian class capable of leadership in the new world. Therefore, he assigned the leadership role to the bourgeoisie.

This middle class was to provide the community of the future with managers, engineers, and bankers (especially bankers; he considered credit a key to development), who would in some way transcend their own self-interest to lead the community for its own good. His emphasis on the need for economic development, and the key role that managers and bankers must play, provided ideological fuel for the industrial revolution in France. However, Saint-Simon's dreams of an ideal community did not come true.

Fourier

Another Frenchman, Charles Fourier (1772-1837), who began writing in 1808, was also influenced by the French Revolution. Unlike Saint-Simon, who emphasized the leadership of the middle classes, Fourier was cynical about the ethics of bourgeois society. With wit and sarcasm, he wrote of the differences between the bourgeoisie's philosophy and its practices, and between moral theory and economic reality in bourgeois market society. Fourier's solution, like Saint-Simon's, was to turn away from the destructive relations of the society of his day and create communities he called *phalansteries*, which would provide a setting for economic and social relationships that would be more nearly equal, and that would increase the probability of continued human survival. Someone asked Fourier who would do the menial tasks in his utopian state, such as collecting garbage. Fourier said that the children would, because they loved to play in filth anyway.

Fourier worried about the conflict between the bourgeois property-owning class and the emerging proletarian class. (This placed him closer to Marx than to his contemporary, Saint-Simon.) Furthermore, he recognized and decried the inferior position of women.

Several communities patterned after Fourier's ideals came into being during the nineteenth century. Although some survived for many years, the Fourier brand of utopian socialism was, from a practical point of view, a failure.

Robert Owen

The best known of these early utopians was an Englishman named Robert Owen (1771-1858). Owen, who came from the upper ranks of the working class, was apprenticed at age ten to a linen draper. In 1800, when he was twenty-nine, he became manager and part owner of the New Lanark cotton mills in Scotland. There he created a model community, and applied an entirely new system of labor management. This industrial enterprise became a marvel of its day.

Friedrich Engels, the intellectual junior partner of Karl Marx, writes of Owen:

> A population, originally consisting of the most diverse and, for the most part, very demoralized elements, a population that gradually grew to 2,500, he turned into a model colony in which drunkenness, police, magistrates, lawsuits, poor laws, charity, were unknown. And all this simply by placing the people in conditions worthy of human beings, and especially by carefully bringing up the rising generation. He was the founder of infant schools, and introduced them first at New Lanark. At the age of two the children came to school, where they enjoyed themselves so much that they could scarcely be sent home again. Whilst his competitors worked their people thirteen or fourteen hours a day, in New Lanark the working day was only ten and a half hours. When a crisis in cotton stopped work for four months, his workers received their full wages all the time. And with all this the business more than doubled in value, and to the last yielded large profits to its proprietors. [Engels's remarks are quoted in *The Marx-Engels Reader*, published by Norton.]

What was the key to Robert Owen's thought? He wrote:

> Any general character, from the best to the worst, from the most ignorant to the most enlightened, may be given to any community, even to the world at large, by the application of proper means, which means are to a great extent at the command and under the control of those who have influence in the affairs of men. [These ideas are quoted in *Masterworks of Economics*, Vol. II, published by McGraw-Hill.]

In other words, Owen was convinced that "man's character is made for, and not by, him." He felt that the nature of people and their behavior can be molded for the better by creating a proper community for people to live in.

After running the New Lanark mills for twenty-seven years, Owen concluded that he was being paternalistic and that the people of New Lanark were at his mercy. Furthermore, he saw no need for profits to be siphoned off, profits created by the labor of the workers. He began to advocate the establishment of communist communities, with economic equality. He wrote to Parliament and petitioned it to implement his scheme, especially for the poor of Ireland, but Parliament rejected the idea.

In 1825 he came to the United States and tried to carry out his ideas here, by founding a communist colony: the community of New Harmony, in Indiana. However, it proved far from harmonious, and after two years it collapsed because of internal dissension. Owen lost most of his fortune in the venture.

He returned to England and devoted his remaining years to helping the working class. He became a leader in the consumer cooperative movement, the Chartist movement, the labor-union movement, and the struggle for legislation to ameliorate working conditions in the factories. Although his dream of establishing utopian socialist communities did not come true, Owen was perhaps the most influential figure in the nineteenth-century British socialist and union movements.

From a practical point of view, one could say that the early utopian socialists failed because the communes they established did not succeed. Those communist settlements that did last a long time were based on dissenting religious philosophies. Examples of these religious communes in the United States in the nineteenth century were the Shaker communities, which grew up in the New England states and in Ohio and Kentucky, and the seven villages in Iowa that comprised Amana.

Note: The religious focus of these Iowa towns has gradually given way to an economic one. The seven communities banded together and formed, initially, a corporation to produce mainly refrigerators and air conditioners, under the brand name of Amana. Thus, the twentieth-century descendants of the thrifty, God-fearing German immigrants have raised their eyes from the fires of hell to the profits of ice, and the cohesiveness of the group has suffered not one whit. So this is one example of a communist society that turned capitalist without having to disband to do so.

The Marxists scorned utopian socialism on grounds that it was not scientific. The utopians, said the Marxists, had no conception of the forces that moved history, and therefore could not understand the developments of their own day. None of the utopian thinkers represented the interests of the emerging proletariat. They wished to emancipate all of humanity at once. As Engels put it, "For, to our three social reformers, the bourgeois world ... is quite as irrational and unjust.... If pure reason and justice have not, hitherto, ruled the world, this has been the case only because men have not rightly understood them."

The Kibbutz Movement and A. D. Gordon
But utopian socialism did not die with the nineteenth century. Today, in Israel, the **kibbutz** is a community that operates on the principle of complete income equality. By 1973, there, were 240 kibbutzim, with more than 95,000 people. In the oldest of these communities, the third generation is taking its place as the leaders. Although these voluntary communist settlements were strongly influenced, when they were formed, by nationalistic (Zionist) ideology and less exotic socialist motives, one should not downgrade the influence of utopian socialism. In 1911, A. D. Gordon, an ardent Zionist and writer who believed that man's salvation lay in working the soil, helped found Deganiah, Israel's first kibbutz, or collective community. His influence on the ideology of the founders of the kibbutz movement was strong. His beliefs, which were built around respect for labor, love of nature, and deep humanistic principles, rejected competitive capitalism, and placed a utopian socialist stamp on the kibbutz movement.

B. F. Skinner
An American psychologist, B. F. Skinner, developed, after World War II, the field of behaviorial psychology, which maintains that people's behavior is determined by past conditioning in their social environment. If one can control that conditioning, one can mold the person. This sounds very much like Robert Owen, except that Skinner, through experimentation (mostly with pigeons), was able to lend force to his ideas by basing them on a new science.

In his book *Walden II*, Skinner sets forth his idea of a utopian commune based on a humanistic application of the theories of behaviorial psychology. Although interested people held several conferences in the mid-1960s aimed at carrying out Skinner's ideas, no one has yet attempted a Walden II matching the scope of Skinner's model.

Communes of the 1960s and 1970s in the United States

In the mid-1960s, many young people in the United States rejected both middle-class politics and lifestyles. Out of the ferment, out of this idealistic seeking of alternatives to the way of life of middle-class America, came the commune movement. People who set up these communes challenged the basic premises of the middle class. They directed this challenge not only at the economic foundations of capitalism, but also at

"I don't know, we don't seem to be doing so well as the Jones' commune."

family structure, at technology, at religion, at the use of drugs, at ideas about sex, education, and nearly every aspect of life. Many of these young people found that the way of life best fitted to their needs, both spiritual and physical, was some form of collective living.

The commune movement was not organized; there was no well-defined political ideology. Each collective was different. Groups with a religious base ranged from Christian communes to so-called spiritual ashrams. Some communes were based on drugs (LSD, marijuana) and aimed at breaking down middle-class behavioral conditioning. Some were political and sought to provide an economic base for their members' political activity. Some experimented with different family structure (group marriage, extended family). Some were urban, some rural (including those on farms), and some emphasized organic foods and ecology.

In effect, then, *there was no coherent organizing principle around which the movement could rally.*

The March-April 1974 issue of *Communities* presented a directory that listed more than 250 communes in the United States. Let's look at some of these communes briefly, to get an idea of their variety.

Twin Oaks, in Virginia, one of the oldest communes, has survived for more than ten years; in 1974 it had about sixty members. The directory describes Twin Oaks as follows:

> Designing non-competitive egalitarian social structure. No private income, property held in common. Labor credits, planner-manager government, Walden II orientation. Hammock and construction industries, printing press. Help publish *Communities*, Newsletter. Working toward cooperative network.

Another example is the Communitarian Village in Oroville, California, described as follows:

Communes of the 1960s and 1970s in the United States   631

Forty people living in interim sets in area and in Berkeley. Cooperating on projects to create diverse village of communes and individuals on large piece of land. Soyburger business, experimental organic garden; edit this magazine. Working toward cooperative network of communities.

Although the commune movement in the United States has developed greatly since the mid-1960s, it has problems. Members still exhibit an amazing innocence about what is needed for economic survival. Many communities start out full of idealism and ambition but with very little capital, and find themselves unable to earn enough income to survive. There is still a large turnover of people in many communes, and the average length of life of a commune is relatively short. The very experimentation that characterizes communes prevents the appearance of unifying factors in the movement. It is a middle-class, and primarily a young people's, movement, with little contact with the working class and poor, or with older people who might have had some experience in accounting and banking and insurance. For the poor, it is not practical as an alternative way of life. For older people, it is too radical a departure from customary lifestyles. Yet despite its weaknesses, the commune movement in the United States attracts a great number of people, and new communes are constantly being formed.

Therefore, one might say that although utopian socialism has not proved itself an economic success, it is still alive and kicking in the world of today.

MARXIST SOCIALISM

Karl Marx was a nineteenth-century German revolutionary who emigrated to England and wrote books that set the world on its ear. His book *Das Kapital* provided the foundation for **Marxist socialism**. His followers claim that he gave socialism the scientific basis that was lacking in the works of the utopian socialists.

Dialectical Materialism

The philosophical foundation of Marxism is **dialectical materialism**, a philosophy that views material things as the subject of all change, and technology and the natural environment as the main forces that cause human society to change continually. But let's examine this philosophy one step at a time.

Dialectics emphasizes that all phenomena, natural and human, involve processes of development. The seed grows into the plant. The infant grows into the child, the child into the youth, the youth into the adult. (Darwin's theory of evolution is another example of this dialectical process of reasoning.)

```
Thesis                    Antithesis
Feudalism                 Commercial class
         \               /
          \             /
           \           /
            \         /
             \       /
              \     /
               \   /
             Synthesis
         Mercantile capitalism
```

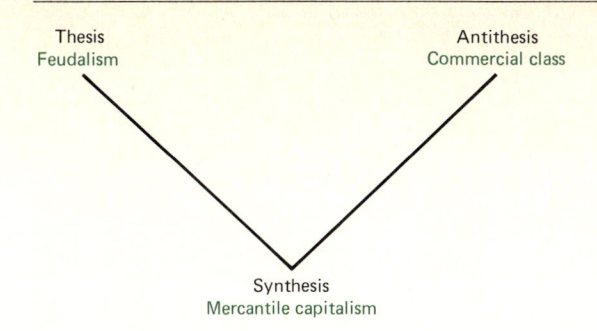

FIGURE 26-1 An Example of Marxian Analysis. Another example would be: thesis = industrial capitalism; antithesis = the proletariat, or laboring class; synthesis (what Marx hoped would occur) = communism.

Marx analyzed this process of development of human society, and used it, as he came to understand it, as the scientific basis for socialism. The first law of this argument is that the foundation of society is materialistic. Technology and the natural environment (climate, resources, geography) are the dominant forces in society's development. The rest (culture, institutions, social classes, and the relations between them) are linked to the economic (materialist) base, and are shaped by that base.

Dialectical materialism is the basic idea behind Marx's concept of **historical materialism**, which holds that human society throughout history has undergone a continual process of change, or development from one form to another: In ancient times, there was slavery; in medieval times, serfdom; then came handicraft and cottage industry, which gave way to factory-oriented capitalism. The guiding factors in this process are changing technology and the natural environment.

Figure 26-1 shows the process of social change according to Marxian analysis for the transition from feudalism to the beginnings of capitalism. The **thesis** (the class system that is dominant at a given time) is feudalism, in which the ruling class is the landed aristocracy. The **antithesis** (the class that is the main force in changing the thesis) is the emerging commercial class. The **synthesis** (the system that evolves after the antithesis has forced changes) is mercantile capitalism, in which the commercial class replaces the landed aristocracy as the dominant class.

Class Conflict

Marxists believe that the most dramatic feature of this process of change is the conflict of classes at each stage of development. In ancient Rome, the slaves were in conflict with their masters. In medieval Europe, the serfs and the emerging merchant class were in conflict with the landed aristocracy. With the development of factories, a new class, the **proletariat** (the workers in the factories), came into conflict with the capitalists, the owners of the factories.

The basis of these conflicts is the effort of one class to dominate and exploit the other classes. A basic tenet of Marxism is that as long as there is private ownership of the means of production, classes will continue to exist, and conflict will result. Division of labor causes a surplus and there is class conflict about who is going to get the surplus.

Marx's revolt of the proletariat? The New York City street-railway strike of 1889 (The Bettmann Archive, Inc.)

Social Production and Surplus Value

Marxists point out that during the Middle Ages, industrial production was primarily based on handicrafts. Machines were simple, and most workers owned their own. Production was individual, and each worker could identify his or her own work. In the eighteenth century, as technology improved and machines became more complex, factories that employed large numbers of workers came into being. As labor became more specialized, these workers performed only a small number of operations in producing a product. They no longer owned their own machines and could no longer point to something and say, "There! I made that." Production was no longer individual, but social. **Social production** means that production of a product requires the cooperation of many workers, and individuals are not able to identify their own contribution specifically.

By the beginning of the eighteenth century, the burgeoisie (capitalists) had gained control of the means of production, and they paid wages to the proletariat (the workers). Marx claimed that these wages were just high enough to enable the workers to subsist, while the value of what the workers produced was greater than the wages paid. The difference was **surplus value**, which measured the degree of exploitation of the proletariat.

Falling Profits and the Reserve Army of the Unemployed

According to Marx, competition between firms and the increasing scarcity of profitable investment opportunities would cause the profits of capitalists to fall. The capitalists could counter this fall in two ways: (1) They could get the workers to work longer hours, and in this way increase surplus value. But the opportunity to do this was limited. (2) They could invest more and improve technology further, thus increasing output per worker and surplus value. However, improving technology meant that more and more machines replaced more and more workers, and this increased unemployment.

The rising number of unemployed caused by increased use of capital and improved technology was called the **reserve army of the unemployed**. This reserve army, Marx said, competed with the employed workers. This competition had the effect of keeping wages down.

Recurring Business Cycles

Marx also maintained that as capitalists increase investment to ward off falling profits, the productive capacity of the economy expands and output increases. But because wages are kept low, workers do not have the ability to buy this expanded output. So, although the economy expands for a while, eventually industry's ability to produce output far outstrips people's ability to buy that growing output. (If you tool up your factory with all the latest equipment, so that you can make 10,000 washing machines a month, but the public has enough money to buy only 5,000 of them, you're soon going to go broke.) Excess capacity is generated, which causes economic crisis and then collapse. Along comes a depression, and firms are forced out of business. Eventually, enough firms are forced out of business so that capacity contracts to a point at which expansion can be renewed, and the process repeats itself. Marx identified the business cycle and the exploitation of labor as the two hallmarks of the capitalist system. Marx was one of the first to introduce the idea of recurring business cycles. In fact, he constructed a theory about them, which constituted an important contribution to economic theory.

Marx's Gloomy Prediction: The Collapse of Capitalism

Marx concluded that capitalism contained within it inherent contradictions that would bring about its end and a movement toward the next stage of development, socialism. He predicted that economic crises would recur, and would become progressively more serious. With more investment and continuing technological change, the reserve army of the unemployed would become larger and larger. Because of their increased investment and ever-greater need to compete against others, firms would get bigger. As this occurred, those among the bourgeoisie who owned smaller firms would be forced into the proletariat and into the reserve army of the unemployed.

Eventually economic crisis and unemployment would become so large that revolution would take place, and capitalism would be overthrown. The proletariat would come to realize that capitalism was against their self-interest; the wastes of resources due to recurring crises would become apparent. The proletariat would therefore seize political power and establish a classless Communist society.

Why Haven't We Had a Revolution?

Marx said that the overthrow of capitalism would take place in the most advanced countries. But to date, Communist governments have been established only in economically backward societies. Has history proved Marx wrong?

Since Marx's prophesy of doom for capitalist societies, there have been four fundamental changes in the advanced economies:

1. The labor movement has organized strong unions that form the active arm of the proletariat. Some people argue that unions have been able to obtain for their members wages high enough that workers have been reaping some of the rewards of greater productivity resulting from increased investment and that the workers' standard of living has risen enough to quiet them.

2. With the development of Keynesian economics, governments have taken an active role in trying to stabilize the economy. To most economists, this seems to have reduced the severity of recurring business crises.

3. Modern capitalist states have developed extensive social welfare programs to help reduce the hardships of the masses.

4. Many workers have themselves become capitalists in a small way. In the United States, 64.5 percent of the population either own or are buying their own homes, and about 18 percent own stocks or bonds. In other words, larger numbers of workers are sharing in the profits of capitalism.

The big question of Marxists today is: Have these four factors (plus others) weakened capitalism's inherent contradictions to the extent that capitalism can survive indefinitely, or have they only postponed its collapse? Or was Marx just plain wrong in his analysis?

Note: This section contains only the barest sketch of the Marxist model. The model is much more complicated, and in order really to understand it, a more detailed study is necessary.

Leninism

Next to Marx himself, the most noted Marxist was V. I. Lenin (1870-1924). To the Russians, Lenin is more of a hero than Marx is. Lenin created the Bolshevik wing of Russia's Social Democratic party and led it in the revolution in 1917, which established the Soviet Union as it is today.

Two of the many contributions of Leninism to Marxist economic and political theory are as follows:

1. Lenin extended Marx's idea of **economic imperialism** and its importance to the development of capitalism. Lenin called economic imperialism "the highest stage of capitalist development." He said that to ward off a fall in profits and lessen the severity of economic crises, the capitalist classes in the developed countries would exploit the underdeveloped countries of the world (in Asia, Africa, and Latin America) in three ways: (a) They would use them as a dumping ground for their excess production, that is, as a source of demand for their output. (b) They would use them as a place to get cheap raw materials, that is, as a source of supply. (c) They would use them as a place in which to invest their excess capital so as to accomplish items a and b, and in the process they would bolster their rates of profit.

In order to carry out these activities at a high enough rate of profit (Lenin said), capitalists would have to obtain direct control (through colonialism) or indirect control of the political and economic institutions of these countries.

Lenin also maintained that economic imperialism is only a temporary measure to ward off the collapse of capitalism; the opportunities for imperialist exploitation are limited, and competition between one capitalist country and another may lead to wars. The colonies themselves will eventually revolt. In the meantime, however, imperialist exploitation provides the basis for prosperity within the capitalist countries, postponing the inevitable confrontation between capitalists and proletariat.

2. Lenin asked *how* a country could bring about a socialist revolution. After all, Lenin's own country, Russia, was an underdeveloped country just beginning its capitalist phase of development. Lenin felt that a well-disciplined, centrally controlled socialist revolutionary party was essential to help create the conditions for socialist revolution. This party had to be prepared to take advantage of a revolutionary situation. In 1902, he succeeded in organizing the Bolshevik (now Communist) party, and in 1917 he and his party were victorious. He warned that although a revolution would establish a dictatorship of the proletariat, only the Communist party would have the correct program and the organizational discipline to lead the proletariat.

Democratic Socialism

Proponents of **democratic socialism** believe in using democratic procedures to gain political power and curtail capitalism. They reject the use of revolutionary violence to seize power, on the grounds that it is both

Democratic socialism in Sweden: Naptime at a state-run day-care center (Courtesy Swedish Information Service)

unrealistic and morally wrong. Although some socialists accept a great deal of Marxist thought, many others reject it.

Democratic socialism is the dominant force in many countries, such as Sweden, Belgium, Denmark, Italy, and Israel. Even when not in a position of top power, democratic socialists are a strong political factor in democratic countries. When the democratic socialists get into power, they concentrate on social welfare, economic development, and curtailing the influence of capitalists. Whether they have been successful or not depends on how one defines success.

ANARCHISM

There are many kinds of anarchists, but there is one belief common to all **anarchism**: it opposes authority, especially when authority is in the hands of the state. The one country that had a strong anarchist movement was Spain, prior to 1939. That was the year that the fascist Francisco Franco became Spain's ruler. Burnett Bolloten, in his book *The*

Grand Camouflage, which deals with the Spanish Civil War of 1936-1939, writes about the anarchists' hostility toward the state:

> Rigidly opposed to the state, which they regarded as "the supreme expression of authority of man over man, the most powerful instrument for the enslavement of the people," the Libertarians [anarchists] were equally opposed to every government whether of the Right or Left. In the words of Bakunin, the great Russian anarchist, whose writings had a far-reaching influence on the Spanish working-class movement, the "people's government" proposed by Marx would simply be the rule of a privileged minority over the huge majority of the working masses. "But this minority, the Marxists argue, would consist of workers. Yes, I dare say, of *former* workers, but as soon as they become rulers and representatives of the people they would cease to be proletarian and would look down upon all workers from their political summit. They would no longer represent the people; they would represent only themselves.... He who doubts this must be absolutely ignorant of human nature." And the Italian anarchist, Malatesta, whose influence on the Spanish Libertarian movement was appreciable, stated: "The primary concern of every government is to ensure its continuance in power, irrespective of the men who form it. If they are bad, they want to remain in power in order to enrich themselves and to satisfy their lust for authority; and if they are honest and sincere, they believe that it is their duty to remain in power for the benefit of the people....
>
> "The anarchists ... would never, even if they were strong enough, form a government without contradicting themselves and repudiating their entire doctrine; and, should they do so, it would be no different from any other government; perhaps it would be even worse."
>
> The establishment of the Spanish Republic in 1931, following the fall of the monarchy and then of the Berenguer dictatorship, did not cause the Libertarians [anarchists] to modify their basic tenets: "All governments are detestable and it is our mission to destroy them." "All governments without exception are equally bad, equally contemptible." "All governments are destroyers of liberty." "Under the monarchy and the dictatorship," wrote an anarchist at the time of the Republican-Socialist coalition in 1933, the workers suffered hunger and a thousand privations and they continue to do so today under the Republic. Yesterday it was impossible to satisfy their most urgent needs and today conditions are the same. We anarchists say this without fear that today any worker will contradict us, and we say more. We say that at all times under whatever type of government, the workers have been tyrannized and have had to wage bitter struggles so that their right to live and enjoy themselves after exhausting hours of labor would be respected." Just as the Libertarians made no distinction between governments of the Left and governments of the Right, so did they make no distinction between individual politicians.

Today there are still anarchists of various persuasions. However, the anarchist movement as a political force exerts little influence.

SUMMING UP

1. A system based on *capitalism* has two essential ingredients: (a) The means of production are privately owned. (b) Economic decisions are expressed through a system of interrelated markets. The two legal elements necessary to achieve these essentials are (a) the right of private ownership, and (b) the legal enforceability of contracts.

2. Under purely competitive capitalism, marginal cost equals price, and there is an efficient allocation of resources, which produces (within the limits of the market) the combination of goods consumers choose. However, some degree of monopoly power usually exists, and so these advantages are often lacking. Some claim that monopoly power is not significant; others claim that the advantages of technological change that monopoly makes possible are worth the misallocation of resources. Still others look to *countervailing power* (power of both buyers and sellers) as the answer to monopoly power. Some justify capitalism on grounds that economic freedom is the best protector of general freedom. As if to prove this point, the economic growth of capitalist countries has been impressive; but so has the growth of communist countries.

3. Even in a society in which there is purely competitive capitalism, the needs of poor people without purchasing power are disregarded in market demand. In addition, firms fail to consider external costs and benefits, especially the costs to the populace of pollution and other forms of environmental damage.

4. The three founders of *utopian socialism*, who all began their work around the beginning of the nineteenth century—the Comte de Saint-Simon, Charles Fourier, and Robert Owen—rejected capitalism as immoral, and urged the establishment of communities where people would live and work without economic distinction.

5. The Frenchman Saint-Simon envisioned the productive classes (the *proletariat* and the bourgeoisie) cooperating to establish a new kind of society, with the bourgeoisie as the leaders. He stressed the need for economic development, and thus provided an ideology that motivated many people during France's industrial revolution.

6. Fourier, also French, wanted communities in which everyone was economically equal. He, however, was cynical about the code of ethics of bourgeois society, and was concerned about conflict between the working classes and the property-owning classes.

7. The Englishman Robert Owen said that "man's character is made for, and not by, him." He created a model industrial village around his New Lanark cotton mills in Scotland and still made money for the company. About 1825, he set up a communist community in the United States, but it failed. Later he became a leader in various progressive movements, such as the Chartist movement, the labor-union movement, and the struggle for legislation to improve conditions in factories.

"I forget whether he calls himself a conservative radical or a radical conservative."

8. Utopian socialism still lives today, both in ideas and in actual organizations. Examples of modern utopian socialism are (a) the *kibbutz* movement in Israel, based on the ideas of A. D. Gordon; (b) the communes proposed by B. F. Skinner in his book *Walden II*, which are to be based on a humanistic application of the theories of behavioral psychology; and (c) the commune movement of the 1960s and 1970s in the United States.

9. The commune movement in the United States today is unorganized, with no well-defined political ideology. The problems of communes include the members' innocence about what is needed for economic survival (they usually start with little capital, and cannot earn enough income to keep themselves going), the high turnover rate of participants, and the short average length of life of individual communes. The commune movement lacks a unifying force. Its membership is middle class and young, and has little to offer the poor.

10. Followers of Karl Marx, the founder of *Marxist socialism,* claim that he gave a scientific basis to socialism. Thus, Marxist socialism is "scientific" socialism.

11. *Dialectical materialism,* the basic principle behind Marx's concept of *historical materialism,* holds that human society throughout history has undergone a continual process of change or development. The social structure evolves from one form to another; the guiding factors in this process of evolution are changing technology and the natural environment.

12. It is basic to Marxist thought that as long as there is private ownership of the means of production, there will be differing classes, and as long as classes exist, conflict will exist, as one class exploits another.

13. Marx said that, in the eighteenth century, as production shifted from handicrafts and cottage industries to manufacturing in factories, individual production became *social production.* Labor became specialized; workers no longer owned the tools and machines they used, and a worker could no longer identify her or his own contribution. Capitalists employed workers and paid them wages that were less than the value of the product produced. The difference between workers' wages and the value of the things produced is *surplus value.*

14. According to Marx, the profits of capitalists eventually began to fall (because of competition and the growing scarcity of profitable investment opportunities). The fall in profits led capitalists to increase their investment to improve technology, and this in turn increased unemployment. This created a *reserve army of the unemployed,* which had the effect of keeping wages down.

15. Marx introduced the idea of recurring business cycles, blaming them on the fact that increased investment and improved technology plus low wages cause producers' capacity to outstrip consumers' demand. These economic crises would become more and more severe, he said, and eventually capitalism would collapse and the proletariat would seize control and establish a classless society. This is what Marx meant by saying that capitalism contained within it inherent contradictions that would bring about its collapse and the advent of socialism.

16. Marx failed to foresee (a) that labor unions would become strong enough to raise the living standards of their members enough to satisfy them; (b) that governments, following Keynesian principles of economics, would step into the picture and reduce the severity of business cycles by manipulating interest rates, taxes, government spending, and even wages and prices; (c) that modern capitalist states would develop extensive social welfare programs; and (d) that many workers would themselves become capitalists, by owning property or stocks and bonds.

17. Lenin, who led the 1917 Bolshevik revolution in Russia, made two major contributions to Marxism: (a) He extended Marx's idea of the *economic imperialism* of capitalism. By the use of economic imperialism, capitalist countries would exploit underdeveloped countries using them as dumping grounds for excess products and as sources of cheap raw materials. In this way the capitalist countries could postpone falling profit rates and forestall economic crises in their own countries. Lenin

said that the opportunities to exploit poor countries are limited, and that eventually capitalism would collapse. (b) He preached the doctrine of having a well-disciplined and centrally controlled revolutionary party to help create and exploit revolutionary situations.

18. *Democratic socialism* is committed to the use of democratic procedures in the quest for political power and in the curtailment of capitalism.

19. Proponents of *anarchism* are against all authority, especially authority on the part of the state. They feel that the state is "the most powerful instrument for the enslavement of the people." They are opposed to *any* government, of either the right or the left.

QUESTIONS

1. As a student of economics, what arguments would you advance for capitalism as a desirable economic system?

2. "Utopian socialism is alive and well in 1977." Do you agree? Why?

3. Sketch the main points of the Marxist model, and give reasons why Marx's predictions about the collapse of capitalism have not come true.

4. Explain the difference between Marxism, Leninism, and democratic socialism.

5. What is the unifying principle that anarchists believe in?

SUGGESTED READINGS

Engels, Friedrich. "Socialism: Utopian and Scientific." In *The Marx-Engels Reader*, edited by Robert C. Tucker. Norton, New York, 1972.

Harrington, Michael. *Toward a Democratic Left*. Macmillan, New York, 1968.

Howe, Irving. *Essential Works of Socialism*. Bantam, New York, 1971.

Owen, Robert. "A New View of Society." In *Masterworks of Economics*, edited by Leonard D. Abbott. McGraw-Hill, New York, 1946. Volume II.

27

Economic Planning: The Soviet Union

Emergence of the Planned Economy

In October 1917, Lenin, in the name of Marxian economics, led the Bolsheviks in the revolution that overthrew the Russian government and made Communism a political reality. Karl Marx had analyzed the development of advanced capitalist countries, such as Great Britain, and had prophesied the collapse of capitalism in these countries. But the Russia that Lenin and the communists inherited was an underdeveloped country that had not yet gone through a capitalist phase, a country, in fact, not fully out of the feudal stage.

The Communist party and the Soviet government (for all intents and purposes the same, since the government had, and has, a one-party rule) were faced with a desperate problem of scarcity. How to achieve economic development was the number-one difficulty. Between 1917 and 1928, the new Russian government had to make a humiliating peace with Germany, put down a long civil war made worse by foreign intervention, and experiment with its New Economic Policy (NEP) that allowed for significant amounts of private enterprise. The government experienced vicious infighting among the Communist leaders—infighting that changed it from a dictatorship by the proletariat to a dictatorship by one person, Joseph Stalin. In 1928, Russia's level of economic activity was lower than it had been in 1914. It was at this point that Stalin launched the first Five-Year Plan, and the Soviet Union became a **command economy**.

A command economy is one in which the problems generated by scarcity are solved by a central planning system.

One thing important about central planning is that to make it work there must be a strong, competent, and incorruptible administration with educated leaders, which is what underdeveloped countries usually do not have.

In this chapter we will explore the way such a centrally planned command economy organizes itself to deal with the problems of what to produce, how to produce it, and who shall receive the output. We will also analyze the problems of central planning and the changes in the process that have taken place recently in the U.S.S.R. Finally, we will try to evaluate the economic successes and failures of the Soviet Union.

After you have read this chapter, you will be ready for Application 27, which concerns the problems of development in the second giant of the Communist world, the People's Republic of China. What is the story behind Red China's development? How does it differ from that of the Soviet Union?

What to Produce: Central Planning

The command economy of the Soviet Union answers the question of what to produce by running it through a system of committees. These groups of people decide on the kinds and amounts of different products the economy will produce by sifting through whatever information is available, and making decisions. Contrast this process with that of a capitalist system, in which production decisions are determined by market prices.

You are aware of how complex the allocation of resources is in a market economy. In a command economy, the problem is just as complex, and, in addition, the planning process itself is equally complex. Let's look at the planning system in the Soviet Union. Figure 27-1 shows the flow of Soviet planning. Follow it as you read about the process.

Setting of Goals and Priorities

The Politburo—the highest decision-making level in the Soviet government—is responsible for the initial setting of goals for the economy during the upcoming planning period. The Russians operate with Five-Year Plans. Their first Five-Year Plan was for 1928-1932; now they are into the tenth Five-Year Plan (1976-1980).

Until the early 1960s, the two kinds of output with the highest priority in Russia were investment in heavy industry to increase productive capacity (tractors and turbines) and production to increase military might. Consumer goods were low on the list. But since the early 1960s, the government has been pressured to increase the production of consumer goods. So, although investment and military production still have top priority, Russian citizens are now beginning to enjoy more of the comforts of life than they had in the past.

The Planning Process

Once the Politburo has established goals and priorities in the broadest sense, a planning body called **Gosplan** translates the objectives into a consistent set of plan targets setting forth how many goods and services of each kind are to be produced, and where. Gosplan uses whatever information is available, and calls in specialists to give further advice.

FIGURE 27-1 The Process of Soviet Planning. Arrows show the flow of information as the plan is composed.

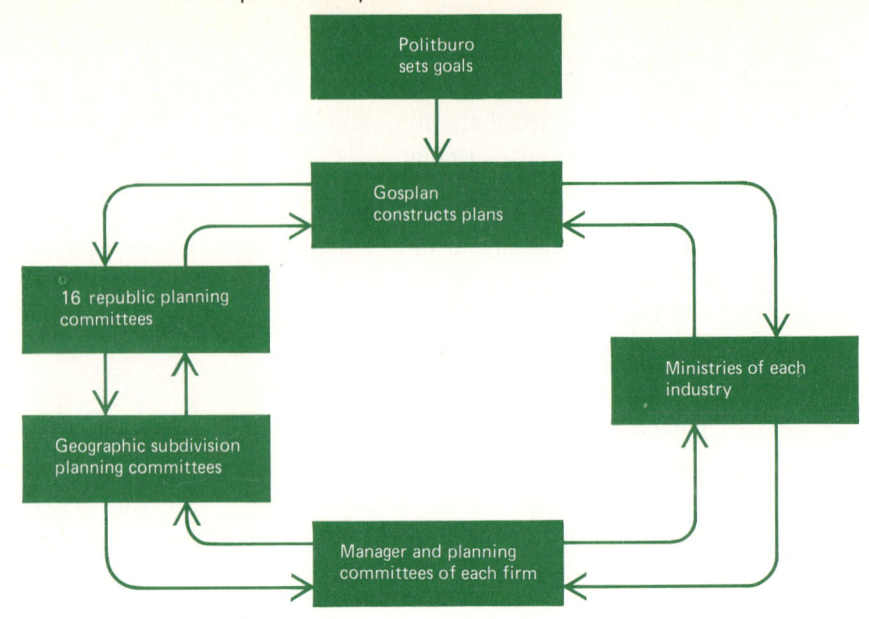

[Flow chart: Politburo sets goals → Gosplan constructs plans ↔ 16 republic planning committees ↔ Geographic subdivision planning committees ↔ Manager and planning committees of each firm ↔ Ministries of each industry ↔ Gosplan constructs plans]

It sets up a Five-Year Plan, breaks it down into yearly plans, and then submits these plans to various units of the bureaucracy for study and criticism. Any criticisms made by these administrative units are fed back to Gosplan. Administrative units are arranged either according to geography or according to industry. A suggested Five-Year Plan is inspected by both kinds of units.

Mattresses are an example. Everybody must have one; a nation that sleeps well works well. But how many mattresses to make, in what sizes, of what materials, in what localities, to sell at what prices? Gosplan ponders the situation: How many extra-firms in Azerbaijan? How many crib mattresses in Kazakhstan?

Gosplan sketches a plan for each geographic unit (Russia is divided into sixteen units, called *republics*, which are like states in the United States). These plans stress decisions about things that flow from one republic to another, and are very complex in the short term (that is, when dealing with periods of one year), since a given plan must spell out millions of instructions to thousands of plants, telling them what to produce, how and when to process, ship, and deliver millions of items of all sizes, materials, and types. The main weakness of the system springs from the sheer volume of decision making that Gosplan must carry out.

After Gosplan sketches a plan, the plan travels down the ladder. The planning committee of the individual republic to which the plan applies studies it and adds its ideas, especially those concerning production in the various subdivisions of the republic. ("Ten thousand extra-softs for those growing tourist centers on the Black Sea. And blued steel for the springs. Springs rust in the salt air, and we've had complaints.")

The republic's planning committee forwards relevant parts of the plan to the planning committee of the local geographic subdivision, which lists what production is needed from each of the firms in its area if national goals are to be met. Then the plan is passed still further down the chain of command, to the manager and planning committees of each individual firm, who study the feasibility of the production targets assigned to it. If the committees or manager has objections, they are passed along the line, back up the planning ladder. ("What do they *mean* blued steel? They said that last year, and the stuff they sent us was already rusty when we off-loaded it!")

When Gosplan approaches a problem by industries rather than regions, the plan travels from Gosplan to the ministries of the various industries in Moscow, and then on down the line to the individual firm. Again it is the manager of a given plant who is responsible for providing feedback about the target assignments given to the firm.

In either case, Gosplan obtains statistics from the industry ministries, from the geographic subcommittees, and from whatever localized sources are available. There is a kind of negotiation or horse trading that goes on between planning bodies and the bottom rung of the planning ladder, the individual firm. The master plan sets forth the goals, and the firm must figure out what it can actually achieve. Interaction between Gosplan and the subcommittees and the local firms tends to lead to more realistic production objectives.

Input, Output, and Planning

The planning process in an economy as sophisticated as that of the Soviet Union is, of course, unimaginably complex. Besides the vast numbers of different finished products, there are huge numbers of intermediary products and raw materials that go into the finished products. In any developed economy there is a complex set of interrelated requirements of inputs needed for the economy to produce various combinations of output. In the U.S.S.R. the planning agencies that set up the master plans must have considerable amounts of information about these **input-output relationships**.

Table 27-1 shows the input-output relationships of a hypothetical economy. Note that the sectors in the horizontal row (those that consume inputs) are the same as the sectors in the vertical column (those that produce output). Each producing entity produces output and consumes input at the same time. For example, sector 1 (steel), in order to

TABLE 27-1 A Simplified Input-Output Table for a Hypothetical Economy

Consumers / Producers	1 Steel	2 Capital	3 Energy	4 Agriculture	5 Labor	6 Output
1. Steel	5	33	5	3	5	51
2. Capital	20	3	18	38	13	92
3. Energy	8	3	3	3	10	27
4. Agriculture	8	5	25	25	250	313
5. Labor	50	100	50	225	25	450

produce 51 units of output, consumes 5 units of its own output, plus 33 units of capital, 5 units of energy, 3 units of agriculture, and 5 units of labor. (We have made the simplifying assumption that all these industries are constant-cost industries.) Trace the inputs the other sectors need to produce their outputs. You can see the interdependence between all sectors even more clearly if you increase the output desired from any one sector.

For example, Gosplan decides to increase shoe production by one million pairs per year over the next five years. To achieve that output, the U.S.S.R. must build more machines to produce shoes and more factories to house these machines, which means more electricity to power the machines, more leather, plastic, rubber, nails, glue, shoelaces, and so forth; which in turn means more machines to produce these increased raw materials and more factories to house them. This will require expansion in agriculture (more cattle for leather) and in mining (more iron for nails), which means still more machines and buildings and equipment to produce the extra machines needed to make more shoes and the raw materials needed to produce them. In other words, there is a resource *rippling effect* that extends throughout the economy.

Thus, you can see that each time an economy decides either to increase or decrease output of a given product, there is a vast, complex set of corollary decisions that must be made. Each decision brings in its wake a host of further decisions.

This set of input-output relationships between raw materials, semifinished products, and finished products is what makes planning so complex.

Implementing the Plan

Given all this complexity of central planning in a developed economy, the Russians set up an ingenious network of agencies to see that the various plans are implemented. The bosses in the Soviet Union can check on the progress of a given plan, and make adjustments where needed, by using a clever system of information-gathering and controls.

1. There are several agencies charged with auditing the books of each firm in the U.S.S.R.

2. The **Gosbank** (the state bank) has branches throughout the country; each firm has an account at the Gosbank and must perform all its financial transactions by checks drawn on it. In this way, the Gosbank has a running account of each firm's activities. This is an important control device.

For example, the government in Moscow sets prices on all resources, including labor. Let's say that a given plan calls for the Marxit Pen Company to produce a million pens this year, and to do the job with x amount of material and x amount of labor, the whole operation to cost no more than 250,000 rubles. The Gosbank extends the Marxit Pen Company credit for the 250,000 rubles. As the firm swings into production, it pays for its resources by check, and its balance at the Gosbank declines. If it meets its quota of a million pens before it has exhausted the 250,000 rubles, then it has exceeded the goals set by the plan. But if Marxit exhausts its credit before it has turned out those million pens, then it is judged inefficient. This system is known as **control through the ruble**.

3. The many branches of the Communist party watchdog firms' production and report any violations of the plan. The secret police also seek out violators.

4. The government brings every citizen into the picture, asking each Soviet citizen to identify and report deviations from the plan, a process called the **criticism and self-criticism program**.

If Gosplan finds out that objectives of the plan are not being attained, it has two courses of action it can take: (1) Thanks to the government's foresight, the U.S.S.R. has stockpiles of various materials; Gosplan can draw on these stockpiles to relieve shortages and enable firms to meet production goals. (2) Since the U.S.S.R. operates under a system of priorities, by which investment in heavy industry and in military production have higher priority than production of consumer goods, when inadequacies develop in carrying out a given plan, the government can cut back on low-priority production and shift resources to production of higher-priority items.

How to Produce: State Ownership

The second problem that all economic systems must deal with is how production is to take place. Under capitalism, enterprises in which production takes place are privately owned, and the profit motive is the driving force behind them. In a command economy, such as the Soviet Union, the state owns most of the resources of production, and all productive enterprises, except for (1) a few retail and wholesale outlets, and (2) **the agricultural sector**.

Although the state does own and operate certain farms, the bulk of Soviet farm products comes from agricultural cooperatives. Most of these cooperatives came into being in the early 1930s, by order of the state, during the period of forced collectivization of agriculture, though some were formed voluntarily by their members.

However, *some* farmland is privately used (an estimated 2 percent of it), because the state gives small plots of land to members of the agricultural cooperatives. Farmers tend these tiny plots in their spare time, spending on them as much time as they can squeeze from their work obligations to the cooperatives, because they are allowed to sell the produce of these plots privately.

Although the Soviet Union's record as far as agriculture in general is concerned is full of failures and inefficiencies, these small plots of privately farmed land are highly productive. Some have estimated that they produce as much as 30 percent of the agricultural output of the U.S.S.R.

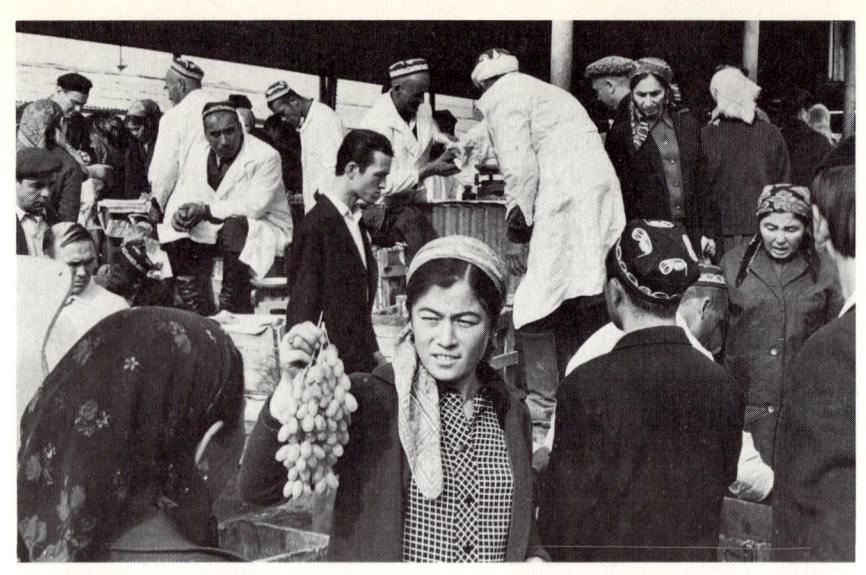

Produce from an agricultural cooperative: Market in Tashkent (Henri Cartier-Bresson/Magnum Photos, Inc.)

(It is hard to pin down the degree of truth in Soviet statistics about their economy, so these figures are, we repeat, estimates.) This amazing productivity of the small percentage of land that is privately used in Russia indicates that private control seems the best method—under either capitalism or Communism—to squeeze maximum production from an agricultural population.

Note: You may be interested to know that in rural areas, most of the homes are privately owned; in urban areas, about one-third are privately owned, the rest are government-owned.

Who Receives Output: The Wage System

The third problem that all economic systems have to face is who is to receive the output of the economy. In both capitalist and communist states, it depends on who has the money to buy it. In the United States, people receive income from wages and salaries, interest on capital, rent on property and homes, and profits from businesses. In the Soviet Union, people receive income only from wages and salaries, plus bonuses given to them to induce them to meet, and even exceed, their production quotas. The extra income acts as an incentive. The state holds the purse strings.

In the Soviet Union, to a far greater degree than in the United States, workers operate by the piece-rate system. There are big differences between wages paid to unskilled and to skilled workers. And among skilled workers, there are considerable wage differences between different grades of skill. When it comes to the managerial grades (both in industry and in government bureaus) and the highly technical or

The difficulty of buying a luxury good in the U.S.S.R. (Henri Cartier-Bresson/ Magnum Photos, Inc.)

professional grades (scientists, doctors, engineers, professors), salaries are relatively high—as much as twenty times higher than salaries of unskilled workers.

The Distribution of Real Income

It is difficult to obtain concrete evidence about the distribution of real income in Russia, but the following discussion seems generally valid.

Because of the great differences between wage rates for unskilled, semiskilled, and skilled workers, and the high salaries paid to professional people, the distribution of money incomes from wages and salaries is probably more unequal in the Soviet Union than in the United States. But when you include Americans' money income from all sources, including profits, interest, and rent, the distribution of money income is more equal in the Soviet Union.

The prices people must pay for consumer goods in the U.S.S.R. are not the cost-of-production prices listed in the Gosbank accounts for the firms that make the goods. Retail prices to consumers are much higher because they include a large **turnover tax**, a tax on goods as they pass through the various stages of production. A turnover tax is similar to a sales tax; the Soviet government imposes the turnover tax to increase the price of the consumer item to such a point that the quantity of the item available (that is, the quantity supplied) is equal to the quantity demanded. This clears the market, and is the equilibrium price. This tax also makes it possible for the government to peg prices of luxury goods higher than prices of necessities, and thereby keep the prices of food, housing, and medical care low.

You can buy a whole wheelbarrow full of cabbages and not pay one kopeck in turnover tax. But if you buy an electric cabbage shredder (if one were indeed available), the tax would be formidable. This would encourage you to eat a lot of cabbage and not to pine for any electrical appliances.

The turnover tax keeps people from trying to buy consumer goods that are in scarce supply, and thus neatly avoids the necessity of direct rationing controls. A final benefit is the income: The Soviet government's main source of income is the turnover tax. You can see why the government is so fond of it.

The turnover tax in the Soviet Union (unlike the sales tax in the United States) tends to be progressive. Ignoring transfer payments, the after-tax income in the Soviet Union tends to be more equally distributed than the before-tax income.

As incentives to efficient production and hard work, the government doles out to properly productive workers bonuses, prizes, special vacations, and access to preferred housing. Since the average per capita income is comparatively low, people work very hard to get these bonuses, which greatly upgrade a winning worker's standard of living.

Prices in the Soviet Union

The Soviet government uses the price system to fulfill two functions:

1. Gosplan attaches prices to raw materials, semifinished products, and labor in order to maintain a Gosbank audit of each firm's progress toward its assigned production target. Gosplan assigns these prices to resources, not to allocate the resources, but to get a concrete cost figure for the average firm in a given industry.

2. Gosplan assigns prices to consumer goods—prices much higher than those credited to the accounts of firms producing these goods. The difference is due, of course, to the turnover tax. These higher retail prices restrict the quantity demanded to the quantity that Gosplan has decreed can be supplied. Thus, the Soviet government uses prices to help implement its overall economic plan, not to allocate resources to the production of those goods it expects consumers to buy (as happens in a market-oriented economy). When an economy has a low per capita income and the stock of consumer goods available is small, this may not cause any trouble. Because of the small supply of consumer goods, citizens buy all of them that are produced. However, when an economy grows to the point at which consumer goods are fairly plentiful, efficiency in the allocation of resources for consumer use becomes a knotty problem. How can any planners really know what the masses of people want to consume? Soviet planners are increasingly plagued by that problem as they allocate more resources to the production of consumer goods. With tractors, you know where you stand, but not necessarily with consumer goods.

For example, if you are planning swim suits for 250 million people (and have no freely operating market to guide you), how are you going to please them all? How are you going to stipulate numbers, sizes, colors, and materials so that the state-run shops are not left holding 50,000 unwanted swim suits at the end of the summer (with a consequent waste of resources)?

Problems of Soviet Planning

Here are some of the flies in the Russians' caviar:

1. The more developed an economy becomes, the more complicated the planning of output becomes. Since each industry (and each firm) uses the products of other industries, at a given time in any economy there is a certain set of input-output relationships. In the early stages of development of a centrally planned economy, these input-output relations are simpler than they are later, when the economy becomes more mature. Three factors increase the complexity of input-output relationships.

First, as the economy grows and output increases, opportunities for specialization occur. For example, a newly emergent economy may not have enough textile mills to justify building special factories to manufacture textile-making machinery. Thus, each factory may need its own workshop to produce and repair its machinery. However, as the economy develops and more textile mills are built, it becomes efficient to create factories that build only textile-making machines. Therefore, an increase in output creates opportunities for firms to specialize and multiplies the number of different kinds of firms.

Second, as an economy develops, it uses more advanced technology, which increases the need for more specialized firms to produce more sophisticated equipment. More firms come into being, more sophisticated relationships evolve, and planners must make more decisions. For example, as a textile firm starts to use more advanced technology, the small workshop attached to the textile plant is less and less likely to be able to produce the improved machines.

Third, the more advanced the Soviet economy becomes, the wider the range of products produced; the wider the range of products, the more complex the planning problem.

2. Soviet planners have a sticky problem: how to state the production goals of a firm. Often in the past they have stated the goals of a firm in terms of volume of output, and then when the firms got into a tight spot, they would skimp on quality. For example, if the planners tell the manager of a nail-making plant to produce a certain number of nails, the firm tends to make small nails. If the planners tell the manager to make a certain gross weight of nails, the firm tends to produce large nails (this is the kind of problem that arises when a firm does not have to try to please consumers).

For example, recently there have been bitter complaints in the Soviet press about the large number of buildings left uncompleted in the U.S.S.R. Construction companies build the shell of a structure quickly and then move on and start another one, without finishing the first. The reason is that the production goals for construction companies are based on the amount of material used. Builders use large amounts of materials when they are putting up the shell of a building, but only small amounts of materials, and lots of labor, when they finish off the interior.

Furthermore, in order to ensure that it will meet its planning target, a firm often hoards materials, understates its supplies, and overstates its costs. As you can imagine, these practices lead to inefficiencies in the economy. So capitalist countries are not the only ones that suffer waste and blunders.

3. Agriculture has always been an ailing limb of the Soviet economy. Although much land in the U.S.S.R. has too little annual rainfall or too short a growing season for highly productive farming, the land that *can* grow crops has been inefficiently used.

Prior to the forced collectivization that began in 1929, Russian agriculture was characterized by small privately owned farms (especially after the breakup of the large estates of the landed gentry in 1917-1918). These small farmers were strongly opposed to the collectivization of agriculture, and feelings ran high, so the agricultural planners were faced at the outset with a resentful labor force. One result has been that despite the mechanization of agriculture, productivity has remained low. Today, about 30 percent of the Russian population remains toiling on farms. In the United States, on the other hand, only about 6 percent of the population is still employed in agriculture, and this 6 percent manages to feed 215 million Americans and have so much left over that food is the number-one U.S. export commodity (which helps our balance of trade considerably). Lately (1973 and 1975), the Soviet Union has made large grain purchases from the West.

Libermanism and Decentralized Decision Making

In the late 1960s, after years of discussion and thought about the flaws in the planning process, Soviet planners undertook reforms in the system. This development in Soviet planning is called **Libermanism**, after Yevsei Liberman, a professor at Kharkov University who suggested the reforms. Libermanism is based on the idea that profitability rather than output should be the measure of success of a firm.

Putting Liberman's ideas into practice required greater decentralization of Soviet planning and more autonomy for managers of individual firms. Under the new ground rules, managers can take orders from the firms to which they sell, orders that specify not only amount, but style, color, quality, size, and so forth. A manager can now "buy" raw materials from other firms. In addition, the manager is given more control than in the past over wages and over prices at which output is to be sold.

As the number of automobiles increases, the Soviet economy must plan for increased output of gas. (Sovfoto)

Now that firms have direct links to suppliers and customers and have some control over prices of resources and finished product, Gosplan can compute the "profitability" of a given firm and award bonuses to the manager and workers, depending on the degree of profitability. Thus, Gosplan is putting the profit motive to work—and it seems to oil the wheels in the U.S.S.R., just as it does in the rest of the world. There is (as you might expect) opposition to Liberman's reforms, especially from the old guard in Gosplan, who fear that their influence will become weaker. Nevertheless, these reforms have been widespread, at times affecting as much as four-fifths of Soviet industry, depending on the political and economic climate.

However, two factors have worked against Libermanism: (1) Despite initiation of plans from below, Gosplan still must approve all the plans of each firm, and Gosplan still has the right to set goals and priorities. (2) In order for the profit motive to work properly, prices must reflect scarcity values and also reflect consumers' tastes. So far, they do neither.

Soviet Economic Growth

Statistical information about the economy of the U.S.S.R. is not the most reliable. However, at present most Russian watchers estimate that Russia's GNP is about half that of the United States. Since the population of the U.S.S.R. is somewhat larger than that of the United States (250 million versus 215 million), Russia's per capita GNP is somewhat less than half that of the United States. This still puts the Soviet Union in the class of affluent developed economies. Furthermore, the rate of growth of Russia's GNP is high and sustained (though it is slowing down). In the 1950s Russia's GNP increased 6 percent to 7 percent per year; in the 1960s, 5 percent to 6 percent per year. And in the 1970s it looks as if its GNP growth rate will be only about 4 percent to 5 percent per year. By comparison, the U.S. GNP since 1950 has had an average rate of growth of only 3 percent to 3.5 percent.

(One must remember that while the industrial revolution in the United States started in the 1860s, the Soviets only came into power in Russia in 1917 and immediately had to fight a disastrous civil war. Also, the productivity capacity of the U.S.S.R. was virtually destroyed or worn out during World War II.)

Basis of Russia's High Rate of Growth
Several factors have contributed to Russia's high rate of growth:

1. *Improved technology.* In 1950 the U.S.S.R. was lagging far behind the Western capitalist countries in technology. However, one advantage the Soviet Union had was that it could adopt new technology brought forth by the developed economies without going to the expense of inventing and perfecting that technology. So the Soviet Union made large gains in productivity quickly by importing advanced technology from the West.

2. *Full employment.* The U.S.S.R. is a command economy and has the power to direct workers to various occupations. Therefore, Gosplan can keep Russia's labor force fully employed, and avoid the recurring business fluctuations of the Western capitalist economies. However, some economists point out that underemployment may run high in Russia, especially in agriculture.

3. *Shift from agriculture to industry.* The level of productivity in Russian agriculture is lower than that in industry. Therefore, whenever labor shifts from agriculture to industry, the overall level of productivity increases. In the Soviet Union about 80 percent of the labor force used to be employed in agriculture. Today that figure is down to 30 percent.

4. *Material resources.* Russia's endowment of natural resources is about as bountiful as that of the United States. This gives the Soviet Union an excellent—and mostly untouched—resource base for economic development.

Russia's Declining Rate of Growth
We said, as you recall, that the rate of growth of Russia's GNP has been slowing down. Some of the factors contributing to this decline are as follows:

1. *Less new technology.* By the 1970s the gap between the level of technology in the U.S.S.R. and that in the West had narrowed. Although this is an indication of Russia's success in copying Western technology, it also means that in the future Russia will make smaller and smaller gains as a result of copying from the West.

2. *Shift from agriculture to industry drying up labor supply.* Russian industry up to now has been able to draw on the agricultural sector for a plentiful supply of labor, but in the 1970s that source is drying up, and a labor shortage is beginning to develop.

3. *Shifts in priorities.* In the early 1960s, Russian leaders made two shifts in goals. The first was a substantial shift to greater military expenditures. Table 27-2 shows that by 1969 Russia devoted about 10 percent of its GNP to the military, only slightly more than the United States did. This naturally held back Russia's growth, because it caused resources to be shifted from investment to military goods.

The second shift in the early 1960s was toward greater amounts of consumer goods. Pressures for increased amounts of consumer goods, from both within and outside political circles, finally succeeded. This probably reduced the amount spent on investment (to some extent, at least) and thereby reduced the rate of growth. Table 27-2 shows that by 1969 Russians spent 51 percent of their GNP on private consumption and 30 percent on investment, versus 63 percent spent on consumption and only 15 percent on investment spent by the United States.

4. *Greater inefficiencies in planning.* Recall that as an economy becomes more mature, input-output relationships become more complex, which makes planning harder for a centrally planned economy. Also, in a planned economy the state's planning committee does not use prices to determine relative scarcity of resources and products, and thus cannot determine the most efficient allocation of resources. That is why, as the U.S.S.R.'s economy develops, its planning becomes less efficient and its rate of growth suffers. Whether using the Liberman method of "planning from below" (allowing individual firms to handle their own affairs) and giving bonuses as profit incentives can increase the efficiency of planning is still unknown.

5. *Depreciation.* When an economy develops, it accumulates a larger and larger stock of capital, which wears out after a while and must be replaced. In the past decade, Russia has had to spend a larger proportion of its gross investment on recovering depreciation (replacing worn-out

TABLE 27-2 Composition of GNP for the United States and the Soviet Union, 1969 (percent)

	United States	Soviet Union
Defense	8	10
Government consumption	14	9
Gross investment	15	30
Private consumption	63	51

Source: Stanley H. Cohn, "Economic Burden of Defense Expenditures," in Joint Economic Committee, *Soviet Economic Prospects for the Seventies,* G.P.O., Washington, D.C., 1973, 151.

capital) and on adding to its total capital stock. The reason was that by the beginning of the 1960s, the capital Russia had accumulated during the period of vigorous growth in the 1950s began to depreciate, and Russia had to use resources for replacement rather than for additions to capital. That is why Russia's rate of capital accumulation and growth has been falling.

SUMMING UP

1. The Soviet Union is a *command economy*, in which the problems generated by scarcity are solved by a system of central planning. Russia's state planning authority is called *Gosplan*.

2. Since the U.S.S.R. is a command economy, the problems of what to produce and how much to produce are solved by means of central planning. First, the Soviet government at its highest decision-making level states certain goals and priorities. In the 1960s, the government gave top priority to investment and military goods, but in the 1970s, it is increasingly emphasizing consumer goods.

3. After Gosplan draws up a plan, using all available data, it channels the plan through the various administrative units, both geographic and industrial (that is, through the planning committees of the sixteen different republics, and through the ministries and planners of the various industries). Eventually, the plan reaches the individual firm and its manager, who comments on the feasibility of the plan and decides whether the firm can fulfill it. The firm has the chance to negotiate the terms and objectives of the plan.

4. Developing and carrying out Gosplan's plan are difficult, especially because the *input-output relationships* (between raw materials, semifinished goods, and finished goods) in any developed economy are complex. Anytime Gosplan decides to increase or decrease output in any one area, a complex set of corollary decisions must be made.

5. In the U.S.S.R., Gosplan keeps a grip on the economic situation by the following means: (a) Each firm is regularly audited by various agencies. (b) The central bank, *Gosbank*, is also the only bank, and it keeps a constant watch on each firm. It can do this because it has all the firm's checks and can keep track of its receipts and disbursements. (c) The secret police, plus each member of the Communist party (which has more than 14 million members) act as watchdogs. (d) The government appeals to each citizen to report any violation of a plan.

6. If firms or industries fail to attain their objectives, Gosplan can (a) use stockpiles of various materials that are in short supply, and (b) shift resources from low-priority to high-priority production.

7. The command economy of the Soviet Union solves the problem of how to produce by having the government own most of the resources of production, except for a few small retail and wholesale enterprises and the cooperative farms, plus small plots of land that the state assigns to each farm family. These private plots (comprising only about 2 percent of Russia's land) account for about 30 percent of its total farm output.

8. In the Soviet Union, as in the United States, who receives the output depends on who has the money to pay for it. The Russian wage system is mainly based on piece rates, which rewards the able worker, and on differences in the level of skill, so that there are wide differences in pay. People receive income only from wages and special bonuses, not from profit, interest, and rents.

9. Despite the greater wage differentials in the U.S.S.R., the distribution of real income tends to be more nearly equal in Russia than in the United States (ignoring transfer payments). First, people in the United States get income not only from wages but from profits, interest, and rent—payments that tend to go to upper-income groups. Second, in the U.S.S.R. prices for necessities (food, housing, medical care) tend to be low because there is a lower *turnover tax* on these than on luxury items. The turnover tax is the difference between the retail price of a good and the price that Gosbank computes as the cost of producing it.

10. The Russian government uses prices for two purposes. First, through the medium of Gosbank it can maintain an audit of each firm's progress toward its assigned production target. Second, the government sets retail prices of products higher than the prices it uses as a cost-of-production price (the difference is the turnover tax). The government does this in order to keep the quantity demanded equal to the quantity that Gosplan has supplied. A high price for a luxury consumer good keeps people from demanding as much of it. Thus, prices help the country's overall plan, but are not used to allocate resources, as happens in a market economy.

11. The planning process in the U.S.S.R. faces three major problems. First, as the Russian economy becomes more developed, the relations between input and output become more complex and planning becomes vastly more difficult for the following reasons: (a) As an economy develops and output increases, firms become more specialized; this increases the number and kinds of firms. (b) Improved technology brings about more complex relationships between firms. (c) The more developed an economy is, the wider the range of products it produces.

12. Second, inefficiencies crop up when firms try to please the Gosplan and not consumers. For example, if production goals are stated in terms of numbers, firms tend to reduce quality.

13. Third, the agricultural sector has proved troublesome to Soviet planners. The productivity of Russia's farms has remained low; 30 percent of the Russian labor force works on farms (as compared to about 6 percent in the United States).

14. In the 1960s, Professor Yevsei Liberman of Russia's Kharkov University recommended that the Soviet planning process be based on profitability rather than productivity. When the government carried out Liberman's ideas, Gosplan began to decentralize the planning process and give more decision-making responsibility to the managers of the individual firms. The new freedom enabled the manager of a firm to take orders for the output of the firm, place orders for raw materials, and to have some leeway in setting wages.

15. *Libermanism*, as practiced in the U.S.S.R., has two limitations: (a) Gosplan retains control, since it still must approve all plans of each firm; it also sets and controls priorities as to use of resources. (b) Prices are still used as tools, and are not allowed to move freely and function as an allocative device.

16. Russia's GNP is somewhat less than half that of the United States. However, the rate of growth of Russia's GNP has been impressive: 6 percent to 7 percent per year in the 1950s, 5 percent to 6 percent per year in the 1960s, and 4 percent to 5 percent per year in the 1970s. The rate of growth of the U.S. GNP has been 3 percent to 3.5 percent per year.

17. Russia's high rate of growth was based on the following factors: (a) The U.S.S.R. was able to borrow superior technology from more advanced economies without having to pay to develop it. (b) Since it is a command economy, it can maintain full employment. (c) A great deal of labor shifted from low-productivity agriculture to higher-productivity industry. (d) The Soviet Union has plentiful natural resources.

18. Russia's rate of growth has been slowly declining since 1960 for the following reasons: (a) The technological gap between the U.S.S.R. and the West has narrowed. (b) By the end of the 1960s the surplus labor available on farms was greatly reduced. (c) The shift of priorities—toward military production in the 1950s and toward more consumer production in the 1960s—reduced investment. (d) As the Russian economy developed into a more complex system, planning inefficiencies increased. (e) When any economy becomes more developed, it must spend larger amounts of its resources on replacing worn-out or depreciated capital.

QUESTIONS

1. Compare ways that Russia's command economy solves the scarcity problems of *what to produce, how to produce,* and *how to distribute the output* with the ways that the United States solves the same problems.

2. How does the government of the Soviet Union use prices; that is, for what purposes? How does this differ from the way prices function in the United States?

3. Which has a more nearly equal distribution of after-tax real income: the United States or the Soviet Union? Why do you think that this is a valid conclusion?

4. What factors were responsible for the high annual rates of growth of the Soviet Union since World War II? Why is this growth rate slowing down?

5. Do you think that the Liberman reforms will solve the Soviet Union's problems of planning? Why or why not?

SUGGESTED READINGS

Bornstein, Morris, and Daniel R. Fusfeld, eds. *The Soviet Economy*, 4th ed. Irwin, Homewood, Ill., 1974.

Campbell, Robert W. *The Soviet-Type Economies*, 3d ed. Houghton Mifflin, Boston, 1974.

Djilos, Milovan. *The Unperfect Society: Beyond the New Class.* Harcourt, Brace, & World, New York, 1969.

Feiwel, George R. *New Currents in Soviet-Type Economies.* International Textbook Company, Scranton, Pa., 1968.

Joint Economic Committee of the U.S. Congress. *Soviet Economic Prospects for the Seventies.* G.P.O., Washington, D.C., 1973.

Application 27

Mainland China: A Different Communism?

Differences Between the U.S.S.R. and the People's Republic of China

The country one tends to think of first in connection with Communism is Russia. The second colossus of the Communist world is the People's Republic of China, with a land area of 3.7 million square miles and an estimated population of about 800 million. Because China's government and people differ from Russia's in a number of ways, it is interesting to compare the development and economic problems of these two vast, populous nations.

First, China became Communist much later than Russia did. Mao Tse-tung led his Communist party to victory thirty-two years after Russia's revolution. In 1949, Peking fell, signaling the birth of the People's Republic of China.

Second, China started from a lower productive base than the U.S.S.R. When Mao came to power, China had just gone through a war with Japan that had lasted more than ten years, and then along came the civil war, climaxed by a Communist victory. China's transportation system was one thing that hampered its development. For example, in 1950 China had only 15,000 miles of railroad and 86,000 miles of highways, while the United States had 400,000 miles of railroad and 3.5 million miles of highways. It is no wonder that China's industrial base was small and that there was high unemployment, inflation, and periodic famine.

Third, Maoism—China's brand of Communism in 1949—differed from the ideology of the Soviet Union. The Russians wanted to change the capitalist system and get rid of government by the czars. Mao was concerned not only with an economic revolution, but also with a revolution in human values. He wanted to change not only the economy but the individual. Only time will tell whether he succeeded.

China's Progress Since the Revolution

China's first Five-Year Plan (1952-1957), like Russia's, gave top priority to the development of heavy industry. It also transformed China's agricultural sector: Collective communes replaced private ownership of farms. This first plan was apparently a success, since China achieved its goals of rapid economic growth. In addition, vast numbers of unemployed entered into productive work, inflation vanished, and (despite increases in population) China's per capita output increased by 4 percent to 5 percent per year.

In 1958, Mao launched the **Great Leap Forward**, a plan much more ambitious than the first Five-Year Plan. The government asked the citizens to curtail personal consumption. But the result was economic disaster. Large numbers of workers were shunted from farms to jobs in industry, with the result that agriculture lagged and food production fell. Planning was poor and execution uncoordinated. Industry churned out poorly constructed and often almost useless products. The government directed millions of people to produce steel in back-yard furnaces; an estimated 600,000 small-scale furnaces were set up.

The result was a 25 percent increase in the amount of steel produced, but the quality of it was poor.

A new plan, set forth in 1961, shifted the priorities and gave primary emphasis to agriculture, ordering those firms producing resources that farmers needed (for example, tractors and fertilizers) to give these items highest priority. Continuing the emphasis on agriculture, the government decreed that light consumer-good industries that made articles needed by the people who lived in the communes had next-highest priority. Much was done to increase the people's incentives to work in farm communes. However, the disasters of the 1958-1960 period were so great that it was not until 1969 (according to some estimates), that both food and industrial production caught up and began to show gains.

In the 1966-1969 period there came the **Cultural Revolution**, apparently an effort (mainly by Chinese teen-agers encouraged by the government) to rid China's citizens of what were considered "bourgeois" influences. Bands of earnest young revolutionists traveled around China, destroying clothing and books they felt were antirevolutionary, sacking private homes, and burning property they considered unproletarian. They preached the spirit of cooperation between workers and explained the character of the socialist man or woman. They ousted newspaper editors, university presidents, and economists. Schools and universities shut their doors in the face of this chaos—just what China did not need at this juncture. Economic efficiency suffered; for example, 400,000 specialists could not complete their training because the schools were closed in 1967-1968.

However, by 1970 the economy had apparently recovered from these disruptions, and China watchers now estimate that its growth in the 1970s is approaching 6 percent per year. (Chinese data are even harder to get and to evaluate than Russian data. Therefore, there is considerable disagreement about growth rates and claims.) The basis of China's newest Five-Year Plan (to cover the years 1976-1980) is the effort to bring about increases in agricultural products and in iron and steel. According to the *New York Times*, recent visitors to China have been told that Peking wants to reach a grain output of 400 million tons per year by 1980. Some think this figure may be more a slogan than an actual goal.

Structure of China's Planned Economy

In mainland China, the agricultural sector, made up of about 80 percent of the population, produces only 40 percent of the nation's output. The main reason why productivity in Chinese agriculture is so much lower than it is in manufacturing is that Chinese farming is very labor-intensive. So manufacturing output, because industry is more mechanized, is growing more rapidly than agricultural output. The government restricts the flow of labor away from farms. The purpose here is probably twofold: (1) to enhance the food supply, and (2) to foster the spirit of socialism in the communes. Agricultural workers who live in these communes have a good deal of latitude in managing their own internal affairs. For example, they decide what the commune will buy with the income it gets from selling its produce. Each family has a small plot for its own use, but (unlike the Russian cooperative-farm workers) they cannot sell privately the produce raised on these little plots.

China is a command economy with a central planning system. Planners control the labor market, and workers have little personal freedom in choosing jobs. ("You will report to Commune 706 two weeks from today.") The government also controls prices, which in the past few years have not only been stable, but may even have fallen somewhat, since the government's policy is to reward productivity not by increasing wages but by lowering prices. Since the disasters of 1958-1961, the government has been trying to decentralize the planning process more and more, on the theory that the closer planners are to the scene of action, the more accurately they will be able to gauge resources needed, probable output, and long-run future needs and achievements.

Although differences in people's incomes still exist, distribution of income is substantially more nearly equal in China than in the Soviet Union. In a hospital in China the average wage for all the staff was 67 yuan a month; for the doctors at that hospital, the average was 85 yuan. The aim of the Maoists is apparently to reduce income differentials even further.

China still has problems, however. The Chinese radio, usually so close-mouthed about internal affairs, candidly admitted in recent broadcasts that the Peking government had to send more than 10,000 troops into factories in the coastal city of Hangchow to quell outbreaks of "bourgeois factionalism" (translation: labor troubles) that were hurting production. And the few travelers coming out of China report that party officials in some factories have been afraid to face workers demanding higher wages or staging slowdowns. As a result officials have sometimes stayed away from their jobs.

It is true that there has been no inflation in China; after all, the government controls both wages and prices. But most workers have not had raises in years. And in 1974 the government took away their bonuses, as part of an effort to prevent backsliding toward capitalism. Stamping out "bourgeois individualism" turns out to be easier said than done.

An Evaluation of China's Experiment

The People's Republic of China, despite mistakes that have bordered on the catastrophic, has developed an economy that is, by its own definition, successful. Apparently there is full employment, price stability, and no more famine. Although the standard of living is low, nobody seems to be starving, and that in itself is a big plus. Economic development continues, and the standard of living is slowly rising.

China's economic structure can be criticized as inefficient: The Chinese give precedence to low-productivity agriculture over higher-productivity industry, and favor lower-productivity light industry (to produce consumer goods) over heavy industry. The government interferes with the process of specialization of workers through training and employment by periodically assigning them to rural communes. But one must bear in mind that the Maoists are apparently not as concerned with "economic development" as Western countries (and the U.S.S.R.) know it. The Maoists want first to create a society imbued with the spirit of cooperation and community service; increases in GNP are only a secondary concern.

Whether the People's Republic of China can continue to increase the standard of living of its people and create a new breed of socialist person who is devoid of "selfish individualism," only time will tell. If it does accomplish all this, will the end be worth the means?

QUESTIONS

1. When the People's Republic of China was founded in 1949, what were the significant economic and ideological differences between it and the Soviet Union?

2. The development of the People's Republic of China has gone through at least four economic stages. Identify them and give a brief description of each.

3. In comparing the economic structure of the People's Republic of China and the Soviet Union, what differences do you see?

4. Do you think that the People's Republic of China has been successful from an economic point of view? Why or why not?

SUGGESTED READINGS

Barnett, A. Doak. *China After Mao*. Princeton, Princeton, N.J., 1967.

Gurley, John. "Maoist Economic Development." *Monthly Review*, 1971.

Reynolds, Floyd G. "Making a Living in China." *Yale Review*, No. 4, June 1974.

Robinson, Joan. *The Cultural Revolution in China*. Penguin, London, 1969.

Schurmann, Franz, and Orvelle Schell. *Communist China*. Vintage, New York, 1967.

Tobin, James. "The Economy of China: A Tourist's View." *Challenge*, March–April 1973.

Application 28

Ideological Convergence: The New Melting Pot?

The United States and the U.S.S.R.: How Far Apart?

Observers of the development of the Soviet Union and the United States in the last few decades have commented on a seeming trend for Communist and capitalist countries to converge, both in their ideologies and in the structure of their economic societies. Some people have even predicted that in the not too distant future, Communist countries will drift slowly away from the left, that capitalist countries (faced by problems arising from the differences between the haves and the have-nots) will drift away from the right, and that the two systems will perhaps meet in the middle. In brief, some people predict that the conflicts and differences dividing East and West will be resolved by changes in both economies, changes brought about by internal forces.

One can reach the same conclusions through Marx's theory of historical materialism. Technology and the material environment (the economic substructure) are dominant and force the superstructure (law, culture, and institutions) to be consistent with them. The technologies of the Soviet Union and the United States are very similar and will probably move even closer in the future. The joint Apollo-Soyuz space mission in the summer of 1975 indicated this trend toward sharing of technological advances, with the official blessing of both governments. Marxists may consider, therefore, that there will be a convergence—an increasing similarity—of the institutions of the two nations.

With their first Five-Year Plan in 1929, the Soviets launched a concerted drive to industrialize. As the United States had done seventy-five years earlier, the Soviet Union shifted its emphasis from a rural to an urban economy. The percentage of Russia's labor force employed in agriculture dropped from 80 percent in 1924 to 30 percent in 1975; quite a drop in fifty years.

In both countries, economic development has created a dominant and highly sophisticated mechanized manufacturing sector, in which the size of each producing unit is largely determined by the needs of technology. From this industrial point of view, the structure of the two countries is very similar.

Chapter 27 discussed the Liberman reforms during the 1960s in the Soviet Union. This "planning from below" greatly decentralized the planning process, giving the managers of Russian firms greater latitude in purchasing, production, and sales. However, this introduction of the profit motive and decentralization of planning is viewed by some as a move toward creating a competitive market, small as this move may be. In Czechoslovakia (before the Russian invasion of 1968), the move toward decentralization of planning and the increase in autonomy of individual plants had gone much further, as it has in Yugoslavia, another Communist country.

An example of a move in the opposite direction is the United States. Since the 1930s, the U.S. government has taken upon itself increased responsibilities in the area of social welfare, regulation of business activity, and changes in discretionary fiscal and monetary policy to correct the instability and what it regards as the inequities of an out-and-out market economy.

In other countries (Great Britain, Denmark, Sweden), governments have gone much further than the United States in social welfare programs (setting up health, housing, and welfare programs to take care of citizens at all ages—the so-called womb-to-tomb security) as well as in programs to regulate and stabilize economic activity.

In France, also a capitalist country, the government has, with fair success, engaged in what is called **indicative planning**, by which it draws up targets for the economy and brings together employers and unions to discuss and modify its proposals. Afterward the employers and unions try—with government support—to implement these plans.

Technology: Pathway to Common Cause

John Kenneth Galbraith, in his book *The New Industrial State*, sets forth a view that one could interpret as being a prediction of convergence.

Drawing by Mary Petty; © 1945, 1973 The New Yorker Magazine, Inc.

"Has anybody ever thought of winning the Communists over to *our* way of life?"

(See Chapter 21, which discusses some of Galbraith's ideas.) In brief, he points out that large corporations are run by committees of technical experts (technocrats) because in our modern technological world the problems of supply, production, and sales are too complex for any individual. Galbraith also argues that the technocrats' chief motives are not profits, but job security, increase in areas of control, and social approval. He extends this argument from the level of large corporations to the operations of government, both in capitalist and so-called Communist countries.

Although Galbraith himself does not explicitly draw an argument in favor of convergence from the above analysis, one can easily do so. In both the United States and the Soviet Union, the complex nature of a highly technological economy shifts decision making into the hands of the technical expert, and away from the profit-maximizing capitalist, on the one hand, and the Marxist politician, on the other.

It may be the technocrats on both sides that have made the détente of the mid-1970s possible.

A Note of Caution

Many observers point out that one can easily overestimate the strength of the factors causing convergence of the economic structures of the United States and the Soviet Union. There are some factors that may stand in the way of convergence:

1. In the United States, private ownership and control of the means of production (resources) is still dominant. In the U.S.S.R., no move is being made toward private ownership, not even in the area of small-scale firms, where there is less controversy about the efficiency of private control.

2. In the United States, the economy is still dominated by market relationships, despite the existence of monopoly power. In the U.S.S.R., the market is rarely allowed to operate, despite the Liberman reforms.

3. In the United States, the role of government in the economy is still restricted, and business fluctuations still occur. Government is still reluctant to interfere directly in the interplay of market forces. In other words, the United States is still mainly a capitalist market-oriented economy.

In the U.S.S.R., Liberman's reforms were designed to strengthen central planning, and Russia watchers see no move toward abandoning central planning or substantially changing it.

So one might say that even if there *are* elements tending toward convergence in both economies, they are not strong enough at this time to enable one to predict a meeting on middle ground in the foreseeable future. There are those, economists among them, who have a plague-on-both-your-houses attitude. These people say that if the United States and the Soviet Union *are* converging, it is not free enterprise converging with socialism, but two bureaucratic, oppressive, concentrated economies acting alike.

QUESTION

Do you think that the economies of the Soviet Union and the United States are changing, so that there will be fewer differences between them in the future? Why or why not?

SUGGESTED READINGS

Lennemann, H., J. P. Pronk, and Jan Tinbergen. "Convergence of Economic Systems in East and West." In *Disarmament and World Economic Interdependence*, edited by Emile Benoit. Columbia, New York, 1967.

Millar, James R. "On The Theory and Measurement of Economic Convergence." *Quarterly Review of Economics and Business*, 12, No. 1 (Spring 1972).

Glossary

Ability-to-pay principle A principle of taxation under which those who have a larger income are deemed capable of paying not only a larger tax but a larger percentage of their income in taxes.

Absolute advantage The ability of a given nation to produce all commodities more cheaply (that is, using up fewer resources per unit of output) than any other nation with which it might trade.

Abstinence theory of interest A theory that people prefer to consume goods and services now, rather than later; therefore, people will save (postpone consuming) only if they are given a reward. That reward is called interest.

Accelerator principle The general rule that changes in the rate of change of consumer demand cause much larger changes in induced investment. The accelerator is positive if a change in the increase in consumer demand causes induced investment to increase. It is negative if the change in induced investment decreases.

Adjustable-peg system A system of exchange in which currencies are pegged, or are not allowed to change in value by more than a specific percentage. The pegs themselves, however, may be changed from time to time.

Administered-price inflation A kind of inflation that occurs when firms with some control over price use that power to raise prices more rapidly than cost increases.

Administered pricing A term used by some economists to refer to prices that are set by the administrators of firms or by government rather than established by independent influences of supply and demand.

Aggregate-demand-equals-aggregate-supply approach An approach to the problem of finding equilibrium income in a simple economic model without government and foreign trade. According to this approach, the equilibrium is at that level at which *aggregate supply*—consumption plus savings $(C + S)$—is equal to *aggregate demand*—consumption plus intended investment $(C + II)$.

Aggregate production function The relationship in physical (nonmonetary) terms between output and employment for a given economy (at a specific time). A "recipe" for output.

Anarchism A school of political thought that holds that all forms of government are oppressive and undesirable. Anarchists oppose all authority, especially when it is in the hands of the state.

Antithesis In Marxist theory, the force arising from a social contradiction that compels a change in the existing thesis (or set of social arrangements).

At factor prices Method of computing national income using the prices paid in the factor markets. This measuring practice excludes indirect business taxes.

At market prices Method of computing national economic accounts using the prices paid in the markets for goods and services. This measuring practice must utilize all market costs incurred in production.

Autarky Economic self-sufficiency.

Automatic stabilizers Structures built into the U.S. economy that have a moderating influence on recessions and inflations. They are automatic in that they operate without being invoked by government policy makers. They are not considered strong enough to prevent, by themselves, the occurence of business fluctuations. Personal income tax is an example.

Autonomous investment Investment that is not affected by changes in the nation's overall level of income and consumption.

Average propensity to consume The percentage of their incomes that people at a given level of income tend to consume:

$$APC = \frac{C}{Y}.$$

Average propensity to save The percentage of their incomes that people at a given level of income tend to save:

$$APS = \frac{S}{Y}.$$

Average revenue Total revenue divided by output.

Average total cost Average fixed cost plus average variable cost.

Backward-bending labor supply curve A graphic illustration of a situation in which the quantity of labor supplied decreases as the wage increases beyond a certain level.

Balanced-budget multiplier The multiplier that makes itself felt when a balanced-budget change in government expenditures and taxes (that is, government expenditures and taxes moving in the same direction and by the same amount) causes the level of national income to change in the same direction and by the same amount as the expenditure-tax change. *See also* Multiplier effect.

Balance-of-payments statement The annual accounting statement disclosing the status of a nation's foreign trade, including its capital and monetary metal transactions. The statement reveals what was bought and sold, and how any difference between the two was financed. (The balance-of-payments account must balance.)

Balance of trade The monetary value of exports minus imports:

$$X - M.$$

Balance to be financed In the balance-of-payments statement, the combination of the basic balance plus the short-term capital account.

Barter A system of exchange that does not involve money; the trading of goods directly for other goods.

Basic balance In the balance-of-payments statement, the balance in the current account plus the balance in the long-term capital account.

Benefits-received principle of taxation The theory of taxation according to which people pay taxes that are commensurate with, or in line with, the benefits they receive from government services.

Bilateral monopoly A market situation in which a single seller bargains with a single buyer.

Bonds Instruments of debt, guaranteeing payment of the investment (face value) plus interest by a certain date. Interest on bonds is a cost of production to a business firm that raises capital by selling bonds.

Bretton Woods conference International monetary conference held in 1944, which established the International Monetary Fund (IMF) and the International Bank for Reconstruction and Development (IBRD).

Budget restraint The limits on purchases of goods imposed by a consumer's income and by the prices of the goods bought.

Burke-Hartke bill Legislation, proposed in 1973 and supported by organized labor, that would have imposed widespread and drastic restrictions on imports of foreign commodities into the United States. (The bill was not enacted.)

Business cycles Variations in a nation's general economic activity; fluctuations in output, income, employment, and prices.

Capital account The account, in a nation's balance-of-payments statement, that is made up of long-term and short-term capital flows.

Capital broadening (constant capital-to-labor ratio) The situation in which capital instruments grow at the same rate as the amount of labor employed.

Capital consumption allowance *See* Depreciation.

Capital deepening The situation in which a nation's employers use more capital relative to the amount of labor used, thus raising the capital-to-labor ratio for the economy.

Capital gains tax A tax placed on the increase in the value of an asset which is realized on sale of the asset. It is considered a tax loophole because the tax rate on such gains tends to be lower than on other forms of income.

Capital-intensive process A production process that uses relatively more capital than labor or land.

Capitalism An economic system with two essential ingredients: (1) the private ownership of the means of production, and (2) the expression of economic decisions through a system of interrelated markets.

Cartel A group of producers who join forces and behave like a monopoly with respect to price and output.

Ceteris paribus In economic analysis, the practice of holding certain variables constant and permitting other, *key* variables to change.

Change in demand A shift in a demand curve (by which more or less of a good is bought at all prices) that results from a change in (1) income, (2) tastes, (3) prices of other goods, (4) number of consumers, or (5) consumers' expectations of future prices.

Change in quantity demanded A movement along a demand curve which results from a change in the price of that good.

Change in quantity supplied A movement along a supply curve which reflects change in the amount of a good offered for sale as only the price of that good changes.

Change in supply A shift in a supply curve which reflects that more or less of a good is offered for sale by a firm at all prices.

Check An order to a bank from the holder of a demand deposit to transfer money from that demand-deposit account and pay it to someone else.

Checking accounts *See* Demand deposits.

Closed shop An employment situation in which workers *must* join a union in order to get or hold a job.

Coins Metal tokens minted by the Treasury and issued through the Federal Reserve Banks; the smallest component of the supply of money.

Command economy An economy in which the problems generated by scarcity are solved by a system of central government planning.

Commercial bank Any bank that holds demand deposits.

Common stock Instruments of ownership of a corporation. People who own shares of common stock can vote on all matters requiring stockholders' consent, and there are no limitations on the amount of dividends they can receive. However, they receive dividends only after all prior claims against the company (interest on bonds, and so on) have been paid.

Comparative advantage A situation in which a nation is relatively more efficient at producing some goods than at producing others, compared with the production capabilities of other nations with which it trades.

Compensatory fiscal policy *See* Functional finance.

Competition The market form in which no individual buyer or seller has influence over the price at which she or he buys or sells. *See also* Pure competition.

Complementary investment An investment that increases the productivity of other investments.

Constant capital-to-labor ratio *See* Capital broadening.

Constant-cost industry An industry in which the cost curves of individual firms remain the same as the output of the industry varies.

Constant GNP *See* Real GNP.

Consumer choice A theory of demand that rests on four assumptions about consumers: (1) Consumers buy competitively. (2) Consumers have limited money incomes and full information. (3)

Glossary 669

Consumers are rational. (4) Consumers maximize their utility or satisfaction.

Consumer price index An index that measures price changes for a certain market basket of goods likely to be purchased by a family of four living in an urban area. Compiled and published monthly by the Bureau of Labor Statistics.

Consumption function Schedule of the quantities that people are willing and able to consume at different levels of income during a given time period.

Contraction phase That part of the business cycle in which the level of economic activity falls.

Control through the ruble Control that the Soviet Union exercises over business firms through the medium of the Gosbank (central bank). A business firm's account at the Gosbank is credited with the value of its assigned production goal. As the firm uses resources, it pays for them by checks on its account. If the firm uses up its account before it achieves its assigned goal, it fails in its assignment.

Corporate profits The return to entrepreneurship in firms that are incorporated. Corporate profits equal dividends plus retained earnings (undistributed corporate profits) plus corporate taxes.

Corporation A legal entity or form of business enterprise, created by the process of incorporation, which functions separately from its owners.

Cost-plus pricing A form of administered pricing in which a firm first computes its variable cost, then its overhead or fixed cost, and finally adds its expected profit per unit. The result is the price it charges to consumers.

Cost-push inflation The kind of inflation that occurs when suppliers of resources increase their prices faster than productivity of manufactures increases. Costs of production then go up, which forces prices up.

Countervailing power The idea that monopoly power often exists on both sides of a market. The monopsony power of buyers is counterbalanced by the monopoly power of sellers.

Coupon economics The system by which a government rations the output of the economy by issuing ration coupons to consumers, which consumers must redeem in order to buy rationed products.

Covert collusion A situation in which representatives of various firms in the same industry meet and decide on prices, shares of the market, and other conditions of the market.

Creeping inflation A kind of inflation in which there is a moderate rise in prices that continues for an extended period of time.

Criticism and self-criticism program A program in the Soviet Union that requires individual citizens to identify and report deviations from the government's economic plan.

Crowding theory A theory that explains the effects of discrimination by tracing the impact that discrimination has in forcing women, blacks, or other minorities into certain kinds of employment and out of others.

Cultural Revolution A mass social movement that took place in the People's Republic of China in 1966-1969, supported by the Chinese government and aimed at rooting out bourgeois and antirevolutionary thought and action.

Currency in circulation Currency (both paper money and coins) that is actually in use, not in the vaults of banks or in the Treasury.

Current account An account in the balance-of-payments statement that is like the income and expense statement of a nation. It includes all current transactions, but excludes short-term and long-term movements of capital.

Customer discrimination Job and wage discrimination resulting from tastes of buyers (for example, diners in restaurants preferring to be served by men or whites).

Decreasing-cost industry An industry in which external economies cause costs of all individual firms in the industry to fall as the output of the industry as a whole increases.

Deflating current GNP The act of decreasing current GNP to take into account a rise in prices; expressing GNP in terms of dollars of constant purchasing power.

Deflationary gap The increase in aggregate demand necessary to make aggregate demand equal to aggregate supply at full employment.

Demand A set of relationships representing the quantities of a good that consumers will buy over a given range of prices in a given period of time.

Demand curve A graphic plotting of the demand schedule, or a set of relationships between various prices of a good and the quantities of it that the public will buy at each of those prices in a given period of time.

Demand deposits Deposits in commercial banks that can be withdrawn "on demand" by one who presents a check.

Demand-pull inflation A rise in prices that occurs when demand for goods exceeds the ability of the economy to supply these goods at existing prices. The result is that the market rations this short supply through the medium of increased prices.

Democratic socialists Those who believe in using democratic procedures to gain political power and to curtail capitalism.

Dependent variable The factor in a two-variable system that changes as a result of changes in the independent factor.

Depreciation An accounting allowance for the capital that "wears out" (either through use or obsolescence) while being used to produce the final goods and services of an economy in a given period of time.

Derived demand A demand for one thing that depends on the demand for something else. (For example, the demand for labor depends on the demand for the goods produced by labor.)

Dialectical materialism A philosophy in which material things are viewed as the subject of all change, and technology and the natural environment as the main forces that cause society to change continually.

Diminishing marginal utility of income The theory that people get less and less satisfaction from each increase in their incomes.

Diminishing rate of transformation The idea that the rate at which one good may be traded off, or transformed, into another decreases.

Discommunication The problems that a large organization encounters in trying to communicate in order to achieve effective decision making; due in part to large size.

Discount rate The rate of interest that the Federal Reserve charges commercial banks when it discounts acceptable short-term debt at the Federal Reserve, to enable the commercial banks to obtain reserves.

Discretionary fiscal policy Day-to-day fiscal policies established by government officials, designed to cope with changing economic conditions.

Diseconomies of scale The disadvantage a firm may encounter when it increases the size of its plant and increases its output, only to find that the cost of each unit produced is greater than before.

Dissavings Consuming more than is produced, or consuming more than one's income.

Double coincidence of demand A system of exchange (or barter) that requires a mutuality of needs; each party to a transaction must want what the other has.

Double taxation A situation that arises when a corporation pays taxes on its gross receipts. Then it distributes its dividends from these receipts to its stockholders, who must then pay income tax on the previously taxed money.

Durable goods Commodities (such as automobiles) that are used up at a very slow rate; that is, it takes a long time to use them up.

Dynamic framework A concept or set of relationships by which one can explain the way certain things change through time.

Economic development A process by which the material well-being of a society's people is significantly improved.

Economic dualism The coexistence within a society of two or more different economies (frequently, one with markets and cash incomes and the other with barter).

Economic imperialism A Marxist concept according to which capitalists ward off a fall in profits and lessen the severity of economic crises by exploiting the underdeveloped countries. Supposedly, capitalists do so by using the underdeveloped countries as a source of demand for their output and supply of cheap raw material and as places to invest capital.

Economic institutions Social institutions through which economic decisions are made (for example, the Federal Reserve System).

Economic loss with production A situation in which a firm's short-run total revenue is less than its total costs, but greater than its total variable costs. The firm minimizes its loss by continuing to produce.

Economic loss without production A situation in which a firm's short-run total revenue is not only less than its total costs, but also less than its total variable costs. The firm loses less by closing down altogether.

Economic profit Profit that is above normal profit. When there is economic profit, total revenue is greater than total cost (including the opportunity cost of entrepreneurs).

Economic rent The payment made to a resource whose supply is perfectly inelastic.

Economics The social science that deals with the analysis of material problems. Economics identifies the various means by which people can attempt to satisfy their unlimited material desires with limited resources.

Economies of scale Achieved by a firm when the cost of each unit produced falls as output increases with larger plant size.

Effective demand The total aggregate demand for commodities and services in an economy.

Elasticity of resource demand The rate at which the quantity of a resource demanded changes as its price changes:

$$\frac{\Delta Q}{Q} \div \frac{\Delta P}{P},$$

where Q = quantity of the resource demanded, P = price of the resource, and Δ (Greek delta) = "change in."

Elasticity of resource supply The rate of change in the quantity of an input supplied as its price changes:

$$\frac{\Delta L}{L} \div \frac{\Delta W}{W},$$

where L = amount of labor, W = wage rate, and Δ (Greek delta) = "change in."

Embargo An absolute prohibition against importing certain goods.

Employment The situation in which a unit of resource (labor, land, capital, entrepreneurship) is used in some economic activity.

Entrepreneurship The function of organizing labor, land, and capital into a firm capable of producing and marketing a commodity or service.

Equation of exchange $MV = PQ$, where M = supply of money, V = velocity of exchange (number of times M changes hands), P = price level, and Q = number of transactions.

Equilibrium exchange rate The rate of exchange between two currencies that clears the market or eliminates excess supply and demand.

Equilibrium income The level of income that results from the central tendency of a model. This level will be maintained as long as the factors in the model (savings and investment) remain the same.

Equilibrium price The market-clearing price, or the price at which quantity demanded equals quantity supplied.

Equity stock *See* Common stock.

Ex-ante investment The amount of investment firms plan to make.

Excess demand The excess of quantity demanded over quantity supplied at a price lower than the equilibrium price.

Excess reserves Assets that banks hold in the form of reserves, but which are over and above that required by Federal Reserve regulations.

Excess supply The excess of quantity supplied over quantity demanded at a price higher than the equilibrium price.

Exchange controls Devices governments use to ration foreign currencies or eliminate excess demand for them.

Expansion The process by which a society's output grows as it uses more and more resources.

Expansion phase That part of the business cycle in which economic activity rises.

Expenditure approach A method of computing national income accounts that is concerned with the kinds of goods people buy, with what kinds of expenditures they make.

Explicit costs Those costs of a firm that result from contracting for resources in the markets.

Exploitation In neoclassical economic theory, a payment to a resource that is less than its value of marginal product.

Exports Commodities and services sold to other nations.

Ex-post investment The investment that firms actually undertake (not simply plan to undertake).

External diseconomies of scale An increase in a firm's costs caused by changes in the output of the industry as a whole.

External economies of scale A decrease in a firm's costs caused by increases in the output of the industry as a whole.

Externalities The differences between privately expressed (market) costs and benefits and publicly expressed (nonmarket) costs and benefits. *See also* Spillovers.

Factor markets Those markets in which the prices of resources like land, labor, capital, and entrepreneurship are established.

Fiat money Money that has greater value as a monetary instrument than as a commodity. It is money because the government issued it and says that it is money, and because people accept it as such.

Final goods and services Goods and services sold to the ultimate user.

Final-value method Method of computing GNP that sums up the prices to final buyers of all goods and services produced by the economy. Avoids double counting by eliminating intermediate production, and leads to the same statistical result as the value-added method of computing GNP.

Financial capital Capital in the form of money; savings that are available for investment in physical capital.

Fine tuning Discretionary changes in fiscal and monetary policy leading to counterchanges in the state of the economy.

Fiscal policy Manipulation of the expenditures and taxes of the federal government to achieve certain economic goals.

Fixed costs Costs that do not vary with output.

Fixed exchange rates A system of international exchange in which the currency of each nation has a certain fixed relationship to the currencies of other nations for exchange purposes.

Foreign-trade multiplier (FTM) The change in GNP resulting from a change in net foreign trade:

$$\text{FTM} = \frac{\Delta \text{GNP}}{\Delta(X - M)},$$

where X = exports, M = imports, and Δ (Greek delta) = "change in."

Fractional reserve requirement A regulation allowing commercial banks to hold reserves that are less than 100 percent of their demand deposits. As a result, such banks can lend out amounts that are a multiple of their reserves.

Free good A good with a price of zero. Supply is greater than demand at any price above zero.

Freely-floating exchange rate A system of international exchange in which the currencies of the various nations are valued according to supply and demand in the international money market. The exchange rate is free to move up or down.

Frictional unemployment Short-term unemployment resulting from workers moving from one job to another.

Full capacity A situation in which a firm or industry is at the low point on its long-run average-cost curve.

Full employment A situation in which everyone in the labor force is employed except those who are frictionally unemployed.

Full-employment budget The budget that balances government expenditures against the level of receipts (taxes) that the government would receive if the economy were at full employment.

Functional distribution of income An approach to the distribution of income that emphasizes the *sources* of income: wages, interest, rent, and profit.

Functional finance A policy that aims at compensating for changes in aggregate demand in the private sector by varying the public sector's expenditures and taxes.

General powers of the Federal Reserve System Powers that enable the Federal Reserve to increase or decrease the amounts of excess reserves that commercial banks need in order to make loans.

General price index Index constructed by the

Commerce Department to convert current GNP to constant GNP.

Giffen goods Goods that are so income-inferior that people buy less of them as their price falls. In such a case, the income effect (inferiority) is stronger than the substitution effect.

GNP gap The difference between potential GNP at 4 percent unemployment and actual GNP achieved.

GNP implicit price deflator *See* General price index.

Gold-flow point The disequilibrium exchange rate at which it is cheaper to buy and ship gold in payment for trade than to buy currencies.

Gold standard The system of international exchange used up until the 1930s, according to which currencies were valued in terms of gold and were convertible into gold, and each nation permitted unrestricted exports and imports of gold.

Gold tranche position The amount of gold a member nation can borrow from the International Monetary Fund (IMF).

Gosbank The state bank in the Soviet Union, used to control and audit individual firms' activities. All firms have accounts with Gosbank, and all their purchases and sales go through the bank.

Gosplan An agency in the Soviet Union that translates overall goals into a comprehensive plan for the economy. Gosplan is the central planning committee of the Soviet Union.

Government expenditures In the national economic accounts, the measure of all goverment purchases of goods and services.

Great Leap Forward Second Five-Year Plan of the People's Republic of China (1958-1962). Execution of the plan was such a disaster that it was abandoned in 1960.

Gross national income (GNI) Total income at market prices generated in the production of all final goods and services during a specific time period. GNI = wages and salaries + rent + interest + proprietors' income + corporate profits + depreciation + indirect business taxes.

Gross national product (GNP) Total dollar value of all final goods and services produced in a given time period. GNP = consumption + gross investment + government expenditures + net foreign investment (export − imports).

Gross private domestic investment Investment including depreciation or capital consumption allowance. *Private* means counting only nongovernment investment; *domestic* means counting only investment made in the United States. Investment is the act of creating capital, manufactured producer goods that aid in producing consumer goods and other capital goods.

Growth The intensive process by which the productivity (output per hour of labor employed or income per capita) increases.

Hedonist One who argues that people act to achieve self-satisfaction.

Historical materialism The view that society throughout history has undergone a continual process of change and development from one form to another. The guiding factors in this process are the natural environment and changing technology.

Historical period A period of time in which technology changes.

Homo communista Communist man.

Homo economicus Economic man.

Homogeneous product A product so standardized that buyers cannot tell the difference between the output of different firms.

Human capital The improvement in labor skills (marginal physical product) attributable to education or other training.

Implicit costs Those costs of the firm that result from using self-owned resources.

Import duties *See* Tariffs.

Imports Commodities and services bought from other nations.

Income approach Computation of the national income accounts based on measuring the kinds of income generated in producing the output of the economy.

Income effect In demand analysis, the change in the quantity of a good that consumers demand as a result of a change in its price and thereby the consumers' purchasing power, or real income.

Income-inferior goods Those goods that consumers tend to buy less of as their incomes increase, and more of as their incomes fall.

Incomes policy A policy that frequently involves wage and price controls by the government. In general, a cooperative effort of labor, management, and government to find mutually agreeable goals for the economy and the means to achieve these goals.

Increasing-cost industry An industry in which individual firms experience external diseconomies (increasing costs) caused by increases in output by the industry as a whole.

Increasing marginal utility of income The assumption that people get more and more satisfaction from each additional increase in their incomes.

Incremental capital-output ratio The additional capital needed to produce additional output.

Independent variable In a two-variable system the factor that changes originally.

Indicative planning The kind of planning one finds in France, where the government draws up targets for the economy and brings together employers and unions to discuss and modify the proposals. Firms and workers, with government support, move to implement these plans.

Indirect business taxes Taxes on goods and services passed on to consumers in the form of higher prices (for example, excise and sales taxes).

Induced investment Investment generated by changes in income and in quantity consumed. An increase in income leads to greater quantities consumed. Then there is an increase in investment to expand capacity in order to satisfy the new demand.

Inflating current GNP Increasing current GNP to take into account a fall in prices; expressing GNP in terms of dollars of constant purchasing power.

Inflationary gap The excess demand at full employment that causes prices, rather than output, to increase

Innovation Introduction of new products or processes.

Input-output relationships The complex set of interrelated requirements for inputs needed by the economy to produce various combinations of output (arranged by industries).

Instantaneous multiplier A multiplier effect that takes place without an intervening period of time. *See also* Multiplier effect.

Interdependence A situation in which economic actions depend on each other (for example, when firms in an industry act on the assumption that their price and output policies are dependent on the actions of other firms in that industry).

Interest The return to the owners of capital. Only interest paid by businesses is included in gross national income. (Interest on the national debt or interest on consumer loans is not included.)

Internal economies of scale Decreasing costs from a firm's increased output in the long term.

Internalizing costs and benefits The process through which the prevention of spillovers or externalities is accomplished by having all costs, private and public included in the price of a good.

Internal rate of exchange The rate at which a nation gives up one good in order to produce another.

International monetary fund (IMF) An organization set up at the Bretton Woods Conference in 1944 to facilitate international trade, especially to assure the financing of such trade.

International reserves Supplies of currency available to finance international trade.

Inverse relationship The relationship in which the dependent variable changes in a direction opposite to that of the independent variable.

Investment function A schedule of the quantities that people are willing and able to invest at various levels of income during a given period of time.

Invisible items Those services, including financial services (as opposed to physical commodities), that are bought and sold in the international marketplace. Items not normally reflected in merchandise exports and imports.

Involuntary additions to inventory *See* Unplanned additions to inventory.

Involuntary reductions in inventory *See* Unplanned reductions in inventory.

Jawboning The use of persuasion on the part of the government to get business and industry to comply with wage and price guidelines.

Glossary 675

Job discrimination A situation in which workers are employed on the basis of some consideration other than their productivity, such as race or sex.

Kibbutz A community that operates on the principle of complete income equality. In Israel in 1973, there were 240 kibbutzim, with more than 85,000 members.

Kinked-demand curve A demand curve that is based on the assumption that firms in an oligopoly follow suit when competitors' prices decrease, but ignore other firms' price increases.

Labor-intensive process A production process that uses relatively more labor than capital or land.

Law of demand The general rule that consumers buy more at low prices than they do at high prices; that price and quantity demanded are inversely related.

Law of diminishing marginal utility The general rule that as more of a particular good is consumed in a given time period, the additional utility of each additional unit of the good will ultimately decrease.

Law of supply The general rule that the quantity supplied rises as price rises, and falls as price falls; that price and quantity supplied are directly related.

Law of variable proportions The general sort-run rule that as a firm uses successive equal units of a variable input in conjunction with a fixed input, additions to output (marginal output) derived from the variable input begin to diminish beyond some point.

Leading indicators Certain kinds of economic activity that lead the business cycle by increasing or decreasing before the rest do. Measurements of these indicators are "weather vanes" for the economy.

Leakages Factors in the multiple creation of demand deposits that reduce the ability of commercial banks to expand the supply of money or demand deposits.

Legal tender Anything that the law requires be accepted in payment of a debt.

Libermanism A development (named after Yevsei Liberman) in Soviet planning in the late 1960s, which emphasizes profitability of firms rather than output goals and gives managers greater latitude in purchasing inputs and in selling products. A strong move toward decentralization in Soviet planning.

Limited liability A legal term that means that those who own the corporation (stockholders) are not responsible for its debts. Stockholders' liability (or the amount stockholders are liable for if the firm goes bankrupt) is limited to the purchase price of their stock.

Liquid assets Assets, such as savings accounts or government bonds, that can be quickly converted into money with little risk of loss.

Liquidate To sell a firm or to convert its plant capacity to producing other goods.

Long-run period A planning period of a firm or industry, in which all inputs are variable. During this period, the firm can choose any plant size permitted by present technology and by its financial limitations.

Lorenz curve A curve that shows the degree of inequality in the distribution of income for a specific year. The percentage of people in different groups is shown on the horizontal axis, and the percentage of income going to each group is shown on the vertical axis.

Loss minimization *See* Profit maximization.

Malthusian specter The nineteenth-century view, advanced by Thomas R. Malthus, that the supply of people (increasing at a geometric rate) would outrun the supply of food (increasing at an arithmetic rate), and that widespread starvation would result.

Marginal cost The cost of producing an additional unit of output.

Marginal efficiency of capital The expected rate of return on capital; the stream of income a business expects to obtain over the life of a piece of capital in relation to the price of that capital.

Marginal physical product The additional amount of product that a firm can produce as a result of hiring an additional unit of input (labor, capital, and so on).

Marginal private cost or benefit Cost or benefit that individuals derive from producing or consuming an additional unit of a good.

Marginal propensity to consume The percentage of any change in income that people tend to spend:

$$MPC = \frac{\Delta C}{\Delta Y},$$

where C = consumption, Y = income, and Δ (Greek delta) = "change in."

Marginal propensity to save The percentage of any change in income that people tend to save:

$$MPS = \frac{\Delta S}{\Delta Y},$$

where S = savings, Y = income, and Δ (Greek delta) = "change in."

Marginal resource cost The amount it costs a firm to hire one more unit of a resource, or factor.

Marginal revenue The change in total revenue due to a small or one-unit change in output.

Marginal revenue product The addition to total revenue attributable to using an additional unit of a resource. One finds it by multiplying the marginal physical product of the resource times the marginal revenue from selling the additional units of product it produces.

Marginal social cost or benefit Cost or benefit to society caused by producing and consuming an additional unit of a good.

Marginal utility The additional satisfaction derived from the consumption of the last unit (or additional unit) of a good purchased.

Marginal utility of income The change in satisfaction derived from a change in income.

Marginal utility of leisure The change in satisfaction derived from a change in leisure time.

Margin requirements Regulation by the Federal Reserve of the percentage of the selling price of stock that a purchaser must put down in cash in order to buy a stock. The purchaser may borrow the rest from a bank or a stockbroker.

Market period The period of time in a firm's economic life in which all its sales come from existing output; no additional output is possible.

Market system The set of means by which exchanges between buyer and seller are made.

Marxist socialism A system of philosophy of government and economics that grew out of the writings of Karl Marx in the nineteenth century.

Materials-balance approach An explanation of environmental problems based on the amount of input used in production and the disposal of waste products created in the consumption of that output.

Means of deferred payment The function of money that is concerned with facilitating lending and the repayment of loans.

Medium of exchange The function of money that deals with exchanging goods for money and money for goods.

Mercantilism A system of economic thought, at its peak from the sixteenth to nineteenth centuries, according to which governments were responsible for the welfare of the economy.

Model A device economists use to create a systematic analogy to actual economic behavior.

Monetarism An approach to economic policy that emphasizes the dominant role of the supply of money. It calls for a fixed and appropriate increase in the money supply each year as the basic policy for economic stabilization.

Monetary policy A government's manipulation of the money supply and the rate of interest to achieve economic goals.

Money Anything that performs the functions of a medium of exchange, standard of values, store of value, and standard of deferred payment.

Money (current) GNP Output of a given year valued at the prices of that year. Data on GNP before being adjusted for price changes.

Money income The number of dollars received in income; does not reflect purchasing power.

Monopolistic competition A market situation with three main characteristics: (1) many firms, (2) differentiated products, and (3) relative ease of entry into and exit from the market.

Monopoly power A firm's ability to influence the price of its product.

Monopsony A market situation in which there is only one buyer.

Moral suasion The use of persuasion by the Federal Reserve to get commercial banks to do what it wants.

Multinational corporations (MNCs) International firms that buy raw materials, sell finished products, and have production facilities in many countries.

Multiplier effect The multiple change in income due to a given initial change in aggregate demand. *See also* Balanced-budget multiplier.

Multiplier formula

$$M = \frac{1}{1 - MPC} \quad \text{or} \quad M = \frac{1}{MPS},$$

where MPC = marginal propensity to consume and MPS = marginal propensity to save.

National banks Commercial banks chartered by the federal government.

National income (NI) Net income of a country using factor prices generated in the production of all goods and services in a given period of time. NI = wages and salaries + rent + interest + proprietors' income + corporate profits.

National income at factor prices Net income of a country obtained by using only market prices of factors rather than market prices of finished commodities or sales on the commodity markets.

Near money Any asset that can be quickly and easily converted into money with little risk of loss.

Negatively sloped Sloping downward, as in a curve.

Negative net investment A situation in which gross investment is less than depreciation. In such a case, the capital stock of the economy is contracting.

Negative savings *See* Dissavings.

Neoclassical economics School of economic thought developed during the late nineteenth century. Many aspects of this thought are considered valid today, and many others have been changed and expanded. For example, Keynesian economics (named after John Maynard Keynes) evolved from a basic change in one aspect of neoclassical economics.

Net foreign trade (NFT) The difference between exports and imports:

$$NFT = X - M,$$

where X = exports and M = imports.

Net national income (NNI) A nation's net income at market prices generated in the production of all final goods and services during a given period of time (excluding depreciation). NNI = wages and salaries + rent + interest + proprietors' income + corporate profits + indirect business taxes.

Net national product (NNP) The net value of all final goods and services a nation produces during a given time period (excluding depreciation). NNP = consumption + net investment + government expenditures ± net exports.

Nondurable goods Commodities, such as food, that are used up fairly quickly.

Nonprice competition Forms of competition between businesses that do not involve price. May include competition in styling, services, advertising, and quality.

Normal profit A profit just large enough to keep the firm producing in the long run. Normal profit is also the firm's opportunity cost (what the firm could earn on other uses of its invested capital). A normal profit is included in total cost.

Normative economics Economic discussions that make judgments about the way things should be.

Official reserve transactions balance In a nation's balance of payments, the account showing how a payment deficit is financed.

Oligopoly An industry characterized by (1) the existence of several firms, each of which can affect the actions of others in the industry; (2) either homogeneous or differentiated products; and (3) significant barriers to entry.

Oligopsony A situation in which there are few buyers in the market.

OPEC An acronym for the Organization of Petroleum Exporting Countries, an international oil export cartel that sets the price of (most) imported oil.

Open-market operations The buying and selling, by the Federal Reserve, of highly liquid, short-term, low-risk government debt.

Opportunity cost The alternative goods one gives up when one chooses to produce a certain thing.

Paradox of thrift An ironic situation in which, if people all try to increase their savings, the equilibrium level of income of the nation and the actual quantity saved decrease.

Paradox of value A situation in which—since people decide to buy a good on the basis of its marginal utility—they are willing to pay a high price for diamonds (whose total utility is relatively low), but a low price for water (whose total utility is very great).

Parity A level for farm-product prices, maintained by governmental support and intended to give farmers the same purchasing power for each product sold as they had in some designated base period.

Partnership A business arrangement in which two or more individuals combine to operate an unincorporated business enterprise.

Per capita real GNP The figure obtained by dividing real GNP by the size of the population.

Perfect elasticity The situation in which price elasticity of demand approaches infinity. This means that as the quantity demanded changes, there is no change in price. The demand curve is horizontal.

Perfect inelasticity The situation in which price elasticity of demand equals zero. This means that as price changes, there is no change in quantity demanded. The demand curve is vertical.

Perfect integration The situation in which units of a resource are paid the same amount in all uses of that resource.

Perfect price discrimination The situation in which a firm charges the same consumer a different price for each unit sold. The price is the maximum that the consumer will pay for each unit.

Periodic multiplier A multiplier effect that takes place over time. *See also* Multiplier effect.

Personal disposable income The portion of personal income that people may either spend or save. PDI = personal income − personal taxes.

Personal income All income received by people, whether from production or from transfer payments. PI = national income − undistributed corporate profits − corporate taxes ± net transfer payments.

Phillips curve A curve that shows the tradeoff between unemployment and price changes. If employment increases, prices will increase; if unemployment increases, price increases will go down.

Physical capital Capital in the form of tools and instruments of production.

Pigou effect An economic reaction whereby, as prices fall, people with savings have greater purchasing power; therefore, savers increase their demand for goods and services.

Positive economics Economic discussions that consist of pointing out what *is*.

Positively sloped Sloping upward, as in a curve.

Positive net investment A situation in which gross investment exceeds depreciation; this means that the capital stock of the economy is expanding.

Precautionary purposes One reason why people want to hold money; they want cash in hand in case of emergencies.

Preferred stocks Stocks that have preference status when it comes to receiving dividends and assets of a given corporation, in case the corporation should have to liquidate. Preferred stocks usually do not carry voting privileges, and the amount of dividends is usually limited.

Price discrimination A situation in which the price of a unit of some good, divided by the marginal cost of that unit, is not the same for all customers. The seller of the good discriminates against some customers.

Price elastic A term describing a market situation in which the quantity of a good demanded changes at a faster rate than the price of the good:

$$\frac{\Delta Q}{Q} > \frac{\Delta P}{P},$$

where Q = quantity demanded, P = price, Δ (Greek delta) = "change in," and $>$ = "greater than."

Price elasticity of demand (E_d) The rate of change in the quantity of a good demanded with respect to the rate of change of its price:

$$E_d = \frac{\Delta Q}{Q} / \frac{\Delta P}{P},$$

where Q = quantity demanded, P = price of the good, and Δ (Greek delta) = "change in."

Price elasticity of supply The rate at which quantity of a product supplied changes as the price of the product changes:

$$\frac{\Delta Q}{Q} / \frac{\Delta P}{P},$$

where Q = quantity supplied, P = price, and Δ (Greek delta) = "change in."

Price index A measure of changes in a price level.

Price inelastic A term describing a market situation in which the quantity of a good demanded changes at a slower rate than the price of the good:

$$\frac{\Delta Q}{Q} < \frac{\Delta P}{P},$$

where Q = quantity demanded, P = price, Δ (Greek delta) = "change in," and $<$ = "less than."

Price leadership In an oligopoly, an arrangement by which the firms in an industry agree to follow the pricing lead of one firm.

Price rivalry The contest in which sellers watch what prices others charge, and then react to those prices.

Primary demand Demand for a commodity (such as cars or refrigerators) by those who have not owned that commodity before: first-time owners.

Private equilibrium The *market* equilibrium between the buyer's privately and noncollusively determined benefits from the sale of a commodity and the seller's privately determined costs (including the profit necessary for entrepreneurship).

Private rates of return Rates of return on investment that do not take into account indirect social costs and benefits (called external costs and benefits).

Production-possibilities curve A useful device derived from the production-possibilities function. *See also* Production-possibilities function.

Production-possibilities function A relationship expressing those combinations of goods that the full-employment use of a society's resources can produce during a particular period of time (using the best available technology).

Profit A return or payment to the entrepreneur.

Profit maximization Profit is said to be maximized or loss minimized when production is at the level at which marginal cost is equal to marginal revenue.

Profit-push inflation *See* Administered-price inflation.

Profits of unincorporated businesses *See* Proprietors' income.

Progressive tax A tax with a rate that increases as the tax base increases.

Proletariat Workers in the factories of the industrial societies developed since the eighteenth century.

Proportional tax A tax with a rate that remains the same as the tax base changes.

Proprietors' income The return to entrepreneurship in firms that are not incorporated.

Protectionism The government's effort to protect domestic firms or industries from free (competitive) international trade by imposing tariffs or quotas on imported commodities.

Public goods Goods that can be used by a person without reducing the amount available for other people to use.

Pure competition A market form that has the following characteristics: (1) No single firm can influence price. (2) There is no collusion. (3) Products are homogeneous. (4) There are no barriers to entry or exit. (5) Prices are flexible. (6) Buyers and sellers have full information.

Pure economic determinism The assumption that the actions of people and institutions are reactions to changing economic reality.

Pure monopoly A market form in which (1) there is just one firm, and (2) there are complete barriers to entry (the firm's product has no close substitutes).

Pure number A number that is independent of the units of measure of the factors involved in compiling it.

Quotas Restrictions on the quantities of goods that may be imported into, or exported from, a country.

Rambouillet conference International financial conference held in France in November 1975, to find a means to prevent huge swings in values of international currencies.

Random variations Variations that cannot be accounted or planned for, since they do not follow any regular pattern.

Rate of exchange The price at which one nation's currency is exchanged for that of another.

Real GNP The output of a nation for a given year,

adjusted for price changes between that year and a given base year.

Real income The value of what one can buy with one's money income.

Regressive tax A tax with a rate that declines as the tax base increases.

Regulated monopoly A market situation in which there is one firm in the industry, but a government regulatory commission sets prices and other conditions that the firm must follow.

Regulation Q A government regulation that empowers the Federal Reserve to set the maximum interest rates that commercial banks can pay on savings accounts and demand deposit (checking) accounts.

Regulations X and W Government regulations that empowered the Federal Reserve to set minimum down payments and maximum length of loans for consumer lending and real estate lending; expired in the 1960s.

Rent In the calculation of gross national income, the payments to owners of land. Includes an estimated rent on homes occupied by their owners.

Replacement demand *See* Secondary demand.

Required reserve ratio The percentage of commercial banks' demand deposits that the Federal Reserve requires these banks to keep in the form of assets called reserves.

Reserve army of the unemployed A Marxist term denoting the number of people who are unemployed in capitalistic societies because of the increased use of capital and improved technology (that is, machines replacing labor).

Reserves Eligible assets (their eligibility determined by the Federal Reserve) that must be held by commercial banks.

Resource externalities Changes in the costs of resources that are not attributable to the actions of a single firm but are due to changes in the industry, or in the natural or political environment.

Resources The inputs (land, labor, capital, entrepreneurship) used to make consumer and producer goods.

Results of historical discrimination The effects on present patterns of jobs and wages attributable to previous economic discrimination.

Retained earnings Undistributed corporate profits.

Savings-equals-intended-investment approach An approach to the problem of finding equilibrium income—in a model without government and foreign trade—according to which the intended investment curve is placed above the x axis (measured income) in relation to the savings function ($S = II$).

Savings function Schedule of the quantities that people are willing and able to save at different levels of income during a given period of time.

Say's law Supply creates its own demand.

Seasonal variations Fluctuations in employment, money supply, and cash flows that occur regularly at certain periods each year.

Secondary demand Demand by consumers for commodities to replace worn-out consumer goods.

Secular trend The expansion or contraction of an economy over very long periods of time. The long-term trend in any time series.

Services Those products of an economy (haircuts, medical attention, and so on) that are not commodities. The value of services is included when GNP is computed.

Short-run period The period of actual production, in which some resources used by a firm are fixed and at least one resource is variable.

Single-tax movement A school of thought in the late nineteenth century, led by Henry George, which proposed taxing away all land rents and using the revenues to fund governments.

Social costs Private costs plus spillovers (externalities). *See also* Externalities; Spillovers.

Socialism A social system in which there is collective or governmental ownership of the means of production and distribution of goods. There are many brands of socialism, encompassing many gradations of political and economic thought. Common to all of them is the idea that control of the means of production should be in public, not private, hands.

Social production A Marxist term that applies to production within modern industrialized societies that requires the cooperation of many workers. This makes it impossible for workers to identify their own work contribution.

Sole proprietorship A form of business enterprise in which one person is the owner, and is solely responsible for that enterprise.

Special drawing rights (SDRs) A system of international reserve assets, the so-called "paper gold"; a market basket of currencies established by the International Monetary Fund (IMF). Nations that are members of the IMF may borrow these SDRs to ease currency crises.

Specific powers of the Federal Reserve Powers of the Federal Reserve to regulate particular areas of lending, such as margin requirements on stock purchases; Regulation Q is, and Regulations W and X were part of these powers.

Speculative purposes One reason why people wish to hold some of their assets in the form of money: they want to be able to take advantage of unforeseen opportunities to invest, to buy bargains, and so forth.

Spillovers Differences between *private* costs and benefits and *public* costs and benefits. *See also* Externalities.

Standard of value The function of money that enables people to place values on goods and services.

State banks Commercial banks chartered by the various state governments.

Stationary state A condition in which a given society has reached the upper limit to its growth in per capita income.

Store of value The function of money that enables holders of money to save by a process of transferring value from the present to the future.

Structural unemployment A kind of unemployment caused by changes in the structure of the economy, either in the composition of demand or in technology. Either one of these types of changes may cause changes in the composition of the demand for labor.

Substitution effect An effect that appears when there is a change in the quantity of a good demanded resulting from a change in its price relative to other goods' prices. This effect comes to light during analysis of demand in a given market. A relatively cheaper good is substituted for relatively more expensive goods.

Supply A set of relationships representing the quantities of a product that a firm (or all firms in an industry) will offer for sale at each possible price in a given period of time.

Supply curve A graphic plotting of the supply schedule, or a set of relationships between various prices of a good and the quantities of it that a firm supplies.

Supply of money All demand deposits in commercial banks, plus all currency and coin in circulation.

Supply of resources The quantities of a resource offered for sale at various prices in a given period of time.

Surplus value Marxist term for the differences between the wages paid to workers and the market value of what the workers produce. Surplus value, to Marxists, measures the degree of exploitation of the proletariat (working class).

Synthesis In Marxist theory, the system that evolves after the antithesis has forced social changes.

Tariffs Taxes on imported goods.

Tax rate With respect to income, the percentage of income a citizen must pay annually in taxes. With respect to property, the percentage of the value of property the owner must pay to the government annually in taxes.

Technocrats Term used by John Kenneth Galbraith to describe those who hold power in large corporations (also used to apply to those who would "manage" the economy).

Technological change Growth in knowledge or advances in techniques that result in more productive capital goods and more efficient organization.

Technostructure Term used by John Kenneth Galbraith to describe the many interlocking committees of people with technical expertise in large corporations, who make the essential corporate decisions.

Terms of trade Relationship between a nation's export prices and its import prices:

$$T = \frac{P_X}{P_I},$$

where P_X = prices of exports and P_I = prices of imports.

Thesis In Marxist theory, the set of social arrangements existing at a given time.

Tight money policy A policy of a nation's central banking authority that aims at reducing aggregate demand by decreasing the supply of money and increasing interest rates.

Time deposits Savings accounts for which banks can require prior notice before the account holder can withdraw the funds.

Total cost Total fixed cost plus total variable cost.

Transactions purposes One reason for holding some assets in the form of money. People do not receive their income at exactly the same time that they need to pay out money. Thus, they want to hold money to be able to meet these day-to-day payments.

Turnover tax A tax on goods as they pass through the various stages of production. The Soviet Union uses turnover taxes to increase prices so that the quantities of goods available (quantity supplied) will be equal to the quantities demanded. It is also employed in some Western European countries.

UNCTAD United Nations Conference on Trade and Development.

Underemployment An employment situation in which units of resources are not employed in their most productive uses.

Unemployment A situation in which a unit of a resource is unable to find use as an input.

Unions Organizations formed by employees for purposes of collective bargaining with employers.

Unit elastic A term describing a market situation in which quantity demanded changes at the same rate as price:

$$\frac{\Delta Q}{Q} = \frac{\Delta P}{P},$$

where Q = quantity demanded, P = price, and Δ (Greek delta) = "change in."

Unit of account *See* Standard of value.

Unlimited liability A situation in which there is no differentiation between the assets of the business and the personal wealth of its proprietor. If the business suffers reverses, the owner is personally liable for all its debts.

Unlimited life A situation in which a corporation can continue to exist no matter who owns its stock.

Unplanned additions to inventory A situation in which a business firm produces more of its product than the public is willing or able to buy, which must then be added to inventory. The result is that the business acts to reduce supplies and reduce amounts produced; income moves toward equilibrium.

Unplanned reductions in inventory A situation in which a business firm does not produce as much of its product as the public is willing and able to buy. The result is that the business acts to increase its orders and increase the amounts produced; income moves toward equilibrium.

Utility theory A theory of demand that assumes that consumers buy things on the basis of their evaluation of the satisfaction to be derived from various combinations of goods, and of their effort to maximize that satisfaction.

Utopian socialism A form of socialism that proposes communities in which people live and work together without economic distinctions. Utopian socialists regard these communities as the solution to economic and social problems.

Value-added method A method of computing GNP in which one adds all additions to the value of a product made at each stage of production; the total of these additions for a given product equals the final value of that product.

Value of marginal product The value to consumers of the output produced by using an additional unit of a resource. One computes this value by multiplying the marginal physical product of the resource times the price of the good produced by the resource.

Variable costs Costs of factors of production (such as labor, raw materials, and so forth) that vary according to variations in the firm's output.

Veblen goods Goods that consumers prefer more of at high prices due to their conspicuous value.

Velocity of exchange The numbers of times the supply of money changes hands in a given period of time.

Visible items Those commodities (such as cars, food, and machinery) that are sold in the international marketplace.

Wage and price controls Mandatory limits on wages and prices established by a regulatory authority and enforced by law.

Wage and price guidelines Suggested rules for levels of wages and prices. The government suggests these rules, but compliance with them is voluntary.

Wage discrimination A form of price discrimination in which employers use, as criteria to determine the wages they pay to their employees, certain characteristics that have nothing to do with the productivity of the employees, such as race or sex. They may pay lower wages to blacks than to whites, to women than to men, and so forth.

Wages and salaries The money income, including social security taxes, that is the return to labor; figured into the computation of gross national income.

Wholesale price index An index that measures change in wholesale prices.

Zero economic growth (ZEG) The idea or belief that an economy's GNP should not increase. ZEG is usually based on a concern for preserving or improving the physical and cultural environment.

Zero population growth (ZPG) The slogan advanced by people who feel that the birth rate should equal the death rate so that population will not increase.

Index

Ability-to-pay principle, 89
Absolute advantage (trade), 576-577
Abstinence theory of interest, 159-160, 162-164, 181
Accelerator principle, 196-197
Accounting, national economic, 104-122
Adjustable-peg system, 610
Advantages (trade)
   absolute, 576-577
   comparative, 576-578, 579-581, 594-595, 597
Advertising, 97
   and competition, 407, 472-473
   for drugs, 509-510
   in monopolies, 446, 472
   as nonprice competition, 495-499
   as product differentiation, 482, 486
   and well-being, 126
Aggregate-demand-equals-aggregate-supply approach, 176, 189, 213-214, 217, 220-221
Aggregate demand function, 187-188
Aggregate production function, 331-333
Aggregate supply function, 188
Agricultural Adjustment Act (1933), 430, 434
Agriculture
   in China, 662-663
   and competition, 405, 430-440
   law of variable proportions in, 375
   prices in, 209, 434-435, 436, 438-439
   in Soviet Union, 649-650, 654, 656, 657
Aid
   for cities, 101-102
   foreign, 436, 437, 596-597

Air pollution, 397-398, 400-403
Albrecht, William, 621
Alcoa, 443, 444, 484, 500, 502
Aluminum industry, 443, 444, 484, 500, 502
American Capitalism (Galbraith), 503
American Motors, 485
American Telephone and Telegraph (AT&T), 84
Analysis (economic), 4-6
   regression, 5
Anarchism, 638-639
Anchovies, 438, 439
Antithesis, 633
Apollo-Soyuz space mission, 664
Armed Services Procurement Regulations, 515
Assets
   of consumers, 170-171
   liquid, 171
Autarky, 576
Automotive industry, 84, 484, 485
   advertising by, 446
   during business fluctuations, 202, 204, 209
   products of, 486, 494-495
   quality in, 494
   styling by, 495
Auto Safety Act (1967), 469
Average propensity to consume, 190-192
Average propensity to save, 190-192
Average revenue, 447-448
Average total cost, 413-416

Backward-bending labor supply curve, 540-541
Bakery industry, 510-512

685

Balance
  basic, 613
  of budget, 224–225, 232–233, 243
  official reserve transactions, 614
  of payments, 611–616
  of trade, 574, 612, 615, 620
Bank Act (1933), 305
Banker's acceptances, 300
Banks, commercial, 264, 276–292, 485
  in depressions, 204–205
  and Federal Reserve System, 286–292, 297, 298, 306–307, 308–309, 311–312
  national, 297
  origins of, 267–269
  state, 298
Banks, savings, 306–307
Baran, Paul, 442, 504
Barriers to entry
  monopolistic, 444–446, 471
  oligopolistic, 486, 511
Barter, 259–260, 599
Baseball, collusive oligopoly in, 492
Beame, Abraham, 99
Beef shortage, 256
Beggar-thy-neighbor argument, for protectionism, 586–587
Behavioral psychology, 630
Beman, Lewis, 155
Benefits
  private, 393
  social, 393, 534–535
  spillover, 393–394
  stream of, 534
Benefits-received principle, 87–89
Bentham, Jeremy, 15
Bethlehem Steel, 446
Bicycle industry, 582–585
Bicycle Manufacturers' Association, 582–583
Bluestone, Barry, 344
Bolloten, Burnett, 638–639
Bolshevik party, 637–644
Bonds, 82, 206, 227–228, 249, 250
Borlaug, Norman E., 36
Borrowing, 266–267, 268
Boulding, Kenneth, 344
Bourgeoisie, 627, 628, 630, 634–635, 662
Brand names, of drugs, 509–510
Bretton Woods conference, 610
Brothers Karamazov, The (Dostoyevsky), 13
Buckley, William F., 9
Budget (federal)
  balanced, 224–225, 232–233, 243
  deficit in, 226–228, 322

  full-employment, 243
  surplus in, 228–229
Budget restraint, 355, 362
Burke-Hartke bill, 621
Burns, Arthur, 604, 610–611
Business cycles, 130–135, 202–209, 239–240, 318–319, 635. *See also* Deflations; Depressions; Inflations; Recessions
Business firms, 71, 80–86
  capital goods of, 73
  demand from, 71–74, 186
  inventories of, 184–187
  investments by, 240–241
  military-industrial, 515–517
  number of, 58, 406, 482, 485
  oligopolistic, 484–504, 508–513
  size of, 457–458, 503
Butler, Samuel, 13

Caesar's Column (Donnelly), 442
Can Cities Survive? (Pettingill and Uppal), 100
Capacity, 339–341
  excess, 204, 423–424, 635
  full, 334–335, 423–424
Capital, 81, 82, 324–325
  broadening, 331
  deepening, 331
  financial, 554
  human, 41, 324, 534–536
  interest rates on, 554–556
  marginal efficiency of, 173–174
  physical, 554
Capital account
  long-term, 613
  short-term, 614
Capital consumption allowance, *see* Depreciation
Capital gains tax, 89
Capital-intensive process, 42, 331
Capitalism, 1, 624–626
  and imperialism, 637
  markets in, 20, 625
  and Marxism, 634–636
  mercantile, 633
  stability of, 132
Capitalists, *see* Bourgeoisie
Carlyle, Thomas, 1
Cartels, 67
Ceteris paribus, 50, 55
Cheap-foreign-labor argument, for protectionism, 586
Checking accounts, *see* Demand deposits
Checks, 263–265, 268, 286–287, 307
Chenery, Hollis, 594

686 Index

Child labor, and GNP, 121
China, People's Republic of, 44, 585, 661-663
Christmas, and currency demand, 308
Chrysler Corporation, 485
Church, and business morals, 97
Circular-flow models, 71-74, 115-116, 157-159, 269-272
Cities, finances of, 99-103
Citizen Nader (McCarry), 468
Citizenship
   and economics, 8-9, 15-16
   and education, 536
Civil Aeronautics Board, 93, 466, 492
Classical economics, 156, 157, 325, 327-328, 593-594
Clayton Act (1914), 442
Closed shop, 548
Club of Rome, 128
Coal Mine Health and Safety Act (1969), 468
Coins, 264, 269, 280-283
Collectives, *see* Communes
Collusion, covert, 491-492, 512-513
Command economy, 551, 644-658, 663
Commodity Credit Corporation (CCC), 438
Communes
   in China, 662
   in England, 628-629
   in France, 628
   in Israel, 630
   in Soviet Union, 649-650, 654
   in United States, 629, 630-632
Communication, in management, 380
Communism, 16, 629, 636, 644, 661-663, 664-666. *See also* Socialism
Communitarian Village commune, 631-632
Communities, 631
Comparative advantage (trade), 576-578, 579-581, 594-595, 597
Competition, 47-48
   in agriculture, 430-440
   and business morals, 97
   and interest rates, 555
   and monopolies, 406, 426, 443, 454-456, 477-479
   monopolistic, 406, 443, 470-479, 481-482
   nonprice, 486, 494-499, 511
   perfect, 406
   and prices, 59-62, 390, 406, 407, 486, 494-499
   pure, 405-427, 477-479, 481
   and supply, 382
   in trade, 581-582
   and wage-price flexibility, 161, 258
Complementarity, of goods, 49, 362
Computer industry, 485, 494
Computers, for money, 269

Congress. *See also* Laws (governmental)
   economic policy by, 240, 321
   and government regulation, 467
Consumer choice, 354
Consumer durables, 108, 133-134, 206
Consumer price index, 119
Consumers
   assets of, 170-171
   and business firms, 71-74
   in capitalism, 626
   income of, 72-73, 74-80
   and monopoly power, 504
   in Soviet Union, 652-653, 657
Consumption, 71, 76
   and business fluctuations, 206, 250, 313
   and demand, 187-189
   and GNP, 108
   and income, 171, 190-192
   and interest rates, 310
   marginal propensity toward, 190-192, 193, 218
   and savings, 168-172, 183-186
   and taxes, 171, 217-222
Consumption function, 166-169, 213-217
Continental Can Company, 443
Contraction phase, of business cycles, 131
Controls
   exchange, 606
   through the ruble, 649
   wage and price, 208-209, 254, 255-258
Cooperatives, *see* Communes
Copyrights, 486
Corporate Power in America (Nader and Green), 504
"Corporate Social Responsibility: Shell Game for the Seventies?" (Henning), 97-98
Corporations, 81-86
   multinational, 85-86, 616
   profits of, 75, 111
   social responsibility of, 97-98
Costs
   in agriculture, 432-433
   and competition, 411-417, 423-424, 477-479
   economic, 369-380
   of education, 534
   explicit, 370-371
   factor, 594
   fixed, 373, 375-376
   of illegality, 387
   implicit, 370-371
   and inflation, 141-142
   of investments, 173
   marginal, 376-377, 411-412, 417, 424
   marginal resource, 523-525, 545

Index   687

Costs (cont.)
  of military-industrial complex, 517
  minimization of, 524
  and monopoly power, 473, 477-479
  opportunity, 28-29, 40, 127, 370, 517
  private, 393
  of production, 57, 369-381
  and profit, 411-417
  psychic, 370
  psychological, 138
  social, 138-139, 393-394, 534-535
  spillover, 393-394
  stream of, 534
  total, 413-416
  of trade, 581
  of unemployment, 138-139
  variable, 373, 375-376, 377
  of wage and price controls, 256-257
Council of Economic Advisers, 240
Countervailing power, 503-504, 626
Coupon economics, 69
Credit cards, 266-267
Creditors, during inflation, 144-145, 154-155. See also Loans
Crimes, economic, 121, 125, 255, 386-388
Criticism and self-criticism program, 649
Crowding out effect, of national debt, 250
Crowding theory, 564
Cuba, 585
Cultural resistance, to economic development, 39
Cultural Revolution, 662
Currencies, international
  pegged, 610
  and trade, 576, 599-611
Currency in circulation, 264, 265-266, 269, 280-282. See also Dollar
  issuance of, 227, 264, 307-308
Current account, 612-613
Curves, 7-8. See also Functions
  cost, 418-422
  demand, 50-54, 58-59, 351-362
  kinked-demand, 488-489
  labor supply, 540-541
  Lorenz, 76-77
  movements along, 53, 58-59
  Phillips, 147-148, 233-234, 319
  production-possibilities (PP), 23-30, 31, 42, 102-103, 577-579
  shifts in, 31, 42, 58-59
  supply, 54, 56-59, 376, 381, 382, 417
  tax-rate, 90
Cycles, business, 130-135, 202-209, 239-240, 318-319, 635. See also Deflations; Depressions; Inflations; Recessions

Daly, Herman, 344
Das Kapital (Marx), 632
Debts. *See also* Liabilities
  individual, 246, 248
  money as, 265-266
  national, 228-229, 239, 244-250, 309, 320-321, 322
  non-interest-bearing, 265
  war, 203, 205, 227, 245-246, 248
Debtors, during inflation, 144-145, 155
Defense expenditures, 87
  and growth, 338-342
  and military-industrial complex, 515-517
  of Soviet Union, 657
  and well-being, 126
Deficits
  balance-of-payments, 614, 615-616
  balance-of-trade, 612, 620-622
  budget, 205, 227-228, 243, 322
Deflationary gap, 222-223
Deflations, 144-145, 146, 607
Demand, 48-54, 350-351
  aggregate, 176, 187-189, 192-193, 217, 220-221, 227, 228-229, 241
  in business fluctuations, 140-141, 206, 209, 222-223
  double coincidence of, 260
  effective, 165-166, 181, 202, 273
  excess, 59-60
  factor, 520-529
  for food, 431, 435-436
  illegal, 387
  and income, 52, 355, 362
  and investments, 186, 187-189, 195-197
  law of, 50, 53, 350-351
  market, 53-54, 59, 358
  for money, 272-273
  and monopolies, 443-444, 447-449
  in monopolistic competition, 474-475
  percentage increase in, 196-197
  price elastic, 359-362, 448-449, 461, 474-475
  price inelastic, 359, 360-361
  and prices, 49, 50-53, 59-61, 350-351
  primary, 202, 204
  and savings, 186
  secondary (replacement), 204
  and unemployment, 135-136, 137
  utility of, 354-358

Demand deposits, 263-266, 268, 269
  interest on, 306
  and loans, 279, 284-286, 287-292
Democratic socialism, 637-638
Denison, Edward, 536
Department of Agriculture, 93, 209, 434, 439
Department of Defense, 515-517
Department of Health, Education, and Welfare, 93
Department of Housing, 93
Department of Transportation, 93
Depleted Society, The (Melman), 126
Depreciation
  and investment, 173
  in national economic accounting, 111-113
  in Soviet Union, 657-658
Depressions, 202, 203-205, 430, 587
  dissavings in, 169
  Keynesian solution for, 161-162
  monetary policy for, 312
  neoclassical solution for, 161
Descriptive stage, of economic analysis, 4-5
Determinism, economic, 36
Development, economic, 32, 35-45. *See also* Growth, economic
  in China, 663
  and income, 79
  resistances to, 39-42
  in Soviet Union, 644
  and trade, 593-597
Dialectics, 632-633
Differentiation, product, 446, 471-476, 481-482
  and advertising, 446, 482, 496
  costs of, 486
  location as, 472, 481-482
  in oligopolistic industries, 486
  quality of service as, 482
Direct relationship, between variables, 7-8
Discommunication, in management, 380
Discount rate, 303-304, 311-312
Discouraged-worker effect, 137
Discrimination, economic, 563-564
  customer, 566
  historical, 563-564
  job, 543, 563-564
  present, 563
  price, 460-462, 467, 481-482, 509
  wage, 543, 563-568
Diseconomies
  external, 418-419
  of scale, 378-380
Disequilibrium, fundamental, in exchange rates, 610

Dissavings, 168-169
Distribution
  functional, 75
  of goods, 22
  of income, 75, 76-80, 249, 366-367, 455, 526, 535
Dollar
  devaluation of, 208-209, 438, 439, 516, 621
  freely floating, 604
  as monetary unit, 261
Donnelly, Ignatseo, 442
Dostoyevsky, F., 13
Dowd, Douglas, 338
Dow Jones Industrial Index, 306
Drug industry
  illegal, 386-387
  legal, 467, 508-510
Drugs, 386-387, 467
  ethical, 508-510
Dualism, economic, 28
Dynamic framework, 23, 323

Ecology
  and economic system, 626
  and GNP, 126, 127
  and government, 397-398
  and growth, 343-344, 401
  price of, 400-403
Economical irrelevance, 79
Economic development, 32, 35-45. *See also* Growth, economic
  in China, 663
  and income, 79
  in Soviet Union, 644
  and trade, 593-597
Economic Report of the President, 240
Economics, 1-9. *See also* Systems (economic)
  classical, 156, 157, 325, 327-328, 593-594
  coupon, 69
  Keynesian, 156-157, 162-176, 182-198, 204, 213-234, 239, 253, 314, 318, 319, 636
  monetarist, 234, 314, 318-319
  neoclassical, 157-162, 181, 213, 225
  normative, 9
  positive, 9
  radical, 1-2, 557
Economics and the Public Purpose (Galbraith), 15
Economics of Public Issues, The (North and Miller), 534
Economies
  external, 381, 418, 421, 595
  internal, 381

Economies *(cont.)*
  of scale, 377-381, 445-446
  zero, 378-380
Economists, 9
Economy
  closed, 344
  command, 551, 644-658, 663
  market, 20-22, 181, 225, 551, 624-626
  open, 344
Education, 533-536
Efficiency
  and costs, 371
  decrease in, 57
  vs. equity, 79-80
  and growth, 325-327
  increase in, 31
Effluents, 343
Ehrlich, Paul, 400-401
Eisenhower, Dwight D., 243, 321, 484, 515
Elasticity, price
  of demand, 359-362, 448-449, 461, 474-475
  infinite, 361-362
  of labor supply, 542-544
  perfect, 474-475
  of resource demand, 525-526
  of supply, 382
  unit, 359, 361
Elderly people, in inflation, 152
Electrical-equipment industry, 491, 512-513
Electric utilities, price discrimination by, 462
Embargoes, 585
Employment, 25-26. *See also* Jobs; Labor; Unemployment
  full, 135, 243, 331-335, 567, 656
  and income, 77, 222-223
  in Keynesian theory, 162-176, 239
  in neoclassical theory, 157-162, 181
  and prices, 146-148, 209
  in Soviet Union, 656
  and trade, 581
Employment Act (1946), 240
Engels, Friedrich, 628
England
  utopian socialism in, 628-629
  wage and price controls in, 255
England, Richard, 344
English Common Law, 84, 442
Entrepreneurship, 39, 556-557, 568
Entry
  into bakery industry, 511
  into competition, 471
  into labor, 543
  into monopolies, 444-446, 471
  into oligopolies, 486
Equal Employment Opportunity Commission, 567
Equal Rights Amendment, 567
Equation of exchange, 270-272
Equilibrium
  exchange rate, 601-605, 610
  income, 166, 183-189, 192-193, 195, 214-217, 219-223, 239
  long-run, 418-423
  price, 59-61, 66, 166, 183, 390-392
  private, 392
  social (public), 392-393, 394-395
Equity, vs. efficiency, 79-80
European Economic Community (EEC), 436
Exchange
  by barter, 259-260
  equation of, 270-272
  mediums of, 259-261
  of money, 260-261, 270-272
  velocity of, 270-272, 314, 319
Exchange rates, 578-579, 599-611
  controls on, 606
  equilibrium, 601-605, 610
  fixed, 604-605, 610
  freely floating, 601-604, 610
  internal, 578
Expansion, economic, 322-325
Expansion phase, of business cycles, 131-132
Expenditure approach, to national economic accounting, 105-106
Expenditures, in GNP, 108-110. *See also* Consumption; Defense expenditures; Government sector, expenditures of
Exploitation, 563
Exports, 206, 572, 600
  agricultural, 438, 439
  and economic development, 594-595
  and GNP, 109-110, 575
  restrictions on, 621
Externalities, 393-398
  and economic systems, 626
  of education, 535-536
  resource, 524-525
  and trade, 582

Factors
  inputs of, 146
  markets for, 72, 518-529
  prices of, 113, 519, 520, 539-557
  of production, 71-72, 520, 534
Federal Advisory Council, 299

Federal Communications Commission, 93
Federal Farm Board, 430
Federal Open Market Committee, 299
Federal Power Commission, 467
Federal Reserve Act (1914), 297, 305
Federal Reserve System, 283-284, 286-292, 297-314
  Board of Governors of, 299, 320, 321
  general powers of, 300
  and international exchange, 309, 605
  and money supply, 209, 227, 264, 283-292, 297, 307, 318-319
  specific powers of, 305-307
Federal Trade Commission (FTC), 93, 442, 469
Feudalism, 633
Final-value method, for GNP, 116
Finance, functional, 226-230, 243, 253-254
Financial institutions, 73. *See also* Banks, commercial; Banks, savings
Fine tuning, 305, 318, 319
Firms, business, *see* Business firms
Fiscal policy, 225-234, 320-322
  adjustments in, 320
  compensatory, 226-230, 243, 253-254
  discretionary, 225-226, 243
  vs. monetary policy, 318-319
  stabilizers in, 240-243, 250, 253
Five-Year Plans
  of China, 662
  of Soviet Union, 644, 645-646, 664
Flexibility
  of military-industrial complex, 517
  of production, 371-380, 382
  and trade, 595
  wage-price, 161-162, 164-165, 181, 258
Fluctuations, business, 130-135, 202-209, 239-240, 318-319. *See also* Deflations; Depressions; Inflations; Recessions
Fluctuations, Growth, and Forecasting (Maisel), 138
Food
  demand for, 431, 435-436
  free, 435-436, 437
  prices for, 152-153, 434-435, 436, 438-439
  supply of, 328, 431-433, 435, 436-440
Food and Drug Administration (FDA), 93, 467
Ford, Gerald, 321
Ford Motor Company, 485
Formulas
  midpoint, 359, 382
  multiplier, 194
Fourier, Charles, 627, 628

France
  socialism in, 627-628
  wage and price controls in, 255
Franco, Francisco, 638
French Revolution, 627-628
Friedman, Milton, 162, 234, 257, 314, 318, 319
Functional finance, 226-230, 243, 253-254
Functions. *See also* Curves
  aggregate demand, 187-188
  aggregate production, 331-333
  aggregate supply, 188
  consumption, 166-169, 213-217
  investment, 167, 172-174
  production-possibilities, 23
  savings, 167, 169-172

Galbraith, John Kenneth, 15-16, 234, 500-501, 503-504, 557, 665
Garment industry, 495
Gasoline. *See also* Oil
  price of, 66-69, 209, 491
  taxes on, 89
Gateway restrictions, 467
General Electric (GE), 512-513
General Motors (GM), 84, 467, 484, 485, 499
General price index, 119-121
General Theory of Employment Interest, and Money (Keynes), 156-157, 162, 233
George, Henry, 553
Germany, 203, 205, 227
GI bill, 78
Giffen, Robert, 353
GNP gap, 138
GNP implicit price deflator, 119-121
Goldberg, Arthur, 119
Gold-flow point, 608
Goldsmith banking, 267-269
Gold standard, 601, 607-610
Gold tranche position, 614
Goldwater, Barry, 119
Goods, 20-21. *See also* Products
  complementarity of, 49, 362
  durable, 108, 133-134, 206
  free, 21, 552
  Giffen, 353
  government, 108
  illegal, 386-387
  income-inferior, 51, 353
  nondurable, 108, 133-134
  private, 398
  public, 398
  Veblen, 51, 352-353

Gordon, A. D., 630
Gorgol, John F., 515
Gosbank, 648-649
Gosplan, 645-647, 655
Government sector, 71, 86-93
   and agriculture, 430, 434-440
   and business firms, 73-74
   and capital market, 555-556
   city, 99-102
   expenditures of, 108-110, 213-217, 224-225, 227, 229-230, 241-243, 310
   and income, 213-234, 367
   and labor, 546, 550-551
   and pollution, 397-398
   regulation by, see Laws (governmental); Regulation, governmental
   size of, 233
   and spillovers, 396-399
   stabilization by, 240-243
   taxes by, see Taxation
Grain
   for Soviet Union, 436, 437, 438-439, 654
   surplus in, 437, 438
Grand Camouflage, The (Bolloten), 638-639
Graphs, 7-8, 24-26
Great Leap Forward, 662
Green, Mark J., 504
Gross national income (GNI), 110-111
Gross national product (GNP), 104, 107-110
   of China, 662, 663
   and defense expenditures, 339-341
   and education, 533
   exclusions from, 121-122
   full-employment, 333-334
   and illegality, 121, 125, 386
   money (current), 119-121
   and national debt, 245-246
   per capita real, 120
   real (constant), 119-121
   of Soviet Union, 655-658
   and trade, 573-575
   and unemployment, 138
   values for, 116-119
   and well-being, 125-129
Growth, economic, 323, 324, 325-336. See also Economic development
   in China, 662, 663
   and defense expenditures, 338-342
   and economic system, 626
   full-employment, 331-333
   and human capital, 536
   and pollution, 343, 401
   in Soviet Union, 655-658
   and trade, 594
   zero, 344
"Growth and Survival" (Heilbroner), 127
Guidelines, wage and price, 254-255
Gulf Oil Company, 491
Gulftane, 491
Gurley, John, 1, 16

Hawley-Smoot tariffs (1930), 587
Hazel-Atlas Glass Company, 443
Hedonism, 15
Heilbroner, Robert, 127
Heller, Walter, 319, 343
Hemenway, David, 466
Henning, Joel F., 97-98
Historical period, 372-373
Homemaker services, in GNP, 121, 125
Homo communista, 16
Homo economicus, 15-16
Homogeneous products, 407, 424, 425, 481, 486
Horizon (planning period), 240
Households, 71-80
Human capital, 41, 324, 534-536
"Human Capital: Policy Issues and Research Opportunities" (Schultz), 535
Humphrey, George M., 493

IBM, 84, 485
Illegality, economic, 121, 125, 255, 386-388
Imperialism, economic, 637
Imports, 572
   duties on, 582-584, 586-587, 621
   and GNP, 109-110
   need for, 575-576
   paying for, 600, 620-622
   restrictions on, 620-622
Income
   in China, 663
   and consumption, 171, 190-192
   and demand, 52, 355, 362
   distribution of, 75, 76-80, 249, 366-367, 455, 526, 535
   elasticity of, 431
   equilibrium, 166, 183-189, 192-193, 195, 214-217, 219-223, 239
   gap in, 38-39, 43-44
   and government, 213-234, 367
   gross national, 110-111
   of households, 72-73, 74-80
   increase in, 39-42
   and inflation, 143-144, 154-155, 209, 243

Income *(cont.)*
  and investment, 175-176, 195-197
  in Keynesian theory, 162-176, 182-198, 213-234, 239
  money, 143-144
  national, 113, 220-221
  and national debt, 248-249
  in neoclassical theory, 157-162, 181
  net national, 112-113
  personal, 114
  personal disposable, 115-116, 218
  proprietors', 111
  real, 143-144, 154-155, 209
  and savings, 190-192
  in Soviet Union, 651-652
  and taxation, 72, 76, 77-78, 89, 115, 217-222, 224-225, 241
  utility of, 366-367, 527, 540-541
  velocity of, 270
  and well-being, 37
Income approach, to national economic accounting, 106
Income effect, 50, 351-353, 540
Income-inferior goods, 51, 353
Income security, 86
Incomes policy, 225, 234, 254-258
Incremental capital-output ratio, 41
Index
  Dow Jones Industrial, 306
  price, 119-121
Industries. *See also* individual industries
  during business fluctuations, 202-204
  in China, 662
  constant-cost, 421-422
  decreasing-cost, 421-422
  durable-goods, 133-134
  increasing-cost, 419-420
  nondurable-goods, 133-134
  oligopolistic, 484-504
  in Soviet Union, 649, 656, 657, 664-665
Inelasticity, price
  of demand, 359, 360-361
  perfect, 361
  and tariffs, 584
Infant-industry argument, for protectionism, 585-586
Inflations, 74, 139-146, 152-155, 181, 240, 321
  administered-price (or profit-push, or sellers'), 142-143, 208, 233
  and budget surplus, 228-229
  cost-push, 141-143, 206, 208, 233
  creeping, 146
  and currency printing, 227
  demand-pull, 140-141, 206, 208, 233, 312
  double-digit, 313
  and income, 143-144, 154-155, 209, 243
  and investment, 242-243
  and military-industrial complex, 516
  monetary policy for, 310, 311-314, 321
  and money supply, 209, 272, 313-314
  and national debt, 249-250
  and prices, 139-146, 152-153, 254-258, 490-491
  and taxation, 153-154, 241, 243, 253
  and trade, 607, 621
  and transfer payments, 230
  and unemployment, 145, 152, 207, 208, 209, 250, 253-254, 311-312
  and wages, 254-258
Inflationary gap, 223
Information, advertising as, 495-496, 497-498
Inland Steel, 493
Innovation, 204, 557. *See also* Technology
Inputs
  factor, 146
  fixed, 372
  in Soviet Union, 647-648
  variable, 372
Instability, economic, 132, 202, 209, 225-226. *See also* Stability, economic
Institutions, economic, 32. *See also* Federal Reserve System
  financial, 73
  nonbanking lending, 314
Integration
  economic, 27-28
  perfect, 27, 42
Interdependency, 42, 485
Interest
  abstinence theory of, 159-160, 162-164, 181
  and consumption, 310
  in GNI, 111
  during inflation, 313
  and investment, 159-160, 162-164, 173, 310, 554-555
  on loans, 303, 304, 554-556
  and money supply, 209
  and national debt, 245-247, 249
  on savings, 306-307
Interest groups, and taxation, 232
Internalization, of externalities, 395
International Monetary Fund (IMF), 596, 605, 610
Interstate Commerce Commission (ICC), 93, 442, 466-467
Inventories
  and government expenditures, 215, 217
  and investments, 186-187

Index 693

Inventories *(cont.)*
  unplanned (involuntary) additions to, 184-185
  unplanned (involuntary) reductions in, 184-186, 215, 220
Inverse relationship, between variables, 7
Investment function, 167, 172-174
Investments, 108
  autonomous, 172-174, 175, 183, 194, 197
  during business fluctuations, 205, 206, 207, 240-243
  complementary, 42
  and consumption, 176
  cost of, 173
  and demand, 186, 187-189, 195-197
  and employment, 333-334
  ex-ante, 186-187
  ex-post, 186-187
  government, 108-109
  gross private domestic, 108, 112
  and income, 175-176, 195-197
  induced, 172, 195-197
  intended, 172-176, 182-186, 197
  and interest, 159-160, 162-164, 173, 310, 554-555
  negative net, 112-113
  net private domestic, 112-113
  positive net, 112-113
  private, 333-334
  rates of return on, 535
  and savings, 159-160, 162-164, 175-176, 182-186
  and trade, 596
  and war, 248
Invisible items
  on balance-of-payments statement, 612
  in international trade, 572-573
Iron, 324
Irrelevance, economical, 79
Israel
  utopian socialism in, 630
  wage and price controls in, 255

Jawboning, 254-255, 257
Jefferson, Thomas, 585
Jewkes, J. P., 503
Jobs. *See also* Employment; Labor; Unemployment
  creation of, 335
  discrimination in, 543, 563-564
Johnson, Lyndon, 162, 207, 257, 321
Joint Economic Committee, 240
Josephson, Matthew, 466

Kaiser Steel, 493
Kefauver, Estes, 467, 493, 498, 508, 510, 511

Kelsey, Frances, 467
Kennedy, John F., 254, 493
Keynes, John Maynard, 2, 15, 156-157, 161-162, 339
Keynesian economics, 156-157, 182-198, 204, 213-234, 253
  and Communism, 636
  on employment, 162-176, 239
  on income, 162-176, 182-198, 213-234, 239
  vs. monetarism, 314, 318, 319
Kibbutz, 630
Kindleberger, C. P., 595
Kissinger, Henry, 596
Kohn, Robert E., 401
Korean War
  business cycles during, 206-207
  debts during, 245
  loan regulations during, 306
  recession after, 207, 312, 321-322
Kuznets, Simon, 43, 44

Labor, 324. *See also* Employment; Jobs; Unemployment; Unions, labor
  child, 121
  in China, 663
  and education, 534
  as factor demand, 521-529
  and GNP, 121
  and protectionism, 586
  in Soviet Union, 650-651, 656, 657
  supply of, 539-544
  as value, 557
  wages for, 75, 539-551
Labor-intensive process, 42, 331
Land, 324
  rents on, 552-554
Laws (economic)
  of demand, 50, 53, 350-351
  of diminishing marginal utility, 355, 357, 358
  of diminishing returns, 374
  Say's, 157-158, 162
  of supply, 57
  of variable proportions, 327, 374-375, 522
Laws (governmental)
  antitrust, 84, 92, 442, 446, 492, 299, 512-513
  against discrimination, 567
  employment, 240
  minimum-wage, 550-551
  regulatory, 92-93, 467-469
Leadership, price, 492-494
Leading indicators, 134-135
Leakages, 290-292
Legal tender, 264

Leisure, marginal utility of, 540-541
Lenders, *see* Creditors; Loans
Lenin, V. I., 1, 636-637, 644
Leninism, 636-637
Lever Brothers, 497
Lewis, W. Arthur, 39
Liabilities. *See also* Debts
    of banks, 278
    limited, 81-82
    unlimited, 80, 81
Liberman, Yevsei, 654
Libermanism, 654-655, 657, 665, 666
Life (business)
    limited, 81
    unlimited, 82
Limits to Growth, The (Club of Rome), 128
Liquidation, of business firms, 411
Liquidity
    of assets, 171
    high, 266
    and interest rates, 554-555
    of national debt, 250
    of near money, 266
Loans
    from banks, 269, 278-280, 281-282, 284-285, 287-292, 312
    and business fluctuations, 144-145, 154-155, 312
    consumer, 306
    from goldsmiths, 268
    interest on, 303, 304, 554-556
    from nonbanking institutions, 314
    real estate, 306
    regulations on, 306
    supply of, 159-160
Location, as product differentiation, 472, 481-482
Long-run period, 372, 377-380
    in monopolistic competition, 476-477
    pure competition in, 417-422
    for pure monopolies, 452-454
Lorenz curve, 76-77
Losses, economic, 411-412, 414-415, 417-418, 452
    minimization of, 411-412. *See also* Profits, maximization of
    by monopolies, 452
    in monopolistic competition, 475, 477

Macroeconomic-employment argument, for protectionism, 586-587
Maisel, Sherman, 138
Malthus, Thomas R., 328
Malthusian specter, 328
Management, of business firms, 80, 81, 82-84, 380
Mansfield, Edwin, 503

Manufacturing, for economic development, 595
Maoism, 16, 662-663
"Maoist Economic Development" (Gurley), 16
Mao Tse-tung, 661-662
Marginal cost (MC), 376-377, 411-412, 417
Marginal efficiency of capital (MEC), 173-174
Marginal physical product (MPP), 522-529
Marginal private benefit, 393
Marginal private cost, 392
Marginal propensity to consume (MPC), 190-192, 193, 218
Marginal propensity to save (MPS), 190-192, 193, 194, 218
Marginal resource cost (MRC), 523-525, 545
Marginal revenue (MR), 411-412, 447-448, 488-489
Marginal revenue product (MRP), 521-529, 563
Marginal social benefit, 393
Marginal social cost, 393
Marginal utility (MU), 355
    of demand, 355-358
    diminishing, 355-358, 366-367
    of income, 366-367, 527, 540-541
    increasing, 366-367
    of leisure, 540-541
Margin requirements, on stocks, 305-306
Marijuana, 386-387
Market period, 372, 373
Markets
    black, 121, 125, 255, 386-388
    capital, 535-536, 555-556, 596
    in capitalism, 625
    factor, 72, 518-529
    oligopolistic, 484-504
    open, 299, 300-302, 311-312
    product, 72, 518
    stock, 204
Market system, 20-22, 181, 225, 551, 624-626
Marshall, Alfred, 15
Marshall Plan, 206
Marx, Groucho, 366
Marx, Karl, 557, 632-637, 644
Marxism, 16, 557, 630, 632-638. *See also* Socialism
Materialism
    dialectical, 632-633
    historical, 633, 664
Materials-balance approach, 401
McCarry, Charles, 468-469
McCracken, Paul 335
McNamara, Robert, 515
McNeil, Neil, 585
Media, and advertising, 496, 498
Melman, Seymour, 126, 515-517
Mercantilism, 165

Mergers, 443
Middle class, *see* Bourgeoisie
Midpoint formula, 359, 382
Military expenditures, *see* Defense expenditures
Military-industrial complex, 515-517
Miller, Roger Leroy, 386, 534
Minorities
　discrimination against, 563-568
　incomes of, 78
　unemployment of, 136, 138
Mobility, of resources, 148, 407, 433
Models, 5
　assumptions of, 30
　circular-flow, 71-74, 115-116, 157-159, 269-272
　Keynesian, 156-157, 162-176, 182-198, 213-234, 253
Monetarism, 234, 314, 318-319
Monetary policy, 225, 234, 310-314, 318-319, 320-322
Monetary systems
　domestic, 259-273
　international, 600-616
Money, 259, 261-263, 269
　banking of, 266-269, 277-292
　as debt, 265-266
　demand for, 272-273
　exchange of, 260-261, 270-272
　fiat, 264
　good, 263
　as income, 143-144
　near, 266-267, 319
　value of, 261-263, 266
Money Lords, The (Josephson), 466
Money supply, 263-265, 266
　and banking, 209, 227, 264, 268, 277-292, 297, 307, 318
　in business fluctuations, 205, 209, 313-314
　changes in, 269-273, 310, 318-319
Monopolies, 442
　in banking, 286
　bilateral, 548-550
　collusive oligopolies as, 491-492
　and competition, 406, 426, 443, 454-456
　laws regulating, 84, 92, 442, 446, 492, 499
　and prices, 148, 164, 233, 257-258, 443, 447-448, 450-452, 460-462
　pure, 406, 442-458
　regulated, 446, 458-460
　and wage and price controls, 257-258
Monopoly Capitalism (Baran and Sweezy), 442, 504
Monopoly Makers, The (Hemenway), 466

Monopoly power, 443, 556-557, 584
　in capitalism, 625-626, 666
　and countervailing power, 504, 626
　exploitation by, 548
　in monopolistic competition, 470-473, 481
　of oligopolies, 508, 510
Monopsony, 504, 515, 546-550
Moore, T. G., 466, 467
Morals, business, 97
Moral suasion, of Federal Reserve System, 307
Mortgages, money for, 306-307
Multinational corporations (MNCs), 85-86, 616
Multiplier effect, 193-195
Multiplier formula, 194
Multipliers, 193-195
　and accelerators, 196-197
　balanced-budget, 224-225, 232-233
　foreign-trade, 573-574
　instantaneous, 194-195
　period, 195

Nader, Ralph, 467-469, 504
Nader's Raiders, 467-469
National Farmers' Organization (NFO), 432
National income (NI), 113, 220-221
National-security argument, for protectionism, 586
National Traffic and Motor Vehicle Safety Act (1966), 467
Nations
　economic development in, 39-45, 79, 593-597, 644, 663
　income in, 76-77, 79
　trade among, 572-588, 593-597
Natural Gas Pipeline Safety Act (1968), 468
Neoclassical economics, 157-162, 181, 213, 225
Net foreign trade (NFT), 573-574
Net national income (NNI), 112-113
Net national product (NNP), 111-112, 270-271
Net worth, of banks, 278
New Economic Policy (NEP), 644
New Industrial State, The (Galbraith), 15, 500, 665
New York City, 99, 492
Nicaragua, 577-579, 581-582
Nixon, Richard M., 104, 162, 208-209, 255, 256, 257, 469
North, Douglass C., 386, 534
Number, pure, 359

Obsolescence, 111-112
Official reserve transactions balance, 614

Oil. *See also* Gasoline; Organization of Petroleum Exporting Countries
   offshore, 324
   shortage of, 66-69, 142, 209, 397, 596
Okun, Arthur, 128-129, 339
Oligopolies, 406, 476, 484-504, 508-513
   collusive, 491-492, 512-513
   kinked-demand, 487-491
   price leadership in, 492-494
Oligopsony, 504
Open-market operations, of Federal Reserve System, 300-302, 311-312
Opportunity costs, 28-29, 40, 127, 370, 517
Organization of Petroleum Exporting Countries (OPEC), 66-67, 142, 209, 249, 595-596
Output, *see* Production
Overproduction, 161, 181
Owen, Robert, 627, 628-630
Ownership
   private, 396-397, 624, 633, 649-650, 666
   state, 649-650, 666

Paradox of thrift, 197-198
Paradox of value, 357
Parity, in agriculture, 434
Partnerships, 81
Patents, 444, 486
   on drugs, 508-509
Payments
   balance of, 611-616
   deferred, 262-263
   interest, 245-247, 249
   international, 599-616
   transfer, 230
Pentagon, 516
Perfection of the innovation stage, 204
Personal disposable income (PDI), 115-116, 218
Personal income (PI), 114
Peru, 438, 439
Pettingill, Robert B., 100-102
Phalansteries, 628
Phillips curve, 147-148, 233-234, 319
Pigou effect, 161
Planning, economic, 644-658, 663, 665, 666
   indicative, 665
Planning period, 240. *See also* Long-run period
Polaroid, 443, 444
Policy (international), trade, 595-597
Policy (national), 240
   balanced-budget, 232-233, 243
   discount, 304

   discount-rate, 304
   easy-money, 312
   energy, 321
   fiscal, 225-234, 240-243, 250, 253-254, 318-319, 320-322
   incomes, 225, 234, 254-258
   monetary, 225, 234, 310-314, 318-319, 320-322
   tight-money, 313
Policy-making stage, of economic analysis, 5-6
Politburo, 645
Politics
   and monopoly regulation, 460
   and taxation, 232
Pollution
   air, 397-398, 400-403
   and GNP, 126, 127
   government intervention with, 397-398
   and growth, 343, 401
   water, 343
Poor people
   in capitalism, 626
   and inflation, 152-153, 154
Population (consumer), 49, 54
Population growth
   of cities, 100
   and economic development, 44
   and economic growth, 328, 329-331, 344
   and pollution, 401
   zero, 344
Postponability, of demand elasticity, 362
Poverty
   in capitalism, 626
   and inflation, 152-153, 154
Precautionary purposes, money for, 272
Presidents, U.S., fiscal policy by, 321. *See also* individual presidents
Price elasticity
   of demand, 359-362, 448-449, 461, 474-475
   of supply, 382
Price index, 119-121
Price inelasticity, of demand, 359, 360-361
Price leadership, 492-494
Price rivalry, 48
Prices, 424
   administered, 501-502
   and advertising, 495
   and city expenditures, 100
   and competition, 59-62, 390, 406, 407, 486, 494-499
   controls on, 208-209, 254, 255-258
   cost-plus, 501-502
   and demand, 49, 50-53, 59-61, 350-351

Index   697

Prices *(cont.)*
   in depressions, 202, 205
   discrimination in, 460-462, 467, 481-482, 509
   and employment, 146-148, 209
   equilibrium, 59-61, 66, 166, 183, 390-392
   factor, 113, 519, 520, 539-557
   for food, 152-153, 434-435, 436, 438-439
   of gasoline, 66-69, 209, 491
   and GNP, 119-121
   guidelines for, 254-255
   and inflation, 139-146, 152-153, 254-258, 490-491
   limit, 500
   market, 110
   and money, 266, 318
   and monopolies, 148, 164, 233, 257-258, 443, 447-448, 450-452, 460-462
   and oligopolies, 487-491
   and quantity, 50, 61, 350-351
   and resources, 255, 369
   and scarcity, 582
   in Soviet Union, 652-653
   and supply, 56-57, 59-61
   value-of-service, 467
   and wages, 161, 164-165, 181, 208-209, 254-258
Prime commercial paper, 300
Principles of Economics (Marshall), 15
Procter and Gamble, 497
Production, 21-30
   aggregate, 331-333
   in agriculture, 433
   during business fluctuations, 145-146, 202-203
   and competition, 408
   costs of, 57, 369-381
   and efficiency, 31
   factors of, 71-72, 520, 534
   illegal, 121, 125
   military, 516
   and money supply, 271-272
   social, 634
   in Soviet Union, 647-648, 653-654
Production-possibilities (PP) curve, 23-30, 31, 42, 102-103, 577-579
Production-possibilities function, 23
Productivity, 30, 72, 369-370, 520
   of agriculture, 433-434
   in city governments, 101
   and growth, 323, 324
   marginal, 374-375, 376, 526
   rate of, 32
Products. *See also* Goods; Services
   differentiation in, 446, 471-476, 481-482, 486, 496
   homogeneous, 407, 424, 425, 481, 486

   marginal physical, 522-529
   marginal revenue, 521-529, 563
Profits, 371, 556
   and business fluctuations, 155, 202-203
   in capitalism, 626
   and Communism, 635, 637
   corporate, 75, 111
   economic (pure), 371, 409, 412-413, 416, 417-418, 421, 450-451, 453, 459, 475-476, 556, 557
   in GNI, 111
   maximization of, 15-16, 62, 411-416, 499-501, 524
   by monopolies, 444, 450-452, 453-454, 459-460
   in monopolistic competition, 475-476
   normal, 371, 410, 412, 413-414, 416, 417-418, 451-452, 454, 459-460, 475-476
   in Soviet Union, 654-655
Progress and Poverty (George), 553
Prohibition, 386-387
Proletariat, 627, 628, 630, 633, 634-635
Promissory notes
   of banks, 303
   of corporations, 300
   for loans, 278-279
Propensity to consume
   average, 190-192
   marginal, 190-192, 193, 218
Propensity to save
   average, 190-192
   marginal, 190-192, 193, 194, 218
Property, *see* Ownership
Proprietorship, sole, 80-81
Proprietors' income, 111
Protectionism, 582-587, 621-622
Psychology, behavioral, 630
Public Interest Research Groups (PIRG), 468
Pure number, 359

Quality
   as nonprice competition, 494-495
   of service, 482, 494-495
   and wage and price controls, 256
Quantity
   of consumption, 170
   in demand, 51-53, 58, 61, 195, 350-351, 444, 447
   and price, 50, 61, 350-351
   and profits, 412-413
   of savings, 170
   of supply, 56, 58
Quotas, 584-585

Race, and economic discrimination, 563-568
Radiation Control for Health and Safety Act (1968), 468-469
Railroads, 442, 466-467, 491
Rambouillet conference, 611
Random variations, in business fluctuations, 131
Rates
   discount, 303-304, 311-312
   of exchange, 578-579, 599-611
   interest, 159-160, 162-164, 173, 209, 246, 303-304, 306, 310, 313, 554-556
   of return, 535
   tax, 89-90, 241
   of transformation, 30, 40-41
   wage, 542-551
Rationality, 354
Ratios
   incremental capital-output, 41
   required reserve, 284, 286, 304-305, 311, 312
Recessions, 145, 146, 205, 206, 207, 208, 240, 312, 321-322
   collusive agreements during, 491
   and durable goods, 134
   functional finance in, 227-228
   and inflation, 142, 145, 146, 152-155
   monetary policy for, 310-311, 312, 314
   taxation during, 241
   thrift during, 197-198
Recycling, of wastes, 344
Regression analysis, 5
Regulation, governmental, 92-93, 466-469
   of banks, 283-284
   on loans, 306
   of military-industrial complex, 515-516
   of monopolies, 84, 92, 442, 446, 458-460, 492, 499
Regulation Q, 306-307
Regulation W, 306
Regulation X, 306
Rent
   economic, 552-554
   in GNI, 111
   relative, 553
Republics, Soviet Union, 646
Research and development
   in oligopolies, 503
   in pure competition, 425-426, 457
Reserve army of the unemployed, 635
Reserves, 284
   decreases in, 302
   excess, 284-286, 292, 300, 304, 311
   fractional, 268, 286
   increases in, 300-301
   international, 604-605
   required, 284, 286, 304-305, 311, 312
   total, 284, 311
Resources, 20-21. *See also* Capital; Labor; Land
   allocation of, 255-256, 478-479, 581, 645
   depletion of, 127-128, 344
   human, 148, 324
   mobility of, 148, 407, 433
   productivity of, 30, 72, 324, 369, 370, 520
   in Soviet Union, 656
   supply of, 323-324, 539, 543
   wasted, 126-127, 344, 495
Revenue
   average, 447-448
   marginal, 411-412, 447-448, 488-489
   in monopolies, 447-448
   and profit, 411-416
   total, 413-416, 447-448
Rhodesia, 585
Ricardo, David, 593
Ridker, Robert, 402
Rippling effect, of Soviet Union resources, 648
Risks
   insurance on, 557
   and interest rates, 554
Robinson-Patman Act (1936), 442
Roche, James M., 401
Roosevelt, Franklin Delano, 130, 205
Russell, Richard, 484

Saint-Simon, 627
Salaries, in GNI, 110-111
Samuelson, Paul, 126
San Francisco school board, 99
Savers, during inflation, 144-145, 154-155
Savings
   and consumption, 168-172
   and demand, 186
   deposits of, 266
   and economic development, 79
   and income, 190-192
   and investment, 159-160, 162-164, 175-176, 182-186
   marginal propensity toward, 190-192, 193, 194, 218
   negative, 168-169
   in recessions, 197-198
   and taxes, 171, 217-222
   in war, 206
Savings accounts, *see* Time deposits
Savings and loan associations, 306-307

Savings-equals-intended-investment approach, 175, 182, 183, 189, 213-217
Savings function, 167, 169-172, 213-217, 219-220
Say, Jean Baptiste, 157, 162
Say's law, 157-158, 162
Scarcity, 21-22
  of beef, 256
  in cities, 102
  of oil, 66-69, 142, 209, 397, 596
  and prices, 582
  in Soviet Union, 644
  value of, 262-263
  and wage and price controls, 255-256
Schultz, T. W., 535
Schumpeter, Joseph, 557
Seasonal variations, in business fluctuations, 131
Secular trend, of business fluctuation, 131
Securities, government, 302, 311. *See also* Bonds; Stocks
Securities and Exchange Commission, 93
Self-interest, economic, 13, 15-16, 97
Services, 108
  government, 108, 225
  homemaker, 121, 125
  as nonprice competition, 494
  quality of, 482, 494-495
  welfare, 100, 437, 636, 665
Sex
  in advertising, 499
  and job discrimination, 563-568
  in utopian socialism, 628
  and wage discrimination, 563-568
Sherman Antitrust Act (1890), 84, 442, 492, 512
Short-run period, 372, 373-377
  in monopolistic competition, 474-475
  in pure competition, 408-417
  in pure monopolies, 449-452
Skinner, B. F., 630
Smith, Adam, 13, 31, 97, 325, 327-328, 593
Smith, Kate, 206
Social costs, 138-139, 393-394, 534-535
Socialism, 1-2, 627
  democratic, 637-638
  Leninist, 636-637
  Maoist, 16, 662-663
  Marxist, 16, 557, 632-638
  utopian, 627-632
Social responsibilities
  of business, 97-98
  of cities, 100
Social science, economics as, 2-3
Social security program, 89, 242
Soil-conservation program, 435, 437

Solow, Robert, 1, 15
Soviet Union
  economic planning in, 644-658
  grain for, 436, 437, 438-439, 654
  and United States, 664-666
Spain, 638-639
Special drawing rights (SDRs), 610
Specialization, and output, 325, 653
Speculative purposes, money for, 272
Spillovers, 393-398
Stability, economic, 132, 209
  of capitalism, 202
  and fiscal policy, 318-319, 320-322
  and monetary policy, 250, 318-319, 320-322
Stabilizers, 225-226
  automatic, 240-243
  and credit cards, 267
  and national debt, 250
Stagflation, 208, 213, 313
Stales clobbering, in bakery industry, 512
Stalin, Joseph, 644
Standard Oil, 442, 444
Static framework, 23, 593
Static principles, of economics, 323
Stationary state, of society, 327-329
Steel industry, 444, 446, 484, 485, 486, 492-494
Stockholders, and management, 82-84
Stocks
  common, 82
  in depressions, 204
  in Federal Reserve Banks, 298
  margin requirements on, 305-306
  preferred, 82
Straight-line labor supply curve, 541
Styling, as nonprice competition, 494
Substitutes, 49
  for factors, 526
  and monopolies, 443
  and price elasticity of demand, 362, 438, 439, 526
  and tariffs, 584
Substitution effect, 50, 352-353, 540
Supply, 48, 54-59, 369
  aggregate, 58, 176, 187-189, 217, 220-221
  costs of, 369-380, 382
  excess, 59-60
  and expansion, 323-324
  of food, 328, 431-433, 435, 436-440
  illegal, 388
  market, 58, 59
  and monopolies, 443-444
  and price, 59-61
  price elastic, 382
  time periods of, 371-380

Surplus
  agricultural, 436-439
  budget, 228-229
  and economic development, 39-40
  rents as, 553
  trade, 622
Surplus value, 557, 633-634
Sweezy, Paul, 1, 442, 504
Synthesis, 633
Systems (economic), 20
  adjustable-peg, 610
  anarchistic, 638-639
  capitalistic, 1, 624-626
  market, 20-22, 181, 225, 551, 624-626
  monetary, 259-273, 600-616
  private-enterprise, 47
  socialistic, 1-2, 627-638

Taconite, 324
Tariff of Abominations (1828), 587
Tariffs, 582-584, 586-587, 621
Tastes, and demand, 53
Taxation
  in business fluctuations, 153-154, 206, 207, 227, 231-232, 242, 243, 253
  on capital gains, 89
  by cities, 101
  and consumption, 171, 217-222
  double, 82
  on households, 72, 76
  and income, 72, 76, 77-78, 89, 115, 217-222, 224-225, 241
  indirect business, 111
  on land, 553-554
  progressive, 89, 241, 243
  proportional, 90, 218
  for public equilibrium, 394-395
  rates of, 89-90, 241
  regressive, 89-90
  and savings, 171, 217-222
  single, 553
  turnover, 119, 651-652
  value-added, 118-119
Technocrats, 15-16, 500, 665
Technology
  in agriculture, 433-434
  and competition, 425-426, 456-458
  and defense expenditures, 341
  and economic development, 40-42
  and growth, 324, 325, 327-328, 329
  and monopolies, 456-458
  in oligopolies, 486, 503
  and pollution, 401

and production flexibility, 372-373, 382
  in Soviet Union, 653, 656, 664
  in United States, 664
Technostructure, 500-501
Television, 496
Tetracycline, 509
Thalidomide, 467
Theorizing stage, of economic analysis, 5
Theory, *see* Economics; Models; individual theories
Theory of the Leisure Class, The (Veblen), 353
Thesis, 633
Thrift, paradox of, 197-198
Time
  and business fluctuations, 229-230
  and multipliers, 194-195
  and production flexibility, 372-380, 382
Time deposits, 266, 306-307
Toynbee, Arnold, 344
Trade, international, 572-588
  absolute advantage, 576-577
  balance of, 574, 612, 615, 620
  comparative-advantage, 576-578, 579-581, 594-595, 597
  and economic development, 593-597
  finance for, 599-616
  free, 585, 588, 594
  net foreign, 573
  terms of, 578-579
Transactions
  money for, 272
  official reserve, 614
  velocity of, 270
Transfer payments, 230
Transformation, diminishing rate of, 30, 40-41
Treasury, United States, 309, 321, 322
Treasury bills, 300
Turgeon, Lynn, 44
Twin Oaks commune, 631

Uncertainty
  in entrepreneurship, 557
  and trade, 595
Underemployment, 26, 656
Unemployed, reserve army of, 635
Unemployment, 74, 135-139. *See also* Employment; Jobs; Labor
  costs of, 138-139
  and defense expenditures, 339
  and demand, 135-136, 137
  frictional, 135
  and inflation, 145, 152, 207, 208, 209, 250, 253, 254, 311-312
  involuntary, 551

Index 701

Unemployment *(cont.)*
  monetary policy for, 311-312
  in neoclassical theory, 157
  and prices, 147-148, 181
  structural, 136, 137, 148, 233
  technological, 520
Union Carbide, 469
Union of Soviet Socialist Republics (U.S.S.R.), *see* Soviet Union
Unions, labor
  in cities, 101
  and Communism, 636
  and discrimination, 568
  and income, 78
  and inflation, 141-142, 144
  and monopoly power, 504
  and monopsony power, 546, 548-550
United Nations Conference on Trade and Development (UNCTAD), 595, 596-597
United Shoe Machinery Company, 444
United States
  in international trade, 572-588
  and Soviet Union, 664-666
Unit of account, 261
Unsafe at Any Speed (Nader), 469
Uppal, J. S., 100-102
Up-to-dateness, and pure competition, 424
U.S. Steel Company, 444, 446, 484, 492-494
Utility, 354
  of demand, 354-358
  diminishing, 355-358, 366-367
  of income, 366-367, 527, 540-541
  increasing, 366-367
  of leisure, 540-541
  marginal, 355-358, 366-367, 527, 540-541
Utility theory, 351, 354-358, 366-367
Utils, 354
Utopian socialism, 627-632

Value
  final, 116
  labor theory of, 557
  of marginal product, 523, 528, 545, 563
  of money, 261-263, 266
  paradox of, 357
  scarcity, 262-263
  standard of, 261
  store of, 261
  surplus, 557, 633-634
Value-added method, for GNP, 116-119
Value-added tax (VAT), 118-119

Variables
  in costs, 373, 375-376, 377
  dependent, 7-8
  independent, 7-8
Veblen, Thorstein, 353
Velocity of exchange (V), 270-272, 314, 319
Velocity of income, 270
Velocity of transactions, 270
Vietnam War
  business cycles during, 207-208, 321
  credit during, 321
  debts during, 245
Visible items
  on balance-of-payments statement, 612
  in international trade, 572
Volunteer work, and GNP, 121

Wages
  controls on, 208-209, 254, 255-258
  discrimination in, 543, 563-568
  in GNI, 110-111
  guidelines for, 254-255
  and prices, 161, 164-165, 181, 208-209, 254-258
  as prices of factors, 539-551
  in Soviet Union, 650-651
Walden II (Skinner), 630
Wall Street Journal, 467, 512, 513
War Economy of the United States, The (Melman), 515-517
Warfare
  advertising, 497
  economic, 444, 486, 489, 491
"War on Poverty," 207
Wars (international)
  business cycles after, 206, 207, 240-241, 312, 321-322
  business cycles during, 205-208, 227, 321
  debts during, 203, 205, 227, 245-246, 248
  growth during, 339
  loan regulations during, 306
Water pollution, 343
Wealth, real, 144-145
Wealth of Nations, The (Smith), 13, 31, 97
Weather, and agriculture, 433
Weinberger, Caspar W., 469
Weisbrod, Burton A., 534
Welfare conditions, 423
Welfare services
  in cities, 100
  and Communism, 636, 665
  for farmers, 437
Well-being, material, 35, 37, 125-129

Westinghouse Corporation, 512-513
"White sale" year, 512
Wholesale price index, 119
Wholesome Poultry Act (1968), 468
Wicker, Tom, 138
Wilson, Charles E., 484
Winkler, Donald R., 535
Women
   in advertising, 499
   and job discrimination, 563-568
   in utopian socialism, 628
   and wage discrimination, 563-568

World War I, debts from, 203, 205, 227
World War II
   business cycles after, 206, 240-241
   business cycles during, 205-206, 227
   debts during, 203, 205, 245
   loan regulations during, 306
   wage and price controls during, 255, 256, 257

Zero economic growth (ZEG), 344
Zero population growth (ZPG), 344
Zimmerman, Erich, 42

Billions of dollars

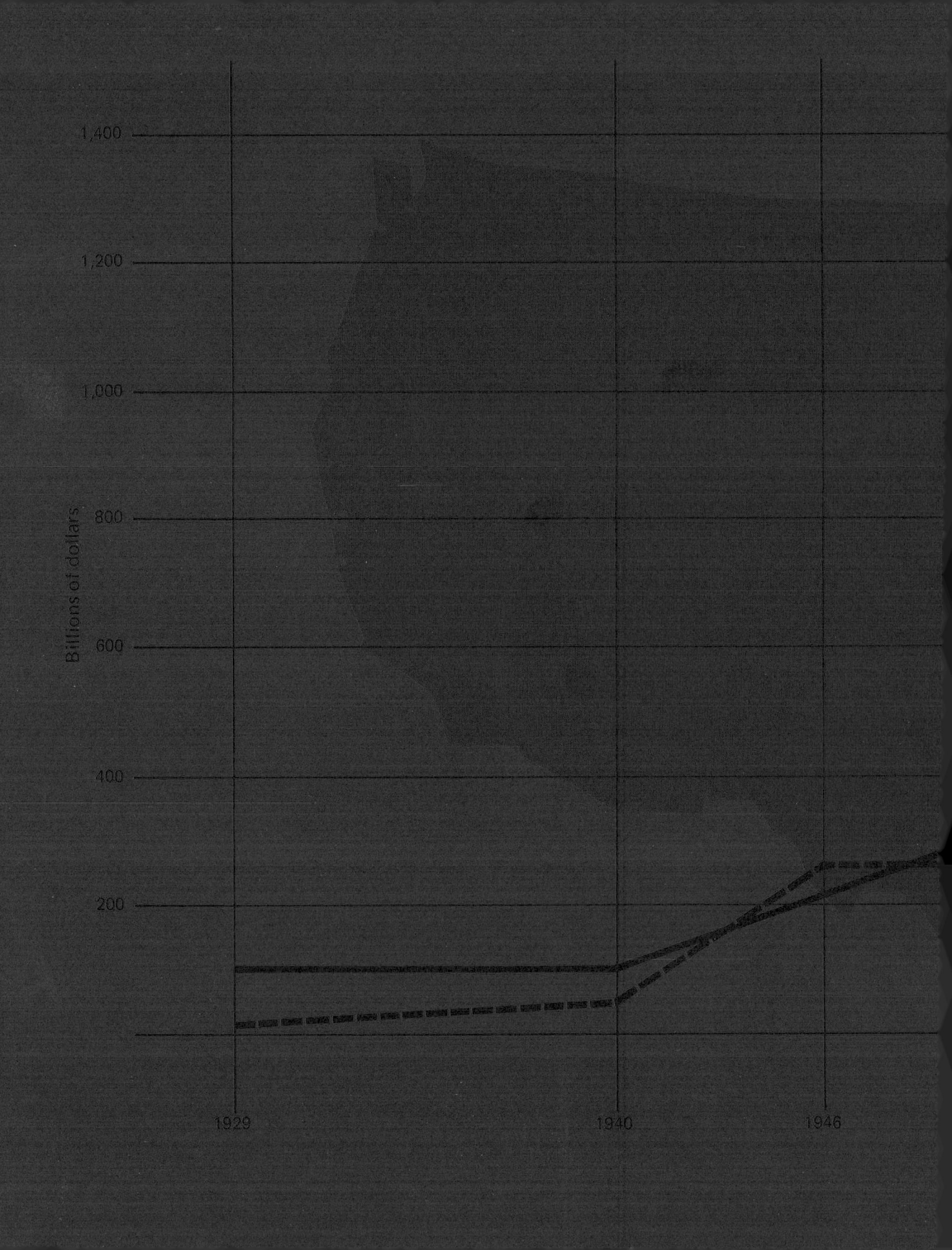

1,400
1,200
1,000
800
600
400
200

1929　　　　　　　　　1940　　　　1946